Guide to scripts used in English writings up to 1500

EXETER MEDIEVAL TEXTS AND STUDIES

Series Editors: Vincent Gillespie and Richard Dance
Founded by M.J. Swanton and later co-edited by Marion Glasscoe

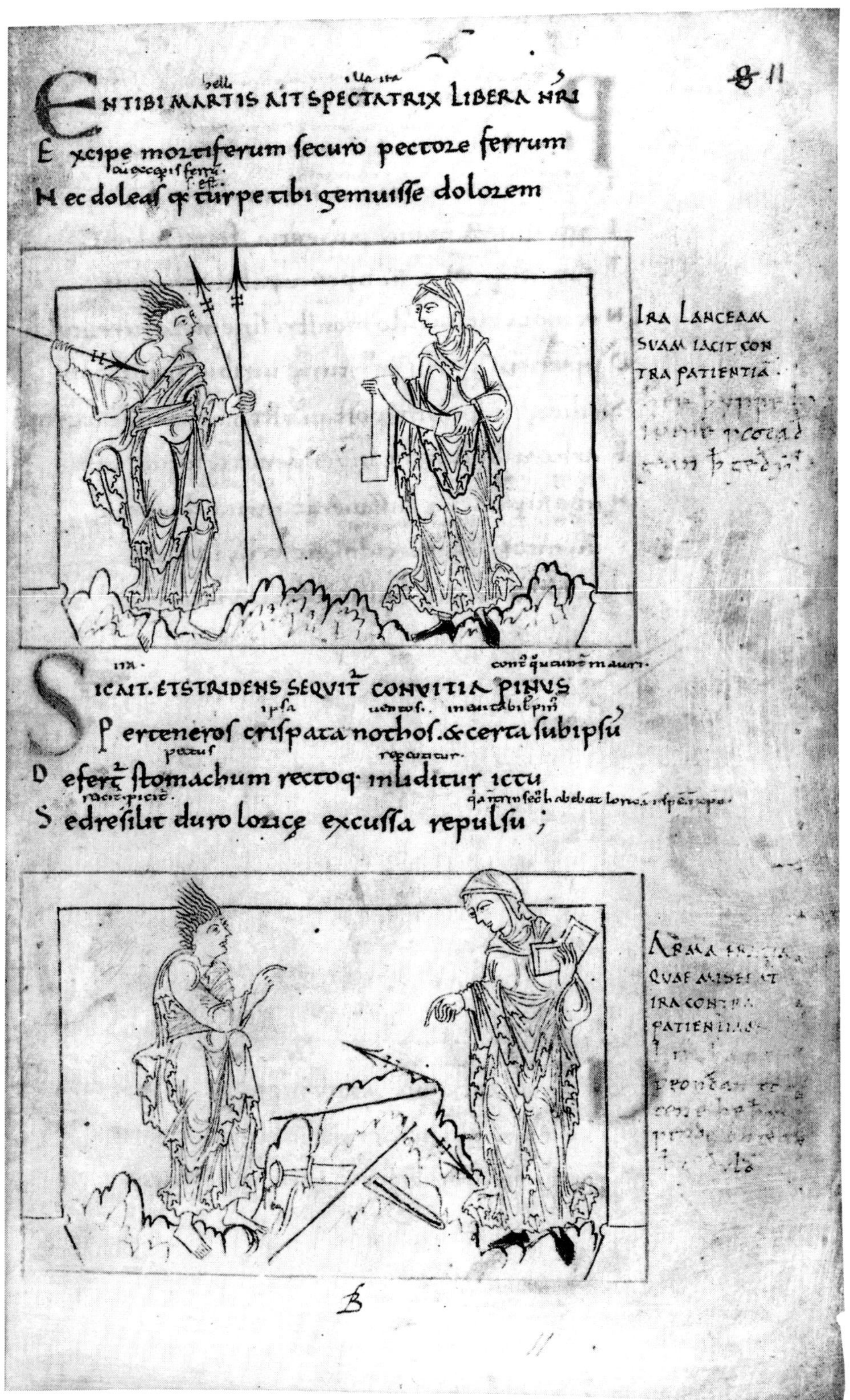

London, British Library, Cotton MS Cleopatra C. viii, f. 11r (formerly 8)
Prudentius, *Psychomachia*, from Christ Church, Canterbury

Patience, shown at the top with a scroll and below with a book, opposes Anger. The drawings, from the turn of the tenth century, derive ultimately from a programme of illustrations inherited from the late Roman world. The text is heavily glossed in Latin for teaching. Note the added English titles in the outer margin.
actual size

GUIDE TO

Scripts

USED IN ENGLISH WRITINGS
UP TO 1500

Jane Roberts

LIVERPOOL UNIVERSITY PRESS

First published 2005 by
The British Library
This corrected edition published 2015 by
Liverpool University Press
4 Cambridge Street
Liverpool L69 7ZU

www.liverpooluniversitypress.co.uk

© Jane Roberts 2005, this edition 2015

British Library Cataloguing-in-Publication data
A British Library CIP record is available

ISBN 978-1-78138-266-0 paperback

Designed by John Trevitt
Typeset in Poliphilus with Blado Italic
Supplemented from Peter Baker's Old English fonts by
Norman Tilley Graphics, Northampton
2015 corrections added by XL Publishing Services, Exmouth
Printed in the UK by
Bell and Bain, Ltd.

Contents

Some symbols used and other miscellaneous information

SOME LETTER-FORMS AND SYMBOLS

þ or 'thorn' is a runic letter, usually indicating *th*.
ƿ or 'wyn' is a runic letter, usually indicating *w*.
ð or 'eth' is a modification of **d** and usually indicates *th*.
Ð is one way of giving prominence to **ð**.
æ or 'ash' is a digraph, in which **a** and **e** are made together.
ȝ or 'yogh' descends from **ᵹ**, the insular form of *g*.
⁊ is the Tironian sign, used in Latin for *et* and in English to represent *and*(-).
& is the ampersand, in origin a ligature of Latin *e* and *t*.

SOME PUNCTUATION MARKS

/ is the virgule, like the . (or point) a versatile marker of pause.
⸮ is the *punctus elevatus*, the forerunner of the colon (the voice rises).
; is used for the *punctus versus*, marking a heavy pause (the voice falls).
¶ is used for the capitulum sign, a marker of new or important material.
§ is used for the paragraphus, a symbol introduced in s. iii Alexandria to mark a new topic.
// marks omission. It is often used where a capitulum sign is to be inserted. In time it came also to be regarded as a paragraph marker. Its role, therefore, is ambiguous.

CONVENTIONS ADOPTED IN TRANSCRIPTIONS

A single vertical | indicates a new line.
The marks \ / enclose letters written above the script line.
The marks / \ enclose letters below the script line.
The marks \\ // enclose letters in the margin.
Round brackets ( ) surround the expansion of abbreviations.
Straight apostrophe ' used where no expansion is offered.
Square brackets [ ] enclose changes made by scribes.
- within square brackets signals some alteration in following letters.
Pointed brackets ⟨ ⟩ to indicate something that is not present in the page reproduced.
→ signals an overrun of text.
g following a line number signifies a gloss line.

MEASUREMENTS

Dimensions are given in millimetres, with vertical measurements preceding horizontals (e.g. 60 mm × 40 mm). Overall page measurements are followed by measurements of the written space, which observe the ruled frames where appropriate. Otherwise, the vertical measurement is taken from the base line for the first line of script to the base line for the last line of script, and the horizontal from the beginning of the text block at the left to what seems to be the general justification achieved at the righthand side. Where a page has a mixture of contents or is incomplete, no written-space measurements are given.

The measurements should serve as a constant reminder that plates are rarely actual size. Moreover, readers should remember that over the centuries many manuscripts have been trimmed, some savagely, and that margins may therefore be considerably less luxurious than originally planned. See, for example, the Peterborough Chronicle (pl. 23), where the added Anglo-Norman chronicle saved at least part of the marginal space in the final pages of the manuscript (look carefully, to see the lines that mark out where the sheets were to have been cut).

DATING

The dating conventions, essentially following those used by Ker, *Cat.* 1957, draw on a mixture of Roman and Arabic numerals, and may be accompanied by further information, some of it superscript:
s. = *saeculo*. Thus s. viii stands for eighth century.
c. = *circa*. Thus *c.* 1000 stands for the turn of the tenth century.
'in.' = the first quarter of a century. Thus s. ix in. = 800-825.
'med.' = the two middle quarters of a century. Thus s. ix med. = 825-75.
'ex.' = the final quarter of a century. Thus s. ix ex. = 875-900.
'1' superscript = the first half of a century. Thus s. xiv^1 = 1300-1350.
'2' superscript = the second half of a century. Thus s. xiv^2 = 1350-1400.
c. 1000 can also be represented by s. x ex. – s. xi in.

ABBREVIATIONS

Add. MSS *Cat.*	The volumes recording additions to the British Library manuscript collections may be found in major libraries, but are most easily accessible through the *Manuscripts On-line Catalogue* at www.bl.uk/catalogues/manuscripts/
As	Analogous text
b.	born
bap.	baptised
CLA	Lowe, E.A., *Codices Latini Antiquiores* (11 vols and Supplement, Oxford, 1934-72)
Coll.	Collated in
d.	died
Disc.	Discussion by
ed./eds	an edited text or collections of papers
ed.	editor or edited
eds	editors
EEMF	Early English Manuscripts in Facsimile
EETS	Early English Text Society
E.S.	Extra Series
f.	folio (i.e. both sides of a leaf)
ff.	folios
Facs.	facsimile (volume)
fl.	*floruit*
Harl. Cat.	Wanley, H., *et al.*, *A Catalogue of the Harleian Collection of Manuscripts ... preserved in the British Museum* 2 vols (London, 1757-62); revised by R. Nares, S. Shaw and F. Douce, 4 vols (London, 1808-12)
Ker, *Cat.* 1957	Ker, N.R., *Catalogue of Manuscripts containing Anglo-Saxon* (Oxford, 1957, re-issued with suppl. 1990)
N.S.	New Series
O.S.	Original Series
Oxford DNB	*Oxford Dictionary of National Biography* (Oxford: Oxford University Press, 2004) at http://www.oxforddnb.com/view/article/6425
pl., pls	plate, plates
Pr.	Printed in
pt	part
r	recto (front side of a folio)
rpt.	reprinted volume or paper
SC	Madan, F. *et al.*, *Summary Catalogue of Western Manuscripts in the Bodleian Library at Oxford*, 7 vols in 8 (Oxford, 1895-1953)
S.S.	Supplementary Series
TH	Tremulous Hand
trsl.	translation
v	verso (back or turned-over side of a folio)

Acknowledgements

Much of the work towards this book was carried out in the library of the University of London, where across the years librarians in the Palaeography Room, Joan Gibbs, Helen Young, Mura Ghosh and Alun Ford were unfailingly generous in providing support, and I am delighted therefore that a University of London manuscript is among the manuscripts illustrated (MS V. 88; see p. 191). Most of the photographic reproductions are from manuscripts in the collections of The British Library, London. I wish also to thank the following for kindly permitting the reproduction of photographs: The British Museum; the Bodleian Library; the University Library, Cambridge; Corpus Christi College, Cambridge; Jesus College, Cambridge; Peterhouse, Cambridge; St John's College, Cambridge; the Dean and Chapter of Exeter; the Dean and Chapter of Lincoln; the Henry E. Huntington Library, San Marino, California; the Royal Library, Stockholm; and the National Library of Russia, St Petersburg. I should like particularly to acknowledge the grant made from the Neil Ker Memorial Fund in support of the colour section.

My thanks go especially to all the students who took part in and asked so many useful questions at weekly graduate seminars held at Senate House in the University of London for students of Old and Middle English, too many to name here. Others who have helped me in drawing this book together include: Ros Allen, Claire Breay, Gill Cannell, Susan Cavanaugh, Andrea Clarke, Catherine Clarke, Justin Clegg, Janet Cowen, Christopher de Hamel, Natasha Eleguina, Warwick Gould, Dorothy Johnston, Martin Kauffman, Matti Kilpio, Erik Kooper, Patricia Lovett, Emma Middleton, Elly Miller, Robert Mullally, Éamonn Ó Carragáin, Paul Vetch, Emma Volodarskaya, Andrew Watson, †Pam Weisweiller, Rudy Weisweiller, Christine Wise, Niamh Whitfield, Paola Zandegiacomo. A special debt of gratitude goes to those who have read and commented on a great deal of the book's contents: Janet Bately, Helen Conrad O'Briain, David Ganz, Pam Robinson, Alex Rumble. At British Library Publications David Way and Kathy Houghton have proved staunch and supportive. Michelle Brown has seen the book through many stages of its development. John Trevitt's wisdom has helped me straighten out ambiguities and his eagle eye has saved me from many stupidities. Norman Tilley has performed miracles, knitting Peter Baker's fonts and Stewart Brookes's ꝭ abbreviation into what must have been a typographer's nightmare. Finally, I must thank my husband, Gerald, for all his help and encouragement.

JUNE 2015

I should like to thank Julia Crick and Vincent Gillespie for their help and encouragement towards this reprinting of the *Guide*. Thanks go also to Debby Banham, Stewart Brookes, Ngaio Hitti, Tadashi Kotake, Francisco José Álvarez López and Eleanor Reem for spotting some errors that have been silently put right.

In memory of
the teaching, generosity and friendship of
Julian Brown and Tilly de la Mare

I General introduction

INTENTION

The general scope of this work is to give an overview of the variety of scripts used in the recording of English literature up to and a little beyond the introduction of print, a period too often broken up into Old English (or English up to and a little beyond the Norman Conquest of 1066) and Middle English (roughly from the Norman Conquest up to 1400 or to 1525 or to some later date, according to the historical stance adopted). Further subdivisions refine on these period terms, for example early Middle English (or Middle English up to *c.*1360), but such terms depend on assumptions made about the history of the English language and its literature, and the divisions indicated are often without particular relevance to the history of script. This book is for readers who want to explore how English was set down in writing before print became general.[1] Its aim is to help readers to identify the sets of letter-forms in use and to understand their place in the history of script. The aim is two-fold because the reading of scripts is helped by understanding changes and developments in the choice of letter-forms from one period to another. The range of samples is taken for the most part from well-known manuscripts.[2] Although illustrations from and facsimiles of these are nowadays far more available than formerly, they are often expensive and rarely widely accessible. I hope that readers will be eager to look for facsimile volumes and recent microfiche, CD-ROM, and web publications (including manuscript descriptions for many major libraries) and that this book will make it easier for them to find and to use such resources efficiently. I have set my eyes on virtually all the manuscripts from which reproductions are taken (not Ellesmere, or the Tanner Bede, which is undergoing rebinding at present), though some very fleetingly in exhibition cases (Lindisfarne Gospels, the Stockholm *Codex Aureus*).

Throughout the centuries covered by this book, the writing of English was, by comparison with the writing of Latin, a minority activity. The Norman Conquest brought huge administrative changes to England and incidentally paved the way for the reception of a second vernacular language, French, in which a great quantity of fashionable Anglo-Norman literature was to be written, but it had little immediate effect on the appearance of books. No more than 1066 is 1476, the year in which Caxton set up his printing press in Westminster, a date that signals immediate change, for the new printed books were not all that different from the manuscripts with which they were at first to co-exist. The codex, or book made up of quires of writing material held together, had already had a long innings since its emergence in the late antique world, and it is proving to have remarkable staying power in a world increasingly dominated by computers. But for England, as far as manuscript studies are concerned, the Middle Ages end with the dissolution of the monasteries in the 1530s.

OVERVIEW OF THE PERIOD

The first Angles and Saxons of Britain came to a Roman province, as fighters to help to defend the country's southern shores against invasion. With the withdrawal of the Roman legions early in the fifth century, the numbers of incoming settlers and raiders must have grown quickly, and the cities and villas of Roman Britain fell into ruin. The new population was largely illiterate, with perhaps only a scattering of the wisest able to incise runes on bone, wood, and stone,[3] and they can have understood little of the Latin memorial stones and inscriptions left by the Romans. How far the Anglo-Saxons came in contact with Romanized Latin-speaking Britons we cannot tell. In the eyes of the Anglo-Saxons, the Britons, speakers of a Celtic tongue, were 'foreign' or *wilisc* (the Old English adjective that gives us the name for the Welsh), and they probably thought them of little account. The Anglo-Saxons liked to think of themselves as receiving Christianity not from their most immediate neighbours, the Britons, but from Rome (Augustine of Canterbury arrived in Kent, A.D. 597, sent by Pope Gregory) and from Iona (some thirty or forty years later Aidan of Lindisfarne, a monk from Iona, taught in King Oswald's Northumbria).

By the age of Bede, learned Englishmen and Englishwomen wrote polished Latin. Whether through direct links with Pope Gregory's Rome or through the influence of Irish missionary activity radiating from Iona, the earliest Anglo-Saxon churchmen were quick to establish links with the late antique world, and they did not, it seems, make much use of their vernacular for the writing down of learned works or scripture. There is little English extant from early Anglo-Saxon

[1] It deals, therefore, with a subset of western historical scripts, for which Brown, M.P. 1990 presents an excellent overview.

[2] Seven of the twelve manuscripts in Skeat 1892 (late ninth to late fifteenth century) are illustrated, eight of the twenty-three chosen by Wright 1960 (twelfth to fifteenth centuries). Only one plate overlaps: Wright also has British Library, Add. MS 36704, f. 46r. Note also Greg 1913.

[3] Parsons 1999 examines the earliest Anglo-Saxon runic inscriptions.

England, for the most part marginalia, glosses to Latin or an occasional runic inscription, the longest of these carved on a stone cross still preserved in Ruthwell, in south-west Scotland. (Runes are illustrated in the photograph of the Frank's Casket on p. 31.) Even the two earliest texts of Cædmon's Hymn were recorded in copies of Bede's *Historia Ecclesiastica* as if by afterthought (for one of these, see pl. 1) rather than as a part of the transcription of the main text, where the Hymn's content is summarized in Latin. The range of manuscripts left by this age is remarkable, but although they are a significant part of the Insular legacy, they show little interest in the vernacular languages of the British Isles.[4]

One manuscript illustrated, the Vespasian Psalter, was later given English glosses (see pl. 2a). In its careful rather artificial Uncials, with Rustic script for display capitals, the Vespasian Psalter is thought to imitate the earliest books brought to Kent by Augustine's mission. Northumbria too, through the travels and baggage of men such as Benedict Biscop and Ceolfrith, was directly in touch with traditions in Rome. Northumbrian scribes, seeking to emulate the imported manuscripts, could create in the stately Uncials of the Codex Amiatinus a Bible so beautiful that it was for a long time thought to be Italian; and they excelled in their use of Half-uncial for gospel-books and psalters.[5] The development of Insular minuscule as a book hand in England is placed in the north, together with the emergence of the hybrid scripts of this early period.[6] Late in the eighth century the first Viking raids began, and many of the early centres of learning disappeared. Despite huge disruption, some manuscripts were saved. The Lindisfarne Gospels codex (pl. 5), arguably the most beautiful of Half-uncial manuscripts from Britain and Ireland, was carried out of the island of Lindisfarne for safety. Less fortunate books were no doubt stripped of their precious bindings and destroyed by the raiders. Yet, even in Mercia, despite heavy settlement by Scandinavian incomers, some semblance of learning remained, and the Book of Cerne (pl. 4), one of four English prayer books extant from the eighth and ninth centuries, shows the continued use there of Insular minuscule as a book hand.

Towards the end of the ninth century, at a time when King Alfred of Wessex had achieved an unsteady peace with the Scandinavians of the Danelaw, there was inevitably a sense of lost ground to be made up. Little Latin literature of any substance was now being produced in England. Through much of the country monasteries lay in ruins. Many manuscripts had been irretrievably lost, though apparently it was possible to get some looted things back. We learn from the inscription of gift written into the Codex Aureus (pl. 3) in the ninth century that this great gospel-book was bought back from Vikings in the 850s or 860s. Late in the century King Alfred paints a gloomy picture of the state of learning in England. In what is the first extant letter written in English, prefaced to his translation of Gregory's *Cura Pastoralis*, he writes to his bishops, presenting himself as the archetypal amateur and putting forward his remedy, an educational programme based on teaching first in English and on further training in Latin for those singled out for advancement. His immediate ambition was to make available in English 'sumæ bec, ða ðe niedbeðearfosta sien eallum monnum to wiotonne', and he reflects sadly how earlier the English had not needed translations.[7] The books associated with Alfred's educational reforms suggest a concern with the basic education of teachers and administrators. Alfred's reign is the period in which books begin to be written in English, if we accept Neil Ker's point that with Oxford, Bodley MS Hatton 20 (pl. 6), the earliest complete manuscript of Alfred's *Pastoral Care*, we see a scribe learning to use Insular minuscule as a book hand for English,[8] in a hand not unlike that seen in a Mercian charter from the first decade of the tenth century (pl. 7). Equally, with the earliest manuscript of the Anglo-Saxon Chronicle (pl. 8), the first scribe is still using **u** and **uu** as well as **p** for 'w'. Because so few of the translations ascribed to Alfred's age are in contemporary manuscripts we have little way of judging when settled ways of writing English first emerged. From before Alfred's time there remain some charters but few English writings of any length. What is extraordinary about his age is the attention given to translation by its men of learning, apparently to the near exclusion of making new works in Latin. Suddenly manuscripts were being copied in English, in significant numbers and for widespread distribution. These books do not necessarily constitute evidence for increased literacy.[9] The illiterate, that is those without Latin and the ability to read Latin, could listen to the new books read aloud. Symptomatic of the sudden importance of the English vernacular as a written language is the dependence of much of Asser's Latin life of the king on a source written in English, the Anglo-Saxon Chronicle.

Despite close links with the Carolingian Empire, England held for a long time to Anglo-Saxon minuscule as its script. Only with the build-up of reformed Benedictine monasteries from the middle of the tenth century did Caroline minuscule script come into use in England, at first for writing Latin. The reformed monasteries continued to use the vernacular in teaching, and new translations were made, for example of rules by which the religious life should be lived and of penitentials. One of those central to the new ways was the great teacher Æthelwold of Winchester, who was scrupulous

[4] For an overview of the early manuscripts see de Hamel 1986 [1994]: chapter 1.

[5] Good introductions to these scripts are to be found in Knight 1984 and 1998.

[6] See in particular T.J. Brown 1993 [1978].

[7] Sweet 1871: I. 7 'some books which are most needful for all men to know'. On Alfred's educational reforms see Bately 1980[1] [1984]; 1988[1].

[8] Ker 1956: 19.

[9] Wormald, C.P. 1977.

to explain in English the Latin books from which he taught.[10] Among his pupils was Ælfric, whose English writings circulated widely in eleventh- and twelfth-century England. Ælfric must have remembered from earlier writings in English phrases and passages that can be identified in his homilies;[11] and translations made into English in King Alfred's age continued to be copied alongside the newer English literature of the reform period, even as late as the twelfth century. Ælfric saw the grammar book he himself wrote (the earliest grammatical work in English) as of use for teaching both Latin and English, and his *Colloquy* (pl. 20), later enlarged by his pupil Ælfric Bata, remained a popular teaching aid. As late as the first half of the thirteenth century a teacher at Worcester, identified by the notes he made in manuscripts in his recognizable tremulous hand (see pls 6, 22, 24), made his own revision of Ælfric's grammar.[12] For a time some scribes must have worked in two alphabets, keeping to the letter-forms derived from Anglo-Saxon minuscule for English, and turning to the new Caroline letter-forms for Latin. Even so, a scribe holding well to the letter-forms of Anglo-Saxon minuscule could in the script's slope give his page a Caroline aspect overall (see pl. 14). Inevitably the distinctions between the two scripts were to become blurred (see pl. 19) once Caroline minuscule was the main working hand for writing Latin, and in time most of the letter-forms distinctive of Anglo-Saxon minuscule dropped out of use in writing English.

The Norman Conquest of 1066 had little immediate impact on the appearance of English books. The introduction of Caroline minuscule had, after all, already come with the Benedictine reforms and had slipped gradually into general use. Codicologically too there is little to distinguish books made before the Conquest from those first made under the Normans.[13] The writing of the main body of the Peterborough Chronicle and, a generation later, the work of its later continuation (pl. 23) take us well into the twelfth century; and there is evidence too for the use of English in annals from early twelfth-century Canterbury (see p. 113). Homilies, Old Testament translations, lives of saints, and even writings from the Alfredian period were still being copied from older manuscripts, and new compilations of English laws and charters were being drawn together. Whereas some scholars remark on inaccuracies in these late copies, emending copiously, others recognize differing levels of accommodation to language change on the part of their scribes. With the latest copies of the Old English Gospels there was some conscious updating in language, so much so that the Hatton text (pl. 29) might better be read as an introduction to the reading of Middle English than as a sample of Old English. Ker, pointing out that no clear line can be drawn between Old English and early Middle English, gathers into his *Catalogue of Manuscripts Containing Anglo-Saxon* any English texts written in scripts that do not share in the rapid developments visible from about 1200.[14] More recently, Margaret Laing's *Catalogue of Sources for a Linguistic Atlas of Early Medieval England* has encouraged a fresh look at how far the term Anglo-Saxon can be stretched beyond the middle of the twelfth century,[15] and new work is going ahead on twelfth-century manuscripts in English under the direction of Elaine Treharne.[16]

It must be emphasized that so far as the history of scripts is concerned, the period terms used in literary studies, Old English and Middle English, are misleading. Similarly, Anglo-Saxon minuscule is often used as a description of hands that still contain most of the distinctive Insular letter-forms well after the Conquest. Whether it remains appropriate for twelfth-century manuscripts in which Caroline letter-forms predominate is another matter. Thus, it seems an inappropriate description for pl. 25, where **f** and **r** are Insular and where both Anglo-Saxon and Caroline forms of **s** are used, as also that of pl. 24, where the letter-forms are essentially Caroline (both are termed Protogothic). Yet with pls 18 and 21, where the scribes are scrupulous in holding to the letter-forms distinctive of Anglo-Saxon minuscule, the description 'Late Anglo-Saxon minuscule' is invoked. That all these manuscripts still have **þ**, **ð**, and **ƿ** is irrelevant to their categorization, because these three letter-forms continued in lively use in the thirteenth century, with **þ** lasting much longer. Even as the use of the Insular-derived letter-forms and the conventions particular to Anglo-Saxon minuscule fell away, Caroline minuscule, the script now generally used for writing Latin, was already slipping into its Protogothic phase. Towards the end of the twelfth century a new development is important: the emergence of more current ways of writing Protogothic script for charters, record keeping, and other administrative purposes.

The proportions of works written and transcribed in Latin and English respectively continued to draw steadily apart. At the time of the Conquest England was unusual in the emphasis placed upon the vernacular for teaching and preaching, for charters, wills, and laws, though even in the century before the Conquest far more manuscripts were written in Latin than in English. Sustained book production may have been largely over in the Benedictine houses by the later twelfth century, but there were in the thirteenth century newer religious orders to set about equipping their libraries. There is little evidence from pre-Conquest England of collections large enough to be regarded as reference libraries,[17] but from late in

[10] This was recorded by Wulfstan Cantor in his life of Æthelwold (Lapidge and Winterbottom 1991: 46). Æthelwold was abbot of Abingdon *c.* 954-63 and bishop of Winchester 963-84.

[11] Whitelock 1962: 59 and n. 18; Godden 1968.

[12] For an account of the activities of the 'Tremulous Hand' scribe see Franzen 1991.

[13] Ker 1960[1].

[14] Ker. *Cat.* 1957: xix.

[15] Laing 1993; see also Laing 1991.

[16] See Treharne 2000.

[17] But see Gneuss 1986 [rpt. 1996: II]; also Lapidge 1985.

the eleventh century the numbers of books increased rapidly.[18] By *c.* 1150 some centres were building up substantial libraries, with scriptoria where secular scribes and illuminators were to play an increasing role.[19] If Bede is the proper context in which to set the Anglo-Saxon period, we should look to such historians as Henry of Huntingdon and William of Malmesbury as the context for English historiography in the twelfth century. Serious works of reference were being written in Latin, but alongside them there sprang up other chronicles elaborating splendid stories from a modicum of historical evidence.[20] Against the rising tide of scholasticism Geoffrey of Monmouth, for example, drew together the heady mix of legend and history that created Arthur. Men such as Wace and Gaimar were quick to translate these histories into Anglo-Norman French for their patrons, but we do not know for whom Laȝamon made his English *Brut* (pl. 33). Saints' lives burgeoned in popularity (pl. 30 is from a life of St Juliana) in both vernaculars as well as in Latin, as did devotional and debate literature (pl. 31 is from the *Ancrene Riwle*, an instructional manual written for three anchoresses of noble birth; and pl. 32, from the debate poem that is *The Owl and the Nightingale*). Although some hands, for example that of the Jesus College copy of the *Owl and the Nightingale* (pl. 32), may retain an old-fashioned look, others, like the Caligula Laȝamon (pl. 33), are highly professional in appearance, at home in the narrow tightly-written Gothic book hands that lie behind the 'black letter' fonts of early printers. Thirteenth-century books containing English are typically written in Gothic *textualis* script, which continued in use in England into the sixteenth century for *de luxe* manuscripts such as liturgical books and considerably later as a display script.

The new Gothic book scripts were slow to write by comparison with the less formal Protogothic hands that continued in use for writing documents. English scribes were soon to find, in their business script, a book hand that was easier to write on a small scale (pl. 36 from the Harley Lyrics manuscript was written by a scribe who is identified as having written some forty charters). The name given to this script, Anglicana, has been extended to comparable documentary hands.[21] Anglicana is, essentially, a script used in England and also therefore in northern France. It is the most typical script of fourteenth- and fifteenth-century English literature and continues in use as a legal hand into the eighteenth century. Whether formal, as in the Ellesmere *Canterbury Tales* (pl. 42), or relatively informal, as in the hand of Robert Thornton (pl. 51), it is the most usual English script of the Middle Ages, and many Chaucer and Langland manuscripts are in Anglicana. From the third quarter of the fourteenth century a second Gothic *cursiva* script, Secretary, comes into use in England, and its distinctive letter-forms infiltrate quickly into Anglicana hands (pls 40, 44, 45). There are by no means so many medieval literary manuscripts containing English in relatively unadulterated Secretary (pl. 52, in Capgrave's hand, and pl. 53 from the official register of the York Plays are good examples) as in good Anglicana. Some of the most stylish fifteenth-century hands draw on a mixture of letter-forms, whether the base is Anglicana (pl. 49) or Secretary (pl. 48), and it is not always easy, and perhaps it is even inadvisable, to distinguish mixed hands as predominantly one or the other. Recent discoveries, in particular by Doyle and Parkes,[22] have led to the identification of professional Privy Seal scribes among those who found time to undertake the copying of English texts among the many commercial scribes at work.[23]

After the thirteenth century few literary manuscripts containing English are in the most formal grades of Gothic *textualis* (but see pl. 43, the Corpus *Troilus*), rather more in the plainer hands of the schools (pl. 37, the *Pearl* manuscript). English texts written in Gothic *textualis* are, indeed, notoriously hard to date (see the commentary for pl. 35) because of the uniform standards achieved across a long period of time. Obviously this is less a problem with the writings of named authors, for whose writings there are firmer notions of likely dates of composition. The letter-forms of Gothic *textualis* were always available to the Gothic *cursiva* scripts for very formal effects, as in pl. 50, where the added title is considerably later than the main text hand. Conversely, the letter-forms of the humanistic scripts of renaissance Italy are on the whole of little concern to the readers of medieval English manuscripts (a hand with humanistic features is seen in the ending added to Chaucer's *House of Fame* in pl. 58). Long before, Anglo-Saxon England had, in King Alfred's reign, held to the letter-forms inherited from Insular minuscule, and as a result even a century later scribes were still using Anglo-Saxon minuscule for writing English at a time when Caroline minuscule had become the main script in use in England. So too early Tudor England for the most part continued in its use of Gothic *cursiva* Anglicana and Secretary scripts, which,[24] it should be remembered, were customarily used by the London scribes who played a part in the emergence of our Standard English from *c.* 1417.[25]

[18] Thomson [1986] 1998: 29-31; Gameson 1999[1].
[19] Thomson [1986] 1998: 32-36. An excellent sense of changing administrative roles in a monastery can be gained from Harvey 2002.
[20] Campbell 1986: 220-21.
[21] Parkes 1969 [1979]: xvi and n. 7.
[22] Doyle and Parkes 1978.
[23] See Parkes 2004 for discussion of one such scribe's output.
[24] Fisher, Richardson, and Fisher 1984 provide a useful collection of relevant Chancery documents, but, as Matheson 1986 points out, their categorization of scripts is misleading.
[25] Samuels 1963 is the starting-point for most subsequent informed discussion of the emergence of Standard English. See further Benskin 1992.

The late 1530s saw the dissolution of the monasteries,[26] with a fairly disastrous effect on the country's ancient libraries. Only a few English cathedrals now retain decent holdings of medieval books: this is more likely if they were 'secular' cathedrals rather than monastic and were therefore spared the summary destruction meted out to most religious establishments.[27] Nevertheless, of English cathedrals to-day, Durham has the biggest collection of surviving medieval manuscripts, and Hereford and Worcester retain sizeable holdings. It should be remembered that the vernacular literary manuscripts of later medieval England were often in private hands and therefore had a better chance of survival than earlier English literature. Yet, because secular owners often willed their books to monastic foundations, these too could have perished at the Dissolution;[28] and by then older texts could already have vanished, their parchment recycled long before the Reformation.

In the early stages of dissolution royal agents were sent out to compile inventories, among them John Leland, who liked to think of himself as the 'king's antiquary'.[29] King Henry VIII's libraries at his three major palaces gained hugely from the depredations made on the monastic libraries, but on the whole, once a religious house was dissolved, its books were given or sold off on the spot to anyone who wanted them or who just wanted the parchment they contained. The lucky books went to devout families or to book lovers, to be appreciated as relics or as the repositories of knowledge, and some were taken overseas for safety's sake. Most remarkably, the Stockholm Codex Aureus had another fortunate escape from destruction. Back in the ninth century it had been redeemed from Viking raiders and given to Christ Church Canterbury, as is recorded in the inscribed ninth-century deed of gift: 'Ic Ælfred aldormon ond Werburg min gefera begetan ðas bec æt hæðnum herge mid uncre clæne feo, ðæt ðonne wæs mid clæne golde' (pl. 3).[30] The Codex Aureus turned up next in seventeenth-century Spain, and it is now in Stockholm. Manuscripts, if they survived, might travel far. There are stories of shiploads of old books and documents sent across the English Channel as scrap;[31] and at home seventeenth-century schoolboys wrapped their books in parchment folders made out of illuminated leaves from psalters.[32] Oxford in the 1540s-1560s, had a glut of books, many of them from neighbouring monasteries and some very possibly imported from far afield. Parchment can after all easily be cleaned down for reuse. College librarians deliberately set about culling outmoded books to make room for the new acquisitions that were pouring from the presses. With so much being printed, why bother to keep the bulky scholastic and patristic volumes that took up so much space? Such rationalization of holdings broke up gifts and bequests built up over a couple of centuries or more, bringing more books on to the market. The 1535 visitation of the universities by commissioners may be thought of as having dragged them into the modern world: the consequences of this visitation for their libraries were disastrous.[33] In the reign of the boy-king, Edward VI, the 1550 Act against 'superstitious books and images' was responsible for further depredations. With it, most older liturgical books disappeared. The effects of the act were savage, and even the Royal Library was purged.[34] Fortunately, many devout people chose to hide books even through the dangerous years. Others too saw the need to hunt out and preserve what remained. John Dee, for example, wrote to Edward's successor, his older sister, Queen Mary, about wanton library destruction, offering to seek out manuscripts for the royal collection; and he set about building up one of the largest collections of manuscripts and printed books in Tudor England.[35]

A brief outline of the life of the playwright and theologian John Bale (1495-1563) should serve to illustrate how unsettled the life of learning became in the middle decades of the sixteenth century.[36] Aged twelve, Bale was a Carmelite in Norwich, but on transferring to Jesus College Cambridge he came under the spell of Cranmer and his circle. Even so, the first forty years of his life were orderly, filled with academic achievement. There were visits to the Low Countries and France, and senior appointments came, first to the Carmelite Friary in Ipswich and then to Doncaster. Bale left monastic life in 1536, and married in 1537. In 1540 he fled across the Channel with his family, probably at first to Antwerp, England having become too dangerous for him. With the accession of Edward VI, he could return to England, to hold a living in Bishopstoke, Hampshire, and to publish books under his own imprint.[37] In 1552 he was appointed bishop of Ossory, where he managed to be consecrated in the revised (i.e., not the Roman) rite. Once Mary Tudor was on the throne, he and his family, but not his books, were in flight again, escaping to safety in Switzerland. Lastly, Queen Elizabeth came to the

[26] See Wright 1951.

[27] See Ker 1967 (rpt. Watson 1985: 293-300).

[28] As, for example, did most of the Anglo-Norman books given by Guy de Beauchamp to Bordesley Abbey (see Blaess 1957).

[29] Carley 1989.

[30] 'I, ealdorman Alfred, and my wife Werburg, obtained this book from the heathen army with our solid cash, that was then with pure gold.'

[31] See Wright 1958[1]: 153-54, who quotes accounts given by John Bale, as does Dorsch 1959: 20.

[32] Mirrlees 1962: 58. See Pickwood 2000: 12, figure 14, for a sixteenth-century schoolbook with sides covered in manuscript waste (Windsor Castle, Library of St George's Chapel M. 169).

[33] See Wright 1958[1]: 168-70.

[34] Carley 1992; 2000: xliii.

[35] See Roberts and Watson 1990.

[36] See Happé 1966 for an overview of his life and writings.

[37] King 1999: 168.

throne, and home he came, ending as a prebend of Canterbury Cathedral from 1560 to his death. The tumultuous years gave way to a degree of calm. Matthew Parker, the new archbishop of Canterbury, could set about amassing the books he was to leave to Corpus Christi College in Cambridge.[38] From 1588 Robert Cotton was acquiring the first books of the collection now in the British Library,[39] and others too were seeking out old books,[40] among them Robert Talbot, a prebendary at Norwich, who was one of the first in modern times to read manuscripts written in Old English.[41] Symptomatic of changed attitudes to the books and other artefacts of the past is the formation of the Elizabethan Society of Antiquaries in *c.* 1585, among its five founder members William Camden (then teaching at Westminster School, the first of his books on the history of the antiquities of Britain appeared in 1586) and Robert Cotton (a generous lender from his ever-growing library).[42] Meetings, held up to *c.* 1608, were attended by men of widely differing interests and political persuasions, many of them owners and readers of old books now prized.[43] It is only too easy for us to forget the changes and reversals of mid-sixteenth-century England. We should not forget the importance of the 1560 proclamation that, in forbidding the defacement of old monuments set up 'for memory' and not out of superstition,[44] helped to usher in the new appreciation of the pre-Reformation inheritance. (The background for much of the vernacular literature of the later fifteenth century and the sixteenth century is very different, with a greater amount of evidence for ownership by individuals.) With Queen Elizabeth I on the throne, religious books from pre-Reformation England again had a fair chance of survival.

Over the following century and a half important new collections of medieval manuscripts formed, for the most part passing eventually to the universities and their colleges or to the British Museum.[45] Some sense of the many adventures undergone by individual manuscripts may be gained by consulting the brief notes on origins and transmission ('Contexts', facing the plates) and the 'People named in the commentaries' index, p. 280. The major movement of English medieval books was largely over by the end of the seventeenth century.[46] Although the 1834 Douce bequest to the Bodleian Library shows that it remained possible to draw together an impressive collection of manuscripts (see pl. 47), the heyday of collecting English medieval manuscripts had come to an end. Towards the end of the seventeenth century the task of publishing library catalogues got properly under way with Thomas Smith's *Catalogus librorum manuscriptorum bibliothecae Cottonianae* (1696),[47] and in the following year Barnard's *Catalogi librorum manuscriptorum Angliæ et Hiberniæ* gave a first overview of the post-Dissolution collections. For Old English manuscripts, and early Middle English as well, Wanley's catalogue (1705) remains an essential tool, particularly for its account of lost and damaged manuscripts. The library and collection catalogues made across the last two centuries are the basic inventories of manuscripts and their contents now in use, even as new and revised listings burgeon on CD-ROMs and web-sites.[48]

THE NAMING OF SCRIPTS

The description of a script is a tricky business. Because scripts change, or evolve, or develop, the words applied to them become slippery; and as palaeographers look for better ways of description, terminologies shift and elaborate. Some very general terms do remain in constant use as essential tools, and their meaning is too often taken for granted. First of all, there are two terms that were taken over into specialized use for handwriting in the early part of the eighteenth century (1710-30), the contrasting terms minuscule and majuscule. Minuscule, a term that could almost be rendered 'lower case' alphabet, is particularly appropriate as a description of italic scripts, whereas majuscule, typically used of capitals, is often thought of as an 'upper case' alphabet.

Ideally, majuscule scripts fit tidily between two horizontal parallel lines, but, if written cursively, the letter-forms of majuscule scripts are likely to have strokes that protrude above (ascenders) or below (descenders) the main body of the script. That is why such examples can be somewhat confusingly described as contained by four lines and contrasted with other instances of 'two-line' majuscule script. It is important to remember that the terms minuscule and majuscule are used in relation to whole alphabets and that, because of their use in defining alphabets, they are also used of individual letters.

38 Page 1993.

39 Tite 1994. For an overview of the restoration of Cotton manuscripts damaged in the 1731 fire at Ashburnham House see Prescott 1997.

40 Wright 1951; Graham 1997².

41 Graham 2000¹; see Graham and Watson 1998 for interesting insights into manuscript ownership in the 1560s.

42 Wright 1958²: 179-90.

43 See Evans 1956.

44 Black 1936: 29.

45 The manuscripts, maps, and book departments were consolidated as the British Library within the Museum in 1973; the new British Library building in Euston Road opened in 1997.

46 Ker 1942-43²; rpt. Watson 1985: 460.

47 This is best approached through Tite 1984.

48 See http://www.palaeography.ac.uk for RSLP Palaeography – Developing the National Resource Project and the Humbul Humanities catalogue http://www.humbul.ac.uk/mss/ for websites related to manuscript studies.

A second pair of contrasting terms is also invaluable for descriptive purposes: cursive and set. A cursive script is written easily and quickly, and it is informal because rapidly produced, with letter-forms made with relatively few strokes. Documentary scripts are often cursive, as for example the *littera documentaria* of the later middles ages (Anglo-Saxon England did not have a separate script for documents). Set scripts are more slowly and deliberately written. Each letter can be made of many strokes, involving much pen-lifting. Set script is essentially formal, and it is usually a book script. For it the later Middle Ages used the term *littera textualis*.[49] Thirdly, a single term, ductus, is used of all aspects of the actual writing of letter-forms. The ductus is not just a matter of the pen-angle and direction and tilt of script, but also of the number of strokes and of the order in which the strokes are made. By angle is meant the angle against the base line of the script: in writing, the pen is rarely held straight, and a change in angle can bring about developments. For example, slanting the pen may mean that feet are more easily produced.

These general terms are widely used and understood. That the terminology now in use for the close description of particular scripts is by no means standardized will be evident from the explanatory sections which serve to alert readers to major changes that lie ahead. The attempt is made to introduce each new major script type as influences from it begin to be glimpsed in the way English is written. In these accounts of particular script types, some reference to alternate and competing terms is inevitable, whether in the synopses themselves or in the discussions that accompany the plates. Here, by way of generalization, it is useful to consider briefly how scripts relate to one another and how they change. Scripts may shift position in hierarchies that are related to function: so, copies of the psalter or the gospels are typically in formal scripts, whereas romances tend to be more cursively written. Or a calligraphically 'good' script can go 'heavy' or 'degenerate', for all good scripts sooner or later suffer progressive elaboration. Again, new scripts may be promoted from 'below', moving from lowly functions to more important contexts. In such movement from below, a script may be purified, shedding cursive features. Late in the eighth century that is what happened with Caroline minuscule in the Carolingian *renovatio*, when a cursive script was 'purified', losing whorls and elaborate strokes. Perhaps 'simplified' provides a less emotive description of the changes involved, for there is something contradictory about the term purified in relation to a script that not only cleaned up the shapes of its letters but also, for aesthetic reasons, adopted some letter-forms from another script (in this case, from Half-uncial). In its turn Caroline minuscule was, by the late twelfth century, becoming elaborate, on the way to transmuting imperceptibly into its Gothic phase, but so gradually that not all palaeographers see the need for Protogothic as a general term. By the middle of the fourteenth century the resultant Gothic script was heavy and ponderous, and late in that century Petrarch was moving towards a simpler script, which marks the beginning of the humanistic scripts of the Renaissance.

Striking changes in the scripts of medieval Europe are therefore associated with these two important renewals of learning, with the Caroline *renovatio* of Charlemagne's empire and with the humanist renaissance in the city states of late-fourteenth- and early-fifteenth-century Italy. The resulting scripts were very influential, and to a great extent they superseded and outlasted the scripts with which they were in competition. Too often, however, it is not possible to make a clear-cut differentiation between scripts. The mix, in relation to the descriptive terms in use, may be an unconscious inheritance, especially where the hand is informal. The interpenetration of letter-forms diagnostic for particular scripts can, in later manuscripts, be so thorough, for example in academic books, as to point to the emergence of university book hands that respond uneasily to attempts to typify them as predominately Anglicana or Secretary.[50] In this book, to help readers develop their own assessment of the difficulties involved, the attempt is made to discuss all samples in relation to a script type, even when choice is difficult and the overall categorization 'Mixed hand' is advanced.

ORGANIZATION

The contents list is the book's main index. After the more general introductory materials, the succession of plates is interrupted by explanatory sections, which describe major phases within the development of scripts used for writing English across eight centuries. Each explanatory section introduces the main features distinctive of a particular script type, indicating their place within the history of script. The groups of plates, ordered for the most part according to approximate date of the main-text hand, can be seen therefore as illustrating variety and change across time.

Each plate is accompanied by transcription and commentary, where details more appropriate to the plates themselves are presented. Three headings are given above the transcription: first, the manuscript's location and pressmark, with the number of the folio illustrated (or page number, if the manuscript is paginated); next, the author and text or some other

[49] The term is discussed by Lieftinck 1954.

[50] See Parkes ([1979] 1969): xxiv for discussion of 'a blend of Anglicana and Secretary which resulted in what was virtually a new kind of book hand'.

identification of the contents of the page; third, a summary script description with date. Below the transcription there follow brief notes, on script, orthographic features, punctuation, and layout, and the abbrevations used. Summary indications of origin and provenance and of page size are also provided, together with introductory bibliography. As far as possible, the illustrations are of whole pages, to allow readers to gain some insight into the entering of text on the page (or the *mise-en-page*). Eight coloured plates are included in a special section between pages 12 and 13, duplicating black-and-white reproductions in the body of the book, to allow readers to gain a fuller idea of the contrasts achieved in manuscript layout and decoration than can be gained from black-and-white reproductions. In addition, some forty supplementary plates are interspersed among the sequence of main plates (see Index of other manuscript pages reproduced, p. 294). Some illustrate or complement aspects of the manuscripts discussed in the main run of plates; others open up issues that readers may wish to explore for themselves.

Indexes at the back of the book serve to draw together some of the discrete information to be found facing the plates. Here will be found an index of the manuscript pages discussed, an index identifying people (principally users and owners in the first centuries following the dissolution of the monasteries) mentioned in the commentaries, an index identifying people and places named in the plates, and a list of references.

A NOTE ON THE TRANSCRIPTIONS

The transcriptions present, as far as is practicable, the letter-shapes, punctuation and layout of the manuscript pages reproduced. Every attempt is made to avoid editorial interference. Yet, because it is incumbent on any transcriber to understand the text as it is read, no attempt is made to reproduce the spaces (or indeed lack of spaces) between words or parts of words. Instead the word divisions that might be expected in a modern critical edition are presented, and ⟨-⟩ is used at line endings where necessary to identify divided words. As far as possible, capitals and other distinctive letter-forms are represented in the transcription, with attention drawn to further significant features in the commentaries.

With a language that is unsettled in its writing system there can be no overall consistency in transcribing its letter-forms. Although the earliest missionaries and teachers of Anglo-Saxon England brought with them long-accustomed ways of writing Latin, the vowel and consonant symbols of their alphabet did not supply obvious counterparts for two English consonants. The Anglo-Saxons had at first to make shifts to indicate the sounds 'th' and 'w' from among the characters available in the alphabet used for writing Latin, for example **d** with a stroke through its ascender (**ð** 'eth') or sometimes **th** for the former, and **u** or **u(u)** ('double **u**') for the latter. As more settled ways of writing English emerged they also incorporated two of the letter-forms they had brought with them from the Continent, that is two of the angular letters or 'runes' they used for making inscriptions on hard surfaces such as wood and stone, into the inventory of letter-forms taken over from Latin: **þ** ('thorn', then as now an English word for the thorn bush and for its prickly thorns) and **ƿ** ('wyn', a word with the meaning joy or happiness).[51] Most editors of Old English texts use **w** for **ƿ**, and, although it is argued that **ƿ** should be used in palaeographical transcriptions,[52] because the aim is to ease understanding of the text, in this book **w** is generally substituted. With the falling away of Anglo-Saxon conventions for writing English, **u(u)** came back into use, together with the pointed letter-forms of the **v(v)** sequence, often ligatured, and sometimes alongside **ƿ**. Similarly, **th** reappears, at first in competition with **þ** but eventually succeeding it. Such changes require discussion, whether according to period or to text, and attention will be drawn to them in the descriptions that accompany the transcriptions.

Letter-forms often have more than one function, as, for example, is the case with **g** in most of the early plates (for example, in pl. 18 'god' (l. 25) is 'God' and 'gearu(m)' (l. 20) is a plural form of *year*, but the initial letter is the same in both words). As is usual now in representing Old English, **g** is used in the facing transcriptions for the Insular letter-form **ᵹ**, and only once two competing letter-forms are in use for separate sounds does it become appropriate to distinguish them in the transcriptions. So in pl. 19, where we see a scribe attempting to keep apart the letter-forms distinctive of the Insular and Caroline scripts, using Insular letter-forms for the English version of the Benedictine Rule and Caroline letter-forms for Latin, one shape only, **g**, will appear in the transcriptions, and the commentary will point to failures on the part of the scribe to keep the two sets of letter-forms apart. Where, however, separate letter-forms begin more or less consistently to indicate different sounds, it becomes important to reflect such changes in the transcriptions. For example, the inventory of letter-forms in pl. 29 is derived from Caroline minuscule, but in addition to the normal Caroline **g** the scribe draws on a

[51] So too the Ostrogoths of Italy had used some runes, including these, in vernacular subscriptions to charters, and Gregory of Tours records that thorn and wyn were two of the runes that Chilperic I introduced into Merovingian scripts. See Chaplais [1969] 1973: 96 fn. 58. Good accounts of English runes and their use are to be found in Derolez 1954, Elliott 1989 [1959], and Page 1973. See also Parsons 1994.

[52] Rumble 1994: 42; but see also Gneuss 1994 (rpt. of 1973): 17.

descendant of the Insular letter-form to indicate the final sound of 'weiȝ' (or *way*, l. 1). This descendant of the Insular **g** is generally called 'yogh'.[53] It has virtually disappeared from modern English, for few people sound its last survivals, the **z** of some proper names (like Menzies or Dalziell) and of some Scottish place names (for example, Culzean) in the traditional way.[54] Although the rounded shape **u** and the pointed **v** are mere positional variants in some alphabets, these are kept apart in the transcriptions, because in English they can mark meaningful distinctions between sounds. Conversely, where the **y** shape is used both as a vowel and for the older **þ**, these are not given separate letter-forms in the transcriptions (see pls 51-54). To do so would be a matter of editorial interference; but to help readers the **y** is italicized where we might expect **th**. It is important for the writing of English to recognise where **y** carries these two very different functions and how eventually even the residual understanding of **y** accompanied by superscript **e** (y^e for *the*) is lost.[55] These are matters of spelling, and as far as possible they are reflected in transcriptions.

At any one time there may be two or more competing shapes in use for particular letters. So far as meaning is concerned it matters little whether a long **s** is used initially and a round **s** finally, just as long as the reader recognizes these different letter-forms as **s**. This distribution of the different shapes of **s** is still familiar from early printed books. Such positional variants may sometimes have been chosen on calligraphic grounds, the taller form at the beginning of a word and the shorter at the end: for some scribes it mattered that a tall letter should lead a string of letters and that it should not poke its head above the line of script at a later point. A scribe's care in choice can say a lot about his attitude to the task in hand, and may be discussed in the commentaries. Positionally determined choices can help in dating hands: the round **r** is, for example, at first restricted to use after **o**, but later it appears after other bowed letters or more generally (see pl. 30, where the round **r** appears after **b**, **p** and even **þ** as well as after **o**, at a time when the use of round **r** is being generalized). Sometimes a sporadically-used letter-form may seem to be an intruder from some other alphabet than the prevailing norm. Thus, Anglo-Saxon square minuscule may draw on Half-uncial features, for example the 'oc' form of **a** (as pl. 11, 'womma' l. 21) or round **s** (pl. 12, 'acennednysse' l. 3), perhaps chosen as an index of greater formality, perhaps carried over from an exemplar or from earlier writing practices. Or the minims of English Caroline minuscule take on the little feet found in contemporary Anglo-Saxon minuscule. Or Secretary hands may adopt the cursive Anglicana **s** as a saving in time (as commonly at the ends of words in the second hand of pl. 55, ll. 9, 10, 14, etc.). Very often the mix is an unconscious inheritance, especially where the hand is informal. Letter-forms, where they are diagnostic for distinguishing between scripts, are identified according to parent scripts in the descriptions, but they are not distinguished in the transcriptions.

As far as possible, each line of script is given a separate line in the transcriptions; otherwise a new line is indicated by means of a vertical stroke. Abbreviations are normally expanded within round brackets, except for the customary symbols & (the ampersand) and ⁊ (the Tironian sign) for both Latin *et* and English *and*. Although by longstanding convention when Latin is transcribed, expansions are usually made silently (i.e. without italics or brackets), in these transcriptions brackets are used, to help acclimatize readers to the system. Most marks of abbreviation have generally accepted values in Latin, where the orthography is relatively stable, but in English an accommodation may be made between the expansion that might be expected in Latin and the norms of spelling of the English text itself. Sometimes there are strokes that cannot easily be understood. This is particularly the case in post-Conquest texts, where unidentifiable pen-strokes can be ambiguous, seeming to some readers a mark of abbreviation, to others mere flourishing of the pen. If no expansion is offered a straight apostrophe is used (the transcript facing pl. 51 has a rash of such apostrophes). Other possibly otiose strokes are discussed according to the difficulties of interpretation presented by a particular text.[56]

A NOTE ON ABBREVIATIONS

When writing English, scribes automatically drew on the repertoire of abbreviations customarily used in writing Latin. This note begins therefore with a few generalizations about the use of abbreviations in Latin manuscripts. First, it is well said: the more solemn the text, the fewer the abbreviations. How far a scribe uses abbreviations, and what sorts of abbreviations, depends on his attitude to the task in hand. Thus, a great bible or psalter may have little or no abbreviation apart from the special forms of the *nomina sacra* or 'sacred names' developed for displaying some twelve or fifteen sacred concepts. The *nomina sacra* carry a huge symbolic value. With them, it is not a matter of saving space or time. So, in pl. 2a, from the Vespasian Psalter, the only words abbreviated by the main hand are forms of *dominus*, *deus*, *sanctus*, and *noster*.

[53] Some such name, variously spelled, was in use in the thirteenth and fourteenth centuries; see *OED* under *yogh*.

[54] i.e. pronounced not as 'zed' or 'zee', but rather like the first sound of *year*.

[55] Few today, as they read out such notices as 'ye olde tea shoppe', begin with 'the'.

[56] Dahood 2000 draws attention to a distinction between final -*r* and final looped -*r* in Southwell Minster, Nottinghamshire, MS 7.

Given that Latin was to remain the language of the liturgy in England through to the Reformation, this is not a convention that feeds over into vernacular manuscripts. On occasion, however, some particular book is given an exceptionally formal treatment, as is the case with the Corpus *Troilus and Criseyde* (pl. 43), where the page illustrated has only two abbreviations, one of them probably made automatically and by mistake and meant to be erased, for the letter it signifies is also written and not needed twice. In the transcriptions that accompany plates, round brackets mark the expansion of abbreviations. Two signs are not expanded: the Tironian sign ⁊ used in Latin for *et* and therefore in English for forms representing *and*; and the ampersand &, in origin a ligature of Latin *et*; and there are two practical reasons why I have not done so. First, in Latin it is a simple enough matter to substitute *et*, but in English there are difficulties of choice, not just between *ond* or *and* but sometimes among a range of forms, for example *on* and *ant*, as well. Second, I have tried as far as possible to replicate in the transcriptions the lineation of the originals, and the substitution of letters in brackets for ⁊ and & would, at the same time as removing from the page a reminder of just which sign was in use, often lengthen lines inconveniently. Otherwise, a straight apostrophe is used in cases of uncertainty where no expansion of a mark of abbreviation is offered.

Some sense of how the methods of abbreviation operate can be gained by looking through six plates in particular. In two of these the main text is Latin, pl. 1 (the St Petersburg Bede) and pl. 20 (Ælfric's *Colloquy*), and in a third, pl. 19, the Latin of the Benedictine Rule alternates, chapter by chapter, with an English version. Two plates from early in the fifteenth century supply Latin apparatus for English texts: the Ellesmere *Canterbury Tales* (pl. 42) and the Harley 674 *Cloud of Unknowing* (pl. 46). And a significant amount of Latin is to be found in the twelfth-century explanatory notes added to explain the story of Abraham and Isaac (pl. 17). These are by no means the only examples of Latin to be found in the plates in this collection, for it seems that Latin can crop up virtually anywhere, in words and phrases, in citations from the Bible or specifying sources, in titles or appeals to an audience; and all such instances provide the corpus from which as far as possible my examples of abbreviations in Latin are taken. Because abbreviated words are used often in glossing texts, Latin glosses also furnish good examples, as, for example in pl. 24, which has shakily written glosses ascribed to the early-thirteenth-century scribe known as the 'Tremulous Hand' scribe. It must be stressed that the selection of examples is made to help in the reading of English.

Abbreviation involves omission, to save space and/or time. Latin orthography was, except for the seventh and eighth centuries, generally stable, which meant that the reader could tolerate accustomed methods of abbreviation with little difficulty, but early vernacular texts, because of the relative instability of their orthography, tend not to use many abbreviations; some examples are noted in the second columns of the following two tables. Words may include more than one form of abbreviation, as in 'Cont(r)arior(um)', pl. 31, l. 21a, though this is less likely to be the case in vernacular texts. It is customary to use the term contraction of omission from the middle of words and suspension of omission at the end. Many abbreviations depend on the omission of a single letter (table 1).[57]

Standard ways of marking the omission of whole syllables are also frequent (table 2). These are the sorts of abbreviations that occur most often in English in the plates in this book. In Old English the most frequent suspension is of the dative plural. Pl. 15, for example, has 'oþru(m)', l. 3a, 'dunu(m)', l. 5a, 'heardu(m)', l. 5a, 'stowu(m)', l. 5a, 'mædu(m)', l. 6a, 'beganu(m)', l. 6a, 'sandigu(m)', l. 7a, in its brief first column, but one spelled-out form 'landun', l. 7a, shows how dangerous it would be to expand these forms silently, and the curious 'drenceo(m)', l. 7, in its second column gives further grounds for retention of brackets. Separate endings for the dative had more or less vanished, together with grammatical gender, by the later twelfth century, so that in Middle English the possessive and plural endings of the noun are, apart from final -*e*, the inflexions most frequently abbreviated. Thus, ꝭ is expanded as -*es* in pl. 40 ('kyng(es)', l. 2, 'moder(es)', l. 5, 'god(es)', l. 10, 'legg(es)', l. 17, 'spor(es)', l. 18), but -*ys* in pl. 57 ('knyt(ys)', l. 5), where other norms obtain. The markers of abbreviation take their values from their use in Latin, and the scribes depend on their use in Latin. How far we bend them in the expansions we make in English texts is open to question.

The settled orthography of Latin allowed also for the use of quite a number both of variable and invariable words. Common invariable words found in the Latin in the plates include: 'q(uo)d' 17:2g, 20:4 (used as English in 41:3, 5 and 56:9, 22, 26), 'u(er)o' 17:8g, '(ve)l' 26:21, '*Incip(it)*' 32 (title), 'no(t)a' 45 (margin), '(et) c(eter)a' 31:17b, '(et) c(etera)' 42:7g, 9g, 17g, 'M(emoran)d(um)' 42:35g, 'ca(pitul)o' 42:36g, '(er)go' 42:39g, 's(i)c' 46:16g, 'Sic(ut)' 17:6g, 'q(u)a(s)i' 46:27g, 28g. Some of these are adopted by English. A group of invariables in which : or ; or ʒ serve to mark abbreviation should be noted: 'Atq(ue)' 20:3, 'atq(ue)' 26:8, 42:41g, 'quoq(ue)' 42:25g, 31g, 'n(eque)' 46:22g. In contrast, English has few invariable words. During the period in which late West Saxon was fairly stable, *þ(æt)* and *þon(ne)* seem to have been invariable, the one using the stroke of abbreviation though its ascender, the other showing suspension by the overline

57 In these two tables and in the discussion that follows them, plate numbers stand before the colon, and line numbers after. Note also: a and b (to indicate columns), and g (form in gloss).

Table 1: letter abbreviations

signalled principally by an overline making m *or* n: die(m) 17:8g, disru(m)pa(n)t 46:26g, i(n) 17:2g	y(m)b 8:14, co(m) 18:8, la(m)masse 23:20, geswu(n)gen 20:10g, ge(n)til 40:13
or, when over g, *making* e:	g(e)feran 8:17, cyning(e) 8:17
by a stroke through an ascender indicating a vowel omitted: capit(u)lo 46:14g	ħ(e) 8:17, cwanȝ(e)liste 30:4, fressh(e) 48:4, all(e) 55:5
by a stroke or flourish, esp. after r *or* m, *making* e	cum(e) 23:24, mor(e) 41:11

Table 2: syllable abbreviations

by superscript vowel for r *to be included*: p(r)imo 42:45g; cont(r)a 42:45g, lib(r)o 50:20	p(r)ior 23:5, g(r)ene 32:18a, c(r)ist 34:21, g(r)ases 36:36b
or u *after* q: q(u)e 17:3g; loq(u)i 46:27g *or* u *after* g: ling(u)am 31:14a	q(u)antite 38:28
overline over t *or* c *making* i (*plus later* n *in syllable if needed*):	pos|sess(i)ou(n) 46:15, sauac(i)ou(n) 50:1
by special signs: 9 (con):	(con)clusiou(n)s 38:4, (con)tene 38:6, (com)pas 38:17
ʼ (er/re *or other vowel with* r): u(er)bo 31:17b	æft(er) 8:10, mynst(re) 23:12, lau(er)d 30:7, oþ(er)eȝ 37:18, bet(er)e 41:23. *The marker may go through an ascender as in* s(ir) 37:7
p *with* ʼ *or overline above* (pre)	p(re)chi(n)g 39:7b, p(re)yȝede 41:18
ꝑ (per): p(er)fecta 19:3 (*may also unpack as* -er-, -or-, *or* -ur-)	p(er)chit 40:20, p(er)petuel 38:22, p(ur)posed 46:24, p(er)sone 48:6, p(ar)ty 55:2
ꝓ (pro): p(ro) 20:10	p(ro)perty 37:14, p(ro)ces 38:21, p(ro)fete 39:44a, p(ro)phete 50:29
ꝭ (-es *etc.*)	kyng(es) 40:2, beest(es) 50:23, among(is) 52:5, Berd(ys) 57:6
^{2} (ur)[58]	co(ur)t 37:13, flo(ur) 40:6, bet(ur) 41:4, creatu(ur) 57:22
ꝰ (us): loc(us) 17:4g, scim(us) 20:10	Prothesela(us) 42:26, cheualro(us) 51:29, syr(us) 57:3, Cyr(us) 57:10
-:, ȝ, *or* ⁊: *in* -bus: fratrib(us) 20:13; praecib(us) 18.1	weorþ(us)te 8:15

(usually called the 'common mark of abbreviation', an overline is the commonest mark of abbreviation). But *þon(ne)* appears in many forms (it may, for example, begin with ð or Ð, or *-on-* may be spelled *-an-*) before the eventual emergence of today's 'then' and 'than'. In time *þæt* gives way to other spellings (*þet, þat*). And understanding of even the abbreviation ꝥ changes:[59] the commonest function of a line through an ascender could lead to its re-interpretation as *þ(e)*. At Peterborough in the middle of the twelfth century the Second Continuator of the Chronicle (pl. 23) uses ð instead of ꝥ (he had little need of ð as a letter symbol, for he was using **th** as well as **þ**).[60] Before **þ** disappears from the inventory of letter-forms used for writing English, it serves as the base for new near-abbreviations such as **þ**^{e} (and later **y**^{e}) for 'the',

[58] A Carolingian monastic invention *c.* 820 at Tours, its use reaches England by the middle of the ninth century (Lindsay 1915: 373, 378-39).

[59] McIntosh 1947-48.

[60] Interestingly, an alphabet in London, British Library, Stowe MS 57, f. 3v, from the Peterborough area in the second half of the twelfth century, ends 'Anglicę litterę Ƿ wen Ð ðet Þ þorn ⁊ ⁊ and'. Robinson 1973 argues that ð had 'that' as its English name, but the coincidence suggests a local development.

widely understood as late as the eighteenth century. The case for regarding **w**[t] as an abbreviation for an invariable 'with' is best beyond the middle ages, when English orthography has settled.

Variable words using either the overline or a line through an ascender include: 'ang(e)l(u)s' 29:25, 'ec(c)lesie' 46:1g, 'lib(r)i' 42:41g, 'n(ome)n' 17:1g, 'no(m)i(n)e' 46:11g, 'N(OSTR)I' 2a:11, 'N(OSTR)O' 2a:14, 'om(n)i' 20:13, 31:16b, 'om(n)es' 42:36g, 'u(est)ri' 46:8g, 's(an)c(tu)s' 50:11, 's(an)c(t)ae' 18:2, 's(an)c(tu)m' 46:21g, 'sp(iritu)s' 46:11g, 'sp(irit)u' 46:27g and with *c* for *s* in 'sp(iritu)s', 46:7g. The abbreviations used for the sacred name Jesus Christ make use of Greek letters, as can be seen in the opening words of the upper inscription 'ie(s)v cr(ist)i' of pl. 3. There the **h** stands for **H** or *eta* and is transliterated as *e*; only in the thirteenth to fifteenth centuries do *ihesus* forms alternate with *iesus*. The *rho* or **x** is transliterated as *r* and no -*h*- need be supplied.[61] Old English, also an inflected language, developed no analogous abbreviations of its own, except in loanwords: for example, *sanct* is often contracted ('s(an)c(t)e' 18:8, 12, 21:16), and *abbod* (see 21:2) can follow the abbreviation pattern of its source language. By the Middle English period the former has given way to *S'* for *seint*, *saint*, *seynt*, etc. (a possible expansion rejected for 'S(ancte)' 23:1, 18, 19, 25), and *abb* with a line through the ascenders makes *abbot* ('abb(ot)rice' 23:17, 18).

Throughout the medieval period most scribes knew and understood the abbreviations usual for Latin, and they transferred to English some of the commonest and best-known abbreviations. There were circumstances in which they went beyond the customary small number of conventional signs normally used for writing the vernacular. In glossing, words could be cut unusually short, as in pl. 2a ('dryht(ne)' 2a:2g, 'dryht(en)' 2a:3g). Or they felt little need always to finish well-known place-names or proper names, for example in pl. 23 'linc(olne)', l. 13, 'norm(andi)', l. 25, 'englel(and)', l. 27, and 'H(enri)', l. 20.[62] At any point, a scribe could choose a capricious abbreviation, like *b'* for *b(iscop)*, *b(yscop)*, etc., as at 23:13, or 'IER:' for 'IER(ominus)', 17.1g. Words may be suspended radically in titles (see 'mortal(ibus)' in the added title in pl. 50). Abbreviation was used for many reasons: to save time; to avoid word division at the end of the line; to justify lines; to give emphasis to particular words. These introductory remarks introduce only the commonest abbreviations that are likely to be encountered when reading Old and Middle English. Specialized dictionaries that should be consulted when in difficulty include Cappelli 1929;[63] Martin 1910; Lindsay 1915; and see Bischoff 1990 [1979] and M.P. Brown 1990 for introductions to abbreviations in western manuscripts.

[61] The -*h*- is needed only under humanist influence. See Chaplais 1987.

[62] This is probably a habit more of scribes accustomed to writing documents.

[63] Heimann and Kay 1982 provides an English translation of Capelli's 'Brachigrafia medioevale' (1929: xi-lxviii).

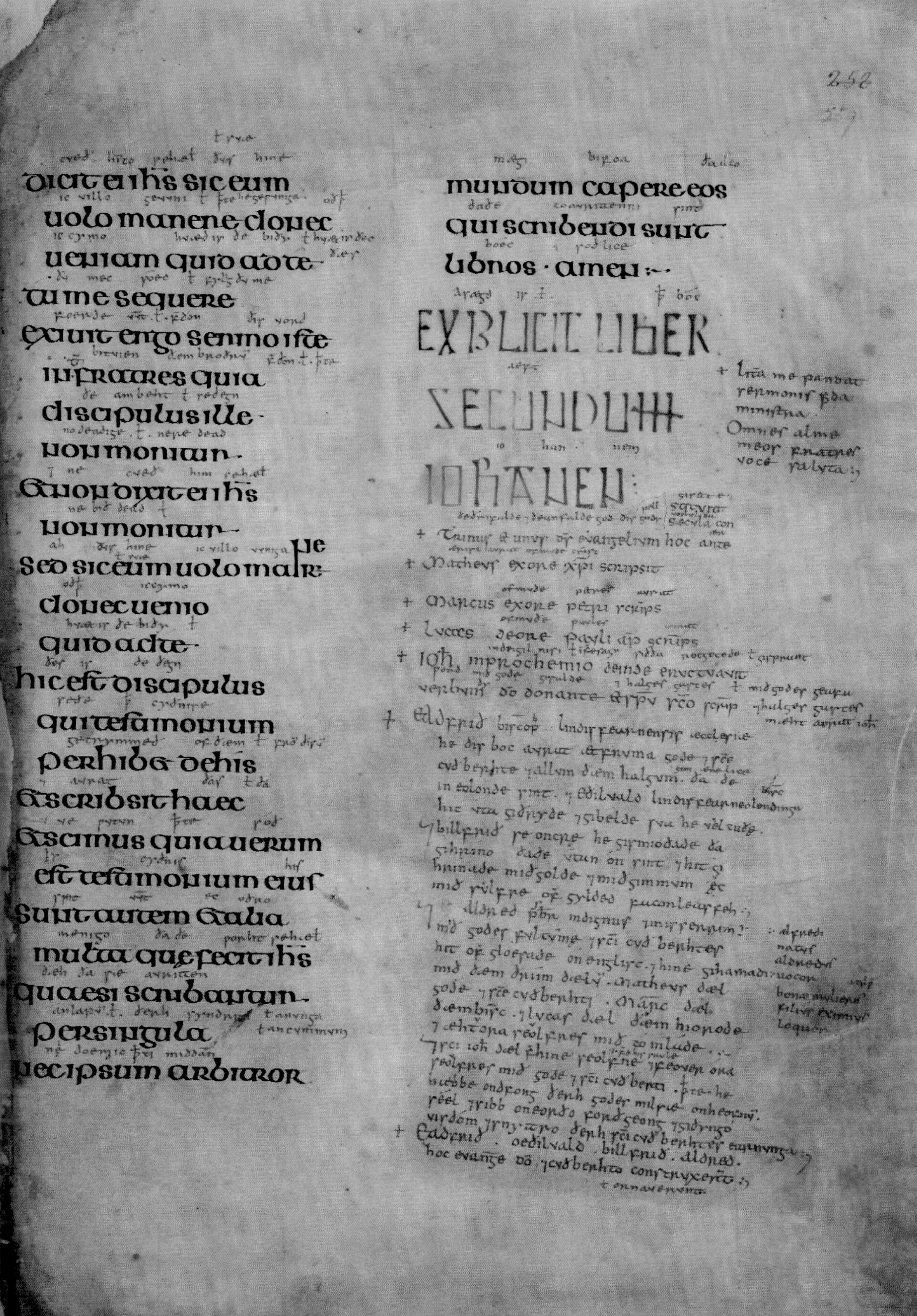

C1 (pl. 5). London, British Library, Cotton MS Nero D. iv, f. 259r
Lindisfarne Gospels, John 21: 22–25, with Aldred's additions
reduced to 68%

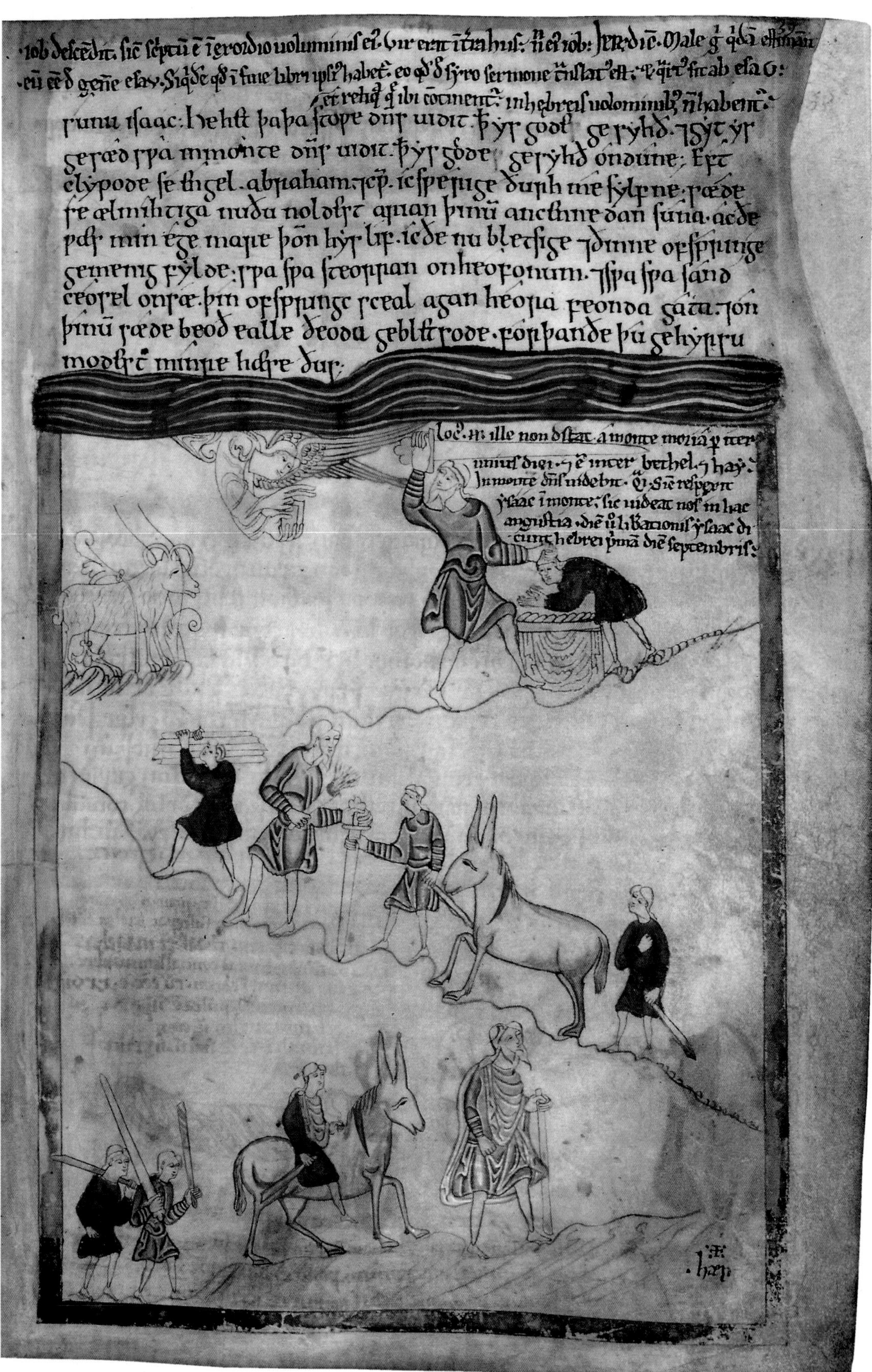

C2 (pl. 17). London, British Library, Cotton MS Claudius B. iv, f. 38r
Translation attributed to Ælfric, Genesis 22: 12–18
reduced to 76%

GLORIOSISSIMO REGI CEOLWULFO BEDA FAMULUS XPI ET PRB HISTORIAM GENTIS ANGLORUM ECCLESIASTICAM QUAM NUPER EDIDERAM LIBENTISSIME TIBI DESIDERANTI REX ET PRIUS AD LEGENDUM AC PROBANDUM TRANSMISI.

C3 (pl. 22). Cambridge, University Library, MS Kk. 3. 18, f. 8v
Old English version of Bede's *Historia Ecclesiastica*, opening of Book I
reduced to 72%

to herode ne hƿyrfden. ac hƿo on oþerne ƿeȝ
on hire riche ferden.
Apparuit angelus dn̄i in sompnis ioseph dicens.
accipe puerum & matrem eius.
Ða hƿo þa ferden þa ætefede drihtnes en
gel iosepe on sƿefne. ⁊ þus cƿæð. Aris ⁊
nym þæt child. ⁊ his moder ⁊ fleoȝ on egyp
te land ⁊ beo þær oð þæt ic þe segge. Toƿærd
is þæt herodes secð þæt child to forspillene.
he aras þa ⁊ nam þæt child ⁊ his moder on
niht. ⁊ ferde in to egypte. ⁊ ƿæs þær oððe hero
des forð sið. þæt ƿære ȝe fylled þæt þe fram
drihtne ȝe cƿeden ƿæs. þurh þanne ƿitegan. Of
egypte ich minne sune ȝe clypede. Ða ƿæs he
rodes sƿiðe ȝe bolȝen for þam þe he be fæht
ƿæs fram þam tungelƿitegan. ⁊ he asende þa. ⁊
of sloh ealle þa child þe on bethleem ƿæron. ⁊
on eallen hire ȝe mæren fram tƿiƿintren elde
⁊ binnæn þan æfter þare tyde þe he ȝe axode
fram þam tungelƿitegen. Ða ƿæs ȝe fylled þ ȝe
cƿeden ƿæs þurh ieremiā þam ƿitegan. Stefne
ƿæs on heahnysse ȝe hyrd. ƿop ⁊ michel ƿoþ
rung. rachel ƿeop hire bearn. ⁊ hye nolde be
on ȝe frefred. for þam þe hyo næren.
Defuncto autem herode ecce apparuit angl̄s

C4 (pl. 29). Oxford, Bodleian Library, MS Hatton 38, f. 80r
Gospels, Matthew 2: 12–18
actual size

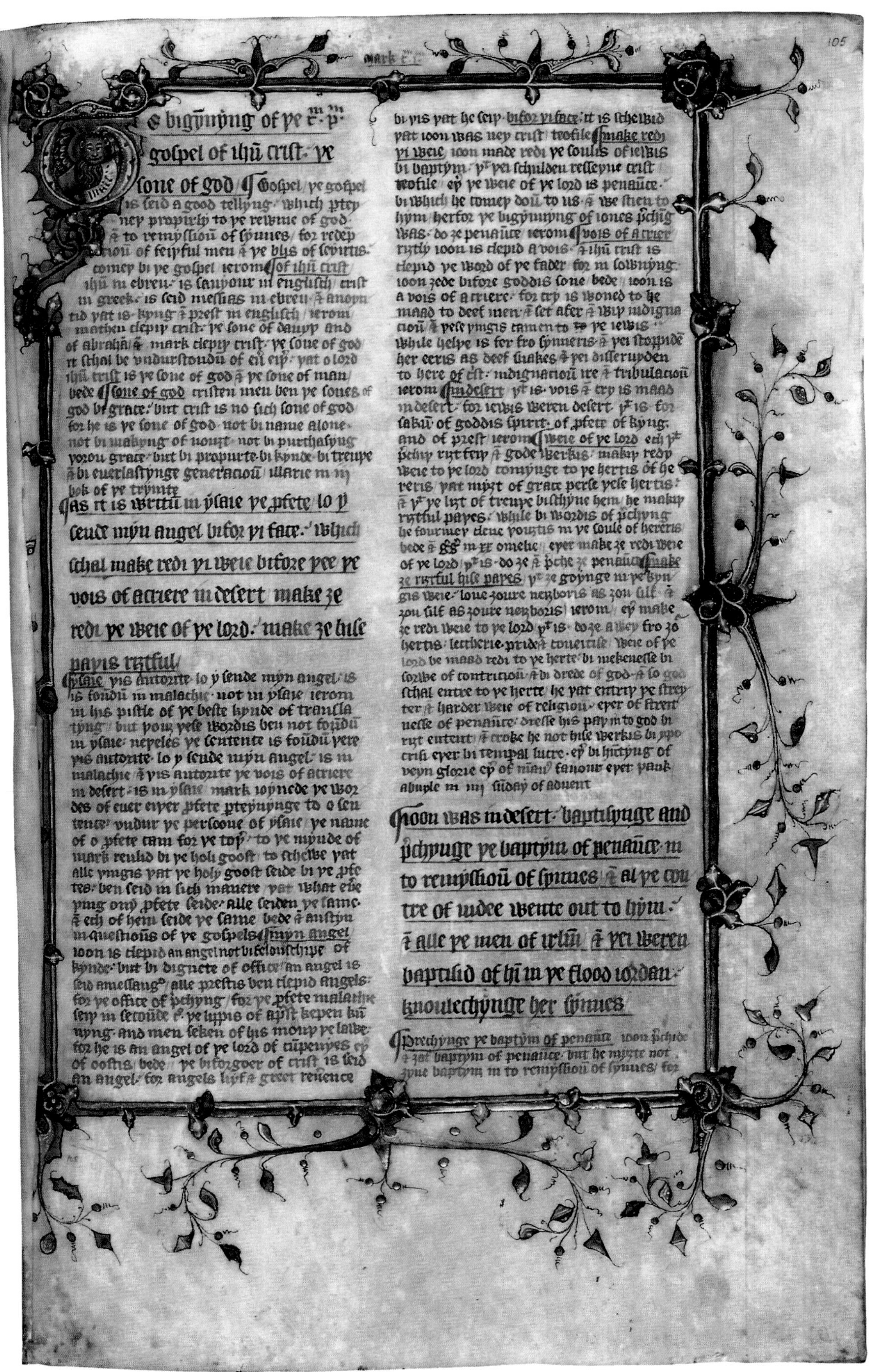

C5 (pl. 39). London, British Library, Additional MS 41175, f. 105r
Glossed Gospels, Mark with commentary, 1: 1-5
reduced to 62%

And ouer al this, full muchel more he thoughte
What for to speke & what to holden inne
And what to arten hym to loue he soghte
And on a song anon right to begynne
And gan loude on his sorwe for to wynne
For wt good hope he gan fullyche assente
Criseide for to loue and naught repente

And of his song nat only the sentence
As writ myn auctour called Lollius
But pleynly saue oure tonges difference
I dar wel sayn in al yt Troilus
Seyde in his song loo euery worde right thus
As I shal seyn and who so list it here
Lo next this verse ye may it fynden here

[illegible] The Songe of Troilus:

Yif no loue is o god what fele I so
And yif loue is/ what thing & which is he
Yif loue be good/ from whennes cometh my wo
Yif it be wikke a wonder thinketh me
Whenne euery torment & aduersite
That cometh of hym may to me sauory thinke
For ay thurst I the more yt ich it drynke

And yif yt at myn owne lust I brenne
From whennes cometh my waylynge & my pleynte
Yif harm agree me I wher to pleyne I thenne
I noot ne whi vnwery yt I feynte
O quyke deth o swete harm so queynte
How may of the in me be swich quantite
But yif that I consente yt it be

And yif yt I consente I wrongfully
Compleyne I wis thus possed to & fro
Al stereles wt inne a boot am I
Amydde the se betwixen wyndes two
That in contrarie stonden euere mo
Allas what is this wonder maladie
For hete of cold for cold of hete I dye

C6 (pl. 45). Cambridge, St John's College MS L. 1, f. 6v
Chaucer, *Troilus and Criseyde*, I. 386-420
reduced to 91%

C7 (pl. 46). London, British Library, Harley MS 674, f. 17v
The Cloud of Unknowing, with continuous marginal gloss in Latin
actual size

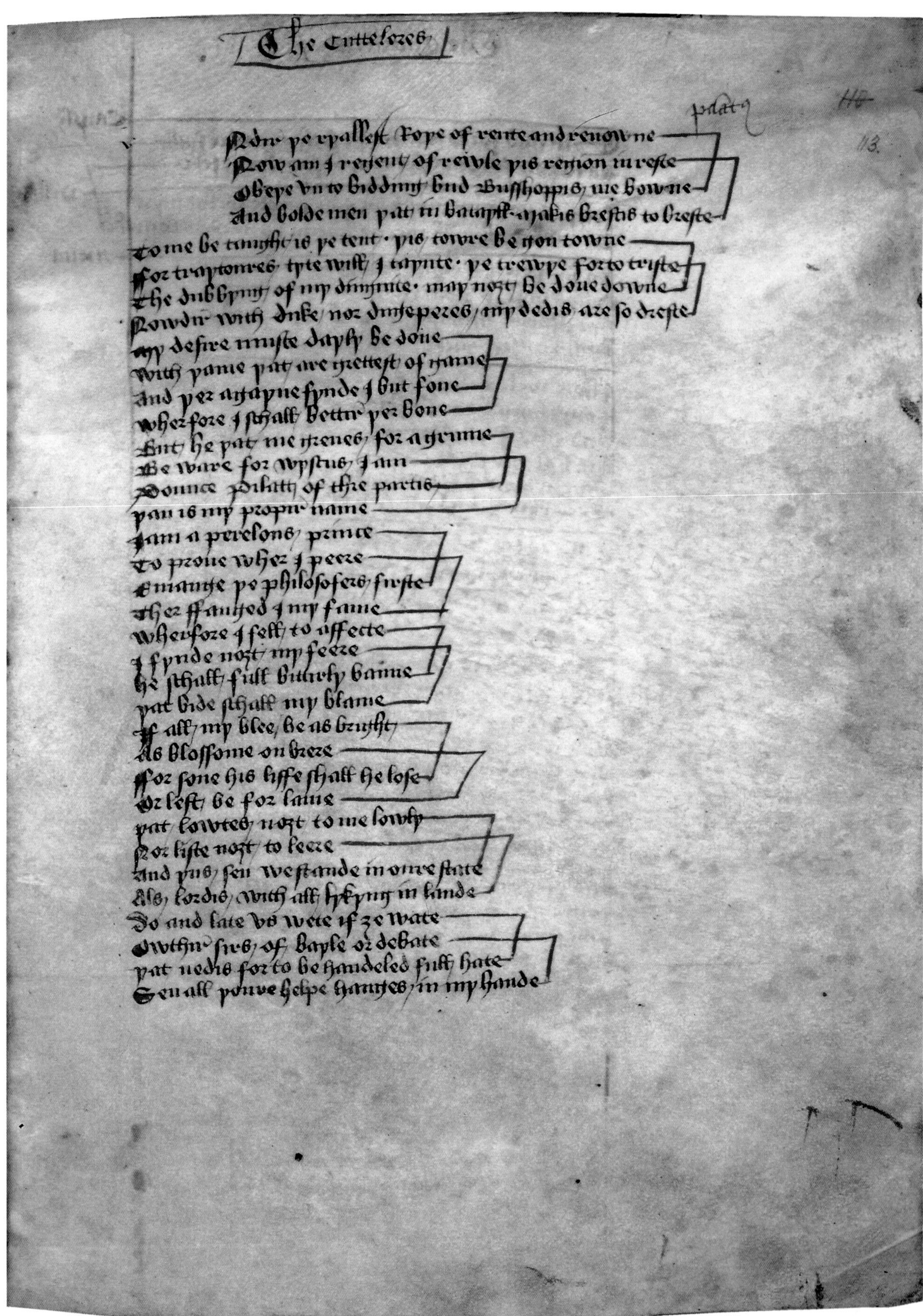

The Cutteleres

Pilatus

Vndir þe ryallest roye of rente and renowne
Now am I regent of rewle þis region in reste
Obeye vnto biddyng bud busshoppis me bowne
And bolde men þat in batayll makis brestis to breste
To me betaught is þe tent þis towre be gon towne
For traytoures tyte will I taynte þe trewþe for to triste
The dubbyng of my dingnite may noȝt be done downe
Nowdir with duke nor dugeperes my dedis are so dreste
My desire muste dayly be done
With þame þat are grettest of game
And þer agayne fynde I but fone
Wherfore I schall bettyr þer bone
But he þat me greues for a grume
Be ware for wyscus I am
Pownce Pilatt of þes partis
Þat is my propir name
I am a perelous prince
To proue wher I peere
Emange þe philosoferes firste
Ther frayned I my fame
Wherfore I fell to affecte
I fynde noȝt my feere
He schall full bitterly banne
Þat bide schall my blame
If all my blee be as bright
As blossome on brere
For sone his liffe shall he lose
Or left be for lame
Þat lowtes noȝt to me lowly
Nor liste noȝt to leere
And þus sen we stande in oure state
Als lordis with all lykyng in lande
Do and late vs wete if ȝe wate
Owthir sirs of bayle or debate
Þat nedis for to be handeled full hate
Sen all youre helpe hanges in my hande

113

C8 (pl. 53). London, British Library, Additional MS 35290, f. 113r
York Plays, 'The Cutteleres, "The Conspiracy"'
reduced to 81%

II Insular background

The traditional date for the coming of Christianity to Anglo-Saxon England is A.D. 597, the year in which St Augustine, sent by Pope Gregory, arrived in Kent. It must, however, be remembered that in northern Britain, among the Picts, the Irish monastic foundation of St Columba had been functioning on the island of Iona since 563. Both the Roman and the Irish missions influenced the development of learning among the English directly, whereas links with the churches and monasteries of the Britons seem to have been by far less important. Missionaries from Kent, led by St Paulinus, first took Christianity into Northumbria to the court of King Edwin in 627, but that mission failed when Edwin was defeated in 633 by Penda of Mercia. A couple of years later Oswald, who had grown up in exile 'in the faith as the Irish taught it',[1] seized Northumbria. Given his upbringing, Oswald sent to Iona for teachers, foremost among them St Aidan, rather than south to Kent. Thus, the Roman church, its influence fanning out from Canterbury, and the Columban church, through the work begun by Aidan of Lindisfarne, were both instrumental in the christianization of the English. The books brought by Augustine and his companions from the Roman world came from within the living tradition of the Roman system of scripts, whereas the books of Oswald's missionaries must have shared in divergent traditions that had developed in Britain and Ireland.

Overall, the Roman system of scripts extends from the reign of the Emperor Augustus (31 B.C.-A.D. 14) at least up to the time of Pope Gregory (died 604) and possibly into the eighth century. Literacy was widespread in the Roman world, and the production of manuscripts a professionalized activity. Square capitals, highly suitable for carving in stone (hence they are also called monumental capitals) but also painted on walls and used in ink on papyrus, were not really a book script. Although we see them as at the top of the Roman hierarchy of scripts and recognize their continuing importance as a part of display script (see pl. 3, and later, for example, pl. 11), few books were written entirely in square capitals. The narrower and more condensed capitals termed 'Rustic' served typically as the formal book script of the antique world, and they came also to be used on monuments. In the eighteenth century these more easily written, more fluid, narrow capitals were mistakenly considered a cheap version of square capitals, and early palaeographers began then to describe them as 'rustic'. Rustic capitals were not in use as a book script in medieval England: pl. 2b from the Vespasian Psalter is an archaizing attempt to reproduce the script as a book script rather than a book script in a living tradition. Like square capitals, rustic capitals play an important part in text layout, although this is more typically a feature of later Anglo-Saxon manuscripts (see, for example, pl. 18). Rustic capitals are not used in the Codex Aureus and they are not found in the other manuscripts closely related to the Vespasian Psalter,[2] despite their use for headings and prefaces in a number of Insular manuscripts. There was as well a third script in the older Roman system of scripts: 'Old Roman Cursive'. This informal script, again descended from capitals, was an everyday script, used for administrative documents, for writing notes, for scribbling on walls; when written more formally, it is dignified with the description 'Literary Cursive'.[3]

By the early fourth century the 'Old Roman system of scripts' had become part of what may, from this point, be termed the 'New Roman system of scripts'. A new formal bookscript, Uncial, appears in the Roman system of scripts from the fourth century, although its origins may lie as far back as the second century. Roman Uncial is a script employing full, rounded letters. Its history is obscure. Suspended between the Old Roman and New Roman systems, its emergence is ascribed to the influence both of Old Roman Cursive and of Greek Uncials. The letter-forms essentially represent a modification of square capitals, influenced by cursive scripts. It is a formal script in which curves have substituted for angles, a script for quill and membrane rather than chisel and stone or reed pen and papyrus. Despite having a few ascenders and descenders, it may be termed a majuscule script. Even its name, Uncial, gives rise to controversy. Some argue that at first the letters were an inch tall, or that they came twelve or sixteen to the column.[4] Uncial appears first in inscriptions in third-century north Africa, and it is found, fully developed, in late-fourth-century Rome, where it continued in use into the eighth century. This script was influential in the development of the Uncial script of the twin monasteries of Monkwearmouth and Jarrow. Under Abbot Ceolfrith (689-716) three Pandects (complete bibles) were made there, one for each of the houses and a third to be given to the pope. Ceolfrith died on his way to Rome with this third Pandect, and the manuscript, now known as the Codex Amiatinus, somehow ended up in Florence, where it is in the Biblioteca Medicea-Laurenziana. There are no Irish manuscripts written in Uncials, and palaeographers were for a long

[1] Bede III.1. See Colgrave and Mynors 1969: 213-14, 'ad doctrinam Scottorum cathecizati'.

[2] Wright and Campbell 1967: 60.

[3] See pls 1-4 in Brown, M.P. 1990.

[4] Jerome seems first to have used the phrase *litterae unciales*; for discussion of its meaning see Meyvaert 1983.

time unwilling to recognize the Codex Amiatinus as a Northumbrian manuscript, thinking so fine a hand must be Roman. The main text hand of pl. 2a (Vespasian Psalter) is an example of Uncial from eighth-century Kent.

Half-uncial can be regarded as a less formal version of Uncial. Written more rapidly and therefore with fewer strokes, Half-uncial was in use from the second century and it may have been influenced by New Roman Cursive in the early fourth century. In Half-uncial the ascenders and descenders became more visible, and loops developed as a time-saving device. In fifth- and sixth-century Rome Half-uncial was used as a book hand: Uncial was the more professional script, but Half-uncial was more usual as the script of the ecclesiastical scriptoria that began to appear in the sixth century. With the gradual disintegration of the Roman empire, local national hands developed, for the most part the inheritance of some admixture of New Roman Cursive and Half-uncial. Of particular importance to the history of scripts for the writing of English are the Insular letter-forms of the British Isles and, later, the Caroline letter-forms that succeeded and to some extent depended upon the administrative scripts of Merovingian Gaul. The term Quarter-uncial is sometimes used of markedly cursive Half-uncial hands: although invoked as a formative stage present in the emergence of the Insular system of scripts, Quarter-uncial does not seem particularly helpful as a script term.

An Insular system of scripts, ultimately descended from the Roman system, came into use in Britain in the early Anglo-Saxon period, where it continued in use up to *c.* 850. (The term 'Insular' is also used to contrast what is distinctive of the British Isles as opposed to what is pan-European. Thus Ireland has retained its distinctive Insular letter-forms at least for writing Irish Gaelic, whereas the descendants of Caroline minuscule are general elsewhere.) With the break-up of the Roman empire, the British Isles were more or less isolated from the old centres of tradition and learning. Although Ireland was never part of the Roman world, missionaries had already begun to work there, mainly from Britain but also from other parts of the sub-Roman world; and literacy did not vanish among the Britons. It seems that the foundational script for the distinctively Insular system of scripts was Half-uncial, the literary script of sixth-century churchmen. A Half-uncial script is used in the earliest piece of writing to survive from Ireland, verses from the psalms on a late-sixth-century set of wooden writing tablets preserved in marshland in County Antrim (the Springmount bog tablets, National Museum of Ireland).[5] In the first extant manuscripts, from the seventh century, two tendencies can be seen: a more formal script that even so looks untidy by comparison with Roman Half-uncial; and a cursive minuscule for everyday purposes. Among the more striking diagnostic criteria are the 'diminuendo' after initials (i.e. an opening sequence of letters that diminish gradually in size), decorative red dots, and a quite lavish use of wedges at the onset of strokes. This is the initial phase in the emergence of the Insular system. Aldred was still using the diminuendo at Chester-le-Street in the middle of the tenth century (see pl. 5, ll. A5b, A7b), where to the north of the Danelaw old practices seem to have lingered, although generally its use was disappearing from English manuscripts by the end of the ninth century (but see pl. 6, l. 1). The decorative use of red dots was adopted into the layout of the Vespasian Psalter (see pl. 2a). Insular Half-uncial at its peak (see pl. 5) is often and confusingly described as 'Insular majuscule', a description that recognizes its achievement more than its origins.[6]

Cursive Insular minuscule scripts can be seen as falling into three groups: Irish (the longest-lived of the group); Northumbrian Phase I or Type A; and Southumbrian Phase I or Type B. (An example of Southumbrian Insular minuscule can be found on p. 21.[7]) In England Phase I ends *c.* 700. Yet, certain abbreviations, distinctive of this group of Insular scripts, for example the Tironian sign ⁊ for *et* 'and', ÷ for *est* 'is', ⁹ for *con-* 'with', and ꝉ for *uel* 'or', feed back into more general use. Phase II emerges towards the end of the seventh century and lasts into the early ninth century, longer in the north. A full hierarchy of scripts is in use in this period, with as many as seven grades recognized.[8] At the bottom are the minuscule grades, all written with a slanted pen. In the least formal of these, the current minuscule, the pen is not lifted between minims: there are many links and ligatures, and the **a** is pointed. Next is cursive minuscule: again the pen is slanted, and it is not always lifted between minims (see pl. 1). Then comes set minuscule, with the pen lifted between minims, but it is so rare as an Insular script as not really to be an effective member of the seven grades. The most formal of the minuscules, Hybrid minuscule, is the main book script of this period: its letters are rounded, and noteworthy is the 'oc' shape for **a**, the form usual in Half-uncial (see the few words in Latin in pl. 4). Half-uncial, written with the pen held straight and very broad, is for much of the Insular script area the topmost book hand; it is the script of some of the greatest manuscripts of this age, for example the Lindisfarne Gospels (main text, pl. 5) and the Book of Kells. More formal again are the decorative grades: display Half-uncial and display capitals. At the very top of the system is English Uncial (main text, pl. 2a), a script that has been described as almost in a class on its own. Despite its small size (the letters are only 3.5 mm in height), the Uncial letter-forms of the Vespasian Psalter are painstakingly built up from careful well-spaced strokes, and the decorative detail is impressive; many strokes end in neatly formed triangular serifs. Uncial script continued

[5] See *CLA Supplement* 1972: no. 1684.

[6] See Doyle 1992: 17-18 for revealing discussion of conflicting applications of this term.

[7] Crick 1997: 70 tentatively identifies the hand as a 'Phase II script showing affinities with Type B'.

[8] Dumville 1999 gives the most substantial recent analysis of the system. See further Brown, M.P. 2004.

in use in Rome into the eighth century, with the latest examples late in that century. Books such as the Vespasian Psalter and the Codex Aureus show Anglo-Saxon England trying to emulate a great period of Roman book hands.

Illustrations are taken from five early manuscripts, a small and unrepresentative sampling of the range and beauty of the books produced in early Anglo-Saxon England. Behind all five manuscripts there lie two identifiable systems of script: the Roman system and the Insular system. Pride of place goes to the St Petersburg Bede (pl. 1), an early Northumbrian manuscript in the Insular tradition, because of its importance for the development of the minuscule script used in Anglo-Saxon England for the writing of English. It is an example of Phase II cursive minuscule as perfected in Monkwearmouth and Jarrow. With the Vespasian Psalter (pl. 2a) and the Codex Aureus (pl. 3), both very likely from Kent, the scribes looked to Roman books for models, whereas the Book of Cerne (pl. 4) shows Phase II minuscule in use in the Midlands. These five manuscripts are by far more important for their main texts in Latin than for the small amounts of English they happen to contain. Perhaps as an afterthought one of the scribes of the St Petersburg Bede (pl. 1) chose to add in the bottom margin the words of Cædmon's Hymn, incidentally therefore leaving evidence for northern English in the early eighth century. Bede did not himself think to cite these lines of poetry, instead summarizing their content in Latin narrative at the appropriate point in the story of Cædmon. From the point of view of the development of the English language, the small glosses later written between the lines of the Vespasian Psalter are an early witness to a more southerly form of English (pl. 2a); and the late-ninth-century Codex Aureus inscriptions in minuscule script (pl. 3), relating to ealdormann Alfred's donation, are sometimes described tentatively as from Surrey rather than Kent because Surrey is where Alfred had large landholdings.[9] So far as script is concerned, these hands, later than the main texts to which they have been added, are examples of the pointed minuscule found in mid-ninth-century Canterbury charters. Small scholarly minuscule probably didn't change much over a long period of time: the type well established in the ninth-century Vespasian Psalter gloss (pl. 2a) is not unlike that used by Aldred for glossing the Lindisfarne Gospels in the middle of the tenth century (pl. 5). As examples of the English language, however, the former the principal witness for Mercian and the latter a major Northumbrian text, both have characteristic non-West Saxon forms that require some discussion in relation to spelling, but this is kept as far as possible to a minimum. Given the primarily incidental nature of English in books extant from before the last decades of the ninth century, the fragmentary 'Exhortation to Prayer' of the Book of Cerne (Cambridge, University Library, Ll.1.10) on what must have been originally the second folio of the manuscript, is particularly interesting (pl. 4). The preceding folio is lost, and signs of wear and tear indicate that this folio, containing what remains of directions as to how to organize individual devotions, very likely written by the main hand,[10] served as the manuscript's outer cover for some time. One or two leaves were, however, often left blank at the beginning of a manuscript to function as protective fly-leaves and could receive later text.[11]

Many by far more beautiful pages might have been chosen from the Lindisfarne Gospels, but the final recto (pl. 5) contains Aldred's correlation of the four authors of the Gospels with the four makers of this newly glossed book.[12] (A reproduction of one of the most splendid pages in the Lindisfarne Gospels can be found on p. 17.) On this page, as in pl. 3, the later additions seem designed to frame the the original text. Indicative here too of the thought that went into lay-out is the careful hardpoint ruling set up for the additions, although it looks as if Aldred had more to say than he at first estimated. In an elaborate conceit Aldred supplies his own closure to the whole book, beginning formally in hybrid minuscule (he may have been aiming at Half-uncial) for four statements about the four evangelists, but above them cramming in a sentence on God as originator of the Gospels. These five sentences, set out with introductory crosses, are themselves glossed in English as if to complement his newly created 'main' text. The following passage in English, again presented in four parts, is also in his usual cursive minuscule, as befits the vernacular. Eadfrith's name, introducing the account of what Aldred knew of the manuscript's history, is given prominence by its alignment with the names of the Evangelists, by the introductory cross to the left, and by the gradation or 'diminuendo' from larger to smaller letters. A seventh cross stands before a sentence in which the four makers of the physical book are remembered, and it rather looks as if the prayer to the right of the Explicit for John's gospel should have followed, for it too is marked out by a cross. Although we do not understand clearly all the words used by Aldred, his is the fullest account of the making of a book that remains from Anglo-Saxon England:

\+ Eadfrith, bishop of Lindisfarne: first of all he wrote this book for God and Saint Cuthbert and all the saints together who are in the island. And Æthilwald, bishop of Lindisfarne, *pressed* and *strengthened* it round about, as he knew well [how to do].

And the anchorite Billfrith, he crafted the metal ornaments that are all over [it] and decorated it also with gold and with precious stones, gilded over with silver, flawless treasure.

[9] For his will, datable to 871-89, see Hoad 1978: 216-18.

[10] Brown, M.P. 1996: 65.

[11] Ivy 1958: 51-54.

[12] See further: Brown, M.P. 2003; Nees 2003; Roberts (forthcoming).

How far the details are be trusted is much debated, not least because of our difficulty with the meaning of 'giðryde' and 'gibelde' (the italics above indicate a need for caution), but the scribe, Eadfrith, was bishop of Lindisfarne (698–721), and the binder, Æthilwald, is known to have returned to Lindisfarne as bishop (721 × 724–40). Moreover, Aldred's wish to be seen as playing his part in adding to the book's worth is not to be doubted. He celebrated the completion of his task with generous gifts:

> And Aldred, an unworthy and most wretched priest,[13] with the help of God and Saint Cuthbert, he glossed it in English and *made himself at home*[14] with these three divisions, Matthew's section for God and Saint Cuthbert, Mark's section for the bishop and Luke's section for the community, together with eight silver ores as *entrance*,[15] and Saint John's section for himself, i.e. for his soul, together with four pieces of silver for God and Saint Cuthbert, so that through God's mercy he may have in heaven acceptance, on earth well being and peace, death and mediation, learning and wisdom through the intercession of Saint Cuthbert.

Here again the meaning of some of the words is unclear and signalled by italics. However, Aldred's use of 'ðis boc' and the pronoun 'hit' (grammatically he should have written 'hi', a feminine pronoun, but already the gender systems of Old English were crumbling in his dialect) shows that, when he was writing, the book carried safely from Lindisfarne was bound in boards splendidly adorned. By contrast, the phrase 'ðas béc' ('these books') used a century earlier in the upper inscription in the despoiled Codex Aureus suggests that it was then in pieces.

There are a few unusual features of Insular book production to be noted. The preparation of membrane was particularly impressive. The pages are thick, can feel almost like suede, and there is surprisingly little colour-contrast difference between the hair and flesh sides of the skin, both of which hold ink well. Sheets were arranged in quires with the hair side following the flesh side, rather than in an alternating sequence that matches flesh with flesh and hair with hair in the two pages of an opening. The quires were ruled after folding, as can be seen from prickings often visible in both inner and outer margins. Only a few English centres are thought to have had substantial collections of books in the pre-Viking age, foremost among them the twin monasteries of Monkwearmouth and Jarrow, York, Canterbury, and Malmesbury. We guess that there were other important centres, for example Hexham in Acca's day, but for our knowledge of them we are dependent for the most part on the writings of Bede, Aldhelm, Alcuin, and Boniface's circle of correspondents.

[13] A *signe de renvoi* directs the eye alongside to the right hand margin where a note contains further information about Aldred: 'Aldred, born of Alfred, is my name: a good woman's son, of distinguished fame [i.e. a good woman]'. (The very appropriate rhyming jingle is the translation of Brown, M.P. 2003: 104.)

[14] This verb, found only here, is paralleled by *hamettan*.

[15] The noun *inlad* occurs twice only in Old English. The customary translation 'for his induction' has prompted ungenerous interpretation of Aldred's intentions.

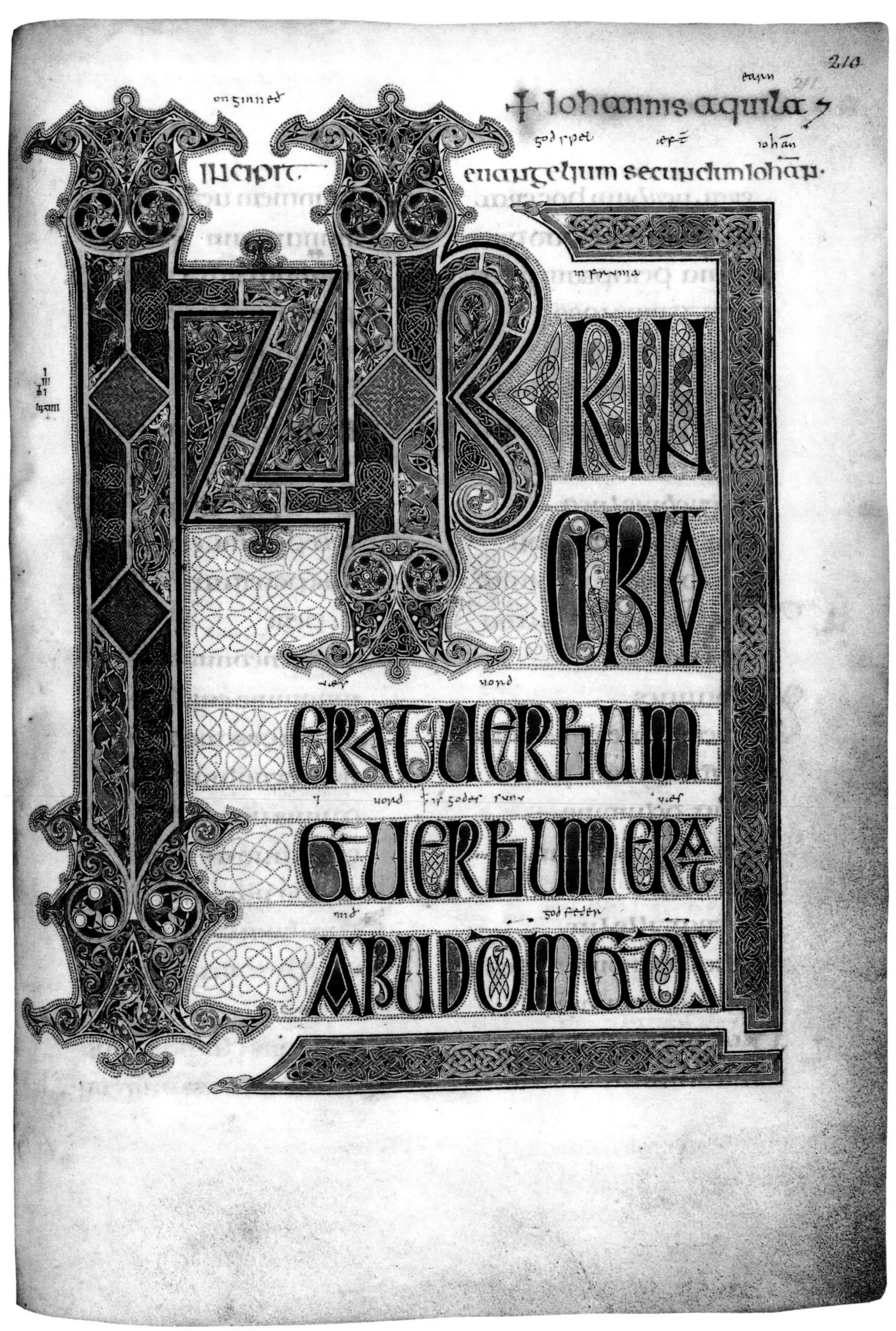

London, British Library, Cotton MS Nero D. iv, f. 211r
Beginning of St John's Gospel, *In principio*
reduced to 65%

I

St Petersburg, National Library of Russia, MS. lat. Q. v. I. 18, f. 107r
Bede, *Historia ecclesiastica gentis Anglorum*, IV: 24
Insular minuscule, current, s. viii med.

TRANSCRIPTION

prouectioris aetatis consti⟨-⟩
tutus . nil carminum aliquando
didicerat , unde nonnumqua(m)
in conuiuio cum esset . lætitiæ
causa decretum . ut omnes
per ordinem cantare deberent ,
Ille ubi adpropinquare sibi
citharam cernebat . surgebat
á media cena . et egressus ad sua(m)
domum[1] repedabat , quod dum
tempore quodam faceret .
et relicta domu conuiuii .
egressus esset ad stabula
iumentorum . quorum ei
custodia nocte illa erat
delegata , Ibiq(ue) hora conpe⟨-⟩
tenti membra dedisset sopori ,
adstitit ei quidam per somniu(m)
eumque salutans . ac suo
appellans nomine . cædmon .
inquit . canta mihi aliquid ,
at ille respondens . nescio
inquit cantare . Nam et ideo
de conuiuio egressus huc
secessi . \\quia cantare .// non poteram .
rursum ille qui cum eo loque⟨-⟩
batur . at tamen ait

mihi cantare habes , quid
inquit debeo cantare ,
Et ille . canta inquit . principiu(m)
creaturarum . quo accepto
responso . statim ipse coepit
cantare in laudem d(e)i conditoris
uersus . quos numquam audierat .
quorum iste est sensus ,
Nunc laudare debemus auctore(m)
regni cælestis . potentiam crea⟨-⟩
toris . et consilium illius . facta
patris gloriæ[2] quomodo ille
cum sit æternus d(eu)s . omnium .
miraculorum auctor extitit .
Qui primo filiis hominum
cælum pro culmine tecti .
dehinc terram cu[p>s]tos humani
generis omnipotens creauit .
Hic est sensus . non a[n>u]tem ordo
ipse uerborum . quæ dormiens
ille canebat . Neque enim
possunt carmina . quam uis
optime conposita . ex alia
in aliam linguam . ad uerbum
sine detrimento sui decoris .
ac dignitatis transferri .
Exsurgens autem á somno

Cædmon's Hymn (added in the bottom margin by the scribe)

Nu scilun herga hefenricæs uard metudæs mehti and his modgithanc uerc uuldurfadur sue he uundra
gihuæs eci dryctin or astelidæ he ærist scop aeldu barnum hefen to hrofæ halig sceppend
tha middingard moncynnæs uard eci dryctin æfter tiadæ firum foldu frea allmehtig .

The St Petersburg Bede, second oldest of the extant versions of the *Historia ecclesiastica*, was completed by *c.* 746 (added marginalia provide the evidence for this date), a decade later than the Moore manuscript, although it is argued that ff. 65-162 might have been produced as early as 732 (Parkes [1982], rpt. 1991: 101 and fn. 40). As well as the pointed **a**, a one-stroke open form is in use. Two separate minims, with wedges, make **u**, but **m** and **n** are generally without pen lifts. High **e** is usual in ligatures, where it is apt to be pushed up to make more room for the following letter, though not always in the **æ** digraph (compare 'æternus', l. 13b, and the first **æ** of 'lætitiæ', l. 4a, with the open form of **a** in 'cælestis', l. 10b, 'gloriæ', l. 12b, 'cælum', l. 16b, 'lætitiæ', l. 4a (second **æ**), 'cædmon', l. 20a, 'quæ', l. 20b). There are few pen-lifts between minims, and the bowl of the open-lobed **p** tends to have the right turn developed for speed in current hands. All nine **æ** forms have high **e** in the Hymn; separately-made **a** and **e** side by side occur also in both the main text ('aetatis', l. 1a) and the Hymn ('aeldu', l. 29). Space-saving vowels sometimes drop below the script baseline, for example 'somniu(m)', l. 18a, 'extitit', l. 14b, a characteristic feature carried over into early Anglo-Saxon minuscule. Note straight-backed **d** in both the main text (e.g. 'decretum', l. 5a, 'deberent', l. 6a) and the Hymn ('metudes', l. 28, 'uuldurfadur', l. 28). Punctuation is by means of the simple *punctus*, sometimes comma shaped (e.g. ll. 3a, 6a, 1b, 2b), and enlarged letters

[1] Note spot of ink before this word.

[2] Pen-hold at end of **æ** should perhaps be read as a punctus.

Plate 1 – reduced to 85%

often sufficiently big to be transcribed as capitals. The first letter of 'Hic', l. 19b, is set out to the left of the script after the summary of the Hymn, a useful indication of where it ends. Together with end-column space and good word division, these devices guide the reader efficiently. The apex sign, signalling stress, can help identify monosyllables, as in 'á media', l. 9a. There are few signs of correction: an insertion is carefully signalled at l. 25a and twice letters appear to be overwritten, in ll. 17b, 19b. Abbreviations are few: the overline signals *m* in 'numqua(m)', l. 3a, 'sua(m)', l. 9a, 'somniu(m)', l. 18a, 'principiu(m)', l. 3b, 'auctore(m)', l. 9b; the syllable of 'Ibiq(ue)', l. 16a, is suspended; and there are two contractions of *deus* ('d(e)i', l. 6b, 'd(eu)s', l. 13b).

The scribe added the early Northumbrian text of Cædmon's Hymn in the bottom margin, outside the usual writing-space, in smaller module (compare the smaller version of his hand seen in the correction to l. 25a). The English text does not use **þ** (see **th** in 'modgithanc', l. 28) or **ƿ** (see **u** in 'uard', l. 28) and its spellings are distinctively northern (e.g. loss of final **n** in 'herga', l. 28). Linguistically, this text is more consistent than the Moore Hymn, a contemporary addition on what was originally the blank last page (f. 128v) of the Moore Bede (Cambridge, University Library, MS Kk. 5. 16).

CONTEXTS

Manuscript probably written in Monkwearmouth–Jarrow. Belonged in the eighteenth century to Achille de Harlay (d.1712), whose son left it to the abbey of St-Germain-des-Prés. Next known in the possession of Peter Dubrovsky in 1791, from whom it was acquired for the St Petersburg Imperial Library in 1805. Known as the Leningrad Bede for much of the last century.

SIZE

c. 270 × 191 mm (*c.* 216 × 160 mm).

BIBLIOGRAPHY

As Colgrave and Mynors 1969: 414-16.
Facs. Arngart 1952.
Disc. Dobiache-Rodjestvensky 1928; Schapiro 1958; Lowe 1958 (rpt. 1972); Blair 1959; Ker, *Cat.* 1957: no. 122; Okasha 1968; Arngart 1973; 1997; Alexander 1978: no. 19; Parkes 1982 (rpt. 1991[1]); O'Brien O'Keeffe 1987, 1990: 23-46; Gneuss 2001: no. 846; Kisseleva in Kahlas-Tarkka and Kilpiö 2001: 29-31.
Cædmon's Hymn. *Pr.* Dobbie 1942: 105. *Facs*: Okasha 1968; Robinson and Stanley 1991: no. 2.3.

London, British Library, Royal MS 4 A. xiv, f. 107v
Felix, *Vita sancti Guthlaci*

End of preface and beginning of chapter titles. This is one of two conjoint folios that survived in the binding of a Worcester manuscript (see pl. 26). Note two glosses: 'referentib(us)', l. 3; and the English word 'foremere', l. 13, above 'De rumigerulo'.
actual size

2a

London, British Library, Cotton MS Vespasian A. i, f. 93v
Vespasian Psalter, with Old English gloss
Main hand: Uncial, s. viii[1]
Psalter gloss: Insular minuscule, current, s. ix med.

TRANSCRIPTION

XCUII PSALMUS IPSI DAUID ·
singað
CANTATE
dryht(ne) song niowne
D(OMI)NO CANTICUM NOUUM
for ðon wundur dyde dryht(en)
QUIA MIRABILIA FECIT D(OMI)N(U)S
gehaelde hine mid ða swiðran his
SALUAUIT EUM DEXTERA EIUS
⁊ earm haligne his
ET BRA[-]CHIUM S(AN)C(TU)M EIUS ···
cuðe dyde dryht(en) hælu his
NOTUM FECIT D(OMI)N(U)S SALUTARE SUUM
biforan gesihðe ðioda onwrah rehtwisnisse
ANTE CONSPECTU GENTIUM REUELAUIT IUS⟨-⟩
his
TITIAM SUAM ···
gemyndig wes mildheortnisse his
MEMOR FUIT MISERICORDIAE SUAE IACOB
⁊ soðfestnisse his gehusscipe[1] israel
ET UERITATIS SUAE DOMUS ISRAHEL ···
gesegun alle endas eorðan haelu godes ures
VIDERUNT OMNES FINES TERRAE SALUTARE D(E)I N(OSTR)I
wynsumiað gode all eorðe
IUBILATE D(E)O OMNIS TERRA
singað ⁊ gefiað ⁊ singað
CANTATE ET EXULTATE ET PSALLITE ···
singað gode uru(m) in citran in citran
PSALLITE D(E)O N(OSTR)O IN CITHARA IN CITHARA
⁊ stefne salmes in hornu(m) gelengdu(m)[2]
ET UOCE PSALMI IN TUB[\L]IS DUCTILIBUS
⁊ stefne hornes hyrnes
ET UOCE TUBAE CORNEAE
wynsumuað in gesihðe cyninges dryhtnes
IUBILATE IN CONSPECTU REGIS D(OMI)NI ···
sie astyred sę ⁊ fynis hire
MOUEATUR MARE ET PLENITUDO EIUS
ymbhwyrft eorðena ⁊ a[n+ll]e ða ðe eardiað
ORBIS TERRARUM ET UNIUERSI QUI HABITANT
in hire
→ IN EA ·

The main-text hand, dated by Wright to *c.* 725, is Uncial. The letters are very regular and must have required much effort, for the script does not flow evenly. Note the small capital rather than Uncial **G** of 'GENTIUM', l. 7 and the space-saving **T** at the end of l. 19. Each verse begins on a new line and ends with three final dots (this arrangement is called *per cola et commata*). Word division is far from complete. Above the ruled lines the *titulus* and psalm number are added in Rustic capitals. The only abbreviations on this page are the customary contracted forms of the *nomina sacra*. Noteworthy is 'NI', l. 11 with overline, a typically Insular abbreviation pointing to the early eighth century (the later *nr-* series comes in early in the eighth century). The overlines are often partially concealed by the later glosses. The erased letter in 'BRA[-]CHIUM', l. 5, was perhaps **C**, and there are signs of other rewritings: the final three letters of 'GENTIUM', l. 7; **I** in the first 'CITHARA', l. 14; 'TUBIS', l. 15, has **B** written over what looks like **L**; the last two letters of 'D(OMI)NI', l. 17. Pricking in both outer

[1] In the space between 'gehus' and 'scipe' there is an erasure.

[2] Something, perhaps the Tironian sign, is erased before this word.

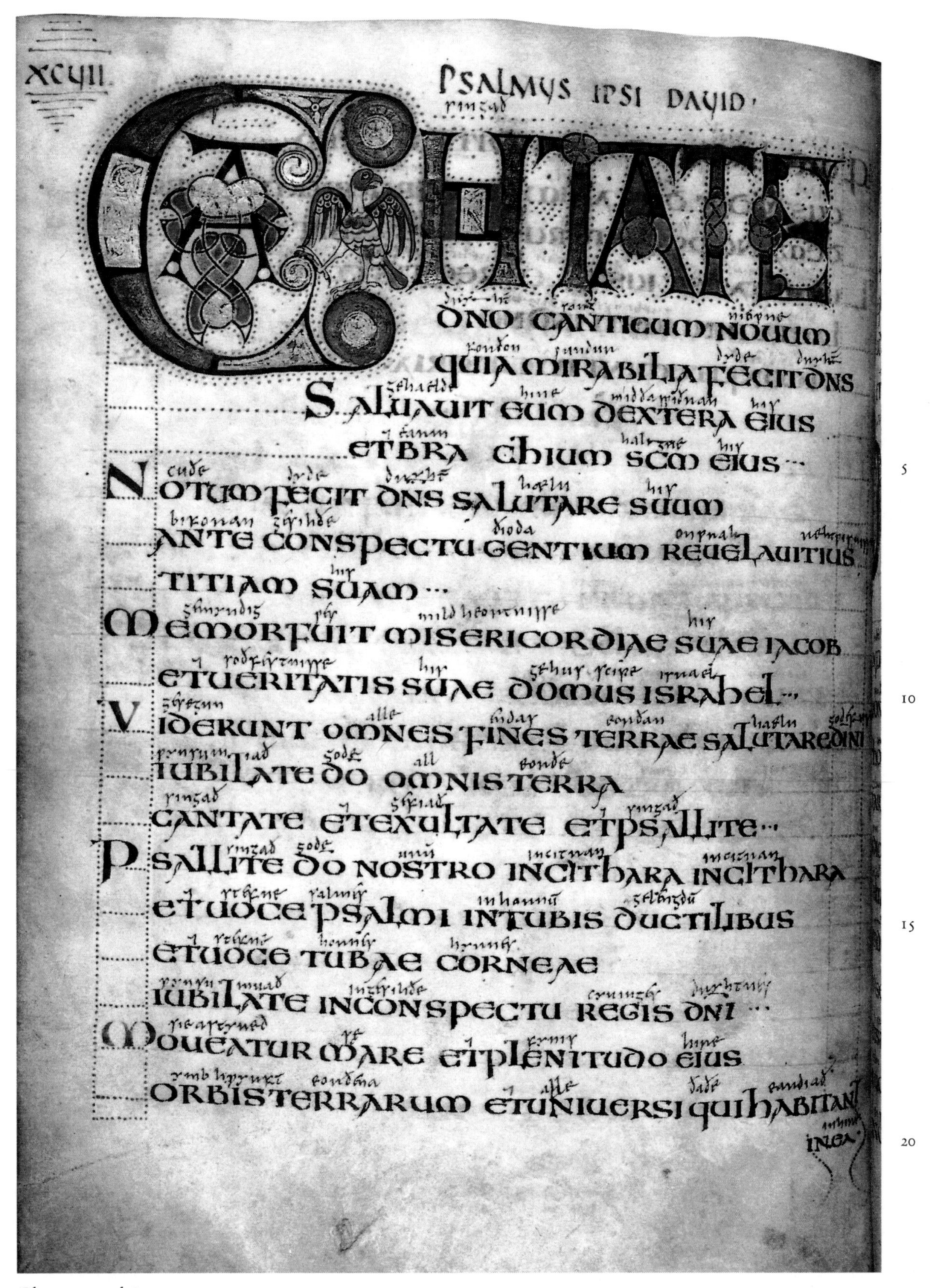

XCVII. PSALMUS IPSI DAVID

CANTATE
DNO CANTICUM NOUUM
QUIA MIRABILIA FECIT DNS
SALUAUIT EUM DEXTERA EIUS
ET BRACHIUM SCM EIUS
NOTUM FECIT DNS SALUTARE SUUM
ANTE CONSPECTU GENTIUM REUELAUIT IUS
TITIAM SUAM
MEMOR FUIT MISERICORDIAE SUAE IACOB
ET UERITATIS SUAE DOMUS ISRAHEL
UIDERUNT OMNES FINES TERRAE SALUTARE DI NI
IUBILATE DO OMNIS TERRA
CANTATE ET EXULTATE ET PSALLITE
PSALLITE DO NOSTRO IN CITHARA IN CITHARA
ET UOCE PSALMI IN TUBIS DUCTILIBUS
ET UOCE TUBAE CORNEAE
IUBILATE IN CONSPECTU REGIS DNI
MOUEATUR MARE ET PLENITUDO EIUS
ORBIS TERRARUM ET UNIUERSI QUI HABITANT
IN EA

Plate 2a – actual size

margins for hardpoint ruling. Miscalculation of space has led to the placing of the last two words as a run-over at the bottom right of the script block.

The gloss is written currently: the pen is not lifted between minims; **ð** can be a single stroke; and **sw** ('swiðran', l. 4) and **ss** (e.g. 'rehtwisnisse', l. 7) are ligatured. Note the tall open **e**; the use of all of **æ**, **ae**, and **ę**; low **s** only; and the short descender of **r**. Wyn is used, but apparently not **þ**, for which note **ð** (sometimes made with a single stroke) only on this page. The gloss is without punctuation. Word division is to some extent affected by the need to avoid the overline abbreviation marks of the main text (e.g. 'haligne', l. 5), but monosyllables tend to attach themselves to the following word (e.g. 'sie astyred', l. 18, and compare 'in citran', l. 14, with the main text). The principal abbreviation is the overline, both for *-m* or *-n* ('uru(m)', l. 14, 'hornu(m)', 'gelengdu(m)', l. 15) and more generally as a mark of suspended words. The latter is common practice in glossing, and the shortened forms of *dryhten* are expanded appropriately. The Tironian sign is to be interpreted as *ond* (compare 'song', l. 2). Words oddly spelled include 'gehusscipe', l. 10 (for 'gehiwscipe'), 'wynsumuað' (for 'wynsumiað'), and 'fynis', l. 18 (for 'fylnis'); and 'alle', l. 19, is emended through overwriting. Linguistically the self-consistency of the dialect has led to the assumption that it may represent the official language of some monastery. The gloss has many non-West Saxon features (e.g. 'gesegun', l. 11), but as the final nasal consonant in 'hornu(m)', l. 15, etc., appears firm, it is Mercian, not Northumbrian. A glossed exemplar is assumed (Gerritsen 1989: 483). A mid-ninth-century dating is now usual.

CONTEXTS
From Kent, whether written at St Augustine's or Christ Church, Canterbury, or at Minster-in-Thanet (Thanet's property was taken to St Augustine's by the eleventh century). Additions (ff. 155-60) were made in Canterbury by Eadui Basan early in the eleventh century. Seen on the high altar in St Augustine's by Thomas of Elmham (*c.* 1414-18) and probably by John Leland (1533-34). Owned by William Cecil, Lord Burghley, from whom Matthew Parker borrowed it (1565). Cotton's signature of ownership (f. 12r) is accompanied by the date 1599. Borrowed by Ussher for collation of psalters (1625). Entered the British Museum with the Cotton Collection in 1753.

SIZE 235 × 180 mm (172 × 145 mm).

BIBLIOGRAPHY
Pr. Sweet 1885: 327-28 (Psalm 97: 1-7); Kuhn 1965: 94-94.
Facs. Wright and Campbell 1967; Pulsiano 1994.
Disc. Sisam 1953: 4, fn. 2, 1956; Ker, *Cat.* 1957: no. 203; Gneuss 1957 [rpt. 1996]; Alexander 1978: no. 29; Pulsiano 1996; Gerritsen 1989; Gameson 1999[2]; Gneuss 2001: no. 381; Tite 2003: 172.

London, British Library, Cotton MS Vespasian A. i, f. 30v

This full-page miniature of David, author of the psalms, with scribes, musicians and dancers, was perhaps originally the manuscript's frontispiece.
actual size

2b

London, British Library, Cotton MS Vespasian A. i, f. 141v
Vespasian Psalter, a prayer by Cassiodorus
Rustic capitals, s. viii

TRANSCRIPTION

TU D(OMI)NE VERVS DOCTOR ET PRAESTITOR ADVOCATUS ET IVDEX LARGITOR
ET MONITOR ET TERRIBILIS ET CLEMENS ET CORRIPIENS ET CONSOLATOR ·
QVI CAECIS MENTIB(VS) DONAS ASPECTVM · QVI FACIS INFIRMIS POSSIBILE
QVOD PRAECIPIS · QVI SIC PIVS ES UT ADSIDVE ROGARE VELIS : SIC MVNIFICVS
VT NEMINEM DESPERARE PATIARIS : DONA QVOD TE PRESTANTE BENE QVAE⟨-⟩
RIMVS · ET ILLA MAXIME QVAE NOSTRA INFIRMITATE NESCIMVS :
QVOD EX TVO DISCIMVS[1] SVSCIPE · QVOD EX NOBIS IGNORANTER PROTVLI⟨-⟩
MVS PARCE · ET PERDUC NOS AD ILLAM CONTEMPLATIONEM · VBI IAM
NON POSSIMVS ERRARE : DONA FACERE QVAE TE INSPIRANTE LOQVI
PRAESUMPSI · DONA CONPLERE · QVAE ALIOS OBSERVARE COMMONVI :
UT QVI PRAESTITISTI[2] PIVM SERMONEM · PROBABILEM QVOQVE CON⟨-⟩
FERAS TVIS FAMVLIS ACTIONEM · LIBERA NOS AMATOR HOMINVM
AB ILLO PERICULO · NE SICVT DICIT APOSTOLVS · DVM ALIIS PRAEDICO IPSE
REPROBUS INVENIAR[3] · QVAM INFIRMI SVMVS TV VERACITER NOSTI ·
QVALI HOSTE DEPRIMIMVR[4] · AGNOSCIS · TE QVAERIT CERTAMEN INPAR TE
EXPETIT MORALIS INFIRMITAS · QVTA MAIESTATIS TVAE GLORIA EST :
SI LEO RVGIENS AB INFIRMA OVE SUPERETVR · SI SP(IRITV)S VIOLENTISSIMVS
A DEBILISSIMA CARNE VINCATVR · ILLE QVI DE CAELO CECIDIT · ET HIC TE
PVGNANTE SVBDATUR · UT SI POTESTATEM IPSIVS AD TEMPVS TVA PER⟨-⟩
MISSIONE PATIMVR · NEQVAQVAM EIVS INSATIABILIBVS FAVCIBVS
SORBEAMVR · FAC ILLVM TRISTEM DE HVMANA LAETITIA · QVI DE OF⟨-⟩
FENSIONE NOSTRA SEMPER EXULTAT :~

This page of Rustic capitals may represent a local development, perhaps even a revived book script. The recto contains the apocryphal psalm 151, written in Uncials and supplied with an English gloss. The scribe of the verso may have been more at home with Uncials than with Rustic capitals: Uncial **f** and **p** are to be noted in this attempt at Rustic capitals as a text hand, for example in 'CORRIPIENS', l. 2, and 'FACIS INFIRMIS', l. 3. It is hard to glimpse any particular distribution in the use of **V** and **U** or indeed to be certain sometimes which is which: both the monumental **V** of square capitals and the round form more usual in Rustics are employed more or less indiscriminately, with **V**, a contamination from display script, predominating. At first glance the text looks as if written in the antique way, with little word division. Yet, there is more punctation than in late antique bookhands. Both a highish point and pairs of points are used; the single points are not distributed at distinct heights as *distinctiones* (i.e. points placed at different heights to signal differing sorts of pause). Some letters following punctuation marks appear significantly enlarged, but in an impressionistic way. The final flourish, typical of Insular manuscripts, was very likely developed originally in Ireland. The abbreviations are few, as befits so formal a piece: its two *nomina sacra* ('D(OMI)NE', l. 2, 'SP(IRITV)S', l. 17); and : makes *-us* in 'MENTIB(VS)', l. 3.

CONTEXTS
Folio 141 is one of four single leaves added to the Vespasian Psalter probably late in the eighth century. Another of these, f. 109, contains excerpts from Cassiodorus, and two, ff. 2 and 3, stand at the outset of the psalter.

SIZE
Ruled as for main text, but using greater width for the writing block (*c.* 158 mm).

BIBLIOGRAPHY
Pr. Kuhn 1965: 308.

[1] For *diximvs*.
[2] 'RAE' on erasure, and the end of the bow on 'P' removed.
[3] The word may be rewritten; note the smaller module.
[4] For *deprimamvr*.

TE DNE UERUS DOCTOR ET PRAESTITOR ADUOCATUS ET IUDEX LARGITOR
ET MONITOR ET TERRIBILIS ET CLEMENS ET CORRIPIENS ET CONSOLATOR·
QUI CAECIS MENTIB: DONAS ASPECTUM· QUI FACIS INFIRMIS POSSIBILE
QUOD PRAECIPIS· QUI SIC PIUS ES UT ADSIDUE ROGARE UELIS· SIC MUNIFICUS
UT NEMINEM DESPERARE PATIARIS: DONA QUOD TE PRESTANTE BENE QUAE
RIMUS· ET ILLA MAXIME QUAE NOSTRA INFIRMITATE NESCIMUS:
QUOD EX TUO DISCIMUS SUSCIPE· QUOD EX NOBIS IGNORANTER PROTULI
MUS PARCE· ET PERDUC NOS AD ILLAM CONTEMPLATIONEM· UBI IAM
NON POSSIMUS ERRARE: DONA FACERE QUAE TE INSPIRANTE LOQUI
PRAESUMPSI· DONA CONPLERE QUAE ALIOS OBSERUARE COMMONUI:
UT QUI PRAESTITISTI PIUM SERMONEM· PROBABILEM QUOQUE CON
FERAS TUIS FAMULIS ACTIONEM· LIBERA NOS AMATOR HOMINUM
AB ILLO PERICULO· NE SICUT DICIT APOSTOLUS· DUM ALIIS PRAEDICO IPSE
REPROBUS INUENIAR· QUAM INFIRMI SUMUS TU UERACITER NOSTI·
QUALI HOSTE DEPRIMIMUR AGNOSCIS· TE QUAERIT CERTAMEN IN PARTE
EXPETIT MORALIS INFIRMITAS· QUIA MAIESTATIS TUAE GLORIA EST·
SI LEO RUGIENS AB INFIRMA OUE SUPERETUR· SI SPS UIOLENTISSIMUS
A DEBILISSIMA CARNE UINCATUR· ILLE QUI DE CAELO CECIDIT· ET HIC TE
PUGNANTE SUBDATUR· UT SI POTESTATEM IPSIUS AD TEMPUS TUA PER
MISSIONE PATIMUR· NEQUAQUAM EIUS INSATIABILIBUS FAUCIBUS
SORBEAMUR· FAC ILLUM TRISTEM DE HUMANA LAETITIA· QUI DE OF
FENSIONE NOSTRA SEMPER EXULTAT·

Plate 2b – actual size

3

Stockholm, Kungliga Biblioteket, MS A. 135, f. 11r
Gospels, Matthew 1: 18
(a) display capitals, s. viii med.
(b) inscriptions: Insular minuscule, pointed, s. ix med. – s. ix^{2}

TRANSCRIPTION

CR(IST)I AUTEM
 GENERATIO
SIC ERAT CVM ESSET DIS⟨-⟩[1]
PONSATA MATER EIVS
MARIA IOSEPH ANTEQVA(M)
CONVENIRENT INVENTA
EST IN VTERO HABENS

Inscription, s. ix med.

† IN nomine d(omi)ni n(ost)ri ie(s)v cr(ist)i , IC aelfred aldormon ⁊ wérburg mín gefera begetan ðas béc[2] æt haeðnu(m) herge
mid uncre claene feo ðæt ðonne wæs mid clæne golde ⁊ ðæt wit deodan for godes lufan ⁊ for uncre saule ðearf[ ]

Deed of gift, s. ix^{2}

Ond forðon ðe wit noldan ðæt ðas halgan béoc lencg In ðære haeðenesse wunaden , ⁊ nu willað heo gesellan Inn to cristes
circan gode to lofe ⁊ to wuldre ⁊ to weorðunga ⁊ his ðrowunga to ðoncunga , ⁊ ðæm godcundan geferscipe to brucen[ne]
ðe Ín cristes circan dæghwæmlice godes lof rærað , to ðæm gerade ðæt heo mon árede eghwelce monaðe for aelfred
⁊ for werburge ⁊ for alhðryðe heora saulum tó ecum lecedome , ða hwile ðe god gesegen haebbe ðæt fulwiht æt
ðeosse stowe beon mote .., Éc swelce Ic aelfred .dux. ⁊ werburg biddað ⁊ halsiað ón godes almaehtiges noman ⁊ on allre
his haligra ðæt nænig món seo to ðon gedyrstig ðætte ðas halgan beoc áselle oððe áðeode from cristes circan ða hwile
ðe fulwiht [s]t[on]da[n mote][3]

Three names appear in the right margin, with loss through cropping of page

Aelfre[d]
Werbur[g]
Alhðryð | eorum [filia][4]

The Codex Aureus, a huge manuscript (each bifolium originally not less than 400 × 600 mm) and splendid in design, is arguably the most lavish book extant from medieval Britain. In format it is almost square, echoing the proportions of late antique books. In script and decoration it resembles the Vespasian Psalter. The Chi-Rho monogram is the most elaborate initial of the Codex Aureus, 'AUTEM' is embellished and the rest of the page is made up of decorated display capitals: more gold leaf than anywhere else in the manuscript. Apart from the opening monogram, the only abbreviation is the overline for inflexional *m* in 'ANTEQUA(M)' at the end of l. 5.

The book opens with a series of purple pages, reflecting late antique practice, and f. 11, the first white leaf, is thus the first page to afford sufficient space for the English additions. These are in a pointed minuscule similar to hands found in Christ Church charters of the middle of the ninth century. English is written confidently: **ƿ** is usual (except for 'saule', l. 2), and **ð** (but not **þ**). The scribe uses both an *æ* ligature and separate letter forms *ae*. Ker suggests that the upper inscription may be a little earlier than the deed of gift to Christ Church, Canterbury in the lower margin. Only the top parts of the last words, which are centred, can now be read. The main mark of punctuation is comma-shaped; two points may precede it for a longer pause followed by a capital; the *i*-longa appears before following minims (as 'In', 'Inn', l. 3); and apex signs help the reader to identify words and syllables that might not otherwards stand out. Overall the layout is carefully planned, with the English of the upper margin written between double rulings in hardpoint, but single rulings for the names and lower addition. The abbreviations in the English additions (apart from the naming of God in Latin

[1] The vowel of the first syllable of *desponsata* is included inside 'D'.
[2] i.e. the four books of the Gospels.
[3] Likely lost letters supplied within square brackets.
[4] Again, cropped letters guessed and given in square brackets. A trace of the third minim of 'eorum' may remain.

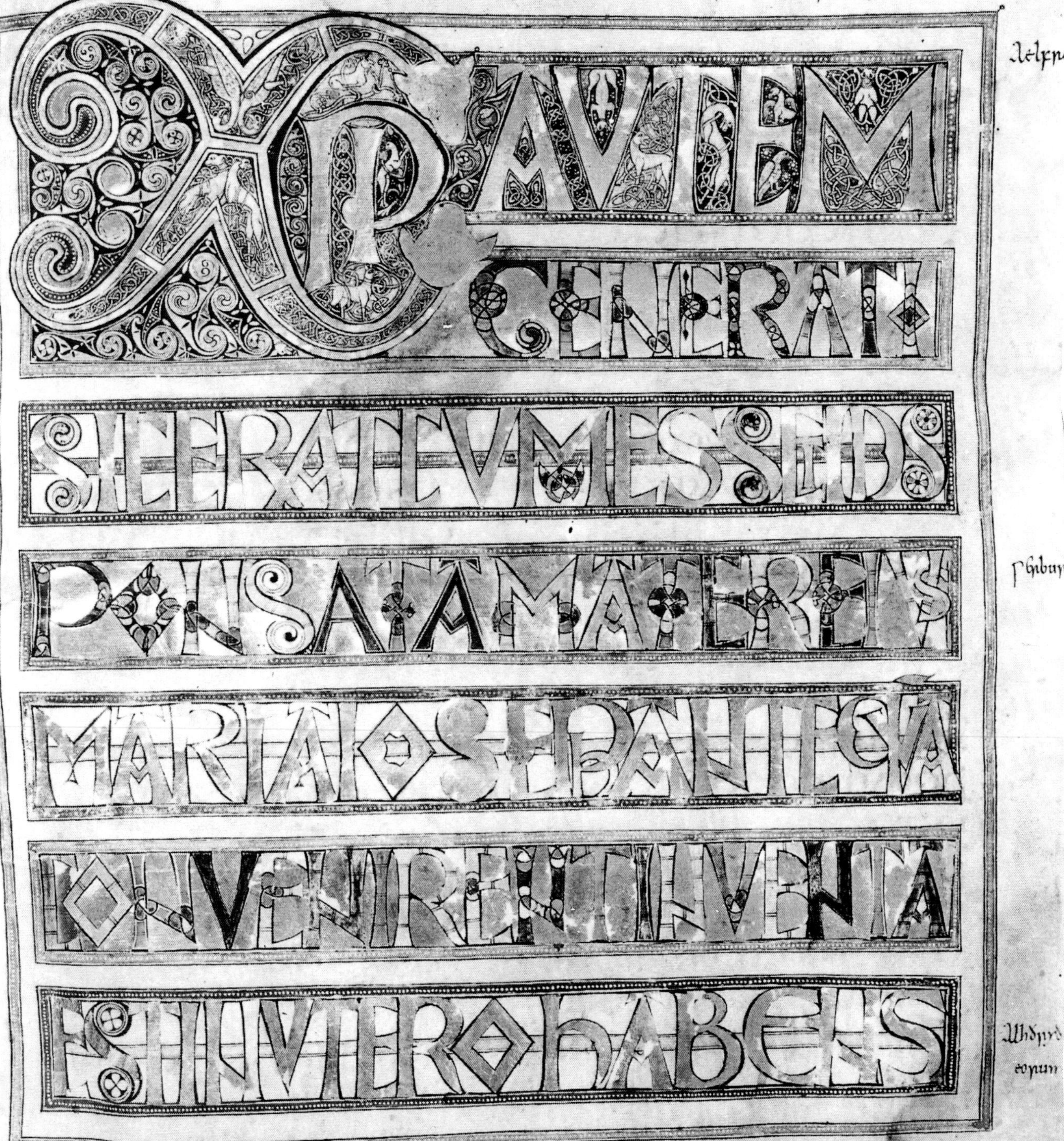

Plate 3 – reduced to 63%

phrases) are the Tironian sign and one use of the overline for *m* in 'haeðnu(m)', l. 2. The cropping of the manuscript has led to the loss of the last letters of the names in the right margin and, presumably, *filia* after 'eorum'.

CONTEXTS

Related to a small group of manuscripts from eastern Kent, whether St Augustine's, Christ Church, or Minster-in-Thanet. The added inscriptions are comparable in script to some mid-ninth-century Canterbury charters. The upper inscription tells of how this book was redeemed from raiders (perhaps during the 850s or 860s). The lower addition, to which the three names in the right-hand margin relate, deeds the book to Christ Church, Canterbury (*c.* 871-889). Sixteenth-century foliation in red is probably not Parkerian (Wormald [1953] 1984: II. 151). Perhaps still in England *c.* 1600, when mangled extracts from the English inscriptions were written into British Library, Arundel MS 504. In 1690 bought 'ex famosa illa bibliotheca Illmi. Marchionis de LICHE Mantuae Carpet(anorum)' in Madrid by John Gabriel Sparwenfeldt for the Swedish royal collections. Known as the Stockholm Codex Aureus.

SIZE

c. 380-95 × *c.* 310-20 mm.

BIBLIOGRAPHY

Pr. (a) Belsheim 1878: 17; (b) Hoad 1978: 115.
Facs. Gameson 2001-02.
Disc. Lowe, *CLA* XI 1966: no. 1642; Wormald [1953] 1984: II. 151; Ker, *Cat.* 1957: no. 385; Alexander 1978: no. 30; Breeze 1996; Campos Vilanova 1997; Gameson 1999[2]: 336-46; Gneuss 2001: no. 937.

London, British Museum, Franks Casket
Titus panel

The Franks Casket, a small box (23 cm × 13 cm × 19 cm) made of whale's bone, was made somewhere in Northumbria or northern Mercia in the first half of the eighth century. This back panel tells the story of Titus's capture of Jerusalem in pictures and words, in both English and Latin. 'Here Titus and the Jews fight' surrounds the storming of the temple (the building in the centre). Start reading sideways along the left-hand side for the beginning of the first sentence, 'her fegtaþ', move to the cross '+' at the top left-hand corner and pick up its ending 'titus end giuþeasu'. 'Here the inhabitants run away from Jerusalem' begins on the other side of the temple, above the people fleeing from Roman soldiers. This second sentence begins in a curious mixture of letter-forms, 'hic fugiant hierusalim', with the subject 'afitatores' in runes along the right-hand side (for 'Hic fugiunt Hierusalim habitatores'). The lower scenes are less easily interpreted, despite the single-word labels in English 'dom' ('judgement', alongside what may be a trial scene at the left) and 'gisl' ('hostage', perhaps indicating the future of the men depicted). (Webster and Backhouse 1991: 101-3.)

4

Cambridge, University Library, MS Ll.1.10, f. 2r
Ending of 'Exhortation to prayer' in the prayer book known as the Book of Cerne
Insular minuscule, s. ix

TRANSCRIPTION

⁊ ðe georne gebide . gece . ⁊ miltse fore alra his
⟨hali⟩gra[1] . gewyrhtum . ⁊ geearningum ⁊ boenum . on
[. . . .]num[2] ða ðe d(omi)no d(e)o gelicedon from fruman
middangeardes , ðonne gehereð he ðec ðorh hiora
ðingunge , do ðonne fiorðan siðe ðin hleor ðriga
to iorðan . fore alle godes cirican . ⁊ sing ðas
fers . d(omi)ni est salus . Saluum fac populum
tuum d(omi)ne praetende misericordiam tuam
Sing ðonne pater noster . gebide ðonne fore
alle geleaffullę menn In mundo . ðonne bistu ðone
deg daelniomende , ðorh dryhtnes gefe alra ðeara
goda ðe ænig monn for his noman gedoeð . ⁊ ðec alle
soðfestę foreðingiað . In caelo et in terra . Am(en) .

This is an example of Phase II Insular minuscule. The scribe uses his normal cursive minuscule for the English injunction: the **a** is pointed, and he does not always raise his pen between minims. The *i*-longa is used before letters made up of minims in 'In mundo', l. 10. Note: the use of **ð** but not **þ**; **ƿ** is usual; variation among **ae, æ,** and **ę**, the last of these twice in inflexions, ll. 10, 13. Latin phrases, because they are in red (now virtually pink), do not show up well in the black-and-white plate. For these, the opening words of prayers to be chanted, the scribe moves to a higher grade of script, hybrid minuscule, which elsewhere he adopts for display purposes. Interspersed in these brief passages are the **a** and round **s** of Half-Uncial, straight-backed **d** and **r** with short descender. The *Exhortation* is now generally regarded as Mercian, although Kentish is also advanced: the spellings lack any pointers to either Northumbrian (final *-m* and *-n* are secure) or West Saxon (not even the distinctive early West Saxon *-ie-*). Note the *-oe-* of 'boenum', l. 2, a feature not found in later West Saxon texts. The punctuation is a simple point, sometimes trailing in a comma-like form, and may be splashed with red; enlarged letters (highlighted with alternating blue and yellow infill) mark new sentences, and only with 'Sing', l. 9, its round **s** set out into the margin, is a differentiated letter-form used. Apart from the Tironian sign (like the punctuation marks, also touched with red), abbreviation occurs in the naming of God ('d(omi)no', l. 3, 'd(omi)ni', l. 7, 'd(omi)ne', l. 8, 'd(e)o', l. 3), and the closing 'Am(en)', l. 13; overlines are shadowed with red. The folio is now the opening of the manuscript, the first folio of the quire being lost, and signs of wear, holes, discoloration, and staining indicate that it must have served as the outer cover for some time. Some letters have been touched up in dark ink: see in l. 8 'tuu', the *dn* of 'd(omi)ne' and *e* and *de* in 'praetende'. Note below the text a roughly-inscribed ?prayer, beginning 'IH'. At the foot of the page a drawing is showing through from the verso, where someone has attempted to copy the head of Matthew at the bottom of the page containing the Matthew miniature.

CONTEXTS

This prayer-book may have been made for or in memory of Æthelwald, bishop of Lichfield (818-30), but both the acrostic poem on f. 21r and name on f. 87v could refer to other bishops so named (the early-eighth-century bishop of Lindisfarne or the ninth-century bishop of Dunwich). The hand is compared (Brown, M.P. 1996) with Bodley, Hatton 93, an early Worcester manuscript, and occasional glossing, extra pointing and other additions, thought by some to be reminiscent of the Tremulous-Hand scribe, point to its having been at Worcester early in the thirteenth century. Earliest certain provenance is in the library of John Moore by 1697, and by this time the ninth-century nucleus of the manuscript (ff. 2-99) was sandwiched between two sets of material relating to Cerne Abbas, Dorset. After Moore's death, King George I bought his library and in 1715 presented it to Cambridge University.

SIZE

c. 230 × 180 mm (*c.* 180 × 140 mm).

BIBLIOGRAPHY

Pr Kuypers 1902: 3; Hoad 1978: 114.
Facs. Doane 2002.
Disc. Ker, *Cat.* 1957: no. 27; Sisam 1956: 9-10; Dumville 1972; Alexander 1978: no. 66; Morrish 1988; Brown, M.P. 1996, 2001[1], 2001[2]; Gneuss 2001: no. 28.

[1] Top of **l** perhaps identifiable, but head of **i** minim lacks definition.

[2] Possibly '[heofe]num'; descender of **f** identifiable.

Plate 4 – actual size

5

London, British Library, Cotton MS Nero D. iv, f. 259r (formerly 252) *Colour pl. C1*
Lindisfarne Gospels, John 21: 22-25, with Aldred's additions
Half-uncial, s. viii in.
Gloss and additions: insular minuscule, pointed, s. x[2]

TRANSCRIPTION

cveð hi(m) to se hæl(end) ðvs 'ł svæ' hine
dicit ei ie(su)s sic eum
ic villo gevvni ł þ(æt)te he gewvniga : oð þ(æt)
uolo manere donec
ic cymo hvæd is ðe bi ðy ł hvæt is ðec 'ðæs'
ueniam quid ad té
ðv mec sóec . ł fylig ðv me
tú me sequere
foerde vvt(udlice) .ł. f(or)ðon ðis vord
exiuit ergo sermo iste
bitvien ðæm broðrv(m) f(or)ðon .ł. þ(æt)te
in\t(er)/ fratres quia
ðe ambeht ł se ðegn
discipulus ille
no deadige .ł. nere dead
non moritur
⁊ ne cveð him se hæl(end)
Et non dixit ei ie(su)s
ne bið dead ł
non moritur
ah [-s] ðvs 'ł svæ' hine ic villo vvniga
Sed sic eum uolo ma\ne/re
oð þ(æt) ic cymo
donec uenio
hvæt is ðe bi ðy ł
quid ad te
ðes is ðe ðegn
Hic est discipulus
se ðe þ(æt) cyðnise
qui testimonium
getrymmeð of ðæm ł fro(m) ðísv(m)
perhibet de hís
⁊ avrat ðas ł ða
Et scribsit haec
⁊ ve wvtvn þ(æt)te sóð
Et scimus quia uerum
Is [-w] cyðnis his
est testimonium eius
synt vvt(udlice) ec oðro
Sunt autem et alia
menigo ða ðe worht se hæl(end)
multa quę fecit ie(su)s
ðæh ða sie avritten
quae si scribantur
ánlapv(m) .ł. ðerh syndrigi ł anvnga 'ł ancvmmvm'
per singula
n[-e\i] doemo ic þ(æt)ti middan(gard)
nec ipsum arbitror

mægi bifoa ða ilco
mundum capere eos
ða ðe to avrittenni sint
qui scribendi sunt
boéc soðlice
libros . amen :~

asægd is .ł. þ(æt) bóc
EXPLICIT LIBER

aeft(er)
SECUNDUM

iohannem
IOHANEN ⁝

ðe ðrifalde ⁊ ðe anfalde god ðis gods\pell/ ær \vorvlda \gisette//
\+ Trinus et unvs d(eu)s evangelivm hoc ante \sæcvla con\stitvit · //
ærist avrat of mvðe crist(es)
\+ Mathevs ex ore cr(ist)i scripsit
of mvðe petres avrat
\+ Marcus ex ore petri scrips(it)
of mvðe pavles avrat
\+ Lvcas de ore Pavli ap(ostoli) scrips(it)
in deigilnisi ł i(n) f(or)esaga siððа rocgetede \\ł gisprant//
\+ IOh(annes) in prochemio deinde ervctvavit
word mið 'ðy' god[-e] gisalde ⁊ halges gastes \\ł mið godes geafa | ⁊ halges gastes | mæht avrát ioh(annes)//
verbvm d(e)o donante et sp(irit)v s(an)c(t)o scrip(sit)

\+ eadfrið bisco[p\b] lindisfearnensis æcclesiæ
he ðis boc avrát æt frvma gode ⁊ s(an)c(t)e
cvðberhte ⁊ allvm ðæm halgvm . ða \gimænelice/ ðe
in eolonde sint . ⁊ eðilvald lindisfearneolondinga \bisc(ob)/
hit vta giðryde ⁊ gibélde sva hé vel cuðę .
⁊ billfrið se oncrę he gismioðade ða
gihríno ða ðe vtan ón sint ⁊ hit gi⟨-⟩
hrínade mið golde ⁊ mið gimmvm ęc
mið svlfre of(er)gylded faconleas feh :7
⁊ [-ic] Aldred p(re)sb(yte)r indignus ⁊ misserim⟨us⟩ \\ælfredi | natvs |
aldredvs | uocor |
i(d est) til w'
⟨→⟩ bonæ mvlieris | filivs eximivs | loquor :7//
mið godes fvltv(m)mę ⁊ s(an)c(t)i cvðberhtes
hit of(er)glóesade ón englisc . ⁊ hine gihamadi
mið ðæm ðríim dælv(m) . Mathevs dǽl
gode ⁊ s(an)c(t)e cvðberhti . Marc(vs) dǽl .

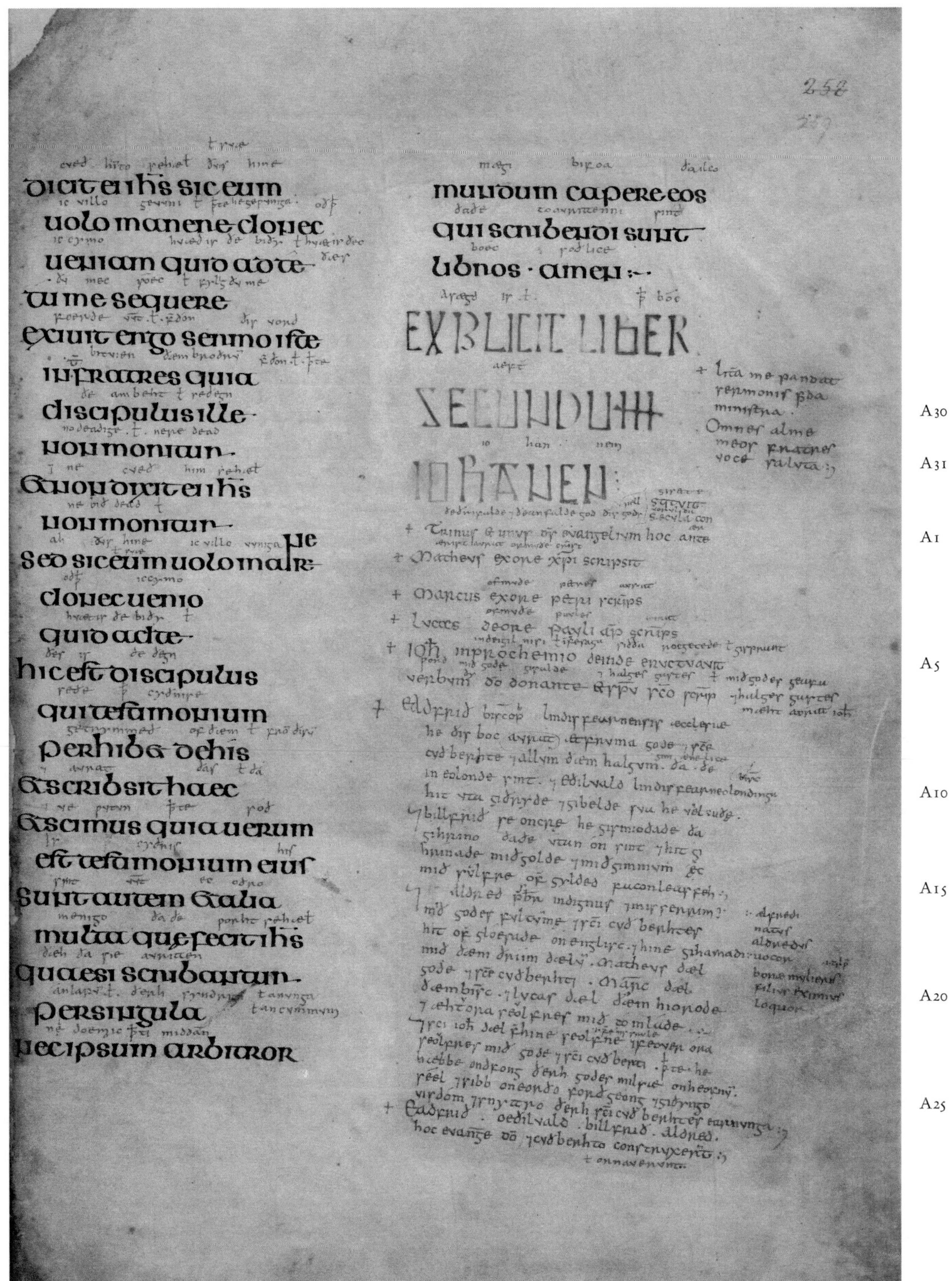

dixit ei ihs sic eum
uolo manere donec
uenio quid ad te
tu me sequere
exiuit ergo sermo iste
in fratres quia
discipulus ille
non moritur
Et non dixit ei ihs
non moritur
sed sic eum uolo mane-re
donec uenio
quid ad te
hic est discipulus
qui testimonium
perhibet de his
et scribsit haec
et scimus quia uerum
est testimonium eius
sunt autem et alia
multa que fecit ihs
quaesi scribantur
per singula
nec ipsum arbitror
mundum capere eos
qui scribendi sunt
libros · amen :-
EXPLICIT LIBER
SECUNDUM
IOHANEN

Plate 5 – reduced to 68%

ðæm bisc(obe) . ꝛ lvcas dæl ðæm hiorode
ꝛ æht\`v′ ora s[eo\\`v′]lfres mið tó inláde .: ~
ꝛ sci ioh(annes) dæl f(or) hine seolfne \`i(d est) f(or)e his savle′ ꝛ feover óra
s[eo\\`v′]lfres mið gode ꝛ s(an)c(t)i cvðberti . þ(æt)te . he
hæbbe ondfong ðerh godes milsæ on heofnv(m) . A25b
séel ꝛ sibb on eorðo forðgeong ꝛ giðyngo
visdóm ꝛ snyttro ðerh s(an)c(t)i cvðberhtes earnvnga :₇
+ eadfrið . oeðilvald . billfrið . Aldred .
hoc evange(lium) d(e)o ꝛ cvðberhto constrvxer(vn)t ′ł ornavervnt .\` :₇
\`\`+ Lit(er)a me pandat | sermonis fida | ministra . | A30b
Omnes alme | meos fratres | voce salvta :ꝛ ′′

Insular Half-uncial was a major book script in early Northumbria. The main script of this splendid manuscript is often described as Insular majuscule, but this is rather a tribute to the scribe's achievement than the true nature of the script. The letters are characteristically round, and wedge serifs, especially on **d**, **g**, and **t**, add to the monumental effect. The main-text letter-forms are generally Half-uncial, but there are some frequently used Uncial alternatives. Compare: the Uncial round **d** of 'quid', l. 3a, and tall Half-uncial forms of 'donec', l. 2a; the Uncial form of **n** in 'donec', l. 2a, with the more usual form in 'manere', l. 2a; the Uncial form of **r** in 'sequere', l. 4a, with the more usual Half-uncial form of 'sermo', l. 5a; the Uncial round **s** of 'sic', l. 1a, with the tall *ſ* of 'iste', l. 5a. A variant for the distinctive Half-uncial **a** does not occur on this page. Note the flat-headed **g** (as in 'ergo', l. 5a); and the Uncial **n** in 'ma\`ne′re', l. 11a, serves as a calligraphic space-saving device, cleverly keeping the word from spilling into the space between the columns. The punctuation is *per cola et commata*, i.e. the positioning of words on lines marks out sense units. Enlarged letters serve as capitals at the beginning of verses, and the end of the gospel is marked with three lines of undecorated elongated capitals, leaving just over half the second column empty.

This space gave Aldred room, once he had completed glossing the gospels, to weave a history of the physical book into his own elaborate ending. The colour plate C1 makes it possible to see Aldred's use of red in this part of the manuscript for glosses. Aldred put a great deal of thought into the layout of these last additions, even setting up careful hardpoint ruling for them, but he did not manage to fit all his material tidily into the second column. Quite where all the additions in the margin fit is debated, but this transcription attempts to present them as a whole; for ease of reference Aldred's additions in the space below the main text begin a new sequence of numbers prefaced by A. Note that ll. A30b-31b could alternatively be positioned before the five sentences at the beginning. The five sentences, set out with introductory crosses, are themselves glossed in English as if to complement the gospel's *explicit* with his own newly created 'main' text. Here Aldred aimed at a more formal script than his usual cursive minuscule, a hybrid minuscule. The script is more slanted than Half-uncial, the minims are fairly freely made and generally slope, and there is a haphazard use of distinctive Half-uncial letter-forms (among them the characteristic Half-uncial **a** of 'Lucas', l. A4b). Compare ll. A28b-29b at the foot of the column. The block in English (ll. A7b-27b) is in cursive minuscule as befits the vernacular. Tironian signs set out to the left of the script block (ll. A12b, A16b and A23b) separate out four main emphases: the original making of the book by bishops Eadfrith and Æthelwald; the craftsmanship of Billfrith the anchorite in adorning it with gold and jewels; Aldred's own act of homage, the provision of an interpretative film of English; and his wish for 'God's mercy in heaven' (l. A25b). For the first two of these, on the original book's history, Aldred used as nucleus an older poem available to him (Roberts, at press). He begins the lower part by muffing the opening, erasing the English pronoun 'ic', l. A16b, perhaps to achieve a formal charter-like effect; has second thoughts too about how to abbreviate *presbyter*, adding *ſ* with the bottom of its stem turning to the left as if constrained by space and neglects to provide the adjective *miserimus* with the necessary abbreviation, unless part of what stands at the end of the line be taken as doing double duty to give *-us* also. Aldred was not always scrupulous about supplying marks of abbreviation; compare the lack of an overline to help the reading of 'sci', l. A23b, as *sancti*. The following mark seems to be a *signe de renvoi*. If read as a question mark (not found anywhere else in Aldred's additions), it acquires significance as a Caroline feature in a conservative small scholarly minuscule otherwise sporting only what Ker ([1943] 1985: 4) describes as 'an *a* which resembles Caroline *a*' among four *a*-shapes used by Aldred. As a *signe de renvoi*, it directs the eye to Latin words not out of place alongside the confessional phrase 'indignus ꝛ misserrim⟨us⟩' (three dots are used a second time, and mark this passage off from the main block). For **a** with stem rising well above the bow see the Hatton *Cura Pastoralis* (pl. 6, 'begá', l. 5) and the first hand of the Parker Chronicle (pl. 8, 'wiecan', l. 6); the head of this protruding stroke bends over in capitals (compare 'Ac', pl. 6, l. 14 and the final letter of 'monna', pl. 7, l. 7). Thus, what has been termed the Caroline-like **a** of Aldred is, like his simplest form of **a** (made from two simple bows open at the top), more likely to have been an inherited feature within his hand. In distribution it is more a capital (see the diminuendo of

'Eadfrið', l. A7b, and the first letter of 'Aldred', ll. A16b, A28b) than a minuscule letter ('allvm', l. A9b) on this page. Also old-fashioned is his habit of tucking vowels beneath the baseline: 'doemo', l. 24ag, 'fida', l. A30b, transcribed from right margin; twice, in 'fylig', l. 4ag, and 'mið', l. A17b, *i* is pushed up. His selection from the special letter-forms in use for writing English is of interest: **ð** is general, with **þ** reserved for the most part for the **ꝥ** abbreviation; **ƿ** (wyn), represented by **w** in the transcription, is relatively infrequent (before vowels in ll. 2ag, 18ag, 21ag, A6bg, and probably A16bg). The pointed form **v** is used for both vowel ('ðvs', l. 1ag) and consonant ('cveð', l. 1ag) and for the two side by side (compare the infinitive 'gevvni', l. 2ag, with the linked finite alternative 'gewvniga'). The forms of English are northern: final -*n* and -*m* are often absent, as in the infinitives 'gevvni' l. 2ag, 'vvniga', l. 11ag, 'bifoa', l. 1bg, or the adverb 'siðða', l. A5bg; 'gisalde', l. A6bg, has Anglian -*a*- rather than the West Saxon -*ea*- ascribed to breaking; and 'feh', l. A15b, rather than *feoh*, shows non-West Saxon smoothing. Although Aldred was based in an area beyond the central belt of Scandinavian settlement, he does not follow the grammatical norms found in Old English from the southern part of the country at this time: thus *ðe* is to be found in subject position as well as the older *se* (see ll. 7ag, 14ag). Whereas the conventional orthography of the south generally has -*e*- for the neutral vowel sound in inflexions, Aldred's tends to have *i* (for a sound made towards the front of the mouth, e.g. 'gihamadi', l. A18b) or *v* in the -*on* ending (for a sound made further back in the mouth, e.g. 'wvtvn', l. 18ag). Yet some of the noteworthy spellings are possibly obsolescent: the *oe* of 'sóec', l. 4ag, 'boéc', l. 3bg, 'of(er)glóesade', l. A18b, etc.; the final -*o* of the first person verb forms 'villo', l. 2ag, 'cymo', l. 12ag, 'doemo', l. 24ag, etc.; and *æ* in *svæ* may be compared with 'suæ' in Hatton 20 (see l. 8, pl. 6). There is some uncertainty with *æ*: the *e* of 'cveð', ll. 1ag, 9ag, can be regarded as a low-stress form, but see also 'ec', l. 20ag (contrast 'ęc', l. A14b), 'ðæh', l. 22ag, and the aberrant inflexions of 'oncrę', l. A12b, and 'milsæ', l. A25b. The abbreviations **⁊**, **ꝥ**, and **ł** are very common. The Tironian sign, if expanded, should be spelt with *on* (see 'oncrę', l. A12b, 'ondfong', l. A25b). Throughout Aldred's glosses in this manuscript, fewer than one in ten instances of **ꝥ** are spelt out. The **ł** abbreviation, not always marked out by surrounding points, is left unexpanded (it should be read as *vel*, but might have been understood as *oþþe* in a vernacular context). The overline customarily makes *m* or *n* (as 'fro(m) ðisv(m)', l. 16ag, and 'i(n)', l. A5bg). As is the way of glosses, it is also used for more radical contractions, for example 'vvt(udlice), ll. 5ag, 20g, 'middan(gard)', l. 24ag, 'crist(es)', l. A2bg, as is the slash through an ascender, for example 'hæl(end)', ll. 1a, 9a, 21a, and 'IOh(annes)', l. A5bg. The expansion of the overline above 'bisc', ll. A10b and A21b (where a plural form could plausibly be advanced), is tricky, given Aldred's emendation of 'biscop', l. A7b to 'biscob'. The *er* mark usually curves a little upwards to the right as in 'of(er)gylded', l. A15b, 'of(er)glóesade', l. A18b, 'Lit(er)a', l. A30b; for its use for *or* see 'f(or)ðon', l. 6a, and 'f(or)esaga', l. A5bg. Note that Aldred should have placed 'middan(gard)', l. 24ag, above the first word of col. b. Some problems of interpretation remain, for example: in 'synt', l. 20ag, the *y* looks like Insular *s*; 'gisprant', l. A5bg, is to be understood as *gesprang*; 'gimænelice', l. A10b, is oddly placed but according to the prompt given by a pair of dots.

The hand of Aldred the priest is found also in Durham, Cathedral Library, A. IV. 19, where he describes himself in 970 (f. 84r) as 'aldred se p(ro)fast', and in occasional Latin glosses added to a copy of Bede's Commentary on the Book of Proverbs written in Wearmouth/Jarrow (Oxford, Bodleian Library, Bodley 819).

CONTEXTS

Aldred states that the manuscript was written by Eadfrith of Lindisfarne (d. 721). Late in the ninth century the community left Lindisfarne with relics and treasures, and after seven years of wandering settled in Chester-le-Street, where Aldred added his glosses and notes in the middle of the tenth century. The community moved to Durham in 995. Manuscript at Durham in twelfth century. A scrawled inscription on f. 211 is no longer identified as by William Turner. Late in the sixteenth century Nowell and Joscelyn excerpted readings from Aldred's gloss, perhaps in London if Nero D. iv was then in William Bowyer's possession. His son, Robert Bowyer (signature f. 2v) owned it by 1605 (Camden's evidence). In Cotton's collection by 1621. Entered the British Museum with the Cotton Collection in 1753. Known as the Lindisfarne Gospels.

SIZE

c. 340 × 250 mm (*c.* 235 × 190 mm). [Liuzza and Doane c.340×240 WS 235-45×185]

BIBLIOGRAPHY

Pr. Skeat 1871-87: 184-88.

Facs. Kendrick *et al.* 1956, 1960; Liuzza and Doane 1995; Brown, M.P. 2002.

Disc. Lowe *CLA*, no. 187; Brown, T.J. *et al.* 1969; Watson 1979, no. 544; Alexander 1978: no. 9; Backhouse 1981, pp. 16, 23 and pl. 12; Dumville 1999; Brown, M.P. 2000, 2003; Tite 2003: 137.

For Aldred: Ker 1942-43[1] [1985]; Ker, *Cat.* 1957: no. 165; Gameson 2001; Gneuss 2001: no. 343; Nees 2003; Roberts forthcoming.

III Anglo-Saxon Minuscule

For Anglo-Saxon minuscule, pointed Insular minuscule is focal (pl. 1, St Petersburg Bede), with ninth-century Southumbrian models like the Book of Cerne (pl. 4) providing the springboard. In adopting Insular minuscule as a book hand in the eighth century, English scribes turned aside from the more widely disseminated scripts in use beyond the British Isles. They are therefore sometimes said to have abandoned using an international script,[1] even though Insular minuscule was used in the continental houses founded by Irish and English missionaries.[2]

In Ireland Insular minuscule continues in use into modern times and in England, too, Insular-derived letter-forms continued to be used long after Caroline minuscule became, from the middle of the tenth century, the script of the reformed Benedictine houses and, increasingly, the script generally in use. From a European perspective the plates representing the Anglo-Saxon period look markedly separate and therefore 'insular', and the term Insular is indeed useful for English manuscripts up into the ninth century, especially in relation to manuscripts without certain provenance (for example, the script of the Book of Durrow or of the Book of Kells can be safely termed Insular when tempers run high). Close links continued between Britain and Ireland. By the middle of the ninth century, however, Viking raids had brought about ever-increasing disruption. In Northumbria most of the ruling familes disappeared, as did many of the great monasteries. Much of Mercia was devastated, and with the death of King Edmund of East Anglia in 869 opposition to the Scandinavian invaders came mainly from western and southern Mercia and from the West Saxons. The ninth century was, for learning and the making of books, more or less a period of stagnation throughout much of England, with standards picking up again in Alfred's reign. The books that survive come generally from far south of the Humber, from Wessex, Kent, and Mercia, suggesting the development of a Mercian script-province in the latter half of the eighth century and the first half of the ninth.[3] Whereas the fifteen or so manuscripts that may be dated to the first half of the ninth century are of good quality and have a finely developed gradation in script styles, by this time the hierarchy of Insular grades had mostly broken down.[4] The earliest manuscripts of King Alfred's educational renaissance look back to older models like the Book of Cerne. A new determination to revitalize learning and to rebuild the religious life of England is signalled by the letter King Alfred (871-99) wrote to his bishops, sent to accompany copies of a translation of Gregory's *Cura Pastoralis* to all the dioceses in the country. Very obviously, the new books in English were not great liturgical volumes. Rather, they were books for reading,[5] and they were to play a part in the education offered in monastic houses at least into the boyhood of Ælfric. Copies of Alfredian translations were made even in the twelfth century,[6] and early in the thirteenth century the Worcester *magister* with the 'tremulous hand' found much to interest him in the translations made by or for Alfred (see pls 6, 22, and 24). The late ninth century, that is to say the period of Alfred's reforms, is to be regarded as the take-off point for Anglo-Saxon minuscule.

There are three phases of Anglo-Saxon minuscule: pointed, square, and round. The major ecclesiastical reforms that got under way in the middle of the tenth century brought with them into the Benedictine monasteries Caroline script, at first for writing Latin, although some of the letter-forms distinctive of Insular script continue in use well into the twelfth century in writing English and are to be found in marginalia as late as the early thirteenth century. The earliest phase of Anglo-Saxon minuscule recognized is typically pointed. It is foreshadowed in charter hands (see the additions in pl. 3) and glosses (pl. 2a). The hand of the Hatton *Pastoral Care* (pl. 6) is important for the emergence of Anglo-Saxon pointed minuscule as a book hand for English. Ker suggests that its scribe was accustomed to using Insular minuscule for charters in English, and is here learning to adapt it as a book hand. This hand, from the beginning of Alfred's renaissance of learning, shows little change from the main script of the Book of Cerne. Even the diminuendo marking the text opening of Hatton 20 looks old-fashioned; and the decoration of the initial capital is reminiscent of the small initials in the Book of Cerne. Like the first scribe of the Parker Chronicle (pl. 8), the Hatton scribe is experimenting with an appropriate choice of letter-forms for the two English consonants foreign to Latin. He seems more accustomed to using **ð** than **þ**, whereas the first Parker scribe depends mostly on **þ**, scarcely using **ð** at all. No more has either the Hatton 20 or the first Parker scribe a settled choice for **w**, the Parker scribe generally using **u** (or **uu**) as well as **ƿ**, and the Hatton scribe retaining **u** in some common words (e.g. *suæ*, *suiðe*). Similar uncertainties are evident in BL, Additional Charter 19791 (pl. 7), one of the

[1] Bishop 1971: xi.

[2] Bischoff ([1975] 1994: 118, 149) points to the use of Anglo-Saxon script at Fulda as late as the middle of the ninth century. See further McKitterick, R. 1989.

[3] Brown, M.P. 1996: 164-78.

[4] Morrish 1988; Brown, M.P. 1998.

[5] Gameson 1995: 201.

[6] Apart from a brief extract in Cotton Tiberius A. iii, ff. 50v-51v, Alfred's free reworking of the *Soliloquia* of Augustine is extant only in the mid-twelfth-century Cotton Vitellius A. xv, ff. 4-59v.

earliest chirographs still extant.[7] The punctuation original to the Hatton scribe is simple; he uses a medial stroke shaped like a comma, though often it is little more than a trailing point. To indicate longer pauses the following letter may be enlarged and tipped with colour. Similar strategies are to be seen in the mid-ninth-century additions to the Codex Aureus (pl. 3), but the running glosses of pl. 2 are without punctuation. The first Parker hand of *c.* 900 is still not unlike the earlier pointed scripts, although it is moving towards the square phase. The scribe still sometimes has low-slung **l** initially, as in 'lond', l. 21, with which compare 'leofusta', l. 1, in the Hatton *Cura Pastoralis* (pl. 6), and **h** is as yet without the second limb's outwards right turn that becomes marked in Anglo-Saxon minuscule from about 900. The use of subscript ligatures, as in 'monna', l. 14, in the first Parker hand, is a relic of earlier practices, for which compare pl. 1, ll. 18a and 14b. At this time the main mark of punctuation is the simple point, complemented by the spacing given to word blocks, words, and parts of words. In both the Hatton *Cura Pastoralis* and the part of the Parker Chronicle written by the first scribe the quires are ruled folded, in the old Insular fashion.

The square phase in its beginnings from *c.* 920, is essentially a tenth-century script, although some distinctive features, for example the use of the 'oc' Half-uncial **a**, especially to be found in Latin texts, probably derive from hybrid Insular minuscule. In English texts Half-uncial **a** is occasional.[8] Examples are found in the plates taken from two of the four codices of Old English poetry (pls 11, 13), all by chance in ordinary words rather than in proper names or cited Latin words, where they are thought to appear most frequently.[9] (The Half-uncial **a** of Caroline scripts, as in pl. 20, where the distinctive **ra** ligature can be seen, was taken over from Half-uncial on the continent.) Early in the tenth century the hand of the Lauderdale Orosius (pl. 9) marks the emergence of the prototype for Anglo-Saxon square minuscule. The script is so like the second hand of the Parker Chronicle as to be thought at least from the same centre and possibly from the same scribe.[10] In addition, similarity of the decorated initials (the starting-point for Wormald's Type I initials)[11] to those found in the Junius Psalter indicates origins in Winchester.[12] There is a generous use of space (this manuscript has not been cropped), and the main mark of punctuation is a point on or a little above the line. The Hatton *Cura Pastoralis,* the first and second Parker scribes and the Tollemache Orosius together provide the evidence for the early West Saxon dialect.[13]

Perhaps the pointed script was not felt to be grand enough, although a striking descendant is to be seen in some important manuscripts. The letters of the Tanner Bede (pl. 10), for example, appear narrow because they are long and well-shaped, but **a**, when following tall **e**, is squarish. From much this time a narrow script, its letter-forms markedly elongated, is in use in the vernacular boundary clauses of charters.[14] Again, there are on the whole few decorated initials in the earliest manuscripts written mainly in English, and those that there are derive mostly from early-ninth-century models. The Tanner Bede, towards the middle of the tenth century, is unusual in having so many elaborate initials.

Anglo-Saxon minuscule is at its most formal in its square phase. Although a simplified script, when formal, Anglo-Saxon square minuscule may have decorative hairline strokes. Overall, the script appears upright, and it has a squarer aspect than pointed minuscule, particularly clear in the open **a** shape completed by a cross stroke. The top of the first stroke of **e** develops a shoulder that protrudes to the left, and the ascender of **d** folds in neatly over the body of the letter. The hand of the Exeter Book (pl. 11) is among the most beautiful to be seen in Anglo-Saxon vernacular manuscripts. This is a stately script, with fine hairline strokes on **g** and **t** and wedges on ascenders and on initial minims. The scribe's occasional use of Half-uncial **a**, an index of his calligraphic ambition, is seen in 'womma' (l. 21). In the plates in this book dotted **y** appears first in pl. 11 (Exeter Book) in straight-limbed forms and thereafter in pls 12, 15, 16, 17, and 18 in this section, but not in pls 13 (except for a later correction in l. 20) and 14.[15] It is worth noting its use also in the mid-tenth-century square minuscule of the main-text hand of pl. 26.

The main hand of pl. 12, from the earliest manuscript of Ælfric's Catholic Homilies, is somewhat stiffer, achieving a heavier appearance largely through the use of round **s** in all positions, though not to the exclusion of the low Insular form or of the long form found in ligatures.[16] A comparable distribution of round **s** is found already in the main-text hand of pl. 26, in a Latin text dated to the middle of the tenth century. Royal 7 C. xii is noteworthy for being the first English vernacular manuscript in which we see the elaborated punctuation system developed in the last decades of the eighth

[7] Chaplais 1968: 315 n. 3 [1973: 63 n. 3].

[8] According to Ker, *Cat.* 1957: xxviii, its last appearance in a datable text is in a 969 Worcester charter.

[9] Muir 1989: 282 gives interesting figures for the appearance of Half-uncial **a** in the Exeter Book: proper names × 37, Latin words × 13, less significant English words × 29.

[10] Dumville 1987 places these two manuscripts in his Phase 1 of square minuscule. His Phase 2, from the 930s, recognises the emergence of a canonical script. But see Ganz (forthcoming). For the second hand of the Parker Chronicle, see p. 51; a third hand is sometimes identified as beginning on l. 22.

[11] Wormald 1945: 120.

[12] Curiously, initials of this type are found also in the Cotton manuscript of the *Heliand*, an Old Saxon poem; the script is English Caroline minuscule, and the manuscript was probably written in the south of England late in the tenth century (see p. 59).

[13] Wrenn 1933 [1967].

[14] Dumville 2001: 8.

[15] Bishop (1954-58: 325) points out that Insular minuscule tends to use undotted **y**.

[16] For these terms see Ker, *Cat.* 1957: xxxi.

century in the Palace School at Aachen. This Ælfric manuscript was almost certainly written and revised at Cerne Abbas in Dorset in *c.* 990, and Ælfric himself can be seen making changes. Once he even marks out a passage to be cancelled, noting that he has used it again elsewhere (see p. 67, in the hand of the manuscript's other main scribe). It is the earliest manuscript in English to use the *punctus elevatus* which, like the point, occurs within what we think of as a sentence;[17] and the *punctus versus* at the end of sentences. Capitals (or enlarged letters) may mark new sentences. Coincidentally, it shows early use of the hyphen, which begins to appear late in the tenth century in English vernacular manuscripts. Occasionally a *punctus interrogativus* is used, though not on the pages reproduced. Similarly, pl. 13 (from Junius 11 or the 'Cædmonian' manuscript) indicates a growing concern with the punctuation of English, the points here serving mainly to demarcate half-line units of verse.[18] So too, frequent points mark units that are paired in Ælfric's rhythmical style (pl. 18, ll. 24-32), in a manuscript that makes little use of the elaborated punctuation system found in his Catholic Homilies. Paradoxically, the light pointing of the Exeter Book (pl. 11), where spacing, supplemented by hard-point dividing lines to help in the identification of verses, may provide a better guide for the reading of poetic texts,[19] even though it cannot be found to be following any systematic principles.[20]

The most admired Old English manuscripts are generally in Anglo-Saxon square minuscule. If the script's occasional incorporation of features derived ultimately from Half-uncial reflects a wish to emulate the greater formality of that script, more immediate models were provided by Insular hybrid minuscule (see pl. 4 from the Book of Cerne). A wish to emulate the simplification of script seen in Carolingian books could have been a contributory factor in the emergence of a more formal Anglo-Saxon minuscule,[21] but the development is based in the Insular way of writing. Soon, however, English square minuscule was to be in competition with Caroline minuscule, which was from *c.* 950 becoming the major script for writing Latin in England. From late in the tenth century the dominance of square minuscule was giving way to rounder hands, unsurprisingly, for it is likely that Caroline minuscule was now the basic script taught, at least in the reformed houses. Its influence is visible even in the first of the two hands of the *Beowulf* manuscript: see p. 63, a page where glossing indicates that this particular text was still being read in the thirteenth century.[22] The effects are plain to see, not just in the forward tilt of pl. 14 (Julius A. x), which reflects the overall ductus of contemporary Caroline scripts, but also in the roundness of the letter-forms and in the lack of a spur to the left of **e**, often a marked feature at the top of the first down-stroke of this letter in Anglo-Saxon square minuscule. By the turn of the century Anglo-Saxon minuscule was typically entering its round phase. In pl. 15 (Vitellius C. iii) the **a** is sometimes square, and both **e** and **c** can have spurs to the left, but the overall appearance of the hand is curiously nondescript for what must have been a handsome book. There are few pointers to date, which could be nearer 1050 than 1000.[23] The double columns are noteworthy as unusual in manuscripts containing Old English, the layout and illustrations being taken over from a Latin original for these medical recipes. Pl. 16 (Nero. A. i) illustrates a famous piece of pulpit-thumping by Wulfstan of York. Relatively small in format, it is from a manuscript that draws together laws, rulings on good conduct, ecclesiastical memoranda, and homilies, seemingly a handbook of useful things used and annotated by Wulfstan himself. Although the script looks rough and the title is in plain black Rustic capitals, these are filled with red, the minims are separately made and the text has the elaborated punctuation seen first in pl. 12.

Quite different in ambition is the Old English Hexateuch (Claudius B. iv, pl. 17), showing the more old-fashioned of the manuscript's two main hands; the other hand may be seen on p. 81. A large book, lavishly illustrated, this was an ambitious undertaking.[24] Its overall design must have been laid out, together with outline sketches of each drawing, before the text was entered. Work continued intermittently on its drawings, almost 400 of them, for a couple of generations or more, but was never completed. An annotator added many explanatory notes in Latin in the middle of the twelfth century. The heavy sprinkling of stress marks, many added later than the main scribal work, also attests to the book's continued use in a living tradition of reading English aloud. In pl. 17, where the Abraham and Isaac story is presented as a succession of events, the typological message is clear: Abraham's willingness to sacrifice his son prefigures the Crucifixion. The use of full-body painting highlights the two servant boys and Isaac, and Isaac is further distinguished by being mounted on a donkey in the central position in the first scene of the story (see colour pl. C2). This mixture of full-body painting with the simple colour outlines of the other elements in the story is an effective mode of emphasis often used in what is termed the 'first style' of Anglo-Saxon drawing.[25] Painting seems to have been completed as a priority in those quires that contain the

[17] Clemoes and Eliason 1966: 24.
[18] O'Brien O'Keeffe 1990: 179ff.
[19] Ker 1933: 228.
[20] Muir 1989.
[21] Wormald 1957: 164; Dumville 1987: 154-55.
[22] Cameron 1974: 221.
[23] Voigts 1976.
[24] The careful abbreviation of the biblical books is discussed by Marsden 2000; 53-63.
[25] Wormald 1952: 26-29.

stories of Abraham, Isaac and Jacob, perhaps because of the great amount of typological significance they carried.[26] What is clear is that the drawings in this manuscript were planned at the outset, with pictures to follow the text illustrated, whereas the illustrations in Junius 11 lack any such regularity.[27]

Greater numbers by far of Anglo-Saxon manuscripts containing Old English survive from the first three-quarters of the eleventh century than from any other period. Although Caroline minuscule was by this time the dominant script, scribes when writing English were accustomed to using the Tironian sign ⁊ instead of the ampersand and the Anglo-Saxon letter forms now distinctive of Anglo-Saxon minuscule, selecting from the single compartment **a**, the round **d**, the spurred **e**, low **f** (its tongue on the writing line), **g** (the Insular ᵹ shape from which yogh is to descend), **h** (its second leg flicking up to the right from *c.* 900), **r**, low **s**, long **s** (descending below the script line) and, less often, distinctive forms of **c**, **o** (both these with a spur to the left, as for **e**), and **y** (for example, the **f**-shaped and the straight-limbed forms). For new work on the script and spellings of eleventh-century English being undertaken at the University of Manchester under the direction of Donald Scragg and Alex Rumble, see http://www.art.man.ac.uk/english/mancass/data/scriptors.php.

The letter-forms of pl. 18 (Julius E. vii) are distinctively Anglo-Saxon, and it would be tempting to categorize the hand as Anglo-Saxon square minuscule, except that in the evenness and in the plainness of ascenders and descenders, the latter straight rather than bending to the left, the underpinning of training in Caroline script may be discerned. The hand is therefore described as Late Anglo-Saxon minuscule, to indicate its transitional nature. As time passed, the ability of scribes to keep consistently to the distinctive Anglo-Saxon letter-forms when writing English diminished, with the Insular-derived **f** and **r** used longest and the Insular-derived **g** taking on a new role (**ȝ** or 'yogh' in contrast to Caroline **g**). The provenance for this manuscript is Bury St Edmunds, which is not known to have had a scriptorium before Cnut's refoundation of the church as a Benedictine house in 1020. As late as 1044, when Leofstan became abbot, he found only ten books, including one copy of a life of Edmund, in the church. There were a few more books in the possession of individual monks and thirty books in one of the monastery's manors, a modest and scattered collection.[28]

[26] See Johnson 2000 for a new assessment of the programme of illumination.
[27] Henderson 1975. For an examination of their disjunctive possibilities see Karkov 2001. A Junius 11 drawing is shown on p. 71.
[28] McLachlan 1986, 16-17.

6

Oxford, Bodleian Library, Hatton MS 20, f. 6r
Opening of Alfred's translation of Gregory, *Cura Pastoralis*
Anglo-Saxon minuscule in the pointed phase, 890-897

TRANSCRIPTION

þv leofusta broður suiðe freondlice ⁊ suiðe fremsumlice ðu me tæl⟨-⟩
desð . ⁊ `mid′ eaðmode Ingeðonce ðu me ciddesð , For ðon Ic min máð ⁊ wolde fleon ða
byrðenne ðære hirdelecan giemenne ðara byrðenna hefignesse , Eall ðæt Ic his
geman Ic awrite on ðisse andweardan béc , ðy læs hi hwæm leohte ðyncen to under⟨-⟩
fónne . ⁊[1] ic eac lære ðæt hira nan ðara ne wilnie ðe hine unwærlice begá ,
⁊ se ðe hi unwærlice ⁊ únryhtlice gewilnige ,[2] Ondræde he ðæt he hi æfre u`n′der⟨-⟩
fenge , Nu ic wilnige ðætte ðeos spræc stigge on ðæt Ingeðonc ðæs leorneres
suæ suæ on sume hlædre stæpmælum near ⁊ near oð ðæt hio fæstlice geston⟨-⟩
de on ðæm solore ðæs modes ðe hi leornige , ⁊ for ðy Ic `hi′ todæle `on′ feower , Án is ða⟨-⟩
ra dæla hu he on `ðone′ folgoð become ·[3] Oðer hu he ðær on libbe · **ð**ridda is hu he
ðær on lære . feorðe is hu he his agene unðeawas ongietan wille . ⁊ hira geðæf
bion . þy læs he for ðy underfenge his eaðmodnesse forlæte , Oððe eft his líf
sie ungelic his ðenunga , Oððe he to ðriste ⁊ to stið sie for ðy underfenge his la⟨-⟩
reowdomes , Ac gemetgige hit se ege his agenra unðeawa , ⁊ befæste he mid his
lifes bisenum ða lare ðæm ðe his wordum ne geliefen . ⁊ ðonne he gód weorc
wyrce gemyne he ðæs yfeles ðe he worhte . **ð**ette sio únrótnes ðe he for ðæm
yflan weorcum hæbbe gemetgige ðone gefean ðe he for ðæm godan weor⟨-⟩
cum hæfde , **ð**y læs he beforan ðæs dieglan deman eagum , sie áhafen on
his mode , ⁊ on ofermettum aðunden , ⁊ ðonne ðurh ðæt selflice his godan
weorc forleose , Ac monige sindon me suiðe ónlice ón úngelæred⟨-⟩
nesse , **ð**eah ðe hi næfre leorningcnihtas næren , wilniað ðeah lareo⟨-⟩

Tremulous hand glosses, etc.

[1] tu
[2] i *over* g; i(n)tent(i)o(n)e
rep(re)hendis
[3] pondera
pastoralis
cur[e>æ]
punctus versus
[4] q(u)ib(us)da(m)
[5] i(n)caute
[6] expetit
punctus elevatus
[7] adeptu(m)
i(n)tent(i)o(n)e
lectoris
[9] *punctus elevatus*
[10] ʔcul(egiu)m
[11] doceat
i(n)firmitate(m)
[12] fugiat
[14] doct(r)ina
te(m)p(er)et
apetitu(m)
[15] magist(er)iu(m)
[16] *punctus elevatus*
[17] (com)paret(ur)
gaudio
punctus elevatus
[18] tumor
[20] similes
i(m)pericia

This is the beginning of the translation, and it follows two folios on which the chapters are listed (Alfred's own prefatory letter, written by a different hand on a separate bifolium, is prefixed to this opening quire). The scribe seems more at home with **ð** than **þ**: apart from the black-line initial of 'þu', l. 1, it appears only in 'þy', l. 12, on this page. Note that as well as using **ƿ** the scribe has **u** after **s** in some common words ('suæ suæ', l. 8, 'suiðe', ll. 1, 20). The head of the straight stroke of **a** sometimes protrudes at the top, as 'begá', l. 5; in capitals it bends over ('Ac', l. 14). Long **s** is found more often before consonants than vowels. Curved strokes are usual in **y**: the **f**-shaped form, with both horns turned to the right, is frequent (e.g. 'ðy', l. 4, 'únryhtlice', l. 6). Long **i** can occur initially before **n** and in the pronoun 'I' (e.g. 'Ingeðonce', l. 2, 'Ic', l. 2). Some spellings are held to be early West Saxon, as for example *-ie-* in stressed syllables ('giemenne', l. 3, 'ongietan', l. 11). The inverted spelling *–sð* for *–st*, reflected in 'tældesð', ll. 1-2 and 'ciddesð', l. 2, occurs sporadically in 'Alfredian' manuscripts (interestingly too in the Vercelli Book). The original punctuation is simple: a medial stroke shaped like a comma and often little more than a trailing point; the following letter may be enlarged and tipped with colour to indicate longer pauses. Over vowels the apex sign indicates stress: on monosyllables 'máð', l. 2, 'béc', l. 4, 'Án', l. 9, 'gód', l. 15, 'ón', l. 20; on prefixes requiring stress 'únrótnes', l. 16, 'áhafen', l. 18, 'ónlice', l. 20, 'úngelæred', l. 20; on the root rather than the prefix 'begá', l. 5. Insertions are positioned above a point or pairs of points in ll. 2, 6, 9, and 10. Hardpoint ruling leaves direct impression on one side only, usually the hair side. Pricked inner and outer margins, so folded before ruling.

[1] As capital: enlarged and touched with colour. Compare ll. 14 and 15.

[2] The scribe's simple punctuation is often modified. Here the additional upper mark makes this an apology for a *punctus elevatus*.

[3] Note show-through of '⁊' from the verso.

Plate 6 – reduced to 81%

Single bounding lines are usual. The decorated initials (see l. 1) follow on from the use of interlace and animal-headed terminals in earlier southern English manuscripts. The only abbreviation used here by the main hand is the Tironian sign. The TH scribe was very likely responsible for supplementing the punctuation (e.g. ll. 6, 9, 16, 17) as well as adding glosses. Underlining, sometimes double, is to be connected with Joscelyn's collection of vocabulary materials.

CONTEXTS

This copy of his translation of Gregory's *Pastoral Care* was sent by Alfred to Werferth, bishop of Worcester. The book remained in Worcester, where notes or scribbles were added in the tenth ('koenwald monachus . ælfric clericus', f. 98v), eleventh (Wulfstan's hand is recognized: see Ker 1971 [1985]) and twelfth centuries ('willimot writ þus oððe bet', f. 53v). Used by the Tremulous Hand in the early thirteenth century. Not in Young's catalogue, *c.* 1622, but probably used at Worcester by Joscelyn, who underlined selected words as far as TH glossing extends. Also used by Junius and Dugdale (note on the recto of f. ii). By 1643-44 belonged to Christopher, Lord Hatton, and after his death acquired by the bookseller Robert Scot, from whom it was bought in 1671 with other Hatton manuscripts by the Bodleian Library, where formerly known as Hatton 88.

SIZE

c. 274 × 215 mm (226-205 × 175-160 mm).

BIBLIOGRAPHY

Pr. Sweet 1871: 22-24 (22, l. 9 to 24, l. 10).
Facs. Ker 1956; Franzen 1998.
Disc. SC 4113; Atkins and Ker 1944: 7, 10, 17; Sisam 1953: 140-147; Ker, *Cat.*1957: no. 324; Temple 1976: no. 1, Watson 1984: no. 517 and pl. 13; Horgan 1986: 108-27.
TH. *Disc*: Franzen 1991: esp. 59-60; Collier 2000; Gneuss 2001: no. 626.

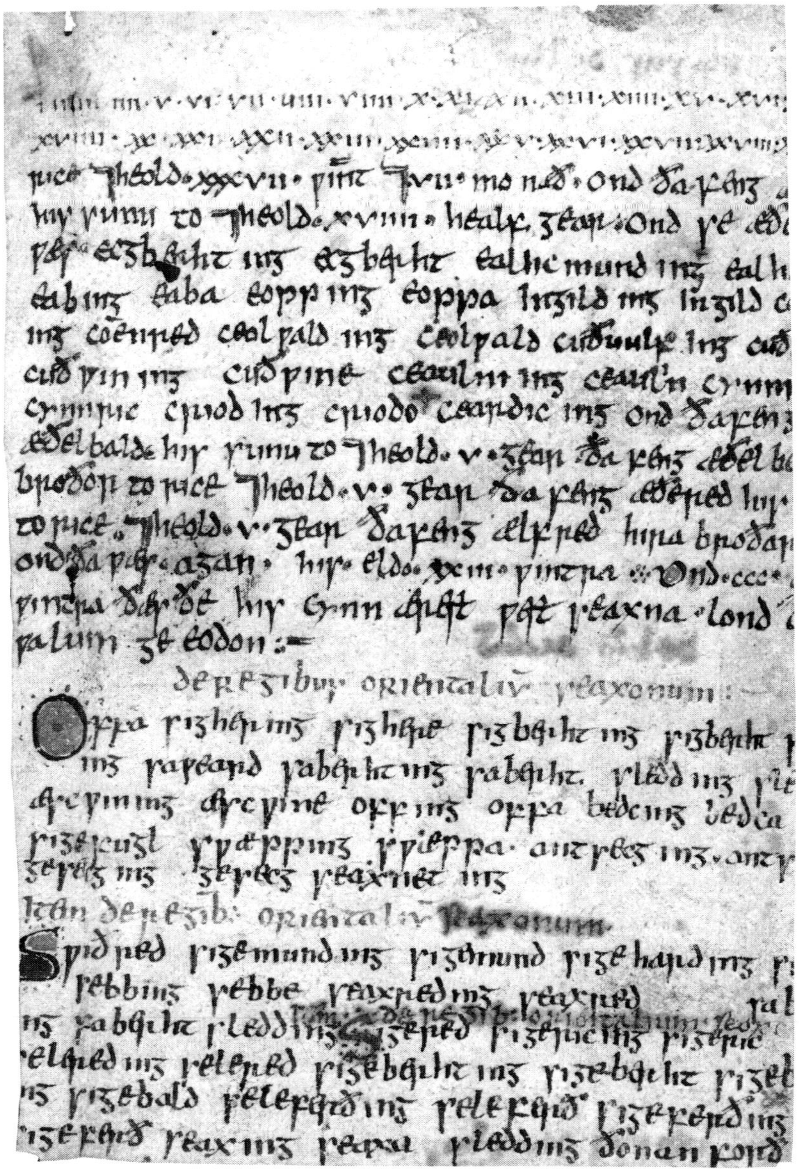

London, British Library, Additional MS 23211, f. 1r
Royal genealogies

These lists celebrate King Alfred's ancestry and the history of his kingdom, which had absorbed the old kingdom of the East Saxons. This fragment, a pastedown lifted from the cover of a printed book, gives the only pre-Conquest regnal lists for kings of the East Saxons: Sigered (l. 25), their last king, was expelled when the East Saxons surrendered in 825 to Egbert, Alfred's grandfather.
actual size

7

London, British Library, Additional Charter 19791
Lease from Werferth, bishop of Worcester, to his reeve Wulfsige
Anglo-Saxon minuscule, in the pointed phase, 904

TRANSCRIPTION

Rixiendum on ecnisse ussum drihtne hælende criste se ðe all
ðing gemetegað ge on heofenum ge on eorðan þæs inflæscnisse ðy gere
þe agen[1] wæs dcccc wintra ⁊ iiii winter ⁊ ðy uii · gebongere · Ic uuerfrid bisco`p′
mid mines arweorðan heorodes geðafuncga ⁊ leafe on weogerna ceastre
sylle wulfsige minum gerefan wið his holdum mægene ⁊ eadmodre her⟨-⟩
nesse anes hides lond on easttune swa swa herred hit hæfde on ðreora mon⟨-⟩
na dæg ⁊ all ðæt Innlond beligeð án dic utane ⁊ þonne ofer ðreora monna
dęg agefe monn eft ðaet lond butan elcon wiðercwide Inn to weogerna ceas⟨-⟩
tre ⁊ ðis seondan ðara monna noman ðe ðæt geðafedon ⁊ mid cristes
rode tacne gefaestnedon + uuerfrið biscop + cynehelm abb(od) + uuerfrið prs'
+ eadmund prs' + berhtmund prs' + tidbald prs' + hildefrið prs' + ecfrið prs'
+ eaduulf prs' + wiglaf prs' + oslac diacon + cynað diacon + berhthelm + wig⟨-⟩
heard + monn + earduulf[2] + uullaf + berhthelm + heahred + cynelaf + uulfred
+ cynehelm + uulfric + cenfrið + hwituc + cynelaf + ceolhelm + uul[l<?f]af + ealh⟨-⟩
mund + earduulf + uulfgar

This assured hand shows the continuance of a lively tradition of charter making into early-tenth-century Mercia. The hand is larger than in charters of the ninth century. The minims of **m** and **n** are cursively made, whereas they are clearly separate in **u**. Long **i** appears not just before **n** (as 'Innlond', l. 7, 'Inn', l. 8) but exaggeratedly so in 'Ic', l. 3. Despite the firm descenders and in particular the sweeping **g**, there is a general unevenness about the letter-forms: both **c** and **e** can seem larger than the norm (as in 'dic', l. 7, or 'eft', l. 8); **y** is small (see 'ðy', ll. 2, 3). As well as **æ**, both **ae** ('ðaet', l. 8, 'gefaestnedon', l. 10) and **ę** ('dęg', l. 8) occur (the **e** of 'elcon', l. 8, is to be put down to Mercian smoothing). Note the low-slung **l** of 'lond', l. 8, and the **r** of Insular hybrid minuscule in the first 'prs'' abbreviation of l. 11 (its descender seems partly obscured by a small stitch). The protruding head of **a** bends over in 'monna', l. 7, a flourish at the end of the line. Of the special letter-forms, **ð** is by far more frequent than **þ**, which occurs, initially only, in 'þæs', l. 2, 'þe', l. 3, and 'þonne', l. 7. The **ð** is sometimes made cursively in a single stroke, but can have two strokes (see 'ðara', l. 9). Some uncertainty is suggested by 'eorðan', l. 2, where **d** has been altered to **ð**, by 'ðæt', l. 8, where the bar is added, and by two spellings for the bishop's name ('uuerfrid', l. 3, and uuerfrið', l. 10). Wyn, represented by **w** in the transcripton, is general, except for the names that begin with **uu-** (*pace* Sisam 1953: 310-11 and fn 2, this charter hardly provides evidence that *u* and *uu* spellings are still preferred at the beginning of the tenth century). The page is carefully ruled in hardpoint, and the opening (copying the invocation phraseology of Latin) is marked by a gentle diminuendo. There are only two points, mid-height, in the whole document, in l. 3, and these are interpreted as standing about the infrequent word 'gebongere' (year of the indiction), otherwise found only in a Mercian charter recorded in Hemming's Cartulary (Cotton Tiberius A. xiii). Numbers are not marked out by points; and the three low-stress words '⁊ ðy uii', l. 3, cluster together. After the preliminaries of invocation and date, the very long **i** of 'Ic', l. 3, draws attention to the beginning of the terms of the agreement. Crosses stand before each witness's name. Note that the ecclesiastical ranks 'bisco`p′', l. 3, and 'diacon', l. 12 (× 2) are not in Latin; I have therefore expanded 'abb' to 'abb(od)', l. 10; and I have not expanded *prs'* to *pr(esbyte)r* because here the abbreviation might have been thought to stand for *preost* (compare Robinson 1982: 395-400 [1994: 160-63]).

[1] An anomalous form.

[2] The **d** is badly rubbed by the folding of the document.

Plate 7 – reduced to 94%

CONTEXTS

This is the lower portion of a chirograph, and there stand at the head the lower parts of the large letters 'COROGRAPHVM' that divided the matching records, roughly dissected. It appears therefore that two copies were made as a record of this lease for three lives of one hide of land at Aston Magna, Gloucestershire. The scribe has noted 'uulfsiges londboc' on the dorse (back or verso), where eleventh- twelfth-century hands have added 'Heastunes boc' and 'Eadward senior'. According to the acquisitions register held in the British Library, Additional Charter 19791 (numbered '5' in the bottom right-hand corner) was acquired as part of the huge Winchelsea Collection (Additional Charters 19788-22613), which was purchased on 12 July 1873 from G. R. Attenborough.

SIZE

c. 158 × 201 mm (125 × 185 mm).

BIBLIOGRAPHY

Pr. Robertson [1939] 1956: 34 (no. 18); Hoad 1978: pp. 220-21.
Facs. Bond 1873-78: III. no. 2.
Disc. Finberg 1961: 52 (no. 90); Sawyer 1968: no. 1281; Dumville 1987: 157-58, 1992: 92;
www.trin.cam.ac.uk/sdk13/chartwww/eSawyer.99/eSawyer2.html

8

Cambridge, Corpus Christi College MS 173, f. 15r (formerly p. 31)
Anglo-Saxon Chronicle (Parker or 'A' version), from the annals for 878-885
Anglo-Saxon minuscule, intermediate in type between pointed and square phase, *c.* 900

TRANSCRIPTION

broþur ⁊ healfdenes on[1] westseaxu(m)[2] on defena scire mid ·xxiii· sci⟨-⟩
pum ⁊ hiene mon þær ofslog . ⁊ dccc· monna mid him . ⁊ xl· mon⟨-⟩
na his heres ⁊ þæs on eastron worhte ęlfred cyning lytle werede
geweorc æt ęþelinga eigge ⁊ of þam geweorce was winnende wiþ þone
here ⁊ sumursætna se dęl se þær niehst wæs þa on þære seofoðan[3]
wiecan ofer eastron he gerad to ecgbryhtes stane be eastan seal⟨-⟩
wyda ⁊ him to co(m)[4] þær ongen sumorsæte alle ⁊ wilsætan ⁊ hamtun⟨-⟩
scir se dęl se hiere behinon sę was ⁊ his gefægene wærun ⁊ he fór
ymb ane niht of þam wicu(m) to iglea ⁊ þæs ymb ane to eþandune
⁊ þær gefeaht wiþ alne þone here ⁊ hiene gefliemde ⁊ hi(m) æft(er) rád
oþ þæt geweorc ⁊ þær sæt ·xiiii· niht ⁊ þa salde se here him fore⟨-⟩
gislas ⁊ micle aþas þæt hie of his rice uuoldon ⁊ him eac geheton
þæt hiera kyning fulwihte onfon wolde ⁊ hie þat gelæston swa
⁊ þæs y(m)b ·iii· wiecan co(m) se cyning to him godru(m) þritiga su(m) þara monna
þe In þa(m) here weorþ(us)te wæron æt alre ⁊ þæt is wiþ ęþelingga eige ⁊ his
se cyning þær onfeng æt fulwihte ⁊ his crismlising was æt weþ⟨-⟩
mor ⁊ h(e) was ·xii· niht mid þa(m) cyning(e) ⁊ h(e) hine miclu(m) ⁊ his g(e)feran mid feo weor\ðude :/
an(no) dccclxxix· Her for se here to cirenceastre of cippanha(m)me ⁊ sæt þær án gear
⁊ þy geare gegadrode on[5] hloþ wicenga ⁊ gesæt æt fullanha(m)me be teme⟨-⟩
se ⁊ þy ilcan geare aþiestrode sio sunne ane tid dæges: ~[6]
aN(no) dccc·lxxx· Her for se here of cirenceastre on eastengle ⁊ gesæt þæt lond ⁊ gedęlde
⁊ þy ilcan geare fór se here ofer sę þe ær on fullanho(m)me sæt
on fronclond to gend ⁊ sæt þær an gear : ~
an(no) dccc·lxxxi· Her for se here ufor on fronclond ⁊ þa francan hi(m) wiþ g(e)fuhton
⁊ þær \þa/ wearþ se here gehorsod æft(er) þa(m) gefeohte : ~
aN(no) dccc·lxxxii· Her for se here up onlong mæse feor on fronclond ⁊ þær sæt
an gear ⁊ þy ilcan geare fór ęlfred cyning mid scipu(m) ut on sę .
⁊ gefeaht wiþ feower sciphlæstas deniscra monna ⁊ þara
scipa tu genam ⁊ þa men ofslægene wæron þe ðęr on wæron ⁊ tue⟨-⟩
gen scipheras him on hond eodon ⁊ þa wæron miclu(m) forslæge⟨-⟩
ne ⁊ forwundode ær hie on hond eodon : ~
aN(no) dccc·lxxxiii· Her for se[7] here up on scald to cundoþ ⁊ þær sæt án gear : ~
aN(no) dccc·lxxxiiii Her for se here up on sunnan to embenum ⁊ þær sæt án gear : ·
aN(no) dccc·lxxxv· Her todęlde se foresprecena here on tu oþer dęl east oþer dęl
to hrofesceastre ⁊ ymbsæton ða[8] ceastre ⁊ worhton oþer
fæsten ymb hie selfe ⁊ hie þeah þa ceastre aweredon oþ þæt \\ęlfred//[9]

This is the first hand of the Parker Chronicle, dated to late in the ninth century or early in the tenth century. The separately made minims thicken and tend to turn up at the foot. Long **i** sometimes appears initially, especially before **m** or **n** ('In', l. 15), as does low-slung **l** ('lond', l. 21). The first stroke of **a** is rounded, with the second protruding at the top. The **e** is tall in the ligatured **æ** (**ę** is also used) and sporadically elsewhere. Similarly **c** may be enlarged initially (it is not therefore transcribed as a capital in place-names, for example 'cirenceastre', l. 18, 'cundoþ', l. 32). The Uncial form of **t** is used

[1] The **o** is altered.
[2] The **s** changed from low to long form.
[3] The **f** may be corrected from **þ**.
[4] '\mon/' is added in later hand to agree with plural subject that follows.
[5] For the numeral *ān* 'one'.
[6] The solar eclipse of 29 October 878. At this point dates are one or two years out in the Parker Chronicle.
[7] The tall **s** here may be written over **w**.
[8] The **ð** is on an erasure, and the word occupies unusually generous space.
[9] On turning the scribe missed a few words, thus having to add 'ęlfred' into this page when making good his error on the verso.

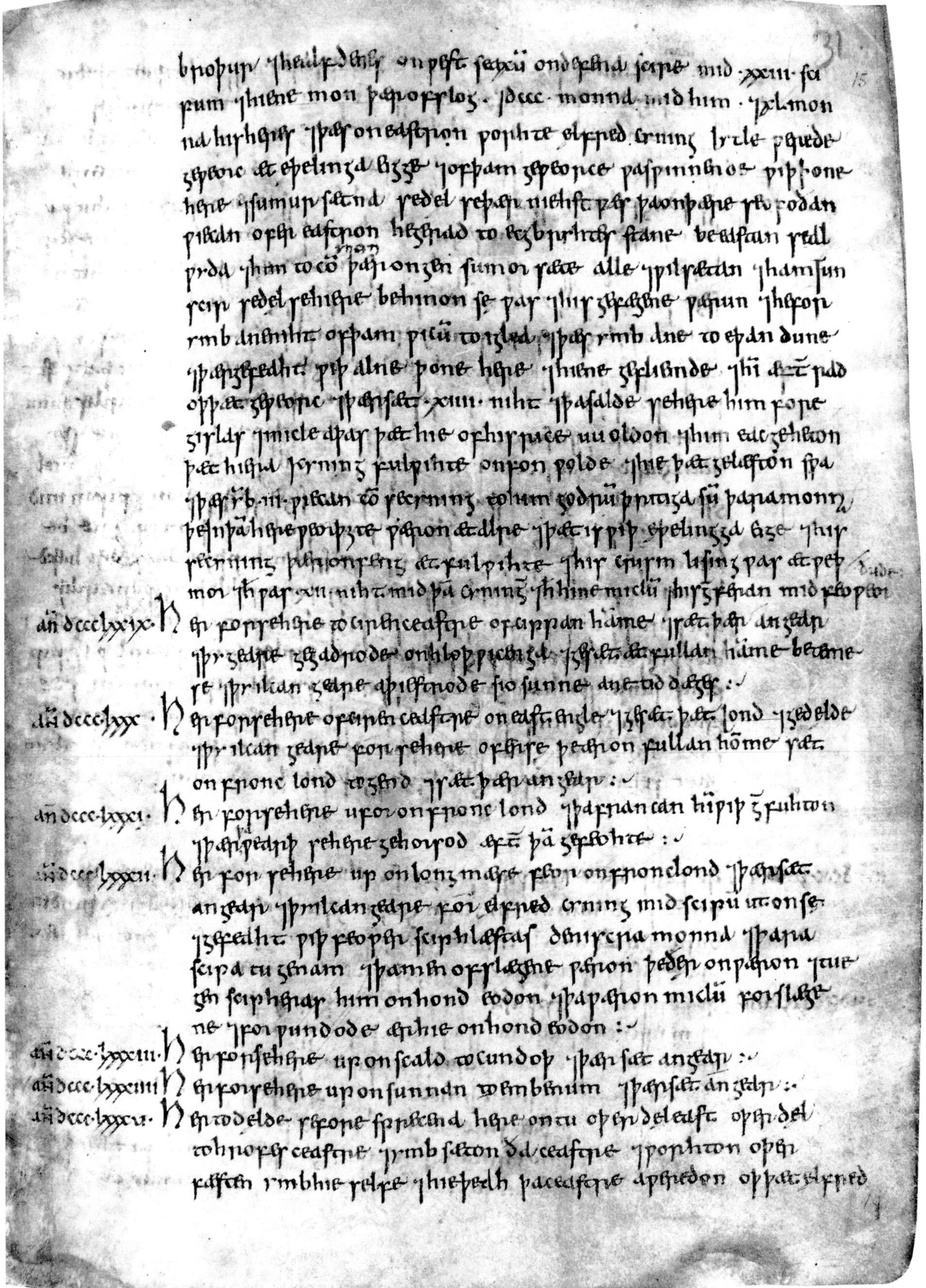

broþur ⁊ healfdenes on west seaxū ond defna scire mid .xxiii. sci
pum ⁊ hiene mon þær ofslog. ⁊ dccc. monna mid him. ⁊ xl. mon
na his heres ⁊ þæs on eastron worhte ælfred cyning lytle werede
geweorc æt æþelinga eigge ⁊ of þam geweorce was winnende wiþ þone
here ⁊ sumursætna se dæl se þær niehst wæs þa on þære seofoðan
wiecan ofer eastron he gerad to ecgbryhtes stane be eastan sealw
yda ⁊ him to cō þær ongen sumorsæte alle ⁊ wilsætan ⁊ hamtun
scir se dæl se hiere behinon sæ was ⁊ his gefægene wærun ⁊ he for
ymb ane niht of þam wicū to iglea ⁊ þæs ymb ane to eþan dune
⁊ þær gefeaht wiþ alne þone here ⁊ hiene gefliemde ⁊ him æfter rad
oþ þæt geweorc ⁊ þær sæt .xiiii. niht ⁊ þa salde se here him fore
gislas ⁊ micle aþas þæt hie of his rice uuoldon ⁊ him eac geheton
þæt hiera kyning fulwihte onfon wolde ⁊ hie þæt gelæston swa
⁊ þæs ymb .iii. wiecan cō se cyning to him godrū þritiga sū þara monna
þe in þā here weorþuste wæron æt alre ⁊ þæt is wiþ æþelinga eige ⁊ his
se cyning þær onfeng æt fulwihte ⁊ his crismlising was æt weþ
mor ⁊ he was xii. niht mid þā cyninge ⁊ he hine miclū ⁊ his geferan mid feo weorðude

an̄ dccclxxix. Her for se here to cirenceastre of cippan hamme ⁊ sæt þær an gear
⁊ þy geare gegadrode on hlop wicinga ⁊ gesæt æt fullan hamme be teme
se ⁊ þy ilcan geare aþiestrode sio sunne ane tid dæges :-

an̄ dccclxxx. Her for se here of cirenceastre on east engle ⁊ gesæt þæt lond ⁊ gedelde
⁊ þy ilcan geare for se here ofer sæ þe ær on fullan hōme sæt
on froncē lond to gend ⁊ sæt þær an gear :-

an̄ dccclxxxi. Her for se here up on froncē lond ⁊ þa francan him wiþ gefuhton
⁊ þa wearþ se here gehorsod æft þā gefeohte :-

an̄ dccclxxxii. Her for se here up onlong mæse feor on froncē lond ⁊ þær sæt
an gear ⁊ þy ilcan geare for ælfred cyning mid scipū ut on sæ
⁊ gefeaht wiþ feower sciphlæstas deniscra monna ⁊ þara
scipa tu genam ⁊ þa men ofslægene wæron þe ðæron wæron ⁊ tue
ge sciphlæstas him on hond eodon ⁊ þa wæron miclū forslæge
ne ⁊ forwundode ær hie on hond eodon :-

an̄ dccclxxxiii. Her for se here up on scald to cundoþ ⁊ þær sæt an gear :-

an̄ dccclxxxiiii. Her for se here up on sunnan to embenum ⁊ þær sæt an gear :-

an̄ dccclxxxv. Her todelde se foresprecena here on tu oþer dæl east oþer dæl
to hrofesceastre ⁊ ymb sæton ða ceastre ⁊ worhton oþer
fæsten ymb hie selfe ⁊ hie þeah þa ceastre aweredon oþ þæt ælfred

Plate 8 – reduced to 79%

occasionally (see 'hamtun⟨-⟩', l. 7), probably to save space. Where **r** follows **o** it may be a simple angled stroke, as in 'geweorc', l. 4, 'sumorsæte', l. 7. Both **þ** and **ƿ** (transcribed as **w**) are in use: **ð** occurs infrequently ('seofoðan'. l. 5, 'weor\ðude', l. 17, 'ðęr', l. 29, 'ða', l. 35); and note 'uuoldon', l. 12. Early West Saxon spellings include the distinctive *ie* ('hiene', l. 2, 'niehst', l. 5, 'wiecan', l. 6, etc.). The letter **k** ('kyning', l. 13) appears only sporadically in Old English; in Latin too it is infrequent, being restricted for the most part to a few words in which the opening letter is used in abbreviation (e.g. 'kł', l. 5, in pl. 18). Word division is by no means complete: articles, pronouns, prepositions, and connectives are often joined to a following word; and compound words are sometimes separated into parts. The main mark of punctuation is the simple point, also used to demarcate numerals, and the space occupied by word blocks, words, and parts of words obviously complements the infrequent points. Some further reading help is given by sporadic stress marks (e.g. 'fór', l. 8, 'rád', l. 10, 'án', l. 33). The annal numbers and opening capitals suggest that care was given to the chronicle's layout, and heavy punctuation marks the end of each annal (the over-run of l. 17 finishes with a pair of points only); adjustments have been made to some annal numbers. Pricking for horizontal lines in both margins, so folded before ruling. On this page the scribe seems to have realized that the space allowed before the next annal number was running out by l. 14, and he resorts to a variety of space-saving devices for the remainder of the annal, for example the subscript **a** of 'monna', l. 14, the final over-run 'weor\ðude/', l. 17, and an unusually heavy use of abbreviations (**ꝫ** in 'weorþ(us)te', l. 15, and the stroke through the ascender of **h** making 'he' twice in l. 17 are rare in Old English). Otherwise the abbreviations on this page are usual in Old English: ⁊ for *ond*; the overline for *m* or *n* and for *e* when above **g** ('g(e)feran', l. 17); and a curving rising stroke for *er* in 'æft(er)', ll. 10, 25.

CONTEXTS

This part of the Parker Chronicle may have been written west of Winchester; in the tenth century it was in Winchester (special prominence is given to Æthelwold and Frithestan). Probably at Christ Church, Canterbury, by *c.* 1070; 'Cronica uetustissima a.' of twelfth-century catalogue (Ker, *Cat.* 1957: xlv). In the sixteenth century Joscelyn notes that it belonged to Nicholas Wotton, dean of Canterbury. Archbishop Parker left it to Corpus Christi College in 1575; consulted in the next century by both Lisle and Whelock.

SIZE

c. 286 × 210 mm (*c.* 245 × 145 mm).

BIBLIOGRAPHY

Pr. Plummer [1952] 1892: 74-78; Bately 1986: 50-52.
Facs. Flower and Smith 1941 [rpt. 1973].
Disc. Ker, *Cat.* 1957: no. 39; Parkes 1976 [1991]; Lutz 1982, 2000; Bately 1988[2]; ~ 1991; Robinson 1988: no. 135, pls 8-13; Dumville 1992; Sato 1997; Gneuss 2001: no. 82.

Cambridge, Corpus Christi College MS 173, f. 21r
Anglo-Saxon Chronicle (Parker or 'A' version), from the annals for 910-916

Hand 2 (cf. pl. 9). Does a third hand begin on l. 22?
reduced to 79%

9

London, British Library, Add. MS 47967, f. 48v (formerly p. 94)
English translation of Orosius, *Historiarum adversum Paganos*, III. xi-IV. i
Anglo-Saxon minuscule, square phase, s. x[1]

TRANSCRIPTION

⁊ nyllað geþencan hwelc hit þa wæs þa nan mon ne
mehte æt oþrum his feorh gebycggan ne furþon
þætte þa wolden gefriend beon þe wæron gebroðor
of fæder ⁊ of meder ; ⁊ her endað sio[1] [w>þ]ridde[2] boc ⁊ on⟨-⟩
ginð seo feorþe ;

AEFT(er)[3] þæm þe romeburg getimbred wæs feower hun⟨-⟩
de wintru(m) ⁊ feower ⁊ siextegum þætte tarenti⟨-⟩
ne þæt folc plegedon binnan tarentan heora byrg
ęt heora þreata[4] þe þær binnan geworht wæs . þa gesa⟨-⟩
won hie romane scipa on ðæm sæ irnan ; þa hrædli⟨-⟩
ce comon tarentine to heora agnu(m) scipu(m) . ⁊ þa oþre
hindan offoran ⁊ hie ealle him to gewildu(m) gedydan bu⟨-⟩
to[5] ·u· ⁊ þa þe þær gefongne wæron hie tawedan mid þæ⟨-⟩
re mæstan unieðnesse sume ofslogon sume of⟨-⟩
swungon sume him wið feo gesealdon ; ða romane
þæt geacsedan þa sendon hie ærendracan to him ⁊
bædon þæt him man g(e)bette þæt him ðær to abylgðe
gedon wæs ; ða tawedan hie eft þa ærendracan mid þæ(m)
mæstan bismere swa hie þa oþre ær dydon ⁊ hie siþþan
ham forleton ; Æfter þæm foran romane on taren⟨-⟩
tine . ⁊ swa clæne hie namon heora fultu(m) mid him
þætte heora proletarii ne moston him be æftan beon
þæt wæron þa þe hie gesett hæfdon þæt sceoldon be
heora wifum bearna strienan þon(ne) hie on gewin foron
⁊ cwædon þæt him wislecre þuhte þæt hie ða ne forlu⟨-⟩
ren þe þær ut fore . hæfde bearn se þe mehte . hie þa
romane comon on tarentine ⁊ þær[6] eall aweston þæt
hie metton ⁊ monega byrg abræcon . þa sendon
tarentine ægwern æft(er) fultume þær hie him æni⟨-⟩
ges wendon . ⁊ pirrus epira cyning him com to

This plate illustrates the emergence of Anglo-Saxon square minuscule. Note that the first stroke of **a** is generally straight and that the top is closed with a straight stroke, but round **a** sometimes follows **e** (compare 'bearna', l. 24 with 'bearn', l. 26). The **e** of **æ** is high; and *e caudata* appears in 'ęt', l. 9. Initially **c** is sometimes enlarged, as in 'cwædon', l. 25, 'cyning', l. 30. The final minim of **m** and **n** can curve inwards. Low **s** is usual, but long **s** appears before **w** in 'swungon', l. 15, 'swa', l. 19, and before **t** in 'strienan', l. 24. The script is very like the second hand of the Parker Chronicle; and the English glosses of Junius 27 (a Latin psalter) are possibly the same hand in a smaller module. Similarities in decorated initials between the Orosius manuscript and Junius 27 also support the assumption that all three manuscripts were at one time in the same scriptorium; perhaps Winchester, because the main hand of the Parker annals for 925-55 is typical of Winchester in the middle of the tenth century. The spellings are still prototypical for early West Saxon, though less markedly so than

[1] Dashes to either side of the **s** perhaps signal some mistake. Note also that the first letter of the following word has been rewritten.
[2] Emendation here involves changing **p** to **þ**.
[3] Note '·I·' to left of text, marking opening of first chapter of fourth book. The sign in the outer margin (**7**, known as the *simplex ductus*), pointing to new material, served to prompt insertion of decorated capital and would have vanished, had the membrane been trimmed along the line prickings.
[4] The loanword for 'theatre' is miscopied.
[5] The final -*n* is missing. Was the scribe trying to decide whether the numeral was *ii* or *v*?
[6] Here wyn may have been altered to thorn, and the subpuncting is now otiose; a discreet word-divider has been supplied after 'eall'.

⁊ nyllað ge þencan hwelc hit þa wæs þa nan mon ne
mehte æt oþrum his feorh gebycgan ne furþon
þætte þa wolden ge freondscipe beon þe wæron gebroðor
of fæder ⁊ of meder. ⁊ her endað sio feowerðe boc ⁊ on
gind sio fifte.

1 ÆFTER þæm þe Romeburg getimbred wæs feowerhun
de wintrum ⁊ feowertig ⁊ siextegum þætte Tarenti
ne þæt folc plegedon binnan Tarentan hiora byrg
æt hiora þeatra þe þær binnan geworht wæs. þa gesa
won hie Romane scipa on ðæm sæ irnan; þa hrædli
ce comon Tarentine to hiora agnum scipum ⁊ þa oþre
hindan offoran ⁊ hie ealle him to gewyldum gedydan bu
to .v. ⁊ þa þe þær gefongne wæron hie tawedan mid þæ
re mæstan unieðnesse sume ofslogon sume of
swungon sume him wið feo gesealdon; Ða Romane
þæt geacsedan þa sendon hie ærendracan to him ⁊
bædon þæt him man gebette þæt him ðær to abylgðe
gedon wæs; Ða tawedan hie eft þa ærendracan mid þæ
mæstan bismre swa hie þa oþre ær dydon ⁊ hie siþþan
ham forleton; Æfter þæm foran Romane on Tarenti
tine. ⁊ swa clæne hie naman hiora fultum mid him
þætte hiora proletarii ne moston him be æftan beon
þæt wæron þa þe hie gesett hæfdon þæt sceoldon be
hiora wifum bearna strienan þonne hie on gewin foron
⁊ sædon þæt him wislecre þuhte þæt hie ðæt ne forlu
ren þe þær ut fore. hæfde bearn se þe mehte hie þa
Romane comon on Tarentine ⁊ þær ealle awestan þæt
hie metton ⁊ monega byrg abræcon. þa sendon
Tarentine æghwær æfter fultume þær hie him æni
ges wendon. ⁊ Pirrus Epira cyning him com to

Plate 9 — reduced to 82%

in pl. 6. The main form of punctuation is a mid to low point; a following capital may mark heavy pauses and the *punctus versus* is used sporadically. Pricking is visible in the outer margin for horizontal ruling across whole sheet; at top of page note two pairs of points to guide bounding vertical lines, and these are often visible at the foot of the page. Apart from the Tironian sign, abbreviation is marked by a slightly rising stroke, for *m* in 'wintru(m)', l. 7, 'agnu(m)', l. 11, 'scipu(m)', l. 11, 'gewildu(m)', l. 12, 'þæ(m)', l. 18, 'fultu(m)', l. 21; for *e* over **g** in 'g(e)bette', l. 17; for -*er* in 'AEFT(er)', l. 6, æft(er)', l. 29; 'þon(ne)', l. 24, is the usual suspension of this form; ꝥ is not used on this page. In the centre of the bottom margin a few strokes, read by some as the name 'abba' but more probably the remains of '·VI·' quire signature, are concealed by a splodge.

CONTEXTS

Probably from Winchester: the script is like the second hand of Parker Chronicle (Parkes 1976: 154 subdivides Ker Scribe 2, identifying as his second scribe ff. 16v-21r apart from last six lines); the decorated initials are comparable with those of Junius Psalter. This Alfredian translation of Orosius includes within its first section reports made by Ohthere and Wulfstan at King Alfred's court. Still in medieval binding: the original Anglo-Saxon boards were newly covered, probably in the fourteenth century (two flyleaves, ff. i are iii, are from documents dated 1347). The name 'Joan Davysun' appears on f. 1r in seventeenth-century hand together with drawings, alphabets and other scribbles, on a folio left blank at the beginning of the Anglo-Saxon manuscript (see p. 55, facing). Noted by Hickes 1689: 167 as in library of John Maitland, duke of Lauderdale, by 1676-78, and as having belonged to John Dee, for which there is no proof. Collated with Junius's transcript of the Cotton Tiberius B. i translation of Orosius by Thomas Marshall (d. 1685). Descended to the Tollemache family of Helmingham, Suffolk, from whom Bosworth had the manuscript on loan (1850-54). On deposit in the British Museum from 1948 and acquired by British Museum in 1953 from the trustees of Lord Tollemache. Foliated as recently as 1968. Formerly Helmingham Hall 46; often known as the Tollemache or Lauderdale Orosius.

SIZE

c. 280 × 190 mm (*c.* 209 × 130 mm).

BIBLIOGRAPHY

Pr. Bately 1980[2]: 83 (ll. 3-28).
Facs. Campbell 1953.
Disc. Bosworth 1858; Add. MSS *Cat.*; Wormald 1945: 118-19; Ker, *Cat.* 1957: no. 133, and p. lix; Temple 1976: no. 8; Gneuss 2001: no. 300.

London, British Library, Additional MS 47967, f. 1r

Drawings of the Four Evangelist symbols were added on this flyleaf in the second half of the tenth century. Among other additions to the page, note under the inscription 'VINEA D(OMI)NI' a rectangle filled with leaf and scroll ornament, part of a Latin alphabet and some runes.
reduced to 82%

10

Oxford, Bodleian Library, Tanner MS 10, 54r (formerly f. 53, p. 105)
Old English version of Bede's *Historia Ecclesiastica*, III: xxiv, xxvii
Anglo-Saxon minuscule, s. x^{1}

TRANSCRIPTION

lib(er) iij[1]

cyning . seofontyne winter ⁊ he hæfde ærest . tru(m)here
biscop him to lareowe be þam we beforan sægdon . se
æftera wæs . gearumon . þridda wæs ceadda . feorða
wynferð . ealle þas wæron endebyrdlice In his dæge
biscophada. brucende In mercna þeode . ⁊ Ca(pitulu)m xxvi ⁄[2]

þA · WÆS · GE ·WORDEN[3] YMB :·
syx hund wintra. ⁊ feower ⁊ syxtig æft(er) drihtnes
menniscnesse . eclipsis solis . þæt is sunnan . aspru⟨-⟩
ngennis . þæt heo sciman ne hæfde . ⁊ wæs eatolice . ón
to seonne wæs þy þriddan dæge . mai þæs monþes . hu⟨-⟩
hugu ymb þa teogðan tíd . dæges . æft(er) þon swylce wæs þy
ylcan geare semninga wool ⁊ aðol . forhergiende ⁊ for⟨-⟩
neomende . ærest þa suðdælas breotone ⁊ swylce eac .
norðanhymbra . mægðe . wæs þreagende ⁊ mid grimme
wæle . longe . feor . ⁊ wide grimsigende micle menigeo mon⟨-⟩
na afylde . ⁊ fornom . þy wiite . eac swylce . tuda cristes
þeow . Se wæs æft(er) colmane . norþanhymbra biscope .
wæs of middangearde genumen . ⁊ wæs arweorðlice . be⟨-⟩
byrged In þæm mynstre þe nemned is . pægina læh . þis
ylce wiite . eac swylce hibernia . scotta ealond . gelíce
wæle sloh . ⁊ cwealmde . wæron þær In þa tiid . monige . of
ongelþeode . ge æðelinga ge oðerra In þara biscopa tíde .
finanes ⁊ colmanes . forleton heora éðelturf ⁊ þider
gewiton . sume for godcundre leornunge . sume for
Intingan forhebbendran liifes . ond sume sona In myn⟨-⟩

This plate illustrates the main hand of the Tanner Bede. The usual Anglo-Saxon letter forms are in use. Letters appear narrow because long and well spaced, but **a** is squarish when following tall **e** ('eatolice', l. 9, 'geare', l. 12, etc.). Note that **þ** usually occurs at the beginning of a word, with **ð** elsewhere. Some long vowels bearing stress are doubled ('wool', l. 12, 'wiite', ll. 16, 20, 'tiid', l. 21). The main punctuation is a point, which varies between being on the line or in mid-position. There are rather a lot of these points, as if to make reading aloud easier (see, for example, l. 15). Proper names are sometimes preceded by points (see ll. 1, 3: after all, initial capitals not used). Heavier punctuation marks the end of a chapter (see ⁊-shaped flourish after 'þeode', l. 5). Word division is by no means complete, but fairly careful – though non-calligraphic – distribution of **þ** and **ð**, together with the use of long **I** (*i*-longa) for **i** where minims follow (as 'Intingan', l. 25) often coincides usefully with the opening of phrases ('In', ll. 4, 5, 19, 21), helping the reader to distinguish words. Stress is indicated occasionally ('ón', l. 9, 'tíd', l. 11, 'gelíce', l. 20, 'tíde', l. 22, 'éðelturf', l. 23). Abbreviation is sparingly used: on this page the Tironian sign for *ond*, the overline for *m* (in 'tru(m)here', l. 1, where the scribe perhaps forgot to complete the name and later added 'h' with '-ere' tucked neatly in at the end of the line) and ' for *er* ('æft(er)', ll. 7, 11, 17). The elaborate initial and line of decorated capitals (Wormald Type 1), marking a major textual division in the Old English Bede, are richly coloured. The human figure is functional, forming the bowed part of the initial **þ** and differing therefore from the gymnastic figures that animate initials in the 'clambering' style found later in the century and particularly popular *c.* 1100 in Canterbury.

[1] Fourteenth-century use of the manuscript is shown by these running titles.

[2] Fourteenth-century cross-referencing to the standard divisions of Bede.

[3] For *geworden*, but lay-out presentation indicated in transcription.

Plate 10 – reduced to 94%

CONTEXTS

Where this manuscript, the 'T' version of the Old English Bede, was written is not known, but decoration may suggest Winchester. Probably at Thorney when parchment from a late-thirteenth-century roll from Thorney Abbey (perhaps serving earlier as a wrapper) was fashioned into leaves pasted to the wooden boards of a (?fourteenth-century) medieval binding. In 1715 Wanley saw in the lodgings of Dr John Smith of Durham a manuscript of the Old English Bede borrowed from Tanner. Could have suffered water damage in 1732, when books belonging to Tanner and in transit between Norwich and Oxford were submerged for twenty hours. Tanner 10 was among Tanner's manuscripts left to the Bodleian Library in 1736. Now in binding of eighteenth or nineteenth century; for what may have been the manuscript's medieval pastedowns, removed in 1898, from a late-thirteenth-century Thorney roll, see Tanner 10*. Known as the Tanner Bede.

SIZE

250 × 162 mm (*c.* 177 × 107 mm).

BIBLIOGRAPHY

Pr. Miller 1890-91, 1898: I. 240-42 (240, l. 14-242, l. 3).
Facs. Bately 1992.
Disc. *SC* 9830; Dodwell 1954: 12n5; Ker, *Cat.* 1957: no. 351; Wormald 1971; Temple 1976: no. 9; Gneuss 2001: no. 668; Gameson 1992.

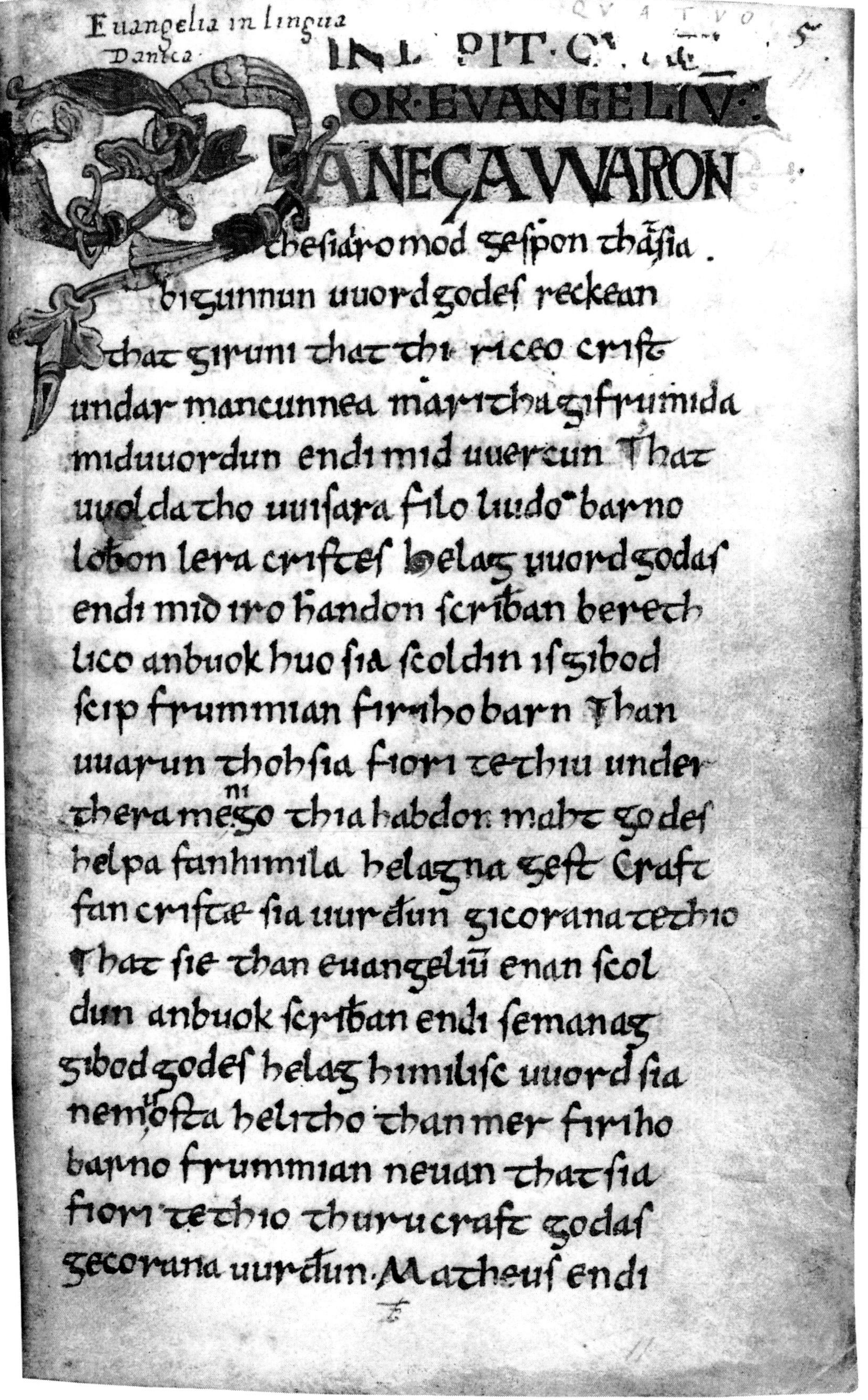

Euangelia in lingua Danica

INCIPIT·QVATVOR·EVANGELIV

MANEGA UUARON
the sia iro mod gespon that sia
bigunnun uuord godes reckean
that giruni that thie riceo crist
undar mancunnea maritha gifrumida
mid uuordun endi mid uuercun That
uuolda tho uuisara filo liudo barno
lobon lera cristes helag uuord godas
endi mid iro handon scriban berech
lico anbuok huo sia scoldin is gibod
scip frummian firiho barn Than
uuarun thoh sia fiori te thiu under
thera menigo thia habdon maht godes
helpa fan himila helagna gest craft
fan criste sia uurdun gicorana te thio
That sie than euangelium enan scol
dun anbuok scriban endi so manag
gibod godes helag himilisc uuord sia
ne moste helitho than mer firiho
barno frummian neuan that sia
fiori te thio thuru craft godas
gecorana uurdun Matheus endi

Because of a, can't be in 11th cent.
Also g
But. You have Caroline r, Caroline d, f
l on baseline (later)

London, British Library, Cotton MS Caligula A. vii, f. 11r
Poem on the life of Christ (*Heliand*) in Old Saxon
actual size

II

Exeter, Exeter Cathedral Library, MS 3501, f. 32v
Guthlac A, ll. 1-29
Anglo-Saxon minuscule, square phase, s. x^2

TRANSCRIPTION

SE BIÐ GEFEANA FæGrast
þonne hy æt frymðe gemetað engel ⁊ seo eadge
sawl . ofgiefeþ hio þas eorþan wynne . forlæteð þas
lænan dreamas . ⁊ hio wiþ þam lice gedæleð . ðon(ne) cwið se
engel hafað yldran hád . greteð gæst oþerne . abeodeð hi(m)
godes ærende . Nu þu most feran þider þu fundadest . lon⟨-⟩
ge ⁊ gelome Ic þec lædan sceal wegas þe sindon weþe ⁊ wul⟨-⟩
dres leoht torht ontyned . eart nu tidfara . to þam
halgan hám þær næfre hreow cymeð . edergong fore yrmþu(m) .
ac þær biþ engla dream . sib ⁊ gesælignes . ⁊ sawla ræst . ⁊ þær
á to feore gefeon motum . dryman mid dryhten þa þe his
domas her æfnað on eorþan he him ece lean . healdeð on
heofonum þær se hyhsta . ealra cyninga cyning ceastru(m)
wealdeð . ðæt sind þa getimbru þe nú[1] tydriað ne þam
fore yrmþum þe þær In wuniað . lif aspringeð ac him
bið lenge hu sel geoguþe brucað . ⁊ godes miltsa . þider
soðfæstra sawla motun . cuman æfter cwealme þa þe
her cristes ·ǽ· lærað ⁊ læstað . ⁊ his lof rærað . Ofer⟨-⟩
winnað þa awyrgdan gæs`tas´ bigytað him wuldres ræste .
Hwider sceal þæs monnes mod astigan . ær oþþe æfter þon(ne)
he his ænne her gæst bigonge þ(æt) se gode mote womma clæne

Though there is now a tendency to move to an earlier date for this manuscript, it is widely thought to have been written a little before the end of the tenth century, say 970-90 rather than 950-70. The script is stately, with fine hairline strokes on **g** and **t** and wedges on ascenders and initial minims. The scribe's occasional use of Half-uncial **a**, an indication of his calligraphic ambition, is seen in 'womma', l. 21. The letters **d** and **ð** are carefully differentiated, with the crossed ascender of **ð** protruding firmly above the script line and the top stroke of **d** flat and curved slighly at the end as in 'abeodeð', l. 5. The **ð** is is not used word-initially, except where enlarged as a capital ('ðon(ne)', l. 4, 'ðæt', l. 14). Three forms are in use for **y**: curved, both dotted ('frymðe', l. 2, and without the dot ('wynne', l. 3), the straight form dotted ('yldran', l. 5) and the **f**-shaped form ('hy', l. 2) which disappears towards the end of the century. Long **i** may appear initially before other minims ('In', l. 15) for clarity (in 'Ic', l. 7, its use before **c** may be as a capital). Pointing is light, with space playing a considerable part in helping the reader (some points in the first few lines of this text have been added, probably by Nowell, e.g. ll. 9, 10, 11); elsewhere in the manuscript points coincide to a very large extent with verse-line endings. Hardpoint dividing lines help the reader separate verses. Square capitals, found as a display script in English manuscripts from the late ninth century, here indicate the opening of *Guthlac A* (the beginning of a second Guthlac poem on f. 44v also opens with a row of square capitals). Stress marks single out some forms for accentuation ('hád', l. 5, 'á', l. 11, and, together with points to either side, 'ǽ', l. 18); for 'nú', l. 14, a negative is needed. There is, in line with the formal nature of the script, little abbreviation apart from the Tironian sign: ꝥ for 'þ(æt)', l. 21; 'ðon(ne)', l. 4, þon(ne), l. 20 (but compare 'þonne', l. 2); and the overline in 'hi(m)', l. 5, 'yrmþu(m)', l. 9, and 'ceastru(m)', l. 13, all towards the end of lines.

The wording of the heading, perhaps added by Nowell, 'Of the Joyes p(re)pared for the(m) that serve god & keepe his com(m)aundeme(n)tes', is reflected in Wanley's description of this item.

[1] The sense requires 'never', suggesting 'ná' should be read.

Plate 11 — reduced to 73%

CONTEXTS

Given to Exeter Cathedral by Bishop Leofric (d. 1072). Where it was written is unknown: somewhere in the west country is assumed, but probably not Exeter, which is likely to have had few books when Leofric made it his see in the 1050s; Glastonbury and Crediton are proposed. Two manuscripts in Latin, London, MS Lambeth Palace 149 and Oxford, Bodleian Library, MS Bodley 319, are also attributed to this scribe. Nowell, who added the title at the top of this page, and Joscelyn were among early users of the manuscript. They may have had access to it in London: manuscript possibly borrowed by Parker or Cecil. Hickes outlined runic passages in the manuscript in pencil. Lent to Edward Lye for a year in 1759 (kept for three) and again to Manning for correcting Lye's work. Known as the Exeter Book.

SIZE

c. 320 × 220 mm (*c.* 240 × 160 mm).

BIBLIOGRAPHY

Pr. Krapp and Dobbie 1936; Roberts 1979; Muir 1994.
Facs. Chambers, Förster and Flower 1933; Muir [2005].
Disc. Ker 1933, *Cat.* 1957: no. 116; Pope 1978; McGovern 1983; Hill 1986, 1988; Muir 1989, 1991; Conner 1986 [2001], 1993; O'Brien O'Keeffe 1990: 155–64; Graham 1994; Gameson 1996[1]; Frank 1998; Gneuss 2001: no. 257.

London, British Library, Cotton MS Vitellius A. xv, f. 102v
Marvels of the East
reduced to 96%

12

London, British Library, Royal MS 7 C. xii, f. 105r (formerly 101r)
Ælfric, In ascensione domini
Anglo-Saxon minuscule, square phase, *c.* 990

TRANSCRIPTION

þrymsetl ⁖ ac he siðode mid þam wolcne of manna gesihþu(m) ;
þær wæron ða gesewene twegen englas on hwitum gyrelu(m) ;
Eac swilce on his acennednysse wæron englas gesewene ⁖
ac þæt halige godspel ne `a´scirde hu hi gefreatewode wæron ⁖
for þan ðe god com to us swiðe eadmod ; On his upstige wæron
gesewene englas mid hwitum gyrelum geglengde ; Blis
is getacnod on hwitum reafe ⁖ for þan ðe crist ferde heo⟨-⟩[1]
-non mid micelre blisse . ⁊ mid micclum þrymme ; On his
acennednysse wæs geþuht swilce seo godcundnyss wære ge⟨-⟩
eadmet . ⁊ on his upstige wæs seo menniscnys ahafen ⁊
gemærsod ; Mid his upstige is adylegod þæt cyrografu(m)
ure genyðerunge . ⁊ se cwyde ure brosnunge is awend ;
ða ða adam agylt hæfde . ða cwæð se ælmihtiga wealdend
him to . þu eart eorðe ⁊ þu gewentst to eorþan ; ðu eart dust
⁊ þu gewentst to duste ; Nu todæig þæt ilce gecynd ferde
unbrosniendlic in to heofenan rice ; ða twegen englas
sædon þæt crist cymð swa swa he up ferde ⁖ for[2] þan ðe he bið
gesewen on þam micclum dome on menniscum hiwe . þæt
his slagan hine magon oncnawan . þe hine ǽr to deaðe
gedydon. ⁊ éác þa ðe his lare forsawon . ðæt hi ðonne riht⟨-⟩
lice onfon þæt ece wite[3] mid deofle ; †[4] we habbað nu ge⟨-⟩
ræd lucas[5] gesetnysse embe cristes upstige ; nu á⟨-⟩
wende we ure smeagunge to þam oþrum godspellere
marcum ⁖ þe cwæð on þissum dæigþerlicum godspelle
þæt se hælend æteowde hine sylfne[6] his apostolum

† þ(æt) halige gewrit cwyð ; tollatur impius ne uideat gloria(m) d(e)i ; si ðam
arleasan ætbroden seo[7] gesihð[-] godes wuldres ; Ne geseoð ða ar⟨-⟩
leasan cristes wuldor þe hine ær on life forsawon ⁖ ac hi ge⟨-⟩
seoð þonne egefulne þone þe hi eadmodne forhigdon ;

This example of a late type of Anglo-Saxon square minuscule is in the stiff, clear hand of the second scribe; for the first scribe see p. 67. The manuscript is localized to Cerne Abbas in Dorset because some of the corrections, for example the lines in the bottom margin on this page, are thought to be by Ælfric himself. The scribe's hand is less stylish than the correcting hand, which is more akin to the hand of the first of the manuscript's scribes. Note the frequent use of round **s**, originally a Half-uncial letter-form and 'relatively uncommon' in Old English manuscripts in all positions (Ker, *Cat.* 1957: xxx). The low Insular **s** is infrequent ('gesewene', l. 3, 'englas', l. 6, 'menniscnys', l. 10, 'is', l. 11) and tall **s** occurs only when ligatured with **w** ('swilce', ll. 3, 9, 'swiðe', l. 5, 'swa', ll. 17, 17) and **p** ('godspel', l. 4, 'godspellere', l. 23, 'godspelle', l. 24). The distribution of **þ** and **ð** is haphazard, although **d** and **ð** are well differentiated. The scribe draws on the elaborated punctuation used in Latin manuscripts, a feature first found in English with any consistency in manuscripts of Ælfric's Catholic Homilies. On this page, in addition to the low point he uses both the *punctus elevatus* (⁖) for incomplete structures and the *punctus versus* (;) for heavier pauses. Capitals generally follow the *punctus versus*, except for the special English letter-forms. These lack capital alternatives, and they are not enlarged (e.g. **þ** in 'þær', l. 2, **ð** in 'ða',

[1] An erased minim is visible; and hyphen to correspond with one at beginning of next line is absent.
[2] Misplaced *signe de renvoi* erased imperfectly above 'for'.
[3] Note erasure.
[4] Note *signe de renvoi*, indicating that text in bottom margin should be inserted here.
[5] The 'c' is on an erasure; a minim or perhaps 'e' was begun.
[6] Note stroke from 'e' to 'y', as if to prevent misdivision of group in reading.
[7] On erasure.

Plate 12 – reduced to 75%

l. 13). Words are presented in blocks to be read aloud from, with the result that parts of words can look strangely stranded (but in 'wite', l. 21, the 'i' and following space are on an erasure). The hyphen at the beginning of l. 8 is not matched by a hyphen at the end of the previous line (hyphens are not used by the first scribe). Apart from the Tironian sign abbreviation occurs only end-line in *-u(m)*, ll. 1, 2, 11. Corrections include the inserted *a-* prefix of l. 4, 'lucas', l. 22, with a third minim overwritten into **c** and 'þissum', l. 24, where the first stroke of **u** is adapted from some other letter (**e**?).

The four lines added for insertion into l. 21 are in a more stylish hand attributed to Ælfric, with **þ** initial and **ð** elsewhere. There is no differentiation of letter-forms between Latin and English. Round **s** appears in 'si', l. 26, and 'geseoð', l. 27. The abbreviations are 'þ(æt)' and 'gloria(m) d(e)i', l. 1.

CONTEXTS

The name 'ælfstan' is in the outer margin of f. 190r alongside l. 14. Some homilies were being read and marked up late in the twelfth century. Probably belonged to Cardinal Wolsey, whose signature is on f. 3 (a fly-leaf); an erased name, read as Robert Beale, is on f. 4 (also a fly-leaf). In royal collections by 1666 (St James's Palace press-mark 'Scrin. xiv. 1' on f. 1v; see 1666 catalogue, f. 16v); probably sequestered after Wolsey's trial (Corley 2000: liii). Entered the British Museum with the Royal Collection in 1757.

SIZE

310 × 205 mm (*c.* 232 × 145 mm).

BIBLIOGRAPHY

Pr. Clemoes 1997: 347-48, ll. 72-97.
Facs. Eliason and Clemoes 1966.
Disc. Warner and Gilson 1921: I. 180-81; Sisam [1931-33] 1953: 171-75; Ker, *Cat.* 1957: no. 257; Watson 1979: no. 877, pl. 24; Gneuss 2001: no. 472.

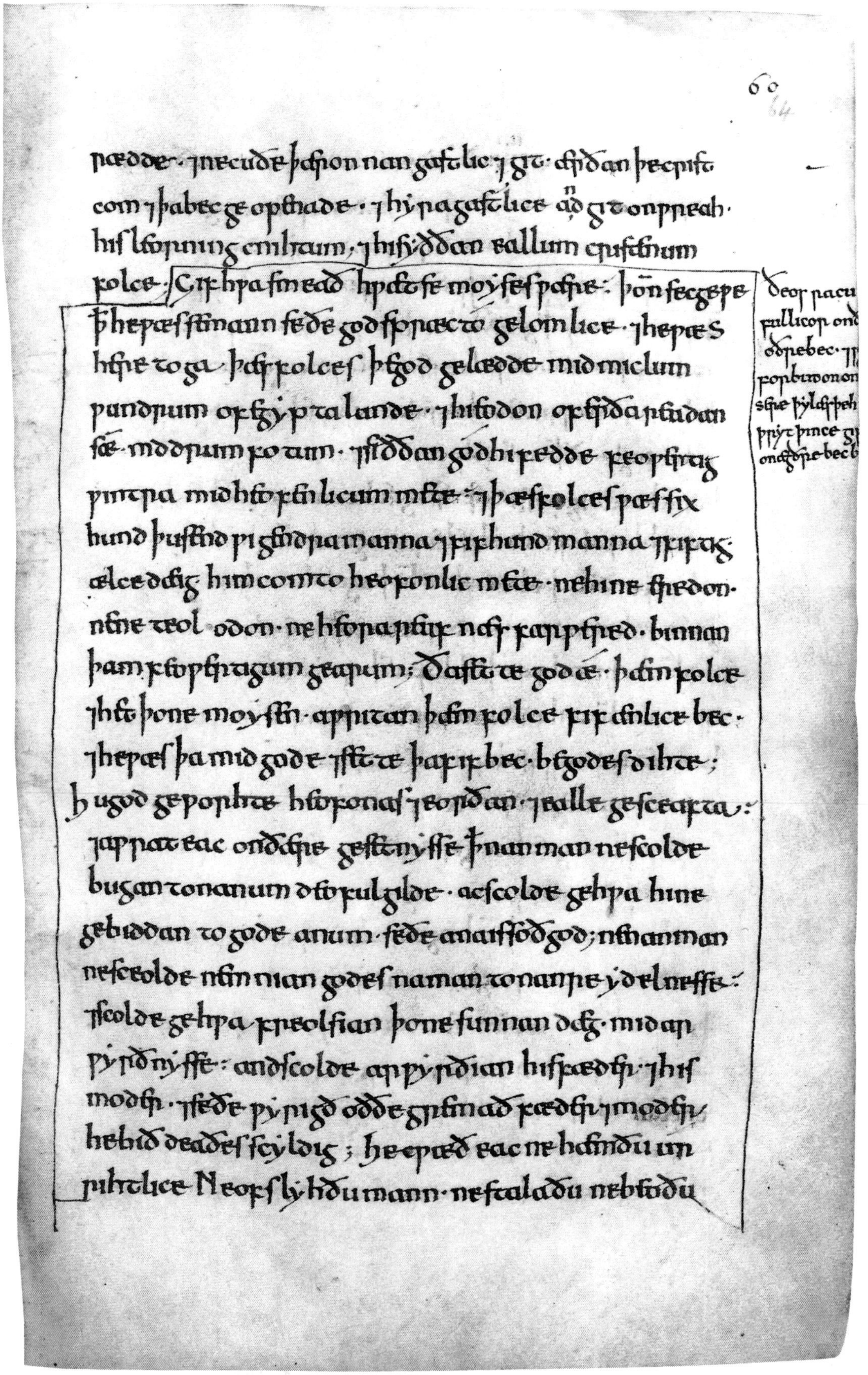

60
64

rædde. ⁊ ne cuðe þæron nan gastlic andgit. ac syððan þe crist
com ⁊ þa bec geopenode. ⁊ hy þa gastlice andgit onwreah.
his leorningcnihtum. ⁊ hi syððan eallum cristenum
folce. Eft hwa sy [illegible] hwæt is se moyses wære: þone secge we
þæt he wæs se mann þe god spræc to gelomlice. ⁊ he wæs
heretoga þæs folces þe god gelædde mid miclum
wundrum of egypta lande. ⁊ hi ferdon ofer ða readan
sæ. mid drium fotum. ⁊ syððan god hi fedde feowertig
wintra mid heofonlicum mete. ⁊ þæs folces wæs six
hund þusend wigendra manna. ⁊ fif hund manna ⁊ fiftig.
ælce dæg him com to heofonlic mete. ne hi ne [illegible].
ne [illegible] teolodon. ne heora reaf ne forwered. binnan
þam feowertigum gearum; Ða sette god æ. þam folce
⁊ het þone moysen awritan þam folce fif ænlice bec.
⁊ he wæs þa mid gode ⁊ sette þa. þæt is þa bec. be godes dihte;
Hu god geworhte heofonas ⁊ eorðan. ⁊ ealle gesceafta:
⁊ þær wæs eac on ðære gesetnysse þæt nan man ne scolde
bugan to nanum deofolgilde. ac scolde gehwa hine
gebiddan to gode anum. se ðe ana is soð god; ⁊ þæt nan man
ne sceolde nemnian godes naman to nanre ydelnesse:
⁊ scolde gehwa freolsian þone sunnan dæg. mid ar
wurðnysse: and scolde arwurðian his fæder ⁊ his
modor. ⁊ se ðe wyrigð oððe gremað fæder oþþe modor,
he bið deaðes scyldig; he cwæð eac ne hæm ðu un
rihtlice. Ne ofslyh ðu mann. ne stala ðu ne [illegible]

high e, insular y

dotted y
[930s→]
no clefts
flat top a
overall boxy
aspect, see C

London, British Library, Royal MS 7 C. xii, f. 64r (formerly 60)
Ælfric, Dominica in media quadragessima
reduced to 75%

13

Oxford, Bodleian Library, MS Junius 11, p. 14
Genesis B, ll. 246-70
Anglo-Saxon minuscule, square phase, s. x ex. – s. xi in.

TRANSCRIPTION

HÆFDE se \e/alwalda . engelcynna . þurh hand⟨-⟩
mægen . halig drihten . t[é\y]ne[1] getrymede . þæm
he getruwode wel . þ(æt) hie his giongorscipe .
fyligan wolden . wyrcean hís willan . for þon hé
h[i\eo]m[2] gewít forgeaf . ⁊ mid his handum gesceop . ha⟨-⟩
lig drihten . gesétt hæfde he híe swa gesǽliglice .
ænne hæfde he swa [w>s]wiðne geworhtne . swá mihtigne
on hís modgeþohte . he lét hine swa micles wealdan .
hehstne to hím on heofona rice . hæfde he hine
swa hwitne geworhtne . swa wynlic wæs his wæwtm
on heofonum . þ(ǽt) him com from weroda drihtne .
gelic wæs he þam leohtum steorrum . lóf sceolde
he drihtnes wyrcean . dýran sceolde he his dreá⟨-⟩
mas on heofonum . ⁊ sceolde hís dríhtne þancian .
þæs leanes þe he him on þam leohte gescerede . þon(ne)
l[-æ>é]te[3] he his hine lange wealdan . ác he \a/wénde hít
hím to wyrsan þinge . óngán hím winn úp \a/hebban .
wið þone hehstan heofnes w\e/aldend . þe síteð on þa(m)
halgan stole . deore wæs hé drihtne ur[e\v(m)][4] . né mihte
him bedyrned w[eo\y]rðan[5] . þ(æt) hís engyl ongan ófermod
wesan . áhóf hine wið hís he\a/rran . sohte hétespræ⟨-⟩
ce . gylpword ongeán . nolde gode þeowian . cwæð þ(æt)
hís líc wære . leoht ⁊ scene . hwit 7 hiowbeorht. né meah⟨-⟩
te hé æt hís hige findan . þ(æt) \he/ gode wolde . geóngerdome .
þéodne þeowian[6] . þúhte him sylfum . þ(æt) he mægyn ⁊ cræft .
máran hæfde . þonne sé halga gód . habban mihte .

The hand, although square and upright, does not keep tidily to the script line any more than it observes a careful page layout. Yet **þ** is usually word initial (except in 'geþohte', l. 8, where it follows the **ge** prefix) and **ð** elsewhere. The **e** element of **æ** rises only a little; **e** is often high in other combinations, for example before **a** (e.g. 'wyrcean', l. 4), **n** (e.g. 'engel', l. 1), **o** (e.g. 'gesceop', l. 5), **r** (e.g. 'weroda', l. 11), **s** ('wesan', l. 21), **t** (e.g. 'getrymede', l. 2, but not 'getruwode', l. 3). One form of **y** is used by the main hand: straight and undotted (note the use of a mistaken single minim as its first stroke in 'getrymede', l. 2). Half-uncial **a** appears twice ('\e/alwalda', l. 1, 'áhóf', l. 21). Low insular **s** only is seen on this page. The spellings are mostly late West Saxon, with corrections moving them further in that direction (e.g. 't[é\y]ne', l. 2, 'h[i\eo]m', l. 5, 'l[-æ>é]te', l. 16). A possible Kentish layer is suggested by such forms as 'mægyn', l. 25, and the original form 'tene', l. 2. *Genesis B* was translated from Old Saxon and, as well as containing unusual words like 'giongorscipe', l. 3, may have seemed clumsy. How far the corrections are to be ascribed to the main hand is debatable. The scribe was certainly responsible for some of the changes, for example the erased **h** visible before **c** in l. 22 and the erasure between the two elements of 'hiowbeorht', l. 23, but he is unlikely to have made some of the correcting letter-forms (e.g. the rounded and dotted **y** of 'w[eo\y]rðan', l. 20, the **v** shape of 'ur[e\v(m)]', l. 19, the rounder **a**/ prefixes of ll. 16, 17). The simple verse pointing, with mid to low points marking of half-lines, is original. The fairly heavily scattered stress marks, frequent on words to be singled out in delivery and many of them serving to pick out pronouns (even over the abbreviated 'þ(æt)', l. 11), were added later; there could be two layers of these stress marks. The opening capital (Wormald, Type I), four lines deep, is followed by three smaller square capitals and uncial **E**, marking a new division of the poem. Note clearly

[1] **e** is subpuncted.
[2] **i** is subpuncted.
[3] First part of ligature **æ** mostly erased.
[4] **e** is subpuncted.
[5] **eo** is subpuncted.
[6] Otiose stroke to right of ascender of **þ**.

HÆFDE se ælƿalda engel cynna þurh hand
mægen. halig drihten. tene getrymede. þæm
he getruƿode ƿel. ꝥ hie his giongorscipe.
fylgan ƿolden. ƿyrcean his ƿillan. for þon he
heom geƿit forgeaf. ⁊ mid his handum gesceop. ha
lig drihten. gesett hæfde he hie sƿa gesæliglice.
ænne hæfde he sƿa sƿiðne geƿorhtne. sƿa mihtigne
on his mod geþohte. he let hine sƿa micles ƿealdan.
hehstne to him on heofona rice. hæfde he hine
sƿa hƿitne geƿorhtne. sƿa ƿynlic ƿæs his ƿæstm
on heofonum. ꝥ him com from ƿeroda drihtne.
gelic ƿæs he þam leohtum steorrum. lof sceolde
he drihtnes ƿyrcean. dyran sceolde he his dream
mas on heofonum. ⁊ sceolde his drihtne þancian.
þæs leanes þe he him on þam leohte gescerede. þon
lete he his hine lange ƿealdan. ac he aƿende hit
him to ƿyrsan þinge. ongan him ƿinn up ahebban.
ƿið þone hehstan heofnes ƿaldend. þe siteð on þam
halgan stole. deore ƿæs he drihtne urum. ne mihte
him bedyrned ƿeorðan. ꝥ his engyl ongan ofermod
ƿesan. ahof hine ƿið his hearran. sohte hete spræ
ce. gylp ƿord ongean. nolde gode þeoƿian. cƿæð ꝥ
his lic ƿære. leoht ⁊ scene. hƿit ⁊ hioƿ beorht. ne meah
te he æt his hige findan. ꝥ he gode ƿolde. geongerdome.
þeodne þeoƿian. þuhte him sylfum. ꝥ he mægyn ⁊ cræft
maran hæfde. þonne se halga god. habban mihte.

Plate 13 – reduced to 78%

visible prickings in the inner margin; outer margin trimmed along dots (see lower part of page); pair of dots visible bottom left-hand margin points to double bounding lines. Abbreviation is sparing and, apart from ⁊ and þ, occurs at the end of lines in 'þon(ne)', l. 15, and 'þa(m)', l. 18. Note that in 'wæwtm', l. 10, the second **w** is read easily as the low **s** to be expected in this word; compare the emendation made in 'swiðne', l. 7. What looks almost like letters in the bottom margin is show-through from p. 13.

CONTEXTS

Elements of Scandinavian ornament identified in the manuscript could derive from English exemplars and need not entail a date in the second quarter of the eleventh century. Probably the 'Genesis anglice depicta' of the early-fourteenth-century catalogue of Christ Church, Canterbury; however, Winchester, Glastonbury, and Malmesbury have been suggested as place of origin. In thirteenth-century binding (Raw 1984). Perhaps in Simonds D'Ewes library *c.* 1637. In the early seventeenth century owned by James Ussher, archbishop of Armagh, who lent it to de Laet and later gave it, *c.* 1651, to Junius. Entered the Bodleian Library with Junius's manuscripts in 1678. Because its contents are compared with Bede's account of Cædmon's poetry, known as the Cædmon Manuscript.

SIZE

c. 323 × 196 mm (*c.* 225 × *c.* 120 mm).

BIBLIOGRAPHY

Pr. Krapp 1931; Timmer 1948; Doane 1991.
Facs. Gollancz 1927; Muir 2004.
Disc. SC 5123; Wormald 1945: 119-21; Ker, *Cat.* 1957: no. 334; Henderson 1975; Temple 1976: no. 58; Raw 1976, 1984; Lucas 1980, 1981; O'Brien O'Keeffe 1990: 179-87; Gneuss 2001: no. 640; Karkov 2001; Lockett 2002.

Oxford, Bodleian Library, MS Junius 11, p. 61
The Translation of Enoch
reduced to 73%

14

London, British Library, Cotton MS Julius A. x, f. 88r (formerly 94)
Old English Martyrology, from entry for St Philip, 1st May
Anglo-Saxon minuscule, round phase, s. x ex. – s. xi in.

TRANSCRIPTION

he getacnað ða gastlican láreowas
godes cyrecena . Ure hælend
geceas ðysne philippu(m) him
to þegne on galilea mægðe
fram bethsaida ðære ceastre .
bethsaida is gereht . domus
uenatorum ðæt þonne is
huntena hus . ðes philippus
æfter þæs ˋhˊælendes uppastig⟨-⟩
nesse he bodade cristes godspell
on sciðia mægðe . ðær he awehte
ðry men of deaðe . ⁊ his lichoma
resteð nu on hierapole þære
ceastre on frygia mægðe . ⁊ his
dohtra twa þa halegestan fæmnan
syndon ðær bebyrgde on twa
healfe his .

Because of its pronounced forward tilt, this hand has a strong Caroline appearance. The letter-forms are, for the most part, distinctively Anglo-Saxon, even in the explication of names in Latin: **a** is in the rounded form; **e** is sometimes horned at the left (see second **e** of 'hælend', l. 2); **y** is straight-limbed; insular **f, g, r,** and low **s** are in use; **d** is round and not differentiated in height from **ð**. Some letters may show incipient Caroline influence, for example the **s** of the **st** ligature hardly descends below the script line (see 'ceastre', l. 5, 'cristes', l. 10), and the final stroke of **h** only occasionally flicks to the right (as in 'bethsaida', l. 5). Both **þ** and **ð** are in use, but without positional distribution; **th** occurs only in the biblical place-name 'bethsaida', l. 5; and **æ** is in use, both with low or high **e**. Word division is almost complete, except that prepositions and sometimes the Tironian sign stand close to the following word. Low points mark pauses; they are faint on ll. 6 and 17. One capital within the text block ('Ure', l. 2) introduces the narrative portion of the entry for St Philip. There are a few stress marks and no hyphens. The use of abbreviations is sparing: ⁊ for 'and' (compare 'fram', l. 5) and the overline for *m* in 'philippu(m)', l. 3. The omitted first letter of 'ˋhˊælendes', l. 9, is neatly positioned, with a caret mark below the line. The name 'philippus' has Latin inflexions in ll. 3 and 8. Note the show-through of capital **O** at the end of l. 1, clearly set out to the left of the script block.

CONTEXTS

A twelfth-century hand alters the text (ff. 153v, 159) and adds some words (f. 160v). A sixteenth-century hand notes names of English saints and occasionally doodles drawings of churches. Otherwise nothing is known of this manuscript before its coming into the Cotton collection. An excerpt was transcribed by Junius into Bodleian MS Junius 101. The twelfth/thirteenth *Vita S. Oswini* in ff. 2-43 is from Tynemouth; and was probably bound with the Old English Martyrology in Cotton's library. Entered the British Museum with the Cotton Collection in 1753.

SIZE

c. 176 × 122 mm (135 × 72 mm).

BIBLIOGRAPHY

Pr. Herzfeld 1900: 70; Kotzor 1981: II. 73.
Disc. Ker, *Cat.* 1957: no. 161; Gneuss 2001: no. 338; Tite 2003: 94.

88 ~~94~~

he getacnað ða gastlican lareowas
godes cyrcean. Ure hælend
geceas ðysne philippum him
to þegne on galilea mægðe
fram bethsaida ðære ceastre.
bethsaida is gereht domus
uenatorum ðæt þonne is
huntena hus. ðes philippus
æfter þæs hælendes upp astig
nesse he bodade cristes godspell
on scitia mægðe. ðær he arærde
ðry men of deaðe. 7 his lichoma
resteð nu on hierapole þære
ceastre on frygia mægðe. 7 his
dohtra twa þa halegestan fæmnan
syndon ðær bebyrgde on twa
healfe his.

Plate 14 – actual size

a + l on baseline
closed bowl of p
forward tilt = carolingian
influence

15

London, British Library, Cotton MS Vitellius C. iii, f. 27r (formerly 23)
Herbal, translation of the enlarged *Herbarius Apuleii*
Anglo-Saxon minuscule, round phase, s. xi^1

TRANSCRIPTION

hreafnes leac :·[2]

Ðeos wyrt ðe man satyrion
ᛏ oþru(m) naman hræfnes leac
nemneð heo bið cenned on hean
dunu(m) ᛏ on heardu(m) stowu(m) ᛏ swa some
on mædu(m) ᛏ on beganu(m) landun ᛏ
on sandigu(m) .
Wið earfoðlice wundela genim þysse
wyrte wyrtruman þe we satyrion
nemdon ᛏ eac sume men priapisci
hatað ᛏ cnuca tosomne hyt þa wunda
aclænsað ᛏ ða dolh gelycð .
Wiþ eagena sár þ(æt) is þon(ne) þ(æt) hwá tornige
sy geni(m) þysse ylcan [-] wyrte
seaw ᛏ smyre þa eagan þærmid

butan y`l´dincge hyt ofgenimð þ(æt) sár[1]

feldwyrt .

Ðeos wyrt þe man gentiana(m)
ᛏ oðru(m) naman feldwyrt
nemneþ heo bið cenned on dunu(m)
ᛏ heo framað to eallum drenceo(m)
heo bið hnesce on æthrine ᛏ bittere
on byrgingce . Nædre

Wið nædrun slite genim þysse
ylcan wyrte gentianam wyrt⟨-⟩
truman ᛏ gedrige hine cnuca

The main text is in a round hand, without character. Some forms of **a** and **u** are not distinct when **a** is more or less square. Both **e** and **c** can have horns. Occasionally **e** is high, but not necessarily in ligature with the next letter. The **d** and **ð** are carefully distinguished. The **y** is dotted, whether curved or straight-limbed. Punctuation is a low point. Each short item is opened by a coloured initial set out to the left of the script block (alternating red, blue, and green). Ruled with double vertical lines in both outer and inner margins, with three verticals separating the columns; the two-column layout, unusual for Old English manuscripts, must echo a Latin exemplar. The drawings, echoing continental models, were inserted after the writing of the text (note the curious shape of the snake in column b). The plant labels were apparently abstracted from the text by the illustrator or colourist, who seems not to have recognized the last letter of 'leac'. For examples of the standard suspensions 'þ(æt)' and 'þon(ne)' see l. 13a. The ending of 'landun', l. 6a, indicates that inflectional expansions of the overline by **m** could misrepresent the language of the text; 'drenceo(m)', l. 7b, also suggests a weakening of inflexions.

Ker dates the script of the plant labels to s. xi med.; Voigts argues for dating the whole manuscript as after 1050.

CONTEXTS

Although Christ Church owned an illustrated Herbal in the Middle Ages, there is no evidence to link this book with Canterbury, any more than for linking it to entries in a thirteenth-century Rochester catalogue. The sixteenth-century owner ('Richerd Hollond thys boke', f. 76) is unidentified; and nothing is known of 'elysabet colmore' of f. 11v. In the Cotton collection by 1621. Borrowed by Le Neve for use by Johannes de Laet (1641). Lent to Dugdale (1653). Suffered shrinkage as result of the 1731 fire in the Cottonian Library, and leaves now separately mounted. Entered the British Museum with the Cotton Collection in 1753.

SIZE

c. 260 × 190 mm (*c.* 222 × 155 mm).

BIBLIOGRAPHY

Pr. de Vriend 1984: 60-62 (ll. 17-10).
Facs. D'Aronco and Cameron 1998; Doane 1994.
Disc. Flom 1941; Ker, *Cat.* 1957: no. 219; Voigts 1976; Temple 1976: no. 63; Gneuss 2001: no. 402; Tite 2003: 162.

[1] Note that shrinkage from fire damage is greater at the top of the folio.

[2] Labels in different hand, s. xi med.

Plate 15 – reduced to 86%

16

London, British Library, Cotton MS Nero A. i, f. 110r (formerly 113)
Wulfstan, *Sermo Lupi ad Anglos*
Anglo-Saxon minuscule, round phase, s. xi in.

TRANSCRIPTION

SERMO LUPI . AD ANGLOS : QUANDO DANI .
MAXIME . P(ER)SECUTI SUNT EOS . QUOD FUIT .
AN(NO) M(IL)L(ESIM)O ·XIIII·[1] AB INCARNATIONE D(OMI)NI
N(OST)RI IE(S)U CR(IST)I :~
Leofan men gecnawað þ(æt) soð is ; Ðeos woruld
is on ofste . ⁊ hit nealæcð þa(m) ende . ⁊ þy[2] hit is .
on worulde áá swa leng swá wyrse . ⁊ swa hit sceal
nyde . for folces synnan . ær antecristes tocyme .
yfelian swyþe ; ⁊ huru hit wyrð þænne .
egeslic ⁊ grimlic . wide on worulde ; Understandað
eac georne . þ(æt) deofol þas þeode nu wela geara .
dwelode to swyþe : ⁊ þ(æt) lytle getreowþa . wæran
mid mannu(m) . þeah hy wel spæcan : ⁊ unrihta
to fela ricsode on lande : ⁊ næs a fela man⟨-⟩
na þe smeade ymbe þa bote . swa georne
swa man scolde : ac dæghwamlice man ihte .
yfel . æft(er) oðru(m) . ⁊ unriht rærde . ⁊ un⟨-⟩
laga manege . ealles to wide . gynd ealle
þas þeode ; ⁊ we eac for þa(m) habbað fela byrsta
⁊ bysmara gebiden : ⁊ gif we ænige bote gebidan
scylan . þon(ne) mote we þæs to gode ernian . bet
þon(ne) we ær þysan dydan ; For þa(m) mid miclan
earnungan we geear`n´edan þa yrmða þe us
on sittað : ⁊ mid swyþe micelan earnun⟨-⟩
gan we þa bote motan . æt gode geræcan :

The manuscript draws together administrative ecclesiastical information, laws, and homilies, mostly in English, very likely as a handbook for the use of Wulfstan, archbishop of York 1002-23, and concurrently bishop of Worcester until at least 1016, who was probably personally responsible for one layer of corrections. The format is small. Although the script (written by one of four main hands over 108 folios) appears informal, the minims are separately made, the first **a** of 'áá', l. 7, is half-uncial, **þ** is not used finally, and **ð** is not used initially. The usual Anglo-Saxon letter-forms are in use, except for low **s**. The ascender of **d** is short and therefore distinct from **ð**; the tail of **g** is normally closed; and the high **e** of **æ** is distinctive. The tags at the top of some ascenders, especially **l** and **þ**, tend towards being split. The spellings are generally normal for late West Saxon, though some levelling of inflexions is evident (note 'synnan', l. 8, 'þysan', l. 22, 'earnungan', ll. 23, 24 where *-um* to be expected; and *-an* for expected *-on* in 'wæran', l. 12, 'scylan', l. 21, 'dydan', l. 22, and in 'spæcan', l. 13, where earlier *-en* might have been expected). The lay-out is assured. The title is in black rustic capitals filled with red, and capitals or enlarged forms (including thickened versions of the Tironian sign in ll. 9 and 19), written by the scribe as he went along, follow the *punctus versus*. Lighter pauses are marked by the *punctus elevatus* or the simple point. The apex sign is sparingly but effectively used (see l. 7, for example). The abbreviations are the normal ones: for English the Tironian sign; crossed **þ** for *þ(æt)*; the overline for *m* in 'þa(m)', ll. 6, 19, 22, 'mannu(m)', l. 13, 'oðru(m), l. 17; 'þon(ne)', l. 21; and 'æft(er)', l. 17; and in the Latin heading note 'per-', the date and the sacred names.

Selected words in ll. 6, 8, 9, 12, 13, 15, 16, 18, 19, 20, 24, and 25 were numbered in connection with Joscelyn's abstraction of words for an Old English dictionary; some words are accompanied by interlinear glosses (e.g. '7 auxit' above 'ihte', l. 16, '13 attayne' above 'geræcan', l. 25).

[1] Number on an erasure; note how second delimiting point has been turned into a *punctus elevatus*.

[2] Note above this word the first of thirteen numbers, some with glosses alongside, entered in an attempt at systematic glossing.

Plate 16 – actual size

CONTEXTS

This homily is from Part B of the manuscript (ff. 70-177); because Wulfstan is thought to have made additions and corrections, it may come from either Worcester or York. Perhaps no longer in a monastic house when in the thirteenth or fourteenth centuries a letter was drafted from a 'Robertus corbet' to 'Magistro Waltero de Driston'' (f. 124). Used by Talbot in mid-sixteenth century. The two present parts were bound together by 1580, when in Joscelyn's possession. Seems next to have been in the hands of Lambarde and Crompton, and, according to Tate, in Cotton's library by 1613 (27 May). Seventeenth-century use by Henry Howard, ? Francis Bacon, Tate, Ussher, and Selden. Entered the British Museum with the Cotton Collection in 1753.

SIZE

167 × 105 mm (*c.* 139 × 69-75 mm).

BIBLIOGRAPHY

Pr. Whitelock 1939 [1952]: 33-35 (ll. 1-20); Bethurum 1957: 267-68 (ll. 1-22).

Facs. Loyn 1971; Wilcox 2000.

Disc. Ker 1948: 71, *Cat.* 1957: no. 164; Watson 1979: no. 538, pl. 28 a-d; Kubouchi 1983 [1995]; Cross 1990; Gneuss 2001: no. 341; Tite 2003: 130.

17

London, British Library, Cotton MS Claudius B. iv, f. 38r (formerly 39) *Colour pl. C2*
Translation attributed to Ælfric, Genesis 22: 12-18
Anglo-Saxon minuscule, round phase, s. xi^{1}

TRANSCRIPTION

Main text:

sunu isaác ; He het þa þa stowe d(omi)n(u)s uidit . þ(æt) ys gode[-s][1] gesyhð . ⁊ gyt ys
gesæd swa in monte d(omi)n(u)s uidit . þ(æt) ys gode[-s] gesyhð on dune ; Eft
clypode se engel . abraham . ⁊ cw(æð) . íc swerige ðurh me sylfne . sæde
se ælmihtiga nu ðu noldest arian þinu(m) ancennedan suna . ac ðe
wæs mín ege mare þon(ne) hys líf[2] . ic ðe nu bletsige ⁊ ðinne ofspringe[3]
gemenigfylde . swa swa steorran on heofonum . ⁊ swa swa sand⟨-⟩
ceosel on sǽ. þin ofspringc sceal agan heora feonda gata . ⁊ on
þínu(m) sæde beoð ealle ðeod[u>a] gebletsode . for þan ðe þu gehyrsu⟨-⟩
modest minre hæse ðus ;

Explication added in the top margin:

. iob descendit . sic(ut) sc(r)iptu(m) e(st) i(n) exordio uoluminis ei(us) . Vir erat i(n) t(er)ra hus ⁖
n(ome)n ei(us) iob ⁖ Ier(ominus) dic(it) . Male ig(itur) q(u)ida(m) estima(n)it[4]
. eu(m) e(ss)e de gen(er)e esav . Si q(u)ide(m) q(uo)d i(n) fine libri ipsi(us) habet(ur) . eo q(uo)d de
syro sermone t(r)anslat(us) est . q(uo)d q(u)art(us) sit ab esav ⁖
§et reliq(u)a q(u)e ibi co(n)tinent(ur) ⁖ in hebreis uolominib(us) n(on) habent(ur) ⁖

Explication added within picture frame:

loc(us) (enim) ille non dstat[5] á monte moriá p(er) iter
unius diei . ⁊ e(st) inter bethel ⁊ hay ⁖
In monte d(omi)n(u)s uidebit . Q(u)a(s)i . Sic(ut) respexit
ysáác i(n) monte ⁖ sic uideat nos in hac
angustia . die(m) u(er)o lib(er)ationis ysaac di-
-cunt hebrei p(r)ima(m) die(m) septembris ⁖

Temple and Gameson suggest a date in the second quarter of the century. Ker describes this handwriting as an 'older type' of script by comparison with the other main-text hand of the manuscript: certainly this scribe, hand 2, is readier to make use of **þ** as well as **ð**, the latter being the usual choice of hand 1, and he is careful to elongate the ascender of **ð**. The **a** is sometimes flat-topped (see 'mare', l. 5, 'ðeod[u>a]', l. 8) and **e** may be high in ligature ('engel', l. 3, 'noldest', l. 4, 'ancennedan', l. 4, 'gebletsode', l. 8, 'gehyrsu|modest', l. 9, 'hæse', l. 9). Both low and long **s** are in use. The spellings are normal for late West Saxon, apart from 'gemenigfylde', l. 6, where -*y*- may point towards the south-east. The distinctive **c**-shaped sign is particularly useful for distinguishing 'God' ('gode[-s]', ll. 1, 2) from 'good'. The principal mark of punctuation is still the simple point; the *punctus versus* here closes heavier sense breaks, and may be followed by a capital (see l. 2). Word division is well developed, except that ⁊ usually joins with the next word; the hyphen is not used; but contrast the practice of hand 1 (see p. 81). Whereas the first scribe uses scarcely any abbreviations other than the Tironian sign, this scribe draws on the forms usual in English, not just 'þ(æt)', l. 2, and the overline ('þinu(m)', ll. 4, 8) but 'cw(æð)', l. 3 and 'þon(ne)', l. 5, as well. The manuscript contains a cycle of some four hundred illustrations. This drawing is to be read from the bottom upwards: it is striking how the few things coloured yellow (see colour pl. C2) draw the eye, in particular the sword-hilt near the centre, the table-top, and again at the top the sword-hilt, this time juxtaposed with a yellow book held out by the angel and contrasting sacrifice under the Old Law and the Law to come. Continued use into the twelfth century is clear from a heavy sprinkling of stress marks, some oddly positioned, as with 'se', l. 4, where the descender of **y**

[1] The final -*s* is erased here and in the next line, leaving 'gode' as subject, instead of the scribe's noun phrase.
[2] Possible earlier stress mark?
[3] False division indicated by twelfth-century mark up?
[4] The **í** suggests that most apex signs from this layer.
[5] For 'd⟨i⟩stat'?

Plate 17 – reduced to 72%

in the line above left little room. I have tried to leave these twelfth-century additions out of the transcription, but to indicate those which seem to remain from a lighter, earlier application of stress marks.

The heavily abbreviated twelfth-century blocks of explication show the continued use of the book. Here the script is Protogothic: note the ligatured **de** and the ticking of single **i**, a feature looking forward to fully Gothic scripts. Note the use of the *paragraphus*, represented by § in the transcription, to mark the overrun of the second line of explication (compare its use at the foot of the first column in pl. 27a). The *signe de renvoi* above '.Hær.' at the bottom right-hand corner refers across to the foot of the facing page (f. 37v), where the explication starts, its opening marked by 'Hwær.' and the same *signe de renvoi*.

CONTEXTS

A selective paraphrase from the opening books of the Old Testament. Identified as a book listed in a late-fifteenth-century catalogue of St Augustine's, Canterbury (James 1903: 201, 516). The Hebrew letters in the bottom margin of f. 125v were written in the thirteenth century or later by someone without much knowledge of Hebrew (information from Stewart Brookes). The chapter number 'xxxvii' was entered on f. 53r by Robert Talbot, probably the first post-dissolution owner. In Cotton's library by 1621, where used by Richard James. Lent to Tate (by 1612), Lisle (1621), Selden (1621 or after), Le Neve (1641), Dugdale (1653). Extracts in Ware's notebook. Entered the British Museum with the Cotton Collection in 1753. Known as the Anglo-Saxon Hexateuch (sometimes Pentateuch).

SIZE

c. 327 × 217 mm (*c.* 267 × 167 mm).

BIBLIOGRAPHY

Pr. Crawford 1922 [1969]: 142-43.
Facs. Dodwell and Clemoes 1974; Doane 2002.
Disc. Ker, *Cat.* 1957: no. 142; Temple 1976: no. 86; Laing 1993: 73; Barnhouse and Withers 2000; Graham 2000; Johnson 2000; Tite 2003: 123; Gneuss 2001: no. 315.

16

he arærde ænne weofod gode · 7 genam of eallum ðam
clænum nytenum · 7 clænum fugelum · 7 geoffrode
gode lac on ðam weofode · God ða underfeng his lac · 7
ðære winsum nysse bræð · 7 cwæð him to · Nelle ic na-
tes hwon awyrigean ða eorðan heonon forð · for mannum
andgyte · 7 geþoht menniscre heortan syndon forð
healde to yfele fram iugoðe · For nostlice ne of slea ic
heonon forð mid wætere ælcðinge cuces · swaswa ic
dyde eallum dagum ðære eorðan · Sæd · 7 ge rip · cyle ·
7 hæte · sumor · 7 winter · dæg · 7 niht · ne geswicað · God
bletsode ða noe · 7 his suna · 7 cwæð him to · Weaxað 7 beoð
gemenifylde · 7 afyllað ða eorðan · 7 beo eower ege 7 oga
ofer ealle nytenu 7 fugelas · 7 ofer ealle ða ðinge ðe on
eorðan styriað · Ealle sæfixas syndon eowrum handum
betæhte · 7 eal ðæt ðe styriað · 7 leofað · beo eow to mete ·
swaswa growende wyrta · ic hi betæce ealle eow butan
ðam anum ðæt ge flæsc mid blode ne eton · Eower blod
ic offange æt eallum wildeorum · 7 eac æt ðam men ·
of ðæs weres handa · 7 his broðor handa ic offange ðæs
mannes lif : swa hwa swa agyt ðæs mannes blod · his
blod byð agoten · witodlice to godes anlicnysse is se man
geworht · weaxe ge nu · 7 beoð gemænifylde · 7 gað ofer
eorðan · 7 gefyllað hi · God cwæð eft to noe · 7 to his sunum
efne nu ic sette minne wed to eow · 7 to eowrum ofspringe ·
7 to eallum libbendum nytenum ðe of ðam arce eodon ·
ðæt ic nateshwon nelle heonon forð eal adydon mid flo
des wæterum · ne heonon forð ne bið flod tosencende ða
eorðan · Ðis bið ðæt tacn mines weddes · ðæt ic do betwux
me · 7 eow · 7 eallum libbendum nytenum · on ecum mægðum
ðæt is ðæt ic sette minne renbogan on wolcnum · 7 he byð
tacn mines weddes betwux me · 7 ðære eorðan · Þonne ic
ofer teo heofonan mid wolcnum · ðonne æteowað min boga
on ðam wolcnum · 7 ic beo gemyndig mines weddes wið eow ·
ðæt heonon forð ne byð flod to adylgienne eall flæsc ·
Bið ðonne se renboga on ðam wolcnum · 7 ic hine geseo ·
7 beo gemyndig ðæs ecean weddes · Ðe geset is betwux gode ·
7 eallum libbendum flæsce ðe ofer eorðan is · Ðis byð
ðæt tacn mines weddes · ðæt ic gesette betwux me

London, British Library, Cotton MS Claudius B. iv, f. 16r

Translation from the Old Testament, Genesis 8:20 – 9:12
reduced to 69%

18

London, British Library, Cotton MS Julius E. vii, f. 203r (formerly 201)
Ælfric, prayer at end of Life of St Martin and opening of Life of St Edmund
Late Anglo-Saxon minuscule, s. xi in.

TRANSCRIPTION

Olim haec trastuli . sicuti ualui . sed modo prae⟨-⟩
cib(us) . constrictus plenius . O martine s(an)c(t)ae .
meritis praeclare . iuua me miseru(m) . meritis
modicum . Caream quo neuis . mihimet nocuus .
castiusque uiua(m) . Nactus iam ueniam . XII · k(a)l(endis)[1]
DECE(M)BR(IS) . PASSIO S(AN)C(T)I EADMVNDI REGIS
S VM SWYÐE GELÆRED MUNUC ET MARTYRIS .
co(m) suþan ofer sæ fra(m) s(an)c(t)e benedictes stówe
on æþelredes cynincges dæge to dunstane
ærcebisceope þrim gearu(m) ær he forðferde .
⁊ se munuc hatte abbo .[2] þa wurdon hi æt spræ⟨-⟩
ce oþ þ(æt) dunstan rehte be s(an)c(t)e eadmunde . swa
swa eadmundes swurdbora hit rehte æþel⟨-⟩
stane cynincge þa þa dunstan iung man wæs .
⁊ se swurdbora wæs forealdod [-.] man . Þa gesette
se munuc ealle þa gereccednysse on anre béc .
⁊ eft ða þa seo bóc com to ús binnan feawu(m) gea⟨-⟩
rum þa awende we hit on englisc . swa swa hit
her æfter stent . Se munuc þa abbo binnan
twam gearu(m) . gewende ham to his mynstre .
⁊ wearð sona to abbode geset on þa(m) ylcan myn⟨-⟩
stre
EADMVND[3] SE EADIGA EASTENGLA CYNINCG
wæs snotor ⁊ wurðful . ⁊ wurðode symble
mid æþelum þeawum þone ælmihtigan god .
He wæs eadmod . ⁊ geþungen . ⁊ swá anræde þurh⟨-⟩
wunode þ(æt) he nolde abugan to bysmorfullu(m)
leahtrum . ne on naþre healfe he ne ahylde his
þeawas . ac wæs symble gemyndig þære soþan
lare . þu[4] eart to heafodmen geset . ne ahefe
þu ðe . ac beo betwux mannu(m) swa swa an man
of him . He wæs cýstig wædlum . ⁊ wydewu(m) swa swa

Although the aspect of the script is Caroline, the scribe is clearly comfortable with the letter-forms used in writing English. Categorization is therefore difficult, and 'late' is used before 'Anglo-Saxon minuscule' to signal a transitional script in which the module is tending towards the rectangular but the insular-derived letters are steady. The **a** is flat-topped, except in **æ**. Tall **e** is occasional in **æ**: 'wæs', ll. 14, 23, 29, 32, 'æfter', l. 19, 'þære', l. 29. The **e** is horned (but not the **c**), and **y**, dotted, is typically straight-limbed (but see 'mynstre', l. 20, 'gemyndig', l. 29, contrast the two forms in l. 7, and note the decorative pen-turn to the right in the bottom line). The letters **þ**, **ð**, and **ƿ** specific to English are all in use: **ð** is not used as an opening letter, and it is noticeably less frequent than **þ**. Note that separate **ae** is used in the Latin whereas **æ** is general in the vernacular text. Word division is incomplete: monosyllables are often attached to a following word, whether singly or in pairs. Punctuation is by a median point, with a capital following to indicate more major pauses. Hyphens do not occur on this page: they do appear elsewhere in the manuscript, sometimes end-line, sometimes at the beginning of the

[1] Should this read 'k(a)l(endas)'? Note that **k** is infrequent in Latin, except for a few words in which, as here, the opening letter is used in abbreviation.

[2] The interlinear translation reads: 'a very learned monk | over sea from seynt benedicts place | in Ethelred Kinges dayes to Dunstane | archbishop three yeeres ere he deceased | & monk hight Abbo'.

[3] The preparation for a larger decorated initial can still be seen.

[4] 'Gif' appears before 'þu' in the Bodley 343 version.

Olim haec quasi uili . sicuti ualui . sed modo p̄prae
cib; . consequetur plenius . Omnia tamen scāe .
meruit p̄praeclare . iuua me in seculū . meruit
modicum . Capiam quo neuis . minime nociuus .
castusque uiuā . Hactus iam ueniam XII . kl
DECEBR . PASSIO SCI EADMUNDI REGIS
SUM SWYÐE GELÆRED MUNUC ET MARTYRIS .
com suþan ofer sæ fram sc̄e benedictes stowe
on æþelredes cynincges dæge to dunstane
ærce bisceope þrim gearū ær he forð ferde .
and se munuc hatte abbo . þa wurdon hi æt spræ
ce oþþæt dunstan rehte be sc̄e eadmunde . swa
swa eadmundes swurdbora hit rehte æþel
stane cynincge þa þa dunstan iung man wæs .
and se swurdbora wæs forealdod man . Þa gesette
se munuc ealle þa gereccednysse on anre bec .
and eft ða þa seo boc com to us binnan feawū gea
rum þa awende we hit on englisc . swa swa hit
her æfter stent . Se munuc þa abbo binnan
twam gearū . gewende ham to his mynstre .
and wearð sona to abbode geset on þā ylcan myn
stre

EADMUND SE EADIGA EASTENGLA CYNINCG
wæs snotor and wurðful . and wurðode symble
mid æþelum þeawum þone ælmihtigan god .
He wæs eadmod . and geþungen . and swa anræde þurh
wunode þæt he nolde abugan to bysmorfullū
leahtrum . ne on naþre healfe he ne ahylde his
þeawas . ac wæs symble gemyndig þære soþan
lare . þu eart to heafod men geset . ne ahefe
þu ðe . ac beo betwux mannū swa swa an man
of him . He wæs cystig wædlum . and wydewū swa swa

Plate 18 – reduced to 85%

following line, and sometimes at the end of a line and the beginning of the following line. The initials, modestly decorated, are red, as is the Latin title spread across ll. 5–7 in rustic capitals (rubrics are underlined in this transcript). A smaller version of this display script marks both the explanatory opening of Ælfric's Edmund homily (l. 7) and the opening of the material drawn from his source, Abbo's life of the saint (l. 23). Some words are marked with an apex sign for emphasis. The abbreviations are the usual ones for Old English, as well as ⁊ and ꝥ, the overline for *m* and the variable *s(an)c(tus)* contraction (in both English and Latin). Further abbreviations are used in Latin: **-b;** for -b*us* (l. 2) and in the title.

CONTEXTS

From Bury St Edmunds, where it was probably bound with other materials relating to Edmund (now Tiberius B. ii, ff. 2–85); a thirteenth-century inscription 'Liber sancti Ædmundi regis ⁊ martyris' is on f. 3. Likely to have been written elsewhere and taken to Bury, where a layer of Old English alterations and insertions was probably added. In Cotton's collection by 1621 ('Thomas Cotton' on f. 3). Note the interlinear translation (ll. 8–12) added by an antiquary. Entered the British Museum with the Cotton Collection in 1753.

SIZE

273 × 185 mm (*c.* 232 × 125 mm).

BIBLIOGRAPHY

Pr. Skeat 1900: II. 312–14; Needham [1966] 1976: 43–44.
Disc. Needham 1958; Ker, *Cat.*1957: no. 162; Torkar 1971; Dumville 1988: 60–61; Gneuss 2001: no. 339; Tite 2003: 99.

IV English Caroline minuscule

Between the period of the decline of the Roman book trade, which continued possibly as late as the death of Pope Gregory the Great (A.D. 604), and the Carolingian renewal (*renovatio*) of learning at the end of the eighth century, important movements in the evolution of national scripts occurred generally across western Europe. Two minuscule scripts in France are to be noted especially, the Merovingian cursive, a tall, narrow, angular script, crabbed and clotted, and heavily decorated with clubs and wedges,[1] together with its more formalized version, associated with Luxeuil (like St Gallen, a house subject to Irish influences) and found first in a lectionary from the end of the seventh century.[2] A more satisfactory book script emerged towards the end of the eighth century at Tours and Corbie,[3] where a tendency to simplify Merovingian can be seen.[4] Crucial to its emergence was the *renovatio* of scripts, dated to the years 780-850 and associated with the educational ambitions of Charlemagne. The *renovatio* scribes were very familiar with late Roman scripts, especially with Half-uncial. At Corbie in north-east France a Half-uncial even seems to have redeveloped in this period as a book script, and from Corbie too comes the first dated example of Caroline minuscule, late in the eighth century. The revival of late antique Half-uncial is therefore seen by some as focal for the development of Caroline minuscule.

At first appearing as a book hand and succeeding several different cursive scripts used throughout Francia,[5] this new script, Caroline minuscule, was not itself used in documents until the end of the ninth century. It is a clear script with few variant letter-forms, and easily read. Most vertical strokes are plain, ending on or just below the line (the descenders are **p** and **q**, and **g** is looped). The overall dates for the script are *c*. 800 - *c*. 1200. Once adopted in England, the plain minims of Caroline minuscule soon acquired feet under the influence of Insular minuscule, a feature that spread into Normandy and France by the late eleventh century. The dates generally accepted for the use of English Caroline minuscule are *c*. 950 - *c*. 1100. Caroline minuscule first appeared in England in the reformed Benedictine monasteries as a script for writing Latin, and it was used alongside Anglo-Saxon minuscule in both its square and round phases. Two main styles of English Caroline minuscule are recognized. The longer-lasting Style II is associated with Glastonbury and Canterbury, where Dunstan played a major part in bringing about reform;[6] the earliest manuscripts are hard to date because of the absence of comparable dated materials. Manuscripts in Style I, connected rather with the influence of Æthelwold, come principally from Abingdon and Winchester,[7] with King Edgar's grant of land to Abingdon Abbey in A.D. 961 providing the first dated charter in English Caroline minuscule.[8] From *c*. 1020 a recognizably generic English Caroline script was in general use for writing Latin, with the result, as Ker observes, that the 'palaeography of the first half of the eleventh century, after the final break down of the Insular hand about the year 1000, is not easy to understand'.[9] After the Conquest English Caroline minuscule was already in decline. The most famous proponent of late English Caroline minuscule was Eadui Basan,[10] a monk at Christ Church, Canterbury, who signed many of his manuscripts. He may have made additions to the Vespasian Psalter (if he did, this is contributory evidence for the early medieval location of that manuscript);[11] and the finely illuminated Arundel Psalter, from which the illustration shown on p. 87 is taken, was written by him. In this full-page drawing St Benedict is an imposing figure, giving the Rule to monks who flock to him from the right with an open book.[12]

Although Caroline minuscule was increasingly the hand of the reformed monasteries of late Anglo-Saxon England, Anglo-Saxon minuscule continued for some time to be the script used for writing English. Thus, Caroline minuscule may be thought of as becoming the dominant script alongside the square phase of Anglo-Saxon minuscule and as being the main script of later Anglo-Saxon England when the native minuscule was in its round phase. Knowledge of the letter-forms distinctive of English Caroline minuscule is particularly valuable for readers of English texts from the eleventh century onwards. Careful inspection should always be made of **a**, **d**, **e**, **f**, **g**, **h**, **r**, and **s** in English hands of this period, and sometimes the shape of **c**, **o**, and **y** can also help towards the categorization of a hand. Whether or not the Tironian sign ⁊ continues in use should be noted, and because Caroline minuscule uses **ę** alongside **æ** and eventually altogether discards the use of both for writing Latin, it also becomes necessary to consider how scribes treat **æ** when writing English.

[1] See Brown, M.P. 1990: pl. 10.
[2] See Brown, M.P. 1990: pl. 13.
[3] See Brown, M.P. 1990: pls 12 and 23.
[4] Ganz 1987.
[5] Ganz 1982 explores analyses of these script types.
[6] Bishop 1971: pl. 10 represents the peak of Style II.
[7] Bishop 1971: pl. 12 is Style I at its grandest.
[8] Sawyer 1968: no. 690: see Chaplais 1995.
[9] Ker 1948: 50.
[10] Bishop 1971: pls 24, 25.
[11] Bishop 1971: pl. 24.
[12] Benedict (*c*. 480-*c*. 550) was abbot and founder of the monasteries of Subiaco and, later, of Monte Cassino, where he put together the final version of his Rule, in the early Middle Ages the most influential blueprint for monastic life.

The neat round script of pl. 19 (Cotton Titus A. iv) allows detailed examination of an attempt to use different script repertoires for Latin and English in a dual-language Benedictine Rule. (A century and a half later the last copy of the bilingual Benedictine Rule, adapted *c.* 1200 for use by the nuns of the Cistercian house at Wintney (see. p. 123), has few of these distinctions.) Although not the earliest extant copy of the bilingual Benedictine Rule, this manuscript may approach most closely to Æthelwold's original translation.[13] The training in Caroline script is dominant, and some inconsistency is found in the English version, for example in the straight **d** of 'standende', l. 24, the long **s** of 'his', l. 15, and the tendency of **a** to develop a head. Otherwise the two sets of letter-forms are distinctive, and it should be noted that the ampersand **&** is used in Latin and the Tironian sign ⁊ in English. (The ampersand, developed from a combination of tall broken-backed **e** with **t**, is not by origin an abbreviation.) For English the scribe makes do with space and the low point as his main way of managing punctuation, whereas in Latin he draws on the elaborated system. Further differences worth comment suggest other ways in which the conventions used for writing English may diverge: for English the scribe retains **æ** (already with a sense of uncertainty as to its role) whereas **ę** is favoured in Latin; and although the three special letter-forms used customarily in Old English, **þ**, **ð**, and **ƿ**, are still in use, there are signs that **ð** will disappear before **þ** (and in pl. 20 too).

The main-text hand of pl. 20 (Cotton Tiberius A. iii) provides a good example of English Caroline minuscule from the middle of the eleventh century.[14] Generous in layout, the words are well spaced and there is little lateral compression. The scribe generally uses simple **e** rather than **ę**, but not in a word common in formulaic phrases, 'sęcula', l. 5. The continuous gloss to Ælfric's *Colloquy* has most of the letter-forms distinctive of Anglo-Saxon minuscule. In modern times, ironically, the gloss has become popular in teaching Old English, whereas the original function of the *Colloquy* was to give practice in speaking Latin.[15] Two major texts in Tiberius A. iii are prefaced by full-page illustrations. Originally the glossed Benedictine Rule stood at the beginning of the manuscript, preceded by a fully painted drawing of St Benedict (see p. 91) in which, as in Arundel 155, monks approach from the right and one monk falls in adoration of the saint. The other drawing (see p. 95) precedes the glossed *Regularis concordia Anglicae nationis*, a code of *c.* 973 designed to establish uniform practices in liturgy and monastic life throughout England. Among the texts associated with the reform was a New Hymnal,[16] for which teaching collections glossed in English were developed. Cotton Vespasian D. xii is just such a book: the page illustrated on p. 99 has at the top the end of a hymn sung 'ad sextum', which is followed by its glossed Latin paraphrase; and the next hymn, on ll. 16-22, is in turn followed by its explication in both languages. Traditionally the composition of the *Regularis concordia* is attributed to Dunstan, although Æthelwold is more likely to have been its compiler. In the picture King Edgar, a palm of peace in his hand, is seated between these two main leaders of the tenth-century Benedictine reform movement in England.[17]

By contrast with the script of Tiberius A. iii, pl. 21, from a section of Cotton Tiberius B. iv written late in the eleventh century, shows the late production of round Anglo-Saxon minuscule of a decent quality. There is, however, something almost artificial in the squarish aspect of pl. 22, a well-designed copy of the Old English Bede in a Worcester hand, even though its scribe holds well to the letter-forms distinctive of Anglo-Saxon minuscule, with round **d** clearly distinguished from **ð** and the distinctive **æ** made in a deliberate way. This is Scribe 2 of Hemming's Cartulary and other Worcester manuscripts and documents (compare the charter in his hand shown on p. 103), with his characteristic triangle of dots above a comma, writing in the last decade of the eleventh century.[18] The Caroline look to the **a** is worth noting and overall the script is becoming more angular. Pl. 23 is particularly instructive, showing contrasting twelfth-century hands in the change-over between the two main scribes of the Peterborough Chronicle. English Caroline minuscule was already losing definition by the end of the eleventh century, its characteristic roundness giving way to the pointed, oval shapes more typical of early-twelfth-century scripts. In the writing of English the letter-forms distinctive of Anglo-Saxon minuscule were to drop away gradually, with **a** and **h** usually the first to lose ground and low **s** losing frequency soon after. The first of the Peterborough Chronicle scribes, writing in *c.* 1131 the last of the annals he added to the 'E' copy of the Anglo-Saxon Chronicle, has a neat round hand, and he is practised in deploying the letter-forms distinctive of Anglo-Saxon minuscule, except that his Caroline **h** gives him away. A generation later the scribe of the Second Continuation writes in a very different way, best described as Protogothic.

[13] Jayatilaka 2003: 151.

[14] A tendency is emerging to date this manuscript to the middle of the century or somewhat later (Gneuss 1997: 13) or to the second half of the century (Turner in Backhouse, Turner and Webster 1984: 47).

[15] See Hill 1998: 146.

[16] Milfull 1996 is the most authoritative account of the hymns of the Anglo-Saxon church.

[17] See Withers 1997, Karkov 2004.

[18] Ker 1948.

London, British Library, Arundel MS 155, f. 133r
Psalter from Christ Church, Canterbury, 1012–1023

St Benedict and the monks of Christ Church, Canterbury
reduced to 76%

19

London, British Library, Cotton MS Titus A. iv, f. 32r
Rule of St Benedict (*Regula sancti Benedicti*), with Æthelwold's translation
English Caroline minuscule, s. xi med.

TRANSCRIPTION

gradibus ascensis ⸵ monachus mox
ad caritatem dei p(er)ueni(et) ⸵ illam
quȩ p(er)fecta foras mittit timore(m) ;
per quam uniuersa quȩ prius
non sine formidine obseruabat ⸵
absque ullo labore uelut naturaliter ex consuetudine incipiet
custodire ; Non iam timore gehen⟨-⟩
ne ⸵ sed amore cr(ist)i & consuetudine
ipsa bona ⸵ & delectatione uir⟨-⟩
tutum ⸵ quȩ d(omi)n(u)s iam [-no>i]n op(er)ari[u+o]
su[u+o][-m] mund[u+o] a uitiis & peccatis
sp(irit)u s(an)c(t)o dignabitur demonstrare ;
Se twelfta stæpæ eadmodnesse
is . Gyf se munuc \inne/[1] on hís heortan
eaþmod byþ ⁊ na þ(æt) an ác eác swilce
utane mid his lichaman eaþmod⟨-⟩
nesse eallum þam þe him on lociað .
symle gebýcnige . þæt si ægþer
ge on weorce . ge on gebedhuse .
ge innan mynstre . ge on weort⟨-⟩
earde . ge on fare . ge on ælcere
stowe . ⁊ swa hwar swa he si . sittende .
standende . oþþe gangende . on⟨-⟩
hnigendum heafde symle his
gesihþa adune on eorþan besette .
⁊ hine sylfne on ælcne timan
scyldigne for his synnum talige

The first impression is of an attempt at differing scripts for Latin (ll. 1-13) and English (ll. 14-28). The upper passage, in Latin, looks less cluttered, largely because only **p**, **q**, and the loop of **g** descend below the line. Note however that the down strokes of **f**, **r**, and **s** can trail below the line (as in the second **r** of 'naturaliter', l. 7, or the **f** of 'foras', l. 3). Letter-forms distinctive of Caroline script by contrast with Anglo-Saxon minuscule are: open-topped **a**, straight-backed **d**, **g** with **o**-shaped top and open tail, short **r**, tall **s** ending on the line (all seen in 'gradibus', l. 1), **h** with second stroke tucking into the left ('monachus', l. 1), tall **f** ('foras', l. 3). Note that **e** in the Latin passage does not have a horn to the left (compare 'sine', l. 5 with 'eác', l. 16) and that the Caroline **st** ligature of 'custodire', l. 8, and 'demonstrare', l. 13, does not occur in English ('stæpæ', l. 14, 'mynstre', l. 21, 'stowe', l. 23, 'standende', l. 24). Again, the more elaborated punctuation system of the Latin passage, with the *punctus elevatus* within the sentence, the *punctus versus* at the end of the sentence and the point all in use on this page, contrasts with the simple point of the English text. The hyphen is used occasionally in the Latin (as in l. 6) but apparently not in the translation. As might be expected, there is a heavier use of abbreviation in the Latin passage: **p** in 'p(er)ueni(et)', l. 2 (in which the ampersand occurs also), and in ll. 3, 11, the overline in 'timore(m)', l. 3, and the *nomina sacra* in ll. 9, 11, 13. Clearly the scribe is accustomed to using Caroline script, for the choice of letter-forms in the Latin text is consistent, even if there seem to have been difficulties with the language (see ll. 11-12). In the English passage the **a** may have a Caroline look to it, as most obviously in 'an', l. 16, straightbacked **d** appears in 'standende', l. 24, the second foot of **h** can appear to drift inwards ('his', l. 17) and **s** ends tidily on line ('hís', l. 15). Note also that in the English passage the scribe attempts to retain the **æ** digraph ('stæpæ', l. 14), but with enthusiasm rather than

[1] This appears to be a contemporary insertion.

32

gradibus ascensis. monachus mox ad caritatem dei perueniet. illam que perfecta foras mittit timorem; per quam uniuersa que prius non sine formidine obseruabat. absque ullo labore uelut naturaliter ex consuetudine incipiet custodire; Non iam timore gehenne. sed amore xpi & consuetudine ipsa bona. & delectatione uirtutum. que dns iam in operario suo mundo a uitiis & peccatis spu sco dignabitur demonstrare;

Se twelfta stæpæ eadmodnesse is. þ se munuc inne on his heortan eadmodnys 7 na þan ac eac swilce utane mid his lichaman eadmodnesse eallum þam þe him onlociað. symle geþycnige. þæt si æt þam ge on weorce. ge on gebedhuse. ge innan mynstre. ge on weortearde. ge on wege. ge on ælcere stowe. 7 swa hwær swa he si. sittende. standende. oþþe gangende. on hnigendum heafde symle his gesihþa adune on eorþan befestte. 7 hine sylfne on ælcne timan scyldigne for his synnum talige

Plate 19 – actual size

s. xi in.

• 2 compartment a in OE
• e w/ spurs in Lat
• horn to left of e

understanding, whereas the Latin has ę ('quę', l. 3). There are signs that ð (found only in 'lociað', l. 18, and not used word-finally in 'byþ', l. 16) is becoming unfamiliar, at least to this scribe. A further example of uncertainty as to the usual forms of English inflexions is 'gesihþa', l. 26. Ruled in hardpoint with vertical double boundary lines. The capitals alternate regularly in red, blue, and green. The only abbreviations in the English passage are the Tironian sign and a single example of 'þ(æt)', l. 16. In the English passage apex signs identify some monosyllables, suggesting it might have been read aloud.

CONTEXTS

Perhaps from Winchester or Christ Church, Canterbury. Contents indicate links with four other manuscripts of the Benedictine Rule, most closely with Cotton Tiberius A. iii, but also with Corpus Christi College Cambridge 57, Cambridge University Library Ll. 1. 14, ff. 70-108, and Harley 5431, ff. 4-126 (Graham 1998: 25). Belonged to Thomas Allen (in his 1622 catalogue). Later acquired by Cotton, very likely with Richard James as intermediary. Transcribed by Junius (MS Junius 52, ff. 1-64). Entered the British Museum with the Cotton Collection in 1753.

SIZE

192 × 118 mm (146 × 73 mm).

BIBLIOGRAPHY

Coll. Schröer 1885-88 [1964]: 31.
Disc. Ker, *Cat.* 1957: no. 200; Graham 1998; Gneuss 2001: no. 379; Tite 2003: 190.

London, British Library, Cotton MS Tiberius A. iii, f. 117v

Monks presenting the rule of St Benedict
reduced to 80%

20

London, British Library, Cotton MS Tiberius A. iii, f. 60v
End of office prayer; opening of Ælfric's *Colloquy*
English Caroline minuscule, s. xi med.

TRANSCRIPTION

diabolo siue inimicis meis uisibilibus tradar . Sed tu potius

bone cr(ist)e in misericordia tua. & non in furore corripe me .

Et ubicumq(ue) oberrauero a te . reuoca me ad te . Atq(ue) reuocatu(m)

paterna pietate semp(er) custodi ad gloria(m) nominis tui . q(uo)d sit

benedictu(m) in sęcula . AMEN .

we cildra biddaþ þe eala lareow þ(æt) þu tæce us sprecan
Nos pueri rogamus te magister ut doceas nos loqui latialit(er)

forþam ungelærede we syndon ⁊ gewammodlice we sprecaþ hwæt wille ge
recte quia idiote sumus & corrupte loquimur . Quid uultis

sprecan hwæt rece we hwæt we sprecan buton hit riht spræc sy
loqui ? quid curamus[1] . quid loquamur nisi recta locutio sit

⁊ behese[2] næs idel oþþe fracod wille beswungen on leornunge
& utilis non anilis aut turpis . Vúltis flagellari in discendo ?

leofre ys us beon geswu(n)gen for lare þonne hit ne cunnan ac we witun
Carius est nobis flagellari p(ro) doctrina quam nescire . Sed scim(us)

þe bilewitne wesan ⁊ nellan onbelæden swincgla us buton þu bi togenydd
te mansuetu(m) esse & nolle inferre plagas nobis nisi cogaris

fra(m) us ic axie þe hwæt sprycst þu hwæt hæfst þu weorkes
a nobis . Interrogo te quid mihi loqueris ? quid habes operis .

ic eom geanwyrde monuc ⁊ ic sincge ælce dæg seofon tida mid gebroþru(m)
P(ro)fessus sum monachu(m) & psallam om(n)i die septe(m) sinaxes cu(m) fratrib(us)

⁊ ic eom bysgod ⁊ on sange ac þeahhwæþere ic wolde betwenan
& occupatus sum lectionibus & cantu . Sed tamen uelle(m) interi(m)

leornian sprecan on ledengereorde hwæt cunnon þas þine geferan
discere sermocinari latina lingua . Quid sciunt isti tui socii ?

sume synt yrþlincgas sume scephyrdas sume oxanhyrdas sume eac swylce
Alii sunt aratores . alii opiliones . quida(m) bubulci . quida(m) etia(m)

huntan sume fisceras sume fugeleras sume cypmenn su⟨-⟩
uenatores alii piscatores . alii aucupes . quida(m) mercatores . qui⟨-⟩

me scewyrhtan sealteras bæceras hwæt
dam sutores . quida(m) salinatores . Quida(m) p[a>i]stores loci . Quid

sægest þu yrþlinge hu begæst þu weorc þin eala leof hlaford þearle
dicis tu arator ? Quomodo exerces opus tuu(m) ? O mi d(omi)ne nimiu(m)

ic deorfe ic ga ut on dægræd þywende oxon to felda ⁊ iugie hig
laboro exeo diluculo minando boues ad campu(m) & iungo eos

to syl nys hyt swa stearc winter þ(æt) ic durre lutian æt ham
ad aratru(m) non est tam asp(er)a hiemps ut audea(m) latere domi

for ege hlafordes mines ac geiukodan oxan ⁊ gefæstnodon sceare
p(ro) timore d(omi)ni mei sed iunctis bobus & confirmato uomere

⁊ cultre mit þære syl ælce dæg ic sceal erian fulne æþer[4] oþþe
& cultro . aratro omni die debeo aratre[3] integru(m) agru(m) aut

The main-text hand is a steady Caroline minuscule, somewhat upright and displaying the ampersand and all the letter-forms that distinguish Caroline from Anglo-Saxon minuscule. Note that **ę** ('sęcula', l. 5) is still in use and **d** is straight-backed. Two of the three characteristic Caroline ligatures are shown: **st** ('custodi', l. 4, 'magister', l. 6) and **ra** with Half-uncial **a** (as in 'tradar', l. 1). The marks of punctuation seen in this page of the *Colloquy* are the low point and

[1] Has been explained as for 'caramus', but could be from *cūro*.

[2] For *behefe*; low **f** misread as **s**.

[3] Thought to show dittography of *t* from the noun 'aratro' a few words earlier, but note Lewis & Short under **ărūtro* 'quod nunc vocant artrare, id est aratrare', *Plin.* 18, 20, 49 §49.

[4] For *æcer*.

diabolo siue inimicis meis uisibilibus tradar. Sed tu potius bone xp̄e in misericordia tua. & non in furore corripe me. Et ubi cumq: oberrauero a te. reuoca me ad te. Atq: reuocatū paterna pietate semp̄ custodi ad gloriā nominis tui. qd̄ sit benedictū in secula. AMEN.

Nos pueri rogamus te magister ut doceas nos loqui latialit̄ recte quia idiote sumus & corrupte loquimur. Quid uultis loqui? quid curamus. quid loquamur nisi recta locutio sit & utilis non anilis aut turpis. Uultis flagellari in discendo? Carius est nobis flagellari p̄doctrina quam nescire. Sed scim̄ te mansuetū esse & nolle inferre plagas nobis nisi cogaris a nobis. Interrogo te quid mihi loqueris? quid habes operis. P̄fessus sum monachū & psallam omni die septē sinaxes cū fratrib: & occupatus sum lectionibus & cantu. sed tamen uellē interim discere sermocinari latina lingua. Quid sciunt isti tui socii? Alii sunt aratores. alii opiliones. quidā bubulci. quidā etiā uenatores alii piscatores. alii aucupes. quidā mercatores. quidam sutores. quidā salinatores. Quidā p̄stores loci. Quid dicis tu arator? Quomodo exerces opus tuū? O mi dn̄e nimiū laboro exeo diluculo minando boues ad campū & iungo eos ad aratrū non est tam aspa hiemps ut audeā latere domi p̄ timore dn̄i mei sed iunctis bobus & confirmato uomere & cultro. aratro omni die debeo arare integrū agrū aut

Plate 20 – reduced to 88%

question mark. Not all short words are separated out (see for example 'Sed tu', l. 1, 'ad te', l. 3, '& utilis', l. 9). The abbreviations are usual in Latin: 'cr(ist)e', l. 2, -**q:** in 'cumq(ue)', l. 3, 'Atq(ue)', l. 3; overline for *m* or *n* in 'reuocatu(m)', l. 3, 'gloria(m)', l. 4, 'benedictu(m)', l. 5, 'mansuetu(m)', l. 11, 'monachu(m)', l. 13, 'om(n)i', l. 13, 'cu(m)', l. 13; 'uelle(m) interi(m)' l. 14, 'quida(m)', l. 16, 'quida(m) etia(m)', l. 16, 'quida(m)', l. 17, 'quida(m)', l. 18, 'Quida(m)', l. 18, 'nimiu(m)', l. 19, 'campu(m)', l. 20, 'aratru(m)', l. 21, 'integru(m) agru(m)', l. 23; **ꝑ** in 'semp(er)', l. 4, 'asp(er)a', l. 21; 'q(uo)d', l. 4; ͛ in 'latialit(er)', l. 6;**ꝓ** in 'p(ro)'; ll. 10, 22, 'P(ro)fessus', l. 13; ꝰ in 'scim(us)', l. 10; -**b:** in 'fratrib(us)', l. 13; the variable form 'd(omi)ne', l. 19, 'd(omi)ni', l. 22. Note 'monachu(m)', l. 13, where -*us* to be expected.

The authorship of the running gloss is often ascribed to Ælfric's pupil Ælfric Bata. The hand, round, neat and forward-sloping, is contemporary with the main text. Although the alternate letter-forms of Anglo-Saxon minuscule are mostly in use, the second stroke of **h** tends to tuck in to the left as in Caroline and there are no examples of low **s** (the mistaken 'behese', l. 9g, suggests that low **s** was in the exemplar). Both **þ** and **ƿ** are usual, but the scribe makes little use of **ð** (no instances on this page). Note the adoption of -**k**- for the back voiceless stop rather than the usual **c** of in the Anglo-Saxon period when **k** is sporadic only, in 'weorkes', l. 12g, and 'geiukodan', l. 22g. Inflectional endings show some departure from late West Saxon norms, for example 'witun', l. 10g, 'oxon', l. 20g; and the final consonant of 'mit', l. 23g, for *mid*, shows unvoicing liable to happen before following *þ* or *t*. The English is only lightly abbreviated, despite its status as a running gloss to the main text. Apart from ⁊ and ꝥ, note the overline in 'gebroþru(m)', l. 13, at the end of the line. The choice of **o** rather than **u** in 'monuc', l. 13, is found sometimes in late Old English where minims might cause confusion. Interestingly, more than half of the manuscript is taken up by texts glossed extensively in English and appropriate for a monastic community.

CONTEXTS

The main text in this compilation is the Benedictine Rule, also with a continuous interlinear gloss. Two names within the manuscript point to use of at least part by Ælfric Bata (f. 117r) and suggest ownership by an 'Eadwi' (f. 164r) perhaps to be identified with Eadui Basan. Both were monks of Christ Church, Canterbury, in the early eleventh century. Manuscript at Christ Church in the 1320s (Eastry's catalogue, no. 296: James 1903: 50, 508). According to Joscelyn, f. 178, a folio that has strayed from Tiberius A. vi, belonged at one time to John Twyne. In Cotton collection by 1621. Used by Selden and Junius. Entered the British Museum with the Cotton Collection in 1753.

SIZE

c. 240 × 177 mm (184-217 × 130-160 mm).

BIBLIOGRAPHY

Pr. Garmonsway 1947: 18-20 (ll. 1-27).
Disc. Ker, *Cat.* 1957: no. 186; Temple 1976: no. 100; Backhouse, Turner and Webster 1984: 47 (no. 28); Watson 1986 [2004[1]]: 137; Gneuss 1997; Gwara 1997; Gneuss 2001: no. 363; Tite 2003: 103-04.

London, British Library, Cotton MS Tiberius A. iii, f. 2v

King Edgar seated between St Æthelwold and St Dunstan
reduced to 80%

21

London, British Library, Cotton MS Tiberius B. iv, f. 68r
Anglo-Saxon Chronicle (Worcester or 'D' version), from the annals for 1016-17
Late Anglo-Saxon minuscule, s. xi^{2}

TRANSCRIPTION

feaht him wið ealle engla þeode . Þa wearð þær ofslægen eadnoð[1]
biscop . ⁊ wulfsie abb(od) . ⁊ ælfric ealdorman . ⁊ godwine ealdorman .
⁊ ulfkytel of eastenglan . ⁊ æþelward ælfwines sunu ealdormannes .
⁊ eall seo duguð of angelcynnes þeode . Ða æft(er) þisum gefeohte
wende cnut cyning úp mid his here to gleawcestrescire þær he
ofaxade þ(æt) se cyning wæs eadmund . Ða gerædde eadric ealdor⟨-⟩
man ⁊ þa witan þe þær gegaderade wæron . þ(æt) þa cyningas heom
betweonan seht geworhtan . ⁊ coman begen þa cyningas togædre
æt ólan íge . wið deorhyrste . ⁊ wurdon feolagan ⁊ wedbroðra
⁊ þ(æt) gefæstnadan ægðer mid wedde . ⁊ eac mid aðan . ⁊ þ(æt) gyld
gesettan wið þone here . ⁊ hi seoððan tohwurfon . ⁊ feng þa
EADMVND cyng to westsexan . ⁊ cnut to þam norðdæle[2] .
Se here gewende þa to scipon mid þam þe hi gefangen hæfdon .
⁊ lundenwaru gryðede wið þone here ⁊ heom fryð bohtan . ⁊
hi gebrohtan heora scypa on lundene . ⁊ hæfdon þær winter⟨-⟩
setl . Ða to s(an)c(t)e andreas mæssan forðferde EADMVND cyng
⁊ is bebyrged mid his ealdan fæder eadgare on glæstinga byri .
MILLE .XVII. Her on þisan geare feng cnut cyng to eall
engla landes rice . ⁊ todælde hit on feower . him seolfan
westsexan . ⁊ þurkylle eastenglan . ⁊ eadrice myrcean . ⁊ éiric .
norðhymbran . On þisum geare wæs eac eadric eaˋlˊdorman
ofslægen . ⁊ norðman leofwines sunu ealdormannes . ⁊ æþel⟨-⟩
ward ægelmeres ˋsunuˊ greatan . ⁊ bryhtric ælfeges sunu on defena
scire . ⁊ cnut cining aflymde ut eadwi æþeling . ⁊ eadwi ceorla

Notes by Joscelyn in a Tudor secretary hand, except that in his additions taken from the Abingdon Chronicle (Tiberius B. i) he attempts to reproduce Anglo-Saxon letter-forms:

8 ?reco(n)ciled show
9 fellowes; frovre bretherne
10 established; othes
12 al. myrcea(n)
13 taken
18 ⁊ on ðam ilcan geare forðferd wulfgar abbud on abbandune ⁊ æðelsige feng to ðam | abbodrice . in lib. m^{r} boyer et hist. petrob.
23 great
24 chorles

For this late copy of the Chronicle it seems best to resort for a second time (compare pl. 18) to the description late Anglo-Saxon minuscule, for this hand also holds well to the distinctive letter-forms. Ker points out that this page is the beginning of supply leaves ff. 68-73 (annals for 1016-1051) written in the 1070s or 1080s, although Dumville argues that the whole was written after 1066 and probably after *c.* 1080. The round hand is comparable to the hands in Worcester charters of the middle of the eleventh century: **a** is rounded and **e** alone is horned (not **c**); **d** hardly rises above the headline, but **ð** is tall and sinuous, and often has a hairline approach stroke at the top of the ascender; low and tall **s** both used, the latter usually in **st** (not ligatured); straight **y**, dotted, is invariable; **þ** is used initially and sometimes medially, **ð** medially and finally, with both enlarged **Þ** (as 'Þa', l. 1) and **Ð** (as 'Ða', ll. 4, 6, 16) as capitals; **g** is closed or nearly so, with the head sometimes starting only at the stem. Descenders mostly taper elegantly to the left; wedges on ascenders solid and roughly symmetrical. Note the use of **k**, relatively unusual in Old English, in the Scandinavian names 'ulfkytel', l. 3, and 'þurkylle', l. 20. Word division is well developed, but with some particles closed up to a following word (e.g. 'Þa wearð', l. 1). Proper names are not given capitals, but note how Rustic capitals draw attention to king 'EADMVND', ll. 12, 16). Occasional accent signs help identification of some stressed syllables (e.g. 'úp', l. 5, 'ólan íge', l. 9). Main pauses are

[1] The subpuncting under *n* looks accidental.

[2] Accidental dot under final *e*.

feaht him wið ealle engla þeode. þær wearð þær ofslægen eadnoð
biscop. 7 wulfsige abb. 7 ælfric ealdorman. 7 godwine ealdorman.
7 ulfkytel of east englan. 7 æþelward ælfwines sunu ealdormannes.
7 eall seo duguð of angelcynnes þeode. Ða æfter þisum gefeohte
wende cnut cyning up mid his here to gleawceasterscire þær he
of axode þ se cyning wæs eadmund. Ða gerædde eadric ealdor
man 7 þa witan þe þær gegaderade wæron. þ þa cyningas heom
betweonan sehte geworhtan. 7 coman begen þa cyningas togædere
æt olan ige. wið deorhyrste. 7 wurdon feolagan 7 wedbroðra
7 þ gefæstnadan ægðer mid wedde. 7 eac mid aðan. 7 þ gyld
gesettan wið þone here. 7 hi seoððan tohwurfon. 7 feng þa
EADMUND cyng to west sexan. 7 cnut to þam norð dæle.
Se here gewende þa to scipon mid þam þe hi gefangen hæfdon.
7 lunden wara griðede wið þone here 7 heom frið bohtan. 7
hi gebrohtan heora scypa on lundene. 7 hæfdon þær winter
setl. Ða to sce andreas mæssan forðferde EADMUND cyng
7 is bebyrged mid his ealdan fæder eadgare on glæstingabyri.
MILLE. XVII. Her on þisan geare feng cnut cyng to eall
engla landes rice. 7 todælde hit on feower. him sylfan
west sexan. 7 þurkylle east englan. 7 eadrice myrcean. 7 eiric
norð hymbran. On þisum geare wæs eac eadric ealdorman
ofslagen 7 norðman leofwines sunu ealdormannes. 7 æþel
ward ægelmeres greatan. 7 brihtric ælfgeres sunu on defena
scire. 7 cnut cining aflymde ut eadwi æþeling. 7 eadwi ceorla

Plate 21 – reduced to 81%

followed by a capital or an Uncial letter. The word 'MILLE', l. 18, which begins the date of the lower annal, is in Uncials, with a one-line initial, in the ink of the text, between the inner bounding lines. The replacement leaves are without colour, unlike the manuscript core. This leaf is ruled with a hard point, apparently on the verso. Pricking for outer bounding lines may be visible at top of leaf. No prickings for horizontal lines are visible, though marks in the gutter look like them at first. There are double bounding lines on both sides of the text, apparently prolonged to the edges; first and last horizontals prolonged to edges. Standard abbreviations are used: ⁊ for '(and)'; ꝥ for 'þ(æt)'; **abb** with slash though ascenders for 'abb(od)', l. 2; **t** with overline in 'æft(er)', l. 4; **sce** with overline for 's(an)c(t)e', l. 16. In l. 23 the description of Æthelweard is bungled, as is clear from the need to insert 'sunu' above: the **g** of his father's name is a late Old English alternative spelling in *Æþel-* names; and 'þæs' might be expected before 'greatan'.

CONTEXTS

In Worcester Cathedral library *c.* 1565 according to Joscelyn. Contents may point to compilation in York (Whitelock 1954: 28-29). Extracts copied by Lambarde and Nowell. Annotated heavily by Joscelyn, who owned it before it entered Cotton's collection. On loan to Tate by 1612 ('Old Saxon story manuscrip. It was Mr Gocelins': Harley 6018, f. 156). Among books borrowed 'upon my bond of 100£' by Wanley in 1709. Entered the British Museum with the Cotton Collection in 1753.

SIZE

c. 281 × 185 mm (238 × 129-140 mm).

BIBLIOGRAPHY

Pr. Classen and Harmer 1926; Cubbin 1996: 62-63.
Disc. Atkins and Ker 1944: 10, 12; Ker, *Cat.*1957: no. 192; Watson 1979: no. 555, pl. 47a-f; Dumville 1983: esp. 33-38; Laing 1993: 81; Lutz 1982, 2000; Gneuss 2001: no. 372; Tite 2003: 106-07.

London, British Library, Cotton MS Vespasian D. xii, f. 111r

Hymns accompanied by glossed explication, s. xi med.
actual size

22

Cambridge, University Library, MS Kk. 3. 18, f. 8v *Colour pl. C3*
Old English version of Bede's *Historia Ecclesiastica*, opening of Book I
English Caroline minuscule, s. xi^{2}

TRANSCRIPTION

GLORIOSISSIMO REGI CEOLWULFO BEDA FAMULUS CR(IST)I ET PR(ES)B(ITER) . HISTORIAM .
GENTIS ANGLORUM ECCLESIASTICAM QUAM NUPER EDIDERAM . LIBEN⟨-⟩
TISSIME TIBI DESIDERANTI REX ET PRIUS AD LEGENDUM . AC PRO⟨-⟩
BANDUM TRANSMISI :·
BREOTON . IS GARSECGES . EALOND . ÐÆT . WÆS
IU GEARA ALBION HATEN IS GESETED BETWYH NORÐDÆLE . AND .
westdæle germanie ⁊ gallie ⁊ hispanie þam mæstum dælu(m) europE
myccle fæce ongegen . þ(æt) is norð ehta hund mila lang . ⁊ tu hund mila brad .
hit hafað fram suðdæle þa mægðe ongean þe mon hateð gallia bellica .
hit is welig þis ealond on wæstmum ⁊ on treowu(m) misenlicra cynna . ⁊ hit is
gescræwe on læswe sceapa ⁊ neata . ⁊ on sumum stowu(m) wingeardas growað .
swylce eac þeos eorðe is berende missenlicra fugela . ⁊ sæwihta . ⁊ fiscwyllu(m)
wæterum . ⁊ wyllgespryngum . ⁊ her beoð oft fangene seolas . ⁊ hronas . and
mereswyn . ⁊ her beoð oft numene . missenlicra cynna weolcscylle . ⁊ muscule .
⁊ on þam beoð oft gemette þa betstan meregrotan ælces hiwes . ⁊ her beoð
swyðe genihtsume weolocas of þam bið gew[-e]orht[1] se weolocreada tælhg . þone
ne mæg sunne blæcan ne ne[2] wyrdan . Ac[3] swa he bið yldra swa he fægerra bið
hit hafað eac þis land sealtseaðas . ⁊ hit hafað hat wæter[4] . ⁊ hat baðo ælcere
yldo . ⁊ hade . þurh todælede stowe gescræpe. Swylce hit is eac berende on
wecga orum ares . ⁊ isernes . leades . ⁊ seolfres . her bið eac gemeted gagates
se stán bið blæc gym . gif mon hine on fyr deð þonne fleoð þær neddran on
weg. Wæs þis ealond eac geo gewurðad mid þa(m) æðelestu(m) ceastru(m) . anes wana
þrittigum . ða þe wæron mid weallu(m) .⁊ torru(m) . ⁊ geatu(m) . ⁊ þam trumestu(m) locum
getimbrade . butan oðru(m) læs\s/an unrim ceastra . ⁊ for ðan þe ðis ealond .
under þam sylfum norðdæle middangeardes nyhst ligeð . ⁊ leohte nihte
on sumera hafað ; Swa þ(æt) oft on middre nihte geflit cymeð þam beheal⟨-⟩
dendum . hwaðer hit si þe æfenglommung ðe on morgen d\e/agung . is on ðon
sweotol ðæt þis ealond hafað mycele lengran dagas on sumera . ⁊ swa eac
nihta on wintra þonne þa suðdælas middangeardes . :· ·I·
Ðis ealond nu on (ond)weardnysse æft(er) ríme fif moyses boca . þam seo godcunde

Glosses were added by Tremulous Hand, but are sporadic after f. 24:

gescræpe, l. 19/ apta
torrum, l. 23/ t(ur)ib(us)
nihte geflit, l. 26/ i(n) questione(m)
æfenglommung, l. 27/ crepusculu(m)
(ond)weardnysse, l. 30/ i(n) p(re)senti

Gloss for ll. 5-15:

Brittannia est occeani insula que fuit
quondam albion uocata est locata inter septentrionem &
occidentem . germanie gallie ⁊ hispanie maximis partibus europe
multo interuallo aduersa que (est) in boream octingentorum milibus passuu(m) longa . ⁊ ducentis milibus lata .
illa habet á meridie illam p(ro)uinciam é (con)tra ∶ quam homines uocant galliam belligicam .
ea est opima hec p(ro)uincia in frugibus atq(ue) arboribus diuersis generibus . ⁊ illa est
apta in pascius ouibus ⁊ íumentis . & in quibusdam locis uínéé cresciuit .
sed ⁊ hec terra (est) ferax diuersarum auium . ⁊ marínaru(m) beluar(um) . ⁊ piscoscis fontib(us)
⁊ fluuiís
capiuntur sepe diuersa genera conchiliorum in q(u)ib(us) s(un)t muscule .
in quibus sunt sepe inuente

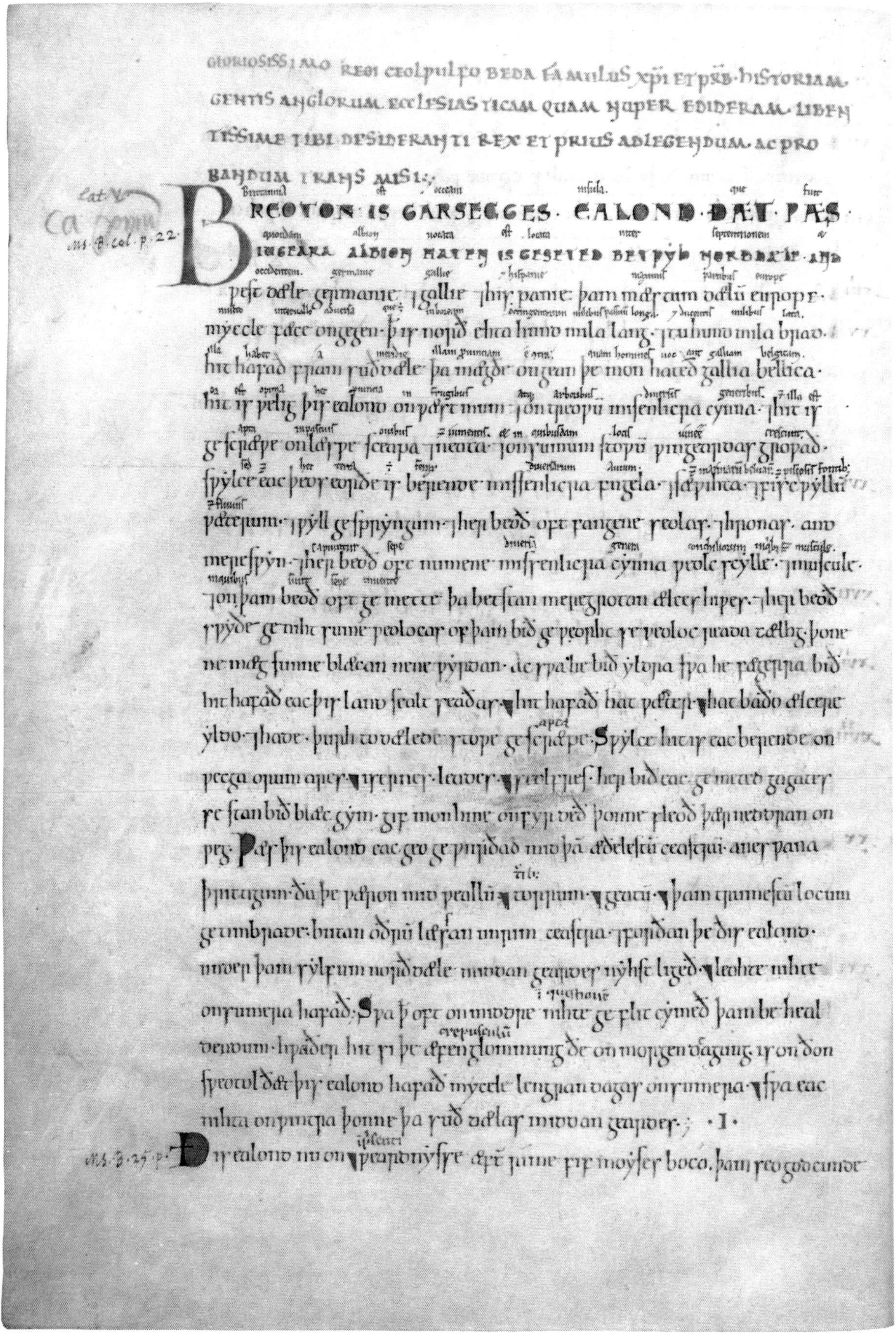

GLORIOSISSIMO REGI CEOLWULFO BEDA FAMULUS XPI ET PRB. HISTORIAM GENTIS ANGLORUM ECCLESIASTICAM QUAM NUPER EDIDERAM LIBENTISSIME TIBI DESIDERANTI REX ET PRIUS AD LEGENDUM AC PROBANDUM TRANSMISI.

BREOTON IS GARSECGES EALOND· ÐÆT WÆS IUGEARA ALBION HATEN· IS GESETED BETWYH NORÐDÆLE AND west dæle germanie 7 gallie 7 hispanie þam mæstum dælum europe· mycele face ongegen· hit is norð ehta hund mila lang· 7 tu hund mila brad· hit hafað from suð dæle þa mægðe ongean þe mon hateð gallia bellica· hit is welig þis ealond on wæstmum 7 on treowum missenlicra cynna· 7 hit is gescræpe on læswe sceapa 7 neata· 7 on sumum stowum wingeardas growað· swylce eac þeos eorðe is berende missenlicra fugela· 7 sæwihta· 7 fiscwyllum wæterum· 7 wyllgespryngum· 7 her beoð oft fangene seolas· 7 hronas· and mereswyn· 7 her beoð oft numene missenlicra cynna weolcscylle· 7 muscule· 7 on þam beoð oft gemette þa betstan meregrotan ælces hiwes· 7 her beoð swyðe genihtsume weolocas of þam bið geworht se weolocreada tælgh· þone ne mæg sunne blæcan ne ne wyrdan· ac swa he bið yldra swa he fægerra bið· hit hafað eac þis land sealt seaðas· 7 hit hafað hat wæter· 7 hat baðo ælcere yldo· 7 hade· þurh todælede stowe gescræpe· Swylce hit is eac berende on wecga orum ares· 7 isernes· leades· 7 seolfres· her bið eac gemeted gagates se stan bið blæc gym· gif mon hine on fyr deð þonne fleoð þær neddran on weg· Wæs þis ealond eac geo gewurðad mid þam æðelestum ceastrum· anes wana þritigum ða þe wæron mid weallum 7 torrum 7 geatum 7 þam trumestum locum getimbrade· butan oðrum læssan unrim ceastra· 7 forðan þe ðis ealond under þam sylfum norðdæle middangeardes nyhst ligeð· 7 leohte nihte on sumera hafað· Swa þæt oft on middre nihte geflit cymeð þam behealdendum hwæðer hit si þe æfenglommung þe on morgen dagung· is on don swiðost ðæt þis ealond hafað mycele lengran dagas on sumera· 7 swa eac nihta on wintra þonne þa suð dælas middangeardes· · I ·

Ðis ealond nu on 7weardnysse æft rime fif moyses boca· þam seo godcunde

Plate 22 – reduced to 72%

Ker describes this Worcester hand as 'regular, stiff, and rather ugly'. It manages most of the distinctive Anglo-Saxon letter-forms well, but the **a** looks Caroline at its head (note especially the form 'anes', l. 22 after a point) and the second stroke of **h** sometimes tends to turn in to the left (e.g. 'hund', l. 8, 'hine', l. 21). Although shapes are mostly rounded, the overall aspect is almost artificially square: note the broken-backed **d.** The **e** is sometimes released in what may be a point; for examples see 'hispanie' and 'europE' in l. 7. There is careful distribution of **þ** and **ð**, with good differentiation of **ð** and **d.** The high **e** of **æ** is mannered. Careful attention is given to layout (see colour pl. C3). The eye is drawn to the capital **B**, three-lines deep, and the gradation from larger to smaller capitals for the first two lines of text, all filled with red (the last letter of l. 7 is also a small capital, but without colour). Above stand four lines in red, taken from the beginning of Bede's preface and serving as a reminder both of Bede and of King Ceolwulf of Northumbria, to whom Bede dedicated his work. Heavy punctuation marks chapter endings, but otherwise, except for the *punctus versus* of l. 26, punctuation is by simple point. Capitals and the Tironian sign following a point may be touched in colour. The hardpoint ruling is supplemented by lead ruling for the gloss to ll. 5-15. Abbreviation is sparingly used: Tironian sign; ꝥ; overline for *m*; rising stroke in 'æft(er)', l. 30. Note that red is applied to '(ond)weardnysse', l. 30, where the abbreviation mark was probably mistaken for the conjunction. Corrections to 'læs\s/an', l. 24, and 'd\e/agung', l. 27, are perhaps by a different hand (the **s** looks Caroline). Note subpuncting in 'gew[e]orht', l. 16, and ƿ written for **p** in 'gescræwe', l. 11.

The Latin continuous gloss to ll. 5-15 is a neat, pointed, early-thirteenth-century hand: note round **d; s** and **f** on line. Using ⁊ (with and without bar) and **&.** Rising strokes over vowels indicate stress; in the transcript they are recorded over **i,** although they might here be interpreted as mere ticking of this vowel. Note in 'beluar(um)', l. 12, a more radical expansion than might be expected in main text; '(est)', l. 12, is expanded from ÷ , a mark of abbreviation that descended from the ancient world. Lines were specially ruled in hardpoint to receive this running text taken from Bede, but the venture may have been discontinued because the main-text ruling skimps on space between ll. 15-16.

CONTEXTS

From Worcester, this is Scribe 2 of Hemming's Cartulary; see his hand also in the character reproduced opposite on p. 103. Coleman, a writer of signed marginalia in eleventh-century Worcester, added chapter titles on ff. 84v, 85, and a signed note on f. 87v. The neat glossing of ll. 5-15 must have been written before the Tremulous Hand glosses, some of which have been erased. In Talbot's hands before given by Archbishop Parker to Cambridge University in 1574. Note the Parkerian red crayon 'Ca(pitulum) p(ri)mu(m)' in the left margin; a smaller hand has added in black ink 'Lat. 1. | MS. B. col. p. 22'), cross-referring to another Cambridge manuscript of the Old English Bede (Corpus Christi College 41). This 'Ca' version of the Old English Bede was the copy text for the edition by Whelock 1643, the first printed text; Whelock may have added some of the interlinear glosses now erased.

SIZE

c. 320 × 225 mm (*c.* 262 × 154 mm).

BIBLIOGRAPHY

Pr. Miller 1890-91, 1898: I. 24-26 (24, l. 29-26, l. 28).
Disc. Ker 1948 [1985], 1949[2] [1985]; Ker, *Cat.* 1957: no. 23; Laing 1993: 46; Graham 1997[1]; Gameson 1999: no. 41; Gneuss 2001: no. 22.

[1] The *e* appears to be subpuncted.

[2] 'regn' left out by scribe.

[3] The curving upper stroke in 'Ac', l. 16, may have been added as part of the rubrication.

[4] The curved stroke over *æ* is otiose.

✠ Her swutelað on ymb þa foreweard þe wæs on geworhte betwux
þam hirede on wihgeraceastre 7 fuldre. þæt is þæt he hæbbe þæt land
æt ludintune III gear for þam ðreom pundum þe he lænde 7 þone
bryce þe on þam lande beo III gear 7 binnon þrym gearum agife
þæt land þam hirede mid swa myclum swa se hired him on hand sette.
þæt synd XII weorc men 7 II gesylhðe oxan 7 I hund sceapa 7
half hundred fodra cornes. And se ðe þas foreward to breke
ne gewurðe hit him næfre forgifen ac beo he forðdemed into
helle wite 7 þær mid deofle wunige oð to domes dæge :;

BRITISH MUSEUM

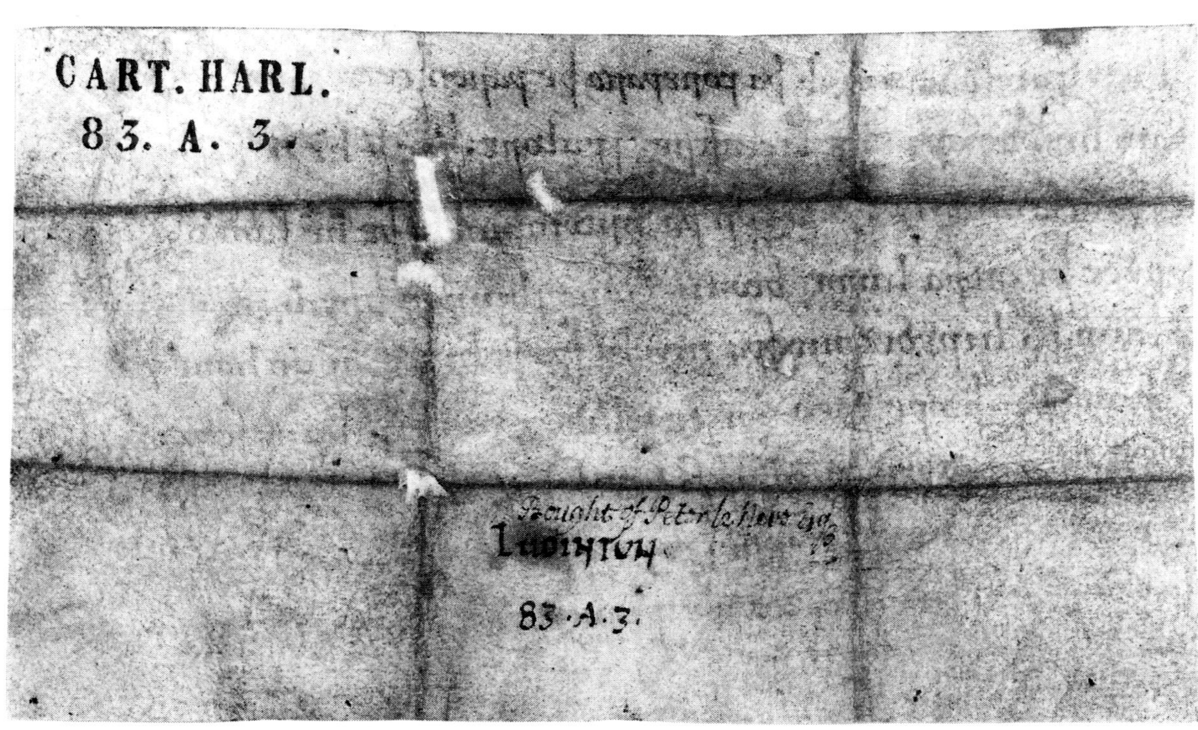

London, British Library, Harley Charter 83 A 3 (Sawyer 1968: no. 1421)

Three-year lease by the community at Worcester to Folder of land at Liddington, Warwickshire
actual size

V Protogothic

From late in the twelfth century Caroline minuscule moves towards the virtual exclusion of curves, foreshadowing the emergence of the more compressed and upright Gothic book script (or *littera textualis*). The writing of script in England in the tenth and eleventh centuries is important for the development of Gothic scripts, and English influence is seen particularly in the treatment of the feet of minims. Although manuscripts that are neither prototypically one nor the other can be called late Caroline or early Gothic, there are good grounds for recognizing a transitional script, its origins traceable to Norman England and Norman and Angevin France in the latter part of the eleventh century and the first half of the twelfth.[1] The term most widely used of this transitional script is Protogothic;[2] alternative terms, whose elements can be mixed and matched, are Primitive Gothic, *praegothica* and *littera minuscula protogothica*, the last of these a salutary reminder that all Gothic scripts are minuscules. The elaborate forms of capital letters typical of the Gothic period, not all of them merely enlarged forms of minuscule shapes, are beginning to develop.[3] So far as English scripts are concerned, from the first half of the twelfth century English Caroline minuscule was transmuting into its Protogothic phase, a change common to the writing both of Latin and of the vernaculars English and Anglo-Norman French. The dates for the use of Protogothic in England are from the first half of the twelfth century (particularly in documents) to the early thirteenth century.

Protogothic minuscule is to be distinguished from those scripts that immediately precede it by its pronounced angularity. Typically its letters are pointed ovals in form. In addition, virtually every stroke possible has a foot. The beginnings of 'biting' can be glimpsed, that is fusions between two adjacent curved letters. This generally appears between **d** and a following **e** first of all: in the first hand of the Peterborough Chronicle (pl. 23) **d** and **e** sometimes touch one another (e.g. 'scolde', l. 4); with the greater compression of the second hand, biting is emergent (e.g. 'sende', l. 12). Letter-forms worthy of note include: the Caroline **a**, still open at the top (the Gothic form is closed at the top); the **ę** (**e** *caudata* or 'tagged **e**'), which disappears from *c.* 1160, where earlier texts have **æ** and Gothic *textualis* generally has plain **e**; the round **r** after **o** (though something like this appears very early in English, for example in pl. 8, ll. 4, 7); and the use of the high **s** in all positions, by contrast with the round **s** of Gothic (at the end of lines first of all, then word final very soon afterwards before becoming general; but some English hands were early to adopt **s** from Half-uncial (see pl. 12). The letter **i**, when doubled, acquires a tick, the forerunner of the dot.[4] By the twelfth century round **d** need no longer be viewed as a distinctively Anglo-Saxon letter-form. Rather, it had continued to be used when writing English and remained because it was identical in form with the round-backed **d** which, in the twelfth century, became increasingly the choice when writing Latin.[5] Because at this time the Tironian sign was becoming used increasingly for 'et' in writing Latin, it also ceases to have a diagnostic value in script differentiation.[6] Thus, Protogothic book hands generally have round-backed **d** and the Tironian sign, whereas documents tend to retain straight **d**, the most formal of them also keeping **&**, the *et* ligature inherited from Caroline minuscule. Earlier, England did not have a separate documentary script, neither in Anglo-Saxon minuscule nor at first in the more recently introduced Caroline minuscule.[7] Now, particularly from the second half of the twelfth century and with a deeply split pointed pen in use, links developed everywhere between minims in documentary hands, occasional loops provided the conditions for the emergence of a single-stroke looped **d**, and ascenders and descenders were decoratively lengthened.[8] This development of a more current form of writing provides the context from which the *cursiva* script Anglicana can take off.

The two main scribes of the Peterborough Chronicle (pl. 23) provide samples dated a generation apart in the twelfth century. The first scribe, who was at work between the years 1122 and 1131, has a neat round hand, with short descenders that turn to the left. Although his **h** is Caroline, he is proficient in the use of the distinctive letter-forms used for writing English and even has examples of the spurred **e**. Yet he is unable to hold convincingly to the grammatical and orthographic norms of late West Saxon. Why should we expect this of him at so late a date in Peterborough? Overall he seems to have done his best, in his 'First Continuation', to observe the conventions of the exemplar he had transcribed, a copy of the Anglo-Saxon Chronicle resembling the Parker version. The hand of the second scribe, who wrote up the annals for

[1] Bischoff 1953: 11.

[2] Derolez 2003 prefers Praegothica.

[3] Johnson and Jenkinson 1915: vol. I provide valuable tables of dated examples of the kinds of letters found in PRO documents from the twelfth century to the fifteenth century.

[4] The dot, an Italian invention, was imported into England *c.* 1500. It can be seen in the late addition to pl. 58.

[5] Ker, *Cat.* 1957: xxix.

[6] Ker, *Cat.* 1957: xxxii.

[7] For late eleventh-century documents using a documentary form of Caroline minuscule see Bishop and Chaplais 1957: pls Va and b.

[8] Brown, M.P. 1990: pl. 27.

1132-54 (the 'Second Continuation') in *c.* 1155, is more compressed. Particularly revealing are the first ten lines of his stint, where there are few descenders, giving the impression of the tidy baseline typical of Caroline-derived hands. With the annal for 1135 he seems to have made an effort to provide a better match visually for the work of the first scribe. His inconsistent use of long **f**, **s**, and **r** forms, which do much to disturb the tidiness of his baseline, owes more to contemporary documentary script than to familiarity with the writing of Anglo-Saxon minuscule. His hold on the letter-forms specific to writing English is weak: **th** is used alongside **þ** and the less frequent **ð**; and **uu** and **u** as well as **w**. When he forgets to use **æ**, his default letter is more often **a** rather than **e**.[9] Whereas the First Continuation is often regarded as Old English, the Second Continuation, by far more removed from Old English in spelling, morphology, syntax and vocabulary, is generally accepted as early Middle English. From much the same time but the other side of the country, the script of the occasional charm entered neatly below the ending of an older Latin text (pl. 26) is also Protogothic. Here the letter-forms mostly derive from the Caroline inventory, and **æ** is not used. Like the second scribe of the Peterborough Chronicle, this scribe too can alternate between **w** and **ƿ**.

The uneasy script of pl. 28, the Royal 1 A. xiv copy of the Old English Gospels, seems constrained by its exemplar to attempt to reproduce the letter-forms of Anglo-Saxon minuscule for the text in English. The scribe manages the Insular-derived forms of **f**, **g**, **h**, and **r** fairly consistently and long **s** usually, with low **s** only occasionally and frequent Caroline high **s**. He uses the Tironian sign, the round-backed **d** (with a link on the right ready to be used as the beginning of a loop, for which see 'drihtnes', l. 3) more often than the straight form, and some letters are touching, so Protogothic seems an appropriate description. The letter-forms of two verses cited in Latin from the Bible indicate that this is basically a Caroline-derived script. The careful ruling and layout are at odds with the air of uncertainty: the scribe is prone to misunderstanding (he does not always recognise **w**), to omission (for example of the particle *þe*), and to introducing Kentish spellings.[10] There is a greater air of confidence about pl. 29, the Hatton 38 copy of the same translation, not least in the attention given lay-out. Symptomatic of the difference between these two manuscripts is the larger amount of abbreviation in the Royal text. In Hatton the Latin verses cited begin on a new line, with an opening red capital for each of the two verses, and they are displayed in a more formal and differentiated script, establishing a firmer sense of hierarchy between the two languages. If this version was copied directly from the Royal text, its scribe must have gone behind the exemplar to find some older spellings that appear in his own version, for example reinstating such obsolescent features as the **ea** of 'bearn, l. 23, and the **æ** of 'wære', l. 12.[11] Despite its lack of lateral compression, this stately and deliberate script is more clearly in the Protogothic phase ('is', l. 9, has ticked single **i**). The scribe is careful to use the distinctive Anglo-Saxon letter-forms for **f** and **r**, but less particular with **h**. Two striking orthographic features mirror spellings beginning to come into use in English at this time: a somewhat inconsistent attempt to give different phonetic values to the Caroline and Anglo-Saxon **g** forms (the latter may be thought of as signalling the emergence of 'yogh'); and the rather more successfully carried through use of **ch** alongside **c**.[12] Although **ch** was to generalize quickly, **k** was not fully established in words like *king* and *keen* until the thirteenth century.[13] Ker points to three other twelfth-century manuscripts in his *Catalogue* as sharing in this move towards the use of **ȝ** for 'only guttural and palatal spirants and not the guttural and palatal stops for which it had previously done duty':[14] the Bodley 343 homily collection (no. 310) throughout; the corrections added to Cambridge, Trinity College B. 15. 34 (no. 86); and the hand 3 additions in Cotton Vespasian D. xiv (no. 209). The supplementary plate on p. 117 shows a changeover between hands 3 and 2 in Cotton Vespasian D. xiv: both these hands use two forms of **g**, by contrast with the manuscript's main hand (see pl. 25).

Orm, the East Midlands author of an ambitious set of Gospel readings and accompanying homilies (pl. 27), is by far more decisive in his attempts to reform English spelling. Central to his approach is the doubling of consonants to signal a preceding short vowel, though not when the vowel is in an open syllable. Refreshingly for Middle English, final syllables are solid: if his *Ormulum* has *-enn* (or *-en* with *n* added fussily above the line), the ending is to be pronounced. Indeed, all syllables are sounded, even final *-e* unless it is elided before an initial vowel or *h*. Once the eye becomes accustomed to the plethora of double consonants (even *cch*, as in 'macche', l. 48a, as well as *ch*, for example 'childe', l. 47a), the helpfulness of these adjustments becomes evident. What remains of Orm's work, perhaps over an eighth of what was planned if not implemented, has all the appearances of a working draft. An untidy volume, it has many irregularly shaped leaves, and added scraps of parchment contain additions and corrections. Little wonder that pages extant as recently as the seventeenth

9 Campbell in Wright and Campbell 1967: 89.

10 Liuzza 1994; Liuzza in Liuzza and Doane 1995.

11 Liuzza (Liuzza and Doane 1995: lxxii) suggests that 'the scribe's own ingenuity rather than another copy of the text . . . provided the motive for alteration and avoidance of dittography'.

12 Liuzza points out (Liuzza and Doane 1995: 162) that alterations in, for example, the presentation of /g/ and /k/ 'do not reflect changing phonology but only changing orthography'.

13 Scragg 1974: 45.

14 Ker, *Cat.* 1957: xxix.

century have since disappeared.[15] Like others of his age, Orm too draws on some of the letter-forms reserved for writing English in the old way, in his case **g**, **h**, and **r**. That he has consciously chosen to use these letter-forms is clear, because elsewhere, when writing Latin as he lists the pericopes for his great work, he uses the Caroline-descended forms that might be expected at this time.[16] But there is more to say about his use of Insular **g**. This is a distinctive form, made with three firmly executed strokes, a flat top, rounded upper part and added tail, by contrast with the two-strokes of the Hatton Gospels scribe's yogh (pl. 29); and innovatively with a fourth stroke Orm completes the circle of the rounded upper part. Thus, for example, he is able to show that his idiolect has two competing forms of the verb *give*: the native 'ȝifenn' ('to give'), l. 11a, and the Norse-descended 'gife', l. 61a ('give', addressed in prayer to God). So, like others writing late in the twelfth and early thirteenth centuries, he experiments with new ways of transposing English to the page, though with far greater rigour, and his *Ormulum* has delighted generations of phoneticians and language historians with its many clues about how the language was changing. Unfortunately therefore discussion of the *Ormulum* tends to be dismissive about its content and appearance, homing in on philological detail. The simple piety of the narratives and homilies that canter on in endlessly near-hypnotic metre are not to modern tastes, and the critics have little to say about Orm's carefulness in laying out his text. They are slow to recognize aspects of layout (spacing, *paragraphus*, simple pointing) that can make this a text from which it is surprisingly easy to read at speaking pace. A relatively tidy page was chosen to illustrate Junius 1, to show the manuscript in a better light than is usual. Even before he set about the extant version of his *Ormulum*, Orm must have put a great deal of thought into devising its conventions.[17] The overall appearance of the manuscript may be off-putting, but the labour put into building up sturdy letters and eliminating variant forms and spellings should not be discounted. Moreover, in its overall dimensions this book can be compared with the Paris Psalter (Paris, Bibliothèque nationale, lat. 8824), although Orm's frugal use of space makes the comparison laughable (see pl. 27, where he manages to squeeze in sixty-four lines of text in his overflowing a column, whereas the Paris Psalter has well spaced narrow double columns of forty-five lines).[18] Both are manuscripts for which the skin was folded parallel to the long side rather than, as is usual, the short side. Tall books, sometimes called holster books,[19] are more often from skins folded twice or three times than from skins folded once.[20]

Some manuscripts containing early Middle English are in a small round script similar to the scripts used in the late twelfth and early thirteenth centuries for the apparatus in glossed books of the Bible. An example is Bodley 34 (pl. 30), a hand probably best considered within the context of Protogothic scripts. Its scribe habitually uses the top ruled line (or writes 'above the top line'), a good indication of a date in the early thirteenth century, for from *c.* 1220 it becomes rare to find script above the top line ruled for writing.[21] (New devotional writing was being written in English on the opposite side of the country too, for example the *Virtues and Vices* dialogue from Essex illustrated on p. 137, also an above top-line text from early in the thirteenth century.) Biting is usually avoided, with **d** and **e** standing closer together but sharing a stroke only occasionally. Yet, although according to Ker the round **r** is restricted to after **o**, this is not true of the whole manuscript: its use also after **b**, **p**, and **ð** is seen in this page. The scribe retains the special letter-forms **þ**, **ð** (these two in good calligraphic distribution,[22] which must have been part of his training), and **ƿ**. He is uncertain in his application of a clumsily written **ȝ** (yogh) as a spelling alternative, which is not always distinguishable from his normal Caroline-derived **g**. The Tironian sign has a cross-bar, a development first seen near the end of the twelfth century.

A distinctively 'twitchy' style is found in some manuscripts from Rochester and Canterbury, for example, pl. 25 (Vespasian D. xiv). Here, as in pl. 29 (the Hatton Gospels), the letter-forms diagnostic for Anglo-Saxon minuscule still in use are down to **f** and **r**; the **a**, **e**, **g**, and **h** are Caroline letter-forms; there are no instances of insular-derived low **s**, but both Anglo-Saxon long **s**, dropping below the line, and Caroline long **s**, ending on the script line, are in use. The hand is easily read, and the minims are separately made. In some ways, it is comparable with the documentary script that was emerging at this time rather than with book scripts: forks are developing on ascenders and descenders and the top of **d** tends to flick to the right. Curiously, someone, perhaps not this scribe, chose to embellish every **g** with a downward-curving tail, as if determined to confer a dash of style. Whereas Caroline **g** prevails in pl. 25, written by the main scribe of Vespasian D. xiv, hands 2 and 3 (see p. 117) show **ȝ** taking on its new rôle as a letter form specific to the writing of English and used alongside the Caroline **g** of the normal scribal repertoire.

The scribe of pl. 24, the Chad homily, draws on none of the distinctive letter-forms often used by his contemporaries for writing English. The contents of this homily derive ultimately from Bede, but there is no agreement as to the date of its

[15] See Ker 1940, Burchfield 1962.
[16] See Parkes [1983] 1991: pl. 34 and discussion.
[17] Burchfield 1956: 69.
[18] See the facsimile volume, Colgrave 1958.
[19] Guddat-Figge 1976: 31-32 gives the fullest list of English holster books I have seen; she does not include Junius 1. See also Robinson (forthcoming).
[20] Gumbert 1993: 228.
[21] Ker 1960.
[22] A calligraphic choice is made on grounds of appearance, as when *þ* is preferred at the beginning of words or blocks of words and *ð* elsewhere.

composition.[23] Unlike the other texts that follow it in Bodley 116, the Chad homily is carefully pointed. Here, apart from the special characters **þ**, **ð** and **ƿ**, the letter-forms generally would not look out of place in a twelfth-century Latin manuscript, and for Thomson it is 'a typical Worcester hand of the first half of the century and with initials in the local style'.[24] Admittedly, by this time the use of **æ** looks old-fashioned, and it too is taking on the status of a letter-form special to the writing of English. Its presence in this homily as elsewhere in the manuscript is probably constrained by its exemplar. The Chad homily is not found in any other manuscript, and in language it is clearly different from the Ælfrician texts that for the most part follow. Whereas they share a basis in late West Saxon, the Chad homily has more in common in vocabulary and syntax with Anglian translations of the Alfredian period. It is therefore possible to argue that *e* for *æ* in the Chad homily reflects the fronting found in some Mercian texts rather than scribal uncertainty as to the functions of **æ**.[25]

The hand of pl. 24, very much in tune with mainstream practice for writing Latin, is presenting English texts without the distinctive letter-forms that were by then the detritus of Anglo-Saxon minuscule. Even so, the scribe with the tremulous hand (TH) adds his own glosses. This Worcester scribe, a 'magister' active in the early thirteenth century,[26] made considerable use of manuscripts containing Old English, as is evident from his numerous glosses, aids towards pronunciation, added punctuation, and apparatus.[27] Examples of his intervention may be seen in three plates (pls 6, 22, and 24). The most heavily glossed of these is pl. 24 (Hatton 116), which has, of the three, the script he must have found it easiest to read. Note how on this page he once supplies yogh above Caroline **g**, whereas more often he is to be seen writing **i** above Insular **g** (i.e. above **ᵹ**). He may have found the script of Hatton 20 (pl. 6) difficult, for apparently he transferred his attentions to the clearer hand of the Corpus Christi College 12 *Cura Pastoralis* instead.[28] Contemporaneous or just a little earlier is the neat pointed hand that glosses in Latin the opening lines of the first book of Bede's *Historia ecclesiastica* (pl. 22), where the TH glosses appear further down on this page. TH glossed two parts of this manuscript fairly heavily, but quite a few of the glosses have been erased. His distinctive backward-sloping hand is best described as Protogothic in these additions.

The term Protogothic is valuable for bringing into focus a distinctive script-type in the long changeover period from English Caroline minuscule to fully developed Gothic *textualis*, with the dates *c.* 1180 - *c.* 1240 defining the central decades of its use. For manuscripts in English the changes are dramatic in this period, which sees both a rapid deceleration in the copying of older English texts and in different dialects at differing speeds the slow pick-up of new writing in English. In Vespasian D. xiv (pl. 25), a manuscript that attests to the continuing popularity of Ælfric's writings as a source of teaching and meditation, materials from the turn of the tenth century are supplemented by pieces newly composed in the twelfth century. Around the end of the twelfth century two new copies of the West Saxon Gospels were made at Christ Church in Canterbury (pls 28, 29). The later of these, clearly abreast of changing spelling conventions, is in a hand that must have retained legibility alongside the closer Gothic scripts about to emerge. The Chad homily too (pl. 24) is dependent on some earlier source, and it stands at the head of blocks of Ælfric texts. It is particularly interesting that this manuscript should come from Worcester, for a disproportionate number of late transcriptions of Old English are from Worcester, where perhaps the old texts continued in use longer than in many parts of the country. Little wonder therefore that the most modern-looking manuscript of Ælfric homilies should come from this neighbourhood and probably from Worcester itself, where the TH scribe used it intensively towards the middle of the thirteenth century. Up in the East Midlands, in the 1120-30s, the main scribe added to the Peterborough Chronicle (pl. 23) entries that cannot have been in his exemplar, and a generation later its second scribe supplied annals about events up to the mid-1150s. Peterborough Abbey's chronicle was being consulted across the thirteenth and fourteenth centuries, for added marginalia supplied aids to finding valued information. With the addition of a short Anglo-Norman chronicle in the margins of ff. 86-90v, complementing the older chronicle with a fashionable epitome of Britain's history, the Peterborough Chronicle became a trilingual manuscript, a reminder of the importance of the French vernacular in England in the middle ages.

23 Roberts 2001: 441.
24 Thomson 2001: xxiv.
25 Campbell 1959, § 168.
26 Ker 1937 [1985].
27 Franzen 1991; Collier 1995, 1997.
28 Collier 2000.

23a

Oxford, Bodleian Library, Laud Misc. MS 636, f. 88v
Anglo-Saxon Chronicle (Peterborough or 'E' version), from the annals for 1131-35
Lines 1-9: Caroline minuscule, *c.* 1131
Lines 10-30: Protogothic *textualis*, *c.* 1155

TRANSCRIPTION

þ(et) hi heafdon forloron S(ancte) Ioh(anni)s mynstre þurh hi(m) ⁊ þurh his mycele sotscipe . þa ne cuþe he hi(m) na betre bote bute behet[1] hem
⁊ aðes swor on halidom þ(et) gif he moste engleland secen þet he
scolde begeton he(m) ðone mynstre of burch . swa þ(et) he scolde
setten þær p(r)ior of clunni . ⁊ circeweard ⁊ hordere ⁊ reilþein
⁊ ealle þa ðing þa wæron wiðinne mynstre ⁊ wiðuten eall he
scolde he(m) betæcen . Þus he ferde into france ⁊ þær wunode eall
þ(et) gear . crist ræde for þa wrecce muneces of burch ⁊ for þ(et)
wrecce `stede'. nu he(m) behofeð cristes helpe ⁊ eall[2] cristenes folces .
M.C ·xxxii· Ðis gear co(m) henri king to þis land. þa co(m) henri abbot
⁊ uureide þe muneces of burch to þe king for þi ð(at) he uuolde underþeden
ð(at) mynst(re) to clunie . sua ð(at) te king was wel neh beþaht . ⁊ sende eft(er) þe muneces . ⁊ þur`h'godes milce ⁊ þur`h' þe b(iscop) of Seresb(yr)i ⁊ te b(iscop) of linc(olne) ⁊ te oþre rice men þe þer wæron þa wiste þe king ð(at) he feorde mid suicdo(m) . Þa he
na(n) mor ne mihte . þa uuolde he ð(at) his nefe sculde ben abb(ot) in burch .
oc xpist[3] it ne uuolde . Was[4] it noht suithe lang þereft(er) þat[5] te king
sende eft(er) hi(m) . ⁊ dide hi(m) gyuen up ð(at) abb(ot)rice of burch . ⁊ faren ut of lande . ⁊ te king iaf ð(at) abb(ot)rice an p(r)ior of S(ancte) neod Martin was gehaten .
he co(m) on S(ancte) PET(res) messedei mid micel wurscipe into the minstre . M.C.[6]
xxxv· On þis gære for se king H(enri) ouer sæ æt te la(m)masse . ⁊ ð(at) oþer
dei þa he lai an slep in scip . þa þestrede þe dæi ouer al landes ⁊
uuard[7] þe sunne suilc als it uuare thre niht ald mone . an st(er)res
abuten hi(m) at middæi . Wur`þ'en[8] men suiðe ofuundred ⁊ ofdred
⁊ sæden ð(at) micel þing sculde cum(e) hereft(er) . sua dide . for þat ilc gær
warth þe king ded . ð(at) oþer dæi eft(er) S(ancte) Andreas massedæi . on norm(andi) .
Þa þestre[9] sona þas landes . for æuric man sone ræuede oþer þe mihte .
Þa namen his sune ⁊ his frend ⁊ brohten his lic to englel(and) ⁊ bebiriend[10]
in Reding(e) . God man he wes ⁊ micel æie wes of hi(m) . durste nan man mis-
don wið oðer on his time . Pais he makede men ⁊ dær . Wua sua bare
his byrthen[11] gold ⁊ sylure . durste na(n) man sei to hi(m) naht bute god .

Peterborough Abbey probably lost its copy of the Chronicle in the fire of 1116: the first of the two main scribes, in about 1121, copied out a version of the Chronicle, interpolating some new materials, and from time to time during the years 1122 to 1131 he added entries. A very similar hand is seen in another Peterborough manuscript of much this time: British Library Cotton Tiberius C. i, ff. 2-42 + Harley 3667. This first scribe's hand is a neat and round script dressed up as Anglo-Saxon minuscule, with short descenders that turn left at the bottom. Most of the distinctive Anglo-Saxon letter-forms are used, and sometimes even the horned **e** (see 'engleland', l. 3). The **h** is generally Caroline, its second stroke turning in to the left, but although the head of **a** can protrude a little, it does not bend over to the left. Sometimes the **d**

[1] Note ascender erased after 'be' and line under resulting gap.
[2] A letter following 'eall' (possibly *e*) was subpuncted and erased.
[3] For 'crist': the first two letters are the Greek letters familiar from traditional abbreviations.
[4] Although **w** stands normally for ƿ in this transcript, here the capital is the Caroline form.
[5] The first letter of 'þat' is on an erasure.
[6] The rest of the date follows at the beginning of the next line. A hand of the thirteenth-fourteenth century has added the note 'burg'| abb'. M`a'r'.' (with a slash through the ascenders of **bb**) as part of the sign-posting of entries specific to the history of St Martin's abbey, Peterborough.
[7] Compare 'warth', l. 25.
[8] Note enlarged ƿ here.
[9] Editors emend to 'þestre⟨den⟩'.
[10] Editors suggest the emendation 'bebirieden'.
[11] The mark below this word is a mistaken dash of red ink.

Plate 23 – reduced to 96%

and **e** touch one another, the beginnings of 'biting', that is fusion between two adjacent curved letters, for example 'scolde', l. 4. Overall, the scribe seems to have done his best to observe the conventions of the Chronicle exemplar he had transcribed, and he keeps **þ**, **ð** (the same size as his **d**), and **p** (the Caroline form **w** can appear for capitals). The use of **i** rather than **g** in both elements of 'reilþein', l. 5, shows the move towards new spellings that reflect more closely contemporary pronunciation. His 'First Continuation' of the Chronicle is as often termed late Old English as early Middle English, but by comparison with late West Saxon, the inflexions look careless, for example *-es* for *-as* ('aðes', l. 3, 'muneces', l. 8) or *-en* or *-on* for *-an* ('secen', l. 3, 'begeton', l. 4, 'setten', l. 5, 'betæcen', l. 7), features sporadic in late Old English but here more pervasive. The Tironian sign, its head curved, has a straight descender in this sample. It is often curved in passages in Latin, and the scribe can resort to the modes of abbreviation customary in Latin but little used in writing Old English, as with 'S(ancte)', l. 1 (possibly 'S(aint)', but he has 'sanct' in the annal for 949), where earlier vernacular manuscripts would have had 's(an)c(t)e'. He knows **ꝥ**, and his preferred spelling for it is 'þet' (see l. 3) rather than 'þæt'. Note that some slightly enlarged letter forms, e.g. 'þus', l. 7, are notionally interpreted as capitals.

The annals for 1132-54 (the 'Second Continuation') were all written at one time, so represent English from a later generation. This is the hand seen also in the London Society of Antiquaries MS 60, ff. 6-71, the *Liber Niger* of Peterborough Abbey; and there are similarities to corrections made in Corpus Christi College Cambridge 134. The letter-forms are Caroline, and the script generally is more compressed, with a greater tendency towards biting (for example, see 'sende', l. 12, 'oc', l. 16, 'p(r)ior', l. 18). As well as **þ** he sometimes uses **ð** ('suiðe', l. 23, 'wið', l. 29, 'oðer', l. 29) and **th** ('suithe', l. 16, 'the', l. 19, 'thre', l. 22, 'warth', l. 25, 'byrthen', l. 30); alongside **p** (e.g. 'was', l. 12, 'wel', l. 12, 'wæron', l. 14) he has **uu** or **u** (e.g. 'uureide', l. 11, 'uuolde', l. 11, 'sua', l. 12). Where **æ** might have been expected in earlier English, he tends to have **a** ('la(m)masse', l. 20, 'uuare', l. 22), though **æ** remains frequent and **e** is occasional ('eft(er)', l. 17, 'messedei', l. 19). After his first ten lines, the scribe appears to be trying, with the annal for 1135, to get nearer to the first scribe's hand. He keeps to a tidy Caroline baseline up to the last line of the 1122 annal, where long **s** trails below the line ('messedei', l. 19, 'wurscipe', l. 19), and with the new annal trailing **s** becomes more frequent, occurring also in ligature (e.g. 'st(er)res', l. 22; compare the **ft** of 'hereft(er)', l. 24), and both **f** (e.g. 'for', l. 20) and **r** ('ouer', l. 20) may descend below the line: perhaps he selected the documentary forms of **f**, **r**, and **s** to approximate to his idea of how to match better the earlier scribe's work. Note that this is the first scribe illustrated for whom **k** is a common letter-form, as for example in 'king', in which **k** is his preferred usage (elsewhere, when copying an exemplar, he has forms of this word in **c**). There is now considerable slippage from the older norms, most strikingly in the unusual use of **ð** as a suspension (otherwise he does not use **ð** at the beginning of words), here interpreted as 'ðat' (compare 'þat', l. 24). Coincidentally (and apparently uniquely), the alphabet found in British Library Stowe 57, f. 3v, a contemporary manuscript with a special interest in Peterborough, gives 'ðet' as the name of **Ð**. He lacks the relative restraint earlier scribes had exercised in the use of abbreviation when writing English. In addition to a rising stroke variously for **m** or **n** (as in 'co(m)', l. 10, na(n), l. 30 (where the numerous assimiliations of the text could point equally to 'na(m)'), for final *-e* ('cum(e)', l. 24), and with rather more curve for **r** and an appropriate vowel (as in 'mynst(re)', 'eft(er)', l. 12, 'Seresb(yr)i', l. 13), this page shows the use of the superscript vowel convention ('p(r)ior', l. 18), a final rising stroke for *-e* ('Reding(e)', l. 28) and syllabic abbreviation in 'abb(ot), l. 15, 'abb(ot)rice', ll. 17, 18 (expanded in accord with the normal Middle English form seen in 'abbot', l. 10). More radical suspensions are used fairly freely: see 'b(iscop)', 'linc(olne), l. 13, 'PET(res)', l. 19 and 'H(enri)', l. 20, 'norm(andi)', l. 25, 'englel(and)', l. 27. Disturbances in the manuscript can be hard to gauge (did the scribe anticipate 'u' at the end of the numeral in l. 10, changing it to 'ii'? is the first vowel of 'namen', l. 27, written over an erasure?).

CONTEXTS

A fourteenth-century ownership inscription is erased and partly missing from f. 1. Marginalia show that the manuscript continued to be read at Peterborough in the thirteenth and fourteenth centuries. Later it was owned by Sir William Cecil, and perhaps by Cotton. Used by Nowell, Parker, Joscelyn, Lisle, and James before eventually coming into the possession of Laud, and thence (gift of 1639) to the Bodleian Library, where formerly Laud E. 80. Borrowed by D'Ewes in 1647. Known as the Peterborough Chronicle.

SIZE

c. 240 × 167 mm (*c.* 168 × 105 mm).

BIBLIOGRAPHY

Pr. Plummer 1892: 262-63; Clark 1970: 53-54; Irvine 2004.
Facs. Whitelock with Clark 1954; O'Brien O'Keeffe 2003.
Disc. *SC* 1003; Bishop 1949-53: 440; Wright 1951, 1960[1]: pl. 1; Ker, *Cat.* 1957: no. 346; Watson 1984: no. 620, pl. 62; Lutz 1982, 2000; Laing 1993: 138-39; Gameson 1999: no. 757; Robinson 2003: no. 149, pl. 11.

23b

Chronicle, *Le Livere de Reis de Brittanie*
Gothic *littera textualis rotunda media*, s. xiii[2]

TRANSCRIPTION

lautre p(ar)tie a poures abbeies . La t(er)ce p(ar)tie a poure clers . La q(u)arte p(ar)tie as engleis[1] ultre mer . iceo
Apres Aluerd receut eduuard sun fiz le regne . P(ru)dome fu e sage ¶[2] fit il tote sa uie .
al regne gou(er)ner . cil auoit tut englet(er)e a sa uolunte . fort fu e uailant . vnke ne fu a bataile
ke il ne venq(u)i . Pur ceo ne se oserent li daneis mes venir en englet(er)e p(ur) mal fere en sun tens . Et[3] ·iii·
femmes out ·v· fiz . e
·ix· filles . dunt le treis
furent en religiun . Elf⸗
led . Edude . e seint Edburg .
Cil fit cinc euekes . e
mit[4] les euesches . Cil rei
auoit vne sue sor elfled
out nun ⁖ la plu sage
ke lem t(r)ouat au secle . e
mut aida a sun frere al
regne guu(er)ner p(ar) sun g(r)ant
sen . si fu apele elfled ⁖
dorlen leuedi . Sun frere[5]
aluered au conte edel⸗[6]
red p(ru)dome e sage dunt
la dame out vn enfant
p(ar) vn couenant k(e) vnk(e)
p(ur) nul home del mund
ne uout a sun seyn(ur) gi⸗
sir . Mes diseit k(e) file de
rei ne deueit pas hant(er)
ne am(er) tel delit k(e) si g(r)ant
anguoisse seut apres .
Cil eduuard regna ·xxiiii·
anz . si morust e gist a⸗
Wincestr(e) .
Apres eduuard receut
Edelstan sun fiz le
regne . mut fu beuas e sa⟨-⟩
ge . il out englet(er)e meuz[7]
ke vnke reis engleis . il
auoit le rei de escoce . e
le rei de Northumb(er)land
a sun comandement . les
reis de Wales venq(u)i tuz
si mist rent sur eus si k(e) il out checun an de Northuuales ·xx· li(ures) de or . e ·ccc· de argent . e ·xx· va⸗
ches . Il auoit vne soer edith out nun . vnk(e) nul home ne vit plu bele fe(m)me . Si loy dire li rei
de f(r)ance hug(e) si enuea se Messages au rei edelstan a abendone . li Messag(er) dist sun Message .
demanda[8] sa soer a loes le rei de f(r)ance . Puys mist auant le presanz . cheuaus[9] couere[10] tut enseles e
enfren[⸗s‵ez′][11] . pieres precioses de tute maneres . le espeie constantin lemperur e sun nun en le espeie od
lettres de or . e vn de clous dunt nostre sein(ur) fu figez en la croiz . la lance charlemain k(e) il soleit
porter encuntre sarasinz . k(e) fu cele dunt nostre sein(ur) fu feru . kar vnk(e) ne leua en bataile ⁖ k(e)

This Anglo-Norman chronicle, commonly described as a short *Brut*, is written in the hand of the First Statute of Westminster of Edward I (1275) of the *Liber Niger* of Peterborough (London, Society of Antiquaries MS 60, ff. 209-19). Only the folios containing this text have escaped savage cropping. The *Livere* has the appearance of a well-planned ancillary text: careful provision is made for the placing of initials (ll. 2, 31) and the seven long lines below the main text contrast pleasingly with the four lines in the upper margin. Biting is frequent with **de**, but occasional otherwise (for example see 'abbeies', l. 1 'daneis', l. 4, 'venit', l. 4, 'aida', l. 14, 'apele', l. 16, 'soer', l. 41). The 2-shaped **r** is not restricted to following **o**. There is little consistency in the distribution of initial **v** and **u**. Round **s** appears only at the end of words, as in 'euekes', l. 9; the superscript sinuous form is also found at the end of words, as in 'treis', l. 6. The main punctuation mark is the point, with the *punctus elevatus* used occasionally to mark apposition (ll. 12, 16, 46). At the end of l. 29 the hyphen shows the phrase broken is regarded as a unit; compare how the preposition stands immediately before the place-name Abingdon in l. 42. The use of capitals to mark proper names is inconsistent. Examples of the customary abbreviations in use are : ˀ in 't(er)ce', l. 1; ² 'p(ur)', l. 4, 'seyn(ur)', l. 23; superscript vowel to signal omission of *r* in 't(r)ouat', l. 13, 'g(r)ant', l. 15; superscript vowel after *q* to signal omission of *u* in 'q(u)arte', l. 1, 'venq(u)i', l. 4; **ꝓ** in 'p(ru)dome', ll. 2, 19; **p** with bar through the descender in 'p(ar)tie', l. 1. A curved overline signals *m* in 'fe(m)me', l. 41; a dot signals *e* over the final letter in each of 'Wincestr(e)', l. 30, and 'hug(e)', l. 42. Note the pervasive use of 'k(e)', l. 21, etc., a form and abbreviation typical of Anglo-Norman French; *vnke* may be similarly contracted. The usual French suspension for 'pounds' is expanded at l. 40 to 'li(ures)'.

CONTEXTS

Written around the main text from f. 86v to f. 90v, where this chronicle ends with the accession of Edward I approximately two-thirds of the way down the left-hand column, also leaving the bottom margin empty. Nearest to this Laud text is Corpus Christi College Cambridge 53, ff. 180v-84r, a text from Peterborough (Clark 1954) and now available in Foltys's edition; Corpus 53, although fuller, is later and is demonstrably not the source for the Laud text. The English phrase 'dorlen leuedi', l. 17, describes Æthelflæd, lady of the Mercians; most of the scribes find it puzzling. Behind the rationalizing reading 'dorlen', shared with the Corpus 53 text, must lie **þeodene* 'of the people', as suggested by Clark (1954: 41). Clark provides the fullest discussion of this phrase, noting that her proposed base form for widely divergent readings is 'not recorded elsewhere'; but see 'Yeodene Lavedi' (Tyson 1975: 16, l. 258, editing the Cambridge University Ee. 1.1 copy). In two places both Laud and Corpus 53 share the same eyeskip (l. 42 'abingdon' occurs once only and l. 43 'or' occurs once only); both have problems with Alfred as brother rather than father of Æthelflæd (see ll. 17-18); both read 'Northumberland' (see l. 37, as against *Cumberland* or *Humberland*); and they agree in many less substantive features. Citations for Corpus 53 are from the Foltys edition; no attempt is made to note all the points of interest in this text.

BIBLIOGRAPHY

As Glover 1865: 16-21; Foltys 1962; Tyson 1975: 16.
Facs. Whitelock with Clark 1954; O'Brien O'Keeffe 2003.
Disc. Clark (in Whitelock 1954): 39-43; Dean with Boulton 1999; Robinson 2003: no. 150, pl. 29.

[1] Corpus 53 also has this mistaken reading instead of *eglises*.
[2] Capitulum sign, separating off run-over placed at end of l. 2.
[3] 'De' might be expected; the interpretation is hesitant.
[4] An adverb (*i* 'there') before the verb is missing also in Corpus 53.
[5] A pinprick with stain follows, not a point. Corpus 53 reads 'Sun frere alfred la dona au conte ...', so the mistaken 'frere' for *pere* must go back to a shared exemplar. Here the clause is incomplete.
[6] The mark below is a stain.
[7] The final letter should be compared with the **s** in the second 'si', l. 40.
[8] The final letter is hesitant.
[9] The second *u* has an extra stroke.
[10] The last letter is an oddly shaped **e**. Corpus 53 has 'covere', but other texts read *cursors* (or *cururs*), which is more likely.
[11] The 's' is subpuncted.

London, British Library, Cotton MS Caligula A. xv, f. 137r
Fragmentary annals from Canterbury

The latest English entry relates to the consecration of Christ Church in 1130, and is in by far the lightest ink on this page.
actual size

24

Oxford, Bodleian Library, Hatton MS 116, p. 5
Chad Homily
Protogothic *textualis*, s. xii[1]

TRANSCRIPTION

licetfeld . in þere he forðferde . ⁊ bebyriged wes .
þe nu git to dege is þ(et) seld eft(er)fylgendra[1] þere
mægðæ biscopa ; He warhte eac degulran
eardungstowe . in þere he synderlicor mid
feawu(m) . þ(et) wes mid seofenu(m) . oððe mid ehta
broðru(m)[2] . swa oft swa he hine fra(m) þa(m) gewinne . ⁊
þes wordes þegnungæ geemetgade . þ(et) he ceadda
þer hi(m) gebed . ⁊ bec redde ; He eac in þere ilcan
megðe on twa(m) gearu(m) ⁊ on halfu(m) gere . þa wulde⟨-⟩
licestan cirican arerde . Þa wes æt seo tíd þa(m)
uplican dóme stihtendu(m) . be þere sprec seo
ciriclice dómbóc ; Tid is stanas to settene .
⁊ to somnienne . þ(et) wes gecweden be þa(m) cwalme
his lichaman . þ(et) he sceolde his þone halgan
gast sendan of þisu(m) eorðlican sældu(m) . to þa(m)
heofonlican getimbru(m) . Mittes þer monige
broðore of þere gesomnunge þes árwurðes-
tan biscopes [3]\\of lich[a<æ]ma[4] atogene weron . þa cóm// his tid ceaddan . þ(et) he sceolde
faran of þysu(m) middangearde to drihtne ;
Ða gelomp hit sume dege . þ(et) he ceadda wu⟨-⟩

Tremulous hand glosses:

[2] fylgendra/ ʒ *above* g

[3] degulran/occult(um)
\\occultu(m)//
[6] gewinne/ labore

[7] þegnungæ/ offitio
geemetgade/ vacar(et)
\\vacaret//

[11] uplican/ sup(er)no
dome/ indi(c)t(i)o
stihtendu(m)/ disponente
\\disponente//
sprec/ dixit

[16] getimbru(m)/ edificiu(m)
Mittes/ cu(m)q(ue)

In contrast with the other major twelfth-century collections of homilies in English, here the letter-forms are essentially Caroline. By this time **æ** is dropping out of use, and in this manuscript where Latin words occur **ę** is preferred and is sometimes used for **e** as well as for older **æ**. The scribe has two forms of **æ**: see 'mægðæ', l. 3, for both. The second of these, with Caroline **a** as its first element, is the more likely to appear throughout the manuscript in aberrant inflexions to be regarded as late hypercorrect spelling. The infrequent occurrence of **æ** in this homily has been put down to an assumed Mercian exemplar in which the Mercian sound change called 'Second Fronting' is invoked to explain the presence of *e* where *æ* might be expected, but *æ* where *a* might be expected is absent. The uncertainty over the use of **æ** is shown in the erasure of the **e** element of the digraph from 'lich[a<æ]ma' (last line in plate).The special characters for writing English **þ**, **ð**, and **ƿ** are all in use. The punctuation is by low point, with *punctus versus* at the end of sentences and following capital (or enlarged letter). There is little such regularity of punctuation in the rest of the manuscript. Some syllables are given stress marks. The main mark of abbreviation is a rising stroke, commonly for *m* and once for *-er-* in 'eft(er)fylgendra', l. 2. Crossed **þ** is expanded as 'þ(et)', the full form found elsewhere in the manuscript. The omission of some words from l. 18 is signalled, and a matching *signe de renvoi* stands before the missing words, which are written below the main text

[1] Note TH's placing of yogh above Caroline **g**.
[2] A verb seems needed here, perhaps 'wunade'.
[3] The *y*-shaped *signe de renvoi* allows the next few words, omitted in error, to be picked up from the bottom margin.
[4] The ending *-n* might be expected in an earlier text.

licet feld. in þere he forð ferde. 7 bebyriged ƿes.
þe nu git to dege is þ feld eft fylgendra þere
occult
megðæ biscopa; He ƿarhte eac degulran
eardung stoƿe. in þere he synderlicor mid
feaƿū. þ ƿes mid seofenū. oððe mid ehta
labore
broðrū. sƿa oft sƿa he hine frā þā geƿinne. 7
affectio vacar;
ƿes ƿordes þegnunga ge emetgade. þ he ceadda vacaret
ƿer hī gebed. 7 bec redde; He eac in þere ilcan
megðe on tƿā gearū 7 on halfū gere. þa ƿulde
licestan cirican arerde. þa ƿes æt seo tid þā
superno iudicio disponente dixit
uplican dome stihtendū. be þere spræc seo
ciriclice dom boc; Tid is stanas to settenne.
7 to somnienne. þ ƿes geƿeden be þā cƿalme
his lichaman. þ he sceolde his þone halgan
gast sendan of þisū eorðlican seldū. to þā
edificiu cuet
heofonlican getimbrū; Mittes ƿer monige
broðore of þere gesomnunge þes arƿurðes-
tan biscopes his tid ceaddan. þ he sceolde
faran of þysū middan gearde to drihtne;
Ða gelomp hit sume dege. þ he ceadda ƿu
ƴ of lichama atogene ƿeron. þa com

Plate 24 — reduced to 90%

block.

The Tremulous Hand glosses are both interlinear and in the margins, some of the latter more or less mirroring the former. There is evidence in the manuscript for the erasure of some marginal glosses. Franzen draws attention to three of her stages of TH glossing (1991:44‑46) on this page: B or the first layer 'occult(um)', l. 3, and 'labore', l. 6; M or with advanced shake 'offitio', 'vacar(et)', l. 7, and 'dixit', l. 11; P or pencil glosses barely visible in the margin and often, though not on this page, in English 'occultu(m)', l. 3, and 'disponente', l. 12 (these cannot be seen in the reproduction).

CONTEXTS

Glosses in the distinctive Tremulous Hand point to use in Worcester in early part of thirteenth century. No. 320 in Young's catalogue of the cathedral manuscripts (*c.* 1622). Belonged to Christopher, Lord Hatton in 1644. Presented by Hatton's son to the Bodleian Library in 1678, where formerly Junius 24.

SIZE

255 × 180 mm (*c.* 198 × 130 mm).

BIBLIOGRAPHY

Pr. Vleeskruyer 1953: 166‑68 (ll. 58‑74).
Disc. SC 5136; Atkins and Ker 1944: 17, 56; Ker, *Cat.* 1957: no. 333; Gameson 1999: no. 730; Treharne 2000: 11‑40; Thomson 2001: xxii, xxiv.
For TH. Franzen 1991: 44‑48.

London, British Library, Cotton MS Vespasian D. xiv, f. 166r
Lines 1–10 from Ælfric's *De dominica oratione*
Lines 11–21 are the opening of a homily on the Phoenix

This plate illustrates hands 2 (ll. 11–21) and 3 (ll. 1–10) of the next manuscript discussed.
actual size

25

London, British Library, Cotton MS Vespasian D. xiv, f. 137r (formerly 132 and 134)
Ælfric, *In Letania Maiore* (Catholic Homilies I. 18)
Protogothic *textualis*, s. xii med.

TRANSCRIPTION

þa nytene fæsten ⁊ ne onbyrigden nanes metes
binnen þreom dagen . Þa þurh þa gecerrednysse
þ(æt) heo yfeles geswican ؛ ⁊ þurh þ(æt) strange fæsten
heom gemiltsode god ⁊ nolde heo fordon swa swa
he ær þa twa burhware sodomam ⁊ gomorram
for heora lehtren mid heofonlice fyre for⸍
bærnde . swa swa we eow gereccen mugen . [⸍þy ða we]
Soð is to secgene[⸍] . þa þa wyreceð on godes w[i>y]lle .
þa becumeð on myrhðe . Ðæt godspell
cweðð . Ælc þære þe forlæt for mine name
fæder oððe moder. gebroðre oððe gesustre . wif
oððe bearn . land oððe gebytle[1] ؛ beo hundfealden
him byð forgolden . ⁊ he hæfð þær to ecan þ(æt) ece
lif . Hundfeald getel is fullfremed . ⁊[2] se þe
forlætt þa ateorigendlice[3] þing for godes na⸍
me ؛ he underfohð þa gastlice mede beo hund⸍
fealden æt gode . Þes cwide belimpð swyðe to mu⸍
nuchades mannen. þa þa for heofone rices my⸍
rehðen forlæteð fæder ⁊ moder ⁊ flæsclice sib⸍
linges . Heo underfoð manega gastlice fæderes
⁊ gastlice gebroðren . for þan þe ealle þæs hades
mænn þe regollice libbeð ; byð him to fæderen

Only two of the letter-forms distinctive of Anglo-Saxon minuscule are consistently employed in this sample of the manuscript's main hand: **f** and **r**. Caroline **s** sits tidily on the script line (e.g. 'swa swa', l. 4) alongside the descending insular form (e.g. 'nanes metes'. l. 1). Round **s** is used occasionally: twice, ll. 5 and 8 (where a capital) on this page. Curious downward-curving tails have been added laboriously to the open-tailed **g**. Note the forks on ascenders and descenders, and the **c** and **e** shapes which accord with the Canterbury and Rochester twitchy style. The straight descender of **p** ends with a stroke turning right ('godspell', l. 9, 'belimpð', l. 17) that helps make it distinct from **p** ('geswican', l. 3, 'swa', l. 4, etc.); compare pl. 30: 'up', l. 1. Both **þ** and **ð** are in use, with **þ** used word-initially; but there is no differentiation in size between **ð**, tagged to the right, and the round-backed **d** (now in general use). The **æ** digraph is retained (the capital of 'Ælc', l. 10, is an angular form found from towards the middle of the twelfth century). In language forms this late copy of an Ælfric homily has acquired many early Middle English features, particularly in unstressed syllables, for example 'dagen', l. 2 (not *dagum*), 'gereccen', l. 7 (not *gereccan*), 'secgene', l. 8 (not *secganne*), 'wyreceð', l. 8 (not *wyrcað*). The most frequent mark of punctuation is the point: for major pauses a capital or enlarged letter (some touched with colour) may follow; and the *punctus elevatus* is also used for minor pauses. The proper name 'sodomam', l. 5, linked with 'gomorram', begins with a round **s**, which need not always be viewed as a capital in this hand. The hyphen is a single rising stroke. Word division appears to be complete. Ruled in pencil. Large initials are alternately red and green. There is little abbreviation: only ⁊ and ꝥ are found on this page. Careful correction is evident: see for example the end of l. 7, and the beginning of l. 8 where the *punctus elevatus* seems to have been written over an erasure. Two words are underlined with underdotting in ll. 12, 15, for abstraction into Nowell's glossary.

[1] Word underlined for inclusion in Nowell's dictionary.
[2] Tironian sign sufficiently enlarged as to serve as capital.
[3] Word underlined for inclusion in Nowell's dictionary.

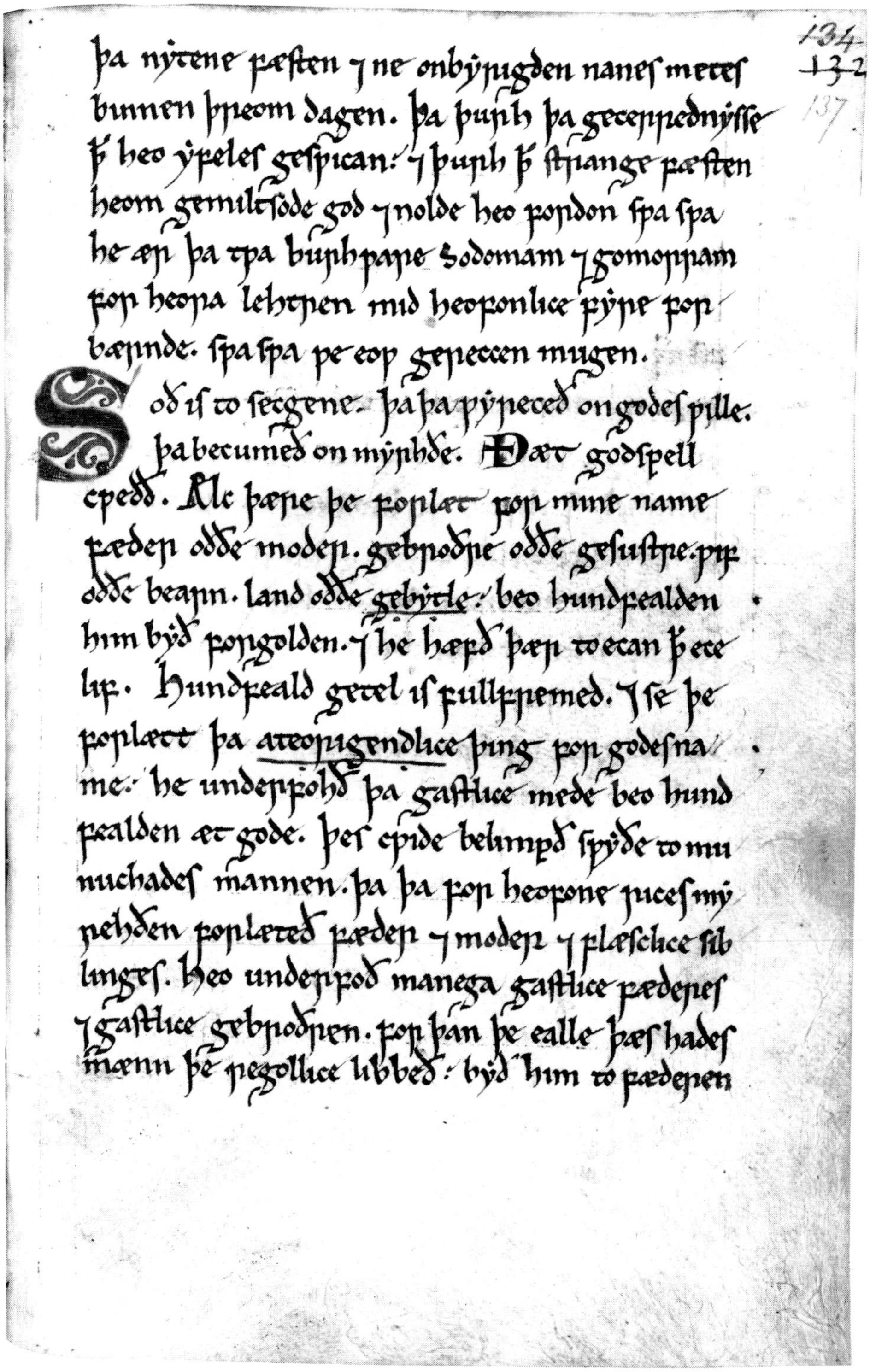

þa nytene fæsten ⁊ ne onbyrigden nanes metes binnen þreom dagen. þa þurh þa gecerrednysse þ heo yfeles geswican: ⁊ þurh þ strange fæsten heom gemiltsode god ⁊ nolde heo fordon swa swa he ær þa twa burhware sodomam ⁊ gomorram for heora lehtren mid heofonlice fyre for bærnde. swa swa we eow gereccen mugen.

Soð is to secgene. þa þa wyrceð ongodes wille. þa becumeð on myrhðe. Þæt godspell cweð. Ælc þære þe forlæt for mine name fæder oððe moder. gebroðre oððe gesustre. wif oððe bearn. land oððe gebytle. beo hundfealden him byð forgolden. ⁊ he hæfð þær to ecan þ ece lif. Hundfeald getel is fullfremed. ⁊ se þe forlæt þa ateorigendlice þing for godes name. he underfohð þa gastlice mede beo hundfealden æt gode. þes cwide belimpð swyðe to munuchades mannen. þa þa for heofone rices myrelðen forlæteð fæder ⁊ moder ⁊ flæslice siblinges. heo underfoð manega gastlice fæderes ⁊ gastlice gebroðren. forþan þe ealle þæs hades mænn þe regollice libbeð: byð him to fæderen

Plate 25 – actual size

CONTEXTS

From a compilation, for the most part of late versions taken from both series of Ælfric's Catholic Homilies together with new early Middle English homiletic materials and additional short entries. The script suggests this manuscript originated at either Rochester or Canterbury, as does the presence of a translation of a homily by Ralph d'Escures, bishop of Rochester 1108–14 and archbishop of Canterbury 1114–22. The phrase 'ego ancilla tua' in a prayer added late in the twelfth century on f. 4 indicates the manuscript was then in a woman's hands. Used by Nowell, who abstracted from it for his dictionary of Old English, by Robert Talbot and Matthew Parker (whose secretary Joscelyn also added annotations). In Cotton's collection by 1621 (used also by L'isle and James).

SIZE

c. 191 × 122 mm (147 × 93 mm).

BIBLIOGRAPHY

Pr. Warner 1917: 120–21. *Coll.* Clemoes 1997: 317–18 (ll. 14–39).
Facs. Wilcox 2000.
Disc. Ker, *Cat.* 1957: no. 209; Handley 1974; Laing 1993: 83; Treharne 2000; Tite 2003: 183.

26

London, British Library, Royal MS 4 A. xiv, f. 106v
a. End of Sermon on Numbers 20: 10 attributed to Jerome
Anglo-Saxon square minuscule, s. x med.
b. Charm against a growth, 'Wenne wenne'
Protogothic *textualis*, s. xii med.
c. Couplet, added perhaps s. xiii[1]
d. Post-medieval index

TRANSCRIPTION

Adoperuit ergo eos nubes tabernaculi
testimonii . et inruit synagoga sup(er) moysen
et ááron . et apparuit gloria d(omi)ni ; Qua(m) uis
magnus sit uitæ merito moyses et aaron .
qua(m) uis animi uirtutib(us) polleant . appa⟨-⟩
rere Tamen eis gloria non potuisset .
nisi in p(er)secutionib(us) . In tribulationibus .
In periculis . atq(ue) in ipsa poene morte iam
positis ;
wenne wenne wenchic`h´enne her ne scealt þu timb`r´ien ne nenne
tun habben ac þu scealt nort `h´eonene to þan nihgán berhge
þer þu hauest ermig[1] enne broþer he þe sceal legge leaf et
heafde under fot uolmes[2] under ueþer earnes under earnes
clea á þu geƿeornie clinge þu alsƿa col on heorþe scring'
þu alsƿá scésne[3] a ƿage . ⁊ ƿeorne alsƿá ƿeter on anbre[4] . sƿa litel
þu geƿurþe alsƿa linsétcorn ⁊ miccli lesse alsƿa anes hand-
ƿurmes huƿeban ⁊ alsƿa litel þu geƿurþe ƿet þu naƿiht
geƿurþe :⁊

. Si p(er) diuitias possemus morte carere ∵
Tunc p(ro)desset eas indeficient(er) Habere .

Monasteriu(m) 143 . (ve)l 144 . ante tine(re) . fo .77.
Vere caro cr(ist)i .81.
Consolatio in afflicc(i)one .80.
Psalm(us) (quattu)or versuu(m) .102.
Cibus animæ .39.a .

Short poems are sometimes recorded in empty space, as here on the last page of a tenth-century manuscript. The charm is written neatly below the last line of the Latin text, holding to the ruling for the main text. Its scribe's letter-forms derive from Caroline minuscule; **æ** is not retained (see 'et', l. 12, 'ƿeter', l. 15, 'ƿet', l. 17). The minims are clearly made, with frequent pen-lifts, even as the script becomes larger and more cursively written. The ascenders have firm wedges, the descenders flick to the left, and few letters overlap (**de** in 'heafde', l. 13). The descender of **ƿ** turns to the left, a feature first of documentary script (see 'huƿeban', l. 17, and contrast the book-hand form with a right turn in pl. 30, 'up', l. 1). Round **r** appears only after **o** ('geƿeornie', l. 14, 'heorþe', l. 14, 'ƿeorne', l. 15). Note both round-backed **d** ('heafde', l. 13, 'under', l. 13) and straight **d** ('under', l. 13). Of the special letter-forms for English, **þ** is secure; **ð** is not used; and **ƿ** (retained for this transcription) is used alongside alternatives. At the outset of this short text **w** appears in the first three words, where the scribe may not have had his eye on the exemplar, but **ƿ** thereafter. Voicing is reflected in the *u* of 'hauest', l. 12, and 'ueþer', l. 13, where earlier *f* would have been the usual spelling, and mistakenly in 'uolmes', l. 13, as if a form of *folm* 'hand' is meant. The scribe's hesitation over using wyn may help explain this crux. After the three opening words with **w**, he settles down to **ƿ** only with 'geƿeornie', l. 14; thus the substitution of a single *u*, compounded by a misreading

[1] For 'erming' (= 'wretch').
[2] A crux. Sense requires *wolues* or *ƿolues* (= 'wolf's').
[3] For 'scerne' (= 'muck, dirt'); the scribe may have misread the Insular **r** of his copy text.
[4] Or 'ambre' (= 'pitcher'). This word is spelled with either *m* or *n*.

[C]ooperuit igitur eos nubes tabernaculum testimonii. Et irruit synagoga super moysen et aaron. Et apparuit gloria domini; quia quamuis magnis sit uitae meritis moyses et aaron. quamuis animi uirtutibus polleant. apparere tamen eis gloria non potuisset. nisi in persecutionibus. in tribulationibus. in periculis. atque in ipsa pene morte iam positis;

Wenne wenne wenchichenne her ne scealt þu timbrien ne nenne tun habben ac þu scealt north eonene to þan nihgan berhge þer þu hauest ermig enne broþer he þe sceal legge leaf et heafde under fot wolmes under weþer earnes under earnes clea a þu geweornie clinge þu alswa col on heorþe scring þu alswa scerne awage and weorne alswa weter on anbre swa litel þu gewurþe alswa linset corn and miccli lesse alswa anes handwurmes hupeban and alswa litel þu gewurþe þet þu nawiht gewurþe:;

Si per diuitias possemus morte carere:
Tunc possessor eas indeficienter haberet.

MVSEVM BRITANNICVM

Monasterium 143 et 144 ante finem fo. 77.
Vere caro xpi. 81.
Consolatio in afflictione. 80.
Psalmus 4or versuum. 102.
Cibus animae. 39.a.

Plate 26 – reduced to 83%

of two minims as three in the middle of whatever form was in his exemplar, maybe *pulues* for *pulfes*, seems to have resulted in 'fot' (foot) being followed by 'uolmes' (of hand). Word division is almost complete (note the attached negative particle 'ne', l. 10, and the attached adverb 'á', l. 14). Within this short poem a low point occurs twice in l. 15, and heavy punctuation clearly marks its ending. A hyphen marks a divided compound (l. 16). There are no abbreviations other than the Tironian sign, unless the final stroke of 'scring'', l. 14, is for -*e*. Caret marks signal corrections in ll. 10 (twice) and 11 (where *h* might belong to the preceding word rather than to '\h/eonene', but a western unvoiced *þ* is assumed for 'nort'; and 'myccli', l. 16, indicates some uncertainty about endings. Occasional short pieces in early Middle English may show marked inconsistency in letter-forms. Compare the Godric hymns (p. 133): the scribe's usual choice is **ƿ**, but he has **w** once, in the last line; and note **th** once in 'burth', although otherwise a fairly formal distribution of **þ** and **ð** is apparent.

The main hand is Anglo-Saxon square minuscule of the mid-tenth century. Round **s** is used in all positions. Note that part of a lifted paste-down is visible at the right: this is an up-side down fragment from Felix's *Vita sancti Guthlaci*, in Insular minuscule, s. viii²/ix¹; a page from this fragment is reproduced on p. 21.

why??

CONTEXTS

The manuscript is thought to have been written at Winchester (Hyde, formerly New Minster, see Ker 1964: 104), may have circumstantial links with Christ Church, Canterbury, but was in Worcester from the twelfth century. It matches a description in Patrick Young's catalogue of the manuscripts of Worcester Cathedral (*c.* 1622: no. 5). Belonged to John Theyer between 1644-46. Theyer's books went to his grandson, and on to a London bookseller, Robert Scott. Bought *c.* 1678 for the Royal Library. Entered the British Museum with the Royal Collection in 1757.

SIZE

276 × 181 mm.

BIBLIOGRAPHY

Pr. (b) Dobbie 1942: 128.
Facs. Robinson and Stanley 1991: no. 19.11; Pulsiano 1996².
Disc. Warner and Gilson 1921: I. 81-82; Atkins and Ker 1944: 18, 32, 63; Ker, *Cat.*1957: no. 250; Laing 1993: 100; Gneuss 2001: nos 455, 456.

London, British Library, Cotton MS Claudius D. iii, f. 78r
Bilingual Benedictine Rule from Wintney, Hampshire
reduced to 65%

27a

Oxford, Bodleian Library, MS Junius 1, f. 72r (formerly cols. 225-226)
Orm, *Ormulum*, ll. 9030-34, 9063-9159, from XV (end of homily) and XVI (preface)
Protogothic *textualis*, s. xii ex.

TRANSCRIPTION

derr weddedd . ⁊ c(r)istess faderr rihht
inoh ∴ þatt wass himm sett to
fosstrenn . þohh þ(att) he stre[o]⟨-⟩[2]
nedd nohht ne wass ∴ þurrh
hi(mm) . ne þurrh nan oþerr . Θ[3]
7 § ⁊ tatt te laferrd iesu crist .
Wass herrsu(mm) till hemm baþe . ⁊ ædmod aȝȝ . ⁊ bliþe . ⁊
fus . To follȝ^{h}enn he[o]re wille ∴
þatt dide he forr he wollde swa .
Vss alle ȝifenn bisne . To cwem(enn)
ure faderr wel. ⁊ ure moderr
baþe . To lutenn hemm . to leff-
tenn hemm . To serrfenn he(mm) well
ȝerrne[5] . To findenn hemm þ(att)
hemm iss ned ∴ Aȝȝ afft(err) ure
mahhte . Forr ȝiff þ(att) tu forr-
werrpesst her . þin faderr . ⁊
tin[6] moderr ∴ þu best forr-
worrpenn att te dom . Butt
iff þűt muȝ^{h}e betenn ·; § Off þ(att)
tatt sannte Marȝe toc . All
þ(att) ȝho sahh . ⁊ herrde . Off hire sune iesu crist . ⁊ off hiss
goddcundnesse . ⁊ leȝȝde itt
all to samenn aȝȝ . To þennkenn
þær abutenn . Forr þatt ȝho
wisste mare off himm . þann
aniȝ mann o life ∴ Off þ(att) icc
habbe shæwedd her . Biforenn
o þiss lare . þær þær þe goddspell wrihhte seȝȝþ . Onn hiss godd-
spelless lare . þatt hirdess fun-
denn iesu crist . I beþþleæmess
chesstre . Vppo þ(att) ilke nahht
tatt he . Wass borenn her to
manne . Forr þære uss seȝȝþ
þe goddspell boc ∴ ⁊ wel uss
birrþ itt trowwenn . þatt ure
laffdiȝ Marȝe toc . All þ(att) ȝho
sahh . ⁊ herrde . Off hire sune
iesu c(r)ist ∴ ⁊ off þa miccle tac-

Nu cumeþþ[1]
me to tel-
lenn forþ ∴
Off sannt
iohan bapp-
tisste . ⁊ tærrihht
tær i le̋t off himm ∴
þær wile i nu bigin-
nenn . To tellenn . ⁊ to
spellenn ȝuw ∴ Off him(m) . ⁊ off
hiss lare . § þiss illke
were[4] sannt iohan ∴ Wass
haliȝ mann wiþþalle .
Forr son summ he wass
waxenn swa . þurrh hise
fre[o]ndess fode . þatt he
þa mihhte hi(mm) sellf[-en] \`wel´
be[o]n . Hiss aȝ^{h}enn hell-
pe ⁊ hirde . ⁊ tatt he
cuþe hi(mm) ane be[o]n . ⁊ lo-
kenn till hi(mm) sellfenn ∴
Forrþrihht anan he
flæh aweȝȝ . Fra faderr
⁊ fra moderr . ⁊ flæh
hi(mm) i(nn)till wessteland ∴ þær
itt wass all unnbiggedd . ⁊
shadde hi(mm) all þwerrt űt
fra menn ∴ Forr þ(att) he wollde hi(mm) ȝemenn . Swa þ(att) he
þurrh an idell word ∴ Ne
shollde hi(mm) nohht forrgill-
tenn . ⁊ tære he ledde
himm ane hiss lif ∴ Fra
þ(att) he wass full litell .
Till þ(att) he waxenn wass . ⁊
neh ∴ Off þrittiȝ winnt(err)
elde . ⁊ siþþenn toc he þær
þe follc . To spellenn . ⁊ to fullh-
tnenn ∴ Forr þ(att) he wollde
ȝarrkenn[7] hemm . Onnȝæ-
ness cristess come . ⁊ here icc wile off hiss fullhht ∴

[1] Here space is left for the pericope 'XV | anno q(u)into⟨-⟩ | decimo i(m)p(er)ii | tyberij cesa⟨-⟩ | ris'.

[2] In this transcript square brackets about **o** point to its erasure from **eo**. Strokes may attempt to stretch across the resulting space; the **o** has sometimes been inked in by a later hand.

[3] The symbol here, with line trailing to left, indicates where text from an inserted slip is to be read. See 27b.

[4] On erasure.

[5] Holm 1922: 93 points out that this should read 'ȝerne', an unusual error.

[6] The superscript **n** seems to be written over a partially erased double overline.

[7] The **k** is on an erasure, perhaps of **c**.

Plate 27a – reduced to 46%

ness . Þatt comenn i þiss middell
ærd . Son su(mm) he co(mm) to manne .
⁊ tatt ȝho leȝȝde itt samenn all :
To þennkenn aȝȝ þær ummbe .
Hu ȝho wiþþ childe wurrþenn wass :
Wiþþutenn iwhillc macche . ⁊
hu ȝho barr þ(att) ilke child : Wiþþ(-)
utenn iwhillc pine . Swa þ(att) ȝho
moderr wurrþenn wass : ⁊ wass
7 þohh maȝȝdenn clene . § ⁊ tatt
te laferrd iesu crist . Wel
wex ⁊ þraf onn elde : Þatt wass
o þ(att) hallf þ(att) he wass . Soþ mann i
goddcunndnesse . § ⁊ tatt tatt
he wass swiþe wis . ⁊ godd . ⁊ menn
full cweme : Þatt wass forr þi
þatt he wass godd . ⁊ god onn alle wise . § ⁊ godd allmahhtiȝ
gife uss rihht[8] . To follȝ^{h}enn
cristess lare . Swa þ(att) we
motenn alle imæn :
Be[o]n borrȝ^{h}enn þurrh hiss
§ are . AM(ÆN) ·;

⁊ off hiss lare spellenn .
⁊ off þatt he wass sennd
þurrh godd : Biforenn
cristess come . Rihht
allse bidell birrþ
be[o]n sennd . To
ȝarrkenn . ⁊
to greȝȝ-
þenn . Onn-
ȝæn hiss
laferrd
þær
þær
he

For this curious manuscript, the working draft of its author, the overall measurements of this folio provide a rough indication of the optimum size of page. Here, frugally, the form of the animal skin is visible at the right-hand side. The module of the script is large in relation to the ascenders and descenders, the lines lie quite close together, and words sometimes cluster in reading blocks (as 'att te dom', l. 20a, or 'itt trowenn', l. 39a). The **o** is a pointed oval, and most down-strokes end in feet that flick sharply to the left. The **h** is likely to be a conscious choice of the Anglo-Saxon form, for elsewhere (f. 7r, for example, where short **r** is also the norm) Orm uses the Caroline form when writing Latin. So too the **r** may be a choice of the alternative letter-form by this time falling out of use for writing English, and in shape it very often resembles the **r** found in twelfth-century documents; the **r** placed above the main line of script to indicate the doubling of the letter is generally the short Caroline form. The yogh is very carefully made with three strokes (for example, the East Midlands pronoun 'ȝho' (she), ll. 23a, 27a, etc.); and Orm modifies this form for the stop consonant (represented by **g** in the transcription, as in 'godd' (God) and 'god' (good), l. 59a). Occasionally, though not on this page, he does use the Caroline-derived shape, his usual form when writing Latin, in words such as *egge* (edge) and as a single consonant once only in the whole *Ormulum* in the French loan-word 'gyn' (trap or gin), l. 7087. Of the special letter-forms needed by English, thorn and wyn (transcribed here as *w*) are used, but **ð** is a fringe form (not on this page, but there are 117 instances in all). The digraph **æ** (absent in Orm's Latin) is retained, most of all in the adverb *þær* (or *tær*) and the article *þære*, but see also 'imæn', l. 63a; often this represents Old English *ea*, as in 'æddmod', l. 8a, 'shæwedd', l. 30a, 'ærd', l. 44a, 'flæh', ll. 23b, 24b, 'Onnȝæness', l. 40b and 'Onnȝæn', l. 51b. Note its use also in 'beþþleæmess', l. 34a, perhaps to help signal a new syllable, and its expansion into 'AM(ÆN)' because that is the spelling used by Orm elsewhere. Note how the **o** of **eo** has generally been erased (although often later redrawn in a different ink), for example 'heore', l. 9a; later in the manuscript **eo** gives way to **e**, and at much the same point the infrequent **ð** is given up. The usual choice of **f**, and even in voiced surroundings where by this time *u* and *v* were frequent spellings, for example 'serrfenn' (to serve), l. 14a, is conservative. Round **s** is used only as a capital.

Orm is noteworthy for his attempt to discipline English spelling, and this may well be the first English manuscript to have *wh-* for earlier *hw-* and *sh-* for earlier *sc*. Central to his practice is the doubling of consonants to signal a preceding short vowel, except when the vowel is in an open syllable. Often the second of a pair of consonants is added above the line, indicating that Orm monitored the spellings carefully. All syllables are to be pronounced, except where elision is possible before an initial vowel or *h* (as in 'þære uss', l. 37a, and 'tære he', l. 32b, 'ane hiss', l. 33b). Orm keeps pretty strictly to his chosen line of fifteen syllables: four feet ending with a stressed syllable (eight syllables); and three feet plus a final unstressed syllable (seven syllables). In 'Þatt he | þa mihhte hi(mm) sellf[-en] \`wel' | be[o]n', ll. 16-18b, something seems to have

[8] The mark above **r** seems without function.

gone wrong; *enn* is obscured by ink, and the added adverb should be in its low stress form *well*. Is elision across initial *w-* being signalled? Incidentally, therefore, his spellings have much to tell us about the English of his time in an area of the country from which little contemporary evidence remains. For example, in this text 'crist', ll. 6a, 24a, etc., must have a long vowel and therefore reflect borrowing from French rather than the continuance of the Anglo-Saxon form; and the analogical *-e* of 'hise', l. 15b, seems required by the metre. Linguistically, the *Ormulum* is an East Midlands text, from south-west Lincolnshire, and there is a strong Norse element in the vocabulary, not just loans such as 'toc', l. 22a, already absorbed into late Old English, but more recent adoptions such as 'baþe' (both), ll. 7a, 13a, 'summ' (as), l. 14b, 'unnbigged' (unbuilt upon, uninhabited), l. 26b, *Fra* or *fra*, ll. 23b, 24b, 28b, 33b, *aȝȝ* or *Aȝȝ* (aye), ll. 8a, 16a, 26a, 46a, *þohh* or *þohh*, ll. 3a, 52a. Grammatical gender has gone, and *þe* (the), ll. 31a, 38a, 38b, is the general form of the definite article, used equally with nouns historically of all three genders. The superposed letters, often corrections, are for the most part random, except for the superscript *-h-* that follows ȝ. Here Orm distinguishes the medial gutteral sounding *-ȝ*^{h}- from the palatal sound of initial *ȝh-* in the pronoun *ȝho* from Old English *hēo*. Note also the choice of *t-* (not *þ-*) where a word that begins with the letter *þ* follows a word that ends in *d* or *t*.

This folio presents a relatively tidy appearance, but the first column extends to the second of the central vertical lines, with the hyphens that stray beyond making the left-hand side of the narrow second column bend curiously; from about l. 27 the columns no longer match. Traces of ruling in lead are visible, and the top ruled line is still being used. Large capitals mark major divisions, as at the top of the second column (very occasionally these are green); and where the *paragraphus* (its first appearance in main-text hand in the sequence of plates), represented by § in the transcript, is accompanied by capitals or enlarged letters, space to help establish the break may be opened on the following line (see ll. 21a, 53a); note also the use of a special sign **7** (known as the *simplex ductus*) in the left-hand margin by ll. 6a and 52a to help the eye separate materials. The *paragraphus* also marks the overrun at the end of the first column. Lines and half-lines are easily recognized in this highly regular metre. Each half of the verse line as often as not opens with a capital or enlarged letter or the enlarged Tironian sign, and in addition the usual presence of function words at the outset of each verse line helps towards their recognition. So too a word ending in an unstressed syllable together with following punctuation mark signals the line end of the second half of the verse line. A low point serves as the main punctuation mark. The *punctus elevatus* frequently marks the end of the first part of the line (20 out of 50 or under half of the full lines on this page), though sometimes at the end of the second part it signals a continuing sentence (ll. 9a, 19a, 29a, 54a, 58a, 21b, 39b). The hyphen is used punctiliously, and noteworthy also is the old-fashioned heavy end-punctuation seen in ll. 21a and 65a. Other occasional diacritics are used. On this page doubled accents warn of possible local difficulties in understanding quickly what is written: 'þűt' (elision of *thou* and *it*), l. 21a, 'le̋t' (left), l. 7b, where the first person pronoun stands immediately before the verb, and 'űt' (out), l. 27b, where the need to stress the adverb is made clear. Prominence is given to the Virgin Mary's name by the inclusion within 'MaRȝe', l. 22a, of the capital letter-form for **r**. Standard abbreviations are used, for example the superscript vowel in 'c(r)istess', l. 1a; but they are often modified. Thus the double overline is to be understood as *mm* or *nn*, as in 'he(mm)', l. 14a, or 'i(nn)till', l. 25b, and it seems appropriate therefore to expand ' by *err* in 'afft(err), l. 16a, and 'wint(err)', l. 36b. So too the crossed **þ** is transcribed as *þ(att)*. At l. 11a the double overline is treated as allowing *-enn* in 'cwem(enn)'. The *signe de renvoi* at the end of l. 5a shows that text is to be supplied from a curiously shaped slip (*c.* 159 mm × 106 mm), visible lying over the facing verso. This is reproduced in real size as pl. 27b; in it the script module is a little larger than in f. 72r.

The hand of the added Latin pericopes (these draw on the pericopes listed on ff. 5r-8v and 9v) is dated by Parkes to early in the last quarter of the twelfth century. Note that ticks are given to double but not single **i**. A seventeenth-century hand adds the reference to Luke 3:1.

CONTEXTS

The book, by far longer than it is wide, is roughly bound in heavy card. The preface opens with the line 'Þiss boc iss nemmnedd Orrmulum Forr þi þatt Orrm itt wrohhte' (This book is called the *Ormulum* because Orm wrote it), generally accepted as written in Orm's own hand. An incomplete list of pericopes, positioned between Orm's Dedication and Preface, indicates that at least 242 biblical narratives were planned, each to be followed by a homily, and much of the first thirty-two readings and homilies is extant. The last twelve pericopes listed in the preliminary folios are from the Acts of the Apostles and, because the five final planned readings concentrate on Peter and Paul, Parkes argues that this concentration may point to an Augustinian house where these saints had a particular importance, noting that the Arroaisian Abbey at Bourne is the only house in the Stamford-Crowland area dedicated to Peter and Paul. The first known owner of the *Ormulum* in modern times, van Vliet, wrote extracts from parts now missing into London, Lambeth MS 783. The next owner was Junius, who numbered the columns with Arabic numerals at the bottom of the page; 108 columns have since disappeared. For the most part the superscript word dividers were added by van Vliet, though Junius may have added to them. Entered the Bodleian Library with Junius's manuscripts in 1678.

SIZE

526 × 192 mm (462 × 170 mm).

BIBLIOGRAPHY

Pr. Holt 1878. I. 9030-9159.

Disc. SC 5113; Skeat 1892: pl. 4; Holm 1922; Sisam [1931-33] 1953: 188-95; Matthes 1933, 1951; Ker 1940; Turville-Petre 1947; Burchfield 1953, 1956, 1962, 1994; Wright 1960[1]: pl. 2; McIntosh [1963] 1969: 400; Scragg 1974: 29-31, 50; Parkes [1983] 1991: 187-200; Laing 1993: 135-36; Solopova 1996; Johannesson 1997; Morrison 2001.

Web 'The Ormulum Project' at <http://www.english.su.se/nlj/ormproj/info/news.htm>.

27b

Oxford, Bodleian Library, MS Junius 1, f. 71r
Orm, *Ormulum*, ll. 9035-62

TRANSCRIPTION

Θ § ⁊ ȝe̋́t forr all an oþerr whatt . Seȝȝ⟨-⟩
de þe laffdiȝ MARȜe . Þatt iosæp cristess
faderr wass . Ȝhő́t seȝȝde wiss to soþe . Forr
þi þ(att) ȝho ne wollde nohht . Kiþenn off crist .
ne shæwenn . Nan þing . whatt gate he
borenn wass . Off haliȝ gast to manne .
Acc all swa su(mm) ȝho wisste wel . Þatt all þe
lede wennde . Annd all swa summ ȝho
wisste wel . Þatt laþe gastess
wenndenn . Þatt [-][9] hire
sune iesu crist . Iosæp-

f. 71v

-pess sune wære ⁖ All swa ȝho spacc . rihht
alls iff he . Iosæpess sune wære . Forr þ(att) ȝho
nollde nohht off crist . Þurrh hĭre[10] sellfenn
shæwenn ⁖ Butt all swillc summ þe laþe gast :
⁊ ec þe follc wel wennde . Swillc durrste
ȝho shæwenn off crist . ⁊ all forr þi ȝho seȝȝde . Lef sune icc . ⁊ tin fæderr þe . Sohht ha-
fenn mikell baþe . Forr þ(att) ȝho wollde læ-
tenn [-n] wel . Hi(mm) sellfenn off hi(mm) sellfenn
All shæwenn whatt he wass . ⁊ hu
he cumenn wass to manne .

[9] Ink covers a false start.

[10] The diacritic shows **i** is short.

Ƿ[illegible] 7 ȝet forr all an oþerr þhatt. Segg- 71
de þe laffdiȝ marȝe. Þatt ioseph cristess
faderr wass. ȝho seggde þiss to soþe. Forr
þi þatt ȝho ne wollde nohht. kiþenn off crist. Forr
ne shæwenn. Nan þing. þhatt gate he
borenn wass. Off haliȝ gast to manne.
Acc all swa sum ȝho wisste wel. Þatt all þe
lede wennde. Annd all swa summ ȝho 71
wisste wel. Þatt laþe gastess
wenndenn. Þatt [illegible] hire
sune iesu crist. Iosep

þess sune wære. All swa ȝho spacc rihht
all iff he. Iosæpess sune wære. Forr þatt ȝho
nollde nohht off crist. þurrh hire sellfenn
shæwenn. Butt all swillc summ þe laþe gast.
7 ec þe follc wel wennde. Swillc wisste
ȝho shæwenn off crist. 7 all forr þi ȝho seg- 5
de. Lef sune icc. 7 tin faderr þe. Sohhtenn ha-
fenn mikell bare. Forrþi þatt ȝho wollde læ-
tenn [illegible] wel. hisellfenn off hisellfenn
All shæwenn þhatt he wass. 7 hu
he cummenn wass to manne.

Plate 27b — actual size

28

London, British Library, Royal MS 1 A. xiv, f. 35r
Gospels, Matthew, 2: 12-19
Protogothic *textualis*, s. xii²

TRANSCRIPTION

ferdon . Apparuit angelus d(omi)ni in sompnis
Ioseph dicens . accipe pueru(m) ⁊ matre(m) eius . .
ða hy þ[o>a] ferden þa ætyrde[1] drihtnes
ængel iosepu(m) on swefnum . ⁊ þus cwæð .
Aris ⁊ nim þ(æt) cild . ⁊ his modor ⁊ fleog on egypte
land ⁊ beo þær oð þ(æt) ic þe segge . Toward is þ(æt) he⟨-⟩
rodes secð þ(æt) cyld to forspillenne . He aras þa ⁊
nam þ(æt) cyld ⁊ his modor on nyht ⁊ ferde on
egyptum . ⁊ wæs þær oð herodes forðsyð . þ(æt)
ware gef[e>y]ld þ(æt) þe from drihtne gecweðen wæs
þurh þonne witegan . Of egypte ic mine sune
geclypode . Đa was herodes swyðe gebolgen
for þam \`þe´ he beþæht wæs fra(m) þam tungelwite⟨-⟩
gan . ⁊ he asende þa. ⁊ ofslog ealle þa cyld þe
on bethleem wæron . ⁊ on eallu(m) hire gemæru(m)
fram twywintru(m) ealde ⁊ binnan þam æfter
þare tyde þe he geacsode fra(m) þa(m) tungelwitegu(m) .
ða wæs gefylled þ(æt) gecweþen wæs þurh ieremia(m)
þam witegan . Stefen wæs on hehnysse gehyrd ⁖
wop ⁊ mycel þotorung . Ræchel weop hyre b[æ>e]rn .
⁊ hyo nolde beon gefref[e>r]ed . for þa(m) \`þe´ hyo næron .
Defuncto aute(m) herode ecce apparuit angelus d(omi)ni
in sompnis ioseph in egipto dicens .
Soðlice þa herodes wæs forðfaren ⁖ witodlice
on s[o>w]efne drihtnes ængel ætyrde Iosepe on .

Although this page, when compared with the closely related pl. 29, suggests little attempt to differentiate between Latin and English, there are some distinctions in choice of letter-forms between the Latin of ll. 1-2 and 21-22 and the English text: **a**, **f**, **g**, **r** (but note Insular form of **r** in 'matre(m)', l. 2), and **s** are Caroline in shape; round and straight **d** are both used; but the second stroke of **h** turns to the right and the Tironian sign is used. In English the scribe generally has the Insular-derived **f**, **g**, **h** (though not in 'bethleem', l. 15 or 'þurh', l. 18), **r**, and, occasionally, long **s** (e.g. 'forspillene', l. 7). Low **s** does not appear on this page, unless in 'secð', l. 7, where the shape seems more like a documentary **s**. The **d** of 'drihtnes', l. 3, is looped as in documentary script of this time, and elsewhere the upper stroke flips neatly to the right. The **o** is typically pointed. Two of the special letter-forms for English, **þ** and **ð**, are carefully used (with **ð** non-initial unless enlarged as a capital); but **w** is misread in a verb perhaps obsolescent ('ætyrde', ll. 3, 25). Even though the scribe seems to be copying doggedly word by word he is prone to Kentish spellings (e.g. 'gef[e>y]ld', l. 10). Occasionally there are hints of the 'prickly' style found in Canterbury and Rochester, whether at the top of **c**, as in 'ic', l. 6, 'secð', l. 7, 'ecce', l. 22, and **e**, as in 'asende', l. 14, or at the side as a result of angularity (e.g. **e** in 'he', l. 17), although overall the appearance is of a round script. The usual punctuation is a simple point (two points at the end of l. 2 may be an attempt to fill out the line), sometimes curled, on the line, with a capital letter following for new sentences, but note the *punctus elevatus* is used in ll. 19, 24. Hyphens are not used. Ruled in pencil on hair side; single bounding lines. Red and green initials alternate. Ker's description, 'a rough untidy hand', is well deserved, for corrections are frequent, with clear signs of a fair amount of erasure. A few abbreviations are used in the English text (the Tironian sign, the crossed **þ**, and the overline for final *-m*); note in the Latin the retention of ⁊. On this page the particle *þe* is omitted twice (ll. 13, 21); 'þonne', l. 11, stands for conventional *þone*; and 'ætyrde', ll. 3, 25, is written twice for *ætywde*, the wyn shape being misread as Insular **r**. The erratic closeness of

[1] Some signs of correction, although the resulting **r** should be **w**.

1100 – 1150

35

ferdon. Apparuit angelus dñi in somnis ioseph dicens. accipe puerū 7 matrē eius. Ða hyo þa ferden þa ætywde drihtnes ængel iosepū on swefnium. 7 þus cwæð. Aris 7 nim þ cild. 7 his modor 7 fleoȝ on egypte land 7 beo þær oð þ ic þe segge. Toward is þ herodes secð þ cyld to forspillenne. He aras þa 7 nam þ cyld 7 his modor on nyht 7 ferde on egyptum. 7 wæs þær oð herodes forðsyð. þ ware ge fyld þ þe from drihtne ge cweðen wæs þurh þonne witegan. Of egypte ic mine sune ge clypode. Ða wæs herodes swyðe ge bolȝen for þam þe he be pæht wæs fram þam tungel witeȝan. 7 he asende þa. 7 of sloȝ ealle þa cyld þe on bedleem wæron. 7 on eallū hire ge mærū fram twy wintrū ealde 7 binnan þam æfter þare tyde þe he ge acsode fram þā tungel witegū. Ða wæs ge fylled þ ge cweðen wæs þurh ieremiā þam witegan. Stefen wæs on heanysse ge hyrd wop 7 mycel þotorung. rachel weop hyre bearn. 7 hyo nolde beon ge frefred. for þā þe hyo næron.

Defuncto autē herode ecce apparuit angelus dñi in somnis ioseph in egipto dicens.

Soðlice þa herodes wæs forð faren. witodlice on swefne drihtnes ængel ætywde iosepe on.

Plate 28 – actual size

letters is to be noted, especially in the fusion of -**pp**- in ll. 1, 22. Note also the mark left by the scribe's knife (l. 6, to the right of the line of script), made when it served to hold down the membrane during writing (Ivy 1958: 63n54). The reading 'ealde', l. 16, replaces 'cilde' of earlier manuscripts and might have been understood as meaning 'age' (the Old English noun *ældu* was feminine).

The Latin headings, which do not appear in the earliest manuscripts of the Old English Gospels, may have been introduced as 'reference points to allow the Old English to be read in parallel with the Latin' (Liuzza 1998: 12).

CONTEXTS

A medieval pressmark of Christ Church, Canterbury, appears on f. 3, and the manuscript is identified as 'Textus iv euangeliorum anglice' in Henry of Eastry's 1337-38 catalogue of holdings. Belonged (names on f. 3) to Cranmer and to Lord Lumley, to whom many of Cranmer's books came through Henry FitzAlan. Lumley made a gift of his library to Henry, Prince of Wales (Jayne and Johnson 1956: 15-16). Entered the British Museum with the Royal Collection in 1757.

SIZE

218 × 145 mm (*c.* 157 × 106 mm).

BIBLIOGRAPHY

Coll. Liuzza 1994: 5.
Facs: Liuzza and Doane 1995.
Disc. Warner and Gilson 1921: I. 5; Ker, *Cat.* 1957: no. 245; Laing 1993: 99-100; Liuzza 1998, 2000.

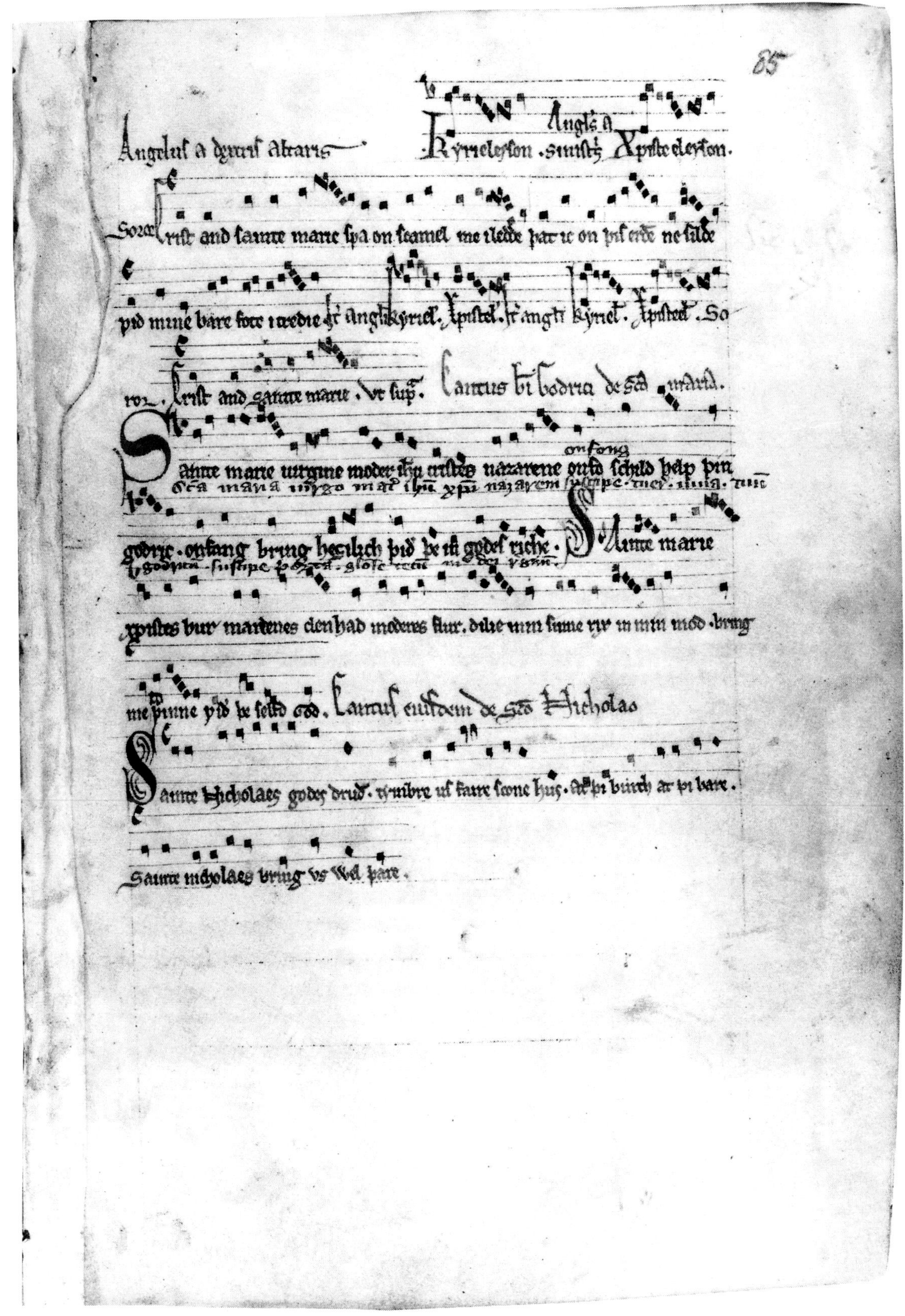

London, British Library, Royal MS 5 F. vii, f. 85r
St Godric's Hymns ('B', 'A' and 'C'); *Kyrie eleison*

This leaf, written early in the thirteenth century, is inserted into the Latin life of Godric by Geoffrey, a monk of Durham. The hymns are in early northern Middle English. Hymn 'C' occurs only in this manuscript. The Latin translation written below 'A' is in a fourteenth-century hand. (See Dobson and Harrison 1979; Laing 1993: 101.)
reduced to 86%

29

Oxford, Bodleian Library, Hatton MS 38, f. 80r *Colour pl. C4*
Gospels, Matthew 2: 12-18
Protogothic *textualis*, s. xii/xiii

TRANSCRIPTION

to herode ne hwyrfden . ac hyo on oþerne weiȝ
on hire riche ferden .
Apparuit angelus d(omi)ni in sompnis ioseph diceNs[1].
accipe puerum & matrem eius .
þA[2] hyo þa ferden þa atewede drihtnes engel iosepe on swefne. ⁊ þus cwæð . Aris ⁊
nym þæt child. ⁊ hys modor ⁊ fleoȝ on egypte land ⁊ beo þær oð þæt ic þe segge. Toward
ís þæt herodes secð þæt child to forspillene .
He aras þa ⁊ nam þæt chyld ⁊ his moder oN[3]
niht . ⁊ ferde in to egypte . ⁊ wæs þær oððe herodes forðsið. þæt wære ȝefeld þæt þe fram
drihtne ȝecweðen[4] wæs . þurh þanne witeȝan . Of
egypte ích minne sune ȝeclypede . Ða wæs herodes swiðe ȝebolȝen for þam þe he befæht[5]
wæs fram þam tungelwitegan . ⁊ he asende þa . ⁊
ofsloh ealle þa chyld þe on bethléém wæron . ⁊
on eallen hire ȝemæren fram twiwintren elde
⁊ binnæn þan æfter þare tyde þe he ȝeaxode
fram þam tunȝelwiteȝen . Ða wæs ȝefylled þ(æt) ȝe⟨-⟩
cweðen wæs þurh ieremia(m) þam witeȝan . Stefne
wæs on heahnysse ȝehyrd . wop ⁊ michel þotorung . rachel weop hire bearn. ⁊ hye nolde beon ȝefrefred . for þam þe hyo næren .
Defuncto autem herode ecce apparuit ang(e)l(u)s

This angular script uses Insular **f** and **r**. Good practice is observed in the distribution of **þ** and **ð** (note **th** in English only in the place-name 'bethléém', l. 17), round-backed **d** and **ð** are carefully distinguished, and **w** retained. Both Caroline **g** and Insular **ȝ** are in use, the former usual before back vowels and in proper names, suggesting a systematic phonetic distinction in the making; the two are differentiated in the transcription. Both Insular and Caroline forms of **h** are used (compare 'herode', l. 1 with 'herodes', l. 9). For **s** the round form is most often found (e.g. finally 'drihtnes', l. 5, 'hys', l. 7, initially 'sune', l. 14); the low Insular form does not occur on this page, but long **s** with stem flicking to the left is frequent, as in 'iosepe', l. 6, 'swefne', l. 6, 'þus', l. 6; and the Caroline form appears in the ligature 'ofsloh', l. 17. The Tironian sign, whether curling to the left (see l. 6) or not (see l. 10), is without the cross-stroke that comes into use *c.* 1200; contrast the ampersand of l. 4 for Latin. Overall the script is drifting towards the more clearly Protogothic forms of the Latin (ll. 3-4 and 25, in italics in transcript), in which Caroline letter-forms prevail (as well as **s** on line, as in 'sompnis', l. 3; note round **s** in 'wæs', l. 13, 'sune', l. 14, pointing towards Gothic scripts). The straight-backed **d** suggests formality at a time when the round-backed form was also in use. Apart from the attempt to give different roles to **g** and **ȝ**, the most striking orthographic feature is **ch**, where the sequence seems generally to trigger the Caroline form of **h** as in 'riche', l. 2, 'child', l. 7. Interestingly, ticks, like those in 'bethléém', l. 17, pick out the monosyllables 'ís', l. 9, and 'ích', l. 14, perhaps indicating that 'ic', l. 8, is unstressed. Note late Old English inflexional levelling (*-en* is pervasive), 'hyo', ll. 1, 5, and 'hye', l. 23, for 'they' and the Kentish look to 'ȝefeld', l. 12 (compare 'ȝefylled', l. 20). Great care has been given to word division (some prefixes are separate, as 'ofsloh', l. 17), and the end-line hyphen is used. The main marker of punctuation is the simple point, with following capitals for new sentences. The large round **d** (l. 25) serving as capital is comparable with the

[1] Note space-saving **N**, sharing second vertical stroke with **s**.
[2] The five-line space for the body of the decorated **þ** has been carefully calculated.
[3] Note elongated letter to fill space.
[4] Spelling here and in l. 21 suggests levelling of **ð** to past participle.
[5] For *beþæht*. Compare pl. 28, l. 13, where **p** is close to the following **æ**.

to herode ne hƿyrfden. ac hyo on oþerne ƿeiʒ
on hire riche ferden.
Apparuit angelus dñi in sompnis ioseph dicens.
accipe puerum & matrem eius.
Ða hyo þa ferden þa ætedeƿde drihtnes en
gel iosepe on sƿefne. 7 þus cƿæð. Aris 7
nym þæt child. 7 his moder 7 fleoʒ on egyp
te land 7 beo þær oð þæt ic þe segge. Toƿard
is þæt herodes secð þæt child to forspillene.
he aras þa 7 nam þæt chyld 7 his moder on-
niht. 7 ferde in to egypte. 7 ƿæs þær oððe hero
des forð sið. þæt ƿære ʒe feld þæt þe fram
drihtne ʒe cƿeden ƿæs. þurh þanne ƿitegan. Of
egypte ich minne sune ʒe clypede. Ða ƿæs he
rodes sƿiðe ʒe bolʒen for þam þe he be fæht
ƿæs fram þam tungelƿitegan. 7 he asende þa. 7
of sloh ealle þa chyld þe on bethleem ƿæron. 7
on eallen hire ʒe mæren fram tƿiƿintren elde
7 binnæn þan æfter þare tyde þe he ʒe acode
fram þam tungelƿitegen. Ða ƿæs ʒe fylled þ ʒe
cƿeden ƿæs þurh ieremiā þam ƿitegan. Stefne
ƿæs on heahnysse ʒe hyrd. ƿop 7 michel ƿoþ
rung. rachel ƿeop hire bearn. 7 hye nolde be
on ʒe frefred. for þam þe hyo næren.
Defuncto autem herode ecce apparuit angl̄s

Plate 29 – actual size

shape shown in Johnson and Jenkinson 1915: 13 for 1225; compare the enlarged ð in l. 3 of Royal 1 A. xiv (pl. 28). Ruled with pencil on both sides for twenty-five long lines, with single bounding verticals; irregular as to which lines extend across whole page. The decoration of the large capitals, in particular the flourishing, points towards the early thirteenth century. Red and blue alternate for the initials, with some survival of green suggesting the late twelfth or possibly the early thirteenth century. Abbreviation, apart from the Tironian sign, is sparing in the English text: only 'þ(æt)', l. 20, and the overline of 'ieremia(m)', l. 21. Linguistically, this version of the Old English Gospels is an interesting mix of conservatism and innovation, a context in which the double *n* of the possessive adjective 'minne', l. 14, looks historically correct by contrast with the article form 'þanne', l. 13 (*þone* is the expected form of late West Saxon). The form 'befæht', l. 15, suggests that the scribe did not immediately understand 'bepæht' in his exemplar. Note the reading 'elde', l. 18, with which compare pl. 28, l. 16. The sixteenth-century title in the upper right-hand margin is in the red crayon found in many manuscripts then owned or consulted by Archbishop Parker or his son John; words in ll. 18, 19, 22 are underlined in the same crayon.

CONTEXTS

A copy close to Royal MS 1 A. xiv (see pl. 28), a Christ Church, Canterbury, book. Belonged to 'Matthæus Cantuar: 1574' (f. 3r). At one time in possession of John Parker: signature on f.1v, and to be identified with 'Evangelia 4 saxonice' in John Parker's book-list in Lambeth Palace 737, f. 153v. In Hatton's library (signature on f. ii recto) when used by Junius for his 1665 edition of the Anglo-Saxon gospels. Sold at Hatton's death to London bookseller Robert Scot. Bought by the Bodleian Library in 1671, where formerly Hatton 65.

SIZE

236 × 158 mm (165 × 107 mm).

BIBLIOGRAPHY

Pr. Skeat 1871-87: 32. *Coll.* Liuzza 1994: 5.
Facs. Liuzza and Doane 1995.
Disc. SC 4090; Ker, *Cat.*1957: no. 325 and p. xix; Laing 1993: 133; Liuzza 1998, 2000.

32

mine mannischnesse ⁊ mine ȝekynde ƿpa soðliche ic scal cumē to 61
hī. ⁊ underfon of his godcundnesse ⁊ of his ȝekynde ðurh his
michele mildce. Gif ic hī ƿile hleste. ⁊ his rad folȝī. For his lu
ue ic ȝeu bidde ðat ȝe me forberē ⁊ ƿpa ƿillē ⁊ ƿpa stierē ðat ic mo
te folȝī ⁊ buhsū biē. Ȝing ƿam on alle gode ƿerkē. Ƿe ƿiete
NU. andsƿered Ratio ⁊ dus. Ƿhile ðe ƿe tegedere ƿuneð. Ratio.
seid. Ƿe ƿenche ðe no seldum ðat ic ðe badd habbē pais
on ðe ⁊ on ðire saule. Ic ƿit ƿat ƿel ðat godd ne mai biē ƿu
nīgende on none saule ðat unfrid is of senes. Herof beð ƿit
nesse ðe ƿrofiete ðe seid. In pace factus est locus eius. On sibsūnesse is
maked his stedel ðe he on scal ƿunigē. Ic ƿot ƿel hƿat
ðe Apostel seid be ȝeu bade. Caro concupiscit adversus spiritum.
⁊ spiritus adversus carnē. Ðe flæsch he seid hit ȝirnið aȝēn ðe goste
⁊ ðe gost aȝēn ðe flesche. ⁊ nadelas ȝit muȝē habbe pais. For
ðan he seid after. Ut non quecumque vultis ita faciatis. For ði he seid
ȝit ƿined ȝung betƿen ðat ȝuker noðer ne scal habbe
his ƿill. Ac ȝit sculē bade ðurh ðese ȝeƿiñe folȝī godes
ƿille. Ðane is sone pais over al ðine lode. Ac help nu all ðat
ðu miht ðat ðin saule hadde a litel reste. ⁊ ðat ðis hali tēple
ðe is arard on ȝiu ðat godd ȝinker sceppend mihte ðarīne ƿunien
ðanne bie ȝit ƿisli sali. ƿit mote ȝiet a litel ƿile ðat hit
bie mid godes fultume ȝiet bet astored. Of sibsumnesse. Of Peace
Siene saule ƿies ilche mihte ðe is icleped pax ðe ƿe nu embe
speked. Hie is sƿiðe niedfull ðe to healdē ⁊ to habbe for

London, British Library, Stowe MS 34 (formerly 240), f. 32r
Vices and Virtues
actual size

30

Oxford, Bodleian Library, Bodley MS 34, f. 42r (formerly 45)
Seinte Iuliene
Protogothic *textualis*, s. xiii in.

TRANSCRIPTION

hat hehe up on hire heaued . þ(at) hit urne end⟨-⟩
delong hire leofliche lich adun to hire he[-a]⟨-⟩[1]
len . Me dude al as he het . Ah þe worldes weal⟨-⟩
dent þ(at) wiste sein iuhan his ewanȝ(e)liste unh⟨-⟩
urt i þe ueat of wallinde eoli þer he wes idon
in. þ(at) ase hal com up þrof ⁖ as he wes hal mei⟨-⟩
den. þe ilke liues lau(er)d . wiste him unwemmet .
His brud of þe bres þ(at) wes wallinde . swa þ(at) ne
þuhte hit hire buten ase wlech weater al þ(at)
ha felde . Eleusius wod þa nuste hwet seȝen .
Ah hehte swiðe don hire ut of his ehsihðe . ⁊
dreaien into dorc hus to prisunes pine ant
swa ha wes idon sone .
⟨H⟩eo[2] as ha þrinne wes i þeost(er)nesse hire ane . feng
to cleopien to c(r)ist . ⁊ bidde þeos bone . lau(er)d
godd almihti mi murhde[3] ⁊ mi mede . mi
sy ⁊ al þe selhðe . þ(at) ich efter seche þu sist al
hu ich am bisteaðet ⁊ bistonden. festne mi
bileaue . Riht me ⁊ read me. for al mi
trust is on þe . Steor me ⁊ streng me for
al mi strengðe is of þe . Mi feader ⁊ Mi moder
for þi þ(at) ich nule þe forsaken ⁖ habbe forsake me .
⁊ al mi nestfalde cun . þ(at) schulde beo me best fre⟨-⟩
on[ð>d] ⁖ beoð me meast feondes . ⁊ mine inhinen ⁖
alre meast heamen. herewurðe healent . habbe

The small round script, still using the top line, is similar to that used in the later twelfth and in the thirteenth century for apparatus in glossed books of the Bible. The older special letter-forms for writing English are still in use: **þ** and **ð** (in good calligraphic distribution); **ƿ** (note Caroline **w** in ‘ewanȝ(e)liste’, l. 4, a word in which even Old English generally has -**u**-, in a phrase headed by the newish French loan-word ‘sein’). Insular **ȝ** and Caroline **g** are not always clearly distinguished (see ‘godd’, l. 16, where the absence of a head-stroke to the left allows identification as **g**, and the awkwardly written and adapted **ȝ** of ‘ewanȝ(e)liste’, l. 4). The **g**, when clearly written, sometimes has an end-word flourish (‘enddelong’, ll. 1-2, ‘feng’, l. 14).The descender of **ƿ** turns to the right as in book hands (**ƿ** with flip to the left at the foot is a feature rather of documentary scripts). There are few bitings. The 2-shaped **r** appears after **b, p,** and **þ** as well as **o**; single *i* is ticked. The three saints’ lives of this manuscript are in the same dialect (‘AB’ language) as the *Ancrene Wisse* text in Cambridge, Corpus Christi College 401. Note that **u**, representing the voicing of **f**, is frequent, both within words, as in ‘heaued’, l. 1, or initially, as in ‘ueat’, l. 5. By this time **k** has become a normal letter-form in the writing of English (compare its use in that part of the Peterborough Chronicle, illustrated in pl. 23, written in the middle of the twelfth century, and contrast its absence from pls 24, 25, 26, 28, 29). The principal mark of punctuation is the point, both for major pauses followed by a capital or enlarged letter (note the enlarged ⁊ in l. 24) and for minor pauses; the *punctus elevatus* is also used for minor pauses. The hyphen is not used, and there are few enlarged letters or capitals. The sheets have pricks or knife slashes in the outer margins for horizontals, pairs of pricks at top and bottom for double bounding verticals, and are ruled in pencil for twenty-five lines, with the first, third, twenty-third, and twenty-fifth lines drawn right across the sheet. Abbreviation too is sparing: **ꝥ** and ˜ on this page; the slashed **l** of ‘ewanȝ(e)liste’, l. 4, and the superscript vowel of

[1] Note subpuncted **a**. The scribe may have begun to write ‘heauet’.
[2] Note small guide-letter to left of writing block for missing **H** and space left for it.
[3] Note **d**, where **ð** might be expected.

Plate 30 – actual size

'cr(i)st', l. 15 (allowing the understanding of -r- before the superscript vowel) may help to save space. The Tironian sign now has a crossbar. Four dots are stranded far to the right of l. 2, as if the scribe planned to note an insertion but decided against it.

CONTEXTS

From the group of writings labelled 'AB' (or 'Katherine') Group, often linked with Wigmore. The book was in a law-office in Herefordshire in the sixteenth century: names in marginal scribbles (Altermonger, clynton, Ewyne, Hauard, Sebourne, Vnet, Wyssham) are associated with Ledbury, Godstow, and Much Cowarne; and incomplete regnal years on ff. 6r, 53v indicate the period 1547-1562. Additions on f. 52r in later-sixteenth-century hand show understanding of the text (a paraphrase of some lines is signed 'Q(uod) Maidwell'). Given to Bodley by Thomas Twyne in 1612.

SIZE

154 × 108 mm (*c.* 115 × 77 mm).

BIBLIOGRAPHY

Pr. d'Ardenne 1936: 25-27 (ll. 257-81).

Facs. Ker 1960[3].

Disc. SC 1883; Watson 1986 [2004[1]]: 144 and n. 39; Laing 1993: 124-25.

VI The Gothic system of scripts: Gothic *textualis*

The Gothic system of scripts came into use gradually, overlapping with Protogothic across the years from the end of the twelfth to the middle of the thirteenth century. It must be stressed that development was continuous, but for practical descriptive purposes divisions are made. The origins for the system lie in the plain vertical strokes distinctive of Caroline minuscule, some with descenders which usually end on the line or just below. These features are, in Caroline hands, combined with the use of curves wherever possible. The increasing angularity in the writing of this script, accompanied by the pointed oval formation of the body of many letters, marks the transmutation into Protogothic, a phase in which feet proliferate and fusions between curved letters begin to appear. A new book script evolved around the turn of the twelfth century. The type that appeared first in Paris came to dominate throughout Europe, except for Italy where at much the same time a somewhat different Gothic minuscule script appeared. The Gothic scripts of northern Europe remained in general use into the sixteenth century. New cursive book hands were to develop also as part of the Gothic system of scripts: two of these, Anglicana and Secretary, are important for the history of the book in England and are therefore given separate introductory sections.

In Gothic *textualis* (or book hand) the curves of Caroline have been almost completely ironed out. The script is typically compressed and upright, and its ascenders and descenders are shorter. Carefully-made minims lie close together, and the pointed oval shapes of Protogothic have given way to a lozenge-like form. The narrowness of the script and its increased recourse to fusions or biting (not just the **de** and, later, **pp** fusions of Protogothic, but **bo, pa, do**, and many more letters are fused together), along with a lessening of space between ruled lines, allows more text to be crammed into the page, especially if a two-column layout is adopted. Very obviously, the more dense the block of writing, the more necessary it became to divide the page into columns, allowing the eye to absorb at a glance a manageable amount of material. It has been calculated that nearly a two-thirds saving of space is possible where the use of abbreviations flourishes. Overall the format can take on a tightly woven appearance, which makes it easy to understand why the description *textura* 'woven' is often used of the script and why it became desirable to give individual space to each word. Heavy use of abbreviations is found, particularly in scholastic texts. Abbreviations, adapted from those in use in writing Latin, are on the whole sparingly used in writing English. So, in pl. 31, an *Ancrene Riwle* manuscript, the small pieces of Latin cited are more heavily abbreviated than is the main text in English.

The emergence of the Gothic system of scripts is accompanied by a growing professionalism new to the writing of manuscripts in medieval Europe. Previously the main centres of learning were the great religious houses, where scribes for the most part performed as best they could according to the task in hand, although already, with the divergence of the kind of handwriting used in books and that used in documents, not all scribes were necessarily adept in both. From *c.* 1200, as universities, guilds, and opportunities for legal training multiplied, an explosion in book production created a greater need for scribes, illuminators, and others associated with the making of books than could be supplied by religious houses. To state the change in the simplest of terms, lay workers had to be paid; and religious too might seek payment. Consequently, commercial competition got properly under way, bringing with it critical evaluation of the products. The quality and worth of script was quantifiable. By employing a separate set of evaluative terms as well as the descriptive terms that identify script types, we can at one and the same time particularize a script and its grade. Grading systems vary in the number of terms used, either allowing for the recognition of a greater or lesser degree of formality (for example, whether or not *formata*) or catering for a wider range of perceptible difference. A two-term set of terms can seem unduly reductive, a four-term set over-elaborate.[1] Yet the four-term set of evaluative terms put forward by Julian Brown makes it possible to generalize assessments of scripts, not just within a script type but across types. The four terms are not script-specific: *currens*, *media*, *formata*, and *formata hybrida*. Because I have found these terms helpful in getting a feel for the hands in which Middle English texts are written, I shall be making use of them from this point, that is, forwards from the period in which writing becomes again a professionalized activity. For the most part I shall invoke the *media* and *formata* grades, and I find it reassuring to realize both that this is a restriction imposed by the manuscripts themselves and that it allows them to be positioned within a larger evaluative framework. The grade *formata hybrida*, applicable for the most part to superlative-plus *cursiva* scripts, is rarely appropriate for English vernacular manuscripts (some such element is present in pls 49 and 53). Gothic *textualis*, by nature a set script, is unlikely to attract the term *currens*.

[1] Work on elicitation theory suggests that a three-term set of evaluators is most efficient; and Brown's descriptors can be viewed as essentially a three-term set (*currens*, *media* and *formata*, with room at the top for an aberrant but starred performance *formata hybrida*). The three categories proposed by Gumbert 1976 as fitting fifteenth-century Dutch manuscripts (*textualis*, *cursiva*, *hybrida*) are script categories, not evaluative terms. New categorizations (too recent for incorporation here) are suggested by Derolez 2003.

Four types of Gothic *textualis* are distinguished, and are graded according to how minims are made.[2] Two styles are formal (therefore *formata*): *prescissa* and *quadrata*. The feet are entirely cut off in *littera prescissa*, which has therefore the alternative description *sine pedibus* 'without feet'. This, the earliest of the four types, is a highly formal script, much used in psalters, and it has close parallels in Protogothic of the twelfth century. With the pen held at a slant, the bottoms of the minims could be filled in neatly, a time-consuming and therefore expensive exercise. In *quadrata* the minims are squared off, with diamond-shaped wedges at top and bottom, giving a script that should be graded *formata*. (Overall the jagged appearance of *quadrata* has sometimes led to its also being described as *fracta* or even *fractura*.) *Semi-quadrata* can also be viewed as a formal script, although it is somewhat less formal than *quadrata*, from which it is distinguished by having wedges consistently only at the top; the minims often end with simple hairlines from the turn of the pen. Finally, a decent plain everyday style, in use, as are the others, throughout the period of the Gothic system of scripts, is termed *rotunda*, obviously from its more rounded aspect. In this Gothic style the minims end in hairline strokes at both the top and bottom. Perhaps because of the closeness of letters in Gothic *textualis*, word division is, in our terms, much improved, with even monosyllables allowed to stand alone. The letter-forms showing noteworthy changes include: **a** now closed, making two compartments; plain **e** for **æ** or **ę** is usual; the round **r** which in Protogothic appeared mostly after **o**, is found after many bowed letters; round **s** replaces straight **s** finally. Round **d**, already generalized in Protogothic documentary scripts, becomes general in Gothic *textualis*, and single as well as double **i** may be given the tick that is the forerunner of to-day's dot. The ampersand **&** gives way to the Tironian sign **⁊**, which takes on a bar.

Although a major script from the late twelfth to the sixteenth century, there are relatively few literary manuscripts containing Middle English in Gothic *textualis*. There are more, proportionately, in the thirteenth century, that is before the development of Anglicana as a book script, than later, but these are on the whole disappointing aesthetically when considered alongside the range of contemporary manuscripts written in Latin or indeed in French. For a chronicler like Matthew Paris, Latin was his normal written language, and he might use French occasionally, for example for saints' lives as well as in headings in maps and other illustrations. (Only a few scraps of English occur in the large body of his writings: the illustration of his hand on p. 149 includes jeering words sung by soldiers in Henry II's reign (col. b, ll. 35-36).) Pl. 31, the Titus D. xviii *Ancrene Riwle*, shows a transitional script: the minims look prickly and the **a** is not yet closed at the top. In its lateral compression, development of more bitings than **de** and **pp** (**pe** for example) and ticking of single **i**, it has moved on from the Protogothic phase. In the distribution of **þ** and **ð**, the scribe follows the formal calligraphic practice established for writing English. By contrast with the Bodley 34 scribe (pl. 30), the Titus D. xviii scribe's **ȝ** or 'yogh' (descended from the earlier **ᵹ** of Insular and Anglo-Saxon scripts) is fully distinct from Caroline **g**, and he is better able to differentiate their roles. This is a workmanlike sample of *textualis semi-quadrata*, a difficult script to produce on so small a scale. The date *c.* 1225 takes account of the 'below top line' dating criterion: the scribe leaves the ruled top line bare of script, a practice to be found suddenly throughout Europe from *c.*1220–40.[3] In its relative lack of bitings, this dating falls within the 1210-1230 decades in which the diffusion of biting takes off.[4]

There is an old-fashioned look to the script of pl. 32, the Jesus College *Owl and the Nightingale*, where the only bitings are with **d**, by contrast with pl. 33 (the Caligula *Brut*) of much the same date, a thoroughly professional performance. The latter is in a fully developed Gothic script, close and solid, with many fusions, yet in its distribution of **þ** and **ð** still in touch with a calligraphic choice passed down from the writing of English late in the tenth century. A much remarked feature of the Caligula *Brut* is the distinctive **æ**. That this digraph should appear so late, and in such numbers, suggests that it was in the author's copy text.[5] Some ten or twelve times instances of **æ** occur still in the other version of Laȝamon's *Brut* (Cotton Otho C. xiii, illustrated on p. 153), even though its redactor got rid of many archaic linguistic features. By the late thirteenth century few scribes had **æ** in their normal repertoires of letter-forms, but as a distinctive trait of older English documents **æ** remains pervasive in copies and forgeries of Anglo-Saxon charters. The script of pl. 34 (the Arundel 292 *Bestiary*) is less laterally compressed, biting is restrained, and the overall impression is of a *rotunda* script. Although some attention is given to the head of the minims, the approach strokes, loops, and forking of ascenders suggest a scribe accustomed to writing documents and perhaps ill at ease with Gothic *textualis*. The scribe generalises **ð**, against the trend under way from the early eleventh century; and because he does not use **þ**, there is little possibility of misreading his **p** with its distinctive rectangular body. Unusually, he differentiates **ȝ** from **g** by using a final head-stroke only for the latter.[6] Both the *Brut* and the *Bestiary*, although poetry, are written continuously: for the former the more or less consistent alternation of *punctus elevatus* and simple end-line point guide the reader helpfully; but the simple point of the *Bestiary* is less efficient in a

[2] Van Dijk 1956 shows these terms in use in the fourteenth century.

[3] Ker 1960[2]. Palma 1988 points out that below-top-line script is found as early as 1176 in glossed manuscripts.

[4] Bischoff 1953, p. 11, fn. 4.

[5] Stanley 1969. For an overview of spelling conventions in early Middle English see Scahill 1994.

[6] Gumbert and Vermeer 1971.

text where a multiplicity of metres is in play. With the use of separate lines for each verse,[7] as in both *Owl and the Nightingale* manuscripts, end-line space becomes the most important visual signal of verse units. Both Jesus 29 and Arundel 292 are trilingual miscellanies, as are Harley 2253 (pl. 36), Digby 86 (p. 165) and Harley 913 (p. 169); Caligula A. ix contains texts in both vernaculars. From the middle of the thirteenth century to the middle of the fourteenth century such miscellanies play an important part in increasing the representation of English writings that have come down to us.[8]

The plates representing the use of Gothic *textualis* in the fourteenth and early fifteenth centuries come from a period when new book-scripts were well established. The earliest of these plates is the Laud *Havelok* (pl. 35), though the script, as is so often the case with Gothic *textualis*, gives few firm clues for dating. Equally, the decoration is of little help in fixing any firmer date than towards the middle or late in the fourteenth century. The script is assured, despite the small module, and sufficiently professional for quick adjustments when glaring mistakes were picked up during writing. For example, the scribe cancels with a neat note of omission rather than erases a line mostly filled (l. 4b) and he adds a forgotten word in the outer margin with a *signe de renvoi* (l. 33b). Of the special letter-forms in use for writing English at this time he uses **þ** but not **ȝ**. One of the two forms for **y** is identical to his **þ** and not always distinguished by having a dot: scribes in the eastern part of the country often used **þ** in both these functions, whereas western manuscripts were more likely to keep them apart.[9] The script of pl. 37 (the *Pearl* manuscript) is very basic, round and plain, and generally dated to late in the century, which is when the *Pearl* poet is thought to have been active. It looks totally uncalligraphic, but the minims are separately written and the expected distribution of **v** (word initial) and **u** (elsewhere) is observed, by contrast with the uncertainty as to the function of **v** evident in the earlier plates illustrating Gothic *textualis*. As with the Jesus College *Owl and the Nightingale*, the word 'old-fashioned' again seems an appropriate descriptor, and parallels for both these hands should perhaps be sought among Anglo-Norman manuscripts.[10] The lack of any evidence for a fifteenth-century dating supports a convergence of pointers towards the late fourteenth century: the manuscript decoration; the costumes in the illustrations; even the motto at the end.

By this time a *cursiva* script was the norm for Middle English literary texts. Even more surprising therefore is the highly formal *quadrata* script of the Corpus *Troilus and Cryseide* (pl. 43), in a manuscript of splendid design where space is used most luxuriously and abbreviations are few. Again the formal **v** ~ **u** distribution is observed. Both the *Pearl* manuscript and the Corpus *Troilus and Cryseide* have illustrations. In the former the drawings,[11] roughly coloured, are added on leaves separate to the quires in which the poems were written or on pages left empty between separate poems, and, relatively unusually,[12] present narrative scenes, perhaps drawn by a regional artist at the request of the owner (see p. 173 for one of these illustrations).[13] In the latter an ambitious integrated programme of some ninety illuminated miniatures was planned but not carried through. The Corpus *Troilus* is a showy and fashionable book, written in a high-grade and costly script with few bitings. The poem has recently been categorized as a lyric compilation abreast of developments in thirteenth- and fourteenth-century French literature, 'a self-consciously authorial compilation of distinct modes of writing'.[14] Set-piece songs and letters, juxtaposed with narrative, are often signalled carefully within the overall presentation of text. Although its only actual illustration is the frontispiece, it is interesting that 'some twenty' of the twenty-five or so songs, letters, and complaints in the Corpus *Troilus* 'correspond with gaps for illustrations'.[15] Tantalisingly, who commissioned it remains unknown.[16] The frontispiece (f. 1v, see p. 195) is of a man popularly identified as Chaucer reading aloud to an audience, but the man does not hold a book and his gestures suggest that he is teaching or preaching.[17] Others argue differently, for example that the picture may be intended to represent Criseyde's parting from Troilus and first meeting with Diomede. Among English vernacular manuscripts the Corpus *Troilus* is in a class of its own, attempting to 'emulate the standard and style of early fifteenth-century books for the French court'.[18] Otherwise, the most lavishly-illustrated Middle English texts are to be found in manuscripts written in the newer *cursiva* book scripts, Anglicana and Secretary, and some of the last supplementary pictures have been selected to indicate the growing range of illustration in books in English, not just in the margins (contrast the rough drawings added to *Dame Siriz*, p. 165, with the care given to the miniatures in the copy of *Mandeville's Travels* illustrated on p. 199) but fully integrated into overall page design (see pp. 243, 247, 251).[19]

[7] By this time poetry is more often than not presented line by line: see Geneviève Hasenohr in Martin and Vezin 1990: 235-38. Huisman 1998: 99-126 discusses English vernacular poetry 1100-1300.

[8] See further Scahill 2003.

[9] Benskin 1982. Benskin 1991: 256, n. 15, points out that the regional distribution would be clearer cut if Gothic *textualis* were excluded.

[10] Doyle 1982: 92 compares British Library MS Egerton 3082 with the *Pearl* manuscript; it is 'of similar ductus and size' but from the early to mid twelfth century.

[11] See the discussions by Lee 1977 and Edwards 1997.

[12] Scott 1989: 46.

[13] Scott 1996: no 12, dating the manuscript *c.* 1375-1400 and the illustrations *c.* 1400-10.

[14] Butterfield 1995: 80.

[15] Butterfield 1995: 55.

[16] Interesting possibilities are discussed by Harris 2000 and Scott 2000.

[17] Pearsall 1977; Salter in Parkes and Salter 1978: 17.

[18] Doyle 1983: 175. Parkes in Parkes and Salter 1978: 6 sees in the Hand 1 script of pl. 43 'a close acquaintance with developments in French *textura* of the late fourteenth century'.

[19] See the survey of book illustration 1390-1490 by Scott 1996.

Other impressive vernacular manuscripts in Gothic *textualis* were being written at this time, notably of the English translation from the Bible made late in the fourteenth century by John Wycliffe and his Oxford associates.[20] Wycliffe moved in royal circles at least to the extent of serving John of Gaunt on ambassadorial missions, and two sumptuous bibles owned by relations of John of Gaunt are extant.[21] From 1409, however, when the reading of unlicensed biblical translations was prohibited, ecclesiatical controls hampered the free production and dissemination of Wycliffite bibles. Pl. 39 (Add. 41175) from a Wycliffite 'Glossed Gospels' manuscript, presenting text together with commentary in a well designed *mise-en-page* (see pl. C5), has been described as among the most professional of Lollard manuscripts.[22] (A less showy Lollard book can be seen on p. 181.) The biblical text is displayed in large script, an arrangement apparently standardized for the Glossed Gospels.[23] Commentary follows, keyed to gospel phrases that are underlined in red and introduced by capitulum signs. In his preface the compiler is scrupulous to explain his sources, pointing to the *Catena Aurea* of Aquinas as his principal authority, unless 'Whanne y telle in what omeli of Gregor eþer of Bede, þanne y my silf se þat origenel of Gregor eþer of Bede' (f. 1v). Add. 41175 contains the gospels of Matthew and Mark, each gospel beginning with a handsome framed page. The symbol of St Mark, his name on a scroll before the lion, is contained in the opening capital. A similar pairing of Luke and John's gospels, as in Bodley 243, would have made up a set.[24] Archbishop Arundel could well have had in mind some such collection when he spoke, in his 1394 funeral oration for Anne of Bohemia, Richard II's wife, of having read and approved for her use an English version of the gospels with glosses upon them.[25]

[20] An excellent overview is provided by de Hamel 2001: 166-89.

[21] de Hamel 2001: 173-74 and pl. 122.

[22] Hudson 1989: 132.

[23] Hargreaves 1979: 173.

[24] Hudson 1989: 141-42, n. 36, suggests this might have been a companion volume.

[25] Hargreaves 1969: 392, 409 'al the foure gospeleris in Engliche with the docturis vpon hem'. Hudson (1985: 154) points out that Wyclif earlier refers to Anne's having the gospels in Czech, German, and Latin.

31

London, British Library, Cotton MS Titus D. xviii, f. 23r
Ancrene Riwle, from Part II
Gothic *littera textualis semi-quadrata formata*, *c.*1225

TRANSCRIPTION

Hope haldes herte hal . hwat se þe
flesch drehes as mon seis . 3if hope nere herte tobreke . A ie(s)u þin
are hu stond ha(m) þ(et) arn þer as alle wa ꝧ weane is wiðute(n) hope of
vtcume ꝧ herte ne mai tobre⟨-⟩[2]
sten ? for þi as 3e wille(n) halden
i(n) wið ow hope . ꝧ te swete breað
of hire . þ(e) 3iues te sawle mihte .
wið muð . ituined cheowes hire inwið owre herte . ne blawe
3e hit nawt ut wið maðelinde
\\muðes//[-wordes] . wið 3eoniende tuteles .
Non habeatis ling(u)am uel aures
prurientes . Lokes seis Ierome
þ(et) 3e ne habben 3icchinde nowðer tunge ne eare . Þ(et) is to seie
þ(et) ow ne luste nowðer speke(n) . ne her-
cni worldli speche . H\id/erto is ise-
id of owre sile(n)ce . ꝧ hu owre speche
schal beo seldscene . Cont(r)arior(um)
eade(m) (est) disciplina . Of silence ꝧ
speche nis bute(n) al are . ꝧ for þi
i writunge ho eornen togede-
res . Nu we schule(n) su(m)hwat speke(n)

of owre heringe a3ain uuel speche . þ(et) 3e þer to3aines tuinen
owre eares . ꝧ 3if ned is ∴ weren owre eheþurles . [-Or][1]
For alle uuele speches mine
leue sustre stoppes owre
eares . ꝧ habbes wlatinge of þe
muð þ(e) speowes ut attre . Vuel[3]
speche is þrefald . Attri . ful . ꝧ
idel . Idel speche is uuel . ful speche
is wurse . Attri ∴ is te wurste . Idel
is ꝧ vnnait al þ(e) god ne cumes
of . ꝧ of þulli speche seis vre la-
u(er)d . schal euch word beo reknet
ꝧ i3eouen reisun . hwi þ(et) ani seide
hit ꝧ tat oðer ilustnede . De om(n)i
u(er)bo ocioso ꝧ c(eter)a . And tis is þah þ(e)
leaste uuel of þe þre vueles .
Hwat ? hu þenne schal mon 3el-
de reisun of þe wurste . þ(et) is of þe
attri ꝧ of ful speche . Nawt ane
þ(et) hit spekes . ah þ(et) hit hercnes .
Ful speche is as of leccherie ꝧ
of oðre fulðes þ(et) unwaschene mu-
ðes speke(n) oðerhwiles. Þeos arn alle
ischraped vt

An early example of Gothic *textualis*, close but still relatively sparing of bitings other than **de** and **pp** (note 'þe', l. 1a, 'speowes', l. 8b, 'speche', l. 23b), this is very much a transitional script, now generally dated to the second quarter of the thirteenth century. It is written below the top ruled line, and 2-shaped **r** is found after **o** and other rounded letters ('breke', l. 3a, 'breað', l. 8a). The minims retain a Protogothic flavour, the curved head of **a** does not yet close up with the lower bowl, the **t** only infrequently has protrusion above the cross-stroke, single **i** is ticked where possibly ambiguous near other minims, **3** is oddly placed on the line, and **ꝧ** is not always barred. The final round **s** usual in fully developed Gothic scripts appears sometimes (see 'as', l. 4a); the ordinary minuscule form with oblique foot is usual, and the sinuous form characteristic rather of the twelfth century is often used at the end of words (e.g. 'cheowes', l. 10a). The distribution of **v** and **u** is uncertain: **v** initial in 'vtcume ', l. 6a, 'Vuel', l. 8b, 'vnnait', l. 12b, 'vre', l. 13b, 'vueles', l. 18b, 'vt', l. 26b; but **u** in 'ut', ll. 12a, 8b, 'uuel', ll. 1b, 10b, 18b, 'uuele', l. 5b, unwaschene', l. 24b, and in both possible places in Latin 'uel', l. 14a, and 'u(er)bo', l. 17b. The overall impression is of a scriptorium where English has continued to be written: note the retention of good calligraphic practice with regard to **þ**, which is usually word initial (in 'eheþurles', l. 4b, the elements of the compound are separate) with **ð** elsewhere; **ƿ** is retained (**w** in transcript). In 'ituined', l. 10a, and 'tuinen', l. 2b, the *-i-* is a marker of vowel length (*ui* is from Old English *ȳ*). Although retaining some characteristic 'AB' features, the text has absorbed north-west Midlands features transmitted by the scribe (Laing and McIntosh 1995). Note for example the pervasive *-es* as verb inflexion (instead of *-eð*/*-ið*), 'arn', ll. 4a, 25b (rather than *beoð*). The main punctuation mark is the point, with following capital or enlarged letter for longer pauses; the *punctus elevatus* signals emphasis but continuation of

[1] Some letters in smaller module are erased. Note also 'uom' to right of l. 6b.

[2] If there is a hyphen, it is concealed by the overlapping capital in column b.

[3] The scrawled cross may draw attention to omission of verse from Matthew 12: 36 (here cited in ll. 16-17b) after 'ut attre', where it is positioned in the Corpus and Vernon manuscripts. Cleopatra and Nero omit the verse altogether.

Plate 31 – actual size

thought (ll. 3b, 11b); the question mark appears in ll. 7a and 19b. Initial letters touched in red give further guidance. Allowance was made for the two-line deep F, an example of the text's overall articulation. Abbreviation in English is sparing: the Tironian sign (not always barred), the overline for *m* or *n*, ꝥ (now ambiguous between *þet* and *þe*: 'þ(e)' is suggested in ll. 9a, 8b, 12b, 17b); and 'ie(s)u', l. 3a. Apart from the letter-forms needed specifically for English, only the greater amount of abbreviation serves to differentiate the Latin of ll. 14-15a, 21-22a, 16-17b. The careful lead ruling for two columns does not always leave a trace. The two-line capital **F** of l. 5b, marking a sub-division within Part II, was inserted later (note the all but obscured guide-letter within the top of the down stroke); in layout Titus reflects the tradition seen in Corpus Christi College Cambridge 402 rather than Cotton Nero A. xiv.

CONTEXTS

Some link with the diocese of Lincoln or of Worcester in the early sixteenth century is suggested by list from earlier binding, on parchment leaf folded in at the back, of bishops of Lincoln up to Cardinal Wolsey and archbishops of Canterbury up to Walter Reynolds (previously bishop of Worcester). This version of the *Ancrene Riwle*, incomplete at the beginning, incorporates more northerly language features (perhaps S. Cheshire) than are to be found in other early versions and is to a certain extent recast for use by men as well as women. There is ownership evidence for ff. 1-13, a separate booklet within the manuscript and possibly first joined to the block that contains *Ancrene Riwle* in the Cotton library (Davidson, Allen). Entered the British Museum with the Cotton Collection in 1753.

SIZE

c. 155 × 118 mm (*c.* 111 × 90 mm).

BIBLIOGRAPHY

Pr. Mack 1963: 15-16. *As* Kubouchi and Ikegami 2003: 143-46.
Disc. Wright 1960[1]: pl. 5; Wilson 1938: xxx-xxxii; Dahood 1984, 1988; Laing 1993: 81-82; Laing and McIntosh 1995; Millett 1996: 53; Dance 2003; Tite 2003: 200; Edwards 2003.

32

Oxford, Jesus College MS 29, f. 156r
The Owl and the Nightingale, ll. 1-64
Gothic littera textualis rotunda media, s. xiii[2]

TRANSCRIPTION

Incip(it) Alt(er)cacio int(er) filomenam ⁊ Bubonem .

Ich wes in one sumere dale .
In one swiþe dyele hale .
Iherde ich holde grete tale .
An vle and one nyhtegale .
þat playd wes . stif . ⁊ starc . ⁊ stro(n)g .
Sum hwile softe . ⁊ lud am[g<o]ng .
And eyþer ayeyn oþer swal .
And let þat vuele mod vt al .
And eyþer seyde of oþres custe .
þat alre wrste þat hi ywuste .
⁊ hure ⁊ hure of oþres songe .
hi holde playding . swiþe stronge .
þe Nihtegale bigon þo speke .
In one hurne of one beche .
⁊ sat vp one vayre bowe .
þat were abute blostme ynowe .
In ore vaste þikke hegge .
IMeynd myd spire . ⁊ g(r)ene segge .
he wes þe gladd(ur) . vor þe ryse .
⁊ song a veole cunne wyse .
Bet þuhte þe drem . þat he were .
Of harpe ⁊ pipe . þan he nere .
Bet þuhte þat heo were ishote .
Of harpe . ⁊ pipe . þan of þrote .
þo stod on old stok . þar byside .
þar þe vle song hire tyde .
And wes myd ivi al bigrowe .
hit wes þare vle erdingstowe .
þe Nihtegale hi iseyh .
⁊ hi biholdeþ[2] . and ouerseyh .
⁊ þuhte wel ful of þare vle .
For me hi halt .[3] lodlich ⁊ fule .

vnwyht heo seyde awey þu fleo .
Me is þe wurs . þat ic þe iseo .
Iwis for þine wle lete .
wel ofte ich my song furlete .
Min heorte atflyhþ . ⁊ falt my tunge .
hwenne þu art to me iþrunge .
Me luste bet speten þane singe .
Of þine fule . howelynge[1] .
þeos vle abod for hit wes eve .
heo ne myhte no leng bileue .
Vor hire heorte wes so gret .
þat wel neyh hire fnast atset .
⁊ warp a word þar after longe .
hw þynk þe nu bi Mine songe .
Wenes tu þat ich ne kunne singe .
þe ich ne cunne of wrytelinge .
Ilome þu dest me grome
⁊ seist me boþe teone ⁊ schome .
If ich þe heolde on myne vote .
So hit bitide þat ich mote .
⁊ þu were vt of þine ryse .
þu scholdest singe on oþer wise .
þe Nihtegale yaf onsware ;
If ich me loki wiþ þe bare .
⁊ me schilde yit þe bléte :
Ne recche ich nouht of þinre þrete .
If ich me holde i(n) myne hegge
Ne recche ich neuer hwat þu segge .
Ich wot þat þu art vnMilde .
wiþ heom þat ne Muwe fro(m) þe schilde
And þu tukest wroþe ⁊ vuele
hwar þu myht ouer smale vowele

Early Gothic *littera textualis rotunda media*, simple and plain, using only **þ** of the special English letter-forms; the exemplar probably had **p** (see 'yit', l. 25b, for *wiþ* 'against'). In style the script is amateur. The minims are separately made, in *rotunda*-style. Serifs are occasional, and are most prominent on initial minims. There are some exceptions to the expected distribution of *v* and *u*; and it may be more than coincidental that the instances on this page, 'ivi', l. 27a, and 'eve', l. 9b, have non-initial *v* for the voiced sound which it conveys in such words as 'vayre', l. 15a, 'vaste', l. 17a, 'vor', l. 19a, etc. Letter-forms in close contact are on the whole avoided: there are bitings only with **d**, a combination that precedes the general Gothic use of fusion, for example ll. 25a, 26a, 29b, 30b. Note final round **s** in 'wurs' l.2b. The **g** is tight, resembling the Anglicana form; and **m** appears sporadically in capital form. The Tironian sign is barred; and in l. 32a has the form usual in Latin for *etiam*. Ker dates this manuscript to the second half of the thirteenth century, despite pointing out that it is 'not essentially different from a twelfth-century hand'. Here on the opening page space has been left for the enlarged

[1] The scribe may have had difficulty in reading his exemplar: space was left and 'howelynge' written in later; other such examples (cf. 'wiþ þe bare', l. 24b) suggest this copy could be near the author's manuscript.

[2] The unnecessary inflexion is to be queried.

[3] The **t** is released in a point; note hesitant separation marks earlier in line after 'me'.

Incip altercacio inter filomenam ⁊ Bubonem. 229

Ich wes in one sumere dale.
In one swiþe dyele hale.
Iherde ich holde grete tale.
An vle and one nyhtegale.
Þat plaid wes stif ⁊ starc ⁊ strong.
Sum hwile softe ⁊ lud among.
And eyþer ayeyn oþer swal.
And let þat vuele mod vt al.
And eyþer seyde of oþres custe.
Þat alre worste þat hi wuste.
⁊ hure ⁊ hure of oþres songe.
Hi holde plaiding swiþe stronge.
Þe nihtegale bigon þo speke.
In one hurne of one beche.
⁊ sat vp one vayre bowe.
Þat were abute blostme ynowe.
In ore vaste þikke hegge.
Meynd myd spire ⁊ grene segge.
He wes þe gladdur vor þe ryse.
⁊ song a veole cunne wyse.
Bet þuhte þe drem þat he were.
Of harpe ⁊ pipe þan he nere.
Bet þuhte þat heo were ishote.
Of harpe ⁊ pipe þan of þrote.
Þo stod on old stok þar byside.
Þar þe vle song hire tyde.
And wes myd ivi al bigrowe.
Hit wes þare vle erdingstowe.
Þe nihtegale hi iseyh.
⁊ hi biholdeþ and overseyh.
⁊ þuhte wel ful of þare vle.
For me hi halt lodlich ⁊ fule.

Vnwyht heo seyde awey þu fleo.
Me is þe wurs þat ich þe iseo.
Iwis for þine vvle lete.
Wel ofte ich my song forlete.
Min heorte atflyhþ ⁊ falt my tunge.
Hwenne þu art to me iþrunge.
Me luste bet speten þane singe.
Of þine fule howelynge.
Þeos vle abod fort hit wes eve.
Heo ne myhte no leng bileue.
Vor hire heorte wes so gret.
Þat wel neyh hire fnast at set.
⁊ warp a word þar after longe.
Hw þynkþ þe nu bi myne songe.
Wenestu þat ich ne kunne singe.
Þeyh ich ne cunne of wrytelinge.
Ilome þu dest me grome.
⁊ seist me boþe teone ⁊ schome.
If ich þe heolde on myne vote.
So hit bitidde þat ich mote.
⁊ þu were vt of þine ryse.
Þu scholdest singe on oþer wise.
Þe nihtegale yaf onsware.
If ich me loki wiþ þe bare.
⁊ me schilde wiþ þe blete.
Ne recche ich nouht of þine þrete.
If ich me holde in myne hegge.
Ne recche ich neuer hwat þu segge.
Ich wot þat þu art vnmilde.
Wiþ heom þat ne muwe fro þe schilde.
And þu tukest wroþe ⁊ vuele.
Hwar þu myht over smale fowele.

Plate 32 – actual size

flourished opening letter, but elsewhere in the manuscript it can clearly be seen that the scribe holds to the old-fashioned practice of writing on the top ruled line. Punctuation is sparing. Most lines end with a point, and points may separate phrases within the line. Note towards the foot of the second column the *punctus versus* (l. 23b) before speech and *punctus elevatus* (l. 25b) where a sentence continues. Occasional rubricated capitals mark paragraphing, blue and red alternating, and guide letters are still visible in the left-hand column (ll. 1, 13, 25, and 29) but have presumably been cropped at the right-hand side of the page. Special letter-forms often serve as capitals at the beginning of verses, where the opening letter (sometimes merely an enlarged letter of the main script) is set apart in a specially ruled column. Otherwise word division is complete. The fourth line of text is singled out by light underlining, providing identification of the poem in English; the red flourishing of the opening capital (filled in with blue) is in a style not found before the second quarter of the century. Few abbreviations are used: the overline for *n/m* ('stro(n)g', l. 5a, 'i(n)', l. 27b, 'fro(m)', l. 30b); the *-ur-* abbreviation in 'gladd(ur)', l. 19a; and the barred Tironian sign. Note the space-saving superscript vowel **e** in 'g(r)ene', l. 18a, which allows a preceding **r** to be read. The Latin title, in red ink of flourishing, has the customary abbreviation for 'Incip(it)' as well as the crossed Tironian sign and ' for *er*; note also *c* for *t* in 'Alt(er)cacio', a spelling found with increasing frequency in the thirteenth century.

CONTEXTS

In Part II of manuscript; given in 1693 to Jesus College by Thomas Wilkins, rector of Llanvair, Llantrissant, Glamorganshire. (For history of part I and evidence that both parts were already together when acquired by Wilkins, see Hill 2003.) Scribal profile places in east Herefordshire, not far from Worcestershire border. Internal dating for other poems in the collection indicates that compilation was unlikely to be before 1256. There is an interesting overlap in contents, both English and Anglo-Norman, with Caligula A. ix (pl. 33). Housed in the Bodleian Library.

SIZE

185 × *c.* 136 mm (*c.* 144 × *c.* 122 mm).

BIBLIOGRAPHY

Pr. Atkins 1922: 3-9 (ll. 1-64); *as* Cartlidge 2001: 2-3 (ll. 1-64). *Coll.* Stanley 1960: 49-51 (ll. 1-64).
Facs. Ker 1963.
Disc. Coxe 1852: II. 10-11; Hill 1963, 1975, 2003; Laing 1993: 145-47; McIntosh, Samuels and Benskin 1986: I. 25, 153, III. 171 (LP 7440 Herefords.); Cartlidge 1996, 1997, 1998; Fletcher 1999.

London, British Library, Royal MS 14 C. vii, f. 64r (formerly 56, 106 and 53)
Matthew Paris, *Historia Anglorum* (written *c.* 1250–5)
reduced to 63%

33

London, British Library, Cotton MS Caligula A. ix, f. 159r
Laȝamon, *Brut*, ll. 13317-46
Gothic *litera textualis semiquadrata formata*, s. xiii^{2}

TRANSCRIPTION

pet(r)eius

–[1]petreius ihaten . hæh mon of
Rome ∶ mid six þusend kem⟨-⟩
pen . þan Romanisce to helpe(n).
And mid muchelie[3] strenðe ∶
Leopen to þan brutten. And
lute heo þer nomen ∶ Ah mo
monie heo þer sloȝen . Brut⟨-⟩
tes to wude heolde heolden ∶
þa oðere æfter wenden . ⁊
þa Bruttes a uoten ∶ uæste[-n]
aȝan stoden . And þa Roma⟨-⟩
nisce fuhte ridende And
Bruttes heom to heolden ∶ ⁊
sloȝen hors[5] heore . ⁊ monie
þer nomen ∶ And i þene wude
droȝen-] .[6] þa iwræð Petreius
wrað ∶ þat his wes þa wur⟨-⟩
se þer . And he mid his uer⟨-⟩
de ∶ from þan wude wende .
And Bruttes heom to buȝen ∶
And biæften heom sloȝe(n) . þa
Bruttuttes weoren ut of [-f][8]
wude ∶ iȝein to þan felde . þa
atstoden romleoden ∶ mid ræ-
ȝe strenȝe . þa bigon þat muchele fiht ∶ þer ueollen eorl⟨-⟩
les ⁊ moni god cnih[9] . þer ueollen a dæi ∶ fiften þusend . A-
ðelere monnen ∶ ær hit weore æfen . þer he finde(n) mihte ∶
þe his main wolde fondien .

hond aȝan honde ∶ strongne \\aȝei(n) str[[ ]]//[2]
sceld aȝein scelde∶ scalkes þer
ueollen . Vrnen þa streten ∶
Mid blodestræmen . Leien
ȝeond þan ueldes ∶ Goldfaȝe
sceldes .[4] Al þene dæi longe ∶
heo heolden þat feht stron⟨-⟩
ge. petreius an his halue ∶ his
folc heold tosomne. þa iwræð
sone ∶ þat Bruttes hafden þat
wurse . Þat isæh þe eorl heȝe∶
of oxeneuorde . Beof wæs Ihæ-
ten ∶ hæh Bruttisc mon . þat
a nare wise(n) ∶ ne mihte hit i-
wurðen . þat Bruttes ne m[u>o]\\ste(n) //
[-te(n)][7] reosen ∶ Buten heo ræd ha-
ueden . þa eorl þa cleopede ∶ cnih⟨-⟩
tes aðele . Of þan alre Bezste(n) ∶
Of alle þan Brutten . And of
þan kennesten ∶ þe þer quike
weoren . And tuhte hine ut
a þan felde ∶ A neoste þere fer⟨-⟩
de . And þus him iseide ∶ an-
heorte him wes unneðe . cnihtes hercnieð nu to me ∶ drih⟨-⟩
ten us helpe . we beoð hidere
icumen ∶ and þis feht habb\\eoð//
undernumen . Buten arðu⟨-⟩
res rede ∶ þe is ure hexte . ȝif
us oht ilimpeð ∶ we him þa
bet likieð . And ȝif us ilim⟨-⟩

The writing is below the top ruled line. This is a fully developed Gothic script, close and solid, with many bitings. There are bold lozenges at the tops of minims, but at the bottoms they are less marked. Even so, the minim feet not infrequently have serifs like those along the top of the script line. The outer margin is clearly heavily cropped. The Gothic round word-final **s** is sometimes used (see 'petreius', l. 16a, and compare 'petreius', l. 1a), but initial **v** appears once only on the page ('Vrnen', l. 3b), where it may function as a capital. Note the retention of: both **þ** and **ð**, in good calligraphic distribution; **ȝ** alongside **g**; but not **ƿ**. The **æ** may be archaistic, because by this time the digraph is scarcely used; in both **æ** and **ð** a deliberately made diamond-shaped attachment is added to the right of **a** and **d** respectively. Round **r** appears after **b** (ll. 10a, 13a, 20a, 22a, 10b, etc.) as well as **o** ('eorl', ll. 26a, 11b). The words are well spaced, but prepositions may be attached to the following word (e.g. 'a uoten', l. 10a, 'a dæi', l. 28a, 'A neoste', l. 22b). Thus the hyphen, which is in any case used inconsistently, can follow a proposition ('an', l. 23b). The text is pointed as verse: the *punctus elevatus* after the first

[1] The passage is cancelled; its repetition may have been discovered very late.
[2] End of correction lost in trimming of page.
[3] For 'muchelre'?
[4] A new section is indicated in the margin between the columns.
[5] The transposition marks are followed in this transcription.
[6] The cancelled passage ends here.
[7] These letters are subpuncted.
[8] Letter subpuncted.
[9] For 'cniht'.

Petreius ihaten. þah mon of Rome. mid six þusend kempen. þan Romanisce to helpe. And mid muchelen strengðe. Leopen to þan Brutten. and luþe heo þer nomen. ah monie heo þer slozen. Bruttes to wude heolde heolden. þa oðere æfter wenden. ⁊ þa Bruttes anoten. na æften azan stoden. And þa Romanisce fuhte rideinde. and Bruttes heom to heolden. ⁊ hors slozen heore. ⁊ monie þer nomen. And ilene wende drozen. þa iwrað Petreius wrað. þat his weg þa wurse þer. And he mid his uerde. from þan wude wende. And Bruttes heom to buzen. and bi æften heom sloze. þa Bruttes weoren ut of þ wude. izein to þan felde. þa æt stoden rom leoden. mid rūze strenze. þa bi gon þat muchele fiht. þer neollen eorlles ⁊ mon god cniht. þer neollen aðen. fiften þusend. aðelere monnen. ær hit weore æfen. þer he finde mihte. þe his main wolde fondien.

hond azan honde. strongne azein stre seld azein seelde. scalkes þer neollen. urnen þa stretes. and blode streamen. leien zeond þan ueldes. gold fæze scelden. Al þene dæi longe. heo heolden þat feht stronge. Petreius an his halue. his folc heold to somne. þa iwrað sone. þat Bruttes hafden þat wurse. Þat isah þe eorl hæze. of Oxeneuorde. Beof was ihatten. þah Brutisc mon. þat a nare wise. ne mihte hit iwurðen. þat Bruttes ne mosten reosen. buten heo ræd haneden. þa eorl þa cleopede. cnihtes aðele. Of þan alre beste. Of alle þan Brutten. And of þan kenneste. þe þer quike weoren. And tuhte hine ut a þan felde. anoxe þere ferde. And þus him iseide. an heorte him wes unneðe. cnihtes hereneð nu to me. duhten us helpe. we beoð inðere icumen. And þis feht habbeð under nimen. buten ardinges rede. þe is ure herte. zif us oht ilimpeð. we him þa ber likieð. and zif us ilim

Plate 33 – actual size

half-line; the point to mark end-line. The first letters of half-lines are generally touched with red, as are some other capitals, particularly proper names. The use of abbreviation is restrained: on this page only the Tironian sign (still unbarred) and the overline for *m* or *n*. This is a professional piece of work, from an assured scribe who did not feel constrained to follow the spellings of his exemplar, as is clear from a comparison of the cancelled passage with the ending of the previous page, coincidentally the end also of the previous quire. Some idea of the degree of correction needed may be had from the cancel, which has not been fully emended (e.g. 'muchlie', l. 4a, 'mo' without expunctuation, l. 6a, the repeated 'heolde heolden', l. 8a, missing punctuation [and half-line?] in l. 12a). The scribe keeps tidily to the right-hand side of the columns, perhaps choosing even to supply and subpunct 'f', l. 22a, as a line-filler. Unfortunately the subsequent painstaking correction of his work can disrupt this cleanliness of layout.

The opening of Laȝamon's *Brut*, written by the manuscript's first scribe, contains its only miniature, the historiated initial 'A' (see p. 153 opposite).

CONTEXTS

Laȝamon in the Caligula preface says he lived at Areley Kings, some ten or twelve miles from Worcester, which is advanced as the likely place of origin. The *Brut* is followed by shorter English and Anglo-Norman pieces, some shared with Jesus 29 (see pl. 32). There is no clear evidence of how this manuscript entered the Cotton collection. Entered the British Museum with the Cotton Collection in 1753.

SIZE

214 × 152 mm (155 × 116 mm).

BIBLIOGRAPHY

Pr. Madden 1847; Brook and Leslie 1963, 1978.
Disc. Wright 1960[1]: pls 6, 7; Ker 1963; Stanley 1969; Brook 1972; Laing 1993: 69-70; Roberts 1994; Weinberg 1994, 2002; Bryan 1999: 183-90; Scahill 2001; Dance 2002; Tite 2003: 114.

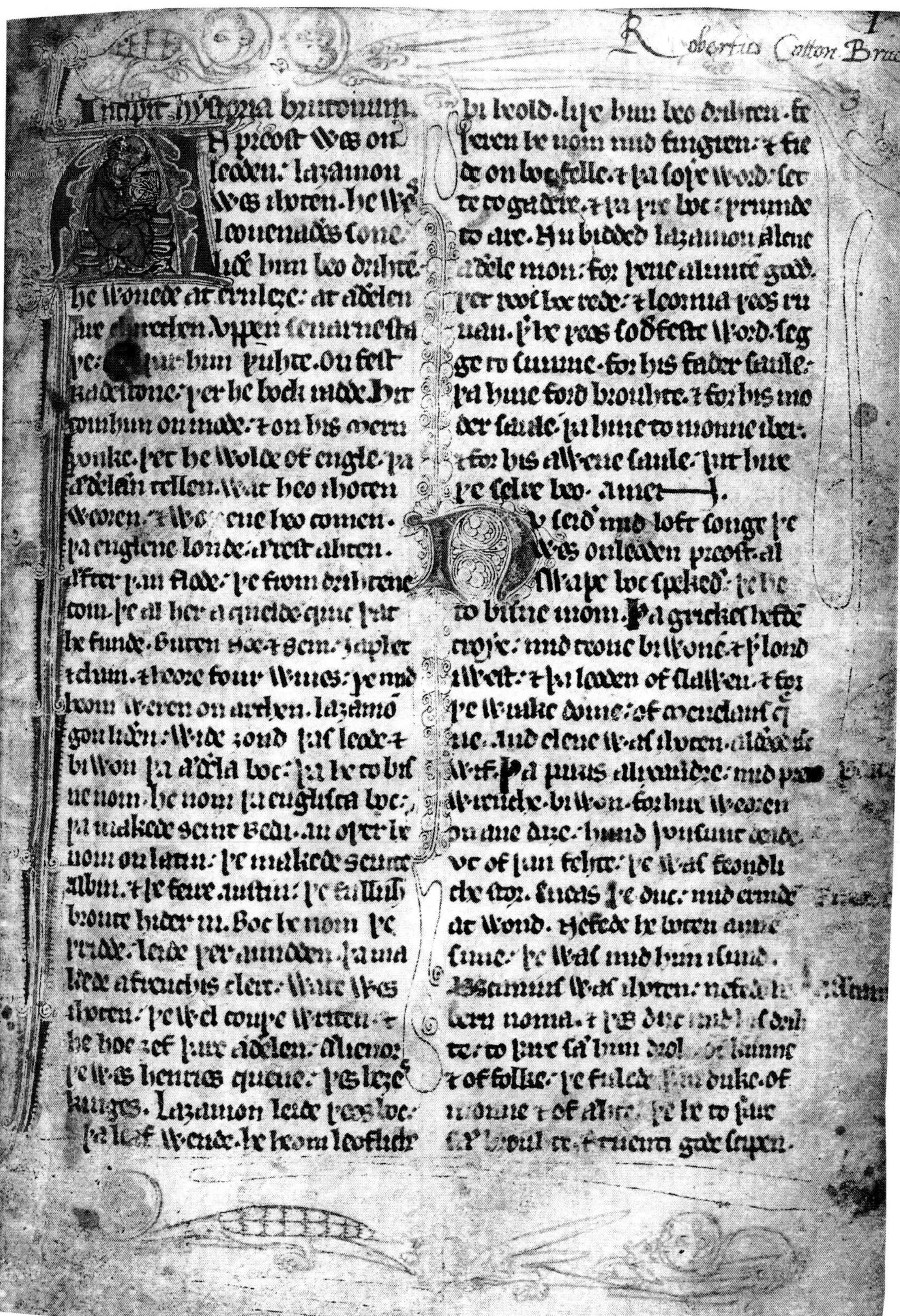

London, British Library, Cotton MS Caligula A. ix, f. 1r
Laȝamon, *Brut*, ll. 1–51
actual size

34

London, British Library, Arundel MS 292, f. 6r
Bestiary, ll. 161-99
Gothic *litera textualis rotunda media*, s. xiii ex.

TRANSCRIPTION

aȝen . caue ȝe haueð to crepen in . ðat wint(er) hire ne
derie . Mete i(n) hire hule ðat[1] . ðat ȝe muȝe bi liuen̄ . ðus
ȝe tileð ðar wiles ȝe time haueð . so it her telleð. oc
finde ȝe ðe wete . corn[2] ðat hire qwemeð . Al ȝe forleteð
ðis oðer seð[3] ðat ic er seide . Ne bit ȝe nowt de barlic beren
abuten . oc suneð it ⁊ sakeð forð . so it same were . ȝet is
wund(er) of ðis wirm . more ðanne man weneð . ðe corn ðat ȝe
to caue bereð . Al ȝet bit otwinne . ðat it ne forwurðe . ne
waxe hire fro . er ȝe it eten wille . *Significacio* . ~~~~~~~
Ðe mire muneð us mete to tilen . Long liuenoðe ðis little wile . ðe we on ðis werld wunen . for ðanne we ofwenden .
ðanne is ure wint(er) . we sulen hung(er) hauen . ⁊ harde sures .
buten we ben war here . do we forði . so doð ðis der . ðanne be
we derue . On ðat dai ðat dom sal ben . ðat it ne us harde
rewe . seke we ure liues fod . ðat we ben siker ðere . so ðis wirm
in wint(er) is ðan ȝe ne tileð nu(m)more . ðe mire suneð ðe barlic
ðanne ȝe fint te wete . ðe olde laȝe we oȝen to sunen . ðe newe
we hauen mote(n) . ðe corn ðat ȝe to caue bereð . all ȝe it bit
otwinne . ðe laȝe us lereð to don god . ⁊ forbedeð us sinne . It
ben[4] us ebriche[5] bodes . ⁊ bekned euelike . It fet ðe licham ⁊ te
gost . oc nowt o ȝeuelike . vre louerd c(r)ist it lene us ðat [-his][6]
his laȝe us fede. nu ⁊ o domes dei . ⁊ tanne we[7] hauen nede .
Ðe hert haueð kindes two . ⁊ forbisnes oc al so . *Natura cerui* .
ðus it is on boke set . ðat man clepeð fisiologet . He draȝeð
ðe neddre of de ston . ðurȝ his nese up onon . of ðe stoc er
of ðe ston . for it wile ðerunder gon . ⁊ sweleð it wel swiðe .
ðerof him brinneð siðen . of ðat attrie ðing . wiðinnen he

Biting is restrained, and there is little lateral compression in this hand. Overall the impression is of a *rotunda* script: some attention is given to minims, but the loops and forking of ascenders are more typical of documentary scripts. Round **u** is general, with **v** shape used once only, after a point and tipped with colour ('vre', l. 21) as against eight instances of word-initial **u** ('us', ll. 10, 14, 19, 19, 20, 21, 22; 'ure', ll. 12, 15; 'up', l. 25). Note **qw** in 'qwemeð', l. 4, a feature more of later than earlier East Anglian manuscripts. Ligatures of **st** are frequent, e.g. 'gost', l. 21. Unusually for so late a hand, the scribe has chosen to use **ð** rather than **þ**; and **d** sometimes appears where **ð** might be expected (e.g. 'de', ll. 5, 25, 'bekned', l. 20). The three-stroke open-topped **ƿ**, used throughout and represented by **w** in the transcription, is in no danger of being read as **þ**. There are two distinct forms of **g**: with cross-stroke from top to right, transcribed as **g**, and without, transcribed as **ȝ**. Initially **h** is unstable ('euelike', l. 20), and absent in many spelling simplifications ('wiles', l. 3, 'wete', l. 4; 'suneð', l. 6, 'sakeð', l. 6, 'same', l. 6, 'sures', l. 12, etc.). Note East Anglian 'ȝe' for 'she'; and the contraction 'ȝet', l. 8, for 'she it'. Assimilations include: 'fint te', l. 17, and '⁊ te', l. 20, '⁊ tanne', l. 22. Although verse, the text is written continuously, with points marking out phrases for the most part co-terminous with verse units. The poet is experimental in the metres used, not to say eclectic, to the distress of modern editors. Overall the layout is careful, with rubrication both of Latin headings and following space-fillers (italicized in the transcript) and of most letters after points. Word division is on the whole well

[1] Editors often argue for the mistaken duplication of the first 'ðat', but it may be understood as for 'so that': 'so that she can live on that'.
[2] The punctuation divides what may be a compound: 'a grain of wheat'.
[3] May not be **ð**, but round **d** crossed by final stroke of **e**.
[4] Often emended to 'bet' in the meaning 'offers'.
[5] Often emended to 'e[rðl]iche'. Otherwise to be understood as 'Hebrew'.
[6] Note 'his' was written twice.
[7] On erasure.

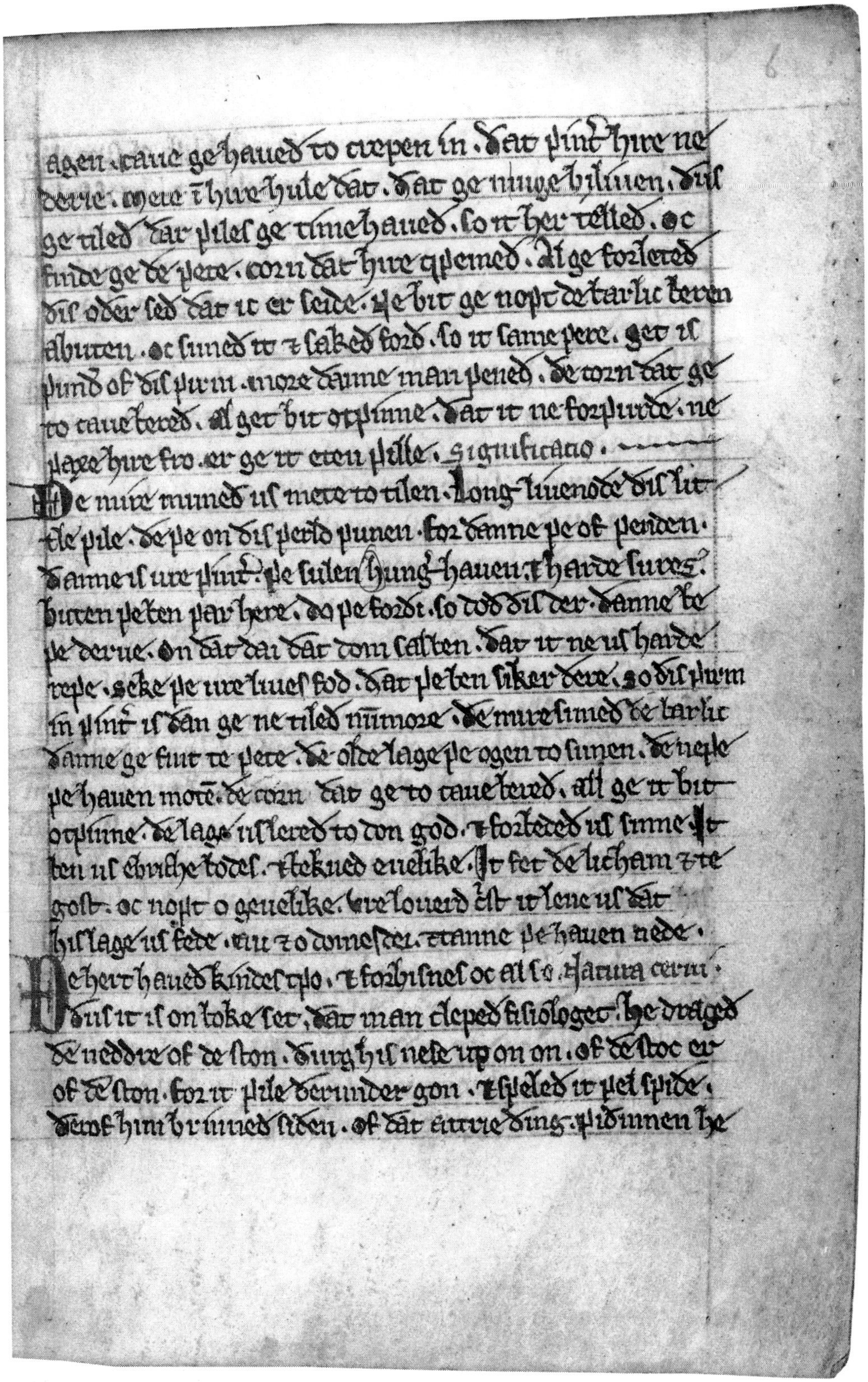

agen. ðanne ge haueð to crepen in. ðat ƿint hire ne derie. mete ⁊ hire hule ðat. ðat ge muge biliuen. ðus ge tileð ðar ƿiles ge time haueð. so it her telleð. oc finde ge ðe ƿere. corn ðat hire cƿemeð. al ge forleteð ðis oðer sed ðat ic er seide. ne bit ge nogt ðe barlic beren abuten. oc suneð it ⁊ sakeð forð. so it same ƿere. get is ƿund of ðis ƿirm. more ðanne man ƿeneð. ðe corn ðat ge to caue bereð. al get bit otƿinne. ðat it ne forƿurðe. ne ƿexe hire fro. er ge it eten ƿille. Significacio.

ðe mire muneð us mete to tilen. long liueneðe ðis little ƿile. ðe ƿe on ðis ƿerld ƿunen. for ðanne ƿe of ƿenden. ðanne is ure ƿint. ƿe sulen hung hauen. ⁊ harde sures. buten ƿe ƿar here. do ƿe forði. so doð ðis der. ðanne be ƿe derue. on ðat dai ðat dom sal ben. ðat it ne us harde reƿe. seke ƿe ure liues fod. ðat ƿe ben siker ðere. so ðis ƿirm in ƿint is ðan ge ne tileð numore. ðe mire suneð ðe barlic ðanne ge fint te ƿete. ðe olde lage ƿe ogen to sunen. ðe neƿe ƿe hauen more. ðe corn ðat ge to caue bereð. all ge it bit otƿinne. ðe lage us lereð to don god. ⁊ forbedeð us sinne. It ben us erðliche bodes. ⁊ eked euelike. It fet ðe licham ⁊ te gost. oc nogt o geneliche. ure louerd crist it leue us ðat his lage us fede. nu ⁊ o domesdei. ⁊ ðanne ƿe hauen nede.

ðe hert haueð kindes tƿo. ⁊ forbisnes oc al so. Natura cerui. ðus it is on boke set. ðat man clepeð fisiologet. he draggeð ðe neddre of ðe ston. ðurg his nese up on on. of ðe stoc er of ðe ston. for it ƿile ðerunder gon. ⁊ sƿoleð it ƿel sƿiðe. ðerof him brinneð siðen. of ðat attrie ðing. ƿidinnen he

Plate 34 – actual size

thought out, but not 'wete . corn', l. 4. Abbreviations: the crossed Tironian sign (the shape of the second instance in l. 22 is a form found from late in the thirteenth century); overline for *m* or *n* (as 'i(n), l. 2; 'nu(m)more', l. 16, etc.) and ʼ for *er* (see 'wint(er), ll. 1, 16, 'wund(er)', l. 7, etc.); the space-saving superscript vowel of 'c(r)ist', l. 21.

CONTEXTS

From a trilingual manuscript, the English suggesting a west Norfolk scribe. Probably written shortly after the 1272 fire in which Norwich Cathedral Priory lost its book collection; has Norwich Cathedral Priory press-mark of *c.* 1300 on ff. 3r and 114v. Owned by Thomas Howard, earl of Arundel in the seventeenth century, and given by his grandson Henry Howard to the Royal Society (stamp on f. 3v) in 1667. Among the Arundel books transferred to the British Museum in 1831.

SIZE

205 × 137 mm (*c.* 152 × 103 mm).

BIBLIOGRAPHY

Pr. Wirtjes 1991: 8-9 (ll. 161-199).
Disc. Ker 1949[1]; Wright 1960[1]: pl. 8; Gumbert and Vermeer 1971; McIntosh, Samuels and Benskin 1986: I. 25; Laing 1993: 67-68.

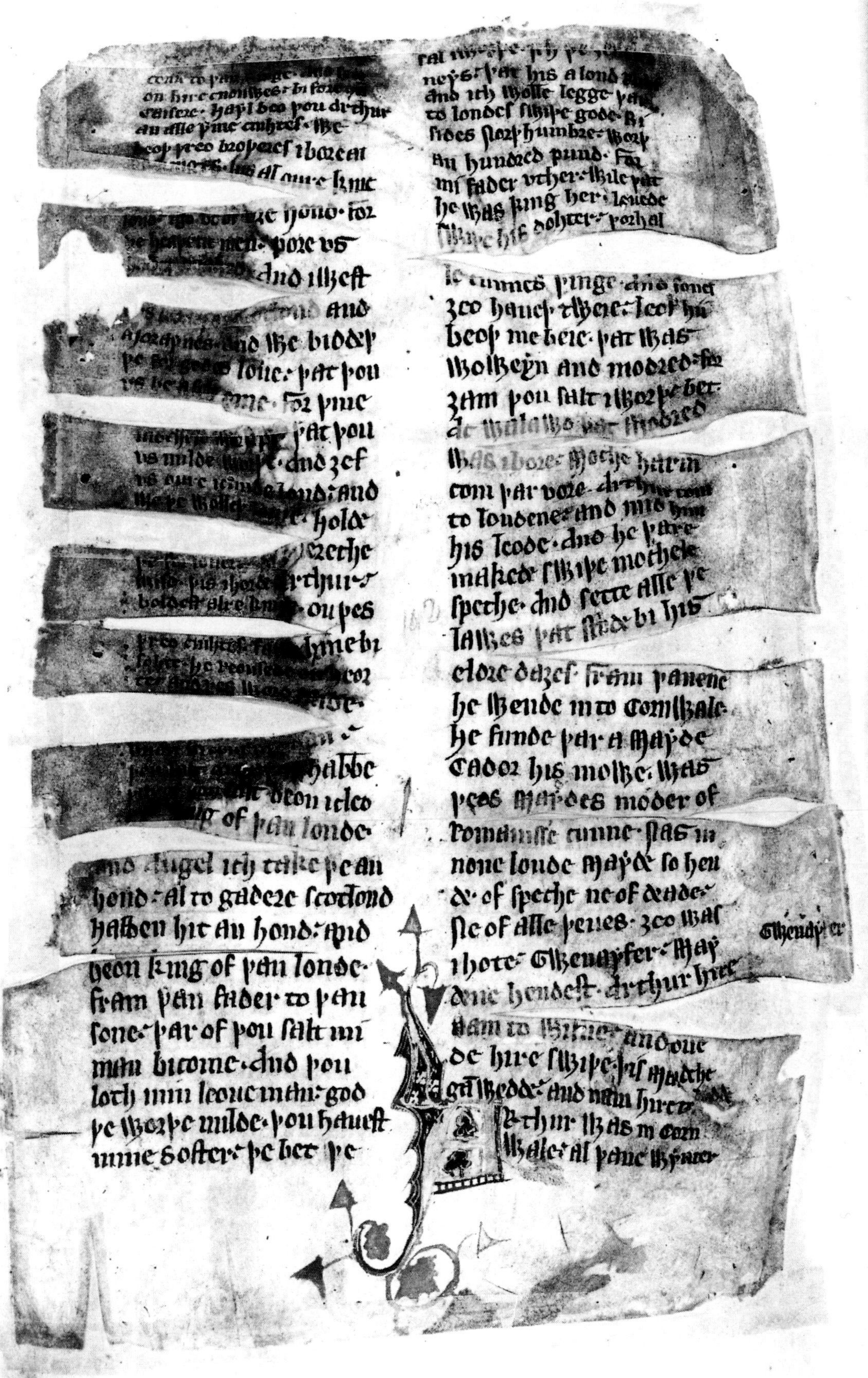

London, British Library, Cotton MS Otho C. xiii, f. 102r
Laȝamon, *Brut*, paralleling ll. 11050–101 of the Caligula version
actual size

35

Oxford, Bodleian Library, Laud Misc. MS 108, f. 219r
Havelock, ll. 2887-975
Gothic *littera textualis semiquadrata formata*, s. xiv[1]

TRANSCRIPTION

Ne of þe spusing seyen nay
But spusede þat ilke day
þat spusinge was god time maked
for it ne were neuere clad ne naked
In a þede samened two
þat cam togidere liuede so
So þey dide al here liue
he geten same(n) sones fiue
þat were þe beste me(n) at nede
þat mouthe ride(n) on ani stede
hwan gu(n)nild was to cestre brouth
hauelok þe gode ne forgat nouth[1]
Bertra(m) þat was þe erles kok
þat he ne dide calle(n) ok
And seyde frend so god me rede
Nu shaltu haue riche mede .
for wissing and þi gode dede
þat tu me dides in ful gret nede
for þa(n)ne y yede in mi cuuel
And ich ne haue bred ne sowel
Ne y ne hauede no catel
þou feddes and claddes me ful wel
haue nu forþi of cornwayle
þe erldom il del withuten fayle
And al þe lond þat godrich held
Boþe in towne and ek in feld
And þerto wile ich þat þu spuse
And fayre bring hire until huse
Grimes douther leuiue þe hende
for þider shal she with þe wende
hire semes curteys for to be
for she is fayr so flour on tre
þe heu is swilk in hire ler
So þe rose in roser
Hwan it is fayr sprad ut newe
Ageyn þe su(n)ne brith and lewe
And girde him sone with þe swerd
Of þe erldom biforn his ferd
And with his hond he made hi(m) knith
And yaf him armes for þat was rith
And dide him þere sone wedde
Hire þat was ful swete in bedde
After þat he spused wore
   wolde þe erl nouth dwelle þore
But sone na(m) until his [-his][7] lond
And seysed it al in his [l>h]ond
And liuede þeri(n)ne he and his wif
An hundred winter in god lif
f ^{ua} or he saw þat he ^{cat}
And gaten mani childre(n) samen
And liueden ay in blisse and game(n)
hwa(n) þe maydens were spused boþe
hauelok anon bigan [-to]`ful′ rathe
his densche men to feste wel
wit riche landes and catel
So þat he weren alle riche
for he was large and nouth chinche[2]
þerafter sone with his here
   for he to lundone forto bere
Corune so þat it sawe
henglishe ant denshe heye and lowe
hwou he it bar with mikel pride
For his barnage þat was unride
þe feste of his corunig[3]
   laste[4] with gret ioying
fourti dawes and sumdel mo
þo bigu(n)nen þe denshe to go
Vnto þe king to aske leue
And he ne wolde hem nouth g(r)eue
for he saw þat he woren yare
Into denemark for to fare
But gaf hem leue sone anon
And bitauhte hem seint Iohan
And bad ubbe his iustise
þat he sholde on ilke wise
denemark yeme and gete so
þat no pleynte come him to
Hwa(n) he ``wore′′ parted alle samen[-t]
   hauelok bilefte wit ioie and game(n)
In engelond and was þe[t>r]i(n)ne
Sixti winter king with winne
And goldeboru quen þat i wene
So mikel loue was hem bitwene
þat al þe werd spak of hem two
he louede hire and she him so
þat neyþer oþe[5] mithe be
fro oþer ne no ioie se
But yf he were togidede[6] boþe
Neuere yete ne were(n) he wroþe
for here loue was ay newe

[1] Did the scribe mistakenly tick and then attempt to cancel marking an *i*?
[2] Rhyme indicates earlier form 'chiche' needed here.
[3] For 'coruni⟨n⟩g'.
[4] Metre suggests need for some such emendation as 'Laste⟨de⟩'.
[5] For 'oþe⟨r⟩'.
[6] Mistake for 'togide⟨r⟩e'.
[7] Dittographed second 'his' is subpuncted.

Ne of ye spusing seyen nay
But spusede yat ilke day
Yat spusinge was god time maked
For it ne were neuere clad ne naked
In a yede samened two
Yat cam to gidere liuede so
So yey dide al here liue
He geten samen sones fiue
Yat were ye beste men at nede
Yat mouthe riden on ani stede
Hwan gunnild was to grimesbi brouth
Hauelok ye gode ne forgat nouth
Bertram yat was ye erles kok
Yat he ne dide callen ok
And seyde frend so god me rede
Nu shaltu haue riche mede
For wissing and yi gode dede
Yat tu me dides in ful gret nede
For yanne y yede in mi cuuel
And ich ne haue bred ne sowel
Ne y ne hauede no catel
You feddest and claddest me ful wel
Haue nu foryi of cornwayle
Ye erldom ilk del withuten fayle
And al ye lond yat godrich held
Boye in towne and ek in feld
And yer to wile ich yat yu spuse
And fayre bring hire un til huse
Grimes douther leuiue ye hende
For yider shal she with ye wende
Hire semes curteys forto be
For she is fayr so flour on tre
Ye heu is swilk in hire ler
So ye rose in roser
Hwan it is fayr sprad ut newe
Ageyn ye sunne brith and lewe
And girde him sone with ye swerd
Of ye erldom biforn his ferd
And with his hond he made him knith
And yaf him armes for yat was rith
And dide him yere sone wedde
Hire yat was ful swete in bedde
After yat he spused wore
Wolde ye erl nouth dwelle yore
But sone nam until his lond

And seysed it al in his hond
And liuede yer inne he and his wif
An hundred winter in god lif
For he saw yat he cam
And geten mani children samen
And liueden ay in blisse and game
Hwan ye maydens were spused boye
Hauelok anon bigan ful rathe
His denshe men to feste wel
Wit riche landes and catel
So yat he weren alle riche
For he was large and nouth chinche
Yer after sone with his here
For he to lundone forto bere
Corune so yat it sawe
Henglishe ant denshe heye and lowe
Hwou he it bar with mikel pride
For his barnage yat was unride
Ye feste of his coruning
Laste with gret ioying
Fourti dawes and sumdel mo
Yo bigunnen ye denshe to go
Unto ye king to aske leue
And he ne wolde hem nouth greue
For he saw yat he woren yare
Into denemark for to fare
But gaf hem leue sone anon
And bitauhte hem seint Iohan
And bad ubbe his iustise
Yat he sholde on ilke wise
Denemark yeme and gete so
Yat no pleynte come him to
Hwan he parted alle samen wore
Hauelok bilefte wit ioie and game
In engelond and was yer inne
Sixti winter king with winne
And goldeboru quen yat i wene
So mikel loue was hem bitwene
Yat al ye werd spak of hem two
He louede hire and she him so
Yat neyyer oye mithe be
Fro oyer ne no ioie se
But yf he were togidere boye
Neuere yete ne were he wroye
For here loue was ay newe

Plate 35 – reduced to 85%

Fusions are restrained, which makes it easier to read a small-module Gothic script. Round **s** appears infrequently, in word final position only. Minims are made with more attention to the top than always to the foot: single **i** generally has a tick; **n** and **u** are not always distinct. The **ȝ** is not used. **þ** appears mostly at the beginning of words, but on this page also within the common words 'Boþe', l. 26a, 'boþe', ll. 7b, 43b (rhymed with and perhaps triggering its use in 'wroþe', l. 44b), 'forþi', l. 23a, 'neyþer oþe', l. 41b, 'oþer', l. 42b). The sequence **th** is hardworking, in 'rathe', l. 8b, 'with', ll. 30a, 37a, 39a, 13b, 17b, 20b, 36b, 'withuten', l. 24a, and, whereas -**ȝ(h)t**- or -**ct**- might seem more usual other than in the Norfolk area, in 'mouthe', l. 10a, 'brouth', l. 11a, 'nouth', ll. 12a, 44a, 12b, 24b, 'douther', l. 29a, 'brith', l. 36a, 'knith', l. 39a, 'rith', l. 40a, 'mithe', l. 41b. The **y** generally has a dot, whether in a form quite similar to **þ** (see 'seyde', l. 15a) or with the descender turning to the right (as 'y yede', l. 19a). The handsome layout is marred by cropping, particularly of the top margin. The large initials are blue, with red pen flourishing; the letters set apart at the head of each line lack the touching in red usual up to 208r but patchy thereafter. The most common mark of abbreviation is the overline for **n** ('þeri(n)ne', l. 2b, 'childre(n)', l. 5b, etc.) or **m** ('Bertra(m)', l. 13a, 'hi(m)', l. 39a, 'na(m)', l. 45a). The line through the ascender of 'ek', l. 26a, might be thought to signal -*e*, but compare its use elsewhere, for example in 'riche', l. 16a, where the stroke is otiose. A superscript vowel saves space in 'g(r)eue', l. 24b. At 4b it seems that the scribe's eye slipped (compare 25b), but he saw his mistake in time to place the superscript warning 'ua[ ]cat' ('it is empty', its two syllables separated, effectively to either side of the words written) to the reader. The stroke apparently added to **d** in 'god', l. 3a, may have resulted from the rewriting of 'day' in the line immediately above, and some words are written over erasures (as 'was', l. 40a, 'in god lif', l. 3b. In 'girde', l. 37a, the last three letters are fudged; compare the final -*e* of 'denshe', l. 16b.

CONTEXTS

Internal linguistic evidence points to south Lincolnshire for author and west Norfolk for scribe of ff. 204-228r, which contain the romances *Havelok* and *King Horn*, a booklet originally independent of the *South English Legendary* materials with which it is bound. The manuscript belonged *c.* 1450-75 to 'Henrico Perueys Testantib(us) Joh(ann)i Rede Presbit(ero) Will(el)mo Rotheley ⁊ Aliis' (f. 238v, where the owner's name is over an erasure). Perueys and Rotheley were London merchants. In Archbishop Laud's library by 1633 (f. 1r has his mark and old pressmark K 60). Given to the Bodleian Library by Archbishop Laud in 1635.

SIZE

c. 277 × 175 mm (230 × 130 mm).

BIBLIOGRAPHY

Pr. Smithers 1987: 79-81 (ll. 2887-2975).
Disc. SC 1486; Görlach 1974: 88-90; Guddat-Figge 1976: no. 87; McIntosh 1976; McIntosh, Samuels and Benskin 1986: I. 25; Laing 1993: 136-37.

VII The Gothic system of scripts: Anglicana

From late in the thirteenth century scribes were trying to find a book hand that was not difficult to write on a small scale. At this time the tightly woven Gothic *textualis* was still the only alternative to a documentary hand, but English scribes seem to have happened upon a way of writing that soon became their ordinary book hand. Late in the twelfth century a semicursive Protogothic had been developing in England into a full-blown *cursiva* script, with its letters linked, loops, and other decorative embellishments, as a business hand (Gothic *littera cursiva anglicana documentaria*). From it emerges Anglicana,[1] first in England, but later as a script local to Britain and extending also into northern France.[2] Yet it was known as a distinctively English script and indeed a Joan Walkyngham, who died in 1346, was aware of its Englishness, for her will notes 'quemdam librum scriptum littera Anglicana'.[3] The dates for usage are from the thirteenth century to the sixteenth century,[4] and even into the eighteenth century for some specialized purposes. About 1375 a new script, termed Secretary and originating in Italy, came from France into use in England, providing competition for Anglicana. Like Anglicana, this too was at first a documentary script (Gothic *littera cursiva* Secretary *documentaria*). Anglicana, like the incoming competing Secretary script, arises from within the Gothic system of scripts. Given their common ultimate origins, the two scripts share many letter-forms. A small number of features is particularly helpful for distinguishing an Anglicana from a Secretary hand: the two-compartment Anglicana **a**; both the pointed **e** and the cursive variety with reversed ductus; the tight **g**, sometimes described as shaped like the numeral 8, which looks rather like a pair of spectacles seen sideways on; the long **r**, descending below the line; the sigma-shaped **s** that looks a little like the numeral **6**; **w** with its two long initial strokes completed by bows; and **x** made with two separate strokes. Also, the Tironian sign continued in use in Anglicana.

The grading terms, introduced already in Section VI, are those put forward by Julian Brown.[5] They are best applied to *cursiva* scripts in relation to the treatment of minims. In both *media* and *currens* scripts minims are linked (the pen is not lifted), but *currens* is below average in both accuracy and style. In *formata* grades the pen is lifted between minims and the style is generally more elaborate than in *media*. The description *cursiva formata hybrida*, which comes under the influence of *textualis*, is used for the highest grade of *cursiva*.[6] Table 3 shows how these terms relate to and build on the descriptions developed by Malcolm Parkes.[7] The essential difference is in the value given the grading term *formata*.[8] For Parkes, the hand shown in pl. 36 is 'a somewhat half-hearted attempt to produce Anglicana Formata', and elsewhere in the manuscript 'the scribe reverts to the less formal version of the script'.[9] Here too, using Brown's grading terms, it is *formata*, and two lower grades cater for a greater degree of differentiation within considerably less whole-hearted attempts at a decent Anglicana script.

Table 3. littera … cursiva anglicana (ss. xiii[1] – xviii)

Parkes	*Brown*
bastard anglicana	*cursiva anglicana formata hybrida*
anglicana formata	*cursiva anglicana formata*
anglicana	*cursiva anglicana media*
	cursiva anglicana currens

Pl. 36 is from a manuscript that Ker describes as written at a critical moment in the history of script.[10] This hand, so well known to readers of the Harley Lyrics manuscript, is an average sample of the new book script, and it provides an excellent introduction to Anglicana book hands (or Gothic *littera cursiva anglicana*). We do not know the scribe's name, but we know that he lived and worked in the area about Leominster and Ludlow from the second decade of the fourteenth

[1] The term has been used in script description from the 1960s, for example in Doyle and Pace 1968: 23. See Parkes 1979, p. xvi, fn. 7.

[2] Derolez (2003: 133-34), in his discussion of a wider European category he calls Cursiva Antiquior, points out that only Anglicana within this grouping, 'precocious and long lasting' and 'a highly idiosyncratic script', developed into 'a canonical book script'.

[3] Friedman 1995: 12.

[4] Parkes [1969] 1979: xvi identifies Oxford, Bodleian Library, Bodley 406, 'copied in 1291', as the earliest example of a book written in Anglicana. Derolez 2003: 140 points to an example in a manuscript datable to *c.* 1264, Oxford, Bodley 91 (Watson 1984: pl. 116), a script certainly tending that way.

[5] Discussed in his Lyell lectures delivered at Oxford in 1977 and widely disseminated in his seminars and lectures.

[6] The grade is similar to the *bastard anglicana* of Parkes (1969); compare Lieftinck's *cursiva bastarda* (1954: 29) or *lettre bourguinonne* (1964: I. xv).

[7] Parkes 1969, 1979.

[8] See further the forthcoming selection from T.J. Brown's writings related to the description of scripts (ed. M.P. Brown and J. Roberts).

[9] Parkes's pl. 1(ii), illustrating f. 134v, is in Brown's terms an example of *cursiva anglicana media/currens.*

[10] Ker 1965: xviii.

century well into the 1340s and that he can be recognized as the scribe of some forty charters as well as of three books.[11] Like Jesus College 29 (pl. 32) and Oxford, Digby 86,[12] also from the Herefordshire area, Harley 2253 contains a wide range of miscellaneous materials, indicating the existence of a flourishing literary culture in the south-west Midlands in the later thirteenth and early fourteenth centuries.[13] Pl. 36 reveals the scribe's documentary training in the marking of the opening of new texts with thick strokes that are lengthened and touched with red. This is a practised hand, skilled in holding steady to a long line of script without ruled lines. Graded *formata*, the formal distribution of **v** and **u** conventional in Gothic scripts is observed, and the pen is lifted between minim strokes so carefully made that **n** and **u** are virtually indistinguishable. Note the distinctive sigma-shaped **s**, essentially a single-stroke Anglicana round **s**. The single-stroke **d** derives from a two-stroke form with the loop turning to the left for increased cursivity. Whereas earlier in his career this scribe had placed forks at the top of some ascenders, loops are now freely used.

By contrast with pl. 36, the script of pl. 40 (Sloane 2593), a small Norfolk songbook from the turn of the fourteenth century, is *media*, being more currently written. There are fewer pen lifts, more abbreviations, and the **e** is the one-stroke cursive form, as yet the looped rather than the round form that had developed by the mid-fourteenth century. Whereas the flat-bottomed **g** of Harley 2253 is made with four strokes, the **g** here is the form more usual in Anglicana. This is the work of a competent writer, whose only Secretary letter-form is the pointed **a**, a more quickly written shape encroaching alongside the two-compartment Anglicana form. Layout is assured, but informal. The dividing lines between stanzas are freehand, and the rhyme braces are roughly drawn. Overall the indications are of an inexpensive book, an *aide memoire* for personal use, made rapidly and without much by way of correction of errors. Although paper was not commonly in use in England for books and pamphlets before the end of the fourteenth century,[14] Sloane 2593 is a small paper manuscript, its leaves now separately mounted. Apparently its scribe's resources did not run to membrane, and he therefore made do with the cheaper alternative, paper, already in use for letters, private correspondence and some local documentary records. East Anglia, the most densely populated and prosperous area of rural England in the later Middle Ages, saw a striking growth of lay literacy, with sustained gentry support for English vernacular writings.[15] Five manuscripts discussed in this book reflect the lively literary tradition of this area (pls 34, 35, 40, 52, 57).

Altogether more consistent is the script of pl. 38 (from Peterhouse 75. I), the first of six pages that give instructions for making an equatory or *equatorium planetarum*.[16] This is a careful rather than a polished performance,[17] and there are only a few current features, for example the occasional use of round **e** at the end of words. Who wrote this English *Equatorie of Planetis* is unknown. Wishful thinking has ascribed both authorship and script to Chaucer, but without convincing proof. The hand seen in pl. 38 is that of the compiler of the manuscript, who probably himself composed this account of how to build an equatory. Indeed, this quire could well once have stood at the head of the compilation,[18] for f. 71r is greatly discoloured. By contrast, pl. 42 is a page from the Ellesmere *Canterbury Tales*, a luxury book widely held to be the most authoritative text for the *Canterbury Tales,* although some prefer the text of the plainer Hengwrt manuscript written by the same scribe, termed the 'B' hand by Doyle and Parkes.[19] The Ellesmere *Canterbury Tales*, more carefully and expensively planned than the Hengwrt compilation, has a greater orthographical consistency. The format is large and the decoration throughout the book is elaborate. A century and a half after its making it was still prized, as is evident from Henry Payne's description of it in his will as 'my Chaucer written in vellum and illumyned w^{t} golde'.[20] The *mise-en-page* is well managed, with capitulum signs keyed to decorated initials in the main text.[21] Yet, by comparison with the apparatus supplied in *Confessio Amantis* manuscripts, the notes seem ad hoc and ill integrated with the text.[22] The earliest extant *Confessio Amantis* manuscripts, Bodleian Library, MS Fairfax 3, makes full and well planned use of an outer column for Latin summaries, notes and speaker markers. In less luxurious copies some of the elements are taken into the text columns: Royal 18 C. xii (see p. 203)[23] manages this more successfully than does Add. 12043, whose scribe gave up supplying summaries and notes

[11] Revard 2000.

[12] See Tschann and Parkes 1996; a page from this manuscript is reproduced on p. 165.

[13] Corrie 2000: 441; see also O'Rourke 2000.

[14] Edwards and Pearsall 1989: 260 note the beginning of the use of paper 'to any extent in the third quarter of the century'. Pamela Robinson tells me that the three earliest datable examples of the use of paper for books and pamphlets in England are from between 1382 and 1414, with 1390 the first firm date, and that two if not all three are from Oxford (Robinson forthcoming).

[15] Beadle 1991.

[16] i.e. an instrument helpful in calculating the positions of the moon and the five planets. The word *equatory* is not in the *OED*; it is recorded by the *MED* as used by Lydgate in the mid-fifteenth century.

[17] The fullest description is by Rand Schmidt 1993: 103-13 especially.

[18] Robinson 1991: 22 points out that it 'would seem to make more sense to have the treatise on the equatorium first'.

[19] Doyle and Parkes 1978. This paper led the way towards a huge increase in the identification of individual scribal hands for the decades to either side of 1400. See for example Mooney 1996 and Blake 1995.

[20] Seymour 1995-97: II. 235.

[21] These are termed 'champie initials' or *littere champide*: see Watson 2003: 22.

[22] Pearsall 1989, 2004.

[23] Both Royal 18 C. xxii (p. 203) and Add. 24194 (p. 187) were written by the early fifteenth-century scribe called 'Δ' by Doyle and Parkes (1978: 206).

shortly after f. 10v (reproduced on p. 221). The notes of the Ellesmere *Canterbury Tales* are sporadic, doubtless the reason why the outer columns were not ruled throughout. It is instructive to see a greater use of abbreviation in these Latin notes than is usual in writing English at this time. Arguments from script have put forward dates in the first decade of the fifteenth century for both Hengwrt and Ellesmere, though the evidence from decoration suggests a possibly earlier date of production for Ellesmere (*c.* 1397 - *c.* 1405) and a date before Chaucer's death for Hengwrt (*c.* 1395 - *c.* 1400).[24] Interestingly, recent work on language suggests both that Hengwrt was made as a text to be read aloud from but Ellesmere for silent reading, and that the scribe worked under Chaucer's supervision at least for Hengwrt.[25] The scribe was perhaps at work in London as early as 1387-88, if the hand of the Mercers' Petition (Kew, National Archives, SC 8/20/997) is his.[26]

The presence of scholarly apparatus seems less surprising in pl. 46 (Harley 674), where the narrower column alongside the main text is ruled in preparation for expected glosses or commentary though this is not forthcoming throughout. The degree of abbreviation in the Latin sources and notes presented in the narrow column is considerably greater than in the opening of the English text. Although the *Cloud of Unknowing*, a work associated with the Carthusian Order, seems to have had a limited circulation,[27] it is accorded a skilled presentation in this manuscript, with some differentiation of scripts according to task: a more formal Anglicana for titles and for the notes a smaller module with the short straight **r** of *textualis rotunda* rather than the long *anglicana* **r** or the round **r** of the main text. The fifteenth century saw a huge expansion in the dissemination of religious literature in English, especially in women's houses, but among men's houses the Carthusians developed an interest in vernacular texts,[28] and these were just the sorts of texts liable to be copied as 'common-profit' books (see p. 229). Even more handsome than Harley 674 is Harley 1197 (pl. 50; the opening of a later copy shown on p. 225 presents a sad contrast), a systematic treatment of the seven capital sins by the Carmelite Richard Lavynham.[29] Lavynham's *Tretis* achieved a far greater currency than his academic work in Latin.[30] The positioning and decoration of large capitals is well designed, many letters are touched in red to help the reader, and Latin citations, clearly underlined in red, are accompanied by source identification. Pl. 41, from an early-fifteenth-century paper manuscript of *Piers Plowman*, is a more modest book, possibly from the London area.[31] Although most early owners of *Piers Plowman* texts seem to have been clerics, the poem was soon to be found in lay hands,[32] gaining a wide audience. Just such a copy might have been owned by William Palmere, rector of St Alphege, Cripplegate, 1397-1400. Interestingly, Palmere left all his books to men, except for 'librum meum vocatum peres plowman'.[33] As with Sloane 2593, the earliest paper manuscript illustrated in this book, the 102 single leaves of Harley 6041 are now mounted on paper guards. The script is a clear and steady *cursiva anglicana media*. The usual Anglicana letter-forms are used, and the initial **s** may be either long (as good calligraphic practice would require) or short. The scribe wrote quickly: the minims are not usually separately made and there are many corrections, but he does not use the cursive round **e** on this page. Space was left for the two-line initial **P** set out into the margin and the title for Passus V is in Gothic *textualis*, a *quadrata* script, somewhat roughly written and therefore also to be graded *media*. Two supplementary plates are from *Piers Plowman* manuscripts, both earlier than this copy and both Anglicana though somewhat higher in grade: British Library, Add. 10574 (p. 177), from the turn of the fourteenth century, in a steady *anglicana formata*, its Latin tags and headings verging on *hybrida* because of the attention given to the head and foot of minims; and University of London, V. 88 (see p. 191), written by Doyle and Parkes hand 'D', coeval with hand 'B' of the Hengwrt and Ellesmere *Canterbury Tales* manuscripts.[34]

As has recently been pointed out, the texts that most people were likely to come across in their daily lives were 'official documents: certificates of good conduct, land-grants, indentures, proclamations, and indulgences'.[35] Overwhelmingly these were in Latin or Anglo-Norman, but John of Langton's agreement to rent land out to Thurstan of Atherton, pl. 44, provides a good example of a land-lease from Lancashire in 1420. The hand is essentially *anglicana*, a decent steady *media* performance from a scribe clearly well accustomed to write such documents. It is interesting to note the choice of the more quickly made Secretary form of **a** as the usual form for this letter, with the Anglicana form serving to mark out names and the beginning of important pieces of information. Pl. 51, from a large folio in paper written by Robert Thornton, is a much more current Anglicana script from the middle of the fifteenth century: the pen is not lifted for minims and the single-stroke **a** with reversed ductus is among the many alternate letter-forms in use. Although the letter-forms are

[24] Scott 1995.

[25] Horobin 2003.

[26] Mooney forthcoming.

[27] Minnis 1984: 70; Gillespie 1989: 322. Hodgson 1982: xvi reports eighteen manuscripts, adding in a footnote a newly found seventeenth-century copy.

[28] Bell 1999: 251.

[29] van Zutphen 1956: xxvii points out that authorship of this text rests on the colophon in Harley 211, f. 46v.

[30] Doyle 1989: 114 points out that the eighteen surviving manuscripts are not confined to East Anglia.

[31] Doyle 1986: 46 suggests a 'line of dissemination' that 'could have run through the London area'.

[32] Wood 1984.

[33] Wood 1984 points out that in three other early wills copies of *Piers Plowman* were left to men.

[34] Doyle and Parkes 1978.

[35] Steiner 2003: 4.

Anglicana, the slope suggests some Secretary influence, as does the angular shape sometimes of **d**. In this manuscript and in British Library Additional MS 31042 Thornton was building up groups for the most part of literary and devotional writings in English, collections that reflect the growing popularity of anthologies in the second half of the fifteenth century.[36] Whereas the miscellanies of the thirteenth and earlier fourteenth centuries gather together English vernacular texts with French and/or Latin works, there is, from the second part of the fourteenth century, a marked growth of collections largely given over to English vernacular writings. Thornton probably spent years begging and borrowing locally the motley materials he shaped into his own volumes, building up sizeable units composed of religious, romance, and miscellaneous texts. He included alliterative poetry in his home-made collections, and but for him we would not know the alliterative *Morte Arthure*, a poem that lends a distinctive quality to some parts of Malory's *Morte.* Alliterative materials do not survive after the first quarter of the fifteenth century in expensive books made in London, nor are they found among the texts copied in a metropolitan context by his near contemporary, John Shirley, for his own use and for use within the Beauchamp household.[37]

Often it is hard to decide between an Anglicana and a Secretary definition. An Anglicana categorization is relatively easy for the St John's *Troilus* (pl. 45). Although the angular appearance of the script suggests Secretary influence and Secretary **s** occurs at the end of words, the scribe otherwise uses the distinctive Anglicana letter-forms. This, like the Corpus *Troilus* (pl. 43) to which textually it is closely related, although making little use of punctuation within the verse line,[38] is a stylish manuscript. Despite the frequent use of the cursive Anglicana **e**, the care taken overall is consistent with a *formata* grading. But sometimes the mix of diagnostic letter-forms is so evenly balanced as to make it necessary to count their relative frequencies. So of two mixed hands, pl. 47 (Douce 335) may be viewed as *anglicana formata* with some Secretary letter-forms (**a**, **g**, **r**, and final **-s** occasional), whereas pl. 48 (Harley 4866) as Secretary *formata* with some *anglicana* alternatives (noteworthy are the **g** and **-s** final). Despite the significant proportion of Secretary letter-forms used as alternatives in the Douce *Master of Game*,[39] there are overall few angular broken strokes in the formation of letters. This, together with the lack of pronounced slope and the absence of horns on letter tops, points towards a mixed hand in which *anglicana* features are well entrenched. Both these mixed script manuscripts are highly formal. The historiated initials of the Douce *Master of Game,* although somewhat plainer than the miniatures of the short text that stands before the *Master of Game* in Cotton Vespasian B. xii (the opening page is reproduced on p. 207), make this an attractive volume. So too, is Harley 4866 (pl. 48), despite the poor quality of its parchment. This manuscript is particularly well known for its single marginal miniature, a portrait of Chaucer, dressed in black, a rosary in his left hand. Pointing beyond the frame to the text where he is memorialized, he has already become the most honoured poet of his age.[40] This Chaucer portrait, endlessly discussed, is thought to share a common model with the Ellesmere painting of Chaucer as pilgrim. Derek Pearsall has suggested that it is possibly the first English non-royal portrait with a claim to be a true likeness.[41]

Many major Middle English texts are written in *anglicana* hands, less often in *anglicana formata* (for example, the Ellesmere Chaucer, pl. 42) than in the *media* grade so well exemplified by the main text hand of pl. 41 (Harley 6041). Sometimes a very sumptuous script deserves singling out as especially even and careful in its letter-forms. Such manuscripts may betray cross-infection as a means of increasing formality, which may be why Julian Brown chose to add *hybrida* almost as an accolade after the grading term *formata.* The text hand of Harley 1197 (pl. 50) is an *anglicana formata hybrida*, verging on *fere-textura* (i.e. 'like' or trying to imitate Gothic *textualis*, in Parkes's terminology this is Bastard Anglicana).[42] In proportions the look is of a *cursiva* script, but the minims are as in *textualis rotunda,* bitings are frequent, and other *textualis* features include the two-compartment **a**, unlooped **d**, the tight form of **g**, short and 2-shaped **r** (the latter general after bows), and final **s**. Harley 2255 too (pl. 49), which incorporates a strong Secretary element, is verging on a *hybrida* grading. The grading of Secretary scripts may be similarly modified by the addition of *hybrida* after *formata.* That comparatively few English vernacular manuscripts attract the description *formata hybrida* reflects the fact that on the whole books in English were given less care and attention by their scribes than were major Latin texts, on which more money was likely to have been spent by those who commissioned them.

[36] See Thompson 1987, Boffey and Thompson 1989, pp. 298-302. Horall 1980 points out that watermark evidence supports the view that Thornton accumulated piles of unbound quires, which were later separated and bound.

[37] A note on Shirley is to be found in the 'People named in the commentaries' index.

[38] Solopova 2001 points to a striking similarity in the use of the virgule in the Hengwrt and Ellesmere *Canterbury Tales* manuscripts, noting that the 'fashion for punctuation' is associated with the ten-syllable line.

[39] Surprisingly little work has been done on this text. Braswell 1984: 343 adds six manuscripts to the earlier total of nineteen. Alexander 1983: 158 notes that in 1421 a scrivener, John Robard of London, was paid for writing twelve books on hunting, asking 'Could these perhaps have been copies of Edward of York's translation of Gaston Febus' hunting book, which had been dedicated to Henry?' It was among the texts copied by Shirley into Add. 16165, the earliest of his compilations (see Connolly 1998: 35-36).

[40] See the discussion by Machan 1992: 284-85.

[41] Pearsall 1994.

[42] See Parkes 1969: pl. 8(ii) for an example.

Oxford, Bodleian Library, MS Digby 86, f. 165r
Dame Siriz
actual size

36

London, British Library, Harley MS 2253, f. 106r
a. 'God þat al þis myhtes may'; b. 'Lustneþ alle a lutel þrowe', ll. 1-18
Gothic *littera cursiva anglicana formata*, s. xiv^{1}

TRANSCRIPTION

¶God þat al þis myhtes may : in heuene ⁊ erþe þy wille ys oo /
ichabbe belosed mony a day : er ant late y be þy foo /
ich wes to wyte ⁊ wiste my lay[1] : longe habbe holde me þer fro /
vol of merci þou art ay : al vngreyþe icham to þe to go /
To go to him þat haþ ous boht : my gode deden bueþ fol smalle /
of þe werkes þat ich ha wroht : þe beste is bittrore þen þe galle
My god ich wiste y nolde hit noht : in folie me wes luef to falle
when y my self haue þourhsoht : y knowe me for þe wrst of alle
God þat de3edest on þe rod[-e][2] : al þis world to forþren ⁊ f[u>y]lle /
for ous þou sheddest þi suete blod[-e] : þ(a)t y ha don me lykeþ ylle
bote er a3eyn þe stiþ y stod[-e] : er ⁊ late loude ant stille
of myne deden fynde y non god : lord of me þou do þy wille
In herte ne myhte y neuer bowe : ne to my kunde louerd drawe /
my meste vo ys my loues trowe : crist ne stod me neuer hawe
Ich holde me vilore þen a gyw[3] : ⁊ y myself wolde bue knowe
Lord merci rewe me now : reyse vp þat ys falle lowe /
God þ(a)t þis world shal hede : þy gode myht þou hast in wolde
on erþe þou come for oure nede : for ous sunful were boht ⁊ solde
when we bueþ dempned after vr dede : a domesday when ryhtes bueþ tolde
when we shule suen þy wounde blede : to speke þenne we bueþ vnbolde
vnbold icham to bidde þe bote : swyþe vnreken ys my réés
þy wille ne welk y ner a fote : to wickede werkes y me chéés
fals y wes in crop ant rote : when y seyde þy lore wes léés /
Iesu c(r)ist þou be mi bote : so boun icham to make my péés
Al vnreken ys my ro : louerd c(r)ist whet shal y say
Of myne deden fynde y non fro : ne noþyng þat y þenke may /
vnwrþ icham to come þe to : y serue þe nouþer nyht ne day /
In þy merci y me do : god þat al þis myhtes may /

¶Lustneþ alle a lutel þrowe	when is lif is hym byreued /
3e þat wolleþ ou selue yknowe	In is rug ⁊ in ys heued
Vnwys þah y be /	he shal foule wormes brede
Ichulle telle ou ase y con	þe fleyhs shal rotie from þe bon
hou holy writ spekeþ of mon	þe senewes vntuen eueruchon
herkneþ nou to me	þe body shal tosye
þe holy mon sayþ in is bok	3e þ(a)t wolleþ þ(a)t soþe ysuen
þ(a)t mon is worm ⁊ wormes kok	vnder g(r)ases þer hue buen
ant wormes he shal vede	byholdeþ wet þer lye

Ker (1965: xviii) describes the hand as 'an average specimen of the admirable kind of writing which English scribes seem to have adopted as their ordinary hand with remarkable suddenness'. Forked ascenders are plain to see in the earlier documents written by this scribe (see the facsimiles in Revard 2000), but not in this sample of his book script. The **a** is made with two strokes. The **g** is not the tight form of later Anglicana, but built elaborately from four strokes and is unusual in having a long flat base. The end-point of long **r** in ligatures joins the next element. The most frequently used form of **s** is the distinctive Anglicana round **s**, made with a single pen stroke and therefore involving little effort (see 'ous' and

[1] On erasure, as is 'y wes', l. 23.
[2] When the scribe came to write 'stod', he erased the last letter from all three rhyming words.
[3] 'Jew', written above by Wanley.

106

Plate 36 – reduced to 79%

'smalle', l. 5). A plain long **s** sometimes appears at the beginning of words and in ligature (as in 'sheddest', l. 10) but more often has a looped descender (see 'sunful', l. 18), getting into position to write the next letter. The starting-point for Anglicana **w** can be seen in 'werkes', l. 6, where two simple bows are completed by a third stroke; and a simplification to two strokes is seen in 'wes', l. 3, 'wyte', l. 3, etc. The distribution of **v** and **u** usual in Gothic scripts is observed; **n** is indistinguishable from **u**; **þ**, in a distinctive form, is retained; and **ȝ** occurs as well as **g**. Initially **h** is unstable ('is', ll. 29b, 30b, 35a, 'ys', l. 30b; and compare 'wet', l. 37b, but 'whet', l. 25) and **f** may be voiced ('vol', l. 4, 'vo', l. 14, 'vede', l. 37a). Some long vowels are written doubled and marked by two **i**-ticks ('réés', l. 21, 'chéés', l. 22, 'léés', l. 23, 'péés', l. 24). Punctuation is light: the capitulum sign marks out the beginning of new texts; capitals or enlarged letters appear often at the outset of lines; the *punctus elevatus* picks out rhymes within the long script lines and the virgule is occasionally used to mark line endings. Word division presents few problems apart from the subject pronoun 'I', where modern editorial choice varies. Thick ascenders, lengthened and touched with colour, are usually restricted to the first line on a page; here they also mark out not just the opening stanza of a new text at l. 29 but continue across the page for the sake of balance. Abbreviations are sparingly used: apart from the Tironian sign, ꝥ for 'þ(at)' in ll. 10, 17, 36a, 35b (× 2), and superscript vowel requiring preceding *r* in 'c(r)ist', ll. 24, 25, 'g(r)ases', l. 36b. This page, the beginning of a new quire, shows some discoloration and wear (e.g. stain mark, perhaps result of a spill, across ll. 1-8; blotchiness of 'ne m', l. 13), as if it had for a time served as the beginning of a booklet.

CONTEXTS

Since the publication of Ker's facsimile volume, much more has been discovered about this scribe, whose hand is to be seen in Ludlow deeds as well as in London, British Library Harley 273 and London, British Library Royal 12 C. xii (Revard 2000). A wrapper used by the scribe, containing accounts (*c.* 1308) from Ardmulghan, co. Meath, and extracts from a Hereford Cathedral ordinal, survives because it was converted into pastedowns; names suggest a west of England household. Samuels ([1984] 1989: 262), argues that 'the evidence for the dialect of the main scribe points clearly to Leominster rather than to Hereford or Ludlow'. Among books of John Batteley bought (1723) for Robert Harley. Entered the British Museum with the Harley Collection in 1753. Known as the Harley Lyrics manuscript, despite miscellaneous range of contents, prose and verse, in English, French, and Latin.

SIZE

293 × 188 mm.

BIBLIOGRAPHY

Pr. (a) Brook 1968 [1948]: 68-69; (b) Furnivall 1901: 511.
Facs. Ker 1965.
Disc. Harl. Cat., Wright 1960[1]: pl. 9; Parkes 1969 (rpt. 1979): pl. 1 (ii); Guddat-Figge 1976: no. 47; Laing 1993: 92-95; Samuels 1989: 256-63 [1984: 39-47]; McIntosh, Samuels and Benskin 1986: I. 23, 111, III. 175 (LP 9260 Herefords.); Fein 2000; Revard 2000: 21-109.

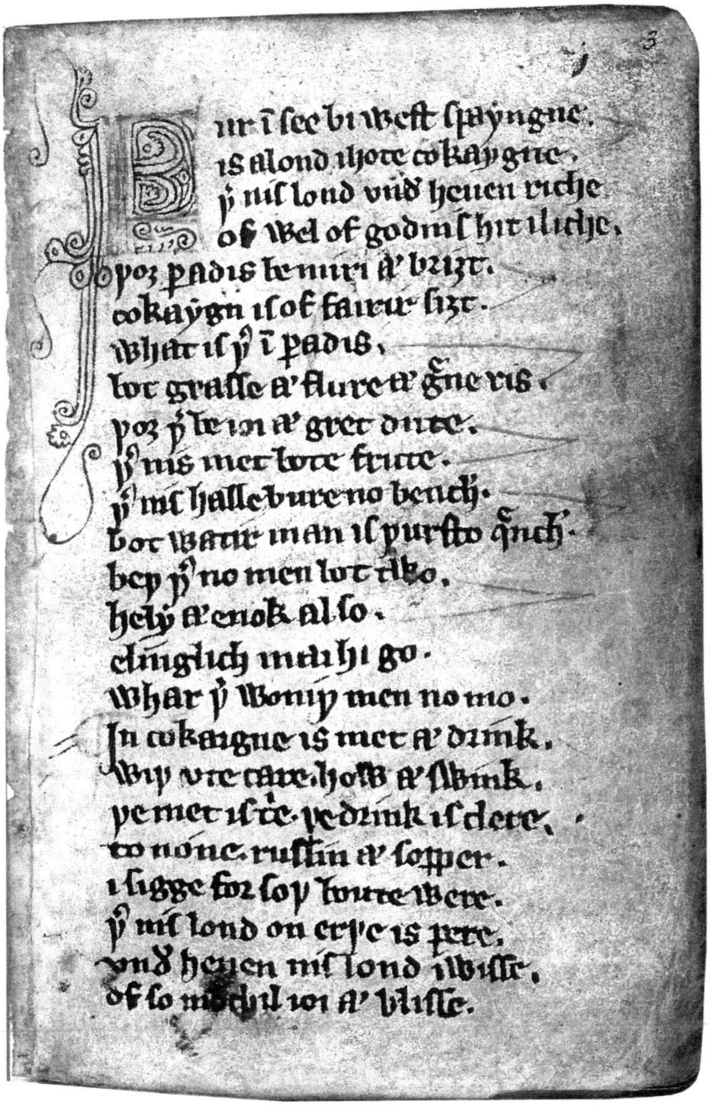

Fur in see bi west spayngne.
Is a lond ihote cokaygne.
Þer nis lond vnder heuen riche
Of wel of godnis hit iliche.
Þoȝ paradis be miri and briȝt.
Cokaygn is of fairir siȝt.
What is þer in paradis.
Bot grasse and flure and grene ris.
Þoȝ þer be ioi and gret dute.
Þer nis met bote frute.
Þer nis halle bure no bench.
Bot watir man is þurst to quench.
Beþ þer no men but two.
Hely and enok also.
Elinglich mai hi go.
Whar þer wonniþ men no mo.
In cokaygne is met and drink.
Wiþ vte care how and swink.
Þe met is trie. þe drink is clere.
To none. russin and sopper.
I sigge for soþ boute were.
Þer nis lond on erþe is pere.
Vnder heuen nis lond iwisse.
Of so mochil ioi and blisse.

London, British Library, Harley MS 913, f. 3r
The Land of Cokaygne, ll. 1–24

This little book, known popularly as the Kildare Lyrics but probably produced in Waterford in the 1330s, is smaller even than the Sloane Lyrics (see pl. 40). A trilingual miscellany from Ireland, most of its contents are in Latin and point to the collection's Franciscan origins. The hand is discussed by Benskin 1990. Note the unusual use of the *autem* abbreviation for *and*.
actual size

37

London, British Library, Cotton MS Nero A. x, Art. 3, f. 49r (formerly 45)
Pearl, ll. 433–68
Gothic *textualis rotunda media*, s. xiv ex.

TRANSCRIPTION

Cortayse quen þe(n)ne syde[1] þat gaye
knelande to grou(n)de folde vp hyr face
makeleȝ moder ⁊ m[u>y]ryest may
blessed by(n)gyner[2] of vch a grace
þe(n)ne ros ho vp ⁊ con restay
⁊ speke me towarde i(n) þat space
s(ir) fele here porchaseȝ ⁊ fongeȝ pray
bot supplantoreȝ none w(i)t(h)i(n)ne þys place
þat emp(er)ise al heue(n)ȝ hatȝ
⁊ vrþe ⁊ helle i(n) her bayly
of erytage ȝet non wyl ho chace
for ho is quen of cortaysye
//The co(ur)t of þe kyndom of god alyue
hatȝ a p(ro)perty i(n) hytself bey(n)g
alle þat may þeri(n)ne aryue
of alle þe reme is quen oþ(er) ky(n)g
⁊ neu(er) oþ(er) ȝet schal depryue
bot vchon fayn of oþ(er)eȝ hafy(n)g
⁊ wolde her corou(n)eȝ wern worþe þo fyue
if possyble were her mendy(n)g
bot my lady of quom Iesu con spry(n)g
ho haldeȝ þe empyre ou(er) v(us) ful hyȝe
⁊ þat dysplese ȝ non of oure gy(n)g
for ho is quen of cortaysye
//Of co(ur)taysye as saytȝ say(n)t poule
al arn we me(m)breȝ of ie(s)u kryst
as heued ⁊ arme ⁊ legg ⁊ naule
temen to hys body ful trwe ⁊ tyste[3]
ryȝt so is vch a krysten sawhe[4]
a longande lym to þe mayster of myste
þe(n)ne loke what hate oþ(er) any gawle
is tached oþ(er) tyȝed þy ly(m)eȝ bytwyste
þy heued hatȝ nauþer greme ne gryste
on arme oþ(er) fynger þaȝ þ(o)u ber byȝe
so fare we alle wyth luf ⁊ lyste
to ky(n)g ⁊ quene by cortaysye

A *cursiva* would be more usual late in the fourteenth century for poetry in English. This is a Gothic *rotunda* script. Although uneven, great care is taken over such details as writing minims separately and observing the expected distribution of **v** (word initial) and **u** (elsewhere). The scribe may have been more at home in *cursiva* than *textualis* (a couple of lines are added in Anglicana above the drawing on f. 129r (see p. 173), but some judge them to be in a hand later than that of the scribe): the **w** is more like the typically Anglicana form (compare pl. 50 and contrast pls 35, 39, 43); and final **s** has its tail prolonged at the top (compare pl. 46). Both **ȝ** and **g** are in use: **ȝ** doubles for the **z** of Anglo-Norman orthography and can thus stand for **s** (note that **tȝ** in 'hatȝ', l. 33, is for voiceless **s**); and **þ** is retained beside **th**. There are no punctuation

[1] For 's⟨a⟩yde'.
[2] Misplaced overline; should read 'bygy⟨n⟩ner'.
[3] For 't⟨r⟩yste'.
[4] Uncorrected, possibly because thought clear enough for *sawle*; endline dot an ink spot rather than point?

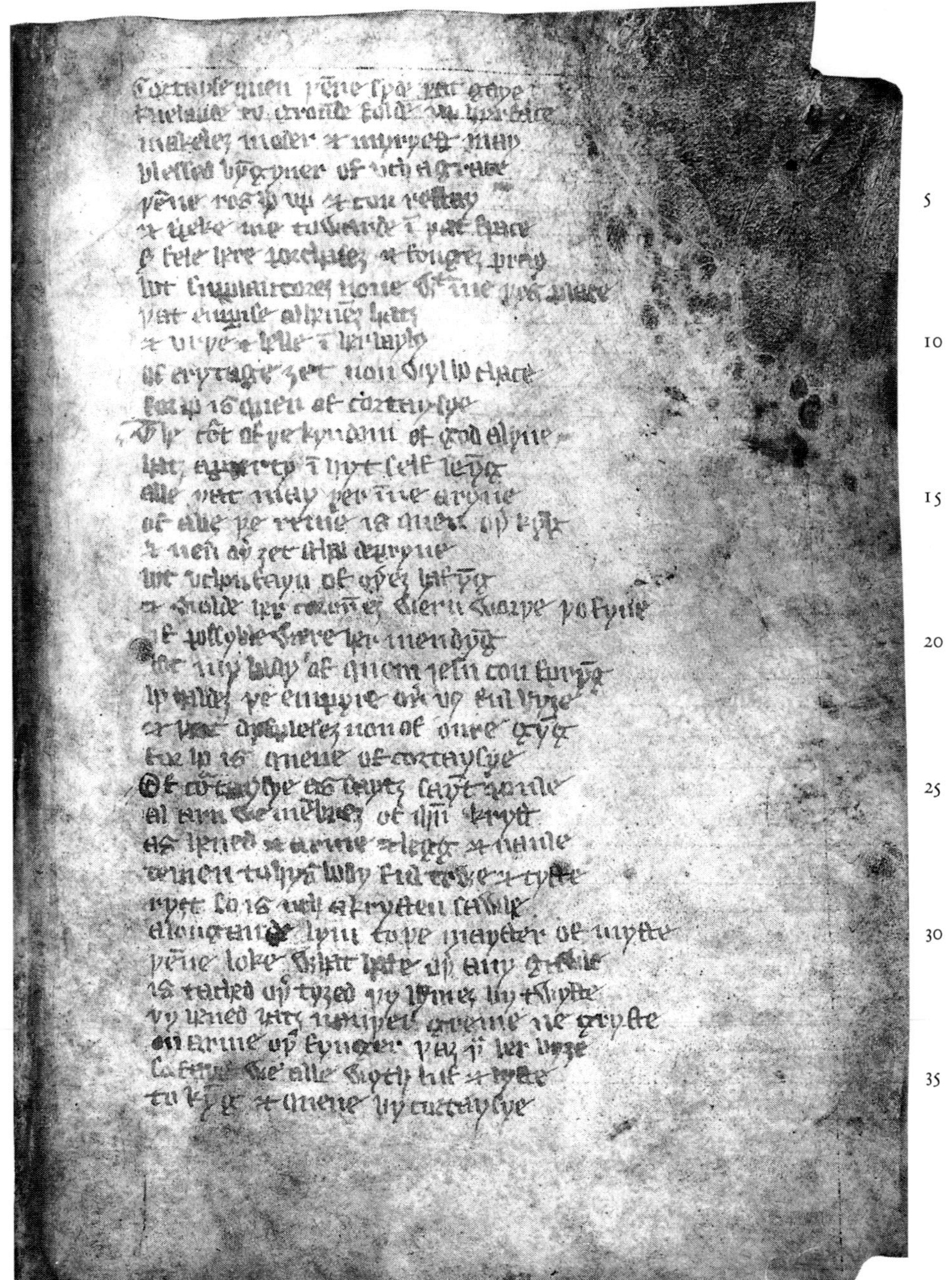

Plate 37 – actual size

markers apart from //, the two small strokes indicating a new paragraph by the beginning of the lower twelve-line stanzas (sometimes also by the first stanza on a page, but not visible here). Customary abbreviations are in use: the overline for *m* ('me(m)breȝ', l. 26, 'ly(m)eȝ', l. 32) or *n* ('þe(n)ne', l. 5, 'grou(n)de', l. 2, etc.), ʹ for *er* ('emp(er)ise', l. 9, 'oþ(er)', l. 16, 'oþ(er)eȝ', l. 18, 'ou(er)', l. 22, etc.); ^{2} for *ur* ('co(ur)t', l. 13, 'co(ur)taysye', l. 25); ꝰ for *us* ('v(us)', l. 22). The Tironian sign is crossed. Note also 's(ir)', l. 7, 'w(i)t(h)i(n)ne', l. 8; 'p(ro)perty', l. 14 and 'ie(s)u', l. 26 (compare 'Iesu', l. 21). The space-saving superscript **u** makes 'þ(o)u', l. 34. Savage cropping means that the drawings which illustrate the poems extend to the page edges; quiring (1^2, 2-8^{12}, 9^4) suggests a complete compilation. These coloured illustrations are atypical of manuscript illumination from England in this period: essentially they are clumsily coloured line drawings, and they need not therefore be seen as an attempt to reproduce a finer exemplar illuminated in a fashionable continental style.

CONTEXTS

The four poems in ff. 41-130 of this manuscript, accepted as of common authorship, are written in the dialect of the north-west midlands, possibly Cheshire. A case that it was written for the Stanley family of Staffordshire and Cheshire has been mounted. The Garter motto 'Hony soyt q(ui) mal penc(e)', added at the end of *Sir Gawain* and coincidentally of the book, suggests a connection with the court of Edward III. Name 'hugo de' in upper margin f. 95r. The manuscript was in the library of Henry Savile of Banke (d. 1617), many of whose manuscripts came from northern monasteries. How it got into Cotton's library (probably by 1621) is unknown. Entered the British Museum with the Cotton Collection in 1753.

SIZE

c. 171 × 123 mm (*c.* 137 × 91 mm).

BIBLIOGRAPHY

Pr. Gordon 1953: 16-17 (ll. 433-86); Andrew and Waldron 1978: 74-76 (ll. 433-86).
Facs. Gollancz 1923.
Disc. Wright 1960^1: pl. 15; Watson 1969 [2004^1]: no. 274; Guddat-Figge 1976: no. 40; Lee 1977; Doyle 1982: 92, 1983: 166; McIntosh, Samuels and Benskin 1986: I. 23-24, 116, III. 37-38 (LP 26 Cheshire); Scott 1996, no. 12; Edwards 1997 [1999]; Tite 2003: 131.

London, British Library, Cotton MS Nero A. x, f. 129r (formerly 125)

Visit of Bertilak's wife to Gawain's bedroom
actual size

38

Cambridge, Peterhouse MS 75. I, f. 71v
Opening of *The Equatorie of the Planetis*
Gothic *littera cursiva anglicana media*, *c.* 1393

TRANSCRIPTION

In the name of god pitos ⁊ M(er)ciable seide [-leyk][1] the largere þ(a)t thow Makest this
instrume(n)t / the largere ben thi chef deuisiou(n)s / the largere þ(a)t ben tho deuisiou(n)s /
in hem may ben mo smale fracciou(n)s / ⁊ euere the mo of smale fracciou(n)s
the ner the trowthe of thy (con)clusiou(n)s / tak therefore a plate of Metal or elles
a bord þ(a)t be smothe shaue / by leuel / ⁊ euene polised § of which whan it is
Rownd ˋby compasˊ / the hole diametre shal (con)tene ·72· large enches or elles ·6· fote of
Mesure / the whiche Rownde bord for it shal nat werpe ne krooke / the egge of
ˋtheˊ circu(m)fere(n)ce shal be bownde w(i)t(h) a plate of yren in Maner of a karte whel /
§ this bord yif the likith may be vernissed or elles glewed w(i)t(h) p(er)chemyn for
honestyte § tak thanne a cercle of Metal þ(a)t be ·2· enche of brede / ⁊ þ(a)t the ˋholeˊ
dyametre ˋw(i)t(h)in this cercle shalˊ (con)tene [-the foreseide][·-72\68·][2] enches / or
·[-6\5] fote ˋ⁊ ·8· enches [-set]ˊ / ⁊ subtili lat this cercle
be nayled vp on the circu(m)fere(n)ce of this bord or ellis Mak this cercle of
glewed p(er)chemyn . / this cercle wole I clepe the lymbe of Myn equatorie
þ(a)t was (com)powned the yer of crist ·1392· (com)plet the laste M(er)idie of dece(m)bre
§ this lymbe shaltow deuyde in 4 quarters by ·2· diametral lynes in Man(er) of
the lymbe of a comune astrelabye ⁊ lok thy croys be trewe proued by
geometrical (con)clusiou(n) / tak thanne a large (com)pas þ(a)t be trewe ⁊ set the ffyx
point ou(er) the Middel of the bord ˋonˊ which Middel shal be nayled a plate of
Metal Rownd § the hole diametre of this plate shal (con)tiene ·16· enches large
for in this plate shollen ben perced alle the centris of this equatorie / ⁊ ek in
p(ro)ces of tyme May this plate be turned abowte after þ(a)t auges of planetes
ben Moeued in the ·9· spere thus[3] may thin instrume(n)t laste p(er)petuel . § tak thanne
as I haue seid byforn the fix fot of thy (com)pas ⁊ set it in the Middel of
this plate ⁊ w(i)t(h) the Moeuable point of thi (com)pas descriue[4] a cercle in the
ferthest circu(m)ference of thy lymbe § ⁊ no(t)a þ(a)t the Middel poynt of this plate
wher as the fix fot of thy (com)pas stondith / wole I calle centre ·aryn· / Mak
thanne a narwer cercle þ(a)t be descriued vp on the same centre aryn but
litel q(u)antite fro the forthest forseid cercle in the lymbe in whiche space
shollen ben deuyde Mynutes of the lymbe / Mak thanne a narwere cercle som
what ferther distau(n)t fro the laste seid cercle / in which shal be deuyded the
degres of the same lymbe Mak yit a narwere cercle som what ferthere
distau(n)t fro this laste seid cercle in which shal ben writen the nombres of

Both authorship and handwriting are ascribed to Chaucer, but this is disputed. There is no other manuscript for this English text, written, from internal date evidence, *c.* 1393. The script, despite its generous proportions and good spacing, is relatively informal. The pen is not lifted between minims and other cursive features include the **y** of ‘lymbe’, l. 25, the tailed round **r** as in ‘byforn’, l. 23, and the occasional use of round **e** finally, as in ‘M(er)ciable’, l. 1. The conventional distribution of **v** and **u** is followed, but the capital shape **M** is frequent word-initially, similarly **R** in ll. 6, 7, 19, and **ff** is found in ‘ffyx’, l. 17, where a capital is inappropriate. Alternative forms are in use for the infinitive *be* or *ben* and for some past participles, for example ‘deuyde’, l. 29, and ‘deuyded’, l. 30. In ll. 23 and 26 ‘fyx’ without expected final –*t* may reflect simplification of consonant cluster. The chief mark of punctuation is the virgule, sometimes with reinforcing point; and the *paragraphus* sign, represented by §, helps to block out the argument clearly. Omissions are carefully positioned, with the

[1] These shadowy letters, firmly cancelled, are much debated. Among suggestions note a transposed Arabic word for ‘it is said’ (see Price 1955: 166) and North's reading (1988: 158, n. 27) ‘Leyc'’ as reference to Robert of Leycester.

[2] The erased *2* is less securely visible than the erased *7*.

[3] A part-written paragraphus may stand to the left of ‘thus’.

[4] The last four letters stand on a clumsy erasure.

In the name of god pitos & merciable seide the leyere the larger þt thow makest this instrument the larger ben thi chef deuisiouns the larger þt ben tho deuisiouns in hem may ben mo smale fracciouns & euere the mo of smale fracciouns the ner the trowthe of thy conclusiouns / tak therfore a plate of metal or elles a bord þt be smothe shaue by leuel & euene polised / of which whan it is rownd by compas the hole diametre shal contene 72 large enches or elles 6 fote of mesure / the whiche rownde bord for it shal nat werpe ne krooke / the egge of the circumference shal be bownde wt a plate of yren in maner of a karte whel / this bord yif the likith may be vernissed or elles glewed wt perchemyn for honestyte / tak thanne a cercle of metal þt be 2 enche of brede & þt the hole dyametre wt in this cercle shal contene ~~the forseide~~ 68 enches or 5 fote & 8 enches / & subtili lat this cercle be nayled vp on the circumference of this bord or ellis mak this cercle of glewed perchemyn / this cercle wole I clepe the lymbe of myn equatorie þt was compowned the yer of crist 1392 complet the laste meridie of decembre / this lymbe shaltow deuyde in 4 quarters by 2 diametral lynes in maner of the lymbe of a commune astrelabye & lok thy croys be trewe proued by geometrical conclusioun / tak thanne a large compas þt be trewe & set the fyx point ouer the middel of the bord on which middel shal be nayled a plate of metal rownd / the hole diametre of this plate shal contene 18 enches large / for in this plate shollen ben perced alle the centris of this equatorie / & ek in proces of tyme may this plate be turned abowte after þt auges of planetes ben moeued in the 9 spere / thus may thin instrument laste perpetuel / tak thanne as I haue seid byforn the fix fot of thy compas & set it in the middel of this plate & wt the moeuable point of thi compas descriue a cercle in the ferthest circumference of thy lymbe / & nota þt the middel poynt of this plate wher as the fix fot of thy compas stondith wole I calle centre aryn / mak thanne a nother cercle þt be descriued vp on the same centre aryn but litel quantite fro the ferthest forseid cercle in the lymbe in which space shollen ben deuyded mynutes of the lymbe / mak thanne a nother cercle som what ferther distant fro the laste seid cercle in which shal be deuyded the degres of the same lymbe / mak yit a nother cercle som what ferther distant fro this laste seid cercle in which shal ben writen the nombres of

Plate 38 – reduced to 63%

caret sign below, in ll. 6, 8, 10, 11, 18. Raised points mark out numbers, though not always to either side (see l. 11), and their use draws attention to the first instance of 'aryn', l. 26, as an unfamiliar word. Unusually for the period but appropriately for such technical material, the numerals are Arabic, though not always shaped as to-day; note for example that the first digit of '·72·', l. 6, is like a capital **A** without its cross-stroke. The abbreviations are standard: the Tironian sign (often with the overline that makes *etiam* in Latin); ˀ (as in 'M(er)ciable', l. 1); the overline for *m* or *n* (as in 'circu(m)fere(n)ce', l. 12); ꝯ for *com-* or *con-* (as in '(con)clusiou(n)s', l. 4 and '(com)plet', l. 14); **p** with barred descender in 'p(er)chemyn', ll. 9, 13, 'p(er)petuel'. l. 22; ꝓ in 'p(ro)ces', l. 21; superscript **a** made with two bows, above **q** giving 'q(u)antite ', l. 28, and in 'no(t)a', l. 25. Note also space-saving **wᵗ** and **þᵗ** (**þ** appears only in the contraction).

The scribe has made many corrections. Sometimes erased readings can be seen, and these are indicated above, for example in ll. 1 and 11, but other erasures are irrecoverable, as under 'dyametre', l. 11, 'tak thanne', l. 17, 'ou(er) t', l. 18, maybe 'this laste', l. 32. Show-through from f. 71r (the opening page of the quire) in the upper margin is from headings written sideways in Gothic *textualis quadrata* for astronomical tables.

CONTEXTS

The manuscript is made up of astronomical tables, instructions for making an equatory (ff. 71v-74r), and, on smaller and more flexible membrane (ff. 75-78), complementary materials that include examples of calculations made in 1391. Of the two main hands, this is Hand C (attributed to Chaucer), who added notes throughout and seems to have drawn the whole together *c.* 1393 (see ll. 13-14 for the completion of 'Myn equatorie' on the 31 December 1392); the more professionally presented tables on ff. 14-62r are in Hand S, and Hand C may here be providing a fair copy of his account of how to make an equatory; by comparison ff. 75-78 have more of the appearance of work in progress. A note by Hand C (f. 5v) links the 31 December 1392 date with the name 'chaucer', but there is no evidence that the translation was made by Geoffrey Chaucer or that it was for his son, 'litel Lowis', for whom he wrote the *Astrolabe*. Yet, the *Equatorie* has been thought a better witness to Chaucer's spellings than any other Chaucerian manuscript, and the *paragraphus* sign distinctive of prose that passed through Chaucer's hands. Calculations seem to relate to London for the most part, but those on f. 63v are attributed to 'I. Somer' of Oxford. A note by Leland in his *Collectanea* makes it likely he saw the manuscript at Peterhouse in 1542, and it is listed in the 1589 catalogue of college books. Currently housed in Cambridge University Library.

SIZE

358 × *c.* 267 mm (300 × *c.* 228 mm).

BIBLIOGRAPHY

Pr. Price 1955; Rand Schmidt 1993.
Facs. Price 1955; Rand Schmidt 1993.
Disc. D[avis] 1958; Petti 1977: pl. 45; Samuels 1983[1] [1988]; Robinson 1988: no. 281, pl. 177; ~ 1991; North 1988: 158-87; Edwards and Mooney 1991; Krochalis 1991; Benson 1992; Partridge 1992; Seymour 1995-97: I. 163; Horobin 2003.

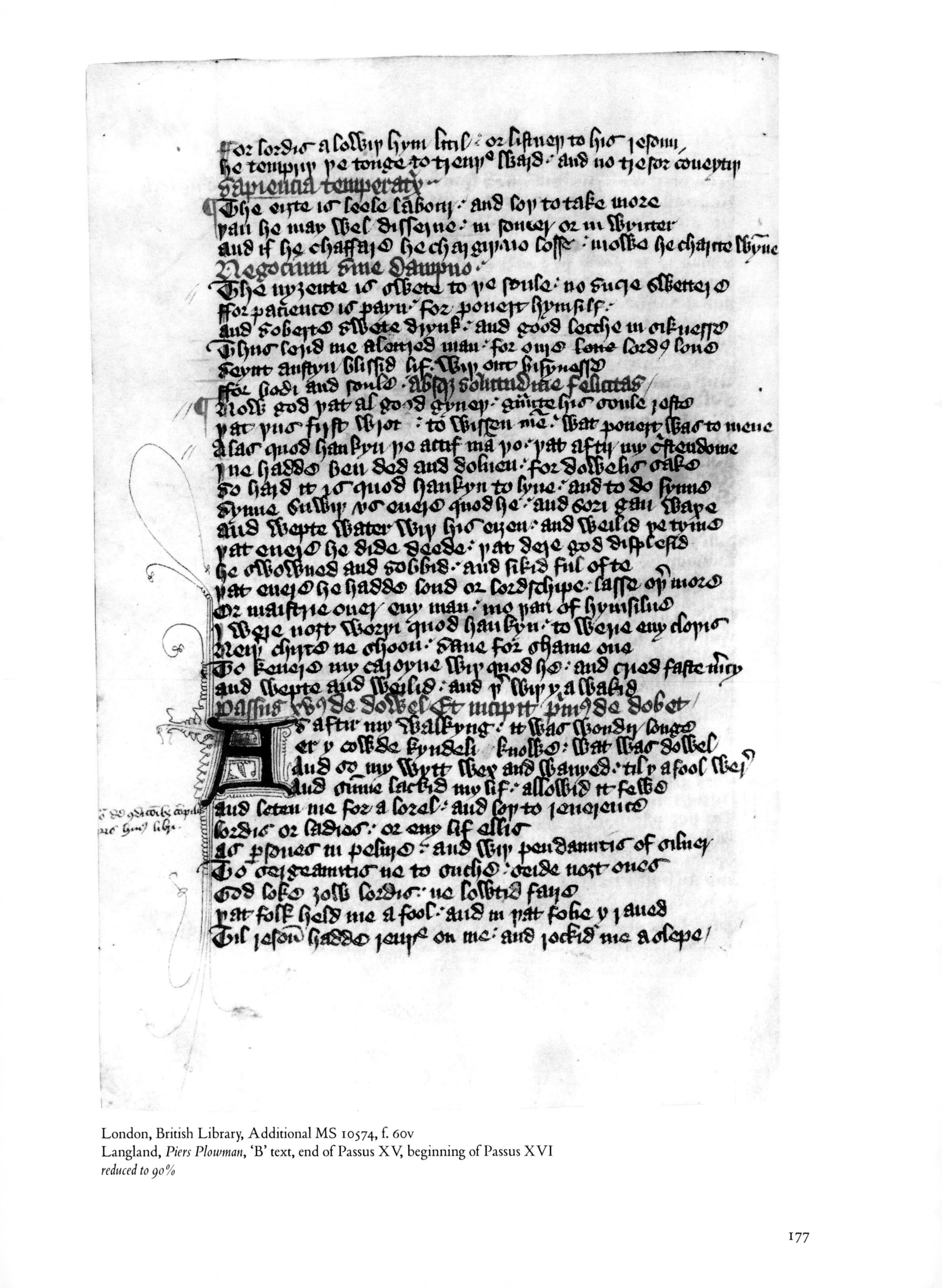

London, British Library, Additional MS 10574, f. 60v
Langland, *Piers Plowman*, 'B' text, end of Passus XV, beginning of Passus XVI
reduced to 90%

39

London, British Library, Additional MS 41175, f. 105r
Glossed Gospels, Mark with commentary, 1: 1⸗5
Gothic *textualis quadrata* and *semi⸗quadrata formata*, *c*. 1400

Colour pl. C5

TRANSCRIPTION

þE bigy(n)nyng of þe c(apitulu)m . p(rologu)m .

gospel of ie(s)u crist ∶ þe

sone of god / ¶ Gospel / þe gospel
is seid a good tellyng ∶ which p(er)tey⸗
neþ propirly to þe rewme of god .
⁊ to remyssiou(n) of synnes / for rede(m)p⸗
tiou(n) of feiþful men ⁊ þe blis of seyntis ∶
comeþ bi þe gospel / ierom ¶ of ie(s)u crist /
ie(s)u in ebreu ∶ is sauyour in englisch / crist
in greek ∶ is seid messias in ebreu . ⁊ anoyn⸗
tid þat is . kyng ⁊ prest in englisch / ierom /
// matheu clepiþ crist ∶ þe sone of dauyþ and
of abraha(m) / ⁊ mark clepiþ crist ∶ þe sone of god /
it schal be vndurstandu(n) of eu(er) eiþ(er) ∶ þat o lord
ie(s)u crist is þe sone of god ⁊ þe sone of man /
bede ¶ sone of gode / cristen men ben þe sones \\of//
god bi grace ∶ but crist is no sich sone of god /
for he is þe sone of god . not bi name alone .
not bi makyng of nou3t . not bi purchasyng
þorou grace ∶ but bi propurte . bi kynde . bi treuþe
⁊ bi euerlastynge generaciou(n) / illarie in ·iij·
bok of þe trynite
¶ as it is writu(n) in ysaie þe p(ro)fete / lo y

sende myn angel bifor þi face ∶ which

schal make redi þi weie bifore þee / þe

vois of a criere in desert / make 3e

redi þe weie of þe lord ∶ make 3e hise

paþis ri3tful /
¶ ysaie / þis autorite · lo y sende myn angel ∶ is
is fou(n)du(n) in malachie . not in ysaie / ierom
in his pistle of þe beste kynde of transla⸗
tyng // but þou3 þese wordis ben not fou(n)du(n)
in ysaie ∶ neþeles þe sentence is fou(n)du(n) þere /
þis autorite . lo y sende myn angel ∶ is in
malachie / ⁊ þis autorite þe vois of a criere
in desert ∶ is in ysaie / mark ioynede þe wor⸗
des of euer eiþer p(ro)fete p(er)teynynge to o sen⸗
tence ∶ vndur þe persoone of ysaie / þe name
of o p(ro)fete cam for þe toþ(er) ∶ to þe mynde of
mark reulid bi þe holi goost / to schewe þat
alle þinges þat þe holy goost seide bi þe p(ro)fe⟨-⟩

bi þis þat he seiþ . bifor þi face ∶ it is schewid
þat ioon was ney crist / teofil ¶ make redi
þi weie / ioon made redi þe soulis of iewis
bi baptym ∶ þ(a)t þei schulden resseyue crist /
teofile // eþ(er) þe weie of þe lord is penau(n)ce ∶
bi which he comeþ dou(n) to us . ⁊ we stien to
hym / herfor þe bigynnyng of iones p(re)chi(n)g
was ∶ do 3e penau(n)ce/ ierom ¶ vois of a crier /
ri3tly ioon is clepid a vois ∶ ⁊ ie(s)u crist is
clepid þe word of þe fader / for in sownyng ∶
ioon 3ede bifore goddis sone / bede // ioon is
a vois of a criere ∶ for cry is woned to [h>b]e
maad to deef men . ⁊ set a fer ⁊ wiþ indigna⸗
ciou(n) / ⁊ þese þingis camen to [-to] þe iewis ∶
while helþe is fer fro synneris . ⁊ þei stoppide(n)
her eeris as deef snakes / ⁊ þei disseruyden
to here of c(r)ist ∶ indignaciou(n) ire ⁊ tribulaciou(n) /
ierom ¶ in desert / þ(a)t is . vois ⁊ cry is maad
in desert ∶ for iewis weren desert . þ(a)t is for⸗
saku(n) . of goddis spirit . of p(ro)fete of kyng .
and of prest / ierom ¶ weie of þe lord / ech þ(a)t
p(re)chiþ ri3t feiþ ⁊ gode werkis ∶ makiþ redy
weie to þe lord comynge to þe hertis of he⟨-⟩
reris / þat my3t of grace perse þese hertis ∶
⁊ þ(a)t þe li3t of treuþe bischyne hem / he makiþ
ri3tful paþes ∶ while bi wordis of p(re)chyng
he fourmeþ clene þou3tis in þe soule of hereris /
bede ⁊ g(re)g(or) in xx omelie // eþ(er) make 3e redi weie
of þe lord / þ(a)t is. do 3e ⁊ p(re)che 3e penau(n)ce ¶ make
3e ri3tful hise paþes / þ(a)t 3e goynge in þe kyn⸗
gis weie ∶ loue 3oure nei3boris as 3ou silf . ⁊
3ou silf as 3oure nei3boris / ierom // eþ(er) make
3e redi weie to þe lord / þ(a)t is. do 3e awey fro 3o(ur)
hertis ∶ lecherie . pride ⁊ coueitise / weie of þe
lord be maad redi to þe herte ∶ bi mekenesse bi
sorwe of contriciou(n) . ⁊ bi drede of god ∶ ⁊ so god
schal entre to þe herte / he þat entriþ þe strey⸗
ter ⁊ harder weie of religiou(n) ∶ eþer of streit⸗
nesse of penau(n)ce ∶ dresse his paþ in to god bi
ri3t entent / ⁊ croke he not hise werkis to ypo⸗
crisi eþer bi temp(er)al lucre . eþ(er) bi hi(n)ctyng of
veyn glorie eþ(er) of ni(m)an(us) fauour eþer þank /
abuyle in iiij su(n)day of aduent

¶ ioon was in desert ∶ baptisynge and

p(re)chynge þe baptym of penau(n)ce . in

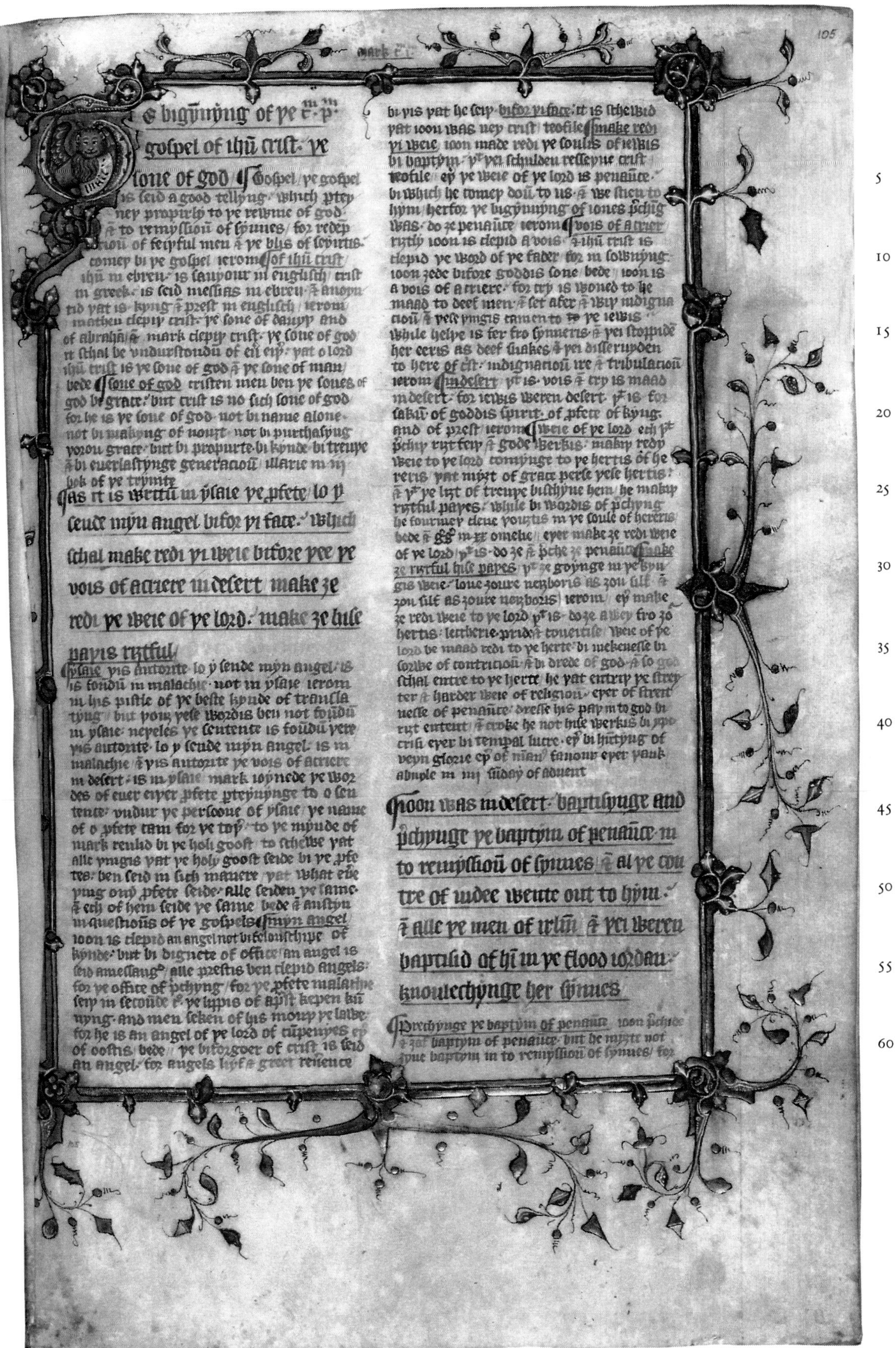

Plate 39 – reduced to 62%

tes ∴ ben seid in sich manere / þat whateu(er)e
þing ony p(ro)fete seide ∴ alle seiden þe same .
⁊ ech of hem seide þe same / bede ⁊ austyn
in questiou(n)s of þe gospels ¶myn angel /
ioon is clepid an angel not bi felouschipe of
kynde ∴ but bi dignete of office / an angel is
seid a messang(er) / alle prestes ben clepid angels ∴
for þe office of p(re)chyng / for þe p(ro)fete malachie
seiþ in secou(n)de c° . þe lippis of a p(re)st kepen ku(n)⟨-⟩
nyng . and men seken of his mouþ þe lawe ∴
for he is an angel of þe lord of cu(m)penyes eþ(er)
of oostis / bede // þe biforgoer of crist is seid
an angel ∴ for angels liyf ⁊ greet reu(er)ence /

to remyssiou(n) of synnes / ⁊ al þe contre of iudee wente out to hym ∴
⁊ alle þe men of i(erusa)l(e)m / ⁊ þei weren
baptisid of hi(m) in þe flood iordan ∴
knoulechynge her synnes /
¶ Prechynge þe baptym of penau(n)ce / ioon p(re)chide
⁊ ȝaf baptym of penau(n)ce ∴ but he miȝte not
ȝyue baptym in to remyssiou(n) of synnes / for

This is a well-spaced *quadrata* script for the passages from the Bible text, tending towards a lower grade in the commentary, where less attention is given the feet of still separately made minims. Ease of reading must have been a requirement, for there is none of the closeness that typifies so many professional hands: bitings are few (**de, pp**), and the round **r** is restricted to following bowed letters. Both **ȝ** and **þ** are in use, the latter, without ascender, accommodating itself neatly to the general tidiness of script. Both pointed **v** and round **u** are positionally distinguished, as are long and round **s**. The indefinite article *a* is usually attached to the following word, for example 'a good', l. 6a, 'a criere', l. 31a (but note 'a fer', l. 13b, which looks like the adverbial phrase *on fear*). By contrast, 'o' meaning *one* is separate, as in ll. 44a, 46a. Features characteristic of central Midlands texts written in the last decades of the fourteenth century include *sich* (as ll. 19a, 49a), *silf* (as 31b, 32b), and *ony* (l. 50a). The pages are carefully ruled, and the simple expedient of allotting two lines to the larger script module is adopted for sections of gospel text, which are underlined in red. A single block of glosses follows, in which each phrase or word selected for comment is introduced by a coloured capitulum sign, red and blue alternating, and underlined in red; words cited incidentally from the gospel are not underlined. The main markers of punctuation are the *punctus elevatus* (sometimes merely a pair of dots and occasionally lacking the lower dot, as in l. 37b) and the point. The virgule, also used to mark pauses, generally stands before the names of authorities. The omission marker (//), signalling the beginning of new information, is sometimes fully obscured by the coloured capitulum sign (see in l. 8b). The abbreviations are customary; 'ie(s)u' in the second line of writing in col. a is expanded from a form usual in the thirteenth and fourteenth centuries. Note the expansion to 'g(re)g(or)' made in l. 28b, the form to be expected in the vernacular, not *gregorius* as might be expected in Latin. Note that 'c(apitul)o', l. 57a, is not expanded for reasons of space. There is some evidence of skilful correction, for example: a few words rewritten in l. 57a; the letter *h* overwritten in '[h>b]e', l. 12b; the repeated 'to' subpuncted in l.14b. One instance of repetition, of 'is', ll. 36-37a, goes unnoticed. The unusual word 'hi(n)ctyng', l. 41b, is probably related to *hinch* and *hincty* (the phrase must mean something like 'with proud arching of the back); and in the next line 'ni(m)an(us)' is to be understood as 'no man's'.

CONTEXTS

The Glossed Gospels take their text from the earlier Wycliffite translation of the Bible; this is the only manuscript extant of the 'Short Mark' glossed gospel. Ownership inscription and notes requesting prayer on ff. 1v, 2, 164, are by a Hugh Blythe (probably of Essex). Further inscriptions on f. 1: John Crowlond, d. 1493, fellow of Queens' College Cambridge 'and person of South Wokyngton [Ockendon] in Essex, Gyver of this boke'; Geoffrey Downes, a fellow of Queens' 1490-94, who gives directions that the book be given after the death of his brother James to the chantry chapel of Pott Shrigley, Cheshire; and the name, erased, of William Grylles, fellow of Exeter College Oxford 1541-51. Bookplate shows it was among the books in the Lee-Dillon library at Ditchley in 1903; given by Harold Lee-Dillon to the British Museum, where examined and foliated 1931.

SIZE

c. 361 × 242 mm (*c.* 255 × 175 mm).

BIBLIOGRAPHY

Disc. Add. MSS *Cat.*; Hudson 1988: 247-59, 1989: 132-34; Hargreaves 1969, 1979; Swanson 2002.

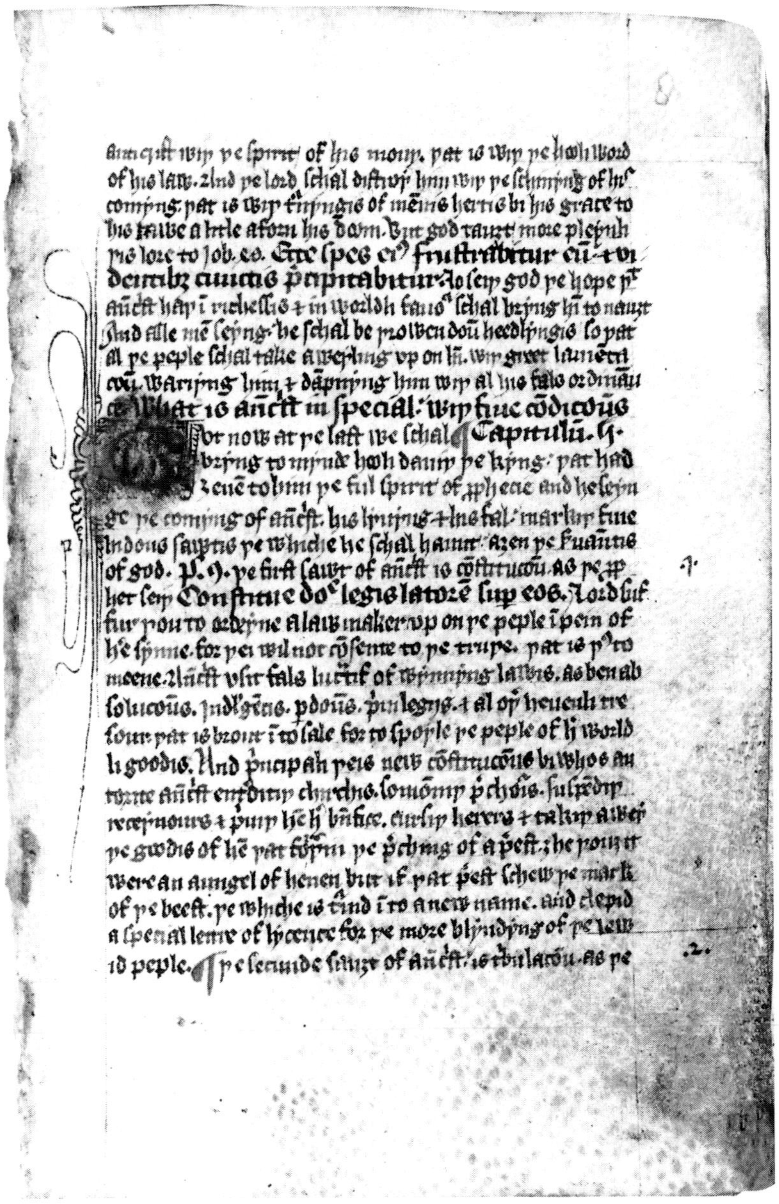

London, British Library, Harley MS 6613, f. 8r
The Lanterne of Liȝt

Not all Lollard books are as handsome as the Glossed Gospels (pl. 39 and colour pl. C5). The *Lantern of Liȝt* was composed after the 1409 Constitutions of Archbishop Arundel (mentioned in l. 24 in this plate). Two manuscript copies of the *Lanterne of Liȝt* survive, both small single-text books. Harley 2324, edited by Swinburn 1917, is a little smaller than Harley 6613 but in a larger-module hand, and the Harley 6613 scribe therefore gets almost twice as much text into each page.

A John Claydon of St Anne's in Aldersgate, London, was brought before Archbishop Chichele in 1415 for possession of books written in English, among them the *Lanterne of Liȝt*. Because he was illiterate, he had his copy read aloud to him by John Gryme, whom he had paid to copy it, and by John Fuller, one of his servants. Claydon was burned as a heretic for possession. As Anne Hudson has pointed out (1989: 125), 'Books were a matter of life and death of Lollards.'
actual size

40

London, British Library, Sloane MS 2593, f. 10v
a. 'I syng a of a myden'; b. 'I haue a gentil cook'; c. 'Omnes gentes plaudite'
Gothic *littera cursiva anglicana media*, s. xiv ex. – s. xv in.

TRANSCRIPTION

¶ I syng a of a myde(n)[1] · þ(a)t is makeles
kyng of alle kyng(es) · to her(e) sone che ches
¶ he ca(m) al so stylle · þ(er) his mod(er) was
as dew in aprylle · þ(a)t fallyt on þe gras
¶ he cam al so stylle · to his moder(es) bowr
as dew in aprille · þ(a)t fallyt on þe flo(ur)
¶ he cam al so stylle · þ(er) his mod(er) lay
as dew in aprille · þ(a)t fallyt on þe spray
¶ Mod(er) ⁊ maydyn · was neu(er) no(n) but che
wel may swych a lady · god(es) mod(er) be

¶ I haue a gentil cook · crowyt me day
he doþ me rysyn erly · my matyins for to say
¶ I haue a ge(n)til cook · comy(n) he is of gret
his comb is of reed corel · his tayil is of get
¶ I haue a gentyl cook · comy(n) he is of kynde
his comb is of red scorel[2] · his tayl is of Inde
¶ his legg(es) ben of aso(ur) · so gen[-i]til ⁊ so smale
his spor(es) arn of sylu(er) qwyt in to þe wortewale
¶ his eyny(n) arn of cristal · loky(n) al in au(m)byr
⁊ eu(er)y niȝt he p(er)chit hy(m) · in my(n) ladyis chau(m)byr

¶ Omnes ge(n)tes // plaudite
I saw myny bryddis sety(n) on a tr(e)
¶ he toky(n) her(e) fleyȝt ⁊ flowy(n) away
w(i)t(h) ego dixi haue good day
¶ Many qwyte feder(es) haȝt[3] þe pye
I may noo(n) mor(e) syngy(n) my lyppis arn so drye

The letter-forms are mostly Anglicana, and the **e** is always the looped Anglicana form. Note the frequent use of pointed Secretary **a** in its early form, with steeply sloping initial stroke of the lobe ('makeles', l. 1, 'alle', l. 2, etc.) and occasional short **r** ('bowr', l. 5, 'for', l. 12, etc.). Secretary influence is betrayed also by the use of broken strokes in the formation of some letters, for example **d** (as in 'dew', l. 4). The minims are written generally without penlifting, so a *media* grading seems appropriate. The **þ** is short, and it is adequately distinguished from **y**, which ends in a right-turning hairline (compare 'doþ' and 'my', l. 12); **ȝ** is in use in the *ght* group ('niȝt', l. 20, 'fleȝt', l. 23) and doubles for *z* in 'haȝt', l. 25, where the last two letters are reversed (i.e. *tȝ* for voiceless *s*); **q** occurs in 'qwyt', l. 18, 'qwyte', l. 25. Note 'che', ll. 2, 9, for *she*. Punctuation is confined to points at mid-line in the first two poems, where the braced pairs of lines are generally laid out as quatrains by modern editors: the pairs of lines are marked by a capitulum sign in the left margin. The third poem is concluded on the next page. Some lines start with a capital or enlarged text letter. Poems are separated by ruled lines. Some layout features may have been added after the writing of the text, but seem to be in the same ink. Some rubrication on ff. 2r-6r. Abbreviations are quite plentifully in use: the overline for *m* or *n*; **r** with tail for *r(e)* ('her(e) ll. 2, 23, 'tr(e)', l. 22, 'mor(e), l. 26); ʼ for *er* (as in 'þ(er)', l. 3, 'mod(er)', l. 7; ² for *ur* ('flo(ur)', l. 6, 'aso(ur)', l. 17); ꝭ for *es* ('king(es), l. 2, 'god(es)', l. 10, etc.); **ꝑ** in 'p(er)chit', l. 20; also **þ**^{t}, **w**^{t}, and the Tironian sign. An unnecessary minim is subpuncted in 'gen[-i]til' l. 17, but some curious readings remain (ll. 1, 16).

[1] For 'maiden'.
[2] Should read 'corel'.
[3] For 'has'.

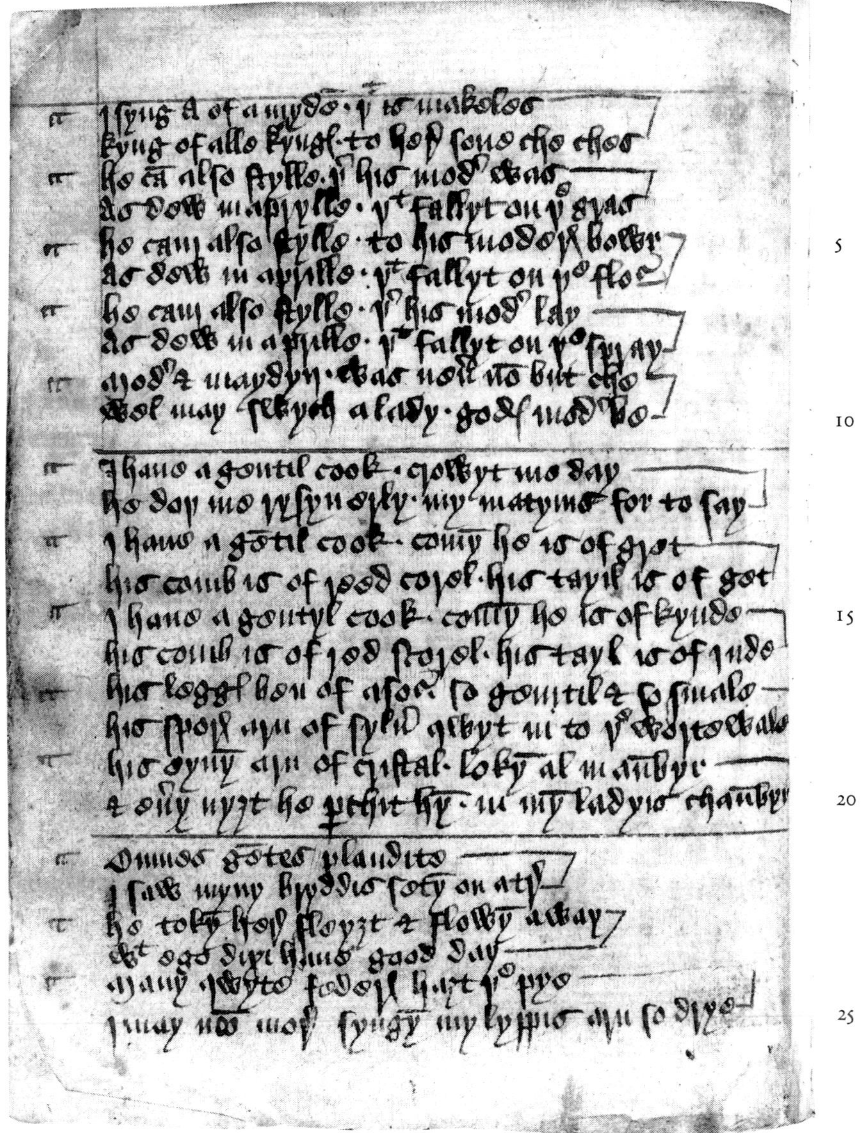

I syng a of a myden þat is makeles
kyng of alle kynges to here sone che ches
he cam also stylle þer his moder was
as dew in aprylle þat fallyt on þe gras
he cam also stylle to his moderes bowr
as dew in aprille þat fallyt on þe flour
he cam also stylle þer his moder lay
as dew in aprille þat fallyt on þe spray
moder & mayden was neuer non but che
wel may swych a lady godes moder be

I haue a gentil cook crowyt me day
he doþ me rysyn erly my matyins for to say
I haue a gentil cook comyn he is of gret
his comb is of red corel his tayil is of get
I haue a gentyl cook comyn he is of kynde
his comb is of red scorel his tayl is of inde
his legges ben of asor so gentil & so smale
his spores arn of syluer qwyt into þe wortewale
his eynyn arn of cristal lokyn al in aumbyr
& euery nyȝt he perchit hym in myn ladyis chaumbyr

Omnes gentes plaudite
I saw myny bryddis setyn on a tre
he tokyn here fleyȝt & flowyn away
with ego dixi haue good day
many qwyte federes hat þe pye
I may noon more syngyn my lyppis arn so drye

Plate 40 – actual size

CONTEXTS

This small paper manuscript (except for f. 12, where the upper part is of parchment) has suffered loss at the beginning: the first remaining poem (f. 2r) is without its opening; and an earlier foliation has been cancelled (present f. 2 was formerly f. 49). The poems are on ff. 2-34; f. 35r is blank; f. 35v has a note on money to be paid 'I(tem) ffor þe dy dye of Cley xxv· s' ⁊ iiij d' | ffor de dye yg''; f. 36r is blank. Notes in at least two late-fourteenth or fifteenth-century hands on f. 36v: 'Ioh(anne)s bardel d(ebet) istu(m) libru(m) þe qweche bradel is of dwellyd In C' (related to the note on f. 36v?); two medical recipes and some scribbles. Commonly but misleadingly termed a 'minstrel book', an internal reference to Lynn (i.e. King's Lynn) accords with linguistic pointers to Norfolk. Although the third lyric on this page might be taken to suggest a paying audience was intended, there are pointers towards connecting the collection with the Benedictine abbey of Bury St Edmunds both because it contains the only medieval carol in honour of St Edmund and because its two carols for St Nicholas may be linked with the Bury custom of giving boy bishops the title 'the bishop of St Nicholas'. In addition, the name of a monk of St Edmunds appears elsewhere as 'Joannis Berdwell'. In the Sloane bequest to the nation. Entered the British Museum among the foundation collections in 1753.

SIZE

c. 146 × *c.* 106 mm (123 × 75-93 mm).

BIBLIOGRAPHY

Pr. (a) Brown 1939: 119; (b) Robbins 1952 [1955]: 41-42; (c) *ibid.*: 5.
Disc. Ayscough 1792: II. 835; Greene 1935: 330, 1962: 173-74; McIntosh, Samuels and Benskin 1986: I. 116, III. 338-39 (LP 4279. Norfolk); Taylor 1991: 60-65.

41

London, British Library, Harley MS 6041, f. 16r
Langland, *Piers Plowman* ('A' text), from Passus IV-V
Gothic *littera cursiva anglicana media*, s. xv^{1}

TRANSCRIPTION

And redyly[1] reson[2] / thow schalt nat wende henne
For as longe as I leue / loue the I wylle
I am redy q(uod) reson / to reste with ȝow eu(er)e
So consience be of ȝour(e) co(n)sel / kepe I no bet(ur)
I g(r)aunte q(uod) the kyng / godes forbode he fayle
As longe as I lyue / libbe we togyd(er)es
Passus quintus de uisione
The kyng and the kniȝt(us) / to the chirche wente
To here matyns and messe / and to mete aft(ur)
Than wakyde I of wynkyng / and wo was withalle
That I ne hadde slepe sadder / and Iseye mor(e)
Or I hadde far(e) a forlong / feyntyse me hadde
That I ne myȝt fe[þ>r]þer a fote / for defaute of slepyng
I sat sotely on my bedis and seide my beleue 14a
and so y babelyd on my bedis[3] that brouth me on slepe 14b
Than sauȝ I muche mor(e) / than I befor(e) tolde
Al þe felde ful of folke / that I furst [-f][4] tolde
And consience wiþ a cros / com for to p(re)che
And p(re)yȝede the peple // haue pyte on hemselue
And prouyde that these pestylences / weren for pur(e) synne
And the southwest(er)ne wynde / on Sat(ur)day at euen
Was ap(er)tly for p(r)ide / and for no poynte ellis
Pyryes and plauntes / wer(e) put to the [-grounde][5] erthe
I ensample sente god / that \`we' schulde do the bet(er)e
Bechis and brode okys / weren blowe to the gro[r>i:u]nde
And turnyde vpward her(e) tayl / in tokenyng of drede
That dedly synne or domesday / schal fordon he(m) alle
Of this mat(er) I myȝt mamele / wel longe
Ac I schal seyȝe as I say / so me god helpe
How consience with a cros / comside to p(re)che
He bad wasto(ur) go werche / what he best couthe
And wynne that he wastide / with su(m) man(er) of crafte[6]

The usual Anglicana forms are in use, but initial **s** may be long or short, and looped cursive **e** is not used; **w** is a tight flower-like shape; **y** sometimes dotted; **ȝ** used as well as **g**; **th** is normal, but **þ** occurs also and is distinguished from **y** by its straight descender. Minims not usually separately made. The title for Passus V, somewhat roughly written, is Gothic *textualis semiquadrata*; the two-line red initial **P**, set out into margin and colliding with l. 9, is surrounded and filled by flourishing of rounded or angular cells containing points. The lines begin with capitals, except for the inserted l. 14b. Word division is largely complete (note 'acros', l. 17, divided in the transcription, and the separated prefix in 'Iseye', l. 11). Virgules are later additions, perhaps in same hand as inserted 'we', l. 23, with Secretary **w**; doubled in line 18 they point to the opening of reported speech. Abbreviations are fairly heavily used: a flourish for final -**e** (ll. 4, 11, 12, 15 (× 2), 19, 22, 25); the overline for *m* or *n* (ll. 4, 26, 31); ʼ for -*er*/*re* (ll. 3, 6, 17, 18, 20, 23, 27, 29, 31); ^{2} for -*ur* (ll. 4, 9, 20, 30). The

[1] Superscript *b*, to indicate order.
[2] Superscript *a*, to indicate order.
[3] Scribe's *signes de renvoi*, caret mark and obelus followed here, but the text remains faulty. Note that the verse dividers have not been added to these lines.
[4] Shaft of letter, possibly **f**, begun mistakenly, and crossed through.
[5] Note subpuncting to mark omission.
[6] The last line is empty, suggesting 14a-14b omission discovered before turning over.

16

And reson redyly thou schalt nat wende henne
ffor as longe as I leue leue the I wylle
I am redy quod reson to reste with ȝow eue
So consience be of ȝour consel kepe I no bet
I graunte quod the kyng godes forbede he fayle
As longe as I lyue lyue we to gyderes

Passus quintus de visione

The kyng and the knyȝt to the chyrche wente
To here matyns and messe and to mete after
Than wakyde I of wynkyng and wo was with alle
That I ne hadde slepe sadder and I seye more
Er I hadde fare a ferlong feyntyse me hadde
That I ne myȝt ferrer a fote for defaute of slepyng
I satt sotely on my bedis that brouȝth me on slepe [interlined: and seide my beleue]
Than sauȝ I muche more than I be for tolde ‸ and so y babelyd on my bedis &c
Al ye felde ful of folke that I first of tolde
And consience with a cros com forto preche
And preyede the peple haue pyte on hem selue
And prouyde that these pestylences weren for pure synne
And the south westrne wynde on Satirday at euen
Was apertly for pride and for no poynte elles
Pyryes and plaumtes were put to the grounde erthe
In ensample sente god that schulde do the bete
Beches and brode okys weren blowe to the grounde
And turnyde up ward her tayl in tokenyng of drede
That dedly synne er domesday schal fordon hem alle
Of this mater I myȝt mamele wel longe
Ac I schal seye as I say so me god helpe
How consience with a cros comside to preche
He bad wastor go werche what he best couthe
And wynne that he wastede with sum maner of crafte

Plate 41 – actual size

superscript vowels make *(r)a* in l. 5 and *(r)i* in l. 21. There are two abbreviated forms of 'quod' (ll. 3, 5), which editors sometimes transcribe as 'quoth', and ꝑ (in 'ap(er)tly', l. 21) is invoked once rather than ᐩ (compare ll. 17, 18, 29). The 9 abbreviation ('kniȝt(us)', l. 8) may, unusually, represent *-es*/*-is*. Corrections are frequent. The second and third words in the first line are marked by superscript *b* and *a* for transposition. A line omitted is carelessly inserted and still presents problems ('sotely', l. 14a, should read 'softely' and 'on my bedis', anticipating the next line, may reflect a mistaken reading in the exemplar). Once the subject pronoun ('we', l. 23) is left out. There is a false start (l. 16), and a word anticipated by eye-skip (l. 22) is subpuncted. Letters are also altered (e.g. ll. 13, 24). This folio, from the second quire of a paper manuscript, has the collation mark 'iiij' in the bottom right-hand corner of the page, as a guide to the binder for keeping the sheets in order. The leaves are now separately mounted. Watermark evidence points to a date in the first quarter of the fifteenth century or not long after.

CONTEXTS

Ff. 1-96 (*Piers Plowman* A Prologue-XI + C XII 297-XXIII) written for one of the Hoo family, Bedfordshire (evidence of shields of arms in margins, though some of these are added and one is perhaps Kentish); passed on to St Augustine's; name of William Holyngborne (monk of St Augustine's, Canterbury, 1510-39) on f. 96v. Related closely to text in Trinity College Cambridge R. 3. 14. Entered the British Museum with the Harley Collection in 1753.

SIZE

c. 225 × 145 mm (180 × 110 mm).

BIBLIOGRAPHY

Coll. Kane 1960: 269-72 (IV: 153-58, V: 1-25).

Disc. Harl. Cat., Kane 1960: 6-7; Doyle 1986; Lyall 1989: 23-26.

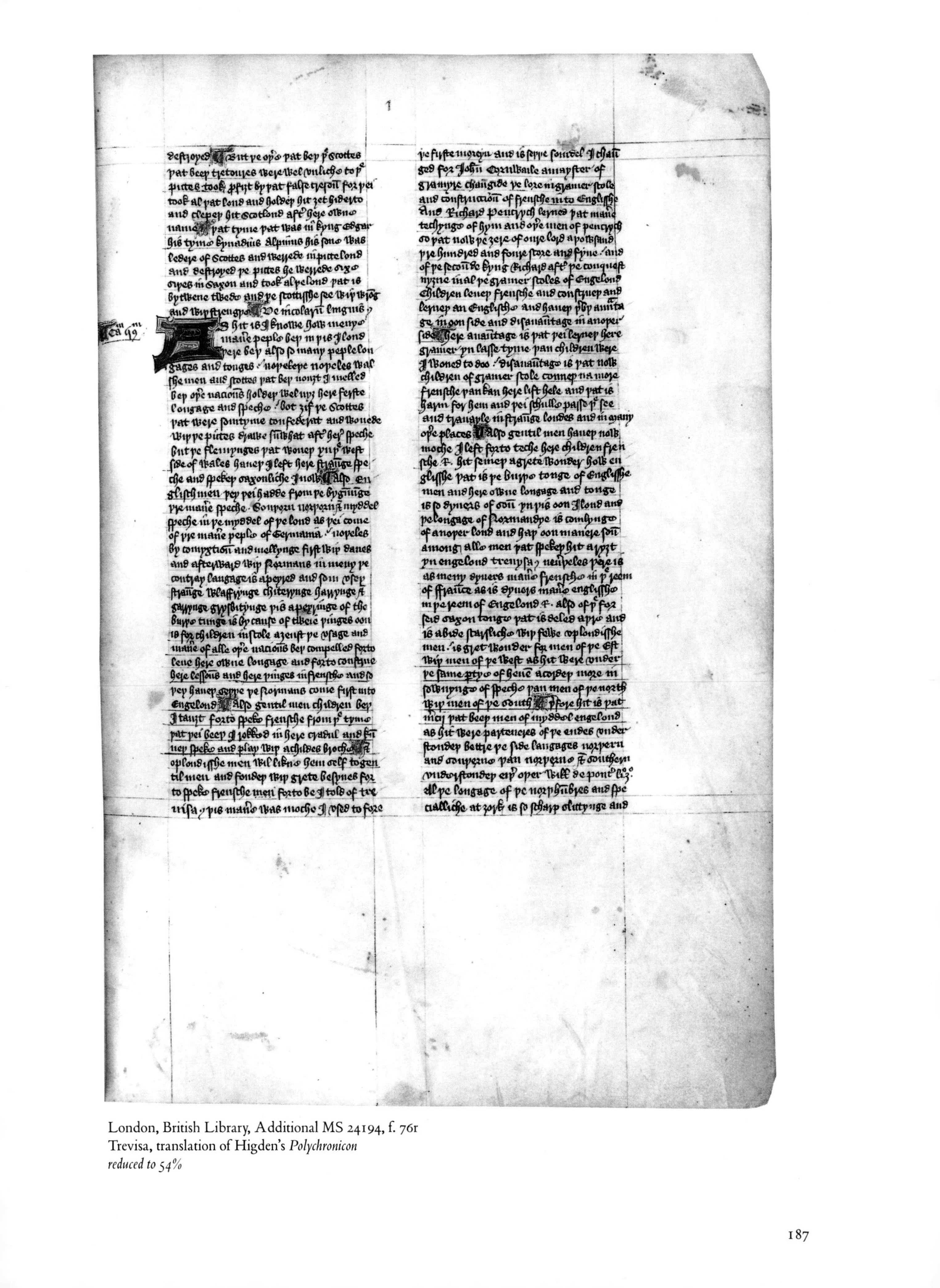

London, British Library, Additional MS 24194, f. 76r
Trevisa, translation of Higden's *Polychronicon*
reduced to 54%

42

San Marino, California, Henry E. Huntington Library, MS EL 26 C 9, 131r
Chaucer, *Canterbury Tales*, 'The Franklin's Tale' and gloss
Gothic *littera cursiva anglicana formata*, s. xv[1]

TRANSCRIPTION

¶ Frankelyn

Wel rather / than they wolde defouled be
I wol conclude / that it is bet for me
To sleen myself / than been defouled thus
I wol be trewe / vnto Arueragus
Or rather / sleen myself in som manere
As dide / Demociones doghter deere
By cause / þ^t she wolde nat defouled be
O Cedasus / it is ful greet pitee
To reden / how thy doghtren deyde allas
That slowe hemself / for which manere cas
As greet a pitee was it / or wel moore
The Theban mayden / that for Nichanore
hirseluen slowe / right for swich manere wo
Another Theban mayden / dide right so
For oon of Macidonye / hadde hir(e) opp(re)ssed
she with hir(e) death / hir maydenhede redressed
What shal I seye of Nicerates wyf
That for swich cas / birafte hirself hir lyf /
How trewe eek was / to Alcebiades
his loue / rather for to dyen chees
Than for to suffre / his body vnburyed be
Lo which a wyf / was Alceste quod she
What seith Omer / of goode Penalopee
Al Grece / knoweth of hir(e) chastitee
Pardee / of Lacedomya / is writen thus
That when at Troie /was slayn Prothesela(us)
No lenger / wolde she lyue / after his day
The same / of noble Porcia telle I may
Withoute Brutus / koude she nat lyue
To whom she hadde / al hool hir herte yeue
The p(er)fir wyfhod of Arthemesie
Honured is / thurgh' al the Barbarie
O Teuta queene / thy wyfly chastitee
To alle wyues / may a Mirour bee
The same thyng' / I seye of Bilyea
Of Rodogone / and eek Valeria
¶ Thus pleyne[3] Dorigene / a day or tweye
Purposynge eu(er)e / that she wolde deye
¶ But nathelees / vpon the thridde nyght
Hoom cam Arueragus / this worthy knyght
And asked hir(e) / why that she weep' so sore
And she gan wepen / eu(er) lenger the moore
¶ Allas quod she / that eu(er)e I was born
Thus haue I seyd quod she / thus haue I sworn
And toold hym al / as ye han herd bifore
It nedeth nat / reherce it yow namoore
¶ This housbonde / with glad chiere in freendly wyse
Answerde and seyde / as I shal yow deuyse

¶ Democionis Ariopagitar(um) p(r)inci(-)
pis virgo filia ⁊ c(etera)
¶ Quo ore laudande sunt Ceda-
sij filie ⁊ c(etera)

¶ Nichanor victis Thebis vnius
capti(n)e[1] virginis amore sup(er)at(us) e(st)
¶ Narrant scriptores Grecie ⁊ alia(m)
Thebanam virginem ⁊ c(etera)

¶ Quid loquar ⁊ ncerati[2] co(n)iuge(m)
pie i(n)pacie(n)s i(n)iurie vir morte(m) ⁊ c'
¶ Alcebiades ille soc(r)atic(us) vict(us) ⁊ c'

¶ Alcesten fabule feru(n)t p(ro) marito
Adameto sponte defuncta(m)/ et
Penolopes pudicia Om(er)i carme(n) e(st)
¶ Lacedomia quoq(ue) poetar(um) ore
cantat(ur) occiso apud Troiam
Protheselao ⁊ c(etera)
¶ Porcia sine Bruto viu(er)e non
potuit

¶ Arthemesia quoq(ue) vxor Mauseoli/ insignis pudiciciis fuisse p(er)hibet(ur) ⁊ c(etera)
¶ Teuta/ Illiricoru(m) Regina ⁊ c(etera)

¶ M(emoran)d(um) strato regulus
¶ Vidi ⁊ om(n)es pene Barbares ca(pitul)o.
xxvj°. p(r)imi
¶ Item Cornelia ⁊ c(etera)
¶ Imitent(ur) (er)go nupte Theanam/ Cle-
obiliam/ Gorgim[4]/ Thymodia(m) Claudias atq(ue) Cornelias/ in fine lib(r)i primi.

¶ Singulas has historias ⁊ plures hanc
materiam conc(er)nentes recitat beatus
Ieromin(us) cont(r)a Iouinianu(m) in p(r)imo suo
Libro ca(pitul)o ·39°·

[1] For *u*? [2] Minim missing. [3] Read 'pleyned'. [4] Or 'Gorgun'.

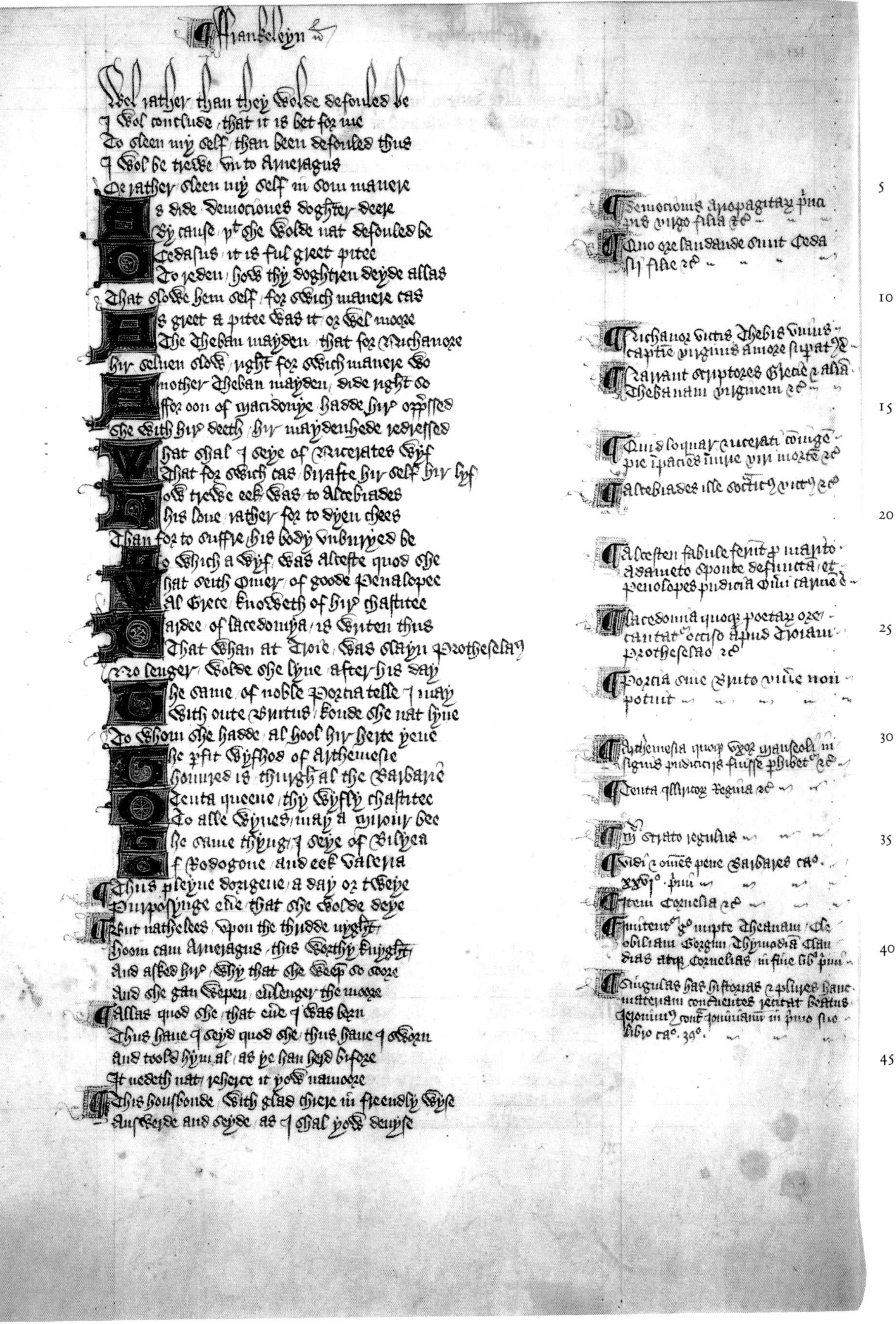
Frankeleyn

Wel rather than they wolde defouled be
I wol conclude that it is bet for me
To sleen my self than been defouled thus
I wol be trewe vn to Arueragus
Or rather sleen my self in som manere
As dide Demociones doghter deere
By cause þt she wolde nat defouled be
O Cedasus it is ful greet pitee
To reden how thy doghtren deyde allas
That slowe hem self for swich manere cas
As greet a pitee was it or wel moore
The Theban mayden that for Nichanore
Hir seluen slow right for swich manere wo
Another Theban mayden dide right so
ffor oon of Macidonye hadde hir oppressed
She with hir deeth hir maydenhede redressed
What shal I seye of Nicerates wyf
That for swich cas birafte hir self hir lyf
How trewe eek was to Alcebiades
His loue rather for to dyen chees
Than for to suffre his body vnburyed be
Lo which a wyf was Alceste quod she
What seith Omer of goode Penalopee
Al Grece knoweth of hir chastitee
Pardee of Lacedomya is writen thus
That whan at Troie was slayn Protheselaus
No lenger wolde she lyue after his day
The same of noble Porcia telle I may
With oute Brutus koude she nat lyue
To whom she hadde al hool hir herte yeue
The parfit wyfhod of Arthemesie
Honured is thurgh al the Barbarie
O Teuta queene thy wyfly chastitee
To alle wyues may a mirour bee
The same thyng I seye of Bilyea
Of Rodogone and eek Valeria
Thus pleyned Dorigene a day or tweye
Purposynge euere that she wolde deye
But nathelees vp on the thridde nyght
Hoom cam Arueragus this worthy knyght
And asked hire why that she weep so soore
And she gan wepen euer lenger the moore
Allas quod she that euere I was born
Thus haue I seyd quod she thus haue I sworn
And tolde hym al as ye han herd bifore
It nedeth nat reherce it yow namoore
This housbonde with glad cheere in freendly wyse
Answerde and seyde as I shal yow deuyse

Democionis Ariopagitarum principis virgo filia etc.
Cum ore laudande sunt Cedasi filie etc.
Nichanor victis Thebis vnius captiue virginis amore succensus est etc.
Narrant scriptores Grecie et aliam Thebanam virginem etc.
Quis loquatur Nicerati coniugem que impaciens iniurie viri mortem etc.
Alcebiades ille socraticus etc.
Alcesten fabule ferunt pro marito Admeto sponte defunctam et Penolopes pudicicia Omeri carmen est
Lacedomia quoque poetarum ore cantatur occiso apud Troiam Protheselao etc.
Porcia sine Bruto viuere non potuit
Arthemesia quoque vxor Mausoli insignis pudicicie fuisse perhibetur etc.
Teuta Illiricorum Regina etc.
Item Strato regulus
Quasi omnes pene Barbaros etc. xxvjo primi
Item Cornelia etc.
Ffuit etiam nupte Theanam Vero bilianam Rodogin Cynuodia Claudias atque Cornelias in fine libri primi
Singulas has historias et plures hanc materiam concernentes recitat beatus Jeronimus contra Jouinianum in primo suo libro capitulo 39o.

Plate 42 – reduced to 58%

The script is a free-running *anglicana formata*, its letters varying in height and slope. The **g** and high 8-shaped final **s** are distinctive (the latter, as in 'Brutus', l. 29a, is found in both the Hengwrt and Ellesmere manuscripts). Positional variants for **s** are the sigma-shaped form at the beginning of words ('she', l. 22, 'seith', l. 23), the long form medially 'asked', l. 41, 'Answerde', l. 48, and in ligatures ('Alceste', l. 22, 'chastitee', l. 33). Linguistically this is London English (Samuels Type III), written by a scribe (Doyle/Parkes Scribe 'B') at work in London *c.* 1400. The hand is identified in four manuscripts: the Cecil fragment of *Troilus and Criseyde*; the Hengwrt *Canterbury Tales*; the Ellesmere *Canterbury Tales* (the present manuscript); and Cambridge, Trinity College R. 32 (Gower's *Confessio Amantis,* copied 1407-09). The *mise-en-page* is well organized, with careful use of one- or two-line capitals and of the capitulum sign to signal reference between the single column of text (set off-centre) and apparatus (a second frame-ruled column in outer writing area). The main mark of punctuation is the virgule, marking pause within the verse line. Proper names are generally given capitals. The abbreviations in the main text are few, unless some of the strokes and flourishes indicated by apostrophe in the transcript are held to require expansion. The stroke through **h** is otiose in ll. 6, 13, 14, 39, 40 and is not therefore expanded in 'thurgh'', l. 32. The curl at the end of 'hir(e)' in ll. 16, 41 is distinct from final **r** elsewhere (compare 'hir', l. 16). The more formal *that* appears eight times, against a single instance of 'þ^{t}', l. 7. By comparison, the notes in Latin look heavily abbreviated, and for reasons of space 'c(etera)' remains unexpanded twice in col. b of the transcript. Note the abbreviated 'capti(n)e', l. 13g, where *u*, not *n*, is needed.

CONTEXTS

This is a large and impressive manuscript, its page size at least 420 × 290 mm before cropping. An early hand (verso of ff. i, vii) suggests a connection with the Paston family. The contents of a poem in a late-fifteenth-century hand (verso of f. ii to recto of f. iv) composed and/or copied '*per* Rotheley' point to the household of the earls of Oxford, the de Vere family. A fifteenth-century inscription names a 'John Hedgeman of Hawkedoun', which is near Hawstead and just twenty miles from Castle Hedingham, seat of the earls of Oxford at that time. Sixteenth-century owners include a Norfolk family called Drury, in the area of Hawstead, Suffolk (*c.* 1528-36 Sir Robert Drury names himself, his two sons and three daughters on f. iv, and other notes are related): Sir Robert was an executor of the thirteenth earl of Oxford. Next owned (f. 130) by Henry Payne, an executor of Sir William Drury's will, who left it to Sir Giles Alington, grandson of Sir Robert Drury's daughter Ursula. Later seemingly in the possession of Roger, Lord North, of Kirtling Court (about six miles away), who added some English poems to the manuscript; and further additions were made by a 'John Neve of Oxenborowe', Norfolk, on f. 48r. Perhaps belonged to Thomas Egerton, Baron Ellesmere; certainly belonged to his son John, first earl of Bridgewater. In London in 1802 for rebinding. On the death of the 3rd duke of Bridgewater in 1803 without a direct heir, the Bridgewater Library passed to a nephew, the earl of Stafford, whose second son Francis Egerton became first earl of Ellesmere in 1846. Entered the Huntington Library with purchase of the Bridgewater Library in 1917. Known as the Ellesmere manuscript.

SIZE

395 × 280 mm (310-22 × 153-55 mm).

BIBLIOGRAPHY

Pr. Benson 1988: 186 (ll. 1442-68).
Facs. Woodward and Stevens 1995, superseding Egerton 1911 and Hanna 1989 (reduced facsimile of the Egerton 1911).
Disc. Samuels 1963, 1983[1], 1983[2] [1988]; Doyle and Parkes 1978 [Parkes 1991]; Ramsey 1982; McIntosh, Samuels and Benskin 1986: I. 25, 91, III. 299 (LP 6400 London); David 1995; Doyle 1995; Parkes 1995; Scott 1995, 1996: no. 42; Hanna and Edwards 1995; Seymour 1995-97: II. 230-35; Solopova 2001; Horobin 2003; Horobin and Mooney at press.

þat iustifiynge suffisance ne seale ȝow þine lettres
Ne no supsidias sende but j assente q(uod) resoun
and j dar legge my lif þat loue wolde lene þe siluer
To wage þin helpe wynne þat þow wilnest aft(er)
More þan all þy marchauntz or þy mytred bisshops
Of lombardz of lukes þat leuen by lone as iewes
The kyng comandede consience þo to congeie all his officers
and receyue þo þat reson louede and right w(ith) þ(at) j wakede

Passus quintus de visione vbi prius

Thus j awaked wot god when j woned in cornhull
kytte and j in a cotell cloped as a loller
And litel y lete by leueth me for sothe
Amonges lollers of london and lewed heremites
ffor j made of þo men as reson me taghte
ffor as j cam by consience wiþ reson j mette
In an hote heruest whan j hadde myn hele
and lymes to labore wiþ and loued wel fare
and no dede to do but drynke and to slepe
In hele and in inwitte on me apposed
Romynge in remembrance þus reson me arated
Can þou seruen he saide or syngen in a chirch
Or koke for my cokeres or to þe carte picche
Mowen or mywen or make bond to sheues
Repe or ben a repereue and arise erly
Or haue an horne and be hayward and ligge þoute a nyghtes
and kepe my corne in my crofte fro pikers and þeues
Or shape shon or cloþ or sheep and kyne kepe
heggen or harwen or swyn or gees dryue
Or eny oþer kynes craft þat to þe comune nedeth
þat þou be betered þerby þat byleue þe fynden
Certes j sayde and so me god helpe

London, University Library, MS V. 88, f. 25v
Langland, *Piers Plowman* ('Ilchester' text), from Passus IV-V
actual size

43

Cambridge, Corpus Christi College MS 61, f. 12r
Chaucer, *Troilus and Criseyde*, I. 386-420
Gothic *littera textualis quadrata formata*, s. xv in.

TRANSCRIPTION

And ouere al this ȝet muchel more he thoughte
What for to speke and what to holden Inne
And what to arten hire to loue he soughte
And on a songe anon right to bygynne
And gan loude on his sorwe for to wynne
For with good hope he gan fully assente
Criseyde for to loue and nought repente

And of his songe naught only the setence[1]
As writ myn auctour called Lollius
But pleinly saue oure tonges difference
I dar wel seyn in al that Troilus
Seyde in his songe loo euery word right thus
As I shal seyn and who so list it here
Loo next this vers he may it fynde here

If no loue is o god what fele I so
And if loue is what thinge and which is he[2]
If loue be good from whennes co(m)meth my woo
If it be wikke a wonder thynketh me
Whenne euery torment and aduersite
That cometh of hym may to me sauory thinke
For ay thrust I the more that ich it drynke

And if that at myn owen lust I brenne
From whennes cometh my waillynge and my pleynte
If harme agree me wherto pleyne I thenne
I noot ne whi vnwery that I feynte
O quik[3] deth o swete harm so queynte
How may of the in me swich quantite
But if that I consente that it be

And if that I consente I wrongfully
Compleyne Iwis thus possed to and fro
Al sterlees withInne a boot am I[4]
Amydde the see bitwixen wyndes two
That Inne contrarie stonden euere mo
Allas what is this wondre maladie
For hote of colde for colde of hote I dye

This is a striking manuscript, apparently intended to contain only *Troilus and Criseyde*, for there are neither running titles nor ruled lines for titles. It opens with a splendid illumination (f. 1v; see p. 195); and many spaces were left for an ambitious programme of miniatures. The parchment is of a good quality, carefully ruled for five stanzas per page, with spaces calculated for expected illustrations, in ink of the same colour as the text. On this page there is see-through only for the fifth stanza because four-fifths of f. 12v was left empty for illustration, with ruling only for the single stanza. Overall this is a surprisingly formal text, with a luxurious sense of space. Decorative strokes are carefully made (short oblique strokes on the heads and feet of minims and on the main strokes of such letters as **f, h, r,** and long **s**; finishing strokes at ascender tops;

[1] For 'sentence'. Overline missed out.
[2] Note in margin 'Canticus | Troili'.
[3] The reading 'quike' of some other manuscripts is better metrically.
[4] The reading 'sterelees' of some other manuscripts is better metrically.

And ouer al this ȝet muchel more he thoughte
What forto speke and what to holden inne
And what to arten hire to loue he soughte
And on a songe anon right to bygynne
And gan loude on his sorwe forto wynne
For with good hope he gan fully assente
Criseyde forto loue and nought repente

And of his songe naught only the sentence
As writ myn auctour called Lollius
But pleinly saue oure tonges difference
I dar wel seyn in al that Troilus
Seyde in his songe loo euery word right thus
As I shal seyn and who so list it here
Loo next this vers he may it fynde here

Canticus Troili

If no loue is o god what fele I so
And if loue is what thinge and which is he
If loue be good from whennes cometh my woo
If it be wikke a wonder thynketh me
Whenne euery torment and aduersite
That cometh of hym may to me sauory thinke
For ay thurst I the more that ich it drynke

And if that at myn owen lust I brenne
From whennes cometh my waillynge and my pleynte
If harme agree me wherto pleyne I thenne
I noot ne why vnwery that I feynte
O quike deth o swete harm so queynte
How may of the in me swich quantite
But if that I consente that it be

And if that I consente I wrongfully
Compleyne iwis thus possed to and fro
Al sterelees within a boot am I
Amydde the see bitwixen wyndes two
That inne contrarie stonden euere mo
Allas what is this wondre maladie
For hote of colde for colde of hote I dye

Plate 43 — reduced to 74%

hairlines especially on final letters). Bitings are few, mostly between **d** and **e** ('holden', l. 2, 'loude', l. 5, 'fynde', l. 14, 'wonder', l. 18, 'deth', l. 26, 'Amidde', l. 32, 'wyndes', l. 32, 'stonden', l. 33, 'colde', l. 35 (× 2); compare 'dar', l. 11, 'be', l. 17). The round **r** follows **o** consistently (e.g. 'for', ll. 2, 5, 7, 'word', l. 12, 'torment', l. 19); and round **s** is word final ('his', ll. 5, 8, 'Lollius', l. 9, 'is this', l. 34). Each line begins with a capital, and proper names are capitalized. No pauses are marked by virgule within the verse line, by contrast with the occasional virgules of the St John's *Troilus* (pl. 45). There is little abbreviation: the overline is omitted once ('setence', l. 8) and once used unnecessarily ('co(m)meth', l. 17). Words are well spaced, and some elements are set apart ('a gree', l. 24, 'vn wery', l. 25, 'I wis', l. 30, 'with Inne', l. 31; but 'euere mo', l. 33, is transcribed as two words).

CONTEXTS

Probably from London or St Albans *c.* 1415-*c.* 1425 (Scott 1996). Four, maybe six, further manuscripts are attributed to the illuminator of f. 1v, who is thought to have completed commissions for a member of the Scrope family. But there is no firm evidence. Such is the quality of this English vernacular manuscript that attempts have been made to identify a royal patron (one suggestion is Charles d'Orléans, indentified with the figure in gold in the f. 1v illumination; see facing page). John Shirley added a couplet by Lydgate to f. 1r, but this is a far more luxurious manuscript than those Shirley owned. Other fifteenth-century inscriptions: 'neu(er) Foryeteth' | Anne neuill'' (f. 101v), and in similar hand 'Knyvett' (f. 108r); 'notnarf Drawde' or Edward Franton on the verso of f. i and ff. 147r, 151r; 'Henrycum Coldvell'' (f. 151r). The name 'Dorote Pennell'' (f. 63r) looks early sixteenth-century. Batman's inscription (f. 150v) records that he got the manuscript from 'Mr Cari' in 1570 and and that he passed it on to Parker. Entered the Parker Library in 1575 as part of Parker's bequest to Corpus Christi College Cambridge.

SIZE

312 × 220 mm (214 × 122 mm).

BIBLIOGRAPHY

Pr. Benson 1988: 478-79; *Pr.* Windeatt 1984: 110-113.
Facs. Parkes and Salter 1978.
Disc. Watson 1965 [2004[1]]: 137, 2004[2]: 4-5; Pearsall 1977; Butterfield 1995; Hardman 1995-96, 1997[1], 1997[2]: 44, 51-54; Seymour 1995-97: I. 59-60; Scott 1996: no. 58; 2000; Parkes 1997: 139-40; Connolly 1998; Harris 2000.

Cambridge, Corpus Christi College MS 61, f. 1v

The frontispiece was the only illustration actually supplied in the manuscript
reduced to 74%

44

London, British Library, Additional Charter 17692
Lease from John of Langton to Thurstan of Atherton, Lancashireshire
Gothic *cursiva anglicana media*, 1420

TRANSCRIPTION

Thys endentur' berus wyttenes þat Ioh(n) of langton' of hyndeley has leton' to ferme to Thurstan of Athirton' ⁊ to hys Ayres ⁊ to hys Assignes þe place þ(a)t was Adam Atkynson' ⁊ þe Newe Marlet lande in hyndeley ffelde in þe towne of hyndeley to terme of lyf of þe forsayd Ioh(n) of langton' ȝelding' be ȝer' xlviij s' ⁊ iiij d to paye at faur' tymes of þe ȝer' þ(a)t is to witte xii s' ⁊ i d at þe fest of Crystonmasse[1] next sewing' þe day making of thes endent(ur)s ⁊ xij s' ⁊ i d at Myde Lenton' next sewing þ(a)t ⁊ xii s' ⁊ i d at þe fest of Myssom(ur) next sewing þ(a)t ⁊ xij s' ⁊ i d at þe fest of saynt Michaell' þe Archang(e)ll'[2] next sewing' þ(a)t ⁊ so paying' xij s' ⁊ i d at four' tymes of þe ȝer' qwyl xlviij s' ⁊ iiij d be payut for all' man(er) sewtus seruis present(us) fre rent(us) Customes falling' þ(er)to safing xlviij s' ⁊ iiij d be ȝer' as h(i)t is beforsayd[3] And all' so þe forsayd Ioh(n) of Langton' grauntes to þe forsayd Thurstan comyne pastur' taurbour' w(i)t(h) all' man(er) of esseme(n)t(us) þ(a)t ane tenaunt or Charterer' has w(i)t(h)in þe towne of hyndeley . And alle so þe forsayd Ioh(n) of [-lan] langton' grauntes to þe forsayd Thurstan þ(a)t if ane mon' distresse þe forsayd Thurstan for ane man(er) of rych' or tytull' claymy(n)g in þ(a)t place safing þe forsayd Ioh(n) of Langton' or hys Ayres or hys Assignes for xlviij s' ⁊ iiij d be ȝer' as h(i)t is beforsayd for alle man(er) sewtus or s(er)uis faling' þ(er)to þen þ(a)t þe forsayd Ioh(n) of langton' schall' Iu þe forsayd Thurstan hys stres agayne or elles þe valewe þ(er)of so þ(a)t þe forsayd Thurstan haue noe harme þ(er)bye And all' so þe forsayd Ioh(n) of langton' grauntes þe forsayd Thurstan to entur' into þe place at Martin⟨-⟩masse[4] next aft(ur) þe day making of þes endent(ur)s In wyutynnysing[5] of þes endent(ur)s we haue sette our' seals wrethun apon' þe Monday next befor þe Natiuite of our' lady[6] Anno regni Regis Henricij qui(n)ti post conques⟨-⟩tu(m) Angl(ie) octauo[7]

A fluent, practised but untidy hand, essentially *anglicana* except for Secretary **a**, which is not always distinct from **o**: see 'lande', l. 2, 'faur'', l. 3 (a form recorded in fourteenth-century use), 'apon', l. 16. The Anglicana form, represented by **A** in the transcript, appears to function as a capital. The *media* grading is indicated by infrequent pen-lifts between minims, and the fairly heavy use of abbreviation is in accord with this grade. There is no distinction in script for the Latin of the final words of dating to the regnal year. Linguistically this is a northern text. Thus, for example, back vowels predominate in inflexions and other final syllables; and *wh-* is strongly aspirated (see 'qwyl' (until), l. 6). Note the distinctive *-ch-* of 'rych'' (right), l. 10, and the unusual *ane* (any) in ll. 9, 10. No punctuation marks are used, except for the haphazardly placed low point in l. 9; thus spelling in full of *And* with following *also* in ll. 8, 9, and 14 signals the arrival of major pieces in information. Note the sporadic use of capitals, usually for names of people (as for the principals 'Ioh(n)' and 'Thurstan'), but not always for place-names (though 'Langton'' in ll. 8 and 11 has a special form of *l*). The 'Newe Marlet lande' (newly manured with marl), l. 2, may have been dignified with capitals as a particularly attractive feature of the property leased. Some dates are given capitals, and there are other occasional capitals. Abbreviations, apart from frequent flourishes represented by the straight apostrophe, do not present problems: ˀ for *er* ('man(er)', ll. 7, 9, 10, 12, 's(er)uis', l. 12, 'þ(er)to', ll. 7, 12, 'þ(er)bye', l. 14, 'þ(er)of', l. 13); ² for *ur* ('endent(ur)s', ll. 4, 15 (× 2), 'Myssom(ur)' (mid-summer), l. 5, 'aft(ur)', l. 15); the slash through ƚ for an omitted vowel (e.g. 'Archang(e)ll'', l. 6); the Tironian sign for *and*; the overline for *m* ('conquest|u(m)', l. 16) or *n* (as in 'Ioh(n)' × 7, 'claymy(n)g', l. 11, 'qui(n)ti', l. 16); by superscript letters as in *þ*^{t} for *þat* (× 10), *w*^{t} for *with* (ll. 8, 9), and *h*^{t} for *hit* (ll. 7, 12); and the pseudo-abbreviation *þ*^{e}. In the transcript the apostrophe is used for likely otiose marks. Both 's'' (with overline) and 'd' (released in such a way as to suggest a point), abbreviations in Latin for *solidi* and *denarii* respectively, are to be understood as standing for shillings and pence, the subdivisions of the pound replaced by decimal currency in 1971. In l. 16 the expansion to 'Angl(ie)' is normal. Apart from its use in the name *Iohn* the long *i* is used twice only: 'In', l. 15, marking the final witnessing of the agreement; and, again before other minims, 'Iu', l. 12, by this time an obsolescent form in the north-west alongside *give* forms.

[1] For *Christenmas*, the usual form of northern dialects; note the otiose overline mid-word.

[2] 29 September.

[3] The *-d* here is released with a final stroke, perhaps meant to indicate a point.

[4] 11 November.

[5] A misspelling (compare 'wyttenes', l. 1) in which a rounded sound after *w-* typical of western texts may be indicated by *-yu-*.

[6] 8 September.

[7] 'after the conquest of England in the eighth year of King Henry V'. Henry V became king in 1413.

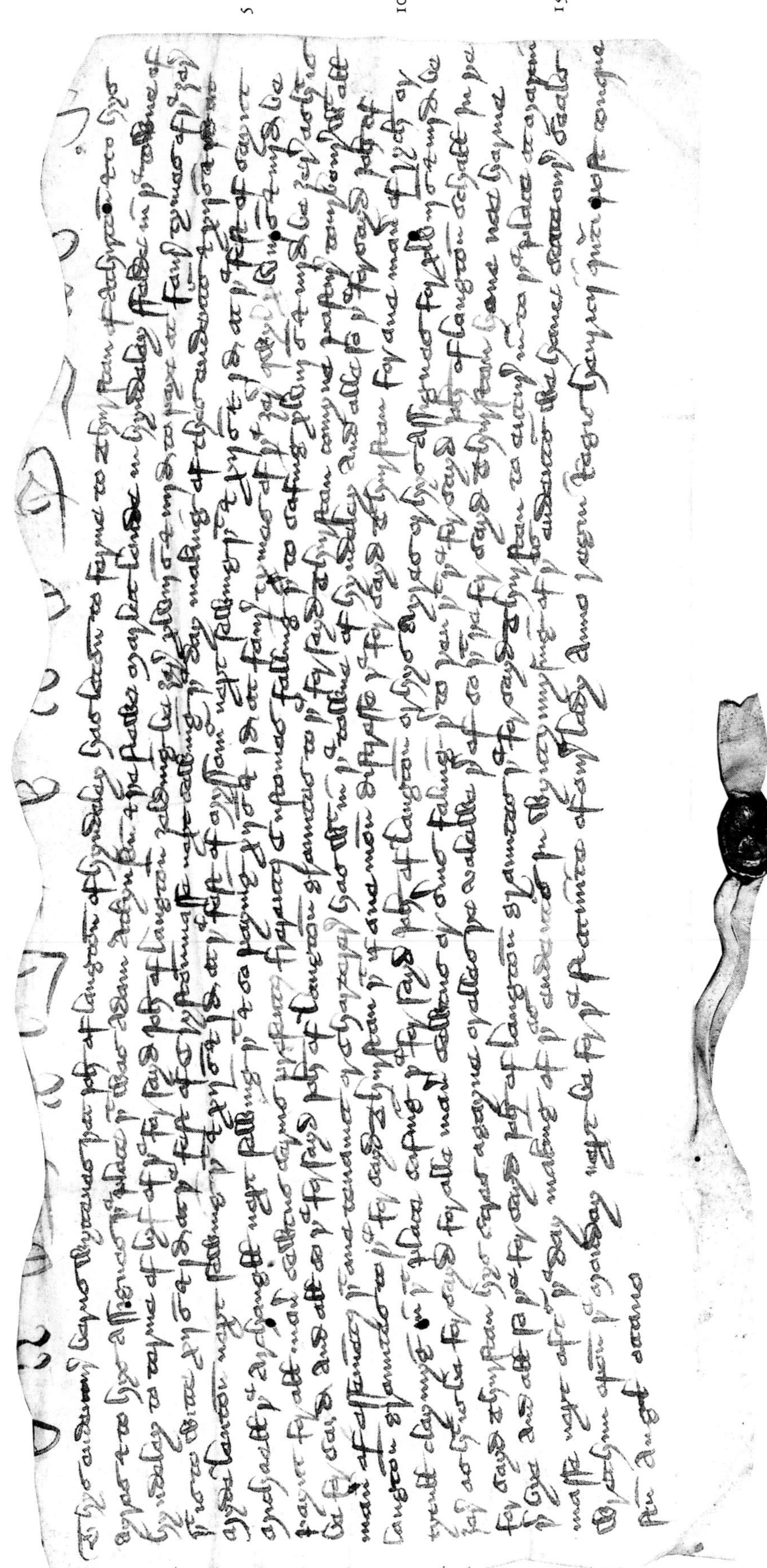

Plate 44 – reduced to 79%

CONTEXTS

This is the lower portion of an indenture (see 'thes endent(ur)s', l. 4), the zigzag cutting at the top splitting records that could be fitted together for validation. It appears therefore that at least two copies were made to record the agreement between John of Langton, near Hyndley, and Thurstan of Atherton, near Manchester, both in Lancashire. There is a well-developed technical vocabulary in use, not all of it recognized in the only edition. For example, 'stres', l. 13, is 'a distraint; also, the chattel or chattels seized in a distraint' (*OED* under *stress* n. II. 10. Law), which, when recognized, makes emendation of the sentence unnecessary. According to the acquisitions register held in the British Library, Additional Charter 17692 was acquired with Additional Charters 17665-17733, all of which were 'Purchased of Miers', 7 Dec. 1868.

SIZE

c. 134 × 285 mm.

BIBLIOGRAPHY

Pr. Morsbach 1923: 6-8 (no. III).

Disc. McIntosh, Samuels and Benskin 1986: I. 104 (LP 87. Grid 362 404. Lancs.), III. 204. Roberts forthcoming.

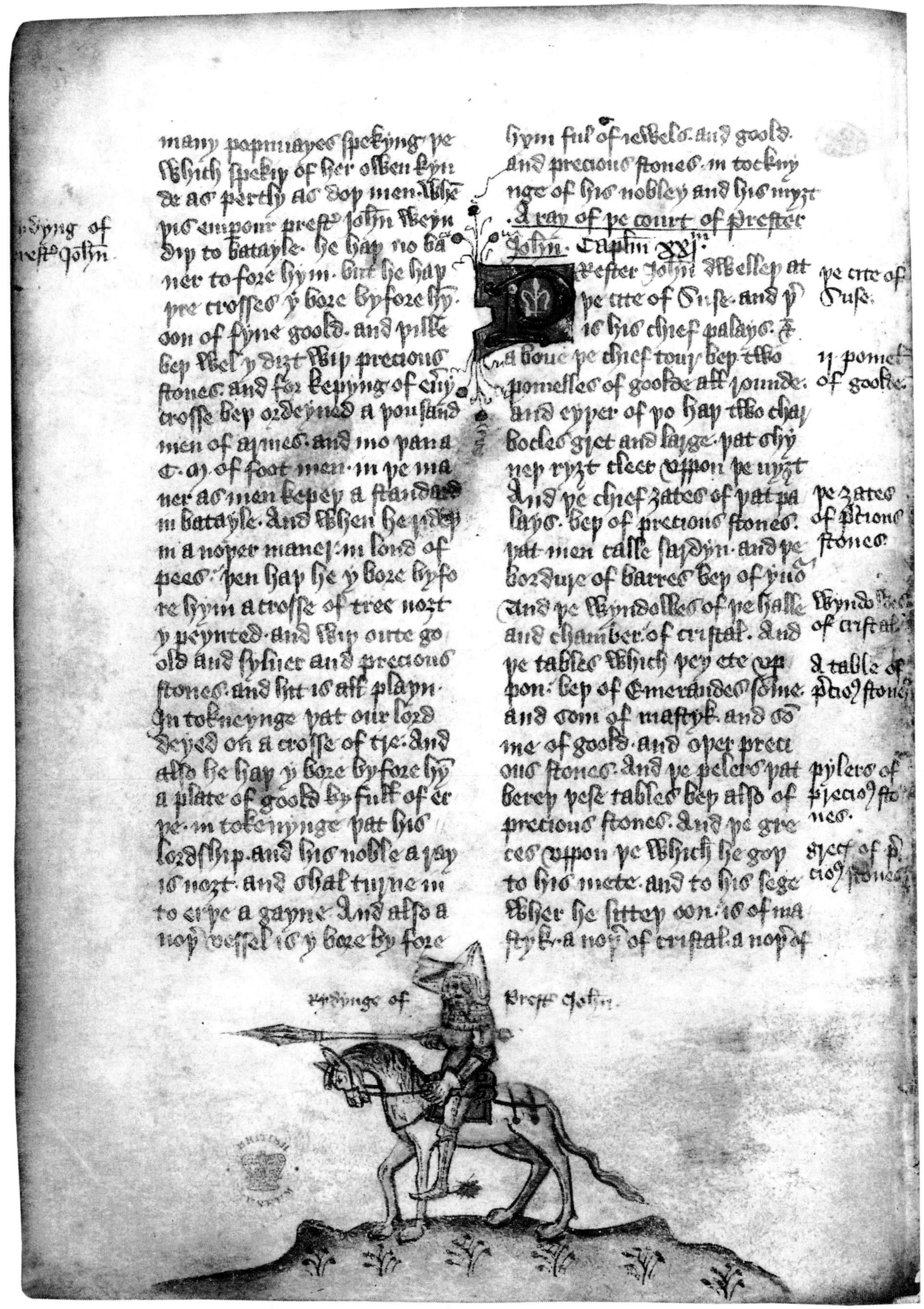
many papinjayes spekyng þe
which spekyn of her owen kyn
de as perfitly as doþ men. Whe
þis emperour prest John wendeþ
in to batayle. he haþ no ba
ner to fore hym. but he haþ
þre crosses y bore byfore hy
m of fyne goold. and þilke
beþ wel y dyzt wiþ precious
stones. and for kepyng of eu
ery crosse beþ ordeyned a þousand
men of armes. and mo þan a
C. M. of foot men. in þe ma
ner as men kepeþ a standard
in batayle. And when he rydeþ
in a noþer maner in lond of
pees. þen haþ he y bore byfo
re hym a crosse of tree nozt
y peynted. and wiþ oute go
old and sylver and precious
stones. and hit is al playn.
In tokenynge þat our lord
deyed on a crosse of tre. And
also he haþ y bore byfore hy
m a plate of goold ful of er
þe. in tokenynge þat his
lordship. and his noblei a [illegible]
is nozt. and shal turne in
to erþe a gayne. And also a
noþer vessel is y bore by fore

hym ful of jewels. and goold.
and precious stones. in tokny
nge of his noblei and his myzt
. A ray of þe court of prester
John. Capitulum xxi.
Prester John dwelleþ at
þe cite of Suse. and þ[er]
is his chief palays. A
boue þe chief tour beþ two
pomelles of goolde al rounde.
and eyþer of þo haþ two char
bocles grete and large. þat shy
neþ ryzt clere uppon þe nyzt.
And þe chief zates of þat pa
lays. beþ of precious stones.
þat men calle sardyn. and þe
bordure of barres beþ of yvo
[ry]. And þe wyndowes of þe halle
and chamber of cristal. And
þe tables which þey ete up
pon: beþ of Emeraudes some.
and som of mastyk. and so
me of goold. and oþer preci
ous stones. And þe pelers þat
bereþ þese tables beþ also of
precious stones. And þe gre
ces uppon þe which he goþ
to his mete. and to his sege
wher he sitteþ on. is of ma
styk. a noþer of cristal. a noþer of

Ridyng of prest John
þe cite of Suse
ii pomels of goolde
þe zates of precious stones
wyndowes of cristal
A table of precious stones
pylers of precious stones
grees of precious stones

Rydinge of Prester John.

London, British Library, Royal MS 17 C. xxxviii, f. 54v
Mandeville's Travels

Prester John mounted, with lance
reduced to 92%

45

Cambridge, St John's College MS L. 1, f. 6v *Colour pl. C6*
Chaucer, *Troilus and Criseyde*, I. 386-420
Gothic *littera cursiva anglicana formata*, s. xv^{1}

TRANSCRIPTION

And ou(er)e al this \`full´ muchel moore he thought
What for to speke / ⁊ what to holden inne
And what to arten hir to loue he soghte
And on a song anon ryght to begynne
And gan loud on his sorwe for to wynne
For w(i)t(h) good hope he gan fullysche assente
Criseide for to loue and naught repente

And of his song nat only the sentence
As writ myn aucto(ur) called lollius
But pleynly saue oure tonges difference
I dar wel say in al *y*^{t} Troilus
Seyde in his song / loo eu(er)y worde right thus
As I shal seyn / And wo[1] so list it heere
lo next this verse ye may it fynden heere

yif no loue is o god what fele I so
And yif loue is / what thing ⁊ which is he
yif loue be good / from whennes comth my wo
yif it be wilke a wonder thinketh me
Whenne eu(er)y torment ⁊ adu(er)site
That comth of hym may to me sauory thinke
For ay thurst I the moore *y*^{t} ich it drynke

And yif *y*^{t} at myn owne lust I brenne
From whennes comyth my waylynge ⁊ my pley(n)te
yif harm agree me I[2] wherto pleyne I thenne
I noot / ne whi vnwery *y*^{t} I feynte
O quyke deth / o swete harm so queynte
how may of the in me \`be´ swich qua(n)tite
But yif that I consente *y*^{t} it \`so´ be

And yif *y*^{t} I consente I wrongfully
Compleyne Iwis thus possed to ⁊ fro
Al steereles w(i)t(h)Inne a boot am I
Amydde the see betwixen wyndes two
That in contrarie stonden e(uer)mo
Allas what us this wondir maladie
For hete of cold / for colde of hete I dye

Overall, this is a formal Anglicana script. The minims are carefully made, with pen-lifts. Secretary **s** is used at the end of words ('his', ll. 5, 12, 'tonges', l. 10, 'Troilus', l. 11, 'this', l. 14, 'is', ll. 15, 16 (× 2), 34, 'whennes', ll. 17, 23, 'Iwis', l. 30, 'thus', l. 30, 'this', l. 34, 'steereles', l. 31, 'wyndes', l. 32, 'Allas', l. 34), and the angular appearance and forward slope also indicate Secretary influence. The cursive Anglicana **e** appears frequently ('moore', l. 1, 'speke', l. 2, 'inne', l. 2, 'arten', l. 3, etc.). The scribe uses *y* in the abbreviation for 'that' (**y** from older **þ** is italicized in the transcript), but his normal choice elsewhere is *th*. The layout is good, making clear the structure of the stanzas (see colour pl. C6): a long *paragraphus* to left-hand side of each stanza (alternating blue and red), and the whole stanza braced at the right-hand side (red). Capital letter-forms are mostly used at the beginning of lines, and the virgule can mark pause within the line. Most proper names are

[1] An alternative spelling for *who*.

[2] Perhaps a mistaken anticipation of 'I' later in the line.

And oue al this full muchel moore he thought
What for to speke & what to holden inne
And what to arten hire to loue he soghte
And on a song anon right to begynne
And gan loude on his sorwe for to wynne
For wt good hope he gan fullyche assente
Criseide for to loue and naught repente

And of his song nat only the sentence
As writ myn auctour called Lollius
But pleynly saue oure tonges difference
I dar wel sayn in al yt Troilus
Seyde in his song loo euery worde right thus
As I shal seyn and who so list it here
Lo next this verse ye may it fynden here

[illegible] The Songe of Troilus

yif no loue is o god what fele I so
And yif loue is what thing & which is he
yif loue be good from whennes cometh my wo
yif it be wikke a wonder thinketh me
Whenne euery torment & aduersite
That cometh of hym may to me sauory thinke
For ay thurst I the moore yt ich it drynke

And yif yt at myn owne lust I brenne
Ffrom whennes cometh my waylynge & my pleynte
yif harm agree me wher to pleyne I thenne
I noot ne why vnwery yt I feynte
O quyke deth o swete harm so queynte
How may of the in me be swich quantite
But yif that I consente yt it so be

And yif yt I consente I wrongfully
Compleyne I wis thus possed to & fro
Al stereles wt inne a boot am I
Amydde the see betwixen wyndes two
That in contrarie stonden euere mo
Allas what is this wonder maladie
For hete of cold for colde of hete I dye

Plate 45 – reduced to 91%

given capitals or enlarged letter-forms (not 'lollius', l. 9). A marginal note points carefully to the opening of Troilus's lament with 'c(itatio) no(t)a k(apitulum)' at l. 15 (the expansion to *citatio* is offered hesitantly), part of apparatus supplied throughout to mark out noteworthy passages. Below a seventeenth-century hand has added 'The Songe | of Troilus : '. The abbreviations, significantly more frequent than for the same passage in the much more formal Gothic *textualis* script of pl. 43, are not unusual: the Tironian sign; ʹ in 'ou(er)e', l. 1, 'eu(er)y', ll. 12, 19, 'adu(er)site', l. 19; ^{2} in 'aucto(ur)', l. 9; the overline for *n* in 'pley(n)te', l. 23, 'qua(n)tite', l. 27; 'w^{t}' in ll. 6, 31. Ruling in brown crayon across top of page and down the left-hand side. Early in the seventeenth century two quires containing *The Testament of Cresseid* were added. The *Testament* was transcribed from Speght's 1602 edition of Chaucer, and some emendations were made to *Troilus*. The shape of **s** in the inserted 'so', l. 28, needed for the metre, suggests that it is a seventeenth-century emendation; so too are 'full', l. 1 and 'be', l. 27 (the *anglicana* round **e** is among the letter-forms used by the *Testament* scribe).

CONTEXTS

Closely related to Cambridge, Corpus Christi College 61 (pl. 43) and probably also from London. Fifteenth-century note on f. 120r, originally a pastedown, identifies as owner a 'Ioh(anni) Trenthall'' (but '-nt-' could be read as *ut* or *nc* or *uc*), who was given it by 'R.C./ M-' (the erasure possibly 'agister'). The word 'kayle' appears at the foot of this page in a hand of the later fifteenth or early sixteenth century. There are inscriptions also on f. 1r (also earlier a pastedown): the name Thomas; and 'William lee ?De B(?k) *et* Johan*nes* [ ] portera*nt* vn br' de Wast.'. Among the scribbles on f. 120v are the names: 'Wyll*i*am', 'Thomas', 'John' (repeatedly), 'Margaret basset', and 'anna basset'. One of fifty books (mostly printed) given to his college by Humphrey Gower, Master of St John's College, in 1683.

SIZE

c. 252 × 170 mm (*c.* 204 × 100 mm).

BIBLIOGRAPHY

As Benson 1988: 478-79. *Coll.* Windeatt 1984: 110-113.
Facs. Beadle and Griffiths 1983.
Disc. James 1913: no. 235; Butterfield 1995; Seymour 1995-97: I. 67-78.

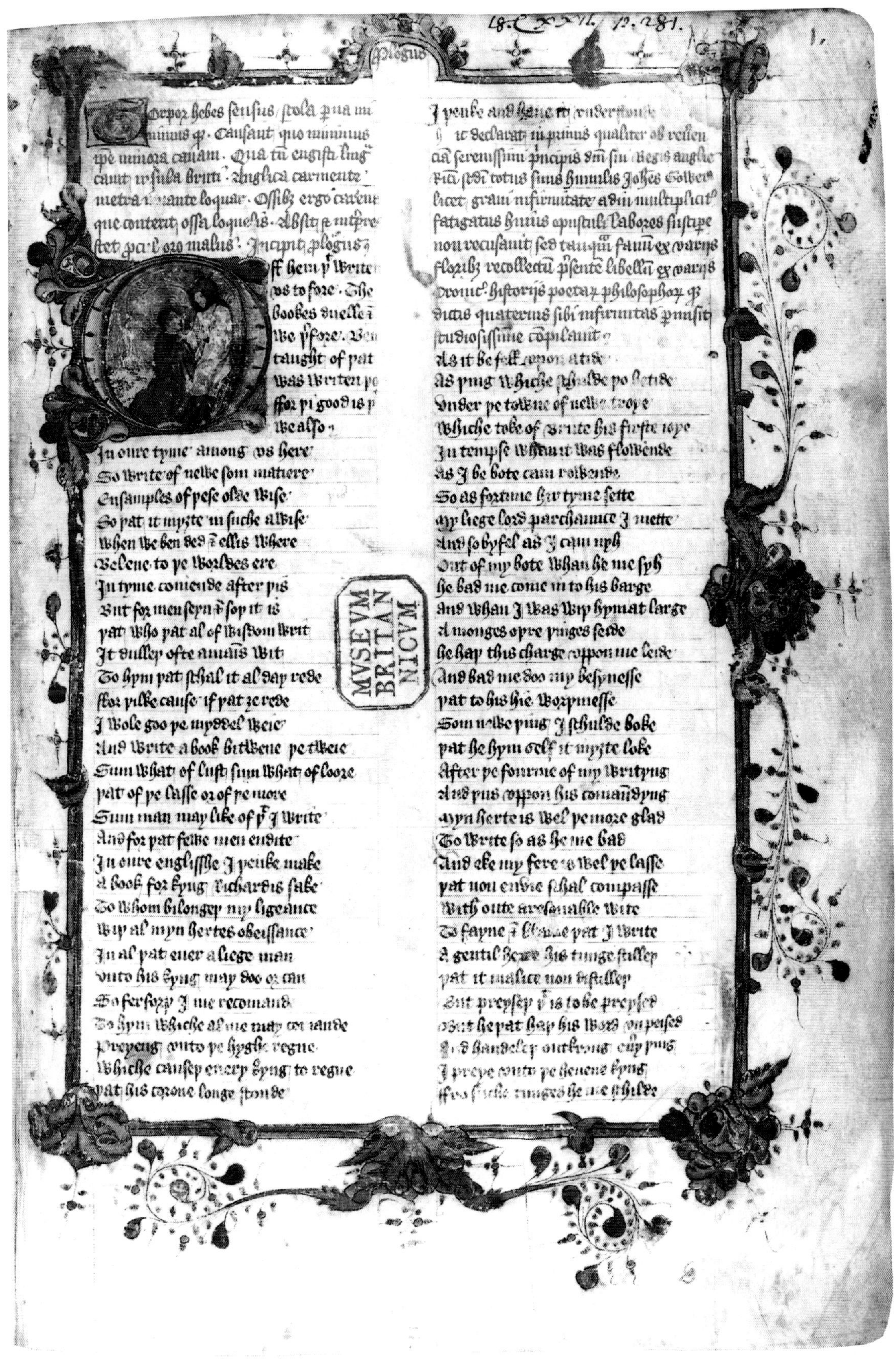

London, British Library, Royal MS 18 C. xxii, f. 1r
Gower, *Confessio Amantis*

Lover kneeling before Confessor
reduced to 61%

46

London, British Library, Harley MS 674, f. 17v

Colour pl. C7

Opening of *The Cloud of Unknowing*, with continuous marginal gloss in Latin

Gothic *littera cursiva anglicana formata*, s. xv^{1}

TRANSCRIPTION

Oracio ec(c)lesie ~ ~
Deus cui omne cor
patet et omnis volu(n)-
tas loquitur et que(m)
nullum latet secre-
tum · purifica per in-
infusionem sp(iritu)s s(an)c(t)i co-
gitatoes cordis u(est)ri ut
p(er)fecte te dilig(er)e ⁊ digne
laudare meream(ur) ame(n)
In no(m)i(n)e p(at)ris ⁊ filii ⁊ sp(iri)t(us)
s[-c]ancti ~ ameN~
Dionisius in sua mis-
tica theologia capit(u)lo
p(r)imo ad thimotheum
talia scribens s(i)c ait ~
Vide ut nullus
indoctorum. ista
audiat ~~~~~~~~~~
Mathei ~ Septimo
Nolite s(an)c(tu)m dare cani-
b(us) n(eque) · mittatis margaritas ante porcos · ne-
forte co(n)culsent eas pe-
dib(us) suis ⸵ ⁊ canes co(n)u(er)-
si disru(m)pa(n)t uos · (Prim)a cor'[1] ·3°·
No(n) potui uob(is) loq(u)i q(u)a(s)i sp(irit)u
alibus · s(ed) q(u)a(s)i carnalib(us) ⁊
i(de)o ta(m)q(u)a(m) p(ar)uul(is) i(n) c(rist)o ⸵ lac
potu(m) dedi · no(n) esca(m) // ~ [uob(is)
ad ebre(os) · 2°· Facti estis

Here bigin(n)eþ þe preyer on þe p(ro)loge ~
God unto whom alle hertes be(n)
open · and unto whom all(e) wille
spekiþ · and unto whom no priue
þing is hid ⸵ I beseche þee so for to cle(n)se
þe entent of myn hert · wiþ þe unspekable ȝift of þi g(r)ace · þat i may p(ar)fite-
lich(e) loue þee · and worþilich preise þee
Amen Here biginneþ þe prolog ~
In þe name of þe fader ⁊ of þe sone
⁊ of þe holy goost · I charge þee
⁊i beseche þee wiþ as moche
power ⁊ v(ir)tewe · as þe bonde of charite is sufficient to suffre · whatsoeu(er)
þou be þat þis book schalt haue in pos-
sess(i)ou(n) · ouþ(er) be propirte · ouþ(er) by keping ·
by bering as messeng(er) · or ell(e)[2] be borowi(n)g
þat in as moche as in þee is by wille
⁊ auisement · neiþ(er) þou rede it ne write it ne speke it · ne ȝit suffre it be
red wretyn or spoky(n)⸵ of any or to any
bot ȝif it be of soche one or to soche one
þat haþ bi þi supposing in a trewe wille
and by an hole entent p(ur)posed him to
be a parfite folower of criste · not o(n)ly
in actyue leuyng ⸵ bot in þe souerei(n)-
nest pointe of conte(m)platife leuing ·
þe whiche is possible by g(r)ace for to
be comen to in þis p(re)sent liif of a p(ar)-
fite soule ȝit abiding in þis deedly
body · and þ(er)to þat doþ þat in hi(m) is ·

This is the opening of a devotional text from the northern part of the central east Midlands. The preceding text is ruled for double columns, as can be seen from the unused double central pricking both at the top and the bottom of the page. Here the single text column is accompanied by a narrow outer column for annotations in Latin. The carefully planned rubrication can be seen more clearly in colour pl. C7. The English titles are in enlarged *anglicana formata* tending to *hybrida*; and the Latin in *textualis rotunda*. Biblical references in the gloss are also in red. Red dashes are used as line fillers, letters after points are often touched with red, and some additional punctuation is supplied in red. The three-line painted initials of the main text are of good quality, in blue flourished with red; the blue one-line initials of the gloss are without flourishing. The Latin text uses only the short straight **r** of *textualis rotunda*, even after **o**, whereas the main text uses either the long *anglicana* **r** or the round **r**. The main text uses **ȝ** ('ȝift', l. 7, 'ȝif', l. 22). The **þ**, without ascender, is clearly distinguished both from **p** and dotted **y**. The round **u** is usual, with the pointed **v** occasional at the beginning of some words ('v(ir)tewe', l. 13). Note ticked double **i** ('liif', l. 29). Word division is almost complete, but note in the main text some attached monosyllables ('atrewe', l. 23, 'aparfite', l. 25, 'comento', l. 29). The usual marks of punctuation are the medial point and, occasionally, the *punctus elevatus*, usually followed by a letter touched with red. Hyphens are used at line ends to mark

[1] For 'corinthios'. Final superscript letters as abbreviations came into use late in the thirteenth century.

[2] For 'elles'.

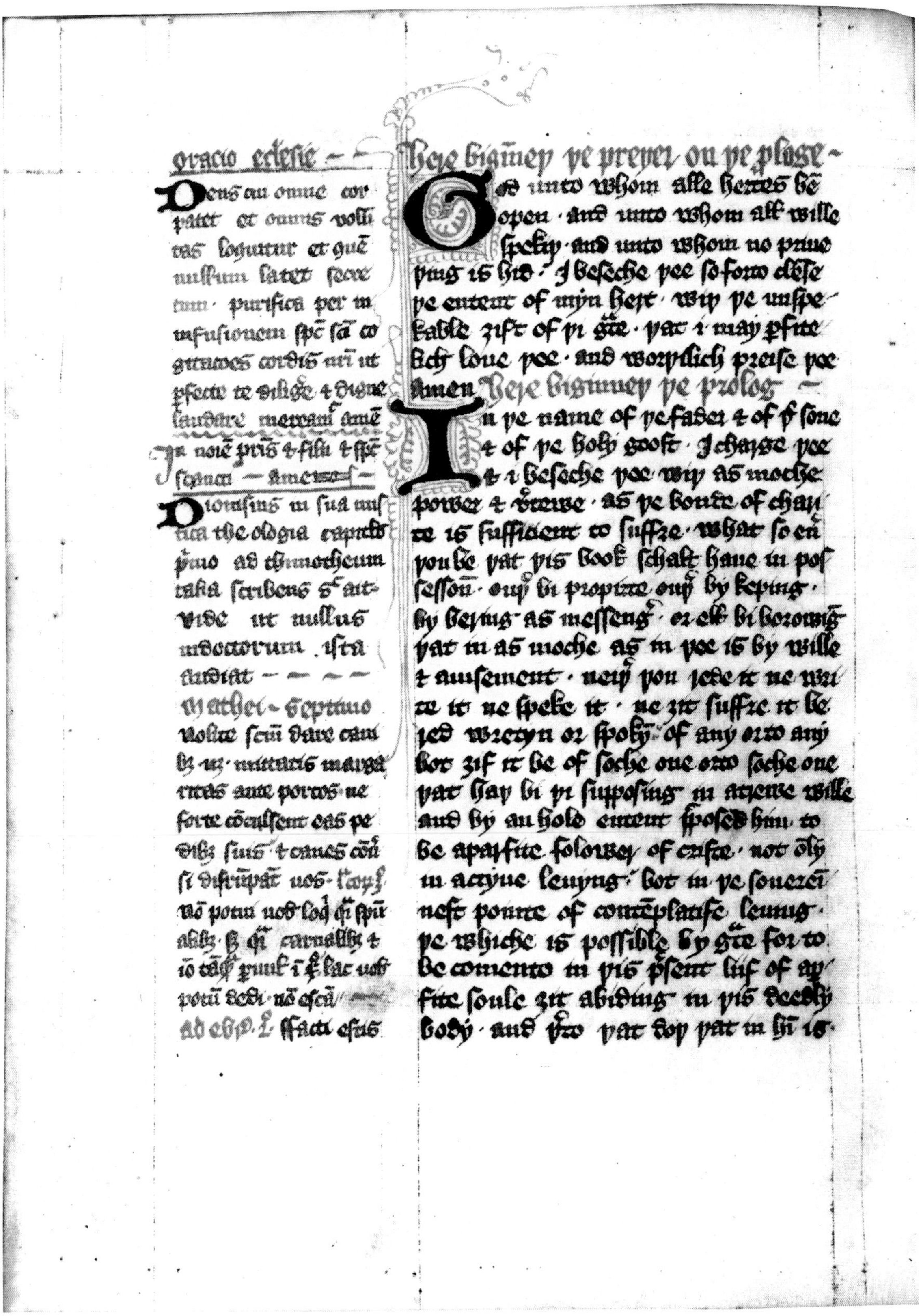

Oracio ecclesie.

Deus cui omne cor patet et omnis voluntas loquitur et quem nullum latet secretum: purifica per infusionem spiritus sancti cogitaciones cordis nostri ut perfecte te diligere et digne laudare mereamur. Amen.

In nomine patris et filii et spiritus sancti. Amen.

Dionisius in sua mistica theologia capitulo primo ad thimotheum taliter scribens sic ait: Vide ut nullus indoctorum ista audiat.

Mathei septimo: Nolite sanctum dare canibus neque mittatis margaritas ante porcos ne forte conculcent eas pedibus suis et canes conversi disrumpant vos. Non potui vobis loqui quasi spiritualibus sed quasi carnalibus tamquam parvulis in Christo lac vobis potum dedi non escam ad ebibendum. ... effacta eius

Here biginneþ þe preyer on þe prologe.

God unto whom alle hertes ben open and unto whom alle wille spekiþ and unto whom no prive þing is hid: I beseche þee so for to clense þe entent of myn hert wiþ þe unspekable 3ift of þi grace þat I may parfiteliche love þee and worþilich preise þee. Amen.

Here biginneþ þe prolog.

In þe name of þe Fader and of þe Sone and of þe Holy Goost. I charge þee and I beseche þee wiþ as moche power and vertewe as þe bonde of charite is sufficient to suffre, what so ever þou be þat þis book schalt have in possession, ouþer bi propirte ouþer by keping, by bering as messenger or elles bi borowing, þat in as moche as in þee is by wille and avisement, neiþer þou rede it ne write it ne speke it, ne 3it suffre it be red, wreten or spoken of any or to any, bot 3if it be of soche one or to soche one þat haþ bi þi supposing in a trewe wille and by an hole entent purposed him to be a parfite folower of Criste, not only in actyve levyng bot in þe sovereinnest pointe of contemplatife levyng þe whiche is possible by grace for to be comen to in þis present lif of a parfite soule 3it abiding in þis deedly body; and þerto þat doþ þat in him is

Plate 46 – actual size

divided words (note in Latin 'ne-', l. 23, treated as attached to next word). Correction by expunctuation can be seen in 'sancti', l. 12; and final *d* is written over an erasure in 'p(ur)posed', l. 24. The abbreviations of the English text are: the overline for *n* ('be(n)', l. 2) and *m* ('conte(m)platife', l. 27) as well as in the *-ion* inflexion ('possess(i)ou(n)', ll. 15-16); ˀ for *-er-* and perhaps *-ir-* and *-ur-* ('v(ir)tewe', l. 13, 'messeng(er)', l. 17, 'p(ur)posed', l. 24, 'p(re)sent', l. 29); ꝑ for *per-* or *par-* ('p(ar)fitelich(e)', ll. 7-8); ꝓ for *pro-* ('p(ro)loge', l. 1); line through ascender for final *-e* ('all(e)', l. 3, 'p(ar)fitlich(e)', l. 8, but 'ell(e)', l. 17, where *elles* required). In the Latin column the abbreviations are numerous and typical; the overline is omitted in 'cogitat⟨i⟩o⟨n⟩es', ll. 7-8. The Tironian sign, barred, is used in both the main text and gloss.

CONTEXTS

Linguistically from north in the east Midlands. The text has strong Carthusian associations: four of the eighteen medieval manuscripts known are of Carthusian provenance, as are the two translations into Latin (Hogg 1980). A note on a torn fly-leaf reads 'Richardus Rolles of Ampuls workes (as Mr. Allyn suppose ...)' and probably refers to Thomas Allen. The ascription to Rolle is mistaken; so too is the late-medieval ascription to Hilton (Sargeant 1976: 237). In the seventeenth century owned by Stillingfleet, whose books were bought in 1707 by Robert Harley. Entered the British Museum with the Harley Collection in 1753.

SIZE

212 × 155 mm (151 × 118 mm).

BIBLIOGRAPHY

Pr. Hodgson 1944: 1-2.
Disc. Harl. Cat.

Alle suche dysport as voydith ydilnesse
It syttyth euery gentilman to knowe
ffor myrthe annexed is to gentilnesse
Wherfore among alle oþer as y trowe
To knowe the craft of huntyng and to blowe
As thys book shall witnesse is one the beste
ffor it is holsum plesaunt and honest
And for to sette yonge hunterys in the way
To venery y caste me fyrst to go
Of whiche .iiij. bestis be that is to say
The hare the herte þe wulfhe the wylde boor also
Of venery for sothe þer be no moe
And so it shewith here in portetewre
Wher euery best is set in hys figure

London, British Library, Cotton MS Vespasian B. xii, f. 3r
Prologue to translation of a hunting treatise by Twety
reduced to 92%

47

Oxford, Bodleian Library, MS Douce 335, f. 45v
Edward, duke of York, *The Master of Game*
Mixed hand: a Gothic *littera cursiva*, s. xv med.

TRANSCRIPTION

what maners an hunter shuld haue

S ire if thu wol teche a man' to be
a gode hunter' he must first be
a childe of vij or viij ȝer' of age
or litel older And if men' wold
sey that I take a childe in to tender'
age for to putte hym to trauaile I answer' That alle naturs
descendith and shorteth and it is wel knowe that a childe
of vij· ȝer' age kan' more now in this time of suche thinges
as hym liketh to lerne than' som time coude[1] a childe of
xij. ȝer' olde / and therfor I put him so[2] ȝonge therto / for o
crafte requireth alle a mannys lyf or he be parfyȝt therof
Also it is seide that a man' lerneth in ȝowthe he wol it
holde in his olde age / And to this childe longeth many
thynges First that he loue wel his maister / and his hert
and besine[s>ss][3] be on' the houndes / and he must be bete whan'
he wol not do as his maister comaundeth' him / on' to the
time that he be drad to faile I shal first teche hym be⟨-⟩
writ al the houndes names and al her' hues til the childe
knowe hem bothe be hue and by name After I shal teche
hym to make clene iche day in the mornyng the houndes
kenel of al foule thinges And to putte to for [-her] hem
ij^{es} in the day faire fresshe clene water' of a welle in a
vessel theras the houndes drinketh / or faire rennyng
water' in the mornyng and in the euenyng /After I wol
teche him that onys in the weke he voide the kenel and
make al clene and renue the strawe and putt in ageyn'
ffressh' new strawe a gret dele and riȝt thik / And ther'

This is a formal script written in a careful clear hand. On balance the choice of letter-forms would allow the categorization Gothic *littera cursiva anglicana formata*, but the proportion of Secretary letter-forms is high. The distribution of **v** and **u** is consistent. The ductus gives the impression of a Secretary hand, and the most consistent Secretary alternative is **a**, but note in the first line of text and at the end of l. 23 forms of **a** that may have been begun as Anglicana letters. Anglicana **s** is used at the beginning of words, the long **s** within words, in the **st** ligature, and where double; and the typically Secretary kidney-shaped **s** is usual at the end of words (but altered to double long **s** in 'besine[s>ss]', l. 16). Note the Anglicana *-s* in the inflection of 'thynges', l. 15. The short **r** is used as well as the long Anglicana form. The Anglicana **g** and **w** are used throughout. Twice **d** ('day', ll. 21, 23) has the angularity found in Secretary hands, but otherwise there is little of the breaking of strokes that might be expected of a Secretary script. The **ȝ** is retained: note also a more informal form with reversed ductus, for example 'ȝer'', l. 9, 'ȝonge', l. 11. The title on the top ruled line, written in red by the main text hand, overruns the writing space. The historiated opening capital, making **S** (beginning 'Sire', l. 2, presumably the Master of Game speaking to a hunter with dog) is six lines deep. Occasional capitals, marking pausing points in the text, are touched in red, but otherwise punctuation, by virgule, is sparing. Abbreviation too is sparing: overlines occur, perhaps in a fairly unthinking way, for expansion seems unnecessary, above some words ending in *n* (ll. 5, 9, 10, 13, 16, 16, 17, 27); final **h** is slashed in ll. 17, 28; and the Secretary final **r** is frequently extended with a curling stroke (see ll. 3, 4, 7, 9, 11, 23, 25, 28). Note how the superscript letters after the numeral in l. 23 prompt the reader to understand '(twi)es', i.e. the adverb *twice*.

[1] The line through the first two letters is show-through from blue initial **M** on recto.

[2] The marks about 'so' are show-through.

[3] Note the change to make clear the *-ness* word element.

What maners an hunter shuld haue

Sire if thu wol teche a man to be a gode hunter he must first be a childe of vij or viij zer of age or litel older And if men wold sey that I take a childe in to tender age for to putte hym to trauaile I answer That alle natures descendith and shorteth and it is wel knowe that a childe of vij zer age kan more now in this time of suche thinges as hym liketh to lerne than som time coude a childe of xij zer olde and therfor I put him so yonge ther to for o crafte requireth alle a mannys lyf or he be parfyzt ther of Also it is seide that a man lerneth in yowthe he wol it holde in his olde age And to this childe longeth many thynges ffirst that he loue wel his maister and his hert and besinesse be on the houndes and he must be bete whan he wol not do as his maister comaundeth him on to the time that he be drad to faile I shal first teche hym be writ al the houndes names and al her hues til the childe knowe hem bothe be hue and by name After I shal teche hym to make clene iche day in the morning the houndes kenel of al foule thinges And to putte to fore hem ijes in the day faire fresshe clene water of a welle in a vessel ther as the houndes drinketh or faire renning water in the morning and in the euenyng After I wol teche him that onys in the weke he voide the kenel and make al clene and renne the stalle and putt in ageyn fresshe new strawe a gret dole and right thik And ther

Plate 47 – reduced to 86%

CONTEXTS

It is likely that Edward, second duke of York, began this translation of the *Livre de Chasse* of Gaston de Foix (or Febus or Phoebus) in 1406, while confined to Pevensey Castle. He dedicated the translation to Henry, prince of Wales, eldest son of his cousin Henry IV. Edward became Master of Game in 1406, having earlier been 'Master of our running dogs called hert houndes'. Illumination suggests a date as late as *c.* 1470–80 and probable London provenance (Scott 1996). Bought for five guineas by Douce at Chauncy sale in 1790 and left by him to the Bodleian in 1834.

SIZE

c. 275 × 182 mm (164 × 114 mm).

BIBLIOGRAPHY

As Baillie-Grohman and Baillie-Grohman 1904: 69.
Disc. *SC* 21910; Rogers 1975: 336; de la Mare 1984; Braswell 1987: 86–87; Scott 1996: no. 122.

VIII The Gothic system of scripts: Secretary

In origin this is very probably an Italian script, descended from Gothic *cursiva*, though it came into late-fourteenth-century England from France. A script analogous to the later English Secretary was in use in Italy in the thirteenth and fourteenth centuries and at the papal court in Avignon in the fourteenth century, at the French royal chancery in the first half of the fourteenth century, and spread through northern Europe by the end of the fourteenth century.[1] It seems likely that the script adopted *c.* 1372 by the Office of the Privy Seal came directly from France.[2] It caught on quickly as the main business script, being quicker to write than Anglicana, and gradually came into more general use, although initial training must more often than not have continued for some time in Anglicana.[3] From about the middle of the sixteenth century scholars and gentlemen took increasingly to humanistic cursive, that is the 'Italic' (or Italian, or as some then called it, 'Roman') script. Many law clerks were still more likely to be using their old 'court' hand, essentially an Anglicana script, both in cursive and set hands. Confusingly, the description 'secretary hand' (or sometimes English Secretary) was given early in the seventeenth century to the script then most generally is use,[4] which had inherited significant Anglicana features.

Secretary script is rather more angular than Anglicana, and its thick and thin strokes are well contrasted. Many strokes are broken, and horns may be found on the heads or sides of letters. The descenders taper. There are three phases of this script, in succession heavy, splayed, and lastly tall and narrow.[5] The distinctive letter-forms that mark it out from Anglicana are: the neat pointed single-compartment **a**; both the **e** with a bow, which may have a horn to the left, and the simple two-stroke alternative; the **g** with its head closed by a separate line and its open tail curling to the left; **r**, footed and sitting on the script line, and often made with a central well when current (sometimes described as the 'v'-shaped **r**); the use of the distinctive tight kidney-shaped form of **s** at the end of words; the three strokes of **w** producing an open form that is to-day instantly recognizable; and **x** cursively written in a single stroke. Table 4 compares the terms used by Julian Brown and Malcolm Parkes.[6] Within Brown's grading terminology, the treatment of minims should be examined carefully. Minims are linked, without lifting of the pen, in both *media* and *currens* grades, with *currens* allowing for hands that are below average in accuracy and style. In more elaborate styles the pen is lifted between minims. Thus, hands graded *formata* have more than average accuracy, and the term *formata hybrida* is available for the highest grade.

Table 4. *littera … cursiva* 'secretary' (*c.* 1375 – s. xviii)

Parkes	*Brown*
	cursiva 'secretary' *formata hybrida*
bastard secretary	*cursiva* 'secretary' *formata*
secretary	*cursiva* 'secretary' *media*
	cursiva 'secretary' *currens*

Pl. 52, in Capgrave's less formal hand,[7] is a good example of Secretary in its first 'heavy' phase. The script is fairly upright, and, although the minims are cursively written, it is a careful hand. Due attention is given to the distribution of **v** and **u**, the sparing punctuation is reinforced by the use of red to mark important opening letters (the single Anglicana letter-form, in 'at', l. 11, is touched with red), and the abbreviations are carefully written. Note the use of Anglicana letter-forms as capitals at the beginning of lines and in the added speech heading in pl. 53, from the official Register of the York play cycle, where the script is of a much higher grade. Here the separately-made minims sometimes have feet, **b**, **h**, and **l** have decorative loops (but not **d**), many letter-forms have horns or a pronounced angularity, word-final decorative strokes or 'hangers' proliferate, as, for example, in pl. 53, and there are few abbreviations. Although a paper manuscript, both the careful construction of the script, in this as in the other two main hands, and the well-considered ruling (fairly uniform throughout the manuscript) indicate that York was prepared to pay for good workmanship for the city record of its plays. One early reference to a York playbook remains. In 1376 a William de Thorp left 'libros meos de ludis' along with an

[1] Parkes 1969 [1979]: xix-xx.
[2] See Derolez 2003, where later more general cursiva scripts, which he terms Cursiva Recentior (or just Cursiva), are examined; and especially pp. 160-62 for the use of this cursiva (or Secretary) in England.
[3] See the discussion of Hoccleve's hand in Burrow and Doyle 2002: xxxiv.
[4] Dawson and Kennedy-Skipton 1968 [1981]: 8.
[5] For 'splayed' see Jenkinson 1927: I. 52.
[6] See further the forthcoming selection from T.J. Brown's writings related to the description of scripts (ed. M.P. Brown and J. Roberts).
[7] Lucas 1982: 229 distinguishes his 'current script of the kind used by university scribes' from a *fere textura*, which he terms 'more chaste'.

'armarialum' to Richard de Yedingham, if Yedingham wanted them, otherwise willing them to St Mary ad Valves, a local parish church; the nearby Augustinian friary, it is argued, 'most readily fills the requirements of a permanent community with a natural interest in the didactic purposes of the play'.[8]

Two more cursive examples of Secretary script are in Scots, as is clear from their orthographical features: the first great piece of Scottish literature in English, Barbour's *Bruce* (pl. 54), and a northern copy of Chaucer's *Troilus* (pl. 56). In the St John's College *Bruce*, a more forward slope is pronounced, splay is developing, and lengthened descenders turn to the left. This is an easy, practised hand, holding for the most part to the letter-forms distinctive of Secretary and following the laid lines of paper. There are no pen-lifts between minims, many ascenders have loops (not just **b**, **h**, and **l**, but often **f**, **s**, **v**, **w**, and **d** as well). The scribe uses both the two-stroke **e** and a more cursive single-stroke form with reversed ductus, harking back rather to the more oval shape than the later round Anglicana **e**. In the more currently written Secretary of pl. 56 (Arch. Selden. B. 24) the two-stroke **e** falls apart, its stem generally attaching to the preceding letter and its head to the next letter or standing alone at the end of a word. In this copy of Chaucer's *Troilus*, the hand's greater use of abbreviation is also an index of its greater speed of writing and less formal script. Literary texts in Scots are written typically in Secretary, an accident of date. Earlier, Scottish business hands had developed analogously to those found in England, but the use of Anglicana seems to have fallen away more quickly in Scotland than in England.[9]

Both Fairfax 16 (pl. 58) and Arch. Selden. B. 24 (pl. 56) are, like the Thornton manuscript, examples of the growing fashion for anthologies of English poetry in the latter part of the fifteenth century. Fairfax 16 has one main scribe, yet it is made up of five separable blocks, each of them foliated by a different hand.[10] Whoever bought this manuscript, perhaps John Stanley, might have made his own selection from sets of booklets according to his taste, commissioning as a suitable frontispiece a splendid full-page painting of Mars and Venus that would not have come cheap.[11] From much this time quite a few similar collections remain, gathering together Chaucer and Chaucerian poems, many of them shorter poems about love and lovers.[12] Two other such manuscripts, Oxford University Bodleian MSS Tanner 346 and Bodley 638, overlap in content with Fairfax 16, even in parallel groupings;[13] together they are called the 'Oxford group'. Not all are necessarily London products. The Findern Anthology, for example, could well have been assembled in the north Midlands;[14] and Arch. Selden. B. 24, from Scotland, can be viewed both as the last major compilation of this group and as 'the first major anthology of vernacular Scottish verse'.[15] Arch. Selden. B. 24 is a book full of surprises, not the least of them that it contains the only copy of the *Kingis Quair* of King James I of Scotland, in language apparently a southern poem given a Scots garb.[16] The page illustrated, from the earlier part of the manuscript containing Chaucerian verse, clearly blends southern English and Scots features.[17]

Once Secretary had come into use in Britain, its distinctive letter-forms must have held a certain cachet. The plain **a** is seen at the turn of the fourteenth century in an anthology of songs from the King's Lynn area, a relatively informal collection (pl. 40, Sloane 2593), as an alternative to the scribe's normal two-compartment form. Early in the fifteenth century the angularity of script in the St John's *Troilus and Criseyde* (pl. 45) betrays Secretary influence, as does its scribe's use of the Secretary final **s**. Secretary **a** is the most consistent Secretary alternative in the well-laid-out *Master of Game* manuscript (pl. 47, Douce 335), which also uses the kidney-shaped **s** at the end of words. The very formal and rather showy script of Harley 2255 (pl. 49) incorporates strong Secretary features: for example, the **g** is Secretary, and short **r** is used more frequently than the long form of Anglicana. Here too the Secretary kidney-shaped **s** is used at the end of words, as if a choice made to mark the hand's formality (the scribe misses only at the end of 'hornys', l. 16). Conversely, it would seem that the most frequently found Anglicana alternatives in reasonably self-consistent Secretary hands are the round **e** and the sigma-shaped **s**, that is the less time-consuming letter-forms among those distinctive of Anglicana when compared with Secretary. So, late in the fifteenth century, the steady near-current Hand B of the Malory manuscript (pl. 55) uses Anglicana **s** at the end of words as does the assured hand of pl. 56 (Arch. Selden. B. 24). The round **e** is, however, avoided in the Secretary *formata* script of Harley 4866 (pl. 48), in which a fashionable twitchiness betrays the influence of newer humanistic script.

By the late fifteenth century the two competing Gothic *cursiva* scripts often seem so intermingled as to have produced a

[8] Johnston 2002.

[9] Simpson 1973: pls 5-7 are Anglicana, 8 and 10 show the encroachment of Secretary letter-forms, 9 is Secretary, as are 11-14, termed by Simpson as 'pre-secretary' and a transitional script, because in his terms (p. 15) secretary as 'a recognisable script' emerged about the 1520s. In the reprint of 1986:14, Simpson adds into his footnote 4 the statement that Parkes 'defines certain scripts as "secretary" as far back as the third quarter of the fourteenth century.'

[10] Norton-Smith 1979.

[11] For discussion of booklets see: Robinson 1978 [1994], 1980; Hanna [1986] 1996: 21-34.

[12] Boffey and Thompson 1989.

[13] Harris (1983) also compares Cambridge University, Ff. 1. 6.

[14] See Beadle and Owen 1977, Harris 1983.

[15] Edwards 1996.

[16] It should be remembered that King James was imprisoned in England from the age of eleven for almost two decades.

[17] See the discussion in Horobin 2003: 131-37.

new cursive book script, typically Secretary in ductus, but using Anglicana round **e** and sigma-shaped **s** as cursive features and liable to adopt other Anglicana letter-forms.[18] Pl. 57, from the early sixteenth-century Digby plays, illustrates just such a hand, in a text copied in the second quarter of the sixteenth century. The *Mary Magdalene* play could indeed have been composed in response to debate about the saint's identity in the years following 1518.[19] It is perhaps pedantic to attempt to continue to identify the elements that come together from the two antecedent *cursiva* scripts, but the exercise is a useful one, helping us to gauge the degree of a scribe's attention to the task in hand.

The everyday hand for writing English in the sixteenth and in the first half of the seventeenth century is essentially a Secretary hand that draws on some of the letter-forms once distinctive of Anglicana, and it presents few problems to those able to read the current hands seen in pls 54-57.[20] By the time these scribes were at work the printing press had come to England, with Caxton's move to Westminster in late 1475 or early 1476,[21] although the first press was not set up in Scotland until 1507.[22] Malory's tales of Arthur (pl. 55) were quick to find their way into print, and the Malory manuscript itself, written very near in time to Caxton's edition, has traces of printer's ink from the 1480s on its pages.[23] It seems likely that Caxton had it at hand while preparing the *Morte Arthure* for the press, alongside a setting copy.[24] Many of the works of the most admired writers of the late fourteenth and the fifteenth century in the English language were made available in ever greater numbers of new printed books, and these, where early manuscripts have been lost, can provide evidence for the early history of texts. The addition of an ending to Chaucer's *House of Fame* in the Fairfax manuscript (pl. 58) is not, however, Chaucer's work, but derives ultimately from Caxton's editorial activities: the scribe copied it from a printed edition of Chaucer's poems. This second hand of pl. 58 is from long after the end of the medieval making of books, and it serves to remind us yet again that later owners did not scruple to make improvements in older manuscript volumes. Similarly, some time after 1602 someone copied Henryson's *Testament of Cresseid* from Speght's 1602 edition of Chaucer's *Workes* to follow after St John's copy of *Troilus*, adding improvements to the main text, for example writing headings such as 'The Songe of | Troilus' (pl. 45). Nevertheless the whole business of scribal copying as the chief procedure within the making of books was to vanish, except at one end of the social spectrum for private use or at the other for *de luxe* presentation volumes. As early as 1465 individually bought printed books were being brought home to Britain and there is evidence that by 1477 books were being imported commercially into London,[25] among them many Books of Hours, the bestseller of the fourteenth and fifteenth centuries.[26] By the early sixteenth century London had become a major city, a centre where the book trade flourished and interesting second-hand books might be bought,[27] and more and more books in English were being printed for an ever-growing niche in the home market, for the numbers of people able to read and write English had increased markedly in the later Middle English period.[28] The target audiences were to be found not just in the court, but in the great houses up and down the land, in the religious houses, the universities and the Inns of Court. In publishing books in English Caxton and his later competitors catered more efficiently than scribes ever could for an ever-wider reading public, often literate only in English, for merchants and women, for far more people than had owned manuscripts.

[18] Parkes 1979: xxiv.

[19] Davidson 1972: 73.

[20] Go to www.english.cam.ac.uk/ceres/ehoc/intro.html for Leedham-Green's online course in reading handwriting 1500-1700.

[21] Hellinga 1999: 67. Earlier in the century London book trade was centred on Paternoster Row, near St Paul's (see Christianson 1987).

[22] Hellinga and Trapp 1999: 14.

[23] Hellinga and Kelliher 1977; Hellinga 1977, 1981, 1983.

[24] See further in Kato 2000.

[25] Harris 1989: 182. See also Sutton and Visser-Fuchs 1995: 64.

[26] Backhouse 1985.

[27] Hellinga 1991: 221.

[28] Trapp 1991: 31.

48

London, British Library, Harley MS 4866, f. 88r (formerly 91)
Hoccleve, *The Regement of Princes*
Mixed hand: a Gothic *littera cursiva*, s. xv^{1}

TRANSCRIPTION

How he þi s(er)uant was mayden marie
And lat his loue floure and fructifie

¶ Alþogh[1] his lyfe be queynt þe resemblaunce
Of him haþ in me so fressh' lyflynesse
Þat to putte othir men in remembraunce
Of his p(er)sone I haue heere his lyknesse
Do make to þis ende in sothfastnesse
Þat þei þ(a)t haue of him lest[2] þought ⁊ mynde
By þis peynture may ageyn him fynde[3]

¶ The ymages þ(a)t in þe chirche been
Maken folk þenke on god ⁊ on his seyntes
Whan þe ymages þei beholden ⁊ seen
Were oft vnsyte[4] of hem causith restreyntes
Of þoughtes gode whan a þing depeynt is
Or entailed[5] if men take of it heede
Thoght of þe lyknesse it wil in hym brede

¶ Yit so(m)me holden oppynyou(n) and sey
Þat none ymages schuld Imaked be
Þei erren foule ⁊ goon out of þe wey
Of trouth haue þei scant sensibilite
Passe ou(er) þ(a)t now blessid trinite
Vppon my maistres so[-\u]le m(er)cy haue
For him lady eke þi m(er)cy I craue

¶ More othir þing wolde I fayne speke ⁊ touche
Heere in þis booke but schuch is my dulnesse
For þ(a)t al voyde and empty is my pouche
Þat al my lust is queynt w(i)t(h) heuynesse
And heuy spirit comaundith st[u>i]lnesse

This upright 'twitchy' formal script, which lends itself to the categorization Gothic *cursiva* Secretary *formata* with some *anglicana* alternatives, makes use of quite a few *anglicana* letter-forms, particularly the two-compartment **a** and the hour-glass shaped **g**, and has many loops (on **d**, **b**, and **h**, for example) and some examples of biting. However, **r** is short throughout and the cursive *anglicana* forms of **e** and **s** are not seen on this page. The **þ** is well distinguished from **y**, which is curly tailed. Some prefixes are allowed to stand on their own, 'be', l. 12, 'I', l. 18, as is 'Al', l. 3. Note the spellings 'were', l. 13, for 'where', and 'schuch', l. 25, for 'such'. There are no markers of punctuation apart from capitulum signs at the outset of new stanzas and capitals for the first letter of each line (**ff** makes **F**, ll. 23, 26). The abbreviations are standard: **p** in 'p(er)sone', l. 6; overline for *m* or *n* (e.g. 'so(m)me', l. 17, 'oppynyou(n)', l. 17); ʼ for *er* in 's(er)uant, l. 1, 'm(er)cy', ll. 22, 23; barred **h** treated as otiose ('fressh'', l. 4); **w**^{t} for 'w(i)t(h)', l. 27; **þ**^{t} for 'þ(a)t', ll. 8, 10, 26 (compare space-saving 'þ^{i}', l. 1). Note that *and* is spelled out both within the line (ll. 2, 17, 26) and at the beginning of the line (ll. 2, 28). The Tironian sign is also used (over an erasure in l. 24). This is a well-designed book, carefully ruled throughout. Capitulum

[1] **g** read as secretary form, possibly damaged.
[2] The Arundel 38 reading 'lost' is better.
[3] Portrait of Chaucer, with hand pointing to verses that describe him. Two other such portraits are extant in *Regement* manuscripts: in British Library, Royal 17. D. vi; and Philadelphia, Rosenbach 1083/30, where the panel is a forgery.
[4] For 'unsight', i.e. 'not seeing': probably an *ad hoc* formation; the word is found otherwise only in Hardy (*OED*).
[5] Meaning 'sculptured'.

How he yi seruaunt was mayden marie
And lat his loue floure and fructifie

Al yogh his lyfe be queynt ye resemblaunce
Of him hath in me so fressh lyflynesse
Yat to putte othir men in remembraunce
Of his persone I haue heere his lyknesse
Do make to yis ende in sothfastnesse
Yat yei yat haue of him lest yought & mynde
By yis peynture may ageyn him fynde

The ymages yat in ye chirche been
Maken folk yenke on god & on his seyntes
Whan ye ymages yei be holden & seen
Were oft vnsyte of hem causith restreyntes
Of youghtes gode whan a ying depeynt is
Or entailed if men take of it heede
Thoght of ye lyknesse it wil in hym brede

Yit some holden oppynyon and sey
Yat none ymages schuld I maked be
Yei erren foule & goon out of ye wey
Of trouth haue yei scant sensibilite
Passe ouer yat now blessid trinite
Uppon my maistres soule mercy haue
For him lady eke yi mercy I craue

More othir ying wolde I fayne speke & touche
Heere in yis booke but such is my dulnesse
For yat al voyde and empty is my pouche
Yat al my lust is queynt with heuynesse
And heuy spirit commaundeth stilnesse

Plate 48 – reduced to 87%

signs introducing each stanza alternate in gold surrounded by purple penwork and in blue surrounded by red. Note that an elaborate display bar with foliage at the top and bottom of the page shows through from the verso. Chaucer's portrait is in the page area reserved for occasional notes in Latin. The leaf signature 'M iij' towards the bottom of the page served to keep the folios within quires in order.

CONTEXTS

Alone in its codex as are twenty-five copies out of forty-three *Regement* manuscripts, this may have been a presentation copy prepared under Hoccleve's supervision. It is an almost exact replica of the *Regement* in British Library, Arundel 38, from which the leaf containing Chaucer's portrait is torn out (its presentation scene is reproduced opposite on p.. 217). Written in London perhaps shortly before Henry V became king (Scott argues for a date span 1411-*c.* 1420), this volume could have been presented to a royal prince, for example Edward, duke of York (d. 1415) or John, duke of Bedford (d. 1435). No known history, however, before entering the Harley Library; the signature 'Oxford E.H.' on the opening page suggests that Edward Harley rather than his father acquired this book. Entered the British Museum with the Harley Collection in 1753.

SIZE

263 × 188 mm (176 × 89 mm).

BIBLIOGRAPHY

Pr. Furnivall 1897: 180-81, ll. 4992-5012. *As* Blyth 1999: 186, ll. 4990-5017.

Disc. Schulz 1937; Mitchell 1968: 110-15; Seymour 1974, 1995-97: I. 157-62; Krochalis 1986; Machan 1992: 284-85; Edwards 1993; Pearsall 1994; Gaylord 1995; Scott 1996, no. 51, pl. 203; Thompson 2000.

Hye noble and myghty Prince excellent
My lord the Prince · o my lord gracious
I humble servant and obedient
Un to ȝour estate hye and glorious
Of whiche I am ful tendre and ful zelous
Me recommaunde unto ȝour worthynesse
With herte entier and spirit of meeknesse

London, British Library, Arundel MS 38, f. 37r
Hoccleve, *De regimine principuum*, 1411–13

Presentation scene, probably Prince Henry of Lancaster (later Henry V) and author (Hoccleve)
reduced to 80%

49

London, British Library, Harley MS 2255, f. 6r
Lydgate, *Horns Away*, ll. 1-24
Gothic *littera cursiva anglicana formata hybrida*, s. xv med.

TRANSCRIPTION

O ff god and kynde / procedith al bewte
Crafft may shewe / a foreyn apparence
But nature ay must haue þ^{e} sou(er)eynte
Thyng countirfet / hath noon existence
Twen gold and gossomer / is gret difference
Trewe metal / requerith noon allay
Vnto purpoos / by cleer experyence
Bewte wyl shewe / thouh' hornes / wer away

§ Riche attires / of gold and perre
Charbonclis / Rubies / of moost excellence
Shewe in dirknesse / liht' wher so they be
By ther natural / heuenly influence
Doubletys of glas / yeue a gret evidence
Thyng countirfet / wil faylen at assay
On this mateer' / concludyng in sentence
Bewte wyl shewe / thouh' hornys wer' away

§ Aleyn remembryth / his compleynt who lyst see
In his book / of famous eloquence
Clad al in floures / and blosmys of a tree
He sawh' Nature / in hir'[1] moost excellence
Vpon hir hed / a keuerchef of Valence
Noon othir richesse / of countirfet array
Texemplefye[2] / by kyndly providence
Bewte wil shewe / thouh' hornys wer away

This mixed script is basically *anglicana*, but with a Secretary slope and strong Secretary alternatives. It can be graded *formata hybrida* because of its incorporation of *textualis* features: the Anglicana two-compartment **a** is usual, though some instances of a straight-sided form occur (for example 'al', l. 1, 'attires', l. 9, 'at assay', l. 14); Anglicana long **r** (e.g. 'requerith', l. 6) occurs less frequently than the Secretary form (e.g. 'apparence', l. 2), but the 2-shaped form of *textualis* uniformly follows **o**. An alternative categorial description is Bastard Anglicana, which also recognizes the high degree of formality achieved. The **x** is the typical Anglicana form (ll. 7, 10, 20, 23). For **w** both the looped Anglicana form (e.g. 'wyl', 'wer', 'away', l. 8) and the Secretary (e.g. 'Bewte', l. 8, 'shewe', l. 8) are used. There are three types of **s**, with what looks like an intended distribution of the kidney-shaped Secretary form at the end of words (but the sigma-shaped Anglicana form appears in 'hornys', l. 16) and tall **s** elsewhere (with the sigma-shaped form used twice at the beginning of words: 'so', l. 11, 'sawh'', l. 20). The Secretary **g** is used throughout. Note that final **f** often has a hanging flourish, as in ll. 9, 10, 13, 18, 21 (× 2). Occasional use is made of lighter final strokes at the end of words, for example 'floures', l. 19, 'hornes', l. 24, 'away', l. 24 (perhaps 'hornes', l. 8, 'glas', l. 13, as well, although transcribed as a virgule). The conventional distribution of **v** and **u** is not always observed (see 'evidence', l. 13), and at the beginning of the line **h**, though enlarged, is not given a distinctive form ('He', l. 20). Yet, this is a very formal hand, making little use of abbreviation. Note 'þ^{e} sou(er)eynte', l. 3, where the space-saving *þ^{e}* for 'the' (**þ** not otherwise in page) together with the ' mark of abbreviation in the following word 'sou(er)eynte' stops the line from straggling. Sometimes **r** is flourished in such a way as to suggest suspension of *-e* ('mateer'', l. 15, 'wer'', l. 16, 'hir'', l. 20), but on comparison of 'wer', ll. 8, 24, no expansion was made. The stroke through **h**, probably without orthographic value, is here marked by the apostrophe (though some might take it as representing *-gh-* in 'thouh'', ll. 8, 16, 24, 'sawh'', l. 20, makes this unlikely). The indefinite article is once attached to the

[1] Compare 'wer'', l. 16.

[2] Note poetic elision.

Off god and kynde procedith al bewte
Crafft may shewe a foreyn apparence
But nature ay must haue þe soueraynte
Thyng countirfet hath noon existence
Twen gold and gossomer is gret difference
Trewe metal requeryth noon assay
Vnto purpoos by cleer experyence
Bewte wyl shewe thouh hornes wer away

Riche attires of gold and perre
Charbonclis rubies of moost excellence
Shewe in derknesse liht wher so they be
By ther natural heuenly influence
Doubletys of glas yeue a gret evidence
Thyng countirfet wil faylen at assay
On this mateer concludyng in sentence
Bewte wyl shewe thouh hornys wer away

Aleyn remembryth his compleynt who lyst see
In his book of famous eloquence
Clad al in flourys and blosmys of a tree
He sawh nature in hir moost excellence
Vpon hir hed a keuerchef of Valence
Noon othir richesse of countirfet array
Texemplefye by kyndly providence
Bewte wil shewe thouh hornys wer away

Plate 49 – reduced to 86%

following word ('a gret', l. 13). The formal layout is well planned and executed: a three-line-deep opening initial with gold leaf on circle of **O** and alternating blue and pink panels; the well-spaced stanzas; the introductory paragraph markers (ll. 9, 17) alternating in blue surrounded by red penwork and gold surrounded by pink. The virgule marks the caesura in most lines and in l. 10 also serves to separate two nouns that follow one another. The red underlining of 'Aleyn' and 'Nature' in ll. 17 and 20 draws attention to Lydgate's reference to Alanus ab Insulis, *De Planctu Nature*; elsewhere in the manuscript matching notes in red are supplied in the generous margins. The numeral '·3·', which has been struck out, specifies that this is third of eleven numbered items at the beginning of the manuscript. The pages are separately ruled, care is taken not to break stanzas across pages and the membrane is of excellent quality: markers of an up-market manuscript.

CONTEXTS

Collection of short poems by Lydgate, copied early in the fifteenth century, possibly in London. The name 'William Curteys' (f. 43v) is that of Lydgate's abbot at the Benedictine house of Bury St Edmunds. First and last leaves, which could have had coats of arms, are missing. History before its appearance in the Harley collection is unknown. Entered the British Museum with the Harley Collection in 1753.

SIZE

269 × *c.* 197 mm (191 × 120 mm).

BIBLIOGRAPHY

Pr. Hammond 1927: 112; *coll.* MacCracken 1934 [1981]: 662-63. *Disc. Harl. Cat.*, Boffey 1996: 71-72; Edwards 2000: 104.

Liber ·i·

His purpose schal ofte faile
In armes he that wol travaile
Or elles loves grace atteigne
His lose tonge he mot restreine
Which bereth of his honoure the keie

Confessor: Forthi my sone in alle weie
Take right goode hiede of this matiere

Amans: I thonke yowe my fader dere
This scole is of gentiel lore
And if there be oght elles more
Of pride which I schal eschiue
Now axeth forth and I wol sue
What thinge that ye me wol enforme

Confessor: My sone yit in other forme
There is a vice of prides lore
Which lich an hauke whan he wol sore
ffleeth upon heght in his delices
After the likinge of his vices
And wole no mannes reson knowe
Til he doun fal and overthrowe
This vice veine glorie is hote
Wherof my sone I the behote
To trete and speke in such a wise
That thou the might the bettre avise

Gloria perpetuos pregnat mundana dolores
Qui tamen est vanus gaudia vana cupit
Eius amicitiam quem gloria tollit inanis
Non sine blandiciis plaudit habere homo
Verbis compositis qui sit strigilare favellum
Grandere sellam [illegible] equus
Sic in amore magis qui blandus sabbat in ore
Verba per hec dominam quos nequit alter habet
Et tamen ornatos cantus varios que paratus
Sepius [illegible] sine lecto aptat amor

Hic loquitur de quarta specie superbie que vana gloria vocatur, cuius condicionem primo describens super eodem in amoris causa confessor amanti consequenter opponit

The prouede vice of veine glorie
Remembreth noght of purgatorie
His worldes ioies ben so grete
Him thenketh of heven no beyete
This lives pompe is al his pes
Yit schal he die natheles
And therof thenketh he but a lite
ffor al his lust is to delite
In newe thinges proude and veine
Als ferforth as he mai atteigne
I trowe if that he might make
His body newe he wolde take
A newe forme and leue his olde
ffor what thinge that he may beholde
The which to comun us is strange
Anon his olde gise change
He wol and fal ther upon
Lich unto the camelion
Which upon euere sondri hewe
That he beholt he most remewe
His colour and thus unavised
ffulofte time stant desgised
More iolif than the brid in may
He maketh him euer fressh and gay
And doth al his arraie desgise
So that of him the newe gise
Of lusti folke al other take
And eke he can carolls make
Rondeal and balade and virelay
And with al this if that he may
Of love gete him avantage
Anon he wext of his corage
So overglad that purgatorie
Ne might abregge his veine glorie
ffor he hath than at al tide
Of love such a maner pride
Him thenketh his ioie is endeles

Confessor: Now schrive the sone in godes pes
And of thi love tell me plein
If that thi glorie hath be so vein

Amans: My fader as touchinge of al
I may noght wel ne noght ne schal
Of veine glorie excuse me
That I ne have for love be
The bettre adressed and arraied
And also I have ofte assaied
Rondeal balade and virelai
ffor hir on whom myn hert lai
To make and also for to peinte
Carolls with my wordes queinte
To sett my purpose al ofte
And thus I sange hem forth fulofte
In halle and eke in chambre aboute
And made mery amonge the route
Bot yit ne ferde I noght the bet
Thus was my glorie in vein beset
Of al the ioie that I made
ffor whan I wolde with hir glade
And of hir love songes make
Sche seide it was noght for hir sake
And list noght my songes here
Ne witen what the wordes were
So for to speke of myn arraie
Yit couthe I never be so gaye
Ne so wel make a songe of love
Wherof I might ben above
And have encheson to be glad

London, British Library, Additional MS 12043, f. 10v
Gower, *Confessio Amantis*
reduced to 56%

50

London, British Library, Harley MS 1197, Part I, f. 9r
Lavynham, *A Little Treatise on the Seven Deadly Sins*
Gothic *littera cursiva anglicana formata hybrida*, s. xv med.

TRANSCRIPTION

De septem mortal(ibus) peccatis .

C Rist þ(a)t deyde vpon a cros for þe sauac(i)ou(n) of mankende ∵ graunte vs grace so to asca= pe þe sly ensaylyng(es) of þe fende . þ(a)t we be nout for synne lost in oure laste ende .

Twey þing(es) I haue p(ur)posid þorwh(e) goddes grace to don in þis litel tretis . Fyrst to schewin schortly þe comoun condic(i)ou(n)s of þe seuene dedli synnes as bi fi= gure and example in gen(er)al . And aftyrward to reherse bi proces and bi ordre what braunchis ⁊ bowis growen out of hem i(n) special . As towchinge þe firste mater an holi man writith in his book Et est s(an)c(tu)s thomas s(e)c(un)d(u)m quosd\`a´m . Secu(n)du(m) quosd\`a´m alios Albertus . The seuene dedly synnes he seyth ∵ arn likenid to seuene sundry bee= stis . As pride is likenid to þe leoun . Coueytise to þe hirchoun . Wrathþe to þe wolf . Enuye to þe hound. Slowȝþe to an asse . Glotonye to a bere . and Leccherie to a swyn . Of whiche figuris ⁊ examplis I þinke to tow= che in eche of þe seuene dedli synnes bi hym self .

P Ride is nout ellis but a badde desyr of heȝy wor= schepe as sey(n)t austin witnessith . et est lib(r)o q(u)arto= decimo . de ciuitate dei. cap(itul)o .xiijº. Therfore I likene a proud man to þe leoun . For as þe leoun lokith þ(a)t alle oþere beest(es) schulde hym worschepen . hym dredin . and to hym bowen ∵ Ryȝt so a proud man þinkith þ(a)t alle oþ(er)e me(n) schulden hym worschepin . hym dredin . and to hy(m) lowten . And þ(er)fore[1] it may weel ben seyd of a proud man ∵ as it is writen in holi scripture . Ecce quasi leo ascendet de sup(er)bia . I(er)emie. quadragesimo nono .c(apitul)o. Loo now seyth þe p(ro)phete ⁊ take hede how he schal as a leoun . arysen vp of his pride . This is a figure þ(a)t distroyȝeth alle v(er)tuys and

The text hand is *anglicana formata hybrida*, verging on *fere-textura* (*fere* 'like'; *textura* = *textualis*). There are loops on **b, h, k,** and **l**; **f** and **s** (except **s** final) are long; **w** in typically Anglicana form. Two-compartment **a**, unlooped **d, g,** short and 2-shaped **r** (the latter general after bows), and final **s** are Gothic *textualis* forms. Fusion is seen in **de, do,** and **pp**. The minims are as in *textualis rotunda*. Note **sc** and **st** ligatures. Closing hairline strokes follow word-final **f** and **t**. Of the special letter-forms **þ** (well differentiated from **y**) is more frequent than **th**; three occurrences of **ȝ**, in 'Riȝt', l. 24, 'Slowȝþe', l. 16, 'heȝy', l. 19, and its analogical appearance in 'distroyȝeth', l. 30, suggest that the exemplar at least had not lost the east Midland articulation of disappearing /χ/. Despite the formality of the script, the scribe uses abbreviation quite heavily for a vernacular work, probably because of its specialized nature: **þ**^{t} ll. 1, 3, 22, 24, 30 for *þat*; overline for *n* in 'i(n)', l. 10, 'sey(n)t', l. 20, 'me(n)', l. 24, for *m* in 'hy(m)', l. 25, and in 'sauac(i)ou(n)', l. 1, 'condic(i)ou(n)s', l. 7; ꝭ for *es* in 'ensaylyng(es)', l. 3, 'þing(es)', l. 5, 'beest(es)', l. 23 ; ꝓ in p(ro)phete', l. 29; ꝰ for *ur* in 'p(ur)posid', l. 5; ʼ for *er* in 'gen(er)al', l. 8, 'oþ(er)e', l. 24, 'þ(er)fore', l. 26; slash through the ascender of **h** in 'þorwh(e)', l. 5; but ⁊ is spelled out (× 8) more often than not (× 3). Doubtless the scribe was accustomed to their use when writing Latin: compare the standard abbreviations used in the three notes of sources (ll. 11-12; 20-21; 27-28); and note the radical suspension of

[1] Note that first letter is adapted from **p**.

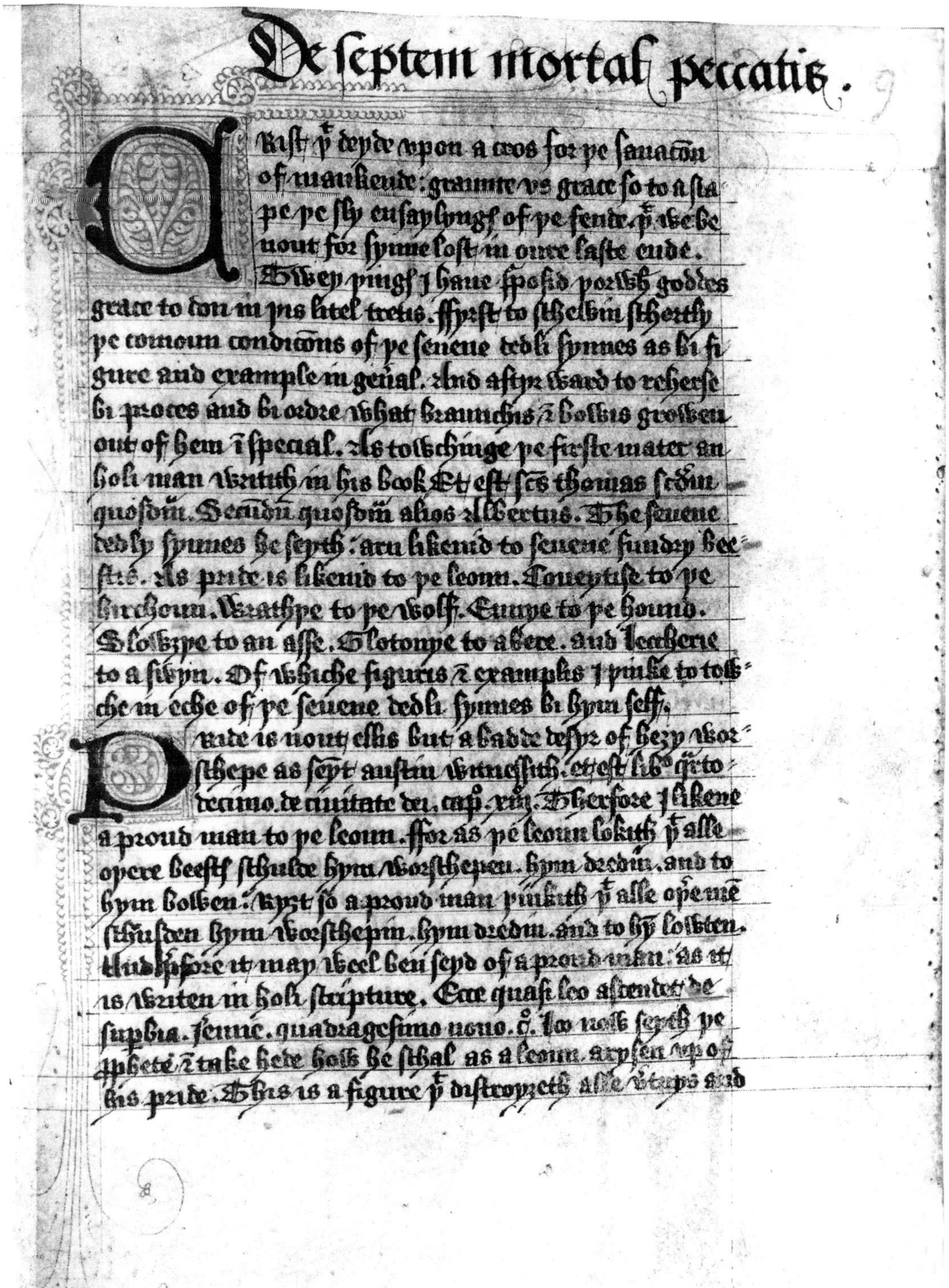

De septem mortal[ibus] peccatis.

[C]rist þat deyde vpon a cros for þe sauacion of mankende: graunte vs grace so to astape þe sly ensaylyngis of þe fende. þat we be nout for synne lost in oure laste ende. Two þingis I haue sposid þorwh goddes grace to don in þis litel tretis. ffyrst to schewin schortly þe comoun condicions of þe seuene dedli synnes as bi figure and exsample in general. And aftyrward to reherse bi proces and bi ordre what braunchis & bowis growen out of hem in special. As touchinge þe firste mater an holi man writith in his book. Et est scs thomas secundum quosdam. Secundum quosdam alios Albertus. The seuene dedly synnes he seyth: arn likened to seuene sundry beestis. As pride is likened to þe leoun. Coueytise to þe irchoun. Wrathþe to þe wolf. Enuye to þe hound. Slowþe to an asse. Glotonye to a bere. And lecherie to a swyn. Of whiche figuris & exsamplis I þinke to touche in eche of þe seuene dedli synnes bi hym self.

[P]ride is nout ellis but a badde desyr of heyȝ worschepe as seynt austin witnessith. et est lib° quarto decimo. de ciuitate dei, cap°. xiii. Therfore I likene a proud man to þe leoun. ffor as þe leoun lokith þat alle oþere beestis schulde hym worschepen. hym dredin. and to hym bowen: Ryȝt so a proud man þinkith þat alle oþere men schulden hym worschepin. hym dredin. and to hym bowen. And þerfore it may wel ben seyd of a proud man: as it is writen in holi scripture. Ecce quasi leo ascendet de superbia. Jeremie. quadragesimo nono. c°. loo now seyth þe prophete & take hede how he schal as a leoun arysen vp of his pride. This is a figure þat distroyeth alle vertus and

Plate 50 – actual size

'mor(t)al(ibus)' in the added title. Punctuation is by point for pauses and *punctus elevatus* to mark continuation. Words divided by the end of the line are marked by pairs of short hairlines (found in manuscripts of the fourteenth and fifteenth centuries). Prickings for horizontal ruling survive in outer margin, and one hole is visible for inner bounding line in bottom margin. The ruling is in ink, with vertical single bounding lines prolonged to edges and first and last pair of horizontals also prolonged to edges. The small capitals of the text are touched with red, and the three Latin notes are underlined in red, as are the English names of the seven sins (ll. 14-16). The opening initial is five lines deep, painted in blue and some red, with red flourishing that runs along upper and inner margins, and incorporates the three-line initial in blue for first main section of text.

The added title is best described as large *cursiva anglicana hybrida*: note the Secretary round **a**, short **r**, and final **s**.

CONTEXTS

Work on the make-up of this manuscript is needed. Part I: ff. 1-76 (membrane) bound with later paper ff. 77-203 (first block ff. 77-141 also on ten commandments and seven deadly sins: top of f. 77r 'Iste liber constat Will(el)mo Jerarde dono'; top of 78r 'Guilielmus Auerelus: | Londiniensis'; f. 140 'Jacoby Sowsch'' among scribbles; ff. 144-203 written by Joh. Pokysfen in the fifteenth century). Part II: ff. 204-413. Red crayon marks of the sort associated with Parker manuscripts occur ff. 1-384 (see the ends of ll. 11, 13, 22 and the underlining of individual letters in 'hirchoun', l. 15, 'lowten', l. 25, and 'figure', l. 30), but not in final booklets. Canterbury connection suggested by note (f. 385) of Parker visitation 7 September 1573. Thus, the contents of the final two booklets (ff. 385-413) could have led to their being added to the preceding materials. Ff. 385-401: 'carmina' from Queen Elizabeth's time with name of Edmund Grindal on f. 385 (name Charles Horn on ff. 385 and 401 also delimits booklet). Ff. 402-13, lacking in the red markings scattered through rest of manuscript, presented by Vossius to Wolsey; these folios may have belonged to Robert Hare. Did these folios go to the Royal Library, to be alienated by Hare? Or were they joined to the rest in the Harley Library? Entered the British Museum with the Harley Collection in 1753.

SIZE

c. 193 × 145 mm (*c.* 141 × 94 mm).

BIBLIOGRAPHY

As. Van Zutphen 1956: ch. xlix. 19.
Disc. Harl. Cat., Wright 1972: 385; Watson 1973 [2004[1]]: 604-05; Watson 2000 [2004[1]]: no. 29.

65

kyste that dyyed one the rode tree to salve mankynd
graunte vs the blysse at olle last endyng Amen.
This tretys that I haue purposyd with goddes grace to do yn this lytyll
tretys. ffyrst to schewe yow the condicions of the .vij. dedely
synnys and by figures and ensampyll yn general And afterwarde
to rehersse hem by processe and by order what braunches gothe
owt of hem. In ensampyll as touchyng to the fyrst mater.
An holy man wrytyth yn his boke and seythe that the .vij. dedely
synnys bethe lykenyd to .vij. sondry bestys. As pride to a lyon
Covetyse to an vrchyn. Wrathe to a wolfe. Envy to an
hounde. Slowthe to an asse. Glotony to a bere. Lechery
to an hoge. of the figures and ensampylsse I purpose to tell
the yn ordre of hem by hem selfe. Pryde. ys nowt
ellys but an evyll desyre of hy worschyppe. Et est in li.
xiiij. de ci. dei. ca. xiij. Ther for he lykenythe a prowde
man to a lyon for ryghte as a lyon lokyth that all bestys
schuld hym worschyppe for drede and to hym bowe. Ryghte so
a prowde man lokythe that all men schulde hym worschyppe
for drede and to hym bowe. And therfor hit may well be seyde
of a prowde man as hit ys wrytyn in holy wrytt. Ecce
qui eos descendit de superbia. Jer. xlix. ca. This ys
a syn that destroyyth all vertues and moste grevythe
god of all vices. In token wherfor. lucyfer. that was
the feyreste Angell yn heven nowe for his pryde he
ys by cum the fowlyste fende of hell and yf yow wolte
wytte whereyn he synnyd I answer and sey yn this
he desyred to haue be pere wythe god for as I seyde
by for pride ys nothe ellis but an evyll desyr of hy
worschyppe And the man of desyr may now a ryse yn
manys herte but by cause of on of these .iij. other hit

ys

In nomine trino hoc opus incipio.

London, British Library, Harley MS 2383, f. 65r
Lavynham, *A Little Treatise on the Seven Deadly Sins*
actual size

51

Lincoln, Lincoln Cathedral MS 91, f. 85v
Morte Arthure (alliterative), ll. 3031–78
Gothic *littera cursiva anglicana media/currens*, s. xv med.

TRANSCRIPTION

I ȝife the in hamptone : a hundreth' pownde large
T he kynge *yan* to assawte : he sembles his knyghtez
With' Somercastell' and Sowe : appon' sere halfes
Skyftis his skotiferis : and skayles the wallis
And iche wa[t>c]he has his warde : with wiese men' of armes
Thane boldly *yay* buske : and bendes Eng[-e]ynes
Payses In pylot(es) : and proues .'[1] theire castes
M[i\y]nsteris and Masondewes : they malle to *ye* erthe
Chirches and chapell's : chalke whitte blawnchede
Stone tepell's[2] full' styffe : in *ye* strete ligges
Chawmbyrs with' chymnes : and many cheefe Inns
Paysede and pelid down' : playsterede walles
The pyne of *ye* pople : was pete for to here
Thane *ye* duchez hire dyghte : with' damesels ryche
The cowntas of crasyn'[3] : with' hir clere maydyns
knelis down' in *ye* kyrnelles : there the kyng houede
On a cou(er)ede [-comlily arayede] horse comlyli arayede
They knewe hym by conten`a´u(n)ce : and criede full' lowde
king crownede of kynde : take kepe to *yese* wordes
we beseke ȝow s(ir) as Sou(er)aynge and lorde
That ȝe safe vs to daye : for sake of ȝoure criste
Send vs some socoure : and saughte with' the pople
Or[4] *ye* Cete be sodaynly : with' assawte wonnen'
he weres his vesere : with' a vowt noble
with' vesage v(er)teuous : this valyante bierne
Meles to hir myldly : with' full' meke wordes[5]
Sall' no m[e\y]sse do ȝow . ma . dame . *yat* to me lenges
I gyf ȝow chartire of pes : ⁊ ȝoure cheefe maydens
The childire and *ye* chaste men' : the cheualro(us) knyghtez
The duke es in dawngere : dredis it bott littyll'
he sall' Ideue[6] *ye* full' wele : dout ȝow noghte ell'es
¶ Thane sent he on' iche a syde to certayne lordez
For to leue *ye* assawte : the Cete was ȝolden'
With' *ye* Erle eldeste son' : he sent hym *ye* kayes
and seside *ye* Same nyghte : be sent of *ye* lordes
The duke to dou(er)e es dyghte : and all' his dere knyghtez
To duelle in dawngere and dole : *ye* dayes of hys lyue
¶ Thare fleede at the ferrere ȝate : folke withowttyn' no(m)m[e>b]yre[7]
For ferde of s(ir) Florent : and his fers knyghtez
Voydes the Cete : and to the wode rynnys
With' vetaile and vessell' : and vesto(ur)e so ryche
Thay buske vpe a banere : abo[u\w]n' *ye* brode ȝates
Of s(ir) Florent in Fay : so fayne was he neu(er)
The knyghte[8] houys on a hyll' : behelde to *ye* wallys
And saide I See be ȝone syngne : the Cete es oures
Sir Arthure Enters anon' : with' hostes arayede
Euen' at *ye* vndron Etles to lenge
In Iche leu(er)e on lowde the kynge did crye

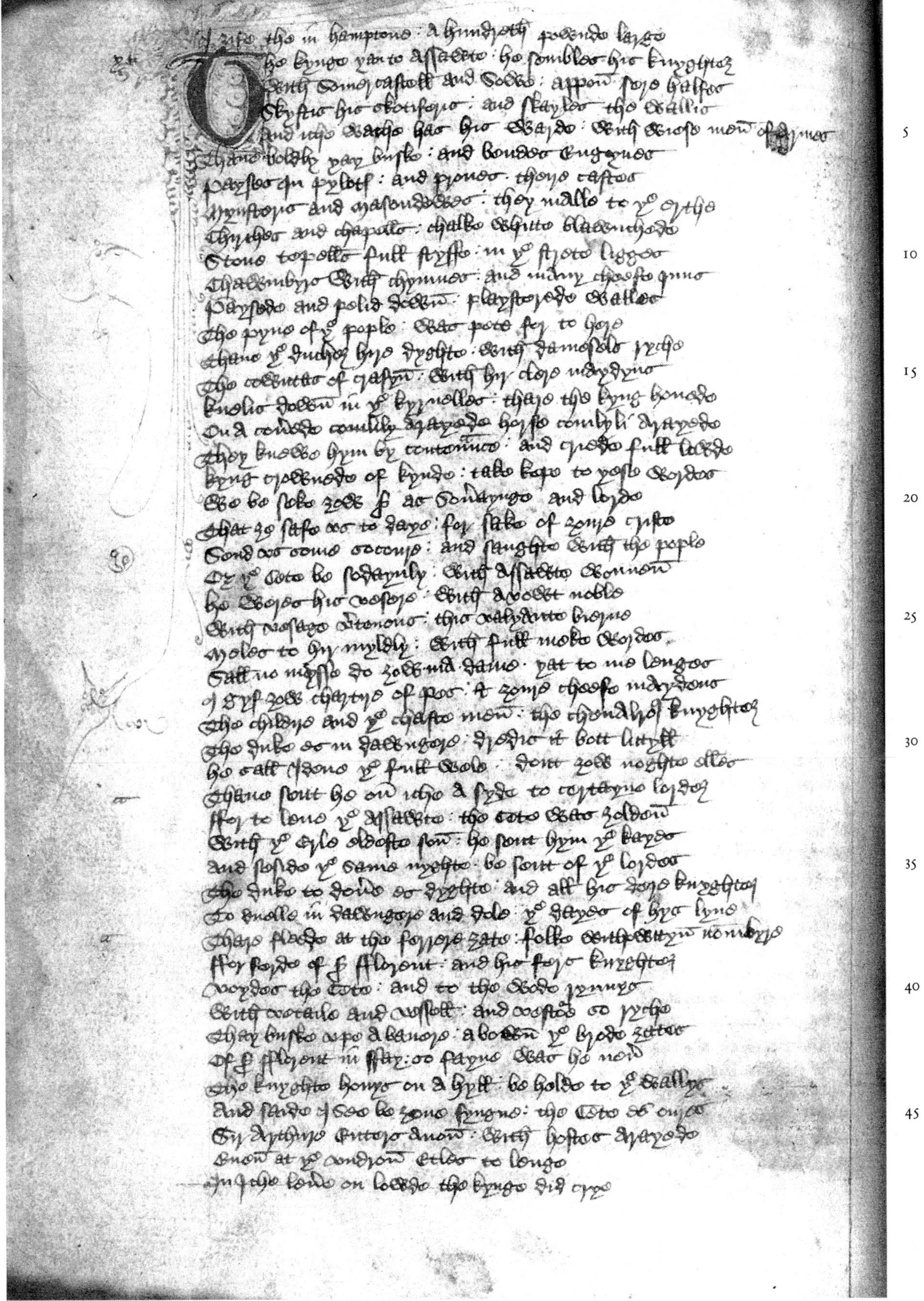

Plate 51 – reduced to 88%

The letter-forms of this almost wholly current hand are Anglicana, although the slope suggests Secretary influence, as does sometimes the angular shape of **d** (although looped). Note the frequent use of a single-stroke **a** with reversed ductus (e.g. 'malle', l. 8, 'assawte', l. 23). The **y** does double duty: where serving for **þ** (mostly at the beginning of words) it is italicized in the transcript; **th** is also in use; and **ȝ** is differentiated from the **z** which appears finally at the end of nouns and verbs (ll. 14, 29, 32, 36, 39). The letter **v** is usually initial and **u** used elsewhere; **w** may interchange with either, resulting in such spellings as 'weres' (raises), l. 24 and 'Masondewes', l. 8. There is little punctuation, beyond the marking of the caesura by a pair of dots. Occasional dots may be mistaken, as in l. 7, or functional, as perhaps at the end of l. 26 before a speech, or in l. 27 to mark out the parts of the French phrase of address. Note the capitulum signs to the left of ll. 32 and 38, to indicate sense breaks. Capitals usually appear at the outset of each line (note that ff. 53r-69r, i.e. the beginning of the poem, are rubricated: a central pair of points are supplied in red with following virgule; and both the first letter of the line and the first letter of the second verse are given a red stroke). Elsewhere capitals are sporadic, marking some nouns, but used more for **e** and **i**, for example 'In', l. 7, 'Ideue', l. 31, 'Enters', l. 46, 'Etles', l. 47, 'Iche', l. 48. Some enlarged letter-forms seem to serve as capitals, for example **s** (though without the extra stroke found in 'Sir', l. 46) and **a** (compare 'And', l. 45, or 'Arthure', ll. 46, with 'and', l. 35). Proper names are not necessarily given capitals (compare 'Florent', ll. 39, 43 with 'hamptone', l. 1, 'crasyn'', l. 15, 'dou(er)e', l. 36). The abbreviations seen on this page include: ᷣ in 'cou(er)ede', l. 17, 'Sou(er)aynge', l. 20, 'v(er)teuous', l. 25, 'dou(er)e', l. 36, 'neu(er)', l. 43, 'leu(er)e', l. 48, and through long **s** in 's(ir)', ll. 20, 39, 43, ꝭ in 'pylot(es)', l. 7, ꝰ in 'cheualro(us)', l. 29; ꝛ in 'vesto(ur)e', l. 41. Frequent overlines and slashing through ascenders, probably otiose, are signalled by the apostrophe, although the expansion is made in 'no(m)m[e>b]yre', l. 38. The Tironian sign occurs only in l. 28, with 'and' otherwise written in full. The scribe has made some corrections, most obviously in ll. 17 and 18, but oddities remain in ll. 10 and 31. Space was left for the filling in of the four-line capital of l. 2, beside which the guide letters 'y' (= *þ*) and 't' as well are both visible. Watermarks correspond to some found in documents dated 1413-61.

CONTEXTS

This is one of two compilations (the other manuscript written by him is British Library, Additional MS 31042) made by Robert Thornton, lord of the manor of East Newton, North Riding of Yorkshire, before 1465 (his widow remarried in that year). Thornton names himself from time to time, for example on ff. 93v, 98v, 176r, 211v, 213r, and 278v. Internal dates narrow transcription to the mid-fifteenth century, after 1422 (internal evidence, f. 250v) and part probably being written in the 1450s (a Thornton birth in 1453 'at Ridayll'' (Ryedale) is noted on f. 49v). Manuscript probably remained in family use up into the late sixteenth century or later and in the East Newton area into the late seventeenth century (other family names are Edward, ff. 75r, 137r, 194r, Eleanor, f. 135v, William, ff. 49v, 144v, and Dorythy, ff. 265r, 266r). Seen at Lincoln Cathedral by Tanner in 1700, and thought to have been acquired while Michael Honeywood was dean. Formerly A. 5. 2. The nineteenth-century binding (that 'good solid attire of Russian leather' paid for by Madden) and some notes are separately conserved. Known as the Thornton Manuscript (confusingly) or the Thornton Romances.

SIZE

291 × 210 mm (*c.* 230 × *c.* 120 mm).

BIBLIOGRAPHY

Pr. Krishna 1976, ll. 3031-78; Hamel 1984, ll. 3031-67, 3112-23.
Facs. Brewer and Owen 1975, em. rpt.1977.
Disc. McIntosh 1962; Owen 1975; Guddat-Figge 1976: no. 27; Stern 1976; Keiser 1979; Horall 1980; Thompson 1982, 1983, 1987; McIntosh, Samuels and Benskin 1986: I. 98; Thomson 1989: 65-69.

[1] Could be a mistaken point.
[2] For 'steeples'.
[3] But 'crafyn'' also read; compare **f** in 'safe', l. 21. Malory has 'Clarysyn'.
[4] Note the tailed form of round **r**.
[5] Note mark; probably not a point.
[6] Hamel (1984): 'i[n]deue', for 'endow, provide for'.
[7] Hamel (1984) acts upon the Gordon and Vinaver (1937) observation that this is the first of sixteen lines used later by Malory and therefore misplaced in Thornton's text.
[8] Editors suggest that Thornton meant to write 'kynge'.

This book was mad of þe
goodis of robert holond for a
comyn p(ro)fite þ(a)t þat p(er)soone þat
haþ þis book co(m)mittid to hi(m) of
þe p(er)soone þ(a)t haþ pow(er) to com-
mitte it ; haue þe vss þ(er)of þe terme of his lijf. p(ra)yinge for the
soule of þe same Robert. And
þ(a)t he þat haþ þe forseid vss of
co(m)missio(u)n whanne he occupieþ
it not ; leene he it for a tyme to
su(m) oþ(er) p(er)soone. Also þat p(er)soone
to whom it was co(m)mittid for
þe terme of lijf ; vndir þe forseid condicio(u)ns deliu(er)e it to a
noþ(er) p(er)soone þe terme of his
lijf. And so be it deliu(er)ed & co(m)mit-

London, British Library, Harley MS 993, f. 38r
Inscription in common-profit book, *c.* 1450

Beginning of inscription that follows, in a larger module in the same hand, Hilton's *Eight Chapters* and the anonymous *Treatise of Discretion of Spirits*. The inscription takes up three further lines over the page: 'tid fro(m) p(er)soone to persoone | man or wo(m)man as longe as | þe book enduriþ / '. The rest of the page is filled by a later owner, James Palmer, who fulminates about the wickedness of seeking prayers for the soul. The making of this common-profit book (or book for general good) was financed from the estate of Robert Holond. It belonged to Sister Anne Colville, a Syon nun, in 1518. (Hodgson 1955: x-xi; on common-profit books see Scase 1992.)
actual size

52

London, British Library, Additional MS 36704, f. 46r
Capgrave, Preface to Lives of Augustine and Gilbert of Sempringham
Gothic *littera cursiva* secretary *media/currens*, *c.* 1451

TRANSCRIPTION

T   o my wel beloued in our(e) lord god
maystir of *ye* order(e) of s[\e/i]mp(r)y(n)gha(m)[1]
whech ordre is entytled on to *ye*
name of seynt gilbert I Frer(e) I· C·[2]
among(is) doctouris lest sende re⸗
uerens as to swech dignyte . desiri(n)g cle(n)nesse
to ȝour(e) soule and helth to ȝour(e) body Now
withinne fewe dayes was notyfied on
to me *yat ye* lyf of our(e) fader seynt augus⸗[3]
tyn whech *yat* I trans[-a]lat into our(e) tu(n)ge
at instau(n)s of a c(er)teyn woma(n) was browt
to ȝour(e) presens whech lykyd ȝow wel as it
is told saue ȝe wold I schul adde *y*(er)to alle
yoo relygyous *yat* lyue vndyr his reule
But to *yis* I answer(e) *yat* it was not my char⸗
ge but if men like for to knowe *yis* mater(e)
diffusely *yei* may lerne it in a s(er)mo(n) *yat* \I/ seid
at cambrig(e) *ye* ȝer(e) befor(e) myn opposiciou(n)
whech s(er)mon vnp[lȝ>h]ap[4] I wil sette in englisch(e)
in *ye* last ende of *yis* werk Than aftir ȝe
had red *yis* lyf of seynt augusty(n) ȝe sayde
to on of my frendes *yat* ȝe desired gretly
ye lyf of seynt gilbert schuld be translat
in the same forme Thus mad he instau(n)ce
to me and I grau(n)ted both ȝour(e) petyciou(n) \\⁊ his// for
I wold not frustrate him of his mediaciou(n)
To *ye* honour(e) of god and of all(e) seyntis *ya*(n)
wil we begy(n)ne *yis* tretys namelych for the
solitarye wome(n) of ȝour(e) religiou(n) whech vn⸗

The choice of Secretary letter⸗forms is assured. Minims are cursively written, yet **v** appears initially, never **u.** There is no clear differentiation between **þ** and **y**, although the form interpreted as **þ**, italicized in the transcript, often has an approach stroke (probably not in '*y*is', l. 20, '*y*e', l. 27, and '*y*a(n)', l. 27); **th** is, by comparison with **y** for *þ*, infrequent ('helth', l. 7, 'withinne', l. 8, 'the', ll. 24, 28, 'both', l. 25, 'Than', l. 20, 'Thus', l. 24). Note that **y** is dotted in 'tyn', l. 10. The yogh is retained. Punctuation is sparing, mainly an occasional point. Split words are signalled by the hyphen. There is a careful application of red to clause⸗ or phrase⸗initial letters, some of which are in distinctive form; the Anglicana **a** in 'at', l. 11, is phrase⸗initial but has not attracted a dash of colour. Some corrections are in red ink: the point in l. 6, the hyphen in l. 9, and the insertions markers in ll. 17 and 25. The abbreviations are carefully written: ꝭ for *is* ('amongis', l. 5); ᷑ for *er* ('c(er)teyn', l. 11, '*y*(er)to', l. 13, and written through the main stroke of **s**, in 's(er)mo(n)', l. 17, 's(er)mon', l. 19; the overline for *n* (e.g. 'desiri(n)g', l. 6, 'cle(n)nesse', l. 6, 'opposiciou(n)', l. 18) or *m* ('s[\e/i]mp(r)y(n)gha(m)', l. 2, which also requires a suspended **r**); flourished final **r**, resolved as *e* ('our(e)', l. 1, 'order(e)', ll. 2, etc.), with which compare 'cambrig(e)', l. 18. The Tironian sign appears only in the marginal addition of l. 25. Capgrave's corrections include: 's[\e/i]mp(r)y(n)gha(m)', l. 2, where **e** is written above **i**; the subpuncting of the second **a** in 'trans[-a]lat', l. 10; '\I/', l. 17; and the partially emended 'vnp[lȝ>h]ap', l. 19.

[1] The recipient of the dedication is identified in the outer margin as 'M(agister) Nicholas| Reysby'.

[2] The underlining of the initials in l. 4 relates to the later identification of 'Iohn' | Capgrave' (perhaps for 'Ioh(a)n(nus)').

[3] Very faint; added in red.

[4] For 'vphap' = 'perhaps, possibly' (this is the latest instance recorded in the *OED*).

46

To my wel beloued in our lord god M. nicholas
mayster of ye ordre of Sempyngham Reysby-
whech ordre is entytled on to ye
name of seynt gilbert I frere J. C. John
a mong doctoures lest sende re Capgrave.
uerens as to swech dignyte desiring clenesse
to your soule and helth to your body Now
with inne fewe dayes was notyfied on
to me yat ye lyf of our fader seynt augus
tyn whech yat I translat in to our tunge
at instauns of a certeyn woman was browt
to your presens whech lykyd yow wel as it
is told saue ye wold I schuld adde yto alle
yoo relygyous yat lyue vndyr his reule
but to yis I answerd yat it was not my char
ge but if men lyke for to knowe yis mater
diffusely yei may lerne it in a sermon yat I seid
at Cambrig ye yere be fore myn opposicion
whech sermon vnhap I wil sette in englisch
in ye last ende of yis werk Than aftir ye
had red yis lyf of seynt augustyn ye sayde
to on of my frendes yat ye desired gretly
ye lyf of seynt gilbert schuld be translat
in the same forme Thus mad he instance
to me and I graunted both your petycyon for
I wold not frustrate hym of his medicacioun
To ye honour of god and of all seyntis yat
wil we begynne yis tretys namely for the
solitarye women of your religion whech vn-

41

Plate 52 – actual size

CONTEXTS

In hand of author, John Capgrave, Augustinian friar at Lynn (King's Lynn, Norfolk), who translated this life of the founder of the Gilbertine order for the nuns of Sempringham (the passage continues 'whech vn| [f. 46v]neth can vndyrstande latyn'); addressing it to the master of the order, he clearly hoped for a wider readership. For the date 1451 see the colophon, f. 116r. Doyle 1989: 118 points to the oddly limited survival of Capgrave's works 'only in autographs and apographs corrected by himself'. Some people for whom prayers were to be said are named on f. 121v: at Reydun (?Reydon, Suffolk) for Joh' Kewe and his wife Matild'; and at Tunsted, Norfolk, for Alicie Curteys, presumably wife of Will(elmu)s. Belonged to Sir Robert Kemp of Gissing, Norfolk, in the seventeenth century (evidence from binding). Afterwards in the Fountaine collection (ownership note 'Andrew Fountaine| Sept 29 1817' on f. 120r). Acquired by British Museum in 1902 (Fountaine sale-catalogue, lot 167).

SIZE

204 × 144 mm (140 × 89 mm).

BIBLIOGRAPHY

Pr. Munro 1910: 61.

Disc. Add. MSS *Cat.*; Wright 1960[1]: pl. 21; Lucas 1972, 1973, 1995, 1997; Watson 1979: no. 376, pl. 515; McIntosh, Samuels, and Benskin 1986: I. 102, III. 333–34 (LP 4057 Norfolk).

London, British Library, Additional MS 61823, f. 123r
Ending of the book of Margery Kempe of Lynn

Margery Kempe's autobiography was written down from her telling of her life and travels. This is the only known manuscript, written in the mid-fifteenth century by a scribe named Salthows.
actual size

53

London, British Library, Additional MS 35290, f. 113r (formerly 110) *Colour pl. C8*
York Plays, 'The Cutteleres, "The Conspiracy"'
Gothic *littera cursiva* Secretary *formata*/*formata hybrida*, 1463–77

TRANSCRIPTION

The Cutteleres

Pilat(us)

⟨V⟩[1] Ndir *y*e ryallest Roye of rente and renowne
Now am I regent of rewle *y*is region in reste
Obeye vnto bidding bud Busshoppis me bowne
And bolde men *y*at in batayll' · Makis brestis to breste
To me betaught is *y*e tent · *y*is towrebegon towne
For traytoures tyte will I taynte · *y*e trew*y*e for to triste
The dubbyng of my dingnite · may noȝt be done downe
Nowdir with duke / nor dugeperes / my dedis are so dreste
My desire muste dayly be done
With *y*ame *y*at are grettest of game
And *y*er agayne fynde I but fone
Wherfore I schall bettir *y*er bone
But he *y*at me greues for a grume[2]
Beware for wyscus[3] I am
Pounce Pilatt of thre partis
*Y*an[4] is my propir name
I am a perelous prince
To proue wher I peere
Emange *y*e philosofers firste
Ther ffanged I my fame
Wherfore I fell to affecte
I fynde noȝt my feere
He schall full bittirly banne
*Y*at bide schall my blame
If all my blee be as bright
As blossome on brere
For sone his liffe shall he lose
Or left be for lame
*Y*at lowtes noȝt to me lowly
Nor liste noȝt to leere
And *y*us sen we stande in oure state
Als lordis with all lykyng in lande
Do and late vs wete if ȝe wate
Owthir sirs of bayle or debate
*Y*at nedis for to be handeled full hate
Sen all youre helpe hanges in my hande

This is f. 123 in Beadle and Meredith 1983. The Secretary script here is higher than a standard *formata* grade (bastard secretary in Parkes's terms): note the separate minims, sometimes with feet, the loops on **b**, **h**, **l** (but not **d**), and the considerable use of final strokes as word dividers. The 2-shaped **r** follows not only **o** ('propir', l. 16, 'proue', l. 18, 'Nor', l. 30) but also **b** ('brere', l. 26), **h** ('thre', l. 15) and **e** ('Ther', l. 20). The doubled **f** is transcribed as the capital form **F** at the beginning of ll. 6, 27 but not within the verse line at the beginning of the word 'ffanged', l. 20. Some Anglicana forms

[1] The guide-letter is largely concealed by the vertical ruled line. The lines visible is this space are show through from braces on the verso.
[2] For 'grone', meaning 'groan'.
[3] Meaning 'vicious'. Beadle 1982 thinks a crux.
[4] The intention is a capital, for **y** is touched in red (see Colour pl. 8).

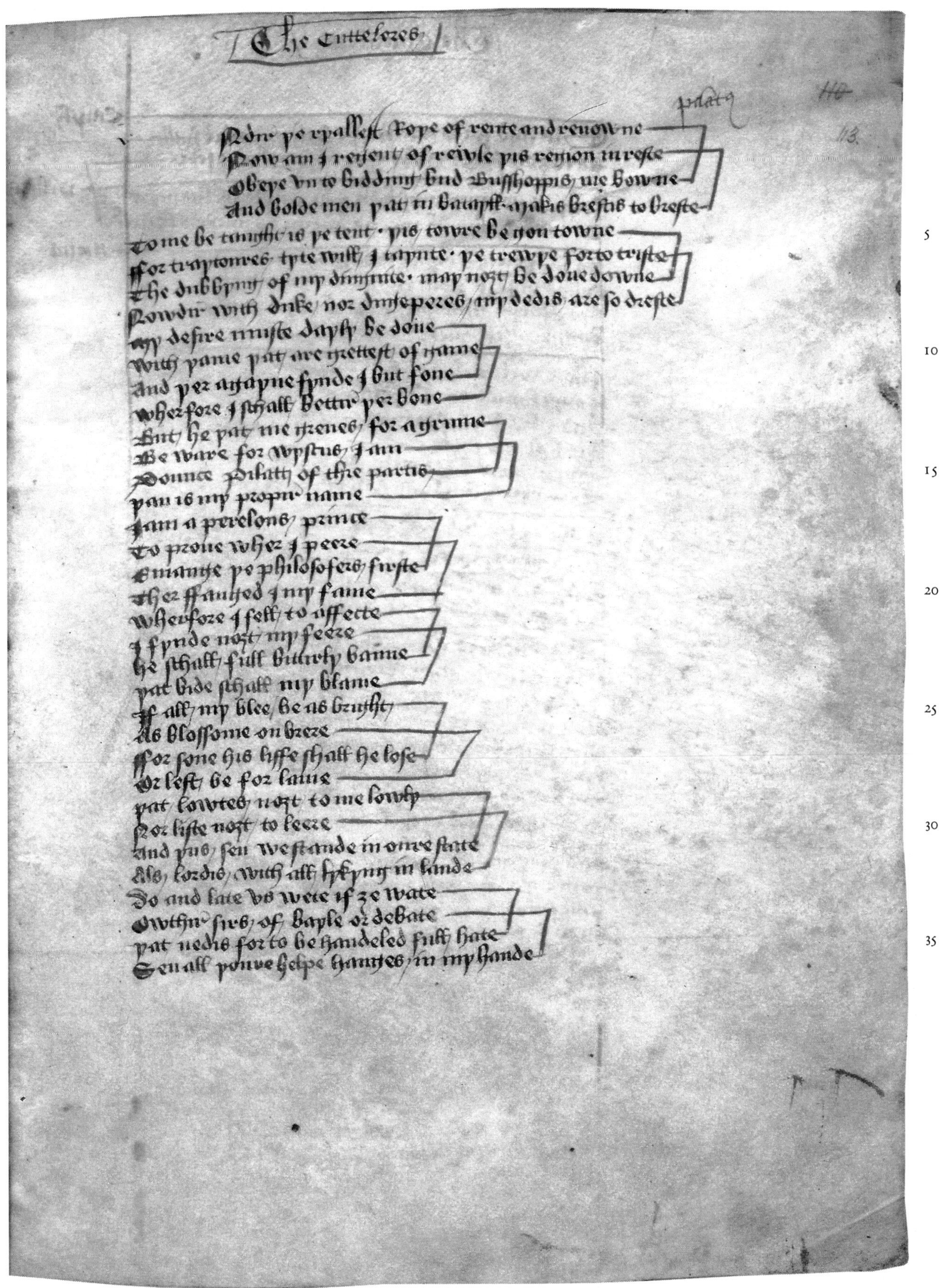

The Cutteleres

Pilatus

Nowe ȝe ryallest rope of rente and renowne
Now am I regent of rewle þis region in reste
Obeye vnto biddyng bud busshoppis me bowne
And bolde men þat in batayll makis brestis to breste
To me be tyghtyng is þe tent · þis towre be yon towne
For traytoures tyte will I taynte · þe trewþe for to triste
The dubbyng of my dygnyte · may noȝt be done downe
Nowdir with duke nor dussepers, my dedis are so dreste
My desire muste dayly be done
With þame þat are grettest of game
And þer agayne fynde I but fone
Wherfore I schall bettir þer bone
But he þat me grenes for a grume
Be ware for wyscus I am
Pownce Pilatt of thre partis
Þan is my propir name
I am a perelous prince
To proue wher I peere
Emange þe philosofers firste
Ther fraunched I my fame
Wherfore I fell to affecte
I fynde noȝt my feere
He schall full bitterly banne
Þat bide schall my blame
If all my blee be as bright
As blossome on brere
For sone his liffe shall he lose
Or left be for lame
Þat lowtes noȝt to me lowly
Nor liste noȝt to leere
And þus sen we stande in oure state
Als lordis with all lykyng in lande
Do and late vs wete if ȝe wate
Owther sirs of bayle or debate
Þat nedis for to be handeled full hate
Sen all youre helpe hanges in my hande

Plate 53 – reduced to 83%

are used as capitals at the beginnings of lines. One letter-form is used for both **þ** (× 18, italicized in transcript) and **y** (× 30): *þ* it is mostly word initial (except 'trewþe', l. 6) and as *y* non-word initial (except 'youre', l. 36; compare 'ȝe', l. 33), so presents few problems of interpretation. Of the eight instances of **th,** four begin words ('The' in the heading and l. 7, 'thre', l. 15, and 'Ther', l. 20), three are in 'with' or 'With' (ll. 8, 10, 32), and only one is mid-word ('Owthir', l. 34). Note **ȝ** in 'noȝt', ll. 7, 22, 29, 30, alongside the **g** of 'betaught', l. 5, 'bright', l. 25. Of the eight long lines which begin the first stanza, ll. 4-7 are divided by points (ll. 15-30, which begin the second of the two stanzas on this page, could also have been presented as long lines), but otherwise the generous use of space obviates the need for punctuation marks. The manuscript was assembled with fairly uniform ruling across the open sheets (but with a certain carelessness in hitting the four points made with knife-point on each page), as the city record of the York plays. The rubricator misplaced the braces to mark rhyme from l. 10; he also framed the running titles; and he usually supplied the speech headings, but not always at the opening of plays ('pilat(us)', added in brownish ink, has an Anglicana **a** and uses the abbreviation 9). There are no abbreviations in the hand of the main text on this page, unless final *-e* is to be supplied in 'batayll'', l. 4.

Another sample of this scribe's hand is included on the facing page, to show the generosity of space allocated to short speeches. Here **þ** and **y** are on the whole kept separate, except finally.

CONTEXTS

Main hand or Hand B of manuscript compiled in the 1460s–1470s as the official Register of the city of York. A scrivener identified as John Clerke entered some plays (4, 18, part of 7) and other substantial additions in the sixteenth century. The date 1583 (f. 4) also suggests continued use. The names Thomas Cutler and Richarde Nandicke occur a few times *c.* 1600 in the opening pages, on the last verso and their initials respectively on ff. 89r and 92r; R Rytchyne man(?ers) on the verso of f. ii; and William Pennell, John Willson on the last verso. Perhaps descended down the Fairfax family for some generations: by 1695 belonged to Henry Fairfax (ownership note f. ix), who gave it to Ralph Thoresby between 1695 and 1708. Documented from 1764 when bought by Horace Walpole in sale of Thoresby's library. With the sale of the Strawberry Hill Library in 1842, passed through the hands of Thomas Rudd, bookseller, and on to B.H. Bright. Sold again at Sotheby's 1844 (Madden very likely responsible for the identification of contents in the catalogue) to Thorpe for Thomas Russell and afterwards to Lord Ashburnham. Bought (1899) by the British Museum at the sale of Ashburnham library.

SIZE

c. 279 × 210 mm (*c.* 180 × 105 mm).

BIBLIOGRAPHY

Pr. Beadle 1982: 220 (ll. 1-28).
Facs. Beadle and Meredith 1983.
Disc. Add. MSS *Cat.*; Petti 1977: pl. 12; Cawley 1980; Beadle and Meredith 1980; McIntosh, Samuels and Benskin 1986: I. 102.

The masonns

With dyntes to dede bes he dight
þat liste not youre lawes forto lowte
his wille

My lorde ser Herowde kyng with crowne (Nunc.)

Pees dastarde in þe deueles dispite (Herod.)

My lorde now note is nere þis towne (Nunc.)

What false harlott liste þe flight
Go bete yone boy and dyng hym downe (Herod.)

Lorde messengeres shulde no man wyte
It may be for youre awne renoune (Miles)

þat wolde I here do telle on tyte (Herod.)

My lorde I mette at morne
Thre kyngis carpand to gedir
Of a barne þat is borne
And þei hight to come hidir (Nunc.)

Thre kyngis for soth (Herod.)

Sir so I say for I saw þaim my selffe all fere (Nunc.)

My lorde appose hym I yow pray (I cons.)

Say felowe are they ferre or nere (Herod.)

Mi lorde þei will be here þis day
þat wote I wele withouten were (Nunc.)

(Herod.)

London, British Library, Additional MS 35290, f. 60v
York Plays, 'The Masouns'
reduced to 83%

54

Cambridge, St John's College MS G. 23, f. 163v
Barbour, *The Bruce*
Mixed hand: a Gothic *littera cursiva*, 1487

TRANSCRIPTION

He that hye Lorde of al thing is
Vp till his mekill blis *y*am(m)e brynge
And grant vs grace *y*at *y*ar ofspryng
Lede weill *y*e Land and ententif
Be to forow[1] in all *y*air liff
*Y*air nobillis[2] eld(er)is gret bounte
Quhar[3] afald god in trinite
Bryng ws hye vp till hevynis blis
Quhar allwayis lestand liking is
Amen

Explicit Liber excellentissimi et
nobilissimi principis roberti de
broys scottorum regis illustrissimi
qui q(ui)d(em) liber scriptus fuit ⁊ finitus
in vigilia sancti Ioha(n)is baptiste
viz decollacio euiusd(em) per manum
I de R cap(ellanu)m Anno D(omi)ni Millesimo
1487 quadringentesimo octogesimo septimo

Epithaphiu(m) regis roberti broys

Hic Iacit i(n)uictus Robertus Rex benedictus
Qui sua gesta legit rep(er)it quot bella p(er)egit
Ad libertatem deduxit per probitatem
Regnum scottorum ∴ nunc viuit i(n) arce polor(um)

Overall this is may be described as Gothic *littera cursiva* Secretary *media*, with some *anglicana* alternatives. The top of the page shows the last nine lines of *The Bruce*. The letter-forms are for the most part Secretary: the single-compartment **a**; **g** (often with horn at top as in 'grace', l. 3); the distinctive tight kidney-shaped form of **s** finally, as in 'is', l. 1, 'his', l. 2, 'vs', l. 3; **e** with its parts tending to separate because cursively written; short secretary **r** usual, but the *anglicana* form sometimes used at end word, as '*y*ar', l. 3; **w** most often cursive secretary form, as 'weill', l. 4, but some looped *anglicana* forms, e.g. 'forow', l. 5, 'allwayis' l. 9, and for the initial vowel of the pronoun 'ws', l. 8. The scribe has some pretensions to style, as shown by decorative hangers, especially after final long **s** (often interpreted as *ss*); because he is writing freely he has a tendency to add loops, as with **d**. Note as well as **th-** (e.g. 'that', 'thing', l. 1), the use of **y** initially, represented by italicized *y* in the transcription (as '*y*a(m)me', l. 2). Even these few lines suggest a cavalier attitude to the distribution of **v** and **u**. The dialect is 'Inglis' (the description the Scots themselves used of their form of northern English up into the sixteenth century, in our terms Scots): distinctive spellings include *qu-* for more southerly *wh-* and *-i-* to mark vowel length (as in 'weill', l. 4). This is a competent steady hand, though perhaps distracted as end of task approaches. In addition to the mistakes noted, perhaps 'his' should be read for 'vs', l. 3. The scribe has, however, given some thought to the layout of this final page of the *Bruce*, setting off his colophon to the right and completing the page in a larger, more formal and upright version of his script (some separate minims, and lengthening of final minim noteworthy) with four lines in praise of Robert the Bruce. The one-stroke **x** of 'excellentissimi', l. 11, is the usual Secretary form.

CONTEXTS

The chaplain 'I de R' of the colophon, dated as completed on 28 August 1487, is not the John Ramsay, prior of Charterhouse at Perth, who made the copies of *The Wallace* (1488) and of Barbour's *Bruce* (1489) to be found in Edinburgh, Advocates' 19. 2. 2 (1). The Cambridge *Bruce*, a small paper volume, was among the books that passed from William Crashaw to Henry Wriothesley and by 1635 from Thomas Wriothesley to St John's College.

[1] Miswritten for 'follow'.
[2] Note dittography of *-is*.
[3] Suggested emendations 'The' or '*Y*e'. May mean 'wherefore'.

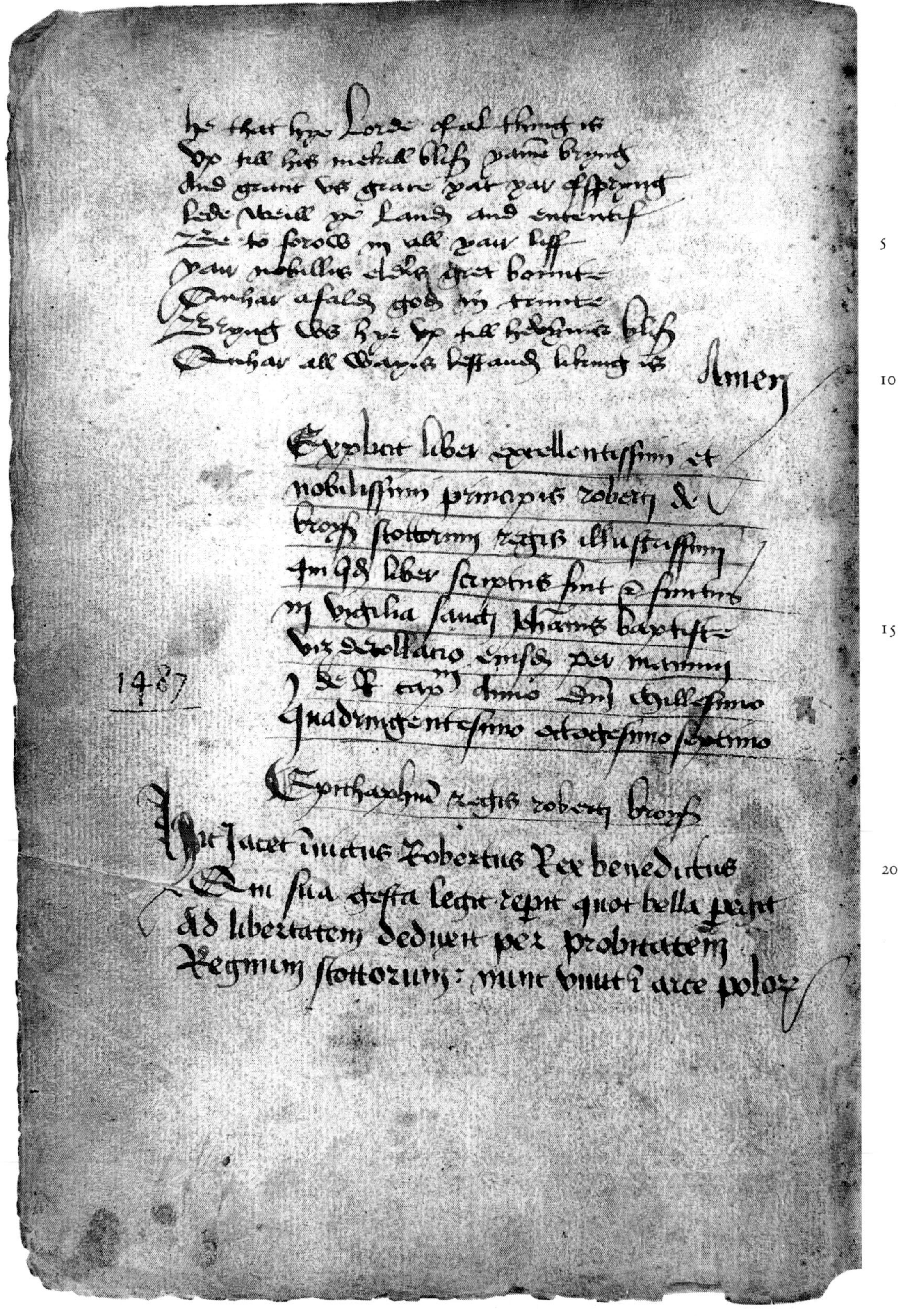

He that hye Lorde of al thing is
Vp till his mekill blis thaim bryng
And grant vs grace that thair offspring
Lede weill the land and ententif
Be to folow in all thair liff
Thair nobillis eldris gret bounte
Quhar afald god in trinite
Bryng vs hye vp till hevynnis blis
Quhar all wayis lestand liking is Amen

Explicit liber excellentissimi et
nobilissimi principis roberti de
broyss scottorum regis illustrissimi
In quo liber scriptus fuit et finitus
in vigilia sancti Johannis baptiste
[illegible] Willelmo [illegible] per manum
J de R [illegible] anno domini Millesimo
quadringentesimo octogesimo septimo

1487

Epithaphium regis roberti broyss
Hic Jacet invictus Robertus Rex benedictus
Qui sua gesta legit repetit quot bella peregit
Ad libertatem deduxit per probitatem
Regnum scottorum: nunc vivit in arce polorum

Plate 54 – actual size

SIZE
c. 210 × 140 mm (usually 158–60 × 80 mm).

BIBLIOGRAPHY
Pr. Skeat 1870–89: 519–20 (xx. 612–20); 1894: II. 196. *Coll.* McDiarmid and Stevenson 1980–85: 3. 263–64.
Disc. James 1913: no. 191; P[revité]-O[rton] 1918; Cunningham 1974; Robinson 1988: no. 307, pl. 330.

55

London, British Library Additional MS 59678, f. 35r
Malory, *Morte Darthure*
Scribe A: Gothic *littera cursiva* Secretary *formata/formata hybrida*
Scribe B: Gothic *littera cursiva* Secretary *media/currens*; s. xv ex.

TRANSCRIPTION

IN the begynnyng of Arthure Aftir he wes chosyn kynge
by aduenture and by grace for the moste p(ar)ty of the barowns knew nat he was
Vther Pendragon son But as Merlyon.[1] made hit opynly knowyn . But
yet many kyngis and lordis hylde hym grete werre for that cause // But well(e)
Arthur ou(er)com hem all(e) the moste p(ar)ty dayes of hys lyff he was ruled by þ^{e} counceile
of Merlyon So hit felle on a tyme kyng Arthur seyde vnto Merlion My ba⸗
rownes woll(e) let me haue no reste but nedis I muste take a wyff ⁊ I wolde none
take but by thy counceile and advice // Hit ys well done seyde Merlyon that
ye take a wyff . For[2] a man of youre bounte and nobles scholde
not be w(i)t(h)oute a wyff . Now is þ(er) ony seyde Marlyon that
ye love more than a noþ(er) . ye seyde kyng' Arthure I love Gwe=[3]
nyvere the kyng(es) doughtir of lodegrean of þ^{e} londe of Came=
lerde the whyche holdyth In his house the table rounde that ye
tolde me he had hit of my fadir Vther And this damesell' is the
moste valyaunte and fayryst that[4] I know lyvyng' or yet that eu(er)
I coude fynde Sertis seyde Marlyon as of her beaute and fayre=
nesse she is one of the fayrest on lyve . But and ye loved hir not
so well' as ye do I scholde fynde you a damesell' of beaute and
of goodnesse that sholde lyke you and please you and youre
herte were nat sette . But there as mannes herte is sette
he woll' be loth to returne . that is trouthe seyde kyng' Arthur
B`ut´ Marlyon warned the kyng' covertly that Gwenyuer was nat
holsom for hym to take to wyff . For he warned hym that laun=
celot scholde love hir and sche hym agayne . And so he turned[5] his
tale to the aventures of the Sankegreal. Than Ma(rlyon) desyred of
the kyng' for to haue men w(i)t(h) hym þ^{t} scholde enquere of Gwenyu(er)
and so the kyng' grunted[6] hym and so Merlyon wente forthe
vnto kyng' lodegean[7] of Camylerde and tolde hym of the desire
of the kyng' þ^{t} he wolde haue vnto his wyff Gwenyu(er) his douȝt(er)
That is to me seyde kyng' lodegreau(n)s the beste tydyng(es) that
eu(er) I herde . that so worthy a kyng of provesse ⁊ noblesse wol wedde
my dougt(er) . And as for my londis I wolde geff hit hym yf I wyste

The upright appearance of Scribe A's opening lines creates the impression of an Anglicana script, and the proper names inserted by him in red ink may be termed *anglicana formata*. The preponderance of letter⸗forms, however, indicates an overall definition of very formal Secretary. The **b** is looped, as is **d** in 'dayes', l. 5, and 'done', l. 8, but not in 'aduenture', ll. 2, 'lordis', l. 4, 'seyde', l. 6, 'nedis', l. 7. Anglicana **r** is occasional (see 'werre', l. 4). The formal distribution of **v/u** is disrupted (compare 'aduenture', l. 2, but 'advice', l. 8). The Tironian sign is used once, l. 7, and ⁺ in 'p(ar)ty'. ll. 2, 5, 'ou(er)com', l. 5. In 'well(e)', l. 4, the stroke through **ll** is clearly without hanger and therefore taken as an abbreviation, but compare 'well', l. 8, 'all(e)', l. 5, 'woll(e)', l. 7. Note space⸗saving **þ** with **e** superscript for 'the', l. 5. The five opening words approximate to Gothic *textualis quadrata* script, with the ascenders elongated. Scribe B (from the last word of l. 8)

[1] This point is in red ink.
[2] The word⸗initial **ff** following a point is here taken as **F**. Compare **For** 23.
[3] Where rubricated names are divided, the hyphens are also in red.
[4] Note separator added to counteract cursive stroke moving from 't' cross⸗bar to 'I'.
[5] Note false stroke before final letter.
[6] For 'graunted'. Did the scribe copy a superscript **a** carelessly as **u** when adding in **r**?
[7] For 'lodegrean'.

IN the begynnyng of Arthure aftir he was chosyn kynge by adventure and by grace for the moste p[ar]ty of the barowns knew nat he was Uther Pendragon son But as Merlyon made hit opynly knowyn. But yet many kyngis and lordis hylde hym grete werre for that cause // But well Arthur overcom hem all the moste p[ar]ty dayes of hys lyff he was ruled by þe counceile of Merlyon So hit felle on a tyme kyng Arthur seyde unto Merlion My barownes woll let me have no reste but nedis I muste take a wyff & I wolde none take but by thy counceile and advice // Hit ys well done seyde Merlyon that ye take a wyff. For a man of youre bounte and nobles scholde not be wᵗoute a wyff. Now is þer ony seyde Marlyon that ye love more than another. Ye seyde kyng Arthure I love Gwenyvere the kyngis doughtir of Lodegrean of þe londe of Camelerde the whyche holdyth in his house the table rounde that ye tolde me he had hit of my fadir Uther And this damesell is the moste valyaunte and fayryst that I know lyvyng or yet that ever I coude fynde Sertis seyde Marlyon as of her beaute and fayrenesse she is one of the fayrest on lyve. But and ye loved hir not so well as ye do I scholde fynde you a damesell of beaute and of goodnesse that scholde lyke you and please you and youre herte were nat sette. But there as mannes herte is sette he woll be loth to returne. That is trouthe seyde kyng Arthur But Marlyon warned the kyng covertly that Gwenyver was nat holsom for hym to take to wyff. For he warned hym that Launcelot scholde love hir and sche hym agayne. And so he turned his tale to the aventures of the Sankegreal. Than M. desyred of the kyng for to have men wᵗ hym þᵗ scholde enquere of Gwenyvere and so the kyng graunted hym and so Merlyon wente forthe unto kyng Lodegean of Camylerde and tolde hym of the desire of the kyng þᵗ he wolde have unto his wyff Gwenyver his doughter That is to me seyde kyng Lodegreauns the beste tydyng that ever I herde. that so worthy a kyng of prowesse & noblesse wol wedde my doughter. And as for my londis I wolde geff hit hym yf I wyste

Plate 55 – reduced to 81%

writes ‘a steady unpretentious secretary’ (Ker). The splay gives a spreading script, less tightly packed and easier to read than Scribe A’s. Scribe B seems inexpert at calculating the space for proper names, but is careful to separate minims when inserting them in red. (That the naming of Merlin may be a special case is argued by Cooper 1997.) Anglicana **s** is usual at the end of words (‘nobles’, l. 9, ‘is’, ll. 10, 14, 17, ‘this’, l. 14, ‘Sertis’, l. 16, etc.). The **d** is without loops. Again standard **v/u** distribution is disturbed (as in ‘provesse’, l. 31), and the scribe may be moving toward the use of **v** as consonant (‘love’, l. 11 (× 2), ‘Gwe=|nyvere’, ll. 11-12, ‘lyvyng'’, l. 15, ‘lyve’, l. 17, ‘loved’, l. 17, ‘covertly’, l. 22, etc.). The **ȝ** appears only in ‘douȝt(er)’, l. 29 (compare ‘doughtir’, l. 12, dougt(er), l. 32); and **þ** only in customary abbreviations (‘þ(er)’, l. 10, ‘noþ(er)’, l. 11), space-saving ‘þ^{e}’, l. 12, ‘þ^{t}’, l. 26). Note ʼ in ‘eu(er)’, l. 15, ‘Gwenyu(er)’, l. 29, ‘douȝt(er)’, l. 29, and ꝭ in ‘kyng(es)’, l. 12, ‘tydyng(es)’, l. 30. The full form is supplied in ‘w(i)t(h)oute’, l. 10, ‘w(i)t(h)’, l. 26. Flourishes are disregarded on **r, m,** and **n** (‘For’, l. 9, ‘man’, l. 9, ‘than’, l. 11, ‘her’, l. 16, etc.), but on **g** indicated by the apostrophe (e.g. ‘kyng'’, l. 11, ‘lyvyng'’, l. 15, etc.). Holding apostrophe also for **ll** with hanger crossing through the letters in ‘well'’, l. 18, ‘damesell'’, ll. 14, 18, ‘woll'’, l. 21, though ‘wol’, l. 31, might support the plainer form. The frame is ruled in ink; a line is ruled for the opening line of text (cf. f. 349r) but otherwise the pricking along the right margin seems not to be used (hardpoint ruling is sometimes visible within the frame elsewhere in manuscript). The curious readings ‘grunted’, l. 27, and ‘lodegean’, l. 28, may reflect misunderstanding of the use of superscript vowels. The letters ‘forte’ in the bottom outer corner are in this scribe’s hand. Identifiable watermarks dated to period 1471-80.

CONTEXTS

Malory, a prisoner (f. 70v) in Newgate, London, completed his *Morte Darthur* between 4 March 1469 and 3 March 1470. Print offset on ff. 159, 186v, 187, and 407 suggests manuscript in Caxton’s workshop *c.* 1480-83. Manuscript in hands of a Richard Followell of Litchborough (signatures f. 348r) before 1535; and a Malory family, living in Litchborough from the fifteenth to seventeenth centuries, sent sons and relations to Winchester College. Thus, the manuscript might have gone to school as a much-loved book. (A less favoured provenance is Winchester Cathedral Library, whose books were scattered twice in the Civil War, with those saved going to Winchester College in 1652. One book which, according to a Register of 1652 donations, opened ‘Here beginneth’, is not among the books returned to the cathedral between 1695-1700; but because the first and last quires of Add. 59678 are lost, the words do not in any case provide proof of identity.) Not in the public eye until identified by Oakeshott in 1934. Formerly Winchester College MS 13; sold to the British Library in 1976. Known as the Winchester Malory.

SIZE

285 × 205 mm (187 × 137 mm).

BIBLIOGRAPHY

Pr. Vinaver 1967 (revised Field 1990): I. 97-8.
Facs. Ker 1976.
Disc. Add. MSS *Cat.*; Oakeshott 1934, 1935, 1963, 1977; Kelliher 1977, 1981; Hellinga 1977, 1981, 1983; Hellinga and Kelliher 1977; Meale 1985; Tieken-Boon van Ostade 1995; Cooper 1997, 2000; Hanks and Fish 1977; Yeats-Edwards 2000; Kato 2000, 2002.

London, British Library, Royal MS 18 D. ii, f. 30v
Lydgate, translation of the *Troy Book*

Wheel of Fortune miniature
reduced to 57%

56

Oxford, Bodleian Library, Arch. Selden. MS B. 24, f. 50r
Chauncer, *Troilus and Criseyde*, III. 624–658
Gothic *littera cursiva* Secretary *media/currens*, s. xv^{2}

TRANSCRIPTION

The bent moon w(i)t(h) hir hornes pale
Saturn and Ioue In Cancro Ioyned were
That suich a rayn from heuen gan auaille
That eu(er)y man or wom(m)an þ(a)t was there
had of that smoky rayn a verray fere
At quhich(e) pandare tho lough and seid thenne
Now were tyme a lady to gone henne

But good nece /. if I my(gh)t eu(er) ples'
3ow any thing /. than preye I 3ow q(uo)d he
To doon my hert as now so grete an(e)[1] es'
As for to duelle here all this ny(gh)t w(i)t(h) me
For nece this is 3o(ur) owen hous' p(ar)dee
And by my treuth I seye It nat a game
To wend' as now to me It were a sham(e)

Criseide quhiche þ(a)t coude as moche good
As half a world' / toke hede of his[2] preyere
And syn It roon / and all was on a flood
She tho(gh)t / as good chepe may I duellen here
And grant it gladely w(i)t(h) a frendes chere
And haue a thank /. as gruche / and than abyde
For hom(e) to gone It nyl nat wele betyde

I wole q(uo)d she / my(n) vncle leef and dere
Syn þ(a)t 3ow list /. It skill is to be so
I am ry(gh)t glad w(i)t(h) 3ow to duellen here
I seid It / but a game þ(a)t I wold' go
Ywis grant m(er)ci / nece my(n) / q(uo)d he tho
Were It a game / or no / sooth for to telle
Now am I glad /. syn þ(a)t 3ow lust to duelle /

Thus all is wele /. but tho bigan ary(gh)t
The newe Ioye /. and all the feste agayn
But Pandarus / if goodly had he my(gh)t
he wold' haue hyed hir to bed fayn
And seid . lord this is an(e) huge rayn
This were a wed(er) for to slepen Inne
And that I rede vs soon to begynne

This is a somewhat currently written Secretary, with an admixture of Anglicana letter-forms, for example final **s** ('his', l. 16, 'this is', l. 33) and occasional **w** (as '3ow', l. 9, 'now', ll. 10, 14, 'world'', l. 16). Possibly showing the influence of French documentary script are the **c** made with two overlapping strokes (e.g. 'chepe', l. 18, 'chere', l. 19) and the exaggerated horns at the top of some letters (e.g. the approach to the upper stroke of **e**; **g** as in 'lough', l. 6; **t** as in 'there', l. 4). The pronoun 'I' has the long letter-form, perhaps for clarity in reading, though initial **i** generally descends below the line (contrast 'if', l. 8). Not all proper names have capitals (e.g. 'pandare', l. 6). The large capital marking the first stanza on the page has been cropped in binding; and capitals are usual at the beginning of each line. Note in this current hand

[1] Interpreting the overline here and in l. 33 as an abbreviation produces the typically Scottish literary form of this article.

[2] The last letter covers a false start.

50

The bent moon wt hir hornes pale
Saturn and Ioue yn Cancro ioyned were
That suich a rayn from heuen gan auaile
That euery man or woman þt was there
Had of that smoky rayn a verray fere
At which pandare tho lough and seid thenne
Now were tyme a lady to gone henne

But good nece if I myȝt euer plese
Yow any thinge than preye I yow qd he
To doon my herte as now so grete an ese
As for to dwelle here all this nyȝt wt me
For whi this is your owen hous parde
And by my trouth I sey it nat agame
To wende as now to me it were a shame

Criseide which þt coude as moche good
As half a world toke hede of his preyere
And syn it ron and all was on a flood
She thoȝt as good chepe may I dwellen here
And graunt it gladly wt a frendes chere
And haue a thank as grucche and than abyde
For hom to gone it myȝt nat wele betyde

I wole qd she myn uncle lief and dere
Syn þt yow list it skill is to be so
I am ryȝt glad wt yow to dwellen here
I said it but agame þt I wold go
Iwis graunt mercy nece qd he tho
Were it agame or no soth for to telle
Now am I glad syn þt yow lust to dwelle

Thus all is wele but tho bigan aryȝt
The newe ioye and all the feste agayn
But pandarus if goodly had he myȝt
He wold haue hyed hir to bed fayn
And said lord this is an huge rayn
This were a wedr for to slepen inne
And that I rede us soon to bigynne

Plate 56 – reduced to 88%

the tendency of **e** to come apart, with its stem attaching to the preceding letter and its headstroke to following letter. Note that **þ** appears only in **þ**ᵗ, with **th** otherwise. Chaucer's poem has acquired typically Scottish spellings, e.g. 'quhich(e)', l. 6, 'roon', l. 17. The punctuation is light: the virgule marking pause within the line is sometimes followed by a point to indicate more major pauses. The only ruling is a single red vertical, thickening in the middle of the page and obscuring in the photograph some of the letters that open lines; the scribe follows the laid lines of the paper. Abbreviations are frequent: 'þ(a)t', ll. 4, 15, 23, 25, 28; 'w(i)t(h)', ll. 1, 11, 19, 24; ˀ in 'eu(er)y', l. 4, 'eu(er)', l. 8, 'm(er)ci', l. 26, 'wed(er)', l. 34; ꝰ in 'ȝo(ur)', l. 12; 'q(uo)d', ll. 9, 22, 26; **ꝑ** in 'p(ar)dee', l. 12. The overline stands for **m** ('wom(m)an', l. 4), **n** ('my(n)', ll. 22, 26), and for final **e** ('an(e)', ll. 10, 33, 'sham(e)', l. 14, 'hom(e)', l. 21). Word-final lengthened final strokes of **n** (e.g. 'wom(m)an', l. 4, 'doon', l. 10, 'roon', l. 17) and **m** ('am', l. 28) are disregarded. A stroke through **h** makes 'quhich(e)', l. 6. Hanger-like flourishes are not expanded: on **s** ('ples'', l. 8, 'es'', l. 10, 'hous'', l. 12) or on **d** ('wend'', l. 14, 'world'', l. 16, 'wold'', ll. 25, 32). For superscript **t** in 'my(gh)t', l. 8, etc., *gh* is supplied (ll. 8, 11, 18, 24, 29, 31; compare 'lough', l. 6). Watermark dates for 1462-85.

CONTEXTS

Troilus makes up the first booklet in a poetic miscellany written *c.* 1488 probably in or near Edinburgh (to be understood from the manner of reporting James IV's birth, f. 120v) for Henry Sinclair, 3rd lord Sinclair (f. 230v mark of ownership; f. 118v his arms, assumed only in 1489), whether inspired out of family piety (his grandmother's brother was James I of Scotland, whose *The Kingis Quair* opens the third booklet on f. 192r) or perhaps in connection with preparations for Sinclair's wedding to Margaret Hepburn, daughter of Lord Hailes, on 4 December 1489 (more attractive in relation to the first booklet than to the whole compilation). This is Hand 1, the main scribe (ff. 1-209v) and scribe of three further manuscripts connected with Sinclair households (Edinburgh, National Library of Scotland MS Acc. 9253; Cambridge, St John's College MS G. 19; and the privately owned Dalhousie manuscript): no longer identified as James Graye. Continued family ownership indicated by 'Maurius Synclar' (f. 79), the names of Henry's daughters 'Elezabeth synclar' (f. 231r), ?'Jen Sinclar' (f. 231v), and various instances of William (ff. 230v) assumed to be family member(s). Unidentified are: 'By me Edward Walker' (f. 155r); 'Mr John Duncan | w(i)t(h) my hand' (f. 229r); 'Agnes Findlason | w(i)t(h) my hand' names (f. 229r), with surname entered again lower on the page; 'villem crvsscanke' (f. 231r); 'Channois 1592' (f. 231v); and on f. 230v 'patrik schiner', 'Lawrence smolo', 'villem schiner', and 'Donald' (perhaps to be identified with the signature in Insular script on f. 231v 'Mis(e) Domnall gorm'.' below two lines of Gaelic). Sometimes called the Sinclair Manuscript. Entered the Bodleian Library with Selden's books in 1659.

SIZE

c. 260 × 182 mm (*c.* 205 × 100 mm).

BIBLIOGRAPHY

As Benson 1988: 522; *coll.* Windeatt 1984: 282.
Facs. Boffey and Edwards 1997.
Disc. SC 3354; Brown 1896: 70-77; MacKenzie 1939: 12, 137; Parkes 1969 [1979]: pl. 13 (ii); Lyall 1989: 250-52; Butterfield 1995; Seymour 1995-97: I. 73-74; Edwards 1996; Boffey 2000.

nesse that was in his maister and seide that he mught not faile to haue the Emperours doughter seyng the tothir ij. of whom ye haue herd mught not be there at and in especiall one that was called le Surnome. which was nouparaill of the world The kynges purveaunce was all redy and abode no thing but the tyme of his departyng Now is it tyme that we retourne to speke of Athis.

It is no doute he was right hevy whan he was allone departed from his company whom he loued so moche but his thought was not like the tothir two for he was not departed ayenst the plesir of his fadir but by his licence & commaundement wherfore he was assured to be right welcome

Thus rode he forth more ioyfully and nought discouerd to noon of his men of his estate nor what he was and whan he came in to Scotland he asked tidynges of the kynge and of his children and where he shold fynde the kynge men told him where the kynge was and all his children in good helthe sauf only for the dethe of his eldest sone that died in the cristen armee that went in to the Reaume of Sizile Than rode he forth til he came to the towne where the kynge was & logged him yn an Inne vnknowen what he was of any body than enquered he what folk there were aboute the kynge of his counseill Than sent he for two or thre of them and whan they came to his loggyng and knewe him they had as grete ioye as coude be thought And than said he to them My frendes the cause that y sent for you is this I drede the grete ioie that the kynge shall haue if he here sodenly of my comyng shold do him to grete an hurt wherfore me thinketh best that it be told him at

London, British Library, Harley MS 326, f. 105v
Romance of the Three Kings' Sons

King with messengers from Prince David; David arrives home
reduced to 93%

57

Oxford, Bodleian Library, Digby MS 133, f. 96r
The Digby Play of Mary Magdalen
Mixed hand: a Gothic *littera cursiva*, *c.* 1525

TRANSCRIPTION

Now have I told yow my hart I am' wyll plesyd
Now lett vs sett don' alle ⁊ make good chyr

¶

Her entyr syr(us) ye fader of mary mavdleyn'

syr(us) ¶ Emp(er)or ⁊ kygg(ys) ⁊ co(n)querors kene
Erlys ⁊ borons and knyt(ys) y^t byn' bold
Berd(ys) in my bow(er) so semely to sen(n)e
I co(m)mavd'[1] yow at onys my hest(ys) to hold
behold my p(er)son' glystery(n)g in gold
semely besyn' of all other men'
Cyr(us) is my name be cleffys so cold
I co(m)ma(n)d yow all obedyent to beyn'
woso woll not in bale I hem bryng'
And kˋnˊett swyche cayftyys in knott(ys) of care
thys castell of mavdleyn' is at my wylddyng'
w(i)t(h) all ye co(n)tre bothe lesse ⁊ more
⁊ Lord of Ie(rusa)l(e)m who agens me don' dare
Alle beteny at my beddyng' be
I am' sett in solas from ˋalˊ syy(n)g sore
and so xall all my posteryte
thus for to leuen in rest ⁊ ryalle
I have her a sone y^t is to me ful trew
No co(m)lyar creatu(ur) of godd(ys) creacyou(n)
to amyabyll dovctors full brygth of ble
ful gloryos to my syth[2] an ful of delectacyou(n)

The overall script description here might be Gothic *littera cursiva* Secretary *currens*, but with many *anglicana* letter-forms, i.e. just the sort of mixture that is often termed Tudor Secretary. It is a hand with few calligraphic pretensions: the impression given is of extreme haste, with interlinear additions picking up some mistakes ('kˋnˊett' l. 13, 'al', l. 18). Note that although **u** does not appear word-initially, **v** can pop up anywhere. Overall the slope of the script suggests that the script is essentially Secretary, as does the use of word-final strokes for example, 'told', 'hart', and 'plesyd' in l. 1 alone). The Secretary **w** is used consistently, and the neat single-compartment **a** is usual (but not in 'hart', l. 1, unless round *e* is read; and in 'And', l. 13, 'Alle', l. 17, the Anglicana **a** form serves as a capital). The scribe uses a somewhat angular 2-shaped **r** (there are two examples of the Anglicana form, 'from', l. 18, 'trew', l. 21), and **d**, although looped, is sometimes angular (as in 'beddyng'', l. 17). The **g** is the Anglicana form, written cursively with the second larger loop in the reverse direction (as 'good', l. 2, 'kygg(ys)', l. 4, etc.), as are the round **e** (general) and sigma-shaped **s** (long **s** appears at the beginning of words), forms preferred in currently written script. The markedly variable spelling includes such distinctive East Anglian features as 'woso' for 'whoso', l. 12, 'xall' for 'shall', l. 19 (the cursively written secretary **x** looking like **y**), and 'syth', l. 24 (compare the hypercorrect 'brygth', l. 23). Having drawn rough lines to mark out separate speeches, which are introduced by red capitulum signs, the scribe largely dispenses with punctuation markers, depending on verse lineation. The margins are lined in brown: a single vertical to the left and head and foot rulings. Common abbreviations are used thickly, perhaps in a slapdash fashion (in 'creatu(ur)', l. 22, he writes 'u' and supplies the *-ur* abbreviation); space-saving forms of *the* and *that* have **y** for *þ* (ll. 3, 15, 21); but flourishes after **m**, **n**, and **g**, probably otiose, are represented by straight apostrophe in the transcription. In l. 21 the need for rhyme indicates the last words should be ordered 'ful trew to me'. The watermark evidence is for paper in use *c.* 1515-25.

[1] For 'co(m)av⟨n⟩d'?

[2] i.e. 'sight'.

Now have I told yow my hart I am wyll plesyd
now lett us sett don alle & make good chere
Her entyr Syrus þe fader of mary maudleyn
Emperor & kyng & conquerour kene
Erle & baron and knyth þat byn bold
Berdys in my bowr so semely to sene
I comaund yow at onys my hestys to hold
Be hold my person glysteryng in gold
Semely besyn of all other men
Cyrus is my name be cleffys so cold
I comaund yow all obedyent to beyn
wo so wyll not in bale I hem bryng
And knett swych caytyvys in knottys of care
thys castell of maudleyn is at my wylddyng
with all þe contre bothe lesse & more
& lord of Jerusalem who agens me don dare
Alle Beteny at my beddyng be
I am sett in solas from al syyng sore
and so xall all my posterite
thus for to leven in rest & ryalte
I have her a sone þat is to me ful trew
no comlyar creatur of goddys creacyon
to amyabyll doctors full bryth of ble
ful gloryos to my syth an ful of delectacyon

Plate 57 – actual size

CONTEXTS

This is Hand D of the manuscript, which contains three plays that were possibly at Bury St Edmunds in the possession of a monk called William (a William Blomefylde was a monk there before the dissolution). Note on f. 157v 'Jhon Parfre ded wryte thys booke' supports putative link with Thetford, Norfolk. Could have passed from William Blomefylde of Bury to Myles Blomefylde ('MB' at top of f. 95r, the beginning of a booklet); or Myles Blomefylde may have got hold of the Chelmsford playbook. On the flimsy identification of John Stow's hand in a very short note (f. 146r) it is argued that the manuscript passed from Myles Blomefylde to John Stow, and possibly from him to Digby. A late-sixteenth or early-seventeenth-century owner William Benson Dewllyns is unidentified; the name Thomas appears twice. Not listed in catalogue of Digby's 1634 bequest to the Bodleian. Mentioned as in Bodley in 1640s surveys (personal notebooks of Gerard Langbaine).

SIZE

209 × 150 mm (176 × *c.* 100 mm).

BIBLIOGRAPHY

Pr. Baker, Murphy and Hall 1982: 25-26 (ll. 47-69).
Facs. Baker and Murphy 1976.
Disc. Baker and Murphy 1967; McIntosh, Samuels and Benskin 1986: I. 147, III. 358-59 (LP 4662 Norfolk); Hunt and Watson 1999: 64.

London, British Library, Cotton MS Julius E. iv Art 6, f. 16v
The Pageants of Richard Beauchamp, Earl of Warwick

Henry V appoints ambassadors to the Council of Constance
reduced to 82%

58

Oxford, Bodleian Library, Fairfax MS 16, f. 183v
Chaucer, *The House of Fame*, with ending added after 1532
(a) Gothic *littera cursiva* Secretary *media/formata*, with some *anglicana* features, s. xv med.
(b) Mixed hand, s. xvii

TRANSCRIPTION

¶The House

That shal not now / be tolde for me
For hit no nede is / redely
Folke kan' synge hit / bet than' I
For alle mote oute / other late or rathe
Alle the sheves / in the lathe
I herde a grete / noyse withalle
In a corner / of the halle
Ther men' of loue / tydyng(es) tolde
And I gan / thiderwarde beholde
For I saugh' rennynge / eu(er)y wight'
As fast as that'[1] / they hadden myght'
And eueryche cried / what thing is that
And so(m)me sayde / I not neuer what
And whan' they were / alle on' an hepe
Tho behynde / begu(n)ne vp lepe
And clamben vp / on' other fast
And vp the noyse[2] / an highen'[3] kast
And troden fast / on' other heles
And stampen' as men' / doon' aftir eles
Atte last / y saugh' a man'
Whiche that y / nat ne kan[4]
But he semed / for to be
A man' of grete / auctorite
   And therewithall' I abrayde
Out of my sleepe halfe afrayde
Remembring well what I had seene
And how hye and ferre I had beene
In my goost , and had great wonder
Of that the god of thunder
Had let me knowen , and began to write
Lyke as yee haue heard me endite
Wherefore to study and rede alway
I purpose to do day by day
   Thus in dreaming and in game
Ended this litel booke of Fame . /

Here endeth the booke
of Fame . / . † . ‡ .

An assured hand, trained in Secretary script. Two Anglicana alternatives are in use: the round **e** (as in 'tolde', l. 1); and sigma-shaped **s** (but not in 'heles', l. 18, which has the distinctive Secretary shape). The final stroke of **g** curls under, and unlooped **w** is cursively made without pen-lifting. Minims are clearly made but not always with pen-lifts. The heading is more formal. Virgules mark pausing positions within the line, sometimes unnecessarily but as if deemed mandatory for

[1] Final *t* on erasure.
[2] Editors generally emend here to 'nose', probably unnecessarily.
[3] A possible reading, though editors often choose to emend the phrase, linking eyes to nose, e.g. 'and yen'.
[4] A line so short that all editors add some word.

The house

That shal not now be tolde for me
For hit no nede is redely
Folke kan synge hit bet than I
For alle mote oute other late or rathe
Alle the shevys in the lathe
I herde a grete noyse withalle
In a corner of the halle
Ther men of love tydynges tolde
And I gan thiderwarde beholde
For I saugh rennynge every wight
As fast as that they hadden myght
And everyche cried what thing is that
And some sayde I not never what
And whan they were alle on an hepe
Tho behynde begunne up lepe
And clamben up on other fast
And up the noyse an highen kast
And troden fast on other heles
And stampen as men doon after eles
Atte last y saugh a man
Which that y nat ne kan
But he semed for to be
A man of grete auctorite
And therwithall I abrayde
Out of my sleepe halfe afrayde
Remembring well what I had seene
And how hye and ferre I had beene
In my goost, and had great wonder
Of that the god of thunder
Had let me knowen, and began to write
Lyke as yee haue heard me endite
Wherefore to study and rede alway
I purpose to do day by day
Thus in dreaming and in game
Endeth this litel booke of Fame. /

Here endeth the booke
of Fame. / . +

Plate 58 – actual size

formal layout. A left-hand margin is ruled, with two lines across both at the top and bottom. Note the return to using the top line for writing. Line-initial capitals are overlaid in red. The abbreviations seen in this short passage are the overline (as in 'so(m)me', l. 13, 'begu(n)ne', l. 15, and ꝭ for *es* in 'tydyng(es)', l. 8. In the transcript the apostrophe marks flourishes on **n** and **t** and the slashed **h** of 'saugh'', ll. 10, 20: in none of these does the metre require a final *-e*.

This plate is placed last because it demonstrates additions being made to a manuscript in a world where printed texts had become the norm. The poem finishes abruptly (and dramatically) at the same place in all three manuscripts. Here the ending supplied by Caxton in his 1483 edition has been copied by a seventeenth-century hand from the version first printed in Thynne's edition of 1532. This last hand gives a glimpse of scholarly script based in humanistic cursive (or 'Italic'), used increasingly from about the middle of the sixteenth century. Note in this mixed hand the use of the curly Greek **e**, an alternative often found in humanistic hands. Final flourishes follow the explicit.

CONTEXTS

An added full-page picture of Mars and Venus (f. 14v) by the Abingdon Missal Master (Digby 227) incorporates the arms of the Hooton branch of the Stanleys. The armorial is attributed to John Stanley, who probably commissioned the manuscript. History of manuscript uncertain from this point until ownership note (f. 321v) by 'Thom[as] Moyelle' (d. 1560). Did it get to Moyelle (or Moyle) through marriage to an Isobel Stanley? Did the Stanley family leave it to Westminster Abbey, from where it was confiscated? Random notes in John Stow's hand, including (f. 82v) mention of Joseph Holland. Three names with mottoes and date 14 October 1612 (Robert Wingfield, Oliver Nicholas, Ferdinando Knyghtly) on f. 333v. Bought (f. 1r) by Charles Fairfax in Gloucester on 8 September 1650; bequeathed to the Bodleian Library by his nephew Sir Thomas Fairfax in 1671.

SIZE

c. 235 × 165 mm (*c.* 153 × 95 mm).

BIBLIOGRAPHY

Pr. Benson 1988: 373 (ll. 2136-58), 1142 ('Caxton ending').
Facs. Norton-Smith 1979.
Disc. SC 3896; Doyle and Pace 1975: 47-49; Doyle 1983: 178; Seymour 1995-97: I. 11-12; Coldiron 2000: 188-89.

IX Afterword

The date 1500 is arbitrary, an indication that this book deals with the scripts in use for writing the forms of English widely categorized as Old English and Middle English. In effect, just as no clear distinctions can be drawn between manuscripts in Old English and Middle English, there is no sharp cut-off point between Middle English and Modern English. So long as texts remained fashionable or of use, they were copied or printed anew. Older manuscripts could continue in use: the late-fifteenth-century Sinclair manuscript (pl. 56), a poetic miscellany, seems to have continued in the family through the next century, with members of the family and friends using its final pages almost as an autograph book; and even later, in 1612, three young men dignified some particular occasion in their lives by entering that year's date and mottoes into the mid-fifteenth-century miscellany, Fairfax 16 (pl. 58). As yet, however, few books in English were read outside Britain and Ireland, unless by exiles. Who else would have read the Vercelli Book of Old English poetry and homilies in northern Italy in the eleventh century? If pieces of English were committed to writing elsewhere in Europe, the circumstances were unusual. A prisoner in Italy with time on his hands took part, it seems, in making a new copy of the English bible he had taken there with him in the hope of demonstrating its freedom from heresy.[1] And Henry V may indeed have encouraged the use of English for his correspondence between France and England across the years 1417-22.[2] But in 1500 the English language was a vernacular little used outside these islands, unless on a battlefield. That was soon to change, when printers on the continent (some of them English exiles) sought to supply the English market with books that printers at home were chary of printing. It remained rare at this time, however, for manuscripts written in Britain to travel beyond the British Isles, unless to be illuminated, as for example books of hours in Bruges or Ghent; and manuscripts in English tended to travel only in special circumstances.[3]

Equally, few works composed in English had as yet been translated into other languages. This is particularly the case for Old English. In Anglo-Saxon times Æthelweard, ruler of the western provinces of England, translated the Anglo-Saxon Chronicle into Latin for his cousin Abbess Matilda of Essen late in the tenth century. They were both descendants of West Saxon kings, and for them the Chronicle contained a great deal of family history. Bishop Asser, too, incorporated ninth-century Chronicle materials into the Latin life of his patron King Alfred that was very possibly aimed at a Welsh audience. English missionaries played an important part in the evangelization of the Scandinavian countries, and it is likely that some Old English writings were adapted there.[4] On the whole, however, such translations as were made were made for home consumption. Translation from English to Latin could arise in the keeping of records. From the middle of the ninth century some documents were written in English, and very often land boundaries in English were positioned carefully within charters otherwise in Latin. In later copies these might be translated into or summarized in Latin. Although there was little lay literacy, land-owners were developing an enthusiasm for the documentation of their holdings,[5] and already in the 1120s laws in Old English were being drawn together and translated into Latin in such collections as the *Textus Roffensis* for the growing bureaucracy of Norman England.[6] In the 1130s Gaimar was turning parts of the Anglo-Saxon Chronicle into Anglo-Norman couplets. Wace too used some text very like the Peterborough Chronicle in his *Roman de Rou*, and Goscelin made use both of Latin and English sources for new lives of the English saints. Gradually, the earliest writings in English slipped out of active use, as they became sources for the writers of Anglo-Norman England.[7]

The twelfth century marks a turning-point in the development of lay literacy, and from this time there is substantial evidence for a surge in new vernacular writing, both devotional and more obviously recreational.[8] The new English writings of Anglo-Norman England co-existed with Anglo-Norman French as well as with Latin,[9] and Latin was as ever overwhelmingly the language of learning and education throughout Europe. The Rule in English (the *Ancrene Riwle*) written for three noble anchoresses was soon translated both into French and Latin, as were some later Middle English devotional writings, the Latin versions conferring on them audiences potentially far wider than mere English speakers. Two translations of the *Cloud of Unknowing* are extant in Latin, but there is no evidence for its circulation on the continent, either in English or Latin, before the Reformation.[10] Throughout the Middle English period, however, French was the

[1] de Hamel 2001, 172-73.

[2] See Blake 1966: 173, 175, and Richardson 1980.

[3] Hellinga and Trapp 1999: 15-16

[4] For example, Kirby 1986: 4, 10, points to *De Falsis Diis* as the immediate source of the Norse Bel and Dragon story in *Hauksbók*. See also the discussion by Blake 1964: 96-97 of a possible translation of a description of the phoenix into Old Norse from Old English.

[5] Lowe 1998.

[6] van Houts 2003: 110-11; Wormald 1999: 228-53.

[7] Cameron 1974: 226.

[8] Parkes 1973; rpt. 1991.

[9] See Short 2003.

[10] Clark 1990:191

vernacular language gaining a European readership. When the monks of Peterborough had an Anglo-Norman *Brut* written into the margins of their Anglo-Saxon Chronicle, they saw it no doubt as an enhancement of their book's worth. Such vernacular histories, first in French and afterwards in English, must by then have provided a more accessible and entertaining digest of Anglo-Saxon history than did the Anglo-Saxon Chronicle. They are, as often as not, part and parcel of the burgeoning writings about King Arthur, popularized first in Latin and in French in the middle of the twelfth century. The earliest major working of these tales extant in English, Laȝamon's *Brut*, came two or three generations after Geoffrey of Monmouth's *Historia* and Wace's *Brut*.

The great English vernacular writers of late-fourteenth-century England were alive to literary developments not just in France but in Italy as well, but they were unlikely to be known on the other side of the English Channel. Chaucer, indeed, in the *Hous of Fame*, widened his sights to emulate not just the great writers of his own age but of Antiquity also. Yet the libraries of lay people in the fifteenth century still ran preponderantly to spiritual writings.[11] Much Middle English literature, even in verse, was aimed at religious instruction,[12] and it should not be forgotten than monastic houses played a large part in the production of books in the century and a half before the Dissolution.[13] For Sir Philip Sydney, looking back from the vantage point of 1579, Chaucer was the outstanding poet of 'that mystie time'.[14] Although Deschamps, *c.* 1385, praised Chaucer as a 'Grant translateur, noble Geffroy Chaucier',[15] Chaucer's contemporary, John Gower, who hedged his bets by writing his three major works in each of Latin, French, and English, may well have had a shrewder eye for immediate fame. Gower's *Confessio Amantis* was translated into both Portuguese and Spanish early in the fifteenth century.[16]

One important sub-set of books in English continued to be particularly influential, writings associated with Lollardy. It is worth drawing attention to the number of manuscripts extant, most notably to the 250 or so manuscripts that contain the whole or part of the Wycliffite translation of the Bible, more copies than of any other work in English from the Middle Ages.[17] These could survive under licence, allowed, for example, to the Brigittine community at Syon.[18] Some had owners above suspicion: Henry VI gave a particularly splendid copy to the Charterhouse in London.[19] They might be brought out even to be signed by an important visitor, just as books of hours then were,[20] or as, in more recent times, Queen Victoria was asked to write her name in the Book of Kells manuscript when visiting Trinity College Dublin. For the most part these bibles remained carefully tucked away, for the ownership of books tainted with Lollardism was suspect and reading or teaching from them dangerous. Nevertheless, there are more copies even today of the standard Wycliffite sermon cycle than of any single version of *Piers Plowman* and almost twice as many as of Chaucer's *Troilus*.[21] The centre of production was at first Oxford, and the forms of English used were based in the speech of the central Midlands, a dialect that if anything dated less than the English of the capital in the late fourteenth century. Many of the Wycliffite bibles are very formal productions, some in *textualis,* a more costly script than the cursive scripts by then customary for texts in English. Ironically therefore, although rejected by those in power, Wycliffite bibles are among the costliest English vernacular books of the late fourteenth and early fifteenth centuries. With other genres of books in English, print overlapped manuscript production. Lollard books continued to circulate quietly, but there was about a century's gap between the making of the Wycliffite bibles and the appearance of the first printed translations from the Bible into English. For England *c.* 1500 the Reformation, and all the changes it brought about, was still to come.

[11] Erler 1999: 495.
[12] Boffey and Edwards 1999: 556-57.
[13] Doyle 1999.
[14] Collins 1907 [1950 impression]: 51.
[15] See Wimsatt 1974: 109.
[16] See Pearsall 2004: 79 (items 83 and 84).
[17] Hudson 1989: 31.
[18] Hargreaves 1969: 414 notes that a Wycliffite translation was given to the brothers at Syon in 1517 (now Manchester, John Rylands Library, English MS 81).
[19] de Hamel 2001: 183.
[20] de Hamel 2001: 188-89.
[21] Hudson 1989: 137.

References

A single general list is presented, to make it easier to find specific items, which are to be found by names and dates.

Abbreviations
EEMF Early English Manuscripts in Facsimile
EETS Early English Text Society
[facs.] Contains facsimile reproductions of full texts

ADAMS, E.N., *Old English Scholarship in England from 1566-1800* (New Haven, London, Oxford, 1917).

ALEXANDER, J.J.G., *Insular Manuscripts 6th to 9th century* (London, 1978).

ALEXANDER, J.J.G., 'Painting and Manuscript Illumination for Royal Patrons in the Later Middle Ages', in Scattergood and Sherborne 1983: 141-62.

ALEXANDER, J.J.G., T.J. BROWN, AND JOAN GIBBS, eds, *Francis Wormald. Collected Writings*, 2 vols (London and Oxford, 1984).

ALLEN, ROSAMUND, LUCY PERRY, AND JANE ROBERTS, eds, *Laȝamon. Contexts, Language, and Interpretation* (London, 2002).

ANDREW, MALCOLM AND RONALD WALDRON, eds, *The Poems of the Pearl Manuscript. Pearl, Cleanness, Patience, Sir Gawain and the Green Knight*, York Medieval Texts, second series (London, 1978).

ARN, MARY-JO, ed., *Fortunes Stabilnes. Charles of Orlean's English Book of Love. A Critical Edition* (Binghamton, 1994).

ARN, MARY-JO, ed., *Charles d'Orléans in England (1415-1440)* (Cambridge, 2000).

ARNGART, O., [facs.], *The Leningrad Bede*, EEMF 1 (Copenhagen, 1952).

ARNGART, O., 'On the Dating of early Bede Manuscripts', *Studia Neophilologica* 45 (1973), 47-52.

ARNGART, O., 'Three Notes on the St Petersburg Bede', in *Names, Places and Peoples*, ed. A.R. Rumble and A.D. Mills (Stamford, 1997): 1-7.

ATKINS, I. AND N.R. KER, eds, *Catalogus librorum manuscriptorum bibliothecae Wigorniensi, made in 1622-23 by Patrick Young, Librarian to King James I* (Cambridge, 1944).

ATKINS, J.W.H., ed., *The Owl and the Nightingale* (Cambridge, 1922).

AYSCOUGH, SAMUEL, *A Catalogue of the Manuscripts preserved in the British Museum hitherto undescribed: consisting of five thousand volumes; including the Collections of Sir Hans Sloane, Bart ...*, 2 vols (London, 1792).

BACKHOUSE, JANET, *The Lindisfarne Gospels* (London, 1981).

BACKHOUSE, JANET, *Books of Hours* (London, 1984).

BACKHOUSE, JANET, D.H. TURNER, AND LESLIE WEBSTER, eds, *The Golden Age of Anglo-Saxon Art 966-1066* (London, 1984).

BAILLIE-GROHMAN, W.A. AND F. BAILLIE-GROHMAN, eds, *The Master of Game by Edward, Second Duke of York. The Oldest English Book on Hunting* (London, 1904).

BAKER, D.C. AND J.L. MURPHY, 'The Late Medieval Plays of MS. Digby 133: Scribes, Dates, and Early History', *Research Opportunities in Renaissance Drama* 10 (1967), 153-66.

BAKER, D.C AND J.L. MURPHY, [facs.], *The Digby Plays (MSS Digby 133 and e Museo 160)*, Leeds Texts and Monographs: Medieval Drama Facsimiles III (Leeds, 1976).

BAKER, PETER S. AND NICHOLAS HOWE, eds, *Words and Work: Studies in Medieval English Language and Literature in Honour of Fred. C. Robinson* (Toronto, Buffalo, London, 1998).

BAKER, DONALD C., JOHN L. MURPHY, AND LOUIS B. HALL JR, eds, *The Late Medieval Religious Plays of Bodleian MSS Digby 133 and e Museo 160*, EETS O.S. 283 (1982).

BANNERMAN, JOHN, 'Gaelic Endorsements of Early Seventeenth-Century Legal Documents', *Studia Celtica* 14-15 (1979-80), 18-33.

BARNHOUSE, REBECCA AND BENJAMIN C. WITHERS, eds, *The Old English Hexateuch* (Kalamazoo, Michigan, 2000).

BARRATT, ALEXANDRA, 'Works of Religious Instruction', in Edwards 1984: 413-32.

BARRON, CAROLINE AND NIGEL SAUL, eds, *England and the Low Countries in the Late Middle Ages* (Stroud, New York, 1995).

BATELY, J.M., *The Literary Prose of King Alfred's Reign: Translation or Transformation?* Inaugural Lecture, King's College, London, 1980[1]. Rpt. *Old English Newsletter* Subsidia 10 (Cemers, Suny-Binghamton, 1984); rpt. with Addenda in Szarmach 2000: 3-27.

BATELY, JANET, ed., *The Old English Orosius*, EETS S.S. 6 (1980[2]).

BATELY, J.M., ed., *The Anglo-Saxon Chronicle: A Collaborative Edition, iii, MS A* (Cambridge, 1986).

BATELY, J.M., 'Old English prose before and during the reign of Alfred', *Anglo-Saxon England* 17 (1988[1]), 93-138.

BATELY, JANET, 'Manuscript Layout and the Anglo-Saxon Chronicle', The Toller Memorial Lecture 1987, *Bulletin of the John Rylands University Library of Manchester* 70 (1988[2]), 21-43.

BATELY, J.M., *The Anglo-Saxon Chronicle: Texts and Textual Relationships*, Reading Medieval Studies: Monographs 3 (Reading, 1991).

BATELY, JANET, [facs.], *The Tanner Bede*, EEMF 24 (Copenhagen, 1992).

BEADLE, RICHARD, ed., *The York Plays* (London, 1982).

Beadle, Richard, 'Prolegomena to a literary geography of later medieval Norfolk', in Riddy 1991: 89-108.

Beadle, Richard, 'Facsimiles of Middle English Manuscripts', in McCarren and Moffat 1998: 319-31.

Beadle, R. and J.J. Griffiths, [facs.], *St John's College, Cambridge Manuscript L. 1. A Facsimile* (Norman [Woodbridge], 1983).

Beadle, R. and P. Meredith, 'Further External Evidence for Dating the York Register (BL Additional MS 35290)', *Leeds Studies in English* N.S. 11 (1980), 51-58.

Beadle, Richard and Peter Meredith with Richard Rastall, [facs.], *The York Play. A Facsimile of British Library MS Additional 35290 together with a Facsimile of the 'Ordo Paginarum' section of the A/Y Memorandum Book* (Leeds, 1983).

Beadle, Richard and A.E.B. Owen, [facs]., *The Findern Manuscript. Cambridge University Library MS. Ff. 1.6* (London, 1977; rpt. with amendments 1978).

Beadle, Richard and A.J. Piper, eds., *New Science out of Old Books. Studies in Manuscripts and Early Printed Books in Honour of A. I. Doyle* (Aldershot, 1995).

Bekkers, J.A.F., *Correspondence of John Morris with Johannes de Laet (1634-1649)* (Assen, 1970).

Bell, David N., 'Monastic libraries: 1400-1557', in Hellinga and Trapp 1999: 229-54.

Belsheim, Iohannes, ed., *Codex Aureus sive quattuor evangelia ante Hieronymum Latine translata.* (Kristianstad, 1878).

Benskin, M., 'The letters <þ> and <y> in later Middle English: and some related matters', *Journal of the Society of Archivists* 7 (1982), 13-30.

Benskin, Michael, 'The Hands of the Kildare Poems Manuscript', *Irish University Review* 20 (1990), 163-92.

Benskin, Michael, 'In reply to Dr. Burton', *Leeds Studies in English* 22 (1991), 209-62.

Benskin, M., Some New Perspectives on the Origins of Standard Written English', *Dialect and Standard Language in the English, Dutch, German and Norwegian Language Areas*, ed. J.A. van Leuvensteijn and J.B. Berns (Amsterdam, 1992), 71-105.

Benskin, Michael and Margaret Laing, 'Translations and *Mischsprachen* in Middle English manuscripts', in Benskin and Samuels 1981: 55-106.

Benskin, Michael and M.L. Samuels, eds, *So meny people longages and tonges. Philological essays in Scots and mediaeval English presented to Angus McIntosh* (Edinburgh, 1981).

Benson, Larry D., ed., *The Riverside Chaucer* (Oxford, 1988).

Benson, Larry, 'Chaucer's Spelling Reconsidered', *English Manuscript Studies 1100-1700* 3 (1992), 1-28.

Berkhout, Carl T., 'Laurence Nowell (1530-ca. 1570)', in Damico 1998: 3-17.

Bernard, Edward, *Catalogi librorum manuscriptorum Angliae et Hiberniae, cum indice alphabetico* (Oxford, 1697).

Bethurum, Dorothy, ed., *The Homilies of Wulfstan* (Oxford, 1957).

Bischoff, B., *Latin Palaeography. Antiquity and the Middle Ages*. English translation by D. Ó Cróinín and D. Ganz (Cambridge, 1990).

Bischoff, Bernhard, *Manuscripts and Libraries in the Age of Charlemagne*, translated and ed. Michael Gorman (Cambridge, 1994).

Bischoff, B., G.I. Lieftinck, and G. Battelli, *Nomenclature des Écritures Livresques du IXe au XVIe Siècle*, Premier Colloque International de Paléographie Latine (Paris 28-30 Avril 1953 (Paris, 1954).

Bishop, T.A.M., 'Notes on Cambridge Manuscripts' Part I, *Transactions of the Cambridge Bibliographical Society*, 1 (1949-53), 432-41; Parts II-IV, 2 (1954-58), 185-92, 192-99, 323-36, Part V-VII 3 (1959-63), 93-95, 412-13, 413-23, Part VIII, 4 (1964-68), 70-77.

Bishop, T.A.M., *English Caroline Minuscule* (Oxford, 1971).

Bishop, T.A.M. and P. Chaplais, *English Royal Writs* (Oxford, 1957).

Black, J.B., *The Reign of Elizabeth 1558-1603* (Oxford, 1936).

Blaess, M., 'L'Abbaye de Bordesley et Les Livres de Guy de Beauchamp', *Romania* 78 (1957), 511-18.

Blair, P.H. with R.A.B.Mynors, [facs.], *The Moore Bede*, EEMF 9 (Copenhagen, 1959).

Blake, N.F., ed., *The Phoenix* (Manchester, 1964).

Blake, N.F., *A History of the English Language* (Houndmills, Basingstoke, 1966).

Blake, N.F., *Caxton and His World* (London, 1969).

Blake, N.F., 'The Ellesmere Text in the Light of the Hengwrt Manuscript', in Stevens and Woodward 1995: 205-24.

Blockley, Mary, 'Further Addenda and Corrigenda to N. R. Ker's *Catalogue*', in Richards 2001: 79-85.

Blodgett, James E.: 'William Thynne (d. 1546)', in Ruggiers 1984: 35-52.

Blyth, Charles R., *Thomas Hoccleve. The Regiment of Princes* (Kalamazoo, 1999).

Boffey, Julia, 'Short Texts in Manuscript Anthologies: The Minor Poems of John Lydgate in Two Fifteenth-Century Collections', in Nichols and Wenzel 1996: 69-82.

Boffey, Julia, 'Bodleian Library, MS Arch. Selden. B. 24 and definitions of the "household book"', in Edwards, Gillespie, and Hanna 2000: 125-34.

Boffey, Julia and A.S.G. Edwards, [facs.], *The Works of Geoffrey Chaucer and 'The Kingis Quair'. A Facsimile of Bodleian Library, Oxford, MS Arch. Selden. B.24* (Cambridge, 1997).

Boffey, Julia and A.S.G. Edwards, 'Literary texts', in Hellinga and Trapp 1999: 555-75.

Boffey, Julia and John J. Thompson, 'Anthologies and Miscellanies: production and choice of texts', in Griffiths and Pearsall 1989: 279-315.

Bond, E.A., [facs.], *Facsimiles of Ancient Charters in the British Museum*, 4 vols (London, 1873-78).

Bosworth, Joseph, *The History of the Lauderdale Manuscript of King Alfred's Anglo-Saxon Version of Orosius* (Oxford, 1858).

BOYD, BEVERLY, *Chaucer and the Medieval Book* (San Marino, 1973).
BOYD, BEVERLY, 'William Caxton', in Ruggiers 1984: 13-34.
BOYD, W.J.P., *Aldred's Marginalia* (Exeter, 1975).
BOYLE, L., *Medieval Latin Palaeography: a bibliographical introduction* (Toronto, 1984); and now see http://www.geocities.com/Athens/Aegean/9891/palaeog.html.
BRASWELL, LAUREL, 'Utilitarian and Scientific Prose', in Edwards 1984: 337-87.
BRASWELL, LAUREL, *The Index of Middle English Prose. Handlist IV A Handlist of Douce Manuscripts containing Middle English Prose in the Bodleian Library, Oxford* (Cambridge, 1987).
BREEZE, ANDREW, 'The Stockholm "Golden Gospels" in Seventeenth-Century Spain', *Notes and Queries* 241 (1996), 395-97.
BREMMER JR, ROLF. H., ed., *Franciscus Junius F.F. and His Circle* (Amsterdam – Atlanta, GA, 1998).
BREMMER JR, ROLF. H., 'Retrieving Junius's Correspondence', in Bremmer 1998: 199-235.
BREMMER, ROLF H., 'The Correspondence of Johannes de Laet (1581-1649) as a Mirror of his Life', *LIAS: Sources and Documents Relating to the Early Modern History of Ideas* 25.2 (1998), 139-64.
BREUKER, PH. H., 'On the Course of Franciscus Junius's Germanic Studies, with Special Reference to Frisian', in Bremmer 1998: 129-57.
BREWER, D.S. AND A.E.B. OWEN, [facs.], *The Thornton Manuscript (Lincoln Cathedral MS. 91)* (London, 1975, rpt. with amendments 1977).
BREWERTON, PATRICIA A., 'Paper Trail: Re-reading Robert Beale as Clerk to the Elizabethan Privy Council', University of London dissertation (1998).
BROOK, G.L., ed., *The Harley Lyrics: The Middle English Lyrics of MS. Harley 2253* (Manchester, 1948; 4th edition 1968).
BROOK, G.L., 'A Piece of Evidence for the Study of Middle English Spelling', *Neuphilologische Mitteilungen* 73 (1972), 25-28.
BROOK, G.L. AND R. F. LESLIE, eds, *Laȝamon: Brut. Edited from British Museum MS Cotton Caligula A ix and British Museum MS Cotton Otho C xiii*, EETS O.S. 250, 277, 2 vols (1963, 1978).
BROOKS, N.P., *The Early History of the Church of Canterbury* (Leicester, 1984).
BROUWER, J.H. AND A. CAMPBELL, 'The Early Frisian Studies of Jan Van Vliet', *Modern Language Review* 34 (1939), 145-76.
BROWN, C., ed., *Religious Lyrics of the XVth Century* (Oxford, 1939).
BROWN, J.T.T., *The Authorship of the Kingis Quair. A new criticism* (Glasgow, 1896).
BROWN, M.P., *A Guide to Western Historical Scripts from Antiquity to 1600* (London, 1990).
BROWN, M.P., *Anglo-Saxon Manuscripts* (London, 1991).
BROWN, M.P., *Understanding Illuminated Manuscripts, a Glossary of Technical Terms* (Malibu and London, 1994).
BROWN, M.P., *The Book of Cerne. Prayer, Patronage and Power in Ninth-Century England* (London, 1996).
BROWN, M.P., '"In the Beginning was the Word": Books and Faith in the Age of Bede', *The Jarrow Lecture* (Newcastle-upon-Tyne, 2000).
BROWN, M.P., 'Female Book-Ownership and Production in Anglo-Saxon England: the Evidence of the Ninth-Century Prayerbooks', in *Lexis and Texts in Early English. Studies presented to Jane Roberts*, ed. Christian J. Kay and Louise M. Sylvester, Costerus New Series 133 (Amsterdam-Atlanta, GA, 2001[1]): 45-67.
BROWN, M.P., 'The 'Tiberius' Group and its Historical Context', in Carol A. Farr and Michelle P. Brown, eds, *Mercia. An Anglo-Saxon kingdom in Europe*, Studies in the Early History of Europe (London and New York, 2001[2]): 278-90.
BROWN, M.P., [facs.], *Das Buch von Lindisfarne: Cotton Nero Ms Nero D.iv der British Library, London = The Lindisfarne Gospels: Cotton MS Nero D.iv of the British Library, London*, 2 vols (Luzern, 2002).
BROWN, M.P., *The Lindisfarne Gospels. Society, Spirituality and the Scribe* (London, 2003).
BROWN, MICHELLE P., 'Fifty Years of Insular Palaeography, 1953-2003: an Outline of some Landmarks and Issues', *Archiv für Diplomatik – Schriftgeschichte Siegel- und Wappenkunde* 50 (2004), 277-325.
BROWN, T.J. *et al.*, [facs.], *The Durham Ritual*, EEMF 16 (Copenhagen, 1969).
BROWN, T.J., 'Palaeography', in *New Cambridge Bibliography of English Literature I* (1974): cols 209-20.
BROWN, T.J., 'Tradition, Imitation and Invention in Insular Handwriting of the Seventh and Eighth Centuries', R.W. Chambers Memorial Lecture, University College, London, 1978, in *A Palaeographer's View*, ed. Janet Bately, Michelle P. Brown, and Jane Roberts (London, 1993): 179-220.
BRYAN, ELIZABETH J., *Collaborative Meaning in Medieval Scribal Culture. The Otho Laȝamon* (Ann Arbor, 1999).
BUDNY, MILDRED, 'The *Biblia Gregoriana*', in Gameson 1999[2]: 237-84.
BURCHFIELD, R.W, 'A Source for Scribal Error in Early Middle English Manuscripts', *Medium Ævum* 22 (1953), 10-17.
BURCHFIELD, ROBERT, 'The Language and Orthography of the Ormulum MS', *Transactions of the Philological Society* (1956), 56-87.
BURCHFIELD, ROBERT, '*Ormulum*: Words Copied by Jan van Vliet from Parts Now Lost', in *English and Medieval Studies Presented to J.R.R. Tolkien on the Occasion of his Seventieth Birthday*, ed. Norman Davis and C.L. Wrenn (London, 1962): 94-111.
BURCHFIELD, ROBERT, 'Line-End Hyphens in the *Ormulum* Manuscript (MS Junius 1)', in *From Anglo-Saxon to Early Middle English: Studies Presented to E.G. Stanley*, ed. Malcolm Godden, Douglas Gray and Terry Hoad (Oxford, 1994): 182-87.
BURROW, J.A. AND A.I. DOYLE, [facs.], *Thomas Hoccleve, A Facsimile of the Autograph Verse Manuscripts*, EETS S.S. 19 (2002).

BUTTERFIELD, ARDIS, '*Mise-en-page* in the *Troilus* Manuscripts: Chaucer and French Manuscript Culture', *Huntingdon Library Quarterly* 58 (1995), 49-80.

C.W.P.O: see Previté-Orton.

CALDWELL, ROBERT A., 'Joseph Holand, Collector and Antiquary', *Modern Phililogy* 40 (1943), 295-301.

CAMERON, ANGUS F., 'Middle English in Old English Manuscripts', in *Chaucer and Middle English Studies*, ed. Beryl Rowlands (London, 1974): 218-29.

CAMPBELL, A., [facs.], *The Tollemache Orosius*, EEMF 3 (Copenhagen, 1953).

CAMPBELL, A., *Old English Grammar* (Oxford, 1959).

CAMPBELL, A., 'The Early Frisian Studies of Jan Van Vliet', *Modern Language Review* 34 (1939), 145-76.

CAMPBELL, JAMES, *Essays in Anglo-Saxon History* (London and Ronceverte, 1986).

CAMPOS VILANOVA, XAVIER, 'The Busy Ups and Downs of An Anglo-Saxon *Codex Aureus* in the Spain of the Habsburgs', *Proceedings of the 9th International Conference of the Spanish Society for Medieval English and Literature*, ed. M. Giménez Bon and V. Olsen (Zaragoza, 1997): 42-48.

CAPPELLI, A., *Lexicon abbreviaturarum: Dizionario di abbreviature latine ed italiane usate nelle carte e codici specialmente del medio evo*, 3rd edition (Milan, 1929).

CARLEY, JAMES P., 'John Leland and the contents of the English pre-dissolution libraries: Lincolnshire', *Transactions of the Cambridge Bibliographical Society* 9 (1986-90 1989), 330-57.

CARLEY, JAMES P., 'The Royal Library as a source for Sir Robert Cotton's collection: a preliminary list of acquisitions', *The British Library Journal* 18 (1992), 52-71; rpt. Wright 1997: 208-29.

CARLEY, JAMES P., 'The Royal Library under Henry VIII', in Hellinga and Trapp 1999: 274-81.

CARLEY, JAMES P. (ed.), *The Libraries of King Henry VIII*, Corpus of British Medieval Catalogues 7 (London, 2000).

CARTLIDGE, NEIL, 'The Date of *The Owl and the Nightingale*', *Medium Ævum* 65 (1996), 230-47.

CARTLIDGE, NEIL, 'The Composition and Social Context of Oxford, Jesus College, MS 29(II) and London, British Library, MS Cotton Caligula A.ix', *Medium Ævum* 66 (1997), 250-69.

CARTLIDGE, NEIL, 'The Linguistic Evidence for the Provenance of *The Owl and the Nightingale*', *Neuphilologischen Mitteilungen* 99 (1998), 249-68.

CARTLIDGE, NEIL, ed., *The Owl and the Nightingale. Text and Translation* (Exeter, 2001).

CAVANAUGH, SUSAN H., 'A study of books privately owned in England 1300-1450', 2 vols, University of Pennsylvania dissertation (Philadelphia, 1980).

CAWLEY, A.C., 'Thoresby and Later Owners of the Manuscript of the York Plays (BL Additional 35290)', *Leeds Studies in English* N.S. 11 (1980), 74-89.

CAYGILL, MARJORIE, 'Sir Frederic Madden: Museum Diarist', *British Museum Magazine* 41 (2001), 35-37.

CHAMBERS, R.W. AND MARJORIE DAUNT, eds, *A Book of London English 1384-1425* (Oxford, 1931).

CHAMBERS, R.W., MAX FÖRSTER AND ROBIN FLOWER, [facs.], *The Exeter Book of Old English Poetry* (London, 1933).

CHAPLAIS, PIERRE, 'Who Introduced Charters into England? The Case For Augustine', *Journal of the Society of Archivists* III, 10 (1969), rpt. in *Prisca Munimenta. Studies in Archival & Administrative History presented to Dr A.E.J. Hollaender*, ed. Felicity Ranger (London, 1973 [1969]): 88-107.

CHAPLAIS, PIERRE, 'The Spelling of Christ's Name in Medieval Anglo-Latin: "Christus" or "Cristus"?', *Journal of the Society of Archivists* 8 (1987), 261-80.

CHAPLAIS, PIERRE, review of Dumville 1993, in *Journal of the Society of Archivists* 16 (1995), 105-07.

CHRISTIANSON, C. PAUL, *Memorials of the Book Trade in Medieval London. The Archives of Old London Bridge* (Cambridge, 1987).

CLARK, CECILY, ed., *The Peterborough Chronicle, 1070-1154. Edited from MS. Bodley Laud Misc. 636 with introduction, commentary, and an appendix containing the interpolations* (London, 1958; 2nd edition 1970).

CLARK, J.P.H., 'Editing the Latin version of the "Cloud of Unknowing" – a progress report', *Analecta Cartusiana* 63. 1 (1990), 191-211.

CLASSEN, E. AND F.E. HARMER, eds, *An Anglo-Saxon Chronicle from British Museum, Cotton MS., Tiberius B. IV* (Manchester, 1926).

CLEMOES, PETER, ed., *Ælfric's Catholic Homilies: the First Series, Text*, EETS S.S. 17 (Oxford, 1997).

CLEMOES, P. AND N. ELIASON, [facs.], *Ælfric's First Series of Catholic Homilies*, EEMF 13 (Copenhagen, 1966).

CLUNIES ROSS, MARGARET, 'Revaluing the Work of Edward Lye, an Eighteenth-Century Septentrional Scholar', *Studies in Medievalism* 9 (1997), 66-79.

COLDIRON, A.E.B., 'Translation, Canons, and Cultural Capital: Manuscripts and Reception of Charles d'Orléans's English Poetry', in Arn 2000: 183-214.

COLGRAVE, B., [facs.], *The Paris Psalter*, EEMF 8 (Copenhagen, 1958).

COLGRAVE, BERTRAM AND R.A.B. MYNORS, eds, *Bede's Ecclesiastical History of the English People* (Oxford, 1969).

COLLIER, WENDY E.J., '"Englishness" and the Worcester Tremulous Hand', *Leeds Studies in English* N.S. 26 (1995), 35-47.

COLLIER, WENDY E.J., 'A thirteenth-century user of Anglo-Saxon manuscripts', *Bulletin of the John Rylands University Library of Manchester* 79 (1997), 149-65.

COLLIER, WENDY, 'The Tremulous Worcester Hand and Gregory's *Pastoral Care*', in Swan and Treharne 2000: 195-208.

COLLINS, J. CHURTON, ed., *Sidney's Apologie for Poetrie* (Oxford, 1907 [1950 impression]).
CONNER, P.W., 'The Structure of the Exeter Book Codex (Exeter, Cathedral Library, MS. 3501)', *Scriptorium* 40 (1986), 233-42; rpt. in Richards 2001: 301-15.
CONNER, P.W., *Anglo-Saxon Exeter: a Tenth-Century Cultural History* (Woodbridge, 1993).
CONNOLLY, MARGARET, *John Shirley: Book Production and the Noble Household in Fifteenth-Century England* (Aldershot, Brookfield USA, Singapore, Sydney, 1998).
COOPER, HELEN, 'M for Merlin: The Case of the Winchester Manuscript', in Kanno *et al.* 1997: 92-107.
COOPER, HELEN, 'Opening Up the Malory Manuscript', in Wheeler, Kindrick, and Salda 2000: 255-84.
CORRIE, MARILYN, 'Harley 2253, Digby 86, and the Circulation of Literature in Pre-Chaucerian England', in Fein 2000: 427-43.
COXE, H.O., *Catalogus codicum MSS. qui in collegiis aulisque Oxoniensibus hodie adservantur*, 2 vols (Oxford, 1852), II. 9-11.
CRAWFORD, S.J., ed., *The Old English Version of the Heptateuch. Ælfric's Treatise on the Old and New Testament and his Preface to Genesis ... with the text of two additional manuscripts transcribed by N.R. Ker*, EETS O.S. 160 (1922).
CRAWFORD, S.J., 'The Worcester Marks and Glosses of the Old English Manuscripts in the Bodleian, together with the Worcester version of the Nicene Creed', *Anglia* 51 (1927), 1-25.
CRICK, JULIA, 'The case for a West Saxon minuscule', *Anglo-Saxon England* 26 (1997), 63-79.
CROSS, J.E., 'Missing folios in Cotton MS. Nero A. I', *British Library Journal* 16 (1990), 99-100.
CUBBIN, G.P., ed., *The Anglo-Saxon Chronicle: a collaborative edition*, vol. 6, MS D (Cambridge, 1996).
CUNNINGHAM, IAN C., '*Bruce* and *Wallace* (National Library of Scotland Advocates' Manuscript 19.2.2)', *Edinburgh Bibliographical Society Transactions* 4 (1974 for 1955-71), 247-52.
DAHOOD, ROGER, '*Ancrene Wisse*, the Katharine Group, and the *Wohunge* Group', in Edwards 1984: 1-33.
DAHOOD, ROGER, 'The Use of Coloured Initials and Other Markers in Early Versions of *Ancrene Riwle*', in *Medieval English Studies presented to George Kane*, ed. Edward Donald Kennedy, Ronald Waldron, and Joseph S. Wittig (Cambridge, 1988): 79-97.
DAHOOD, ROGER, 'Abbreviations, Otiose Strokes and Editorial Practice: The Case of Southwell Minster MS 7', in *New Perspectives on Middle English Texts. A Festschrift for R. A. Waldron*, ed. Susan Powell and Jeremy J. Smith (Cambridge, 2000).
DAMICO, HELEN, ed., *Medieval Scholarship. Biographical Studies in the Formation of a Discipline*, vol. 2, Literature and Philology (New York and London, 1998).
DANCE, RICHARD, 'Interpreting Laȝamon: linguistic diversity and some cruces in Cotton Caligula A. ix, with particular reference to Norse-derived words', in Allen, Perry, and Roberts 2002: 187-202.
DANCE, RICHARD, 'The AB Language: the Recluse, the Gossip and the Language Historian', in Wada 2003, 57-82.
D'ARDENNE, S.T.R.O., ed., *Þe Liflade ant te Passiun of Seinte Iuliene* (Liège, 1936).
D'ARONCO, M.A. AND M.L. Cameron, [facs.], *The Old English Illustrated Pharmacopoeia: British Library Cotton Vitellius C.III*, EEMF 27 (Copenhagen, 1998).
DAVID, ALFRED, 'The Ownership and Use of the Ellesmere Manuscript', in Stevens and Woodward 1995: 307-26.
DAVIDSON, CLIFFORD, 'The Digby *Mary Magdalene* and the Magdalene cult of the Middle Ages', *Annuale Medievale* 13 (1972), 70-87.
D[AVIS], N[ORMAN], note added to review of Price, *The Equatorie of the Planetis*, in *Review of English Studies* N.S. 9 (1958), 180-83.
DAVIS, NORMAN AND C.L. WRENN, eds, *English and Medieval Studies Presented to J.R.R. Tolkien* (London, 1962).
DAWSON, GILES E. AND LAETITIA KENNEDY-SKIPTON, *Elizabethan Handwriting 1500-1650* (London, 1968, rpt. Chichester, 1981).
DEAN, RUTH J. WITH MAUREEN B.M. BOULTON, *Anglo-Norman Literature. A Guide to Texts and Manuscripts* (London, 1999).
DE BEER, G.R., *Sir Hans Sloane and the British Museum* (London, New York, Toronto, 1953).
DE HAMEL, CHRISTOPHER, *A History of Illuminated Manuscripts* (London, 1986; 2nd edition 1994).
DE HAMEL, CHRISTOPHER, *The Book. A History of the Bible* (London, 2001).
DE LA MARE, A.C., 'Development of the manuscript collection', in *The Douce Legacy. An exhibition to commemorate the 150th anniversary of the bequest of Frances Douce (1757-1834)* (Oxford, 1984): 130-39.
DEKKER, KEES, '"That Most Elaborate One of Fr. Junius": An Investigation of Francis Junius's Manuscript Old English Dictionary', in Graham 2000[3]: 301-43.
DEROLEZ, Albert, *The Palaeography of Gothic Manuscript Books* (Cambridge, 2003).
DEROLEZ, R., *Runica Manuscripta*, Werken Uitgegeven door de Faculteit van de Weijsbegeerte en Letteren 118 (Brugge, 1954).
DE VRIEND, HUBERT JAN, ed., *The Old English Herbarium and Medicina de Quadrupedibus*, EETS O.S. 286 (1984).
DOANE, A.N., ed., *The Saxon Genesis. An Edition of the West Saxon* Genesis B *and the Old Saxon Vatican* Genesis (Madison, Wisconsin, 1991).
DOANE, A.N., [facs.], *Books of Prayers and Healing*, Anglo-Saxon Manuscripts in Microfiche Facsimile I (Binghamton, New York, 1994).
DOANE, A.N., [facs.], *Anglo-Saxon Bibles and 'The Book of Cerne'*, Anglo-Saxon Manuscripts in Microfiche Facsimile 7 (Tempe, Az., 2002).
DOBBIE, E.V.K., ed., *The Anglo-Saxon Minor Poems*, The Anglo-Saxon Poetic Records 6 (New York, 1942).
DOBIACHE-RODJESTVENSKY, O., 'Un Manuscript de Bède à Leningrad', *Speculum* 3 (1928), 314-21.

DOBSON, E.J. AND F. LL. HARRISON, eds, *Medieval English Songs* (London and Boston, 1979).
DODWELL, C.R., *The Canterbury School of Illumination 1066-1200* (Cambridge, 1954).
DODWELL, C.R. AND P. CLEMOES, [facs.], *The Old English Illustrated Hexateuch*, EEMF 18 (Copenhagen, 1974).
DORSCH, T.S., 'Two English Antiquaries. John Leland and John Straw', *Essays and Studies* 12 (1959), 18-35.
DOUGLAS, DAVID C., *English Scholars* (London, 1939, rpt. 1943; 2nd edition 1951).
DOYLE, A.I., 'Books connected with the Vere family and Barking Abbey', *Transactions of the Essex Archaeological Society* N.S. 25 (1955-58), 222-43.
DOYLE, A.I., 'The Work of a Late Fifteenth-Century English Scribe, William Ebesham', *Bulletin of the John Rylands University Library of Manchester* 39 (1957), 298-325.
DOYLE, A.I., 'Appendix B. A Note on St. John's College, Cambridge, MS. H. 5', in Curt F. Bühler, ed., *The Epistle of Othea*, EETS O.S. 264 (1970): 125-27.
DOYLE, A.I., 'The Manuscripts', in *Middle English Alliterative poetry and its Literary Background: seven essays*, ed. David Lawton (Cambridge, 1982): 88-100.
DOYLE, A.I., 'English Books In and Out of Court from Edward III to Henry VII', in Scattergood and Sherborne 1983: 163-81.
DOYLE, A.I., 'Remarks on surviving manuscripts of *Piers Plowman*', in Kratzmann and Simpson 1986: 35-48.
DOYLE, A.I., 'Publication by members of the religious orders', in Griffiths and Pearsall 1989: 109-23.
DOYLE, A.I., 'Book Production by the Monastic Orders in England (*c.* 1375- 1530): Assessing the Evidence', in *Medieval Book Production. Assessing the Evidence*, ed. Linda L. Brownrigg, (Los Altos Hills, CA, 1990): 1-19.
DOYLE, A.I., 'A Fragment of an Eighth-Century Office Book', in *Words, Texts and Manuscripts*, ed. Michael Korhammer with the assistance of Karl Reichl and Hans Sauer (Cambridge, 1992): 11-27.
DOYLE, A.I., 'The Copyist of the Ellesmere Canterbury Tales', in Stevens and Woodward 1995: 49-67.
DOYLE, A.I. AND GEORGE B. PACE, 'A New Chaucer Manuscript', *Publications of the Modern Language Association* 83 (1968), 22-34.
DOYLE, A.I. AND GEORGE B. PACE, 'Further Texts of Chaucer's Minor Poems', *Studies in Bibliography* 28 (1975), 41-61.
DOYLE, A.I. AND M.B. PARKES, 'The Production of Copies of the *Canterbury Tales* and the *Confessio Amantis* in the Early Fifteenth Century', in *Medieval Scribes, Manuscripts and Libraries: Essays presented to N. R. Ker*, ed. M.B. Parkes and Andrew G. Watson (London, 1978): 163-210; rpt. Parkes 1991: 201-48.
DUMVILLE, DAVID N., 'Liturgical drama and panegyric responsory from the 8th century. A re-examination of the origin and contents of the 9th-century section of the Book of Cerne', *Journal of Theological Studies* N.S. 23 pt 2 (1972), 374-406.
DUMVILLE, DAVID N., 'English Libraries before 1066: Use and Abuse of the Manuscript Evidence', in *Insular Latin Studies: Latin Texts and Manuscripts of the British Isles*, ed. Michael Herren (Toronto, 1981), 153-78; rpt. with revisions in Richards 1994: 169-219.
DUMVILLE, DAVID N., 'Some aspects of annalistic writing at Canterbury in the eleventh and early twelfth centuries', *Peritia* 2 (1983), 23-57.
DUMVILLE, DAVID N., 'English Square minuscule script: the background and earliest phases', *Anglo-Saxon England* 16 (1987), 147-79.
DUMVILLE, DAVID N., 'Beowulf come lately. Some Notes on the Palaeography of the Nowell Codex', *Archiv* 225 (1988), 49-63.
DUMVILLE, DAVID N., *Wessex and England from Alfred to Edgar* (Woodbridge, 1992).
DUMVILLE, DAVID N., *English Caroline Script and Monastic History, Studies in Benedictinism, A.D. 950-1030* (Woodbridge, 1993).
DUMVILLE, DAVID N., *A Palaeographer's Review: The Insular System of Scripts in the Early Middle Ages*, volume one (Suita, Osaka, 1999).
DUMVILLE, DAVID D., 'Specimina Codicum Palaeoanglicorum', in *Collection of Essays in Commemoration of the 50th Anniversary of the Institute of Oriental and Occidental Studies* (Osaka, 2001).
EDWARDS, A.S.G. ed., *Middle English Prose. A Critical Guide to Major Authors and Genres* (New Brunswick, New Jersey, 1984).
EDWARDS, A.S.G., 'The Chaucer Portraits in the Harley and Rosenbach Manuscripts', *English Manuscript Studies* 4 (1993), 268-71.
EDWARDS, A.S.G., 'Bodleian Library MS Arch. Selden B.24: A "Transitional" Collection', in Nichols and Wenzel 1996: 53-67.
EDWARDS, A.S.G., 'The Manuscript: British Library MS Cotton Nero A.x', in *A Companion to the Gawain Poet*, ed. D. S. Brewer (Cambridge, 1997, rpt. 1999): 197-219.
EDWARDS, A.S.G., 'Manuscript and Text', in McCarren and Moffat 1998[1]: 159-68.
EDWARDS, A.S.G., 'Representing the Middle English Manuscript', in Pearsall 1998[2]: 65-79.
EDWARDS, A.S.G., 'John Shirley and the Emulation of Courtly Culture', in Mullally and Thompson 1997: 309-17.
EDWARDS, A.S.G., 'Fifteenth-century Middle English verse author collections', in Edwards, Gillespie, and Hanna 2000: 101-23.
EDWARDS, A.S.G., 'The Middle English Manuscripts and Early Readers of *Ancrene Wisse*', in Wada 2003, 103-12.
EDWARDS, A.S.G., 'John Stowe and Middle English Literature', in Gadd and Gillespie 2004: 109-18.
EDWARDS, A.S.G., VINCENT GILLESPIE, AND RALPH HANNA, eds, *The English Medieval Book. Studies in Memory of Jeremy Griffiths* (London, 2000).
EDWARDS, A.S.G. AND LINNE R. MOONEY, 'Is the *Equatorie of the Planets* a Chaucer holograph?', *The Chaucer Review* 26 (1991), 31-42.
EDWARDS, A.S.G. AND DEREK PEARSALL, 'The manuscripts of the major English poetic texts', in Griffiths and Pearsall 1989: 257-78.

Egerton, Alex, [facs.], *The Ellesmere Chaucer Reproduced in Facsimile*, 2 vols (Manchester, 1911).

Eliason, Norman E. and Peter Clemoes, [facs.], *Ælfric's First Series of Catholic Homilies (British Museum Royal 7 C.XII, fols. 4-218)*, EEMF 13 (Copenhagen, 1966).

Elliott, Ralph W.V, *Runes. An Introduction* (Manchester, 1959; 2nd edition 1989).

Erler, Mary C., 'Devotional literature', in Hellinga and Trapp 1999: 495-525.

Evans, Joan, *A History of the Society of Antiquaries* (Oxford, 1956).

Fein, Susanna, ed., *Studies in the Harley Manuscript. The Scribes, Contents, and Social Contexts of British Library MS Harley 2253* (Kalamazoo, Michigan, 2000).

Field, P.J.C., see under Vinaver.

Finberg, H.P.R., *The Early Charters of the West Midlands* (Leicester, 1961).

Fisher, John H., Malcolm Richardson, and Jane L. Fisher, *An Anthology of Chancery English* (Knoxville, 1984).

Fletcher, Alan J., 'The Genesis of *The Owl and the Nightingale*: a New Hypothesis', *The Chaucer Review* 34 (1999), 1-17.

Flom, George T., 'On the Old English Herbal of Apuleius Vitellius C III', *Journal of English and German Philology* 40 (1941), 29-37.

Flower, R., 'Laurence Nowell and the Discovery of England in Tudor Times', *Proceedings of the British Academy* 21 (1935), 46-73; rpt. in Stanley 1990: 1-27.

Flower, R. and H. Smith, [facs.], *Parker Chronicle and Laws (Corpus Christi College, Cambridge MS. 173): A Facsimile*, EETS o.s. 208 (1941).

Foltys, Christian, ed., *Brutus Li Rei de Engleterre. Le Livere de Reis de Engleterre* (Berlin, 1962).

Fox, Denton, ed., *The Poems of Robert Henryson* (Oxford, 1981).

Frank, Roberta, 'When Lexicography Met the Exeter Book', in Baker and Howe 1998: 207-21.

Franzen, C., *The Tremulous Hand of Worcester* (Oxford, 1991).

Franzen, C., [facs.], *Worcester Manuscripts*, Anglo-Saxon Manuscripts in Microfiche Facsimile 6 (Binghamton, New York, 1998).

Frantzen, Allen J., *Desires for Origins. New Language, Old English and Teaching the Tradition* (New Brunswick and London, 1990).

Friedman, John B., 'Books, Owners and Makers in fifteenth-century Yorkshire: the Evidence from some wills and extant manuscripts', in Minnis 1989: 111-27.

Friedman, John B., *Northern English Books, Owners, and Makers in the late Middle Ages* (New York, 1995).

Furnivall, F.J, ed., *Hoccleve's Works: The Regement of Princes*, EETS e.s. 72 (1897).

Furnivall, F.J., ed., *Minor Poems of the Vernon MS. Part II*, EETS o.s. 117 (1901).

Gadd, Ian and Alexandra Gillespie, eds., *John Stowe (1525-1605) and the making of the English past* (London, 2004).

Gameson, Richard, 'The decoration of the Tanner Bede', *Anglo-Saxon England* 21 (1992), 115-59.

Gameson, Richard, 'Alfred the Great and the Destruction and Production of Christian Books', *Scriptorium* 49 (1995), 180-210.

Gameson, Richard, 'The origin of the Exeter Book of Old English poetry', *Anglo-Saxon England* 25 (1996[1]), 135-85, pls II-IX.

Gameson, Richard, 'Book production and decoration at Worcester in the tenth and eleventh centuries', in *St Oswald of Worcester: Life and Influence*, ed. Nicholas Brooks and Catherine Cubitt (London and New York, 1996[2]): 194-243.

Gameson, Richard, *The Manuscripts of Early Norman England (c. 1066-1130)*, published for the British Academy (Oxford, 1999[1]).

Gameson, Richard, ed., *St Augustine and the Conversion of England* (Stroud, 1999[2]).

Gameson, Richard, 'The Earliest Books of Christian Kent', in Gameson 1999[2]: 313-73.

Gameson, Richard, [facs.], *The Codex Aureus an eighth-century Gospel book Stockholm, Kungliga Bibliothek, A. 135*, 2 vols, EEMF 28 (Copenhagen, 2001-02).

Gameson, Richard, *The scribe speaks? Colophons in early English manuscripts*, H.M. Chadwick Memorial Lectures 12 (Cambridge, 2001).

Ganz, David, 'Traube on "Schrifttypen"', *Scriptorium* 36 (1982), 293-303.

Ganz, David, 'The Preconditions for Caroline Minuscule', *Viator* 18 (1987), 23-44.

Ganz, David, paper on Anglo-Saxon square minuscule, forthcoming, in 'Cambridge History of the Book in Britain', vol. I.

Garmonsway, G.A., ed., *Ælfric's Colloquy*, Methuen's Old English Library (London, 1939; 2nd edition 1947).

Gatch, Milton McC., 'Humfrey Wanley (1672-1726)', in Damico 1998: 45-57.

Gaylord, Alan T., 'Portrait of a Poet', in Stevens and Woodward 1995: 121-42.

Gerritsen, Johan, 'Correction and Erasure in the Vespasian Psalter gloss', *English Studies* 70 (1989), 477-83.

Gillespie, Vincent, 'Vernacular Books of Religion', in Griffiths and Pearsall 1989: 317-44.

Glover, John, ed., *Le Livere de Reis de Britannie* e *Le Livere de Reis de Engleterre*, Rolls Series 42 (1865).

Gneuss, Helmut, 'Zur Geschichte des MS. Vespasian A.I', *Anglia* 75 (1957), 125-33; rpt. Gneuss 1996: no. VII.

Gneuss, Helmut, 'A preliminary list of manuscripts written or owned in England up to 1100', *Anglo-Saxon England* 9 (1981), 1-60; superseded by Gneuss 2001.

Gneuss, Helmut, 'Anglo-Saxon Libraries from the Conversion to the Benedictine Reform', *Settimane di studio del Centro italiano di studi sull'alto medioevo XXXII (Spoleto 1984). Angli e sassoni al di qua e al di là del mare* (Spoleto, 1986): 643-88; rpt. Gneuss 1996: no. II.

GNEUSS, HELMUT, 'Guide to the Editing and Preparation of Texts for the *Dictionary of Old English*', in Scragg and Szarmach 1994: 7-26 [1973].

GNEUSS, HELMUT, *Books and Libraries in Early England* (Aldershot and Borrkfield, Vermont, 1996).

GNEUSS, HELMUT, 'Origin and Provenance of Anglo-Saxon Manuscripts: the Case of Cotton Tiberius A.III', in Robinson and Zim 1997: 13-48.

GNEUSS, HELMUT, *Handlist of Anglo-Saxon Manuscripts. A List of Manuscripts and Manuscripts Fragments Written or Owned in England up to 1100* (Tempe, Arizona, 2001).

GODDEN, M.R., 'The sources for Ælfric's homily on St Gregory', *Anglia* 86 (1968), 79-88.

GÖRLACH, MANFRED, *The Textual Tradition of the South English Legendary*, Leeds Texts and Monographs N.S. 6 (Leeds, 1974).

GÖRLACH, MANFRED, 'Recent facsimile editions of Middle English literary manuscripts', *Anglia* 105 (1987), 121-51.

GOLLANCZ, I., [facs.], *Pearl, Cleanness, Patience and Sir Gawain, reproduced in facsimile from the unique MS. Cotton Nero A. x. in the British Museum*, EETS O.S. 162 (1923).

GOLLANCZ, I., [facs.], *The Cædmon Manuscript of Anglo-Saxon Biblical Poetry* (1927).

GORDON, E.V., ed., *Pearl* (Oxford, 1953).

GRAHAM, TIMOTHY, 'A Parkerian transcript of the list of Bishop Leofric's procurements for Exeter Cathedral: Matthew Parker, the Exeter Book, and Cambridge University Library MS Ii.2.11', *Transactions of the Cambridge Bibliographical Society* 10 pt 4 (1994), 423-55.

GRAHAM, TIMOTHY, 'Robert Talbot's "Old Saxonice Bede" Cambridge University Library, MS Kk.3.18 and the "Alphabetum Norwagicum" of British Library, Cotton MSS, Domitian A. IX', in James P. Carley and Colin G.C. Tite, eds, *Books and Collectors 1200-1700*, The British Library Studies in the History of the Book (London, 1997[1]): 295-316.

GRAHAM, TIMOTHY, 'The Beginnings of Old English Studies: Evidence from the Manuscripts of Matthew Parker', in Sato 1997[2]: 29-50.

GRAHAM, TIMOTHY, 'Cambridge, Corpus Christi 57 and its Anglo-Saxon Users', in Pulsiano and Treharne 1998: 21-69.

GRAHAM, TIMOTHY, 'Early Modern Users of Claudius B. iv: Robert Talbot and William L'Isle', in Barnhouse and Withers 2000[1]: 271-316.

GRAHAM, TIMOTHY, 'John Joscelyn, Pioneer of Old English Lexicography', in Graham 2000[2]: 83-140.

GRAHAM, TIMOTHY, ed., *The Recovery of Old English. Anglo-Saxon Studies in the Sixteenth and Seventeenth Centuries*, Publications of the Richard Rawlinson Center, Medieval Institute Publications (Kalamazoo, 2000[3]).

GRAHAM, TIMOTHY AND ANDREW G. WATSON, *The Recovery of the Past in early Elizabethan England. Documents by John Bale and John Joscelyn from the Circle of Matthew Parker*, Cambridge Bibliographical Monographs No. 13 (Cambridge, 1998).

GREENE, R.L., ed., *The Early English Carols* (Oxford, 1935).

GREENE, R.L., ed., *A Selection of English Carols* (Oxford, 1962).

GREG, W.W., *Facsimiles of twelve early English manuscripts in the library of Trinity College Cambridge* (Oxford, 1913).

GRIFFITHS, JEREMY AND DEREK PEARSALL, eds, *Book Production and Publishing in Britain 1375-1475* (Cambridge, 1989).

GUDDAT-FIGGE, GISELA, *Catalogue of Manuscripts Containing Middle English Romances* (Munich, 1976).

GUMBERT, J.P., 'A Proposal for a Cartesian Nomenclature', in *Litterae textualis. A series on manuscripts and their texts*, ed. J.P. Gumbert and M.J.M. de Haan, Miniatures scripts collections. Essays presented to G.I. Lieftinck 4 (Amsterdam, 1976): 45-52.

GUMBERT, J. PETER, 'Sizes and Formats', in *Ancient and Medieval Book Materials and Techniques*, ed. Marilena Maniaci, 2 vols, Studi e Testi (1993), I. 227-63.

GUMBERT, J.P. AND P.M. VERMEER, 'An Unusual *Yogh* in the *Bestiary* Manuscript – A Palaeographical Note', *Medium Ævum* 60 (1971), 56-57.

GWARA, SCOTT WITH DAVID W. PORTER, eds, *Anglo-Saxon Conversations. The Colloquies of Ælfric Bata* (Woodbridge, 1997).

HAMEL, MARY, ed., *Morte Arthure. A Critical Edition* (New York and London, 1984).

HAMMOND, E.P., ed., *English Verse between Chaucer and Surrey* (Durham, N. Carolina, London, 1927).

HANDLEY, RIMA, 'British Museum MS. Cotton Vespasian D. xiv', *Notes and Queries* 219 (1974), 243-50.

HANKS, D. THOMAS AND JENNIFER L. FISH, 'Beside the Point, Medieval Meanings vs. Modern Impositions in Editing Malory's "Morte Arthur"', *Neuphilologische Mitteilungen* 98 (1977), 273-89.

HANNA III, RALPH, [facs.], *The Ellesmere Manuscript of Chaucer's Canterbury Tales: a working facsimile*, rpt. 75% size in single vol. of Egerton 1911 (Cambridge, 1989).

HANNA III, RALPH AND A.S.G. EDWARDS, 'Rotheley, the De Vere Circle, and the Ellesmere Chaucer', *Huntingdon Library Quarterly* 58 (1995), 11-35.

HANNA III, RALPH, *Pursuing History. Middle English Manuscripts and Their Texts* (Stanford, 1996).

HAPPÉ, PETER, *John Bale* (New York, 1966).

HARDMAN, PHILLIPA, 'Windows into the Text: Unfilled Spaces in Some Fifteenth-Century English Manuscripts', in *Texts and Their Contexts: Papers from the Early Book Society*, ed. John Scattergood and Julia Boffey (Dublin, 1997[2]): 44-70.

HARDMAN, PHILLIPA, 'Interpreting the Incomplete Scheme of Illustration in Cambridge, Corpus Christi College MS 61', *English Manuscript Studies 1100-1750* 6 (1977[1]), 52-69.

HARDMAN, PHILLIPA, 'Chaucer's Articulation of the Narrative in *Troilus*: the manuscript evidence', *The Chaucer Review* 30 (1995-96), 111-33.

HARGREAVES, H., 'The Wyclyffite Versions', in *The Cambridge History of the Bible*, II, ed. G.W.H. Lampe (Cambridge, 1969): 387-415.

HARGREAVES, H., 'Popularising Biblical Scholarship: The Role of the Wycliffite *Glossed Gospels*', in *The Bible and Medieval Culture*, ed. W. Lourdaux and D. Verhelst (Louvain, 1979): 171-89.

HARPER-BILL, CHRISTOPHER AND ELISABETH VAN HOUTS, eds, *A Companion to the Anglo-Norman World* (Woodbridge, 2003).

HARRIS, KATE, 'The origins and make-up of Cambridge University Library MS Ff.1.6', *Transactions of the Cambridge Bibliographical Society* 8 (1983), 299-333.

HARRIS, KATE, 'Patrons, Buyers and Owners: the evidence for ownership and the rôle of book owners in book production and the book trade', in Griffiths and Pearsall 1989: 163-99.

HARRIS, KATE, 'The Patronage and Dating of Longleat House MS 24, a Prestige Copy of the *Pupilla Oculi* Illuminated by the Master of the *Troilus* Frontispiece', in Riddy 2000: 35-54.

HARVEY, BARBARA, *The Obedientaries of Westminster Abbey and their Financial Records, c.1275-1540* (Woodbridge, 2002).

HEALEY, THOMAS F., *Richard Crashaw*, Medieval and Renaissance Authors 8 (Leiden, 1986).

HECTOR, L.C., *The Handwriting of English Documents* (London, 1958; 2nd edition 1968).

HEESAKKERS, CHRIS L., 'Junius as a Tutor: His *Paraenesis missa Alberico de Vere*', in Bremmer 1998: 93-115.

HEIMANN, DAVID AND R. KAY, *The elements of abbreviation in medieval Latin Palaeography* (Kansas, 1982).

HELLINGA, LOTTE, 'The Malory Manuscript and Caxton', in Hellinga and Kelliher 1977: 91-101.

HELLINGA, LOTTE, 'The Malory Manuscript and Caxton', in Takamiya and Brewer 1981: 127-41.

HELLINGA, LOTTE, 'Manuscripts in the hands of printers', in *Manuscripts in the fifty years after the invention of printing*, ed. J.B. Trapp (London, 1983): 3-11.

HELLINGA, LOTTE, 'Importation of Books Printed on the Continent into England and Scotland before 1450-1520, in *Printing the Written Word. The Social History of Books circa 1450-1520*, ed. Sandra Hindman (Ithaca and London, 1991): 205-24.

HELLINGA, LOTTE, 'Printing', in Hellinga and Trapp 1999: 65-108.

HELLINGA, LOTTE AND HILTON KELLIHER, 'The Malory Manuscript', *British Library Journal* 3 (1977), 91-113.

HELLINGA, LOTTE AND J.B. TRAPP, eds, *The Cambridge History of the Book in Britain*, vol. III, 1400-1557 (Cambridge, 1999).

HENDERSON, GEORGE, 'The Programme of Illustrations in Bodleian MS Junius XI', in *Studies in Memory of David Talbot Rice*, ed. Giles Robertson and George Henderson (Edinburgh, 1975): 113-45.

HERZFELD, GEORGE, ed., *An Old English Martyrology. Re-edited from manuscripts in the libraries of the British Museum and of Corpus Christi College, Cambridge*, EETS O.S. 116 (1900).

HESLOP, T.A., 'The production of *de luxe* manuscripts and the patronage of King Cnut and Queen Emma', *Anglo-Saxon England* 19 (1990), 151-95.

HETHERINGTON, M.S., 'The Beginnings of Old English Lexicography' (issued from Spicewood, Texas, 1980).

HEYWORTH, P.L., ed., *Letters of Humfrey Wanley. Palaeographer, Anglo-Saxonist, Librarian 1672-1726* (Oxford, 1989).

HILL, BETTY, 'The History of Jesus College, Oxford, MS. 29', *Medium Ævum* 32 (1963), 203-13.

HILL, BETTY, 'Oxford, Jesus College MS. 29: Addenda on Donation, Acquisition, Dating and Relevance of the "Broaken Leafe" Note to The Owl and the Nightingale', *Notes and Queries* 220 (1975), 98-105.

HILL, BETTY, 'Oxford, Jesus College MS 29, Part II: contents, technical matters, compilation, and its history to *c.* 1695', *Notes and Queries* 248 (2003), 268-76.

HILL, JOYCE, 'The Exeter Book and Lambeth Library MS 149: A Reconsideration', *American Notes & Queries* 224 (1986), 112-16.

HILL, JOYCE, 'The Exeter Book and Lambeth Palace Library MS 149: The Monasterium of Sancta Maria', *American Notes & Queries* 226 (1988), 4-9.

HILL, JOYCE, 'Winchester Pedagogy and the *Colloquy* of Ælfric', *Leeds Studies in English*, N.S. 29 (1998), 137-52.

HOAD, T.E., ed., *Henry Sweet. A Second Anglo-Saxon Reader. Archaic and Dialectal* (Oxford, 1978).

HODGSON, PHYLLIS, ed., *The Cloud of Unknowing and The Book of Privy Counselling*, EETS O.S. 218 (1944).

HODGSON, PHYLLIS, ed., *Deonise Hid Diuintie*, EETS O.S. 231 (1955).

HODGSON, PHYLLIS, ed., *The Cloud of Unknowing and related treatises*, Analecta Cartusiana 3 (Salzburg, 1982).

HOFTIJZER, PAUL G., 'The Library of Johannes de Laet', *LIAS: Sources and Documents Relating to the Early Modern History of Ideas* 25.2 (1998), 201-26.

HOGG, JAMES, 'Mount Grace Charterhouse and Late Medieval English Spirituality', *Analecta Cartusiana* 82. 3 (1980), 1-43.

HOLM, SIGURD, *Corrections and Additions in the Ormulum Manuscript* (Uppsala, 1922).

HOLT, ROBERT, ed., *The Ormulum, with the Notes and Glossary of Dr. R.M. White*, 2 vols (Oxford, 1878).

HORALL, SARAH M., 'The Watermarks of the Thornton Manuscripts', *Notes and Queries* 225 (1980), 385-86.

HORGAN, DOROTHY M., 'The Old English *Pastoral Care*: the Scribal Contribution', in Szarmach 1986: 108-27.

HOROBIN, SIMON, *The Language of the Chaucer Tradition* (Cambridge, 2003).

HOROBIN, SIMON AND LINNE R. MOONEY, 'A *Piers Plowman* Manuscript by the Hengwrt/Ellesmere Scribe and its Implications for London Standard English' (at press).

HUDSON, ANNE, *The Premature Reformation. Wycliffite Texts and Lollard History* (Oxford, 1988).

HUDSON, ANNE, *Lollards and their Books* (London and Ronceverte, 1985 [1982]).

HUDSON, ANNE, 'John Stowe', in Ruggiers 1984: 53-70.

HUDSON, ANNE, 'Lollard book production', in Griffiths and Pearsall 1989: 125-42.

HUISMAN, ROSEMARY, *The Written Poem: Semiotic conventions from Old to Modern English* (London and New York, 1988; rpt. 1999).

HUNT, R.W. AND A.G. WATSON, *Bodleian Library Quarto Manuscripts IX Digby Manuscripts* (Oxford, 1999).

IRVINE, SUSAN, *The Anglo-Saxon Chronicle 7. MS E* (Cambridge, 2004).

IVY, G.S., 'The Bibliography of the Manuscript Book', in Wormald and Wright 1958: 32-65.

JAMES, M.R., *The Ancient Libraries of Canterbury and Dover* (Cambridge, 1903).

JAMES, M.R., *A Descriptive Catalogue of the Manuscripts in the Library of Corpus Christi College, Cambridge*, 2 vols (Cambridge, 1909-12).

JAMES, M.R., *A Descriptive Catalogue of the Manuscripts in the Library of St. John's College, Cambridge* (Cambridge, 1913).

JAYATILAKA, ROHINI, 'The Old English Benedictine Rule', *Anglo-Saxon England* 32 (2003), 147-87.

JAYNE, SEARS R. AND F.R. JOHNSON, eds, *The Lumley Library. The catalogue of 1609* (London, 1956).

JENKINSON, HILARY, *The Later Court Hands in England from the fifteenth to the seventeenth century*, 2 vols (Cambridge, 1927).

JOHANNESSON, NILS-LENNART, 'Overwriting, Deletion and Erasure: Exploring the Changes in the *Ormulum* Manuscript'. *Jestin'* 2 (1997), 21-29; available at www.english.su.se/nlj/ormproj/Jestin97.htm

JOHNSON, CHARLES AND HILARY JENKINSON, *English Court Hand A.D. 1066 to 1500 illustrated chiefly from the Public Records*, 2 vols (Oxford, 1915; rpt. New York, 1967).

JOHNSON, DAVID F., 'A Programme of Illumination in the Old English Illustrated Hexateuch', in Barnhouse and Withers 2000: 165-99.

JOHNSTON, ALEXANDRA F., 'Traders and Playmakers: English Guildsmen and the Low Countries', in Barron and Saul 1995: 99-114.

JOHNSTON, ALEXANDRA F., 'The *York Cycle* and the Librarians of York', in *Harlaxton Studies XI: The Church and Learning in late Medieval Society, Studies in Honour of Professor R.B. Dobson*, ed. Caroline Barron and Jenny Stratford (Donington, 2002): 355-70.

KANE, GEORGE, ed., *Piers Plowman. The A Version* (London, 1960).

KANNO, MASAHIKO, HIROSHI YAMASHITA, MASATOSHI KAWASAKI, JUNKO ASAKAWA, AND NAOKO SHIRAI, eds, *Medieval Heritage Essays in Honour of Tadahiro Ikegami* (Tokyo, 1997).

KARKOV, CATHERINE E., *Text and Picture in Anglo-Saxon England: Narrative Strategies in the Junius 11 Manuscript* (Cambridge, 2001).

KARKOV, CATHERINE E., *The Ruler Portraits of Anglo-Saxon England*, Anglo-Saxon Studies 3 (Woodbridge, 2004).

KATO, TAKAKO, 'Irregular Textual Divisions in Caxton's *Morte Darthur* in Paraphs and Chapter Divisions', *Poetica* 53 (2000), 15-36.

KATO, TAKAKO, *Caxton's* Morte Darthur: *the printing process and the authenticity of the text* (Oxford, 2002).

KEISER, GEORGE, 'Lincoln Cathedral MS 91: life and milieu of the scribe', *Studies in Bibliography* 32 (1979), 158-79.

KELLIHER, HILTON, 'The early history of the manuscript', in Hellinga and Kelliher 1977: 101-13.

KELLIHER, HILTON, 'The early history of the Malory manuscript', in Takamiya and Brewer (Bury St Edmunds, 1981): 143-58.

KELLIHER, HILTON AND SALLY BROWN, *English Literary Manuscripts* (London, 1986).

KENDRICK, T.D., T.J. BROWN, AND R.L.S. BRUCE-MITFORD, *et al.*, [facs.], *Evangeliorum quattuor Codex Lindisfarnensis*, 2 vols (Olten and Lausanne, 1956, 1960).

KER, N.R., review of Chambers, Förster, and Flower 1933, in *Medium Ævum* 2 (1933), 224-31.

KER, N.R., 'The Date of the "Tremulous" Worcester Hand', *Leeds Studies in English* 6 (1937), 28-29; rpt. Watson 1985: 67-69.

KER, N.R., 'Unpublished Parts of the *Ormulum* Printed from MS. Lambeth 783', *Medium Ævum* 9 (1940), 1-22.

KER, N.R., *Medieval libraries of Great Britain. A list of surviving books* (London, 1941; 2nd edition 1964); for *Supplement to the Second Edition*, see WATSON, A.G. 1987.

KER, N.R., 'Aldred the Scribe', *Essays and Studies* 28 (1942-43[1]), 7-12; rpt. Watson 1985: 3-8.

KER, N.R., 'The Migration of Manuscripts from the English Medieval Libraries', *The Library*, 4th ser., 23 (1942-43[2]), 1-11; rpt. Watson 1985: 459-70.

KER, N.R., 'Hemming's Cartulary', *Studies in Mediaeval History Presented to Frederick Maurice Powicke*, ed. R.W. Hunt, W.A. Pantin, and R.W. Southern (Oxford, 1948): 49-75; rpt. Watson 1985: 31-59.

KER, N.R., 'Medieval Manuscripts from Norwich Cathedral Priory', *Transactions of the Cambridge Bibliographical Society* 1 (1949[1]), 1-28; rpt. Watson 1985: 243-72.

KER, N.R., 'Old English Notes signed "Coleman"', *Medium Ævum* 18 (1949[2]), 28-3; rpt. Watson 1985: 28-30.

KER, N.R., [facs.], *The Pastoral Care: King Alfred's Translation of St. Gregory's Regula pastoralis*, EEMF 6 (Copenhagen, 1956).

KER, N.R., *Catalogue of Manuscripts containing Anglo-Saxon* (Oxford, 1957; re-issued with suppl. 1990).

KER, N.R., *English manuscripts in the century after the Norman Conquest* (Oxford, 1960[1]).

KER, N.R., 'From "Above Top Line" to "Below Top Line": a Change in Scribal Practice', *Celtica* v (1960[2]), 13-16; rpt. Watson 1985: 71-74.

KER, N.R., [facs.], *Facsimile of MS. Bodley 34*, EETS O.S. 247 (1960[3]).

KER, N.R., 'Fragments of Jerome's Commentary on St Matthew', *Medievalia et Humanistica* 14 (1962), 7-14; rpt. Watson 1985: 113-20.

KER, N.R., [facs.], *The Owl and the Nightingale. Reproduced in facsimile from the surviving manuscripts Jesus College Oxford 29 and British Museum Cotton Caligula A. ix*, EETS O.S. 251 (1963 for 1962).

KER, N.R., [facs.], *Facsimile of British Museum MS. Harley 2253*, EETS O.S. 255 (London, New York, Toronto, 1965).

KER, N.R., 'Cathedral Libraries', *Library History* 1 (1967), 38-45; rpt. Watson 1985: 293-300.

KER, N.R., 'The Handwriting of Archbishop Wulfstan', in *England before the Conquest: Studies in Primary Sources Presented to Dorothy Whitelock*, ed. Peter Clemoes and Kathleen Hughes (Cambridge, 1971): 315-31; rpt. Watson 1985: 9-26.

KER, N.R., [facs.], *The Winchester Malory*, EETS S.S. 4 (1976).

KERBY-FULTON, KATHRYN AND STEVEN JUSTICE, 'Scribe D and the Marketing of Ricardian Literature', in *The Medieval Professional Reader at Work: Evidence from Manuscripts of Chaucer, Langland, Kempe, and Gower*, ed. Kathryn Kerby-Fulton and Maidie Hilmo (Victoria, 2001): 217-237.

KERLING, JOHAN, 'Scholar, Antiquary, Factotum: Franciscus Junius Revisited', in *Current Research in Dutch and Belgian Universities on Old English, Middle English and Historical Linguistics: Five Papers Read at the Sixth Philological Symposium Held at Utrecht on 3rd November 1984*, ed. Frans Diekstra (Nijmegen: Katholieke Universiteit Nijmegen, 1984): 33-43.

KILPIÖ, MATTI AND LEENA KAHLAS-TARKKA, eds, *Ex Insula Lux. Manuscripts and hagiographical material connected with medieval England* (Helsinki, 2001): 93-98.

KING, JOHN N., 'The book-trade under Edward VI and Mary I', in Hellinga and Trapp 1999: 164-78.

KIRBY, IAN J., *Bible Translation in Old Norse* (Geneva, 1986).

KISSELEVA, LUDMILA, OLGA BLESKINA AND MARGARITA LOGUTOVA, 'Descriptions of the manuscripts from the National Library of Russia', in Kilpiö and Kahlas-Tarkka 2001: pp. 25-82.

KNIGHT, STAN, *Historical Scripts. A handbook for calligraphers* (London, 1984).

KNIGHT, STAN, *Historical Scripts. From Classical Times to the Renaissance* (Delaware, 1998).

KOTZOR, G., ed., *Das altenglische Martyrologium*, Bayerische Akad. der Wiss., Phil-Hist. Klasse, Abhandl. NF Heft 88/1.2 (Munich, 1981).

KRAPP, G.P., ed., *The Junius Manuscript*, The Anglo-Saxon Poetic Records 1 (New York and London, 1931).

KRAPP, G.P. AND E.V.K. DOBBIE, eds, *The Exeter Book*, The Anglo-Saxon Poetic Records 3 (New York and London, 1936).

KRATZMANN, GREGORY AND JAMES SIMPSON, eds, *Medieval English Religious and Ethical Literature. Essays in Honour of G.H. Russell* (Cambridge, 1986).

KRISHNA, VALERIE, ed., *The Alliterative Morte Arthure. A Critical Edition* (New York, 1976).

KROCHALIS, JEANNE E., 'Hoccleve's Chaucer Portrait', *The Chaucer Review* 21 (1986), 234-45.

KROCHALIS, JEANNE E., 'The Books and Reading of Henry V and his Circle', *The Chaucer Review* 23 (1988-89), 50-77.

KROCHALIS, JEANNE E., 'Postscript: the *Equatorie of the Planetis* as a translator's manuscript', *The Chaucer Review* 26 (1991), 43-47.

KUBOUCHI, TADAO, 'A Note on Prose Rhythm in Wulfstan's *De Falsis Dies*', *Poetica* 15-16 (1983), 57-106; rpt. Kubouchi 1995: no. 3.

KUBOUCHI, TADAO, *From Wulfstan to Richard Rolle. Select Papers on Old and Middle English* ([Tokyo], 1995).

KUBOUCHI, TADAO AND KEIKO IKEGAMI, eds, *The* Ancrene Wisse. *A Four-Manuscript Parallel Text. Preface and Parts 1-4* (Frankfurt am Main, 2003).

KUHN, SHERMAN M., *The Vespasian Psalter* (Ann Arbor, 1965).

KUHN, SHERMAN M., 'Some Early Mercian Manuscripts', *Review of English Studies* N.S. 8 (1957), 355-70.

KUYPERS, A.B., *The Prayer Book of Aedeluald the Bishop, Commonly Called the Book of Cerne* (Cambridge, 1902).

LAING, MARGARET, ed., *Middle English Dialectology: essays on some principles and problems by Angus McIntosh, M.L. Samuels and Margaret Laing* (Aberdeen, 1989).

LAING, MARGARET, 'Anchor Texts and literary manuscripts in early Middle English', in Riddy 1991: 27-49.

LAING, Margaret, *Catalogue of Sources for a Linguistic Atlas of Early Medieval England* (Cambridge, 1993).

LAING, MARGARET AND ANGUS MCINTOSH, 'The Language of *Ancrene Riwle*, the Katharine Group Texts and *Þe Wohunge of ure Lauerd* in BL Cotton Titus D xviii', *Neuphilologische Mitteilungen* 96 (1995), 235-63.

LAPIDGE, MICHAEL, 'Surviving booklists from Anglo-Saxon England', in *Learning and Literature in Anglo-Saxon England. Studies presented to Peter Clemoes*, ed. Michael Lapidge and Helmut Gneuss (Cambridge, 1985): 33-89.

LAPIDGE, MICHAEL AND MICHAEL WINTERBOTTOM, eds, *Wulfstan of Winchester. The Life of St Æthelwold* (Oxford, 1991).

LASS, ROGER, ed., *Approaches to English Historical Linguistics. An Anthology* (New York, Chicago, etc., 1969).

LEE, JENNIFER A., 'The Illuminating Critic: the illustrator of Cotton Nero A.X', *Studies in Iconography* 3 (1977), 17-46.

LEE, STUART, 'Oxford, Bodleian Library, MS Laud Misc. 381: William L'Isle, Ælfric, and the *Ancrene Wisse*', in Graham 2000: 207-42.

LEEDHAM-GREEN, ELISABETH, *English Handwriting 1500-1700: An Online Course*, www.english.cam.ac.uk/ceres/ehoc/intro.html

LEWIS, C.T. AND C. SHORT, *A Latin Dictionary* (Oxford, 1922; rpt. 1966).

LINDSAY, W.M., *Notae latinae* (Cambridge, 1915).

LE SAUX, FRANÇOISE, ed., *The Text and Tradition of Laȝamon's* Brut (Cambridge, 1994).

LIEFTINCK, M.G.I., 'Pour une Nomenclature de l'Écriture livresque de la Période dite Gothique. Essai s'appliquant spécialement aux manuscrits originaires des Pays-Bas médiévaux', in Bischoff, Lieftinck, and Battelli 1954: 15-34.

LIEFTINCK, G. I., *Manuscrits datés conservés dan les Pays-bas*, 2 vols (Amsterdam, 1964).

LIUZZA, R.M., ed., *The Old English Version of the Gospels*, 2 vols, EETS O.S. 304, 314 (1994, 2000).
LIUZZA, ROY MICHAEL, 'Who Read the Gospels in Old English?', in Baker and Howe 1998: 3-24.
LIUZZA, ROY MICHAEL, 'Scribal habit: the evidence of the Old English Gospels', in Swan and Treharne 2000: 143-65.
LIUZZA, ROY M. AND A.N. DOANE, [facs.], *Anglo-Saxon Gospels*, Anglo-Saxon Manuscripts in Microfiche Facsimile 3 (Binghamton, New York: 1995).
LLOYD, L.J., *The Library of Exeter Cathedral* (Exeter, 1967).
LOCKETT, LESLIE, 'An integrated re-examination of the dating of Oxford, Bodleian Library, Junius 11', *Anglo-Saxon England* 31 (2002), 141-73.
LOGUTOVA, MARGARITA, 'Insular codices from Dubrovsky's collection in the National Library of Russia', in Kilpiö and Kahlas-Tarkka 2001: 93-98.
LOWE, E.A., *Codices Latini Antiquiores* (11 vols and Supplement, Oxford, 1934-72).
LOWE, E.A., 'A Key to Bede's Scriptorium: Some Observations on the Leningrad Manuscript of the *Historia ecclesiastica gentis Anglorum*', *Scriptorium* 12 (1958), 182-90. 6pls.; rpt. in Ludwig Bieler, ed., *E.A. Lowe. Palaeographical Papers 1907-1965*, 2 vols (Oxford, 1972): II. 441-49.
LOWE, E.A., *English Uncial* (Oxford, 1969).
LOWE, KATHRYN A., 'Lay Literacy in Anglo-Saxon England and the Development of the Chirograph', in Pulsiano and Treharne 1998: 161-204.
LOYN, H.R., [facs.], *A Wulfstan Manuscript, containing Institutes, Laws, Homilies*, EEMF 17 (Copenhagen, 1971).
LUCAS, PETER J., 'Sir Robert Kemp and the Holograph Manuscript containing Capgrave's *Life of St. Gilbert* and *Tretis*', *British Museum Quarterly* 36 (1972), 80-83.
LUCAS, PETER J., 'Consistency and Correctness in the Orthographic Usage of John Capgrave's *Chronicle*', *Studia Neophilologica* 45 (1973), 323-55.
LUCAS, PETER, 'MS Junius 11 and Malmesbury', *Scriptorium* 34 (1980), 197-220; ~ 35 (1981), 3-22.
LUCAS, PETER J., 'The Growth and Development of English Literary Patronage in the Later Middle Ages and Early Renaissance', *The Library* 4 (1982), 219-48.
LUCAS, PETER J., 'An author as copyist of his own work. John Capgrave OSA (1393-64)', in Beadle and Piper 1995: 227-46.
LUCAS, PETER J., *From Author to Audience. John Capgrave and Medieval Publication* (Dublin, 1997).
LUTZ, ANGELIKA, 'Das Studium der angelsächsichen Chronik im 16. Jahrhundert: Nowell und Joscelyn', *Anglia* 100 (1982), 301-56.
LUTZ, ANGELIKA, 'The Study of the Anglo-Saxon Chronicle in the Seventeenth Century and the Establishment of Old English Studies in the Universities', in Graham 2000: 1-82.
LYALL, R.J., 'Materials: the paper revolution', in Griffiths and Pearsall 1989: 11-29.
LYALL, R.J., 'Books and book owners in fifteenth-century Scotland', in Griffiths and Pearsall 1989: 239-56.
MACALISTER, R.A.S., 'The Colophon in the Lindisfarne Gospels', in E.C. Quiggin, ed., *Essays and Studies Presented to William Ridgeway* (Cambridge, 1913): 299-305.
MCCARREN, VINCENT AND DOUGLAS MOFFAT, eds, *A Guide to Editing Middle English* (Ann Arbor, 1998).
MCCARREN, VINCENT AND DOUGLAS MOFFAT, 'A Practical Guide to Working with Middle English Manuscripts', in McCarren and Moffat 1998: 305-18.
MACCRACKEN, H.N., ed., *The Minor Poems of John Lydgate*, vol. 2, EETS O.S. 192 (1934).
MCDIARMID, MATTHEW P. AND J.A.C. STEVENSON, eds, *Barbour's Bruce*, 3 vols (Edinburgh, 1980-85).
MCGOVERN, D.S., 'Unnoticed punctuation in the Exeter Book', *Medium Ævum* 52 (1983), 90-99.
MCINTOSH, ANGUS, 'The relative pronouns *þe* and *þat* in early Middle English', *English and Germanic Studies* 1 (1947-48), 73-87.
MCINTOSH, ANGUS, 'The textual transmission of the alliterative *Morte Arthure*', in Davis and Wrenn 1962: 231-40.
MCINTOSH, ANGUS, 'A New Approach to Middle English Dialectology', *English Studies* 44 (1963), 1-11; rpt. Lass 1969: 302-403.
MCINTOSH, ANGUS, 'The Language of the Extant Versions of *Havelok the Dane*', *Medium Ævum* 45 (1976) 36-49.
MCINTOSH, A., M.L. SAMUELS, AND M. BENSKIN, with the assistance of Margaret Laing and Keith Williamson, *A Linguistic Atlas of Late Mediaeval English,* 4 vols (Aberdeen, 1986).
MACKENZIE, W. MACKAY, ed., *The Kingis Quair* (London, 1939).
MCKITTERICK, D.J., *The Library of Sir Thomas Knyvett of Ashwellthorpe c. 1539-1618* (Cambridge, 1978).
MCKITTERICK, ROSAMOND, 'Anglo-Saxon Missionaries in Germany; reflections on the manuscript evidence', *Transactions of the Cambridge Bibliographical Society* 9 (1986-90: 1989), 291-329.
MCLACHLAN, ELIZABETH PARKER, *The Scriptorium of Bury St. Edmunds in the Twelfth Century* (New York and London, 1986).
MACHAN, TIM WILLIAM, 'Textual Authority and the works of Hoccleve, Lydgate, and Henryson', *Viator* 23 (1992), 281-99.
MACK, FRANCES M., ed., *The English Text of the Ancrene Riwle, B.M. Cotton MS. Titus D.* XVIII, *and Lanhydrock Fragment*, ed. A. Zettersten, EETS O.S. 252 (1963).
MADAN, F. *et al.*, *Summary Catalogue of Western Manuscripts in the Bodleian Library at Oxford*, 7 vols in 8 (Oxford, 1895-1953).
MADDEN, SIR FREDERIC, *Laȝamons Brut, or Chronicle of Britain*, 3 vols (London, 1847; rpt. Osnabrück, 1967).
MANLY, JOHN M. AND EDITH RICKERT, *The Text of the Canterbury Tales*, 8 vols (Chicago, 1940).

MARSDEN, RICHARD, 'Translation by Committee? The "Anonymous" Text of the Old Testament Hexateuch', in Barnhouse and Withers 2000: 41-89.

MARTIN, C.T., *The Record Interpreter: A Collection of Abbreviations, Latin Words, and Names used in English Historical Manuscripts and Records*, 2nd edition (London, 1910).

MARTIN, HENRI-JEAN AND JEAN VEZIN, eds, *Mise en page et mise en texte du livre manuscrit* ([Paris], 1990).

MATHESON, LISTER M., review of Fisher, Richardson, and Fisher 1984, *Speculum* 61 (1986), 646-50.

MATSUDA, TAKAMI, RICHARD A. LINENTHAL AND JOHN SCAHILL, eds, *The Medieval Book and a Modern Collector. Essays in Honour of Toshiyuki Takamiya* (Cambridge and Tokyo, 2004).

MATTHES, H.C., *Die Einheitlichkeit des Orrmulum: Studien zur Textkritik, zu den Quellen und zur sprachlichen Form von Orrmins Evangelienbuch* (Heidelberg, 1933).

MATTHES, H.C., 'Die Orrmulum Korrekturen', *Journal of English and Germanic Philology* 50 (1951), 183-199.

MAXWELL, MARCIA L., 'The Anglo-Norman prose "Brut": a list of extant manuscripts and their locations', *Analytical & Enumerative Bibliography* N.S. 7. 1 (1993), 15-17.

MEALE, CAROL, 'Manuscripts, Readers and Patrons in Fifteenth-century England: Sir Thomas Malory and Arthurian Romance', in *Arthurian Literature IV*, ed. Richard Barber (Woodbridge, 1985): 93-126.

MEREDITH, PETER, 'Stage Directions and the Editing of Early English Drama', in *Editing Early English Drama: special problems and new directions*, ed. A.F. Johnston (New York, 1987): 65-94.

MEYVAERT, PAUL, '"Unusual letters": Jerome's meaning of the term', *The Journal of Theological Studies* 34 (1983), 185-88.

MILFULL, INGE B., *The Hymns of the Anglo-Saxon Church*, Cambridge Studies in Anglo-Saxon England 17 (Cambridge, 1996).

MILLER, THOMAS, ed., *The Old English Version of Bede's Ecclesiastical History of the English People*, EETS O.S. 95, 96, 110, 111 (1890-91, 1898).

MILLETT, BELLA with the assistance of George B. Jack and Yoko Wada, *'Ancrene Wisse', The Katherine Group, and the Wooing Group*, Annotated Bibliographies of Old and Middle English Literature II (Cambridge, 1996).

MINNIS, ALASTAIR, '*The Cloud of Unknowing* and Walter Hilton's *Scale of Perfection*', in Edwards 1984: 61-81.

MINNIS, A.J., ed., *Latin and Vernacular. Studies in Late-Medieval Texts and Manuscripts* (Cambridge, 1989).

MIRRLEES, HOPE, *A Fly in Amber being an extravagant biography of the romantic antiquary Sir Robert Bruce Cotton* (London, 1962).

MITCHELL, JEROME, *Thomas Hoccleve. A Study in Early Fifteenth-Century Poetic* (Urbana, 1968).

MOONEY, L.R., 'More Manuscripts written by a Chaucer Scribe', *The Chaucer Review* 30 (1996), 401-07.

MOONEY, LINNE R., 'Chaucer's Scribe', forthcoming in *Speculum*.

MORRISH, JENNIFER, 'Dated and Datable Manuscripts copied in England during the ninth century: A Preliminary List', *Mediaeval Studies* 50 (1988), 512-38.

MORRISON, STEPHEN, 'Continuité et innovation littéraire en Angleterre au XIIe siècle: la prédication de la *militia Christi*', *Cahiers de Civilisation Médiévale* 44 (2001), 139-157.

MORSBACH, L., ed., *Mittelenglische Originalurkunden der Chaucer-Zeit bus zur Mitte des XV. Jahrhunderts, in der grossen Mehrzahl zum Erstenmal veröffentlich von L.M.*, Alt.- u. Mitteleng. Texte 10 (Heidelberg, 1923).

MUIR, BERNARD. J., 'A Preliminary Report on a New Edition of the Exeter Book', *Scriptorium* 43 (1989), 273-88.

MUIR, BERNARD. J., 'Watching the Exeter Book Scribe Copy Old English and Latin Texts', *Manuscripta* 35 (1991), 3-22.

MUIR, B.J., ed., *The Exeter Anthology of Old English Poetry: an Edition of Exeter Dean and Chapter MS 3501*, 2 vols (Exeter, 1994), 2nd edn 2000.

MUIR, BERNARD, [facs.], *A digital facsimile of Oxford, Bodleian Library, MS. Junius 11* (Oxford, 2004).

MUIR, BERNARD, [facs.], *The Exeter Anthology of Old English Poetry* [Exeter, 2005].

MULLALLY, EVELYN AND JOHN THOMPSON, eds, *The Court and Cultural Diversity. Selected Papers from the Eighth Triennial Congress of the International Courtly Literature Society* (Cambridge, 1997).

MUNRO, J.J., ed., *John Capgrave's Lives of St. Augustine and St. Gilbert of Sempringham, And a Sermon*, EETS O.S. 140 (1910).

NEEDHAM, G.I., 'Additions and alterations in Cotton MS. Julius E VII', *Review of English Studies* N.S. 9 (1958), 160-64.

NEEDHAM, G.I., ed., *Lives of Three English Saints* (London, 1966; revised 1976).

NEES, LAWRENCE, 'Reading Aldred's Colophon for the Lindisfarne Gospels', *Speculum* 78 (2003), 333-77.

NICHOLS, STEPHEN G. AND SIEGFRIED WENZEL, eds, *The Whole Book. Cultural Perspectives on the Medieval Miscellany* (Ann Arbor, 1996).

NORTH, J.D., *Chaucer's Universe* (Oxford, 1988).

NORTON-SMITH, JOHN, [facs.], *Bodleian Library MS Fairfax 16* (London, 1979).

OAKESHOTT, WALTER F., 'The Text of Malory', *The Times Literary Supplement*, 27 Sept. (1934).

OAKESHOTT, WALTER F., 'Caxton and Malory's Morte Darthur', *Gutenberg Jahrbuch* (1935), 112-16.

OAKESHOTT, WALTER F., 'The Finding of the Manuscript', in *Essays on Malory*, ed. J.A.W. Bennett (Oxford, 1963): 1-6.

OAKESHOTT, WALTER F., 'The matter of Malory', *The Times Literary Supplement*, 18 Feb. (1977), 193.

O'BRIEN O'KEEFFE, KATHERINE, 'Graphic Clues for Presentation of Verse in the Earliest English Manuscripts of the *Historia ecclesiastica*', *Manuscripta* 31 (1987), 139-46.

O'Brien O'Keeffe, Katherine, *Visible Song: Transitional Literacy in Old English Verse*, Cambridge Studies in Anglo-Saxon England 4 (Cambridge, 1990).

O'Brien O'Keeffe, Katherine, [facs.], *Manuscripts containing the Anglo-Saxon Chronicle, works by Bede, and other texts*, Anglo-Saxon Manuscripts in Facsimile 10 (Tempe, Az., 2003).

Okasha, Elisabeth, 'The Leningrad Bede', *Scriptorium* 22 (1968), 35-37 and pl. 1.

O'Rourke, Jason, 'British Library MS. Royal 12 C. xii and the Problems of Patronage', *Journal of the Early Book Society* 3 (2000), 216-26.

O'Sullivan, O., 'The Palaeographical Background to the Book of Kells', in *The Book of Kells. Proceedings of a Conference at Trinity College Dublin 6-9 September 1992*, ed. F. O'Mahony (Aldershot: 1994):175-82.

Owen, A.E.B., 'The Collation and Descent of the Thornton Manuscript', *Transactions of the Cambridge Bibliographical Society* 6 (1975), 218-25.

Page, R.I., *An Introduction to English Runes* (London, 1973).

Page, R.I., *Matthew Parker and his Books*, Sandars Lectures in Bibliography Delivered on 14, 16, and 18 May 1990 at the University of Cambridge (Kalamazoo, Michigan: 1993).

Palma, Marco, 'Modifiche di alcuni aspetti materiali della produzione libraria latina nei secoli xii e xiii', *Scrittura e civiltà* 12 (1988), 119-33.

Parkes, M.B., *English Cursive Bookhands, 1250-1500* (Oxford, 1969; rpt., with minor revisions, London, 1979).

Parkes, M.B., 'The Literacy of the Laity', in *Literature and Western Civilization: The Medieval World*, ed. D. Daiches and A.K. Thorlby (London, 1973): 555-76; rpt. Parkes 1991: 275-97.

Parkes, M.B., 'The palaeography of the Parker manuscript of the Chronicle, laws and Sedulius, and historiography at Winchester in the late ninth and tenth centuries', *Anglo-Saxon England* 5 (1976), 149-71; rpt. Parkes 1991: 143-69.

Parkes, M.B., 'On the Presumed Date and Possible Origin of the Manuscript of the "Ormulum": Oxford, Bodleian Library, MS. Junius 1', in *Five Hundred Years of Words and Sounds: A Festschrift for Eric Dobson*, ed. E.G. Stanley and D. Gray (Cambridge, 1983): 115-27; rpt. 1991[1]: 187-200.

Parkes, M.B., 'The Scriptorium of Wearmouth-Jarrow', Jarrow Lecture (Jarrow, 1982); rpt. Parkes 1991[1]: 93-120.

Parkes, M.B., *Scribes, Scripts and Readers* (London and Rio Grande, 1991[2]).

Parkes, M.B., *Pause and Effect: an Introduction to the History of Punctuation in the West* (Aldershot, 1992).

Parkes, M.B., 'The Planning and Construction of the Ellesmere Manuscript', in Stevens and Woodward 1995: 41-47.

Parkes, M.B., 'Stephen Batman's Manuscripts', in Kanno *et al.* 1997: 125-56.

Parkes, M.B., 'Richard Frampton: A Commercial Scribe *c.* 1390 - *c.* 1420', in Matsuda, Linenthal and Scahill 2004: 113-24.

Parkes, M.B and Elizabeth Salter, [facs.], *Troilus and Criseyde: Geoffrey Chaucer: A Facsimile of Corpus Christi College Cambridge MS 61* (Cambridge, 1978).

Parkes, M.B. and Andrew G. Watson, eds., *Medieval Scribes, Manuscripts & Libraries. Essays presented to N.R. Ker* (London, 1978).

Parsons, David, 'Anglo-Saxon Runes in Continental Manuscripts', in *Runische Schriftkultur in kontinental-skandinavischer und -angelsächsischer Wechselbeziehung*, ed. Klaus Düwel (Berlin, New York: Walter de Gruyter, 1994): 195-20.

Parsons, David N., *Recasting the Runes. The Reform of the Anglo-Saxon Futhorc*, Runrön 14 (Uppsala, 1999).

Partridge, Stephen, 'The Vocabulary of *The Equatorie of the Planetis*', *English Manuscripts Studies 1100-1700* 3 (1992), 29-37.

Pearsall, Derek, 'The *Troilus* Frontispiece and Chaucer's Audience', *The Yearbook of English Studies* 7 (1977), 68-74.

Pearsall, Derek, ed., *Manuscripts and Readers in Fifteenth-Century England: The Literary Implications of Manuscript Study* (Cambridge, 1983).

Pearsall, Derek, 'Gower's Latin in the *Confessio Amantis*', in Minnis 1989: 13-25.

Pearsall, Derek, 'Hoccleve's *Regiment of Princes*: The Poetics of Royal Self-Representation', *Speculum* 69 (1994), 386-400.

Pearsall, Derek, 'The Manuscripts and Illustrations of Gower's Works', in *A Companion to Gower*, ed. Siân Echard (Cambridge, [2004[1]], 73-97.

Pearsall, Derek, 'The Organisation of the Latin Apparatus in Gower's *Confessio Amantis*: The Scribes and their Problems', in Matsuda, Linenthal and Scahill [2004[2]]: 99-112.

Petti, Anthony G., *English literary hands from Chaucer to Dryden* (London, 1977).

Pickwoad, Nicholas, 'The use of Fragments of Medieval Manuscripts in the Construction and Covering of Bindings on Printed Books', in *Interpreting and Collecting Fragments of Medieval Books*, ed. Linda L. Brownrigg and Margaret M. Smith (Los Altos Hills, CA 94022, 2000): 1-20.

Plummer, C., ed., *Two of the Saxon Chronicles parallel*, 2 vols (1892-99; rpt. with additions by D. Whitelock 1952).

Pope, John C., 'Palaeography and poetry: some solved and unsolved problems of the Exeter Book', in Parkes and Watson 1978: 25-65.

Prescott, Andrew, *English Historical Documents* (London, 1988).

Prescott, Andrew, '"Their Present Miserable State of Cremation": The Restoration of the Cotton Library', in Wright 1997: 391-452.

P[revité-]O[rton], C. W., 'The Southampton MSS.', *The Eagle* (June, 1918), 207-13.

PRICE, DEREK J., [facs.], *The Equatorie of the Planetis*, with a linguistic analysis by R.M. Wilson (Cambridge, 1955).
PULSIANO, PHILLIP, [facs.], *Psalters I*, Anglo-Saxon Manuscripts in Microfiche Facsimile 2 (Binghamton, New York, 1994).
PULSIANO, PHILLIP, 'The originality of the Old English gloss of the *Vespasian Psalter* and its relation to the gloss of the *Junius Psalter*', *Anglo-Saxon England* 25 (1996[1]), 37-68.
PULSIANO, PHILLIP, [facs.], *Glossed Texts, Aldhelmiana, Psalms*, Anglo-Saxon Manuscripts in Microfiche Facsimile 4 (Binghamton, New York, 1996[2]).
PULSIANO, PHILLIP, 'William L'Isle and the Editing of Old English', in Graham 2000: 173-206.
PULSIANO, PHILLIP AND ELAINE M. TREHARNE, eds, *Anglo-Saxon Manuscripts and their Heritage* (Aldershot, Brookfield USA, Singapore, Sydney, 1998).
RADEMAKER, C.S.M., 'Young Franciscus Junius: 1591-1621', in Bremmer 1998: 1-17.
RAMSEY, R.V., 'The Hengwrt and Ellesmere Manuscripts of the *Canterbury Tales*: Different Scribes', *Studies in Bibligraphy* 35 (1982), 133-54.
RAND SCHMIDT, KARI ANNE, *The Authorship of The Equatorie of the Planetis* [includes reduced facs.] (Cambridge, 1933).
RAW, BARBARA, 'The Probable Derivation of Most of the Illustrations in Junius 11 from an Illustrated Old Saxon *Genesis*', *Anglo-Saxon England* 5 (1976), 133-48.
RAW, BARBARA, 'The Construction of Oxford, Bodleian Library, Junius 11', *Anglo-Saxon England* 13 (1984), 187-207; rpt. Richards 2001: 251-75.
RAW, BARBARA, 'Alfredian Piety: the Book of Nunnaminster', in *Alfred the Wise. Studies in honour of Janet Bately on the occasion of her sixty-fifth birthday*, ed. Jane Roberts and Janet L. Nelson with Malcolm Godden (Cambridge, 1997): 145-53.
REVARD, CARTER, 'Scribe and Provenance', in Fein 2000: 21-109.
RICHARDS, MARY P., 'On the Date and Provenance of MS Cotton Vespasian D. xiv, ff. 4-169', *Manuscripta* 17 (1972), 31-35.
RICHARDS, MARY P., 'Innovations in AElfrician Homiletic Manuscripts at Rochester', *Annuale Mediaevale* 19 (1979), 13-26.
RICHARDS, MARY P., ed., *Anglo-Saxon Manuscripts. Basic Readings* (New York and London, 2001).
RICHARDSON, MALCOLM, 'Henry V, the English Chancery, and Chancery English', *Speculum* 55 (1980), 726-50.
RIDDY, FELICITY, ed., *Regionalism in late Medieval Manuscripts. Essays celebrating the publication of* A Linguistic Atlas of Late Medieval English (Cambridge, 1991).
RIDDY, FELICITY, ed., *Prestige, Authority and Power in Late-Medieval Manuscripts and Texts* (Woodbridge, 2000).
ROBERTS, JANE, ed., *The Guthlac Poems of the Exeter Book* (Oxford, 1979).
ROBERTS, JANE , 'A Preliminary Note on British Library, Cotton MS Caligula A. ix', in Le Saux 1994: 1-14.
ROBERTS, JANE, 'The English Saints Remembered in Old English Anonymous Homilies', in *Old English Prose Basic Readings*, ed. Paul E. Szarmach (New York and London, 2000).
ROBERTS, JANE, review of Swan and Treharne 2000, in *Notes and Queries* 247 (2002), 267-68.
ROBERTS, JANE, 'Aldred signs off', forthcoming in *Writing and Texts in Anglo-Saxon England*, ed. A.R. Rumble.
ROBERTS, JANE, 'A Lancashire lease', in *Medieval Relationships* (forthcoming).
ROBERTS, JULIAN AND ANDREW G. WATSON, *John Dee's Library Catalogue* (London, 1990).
ROBERTSON, A.J., ed., *Anglo-Charters*, 2nd edition (Cambridge, [1939] 1956).
ROBBINS, R.H., ed., *Secular Lyrics of the XIVth and XVth Centuries* (Oxford, 1952; 2nd edition 1955).
ROBINSON, FRED C., 'Syntactical Glosses in Latin Manuscripts of Anglo-Saxon Provenance', *Speculum* 48 (1973), 443-75.
ROBINSON, FRED C., 'Latin for Old English in Anglo-Saxon Manuscripts', in *Language Form and Linguistic Variation: papers dedicated to Angus McIntosh*, ed. John Anderson (Amsterdam, 1982): 395-400; rpt. in Robinson 1994: 160-63.
ROBINSON, FRED C., *The Editing of Old English* (Oxford UK and Cambridge USA, 1994).
ROBINSON, FRED C. AND E.G. STANLEY, [facs.], *Old English verse texts from many sources: a comprehensive collection*, EEMF 23 (Copenhagen, 1991).
ROBINSON, P.R., 'Self-contained Units in Composite Manuscripts of the Anglo-Saxon Period', *Anglo-Saxon England* 7 (1978), 231-8; rpt. in Richards 1994: 25-35.
ROBINSON, P.R., 'The "Booklet": A Self-Contained Unit in Composite Manuscripts', *Codicologica* 3 (1980), 46-69.
ROBINSON, P.R., *Catalogue of Dated and Datable Manuscripts c.737-1600 in Cambridge Libraries*, 2 vols (Cambridge, 1988).
ROBINSON, PAMELA, 'Geoffrey Chaucer and the *Equatorie of the Planetis*: the state of the problem', *The Chaucer Review* 26 (1991), 17-29.
ROBINSON, P.R., 'The Format of Books: Books, Booklets, Rolls in London Libraries', in *Cambridge History of the Book in Britain, II, 1160-1400*, ed. R.M. Thomson and Nigel Morgan (forthcoming).
ROBINSON, P.R., *Catalogue of Dated and Datable Manuscripts c. 888-1600 in London Libraries*, 2 vols (London, 2003).
ROBINSON, P.R. AND RIVKAH ZIM, eds, *Of the Making of Books. Medieval Manuscripts, their Scribes and Readers. Essays presented to M.B. Parkes* (Aldershot, 1997).
ROGERS, DAVID, 'Francis Douce's manuscripts. Some hitherto unrecognized provenances', in *Studies in the Book Trade in honour of Graham Pollard*, ed. R.W. Hunt, I.G. Philip, R.J. Roberts (Oxford, 1975): 315-340.
ROSTENBERG, LEONA, *Literary, Political, Scientific, Religious & Legal Publishing, Printing & Bookselling in England, 1551-1700: Twelve Studies*, 2 vols (New York, 1965).

RUGGIERS, PAUL G., ed., *Editing Chaucer. The Great Tradition* (Norman, Oklahoma, 1984).

RUMBLE, ALEXANDER R., 'Palaeography and the Editing of Old English Texts', in Scragg and Szarmach 1994: 39-43.

SAMUELS, M.L., 'Some Applications of Middle English Dialectology', *English Studies* 44 (1963), 81-94; rpt. Lass 1969: 404-18.

SAMUELS, M.L., 'Spelling and dialect in the late and post-middle English periods', in Benskin and Samuels, 1981: 43-54.

SAMUELS, M.L., 'Chaucer's Spelling', in *Middle English Studies presented to Norman Davis*, ed. D. Gray and E.G. Stanley (Oxford, 1983[1]): 17-37; rpt. Smith 1988: 23-37.

SAMUELS, M.L., 'The Scribe of the Hengwrt and Ellesmere Manuscripts of *The Canterbury Tales*', *Studies in the Age of Chaucer* 5 (1983[2]): 49-65; rpt. Smith 1988: 38-50.

SAMUELS, M.L., 'The Dialect of the Scribe of the Harley Lyrics', *Poetica* 19 (1984), 39-47; rpt. Laing 1989: 256-63.

SARGENT, MICHAEL G., 'The Transmission by the English Carthusians of some Late Medieval Spiritual Writings', *The Journal of Ecclesiastical History* 27 (1976), 225-40.

SARGENT, MICHAEL G., ed., *De Cella in Seculum: Religious and Secular Life and Devotion in Late Medieval England* (Woodbridge, 1989).

SATO, SHUJI, *Back to the Manuscripts.* Papers from the Symposium 'The Integrated Approach to Manuscript Studies: A New Horizon' held at the Eighth General Meeting of the Japan Society for Medieval English Studies, Tokyo, December 1992. Occasional Papers 1 (Tokyo, 1997).

SATO, SHUJI, 'Back to the Manuscripts: Some Problems in the Physical Descriptions of the *Parker Chronicle*', in Sato 1997: 69-104.

SAWYER, P.H., *Anglo-Saxon Charters. An Annotated List and Bibliography* (London, 1968); www.trin.cam.ac.uk/sdk13/chartwww/eSawyer.99/eSawyer2.html

SCAHILL, JOHN, 'Early Middle English Orthographies: Archaism and Particularism', *Medieval English Studies Newsletter* 31 (1994), 12-22.

SCAHILL, JOHN, 'The Audiences of Medieval Chronicles and of Cotton Caligula A. ix', *The Geibun-Kenkyu* 80 (2001), 142-59.

SCAHILL, JOHN, 'Trilingualism in Early Middle English Miscellanies: Language and Literature', *The Yearbook of English Studies* (2003), 18-32.

SCASE, WENDY L., 'Reginald Pecock, John Carpenter and John Colop's "Common-profit" books: aspects of book ownership in fifteenth-century London', *Medium Ævum* 61 (1992), 261-74.

SCATTERGOOD, V.J. AND J.W. SHERBORNE, eds, *English Court Culture in the Later Middle Ages* (London, 1983).

SCHAPIRO, M., 'The decoration of the Leningrad manuscript of Bede', *Scriptorium* 12 (1958), 191-207.

SCRAGG, D.G., *A history of English spelling* (Manchester, 1974).

SCRAGG, D. G. AND PAUL E. SZARMACH, eds, *The Editing of Old English* (Cambridge, 1994).

SCHRÖER, ARNOLD, ed., *Die angelsächsischen Prosabearbeitungen der Benediktinerregel*, Bibliothek der angelsächsischen Prosa 2 (1885-88; 2nd edition with supplement by H. Gneuss, Darmstadt, 1964).

SCHULZ, H.C., 'Thomas Hoccleve, Scribe', *Speculum* 12 (1937), 71-81.

SCOTT, KATHLEEN L., 'Design, decoration and illustration', in Griffiths and Pearsall 1989: 31-64.

SCOTT, KATHLEEN L., 'An Hours and Psalter by Two Ellesmere Illuminators', in Stevens and Woodward 1995: 87-119.

SCOTT, KATHLEEN L., *Later Gothic Manuscripts 1390-1490. A Survey of Manuscripts Illuminated in the British Isles, volume VI*, 2 vols (London, 1996).

SCOTT, KATHLEEN L., 'Limner-Power: A Book Artist in England *c.* 1420', in Riddy 2000: 55-75.

SEYMOUR, M.C., 'The Manuscripts of Hoccleve's *Regiment of Princes*', *Edinburgh Bibliographical Society Transactions* 4 (1974 for 1955-71), 255-97.

SEYMOUR, M.C., *A Catalogue of Chaucer Manuscripts*, 2 vols (Aldershot, 1995-97).

SHORT, IAN, 'Language and Literature', in Harper-Bill and van Houts 2003: 191-213.

SIMPSON, GRANT G., *Scottish Handwriting 1150-1650. An introduction to the reading of documents* (Edinburgh, 1973; Aberdeen, 1977, 1983 and with corrections 1986).

SIMS-WILLIAMS, PATRICK, *Religion and Literature in Western England, 600-800*, Cambridge Studies in Anglo-Saxon England 3 (Cambridge, 1990).

SISAM, K., 'Anglo-Saxon Royal Genealogies', *Proceedings of the British Academy* 39 (1953[1]), 287-348; rpt. in Stanley 1990: 145-204.

SISAM, KENNETH, *Studies in the History of Old English Literature* (Oxford, 1953[2]).

SISAM, KENNETH, 'Canterbury, Lichfield, and the Vespasian Psalter', *Review of English Studies*, N.S. 7 (1956), 1-10, 113-31.

SKEAT, W.W., ed., *The Bruce; or, The Book of the most excellent and noble prince, Robert de Broyss, King of Scots: compiled by Master John Barbour, Archdeacon of Aberdeen, A.D. 1375*, EETS E.S. 11, 21, 29, 55 (1870-89).

SKEAT, WALTER W., ed., *The Holy Gospels in Anglo-Saxon, Northumbrian, and Old Mercian Versions* (Cambridge, 1871-87; rpt. Darmstadt, 1970).

SKEAT, WALTER W., ed., *The Bruce*, 2 vols, Scottish Text Society 31, 32 (Edinburgh, 1873, 1874; rpt.1894).

SKEAT, WALTER. W., ed., *Ælfric's Lives of Saints*, EETS O.S. 76, 82, 94 and 114 (1881-1900).

SKEAT, WALTER. W., *Twelve Facsimiles of Old English Manuscripts* (Oxford, 1892).

SMITH, J.J., ed., *The English of Chaucer and his contemporaries. Essays by M. L. Samuels and J. J. Smith* (Aberdeen, 1988).

SMITHERS, G.V., ed., *Havelok* (Oxford, 1987).

SOLOPOVA, ELIZABETH, 'The metre of the *Ormulum*', in *Studies in English Language and Literature. 'Doubt wisely': Papers in honour of E.G. Stanley*, ed. M.J. Toswell and E.M. Tyler (London, 1996), 423-39.

SOLOPOVA, ELIZABETH, 'The survival of Chaucer's punctuation in the early manuscripts of the *Canterbury Tales*', in *Middle English Poetry: Texts and Traditions: Essays in Honour of Derek Pearsall*, ed. Alastair Minnis (Woodbridge, Suffolk, 2001): 27-40.

STANLEY, E.G., ed., *The Owl and the Nightingale* (London 1960; re-issued Manchester, 1972; rpt. 1981).

STANLEY, E.G., 'Laȝamon's Antiquarian Sentiments', *Medium Ævum* 33 (1969), 23-37.

STANLEY, E.G., ed., *British Academy Papers on Anglo-Saxon England* (Oxford, 1990).

STANLEY, E.G., 'The Sources of Franciscus Junius's Learning as Revealed in the Junius Manuscripts in the Bodleian Library', in Bremmer 1998: 159-76.

STEINER, EMILY, *Documentary Culture and the Making of Medieval English Literature* (Cambridge, 2003).

STERN, KAREN, 'The London "Thornton" Miscellany', *Scriptorium* 30 (1976), 26-37, 201-18.

STEVENS, MARTIN AND DANIEL WOODWARD, eds, *The Ellesmere Chaucer. Essays in Interpretation* (San Marino, California, and Tokyo, 1995).

STRATFORD, JENNY (formerly Lewis), 'The manuscripts of John, Duke of Bedford, Library and Chapel', in *England in the Fifteenth Century: Proceedings of the 1986 Harlaxton Symposium*, ed. D. Williams (Woodbridge, 1993): 329-50.

STRATFORD, JENNY, *The Bedford Inventories. The worldly goods of John, Duke of Bedford, Regent to France (1389-1435)* (London, 1993).

STRONGMAN, SHEILA, 'John Parker's manuscripts; an edition of the lists in Lambeth Palace MS 737', *Transactions of the Cambridge Bibliographical Society* 7 (1977), 1-27.

STUBBS, E.V., [facs.], *The Hengwrt Chaucer Digital Facsimile* (Leicester, 2000).

SUTTON, ANNE F. AND LIVIA VISSER-FUCHS, 'Choosing a Book in late Fifteenth-century England and Burgundy', in Barron and Saul 1995: 61-98.

SWAN, MARY AND ELAINE M. TREHARNE, eds, *Rewriting Old English in the Twelfth Century*, Cambridge Studies in Anglo-Saxon England 30 (Cambridge, 2000).

SWANSON, R.N., 'A Small Library for Pastoral Care and Spiritual Instruction in Late Medieval England', *Journal of the Early Book Society* 5 (2002), 99-120.

SWEET, HENRY, ed., *King Alfred's West=Saxon Version of Gregory's Pastoral Care*, 2 vols, EETS O.S. 45, 50 (1871).

SWEET, HENRY, ed., *The oldest English texts*, EETS O.S. 83 (1885).

SWINBURN, L.M., ed., *The Lanterne of Liȝt*, EETS O.S. 151 (1917).

TAKAMIYA, TOSHIYUKI AND DEREK BREWER, eds, *Aspects of Malory*, Arthurian Studies 1 (Cambridge, 1981).

TAYLOR, ANDREW, 'The Myth of the Minstrel Manuscript', *Speculum* 66 (1991), 43-73.

TAYLOR, ANDREW, 'Authors, Scribes, Patrons and Books', in J. Wogan-Browne, N. Watson, A. Taylor, and R. Evans, eds., *The Idea of the Vernacular: An Anthology of Middle English Literary Theory, 1280-1520* (University Park, Pa, 1999): 353-65.

TEMPLE, ELŻBIETA, *Anglo-Saxon Manuscripts 900-1066* (London, 1976).

THOMAS, MARCEL AND FRANÇOIS AVRIL, [facs.], *The Hunting Book of Gaston Phébus* (London, 1998).

THOMPSON, JOHN J., 'Textual *lacunae* and the Importance of Manuscript Evidence', *Transactions of the Cambridge Bibliographical Society* 8 (1982), 270-75.

THOMPSON, JOHN J., 'The compiler in action: Robert Thornton and the "Thornton Romances" in Lincoln Cathedral MS 91', in Pearsall 1983: 113-24.

THOMPSON, JOHN J., *Robert Thornton and the London Manuscript* (Cambridge, 1987).

THOMPSON, JOHN J., 'After Chaucer: Resituating Middle English Poetry in the Late Medieval and Early Modern Periods', in Derek Pearsall, ed., *New Directions in Later Medieval Manuscript Studies: Essays from the 1998 Harvard Conference* (Woodbridge, 2000), 183-99.

THOMSON, R.M., 'The Library of Bury St Edmunds Abbey in the Eleventh and Twelfth Centuries', *Speculum* 47 (1972), 617-45.

THOMSON, RODNEY M., 'The Norman Conquest and English Libraries', in P.F. Ganz, ed., *The Role of the Book in Medieval Culture* (1986), II. 27-40; rpt. in R.M. Thomson, *England and the 12th-Century Renaissance* (Aldershot, Brookfield USA, Singapore, Sydney, 1998): no. XVIII.

THOMSON, R.M., *Catalogue of the Manuscripts of Lincoln Cathedral Library* (Cambridge, 1989).

THOMSON, RODNEY M., *A Descriptive Catalogue of the Medieval Manuscripts in Worcester Cathedral Library* with a contribution on the bindings by Michael Gullick (Cambridge, 2001).

TIEKEN-BOON VAN OSTADE, INGRID, *The Two Versions of Malory's* Morte Darthur. *Multiple Negation and the Editing of the Text*, Arthurian Studies 35 (Cambridge, 1995).

TIMMER, B.J., ed., *The Later Genesis* (Oxford, 1948).

TITE, C.G.C., [facs.], Thomas Smith, *Catalogue of the Manuscripts in the Cottonian Library 1696* (*Catalogus librorum manuscriptorum bibliothecae Cottoniae*), Reprinted from Sir Robert Harley's copy, annotated by Humfrey Wanley, together with documents relating to the fire of 1731 (Cambridge, 1984).

TITE, COLIN G.C., '"Lost, Stolen or Strayed": A Survey of Manuscripts Formerly in the British Library', *The British Library Journal* 18 (1992), 107-47; rpt. Wright (1997): 262-306.

TITE, COLIN G.C., *The Manuscript Library of Sir Robert Cotton*, The Panizzi Lectures 1993 (London, 1994).

TITE, COLIN G.C., *The Early Records of Sir Robert Cotton's Library. Formation, Cataloguing, Use* (London, 2003).
TORKAR, R., 'Zu den Vorlagen der ae. Handschrift Cotton Julius E vii', *Neuphilologische Mitteilungen* 72 (1971), 711-715.
TRAPP, J.B., 'Literacy, books and readers', in Hellinga and Trapp 1999: 31-43.
TREHARNE, ELAINE, 'The Dates and Origins of Three Twelfth-Century Old English Manuscripts', in Pulsiano and Treharne 1998: 227-53.
TREHARNE, ELAINE, 'The production and script of manuscripts containing English religious texts in the first half of the twelfth century', in Swan and Treharne 2000: 11-40.
TSCHANN, JUDITH AND M.B. PARKES, [facs.], *Facsimile of Oxford, Bodleian Library, MS Digby 86*, EETS S.S. 16 (1996).
TURVILLE-PETRE, JOAN, 'Studies in the *Ormulum* MS.' *Journal of English and Germanic Philology* 46 (1947), 1-27.
TYSON, D.B., 'An early French prose history of the kings of England', *Romania* 96 (1975), 1-26.
VAN DIJK, S.J.P., 'An Advertisement Sheet of an early fourteenth-century writing master at Oxford', *Scriptorium* 10 (1956), 47-68.
VAN HOUTS, ELISABETH, 'Historical Writing', in Harper-Bill and van Houts 2003: 103-21.
VAN ZUTPHEN, J.P.W.M., ed., *Richard Lavynham, O. Carm.: A Litil Tretys on the Seven Deadly Sins* (Rome, 1956).
VINAVER, EUGÈNE, ed., *The Works of Sir Thomas Malory*, 3 vols (Oxford, 1947; 2nd edition 1967; 3rd edition 1990 with notes pp. 1747-68 by P.J.C. Field).
VLEESKRUYER, R., ed., *The Life of St. Chad: An Old English Homily* (Amsterdam, 1953).
VOIGTS, LINDA EHRSAM, 'A New Look at a Manuscript containing the Old English Translation of the *Herbarium Apulei*', *Manuscripta* 20 (1976), 40-56.
WADA, YOKO, ed., *A Companion to* Ancrene Wisse (Cambridge, 2003).
WALLIS, P.J., 'The Library of William Crashaw', *Transactions of the Cambridge Bibliographical Society* 2 (1954), 213-38.
WANLEY, HUMFREY, *Librorum vett. septentrionalium, qui in Angliæ bibliothecis extant, nec non multorum vett. codd. septentrionalium alibi extantium catalogus historico-criticus, cum totius thesauri linguarum septentrionalium sex indicibus* (Oxford: E Theatro Sheldoniano, 1705); [facs.] rpt. Menston: Scolar Press, 1970. (Vol. II of George Hickes, *Antiquæ literaturæ septentrionalis libri duo.*)
WARNER, GEORGE F. AND JULIUS P. GILSON, *Catalogue of Western Manuscripts in the Old Royal and King's Collections*, 4 vols (London, 1921).
WARNER, RUBIE D.-N., ed., *Early English Homilies from the Twelfth Century MS. Vesp. D. XIV*, EETS O.S. 152 (1917).
WARNICKE, R.M., *William Lambard Elizabethan Antiquary 1536-1601* (Compton Chamberlayne, Salisbury, 1973).
WARNICKE, ROTHA M., 'Note on a Court of Requests Case of 1571', *English Language Notes* 11 (1974), 250-56.
WATSON, A.G., 'Christopher and William Carye, collectors of monastic manuscripts and "John Carye"', *The Library* 5th series, 20 (1965), 135-42; rpt. Watson 2004[1]: V.
WATSON, A.G., *The Library of Sir Simonds D'Ewes* (London, 1966).
WATSON, ANDREW G., *The Manuscripts of Henry Savile of Banke* (London, 1969); rpt. Watson 2004[1]: IX.
WATSON, ANDREW, review article of WRIGHT 1972, *The Journal of the Society of Archivists* 4, no. 7 (1973), 603-09; rpt. 2004[1]: X.
WATSON, ANDREW, 'Thomas Allen of Oxford and his Manuscripts', in Parkes and Watson 1978: 279-314; rpt. Watson 2004[1]: VII.
WATSON, ANDREW, *Catalogue of Dated and Datable Manuscripts c. 700-1600 in the Department of Manuscripts, the British Library* (London, 1979).
WATSON, ANDREW G., *Catalogue of Dated and Datable Manuscripts c. 435-1600 in Oxford Libraries*, 2 vols (Oxford, 1984).
WATSON, ANDREW G., ed., *Books, Collectors and Libraries. Studies in the Medieval Heritage. N.R. Ker* (London and Ronceverte, 1985).
WATSON, A.G., 'John Twyne of Canterbury (d. 1581) as a Collector of Medieval Manuscripts: a Preliminary Investigation', *The Library* 6th series, 8 (1986), 133-51; rpt. Watson 2004[1]: IV.
WATSON, ANDREW G., *Medieval libraries of Great Britain. A list of surviving books* ed. N.R. Ker, *Supplement to the second edition* (London, 1987).
WATSON, ANDREW G., 'Robert Hare's Books', in Edwards, Gillespie, and Hanna 2000: 209-32; rpt. Watson 2004[1]: VI.
WATSON, ANDREW G., *Medieval Manuscripts in Post-Medieval England* (Padstow, 2004[1]).
WATSON, ANDREW G., 'Additional Notes', in Watson 2004[1]: 1-17.
WATSON, ROWAN, *Illuminated Manuscripts and their Makers* (London, 2003).
WEBBER, TERESA, 'Script and Manuscript Production at Christ Church, Canterbury, after the Norman Conquest', in *Canterbury and the Norman Conquest: churches, saints, and scholars, 1066-1109*, ed. Richard Eales and Richard Sharpe (London 1995): 145-58.
WEBSTER, LESLIE AND JANET BACKHOUSE, eds, *The Making of England. Anglo-Saxon Art and Culture AD 600-900* (London, 1991).
WEINBERG, CAROLE, 'The Latin Marginal Glosses in the Caligula Manuscript of Laȝamon's *Brut*', in Le Saux 1994: 103-20.
WEINBERG, CAROLE, 'Marginal Illustration: a clue to the provenance of the Cotton Caligula manuscript of Laȝamon's *Brut*', in Allen, Perry, and Roberts 2002: 39-52.
WHEELER, BONNIE, ROBERT L. KINDRICK, AND MICHAEL N. SALDA, eds, *The Malory Debate. Essays on the texts of* Le Morte Darthur, Arthurian studies 47 (Cambridge, 2000).
WHITELOCK, DOROTHY, ed., *Sermo Lupi ad Anglos* (London, 1939; 2nd edition 1952).
WHITELOCK, D., [facs.], *The Peterborough Chronicle. The Bodleian manuscript Laud Misc. 636. With an appendix by Cecily Clark*, EEMF 4 (Copenhagen, 1954).
WHITELOCK, DOROTHY, 'The Old English Bede', *Proceedings of the British Academy* 48 (1962), 57-90; rpt. Stanley 1990: 227-60.

WILCOX, JONATHAN, [facs.], *Wulfstan Texts and Other Homiletic Materials*, Anglo-Saxon Manuscripts in Microfiche Facsimile 8 (Binghamton, New York, 2000).

WILSON, R.M., ed., *Sawles warde. An early Middle English homily edited from the Bodley, Royal and Cotton MSS.*, Leeds School of English Language Texts and Monographs 3 (Leeds, 1938).

WIMSATT, J.I., 'Chaucer and French Poetry', in *Writers and their Background. Geoffrey Chaucer*, ed. Derek Brewer (London, 1974): 109-36.

WINDEATT, B.A., ed., *Geoffrey Chaucer,* Troilus & Criseyde: *A new edition of 'The Book of Troilus'* (London and New York, 1984).

WIRTJES, HANNEKE, ed., *The Middle English* Physiologus, EETS O.S. 299 (1991).

WITHERS, BENJAMIN, 'Intereaction of Word and Image in Anglo-Saxon Art II: Scrolls and Codex in the Frontispiece to the *Regularis Concordia*', *Old English Newsletter* 31.1 (1997): 38-40.

WOOD, ROBERT A., 'A Fourteenth-Century London Owner of "Piers Plowman"', *Medium Ævum* 53 (1984), 83-90.

WOODWARD, DANIEL AND MARTIN STEVENS, [facs.], *The New Ellesmere Chaucer Facsimile (Huntington MS El. 26 C 9)* (Tokyo and San Marino, California, 1995).

WORMALD, C.P., 'The Uses of Literacy in Anglo-Saxon England and its Neighbours', *Transaction of the Royal Historical Society*, 5th series 27 (1977), 95-114.

WORMALD, [C.] PATRICK, *The Making of English Law: King Alfred to the Twelfth Century*, Vol. I (Oxford 1999).

WORMALD, FRANCIS, 'Decorated Initials in English MSS. from A.D. 900 to 1100', *Archæologia* 91 (1945) 107-35; rpt. Alexander, Brown and Gibbs 1984: I. 47-75.

WORMALD, FRANCIS, *English Drawings of the Tenth and Eleventh Centuries* (London, 1952).

WORMALD, FRANCIS, 'Afterthoughts on the Stockholm Exhibition' [1953], rpt. Alexander, Brown, and Gibbs 1984: II. 147-52.

WORMALD, FRANCIS, 'The Insular script in late tenth century English Latin MSS', *Atti del X Congresso internazionale di scienze storicho, Roma, 4-11 Settembre*, ed. A Ferrabino (Roma, 1957): 160-65.

WORMALD, FRANCIS, 'The "Winchester School" before St Æthelwold', in *England before the Conquest: Studies in Primary Sources Presented to Dorothy Whitelock*, ed. Peter Clemoes and Kathleen Hughes (Cambridge, 1971), pp. 305-12; rpt. Alexander, Brown, and Gibbs 1984: I. 76-84.

WORMALD, FRANCIS AND C.E. WRIGHT, *The English Library before 1700* (London, 1958).

WRENN, C.L., 'Standard Old English', *Transactions of the Philological Society* (1933), 65-88; rpt. as '"Standard" Old English', in C.L. Wrenn, *Word and Symbol. Studies in English Language* (London, 1967): 57-77.

WRIGHT, C.E., 'The Dispersal of the Monastic Libraries and the Beginnings of Anglo-Saxon Studies: Matthew Parker and his Circle', *Transactions of the Cambridge Bibliographical Society* 1 (1949-53: 1951), 208-37.

WRIGHT, C.E., 'The Dispersal of the Libraries in the Sixteenth Century' [=Wright 1958[1]], in Wormald and Wright 1958: 148-75.

WRIGHT, C.E., 'The Elizabethan Society of Antiquaries and the Formation of the Cottonian Library' [=Wright 1958[2]], in Wormald and Wright 1958: 176-212.

WRIGHT, C.E., *English Vernacular Hands from the Twelfth to the Fifteenth Centuries* (Oxford, 1960[1]).

WRIGHT, C.E., 'Humfrey Wanley: Saxonist and Library-Keeper', Sir Israel Gollancz memorial Lecture 1960, *Proceedings of the British Academy* 46 (1960[2]), 99-129.

WRIGHT, C.E., 'Portrait of a Bibliophile VIII. Edward Harley, 2nd Earl of Oxford, 1689-1741)', *Book Collector* 11 (1962), 158-74.

WRIGHT, C.E. AND RUTH C. WRIGHT, eds, *The Diary of Humfrey Wanley 1715-1726*, 2 vols (London: Bibliographical Society, 1966).

WRIGHT, CYRIL ERNEST, *Fontes Harleiani. A Study of the Sources of the Harliean Collection of Manuscripts preserved in the Department of Manuscripts in the British Museum* (London, 1972).

WRIGHT, C.J., ed., *Sir Robert Cotton as Collector: Essays on an Early Stuart Courtier and His Legacy* (London, 1997).

WRIGHT, D.H. AND A. CAMPBELL, [facs.], *The Vespasian Psalter (B.M. Cotton Vespasian A.1)*, EEMF 14 (Copenhagen, 1967).

YEATS-EDWARDS, PAUL, 'The Winchester Malory Manuscript: An Attempted History', in Wheeler, Kindrick and Salda 2000: 367-89.

Names of people and places in the plates

This list is designed both to help identify proper names in plates (except for Jesus Christ/Messiah forms, which are not included) and to supply modern forms. For pl. 7 only those names that occur in the body of the charter are included below; the names in pl. 44 are not included. The list does not present headword forms for English, Latin or French: rather the relevant phrase is given and translated; and occasionally a brief note is added. The order is alphabetical, with **ę** treated as **æ**, initial **i** and **j** taken together, **þ** or **ð** following **t**, and initial **v** and **u** taken together.

ááron 26: Aaron
abendone 23b: Abingdon
abbo 18: Abbo (a monk from the Benedictine abbey of Fleury)
abraham 17, 39: Abraham
abuyle 39: (Johannes Halgrinus of) Abbeville
adam 12: Adam
p(ro) marito **Adamet**o 42g: for her husband Admetus
ægelmeres 21: of Æthelmær (ealdorman of the Western Provinces; ‹g› a late spelling)
ælfeges sunu 21: son of Ælfheah
ęlfred cyning 8: King Alfred (the Great)
ælfric 21: Ælfric (ealdorman of Hampshire)
ælfwines 21: of Ælfwine (D Chronicle agrees with C, whereas E has Æþelsiges)
æt **ęþelinga eig**ge 8: at Athelney
æþelredes cyninges 18: of King Æthelred
æþelstane cynincge 18: about King Athelstan
æt **alr**e 8: at Aller (in Somerset)
æþelward 21 (l. 3): Æthelweard (son of the earldorman of East Anglia)
æþelward 21 (l. 22): Æthelweard (son of the earldoman of the Western Provinces)
Albertus 50: Albertus
ALBION 22: Albion (an older name for Britain)
Alcebiades 42g: Alcibiades
Alceste 42g: Alcestis (wife of Admetus)
Aleyn 49: Alanus (de Insulis, author of *De planctu Naturae*)
Aluerd 23b: Alfred (the Great)
aluered 23b: Alfred (the Great)
to s(an)c(t)e **andreas** mæssan 21: on St Andrew's day
eft(er) S(ancte) **Andreas** massedæi 23: after St Andrew's day (30 November)
of **angelcyn**nes þeode 21: of England (lit. of the people of the English race)
GENTIS **ANGL**ORUM 22: of the people of the English
Ariopagitar(um) 42: of the Ariopagites
Arthemesie 42g: Artemisia
Arthure 51, 55: Arthur (king of Britain)
arðures 33: Arthur's
Arueragus 42: Arveragus (Dorigen's husband)
seynt **augustyn** 52: Saint Augustine (of Hippo)
sey(n)t **austin** 50: Augustine (of Hippo)
austyn 39: Augustine (of Hippo)
Barbares 42g: foreigners
the **Barbarie** 42: heathendom
beda 22: Bede
bede 39: Bede
s(an)c(t)e **benedict**es 18: of Saint Benedict
Beof 33: Beof (an Oxford noble; in Wace's *Brut* he is named Bos, in accord with Geoffrey of Monmouth's Boso)
Bertra(m) 353: (a cook in Godrich's household)
bethel 17: Bethel (a village about eleven miles north of Jerusalem)
bethleem 28: Bethlehem
bethléém 29: Bethlehem
bethsaida 14: Bethsaida
beteny 57: Bethany
Bilyea 42: Bilia (wife of Dullus)
BREOTON 22: Britain
breotone 10: of Britain
Brittannia 22g: Britain
regis roberti **broys** 54: of King Robert (the) Bruce
roberti de **broys** scottorum regis 54: of Robert of Bruce, king of Scots
hæh **Bruttisc** mon 33: a noble Briton
þan **brutten** 33: the Britons
Bruttes 33: Britons
Brutus 42g: Brutus
ðone mynstre of **burch** 23: the monastery of Peterborough
bryhtric 21: Brihtric
Frer(e) I· **C**·52: Friar J[ohn] C[apgrave] (Augustinian friar of Lynn)
cædmon 1: Cædmon (of Whitby)
cambrig(e) 52: Cambridge
Camelerde 55: Camylyard (Lodegraunce's kingdom)
In **Cancr**o 56: in Cancer
Joh(a)n(nus) **Capgrave** 52: (marginal identification of letters) I· C·
ceadda 10, 24: Chad
Cedasus 42g: Scedasus (of Boetia)
CEOLWULFO 22: to Ceolwulf (Bede's dedicatee was king of Northumbria, 729‑37)
to **cestr**e 35: to Chester
charlemain 23b: Charlemagne
seo **ciriclice dómbóc** 24: Ecclesiastes
of **cippanha(m)**me 8: from Chippenham
of/to **cirenceastr**e 8: from/to Cirencester
clunie 23: Cluny
p(r)ior of **clun**ni 23: a prior from Cluny (in France)
Claudias 42g
Cleobiliam 42g
cnut cyning 21: King Cnut (or Canute)
colmane 10: Colman
constantin 23b: Constantine (the Great, Roman emperor)

cor(inthios) 46g: Corinthians
Cornelia 42g: Cornelia
Cornelias 42g
cornwayle 35: Cornwall
The cowntas of **crasyn'** 51: the countess of Crasyn (unusual form; Malory has 'Clarysyn')
Criseide 56: Criseyde
Criseyde 43, 45: Criseyde
cundoþ 8: Condé
Cyr(us) 57: Cyrus (a tyrant, father of Mary Magdalene)
li **dane**is 23b: the Danes (i.e. the Vikings)
dauyþ 39: David
dece(m)bre 38: December
DECE(M)BR(IS) 18: of December
on **defena scir**e 8, 21: in Devonshire (lit. in the shire of the people of Devon)
Demociones doghter 42g: Demotion's daughter
denemark 35: Denmark
deniscra monna 8: of Danish men
denshe 35: Danish
wið **deorhyrst**e 21: near Deerhurst
Dionisius 46g: Dionisius
Dorigene 42: Dorigen (wife of Arveragus)
to **dou(er)**e 51: to Dover
dunstane 18: Dunstan
mid his ealdan fæder **eadgar**e 21: with his grandfather Edgar
eadmund 21: Eadmund (king of England, son of Æthelred)
EADMVNDI REGIS 18: of King Edmund (killed by Viking raiders in 869)
eadnoð 21: Eadnoth (bishop of Dorchester)
eadric 21: Eadric (ealdorman of Mercia)
eadwi æþeling 21: atheling Eadwig (son of King Ethelred)
eadwi ceorla kyning 21: Eadwig, king of the *ceorls* (whoever this curiously named man was, he was exiled a few years later)
eastenglan 21: East Anglia
of **eastengl**an 21: from East Anglia (lit. from the East Angles)
on **eastengle** 8: to East Anglia (lit. into the East Angles)
on **eastr**on 8: during Easter
on **easttune** 7: in Aston (Aston Magna, Gloucestershire)
ad **ebre**(os) 46g: to the Hebrews
ebreu 39: Hebrew
to **ecgbryht**es stane 8: to Egbert's stone (a shire or hundred meeting-place, unidentified)
seint **Edburg** 23b: Saint Edburga (daughter of Edward the Elder)
edelred 23b: Æthelred (governor of Mercia, married to Æthelflæd)
Edelstan 23b: Athelstan (king, son of Edward the Elder)
edith 23b: Edith (but a sister of Athelstan called Eadhild married Hugh)
Edude 23b: Edith (daughter of Edward the Elder, married Emperor Otto I)
eduuard 23b: Edward (the Elder)
in **egipt**o 28: in Egypt
Of **egypt**e 28, 29: from Egypt
on **egypt**e land 28, 29: into the land of Egypt
in to **egypt**e 29: into Egypt
on **egypt**um 28: into Egypt (lit. into the Egyptians)
éiric 21: Eric
Eleusius 30: Eleusius (suitor of St Juliana)
Elfled 23b: Æthelflæd (a daughter of Edward the Elder)
elfled 23b: Æthelflæd (Lady of the Mercians; sister of Edward the Elder)
to **emben**um 8: to Amiens
engelond 35: England
to eall **engla land**es rice 21: to all the kingdom of England
ealle **engla** þeode 21: the whole nation of the English
engleis 23b: (the) English
engleland 23a: England
englet(er)e 23b: England
englisch- 39, 52: English
on **englisc** 18: in English
epira cyning 9: king of the people of Epirus
esav 17: Esau
escoce 23b: Scotland
to **eþandun**e 8: to Eddington
europE 22: of Europe
finanes 10: of Finán (a bishop)
s(ir) **Florent** 51: Sir Florent (Sir Florence in Malory)
þa **franc**an 8: the Franks
france 23(b): France
into **france** 23: to France
fronclond 8: the Frankish empire
on **frygia** mægðe 14: in the country of Phrygia
æt **fullanha(m)**me 8: at Fulham
on **fullanho(m)**me 8: in Fulham
on **galilea** mægðe 14: in the country of Galilee
gallia bellica 22: Belgic Gaul
gallie 22: of Gaul
gearumon 10: Jaruman
gend 8: Ghent
germanie 22: of Germania
seynt **gilbert** 52: Saint Gilbert (of Sempringham, founder of the Gilbertine order)
on **glæstinga byr**i 21: in Glastonbury
to **gleawcestrescir**e 21: to Gloucestershire
godrich 35: Godrich (earl of Cornwall and regent of England)
godwine 21: Godwin (ealdorman of Lindsey)
goldeboru 35: Goldeboru (daughter of Athelwold, king of England)
gomorram 25: Gomorrah
Gorgim 42g: Gorgon
Grece 42: Greece
Grecie 42g: of Greece
g(re)g(or) 39: Gregory
Grimes douther 35: Grim's daughter (Grim was a Danish fisherman who saved Havelok's life)
gu(n)nild 35: Gunnild (a daughter of Grim)
Gwenyvere 55: Guinevere
a **gyw** 36: a Jew
hamptone 51: Hampton
hamtunscir 8: Hampshire
hauelok 35: Havelok (son and heir of the king of Denmark)
hay 17: Hai (or sometimes Ai), to the east of Bethel
healfdenes 8: Halfdane, a Viking leader
hebrei 17: the Hebrews or Jews

in **hebre**is uoluminib(us) 17: in the Hebrew books
henglishe 35: English
henri abbot 23: Abbot Henry (of Poitou, abbot of St Jean d'Angely; abbot of Peterborough)
henri king 23: King Henry (Henry I, king of England and Normandy)
Herod 29: Herod
herode 28: (to) Herod
herodes 28, 29: Herod('s)
herred 7: Herred (previously holder of land being leased)
hibernia 10: Hibernia or Ireland
on **hierapol**e þære ceastre 14: in the city of Hierapolis
hispanie 22: of Spain
to **hrofesceastr**e 8: to Rochester
hug(e) 23b: Hugh (duke of the Franks, married Eadhild, sister of Athelstan)
þurh **ieremia**(m) þam witegan 28: through the prophet Jeremiah
þurh **ieremia**(m) þam witeȝan 29: through the prophet Jeremiah
I(er)emie 50: Jeremiah
ierom 39: Jerome
Ierome 31: Jerome
IER(ominus) 17: Jerome
Ieromin(us) 42g: Jerome
i(erusa)l(e)m 39: Jerusalem
I(erusa)l(e)m 57: Jerusalem
iewis 39: Jews
to **igle**a 8: Iley Oak (now lost)
illarie 39: Hilary of Poitiers
Illiricicoru(m) Regina 42g: queen of Illirica
iob 17: Job
sannt **iohan** 27: St John
sancti **Ioha(n)**is baptiste 54: of Saint John the Baptist
seint **Iohan** 35: Saint John
S(ancte) **Ioh(ann**i)s mynstre 23: Saint John's monastery
iones p(re)chi(n)g 39: John's preaching
ioon 39: John
þe flood **iordan** 37: the river Jordan
Iosæpes 27g: of Joseph
iosepe 29: to Joseph
Iosepe 28, 29: to Joseph
IOSEPH 3: Joseph
ioseph 28: Joseph
Ioseph 28: Joseph
iosepu(m) 28: to Joseph
Ioue 56: Jove or Juppiter
Iouinianu(m) 42g: Jovinianus or Jovinian (adversary of Jerome)
iudee 39: Judea
sein **iuhan** 30: Saint John
isaác 17: Isaac (son of Abraham)
Lacedomya 42g: Lacedomia (for Laodamia)
æt te **la(m)masse** 23: at Lammas (1 August)
leofwines 21: of Leofwine
leyk 38: (mostly erased; possibly an unidentified proper name)
licetfeld 24: Lichfield
linc(olne) 23: Lincoln
lodegrean 55: Lodegraunce (father of Guinivere)
Lollius 43, 452: Lollius (a fictional authority)
lucas gesetnysse 12: Luke's account
on **lunden**e 21: into London
lundenwaru 21: the people of London
to **lundon**e 35: to London
of **Macidony**e 42g: from Macedonia
mæse 8: (river) Meuse
mai þæs monþes 10: of the month of May
malachie 39: Malachy
sannte **MaRhe** 27a: St Mary
þe laffdiȝ **MaRhe** 27a: the lady Mary
MARIA 3: Mary
marie 48: Mary
Marlyon 55: Merlin
to þam oþrum godspellere **marc**um 12: to Mark, the second Evangelist
mark 39: Mark
mary mavdleyn' 57: Mary Magdalen
Mathei 46g: Matthew
matheu 39: Matthew
Martine 18: Martin (of Tours)
thys castell of **mavdleyn'** 57: the stronghold or town of Magdala
vxor **Mauseol**i 42g: wife of Mausolus
Martin 23: Martin (prior of St Neot's)
In **mercn**a þeode 10: among the people of the Mercians
Merlion 55: Merlin
Merlyon 55: Merlin
moriá 17: Moriah (an area of countryside in ancient Palestine; the hill which Abraham and Isaac climbed is traditionally identified with the site of the Temple of Jerusalem)
fif **moyses** boca 22: of the five books of Moses (the first five books of the Old Testament, i.e. the Pentateuch)
moysen 26a: Moses
moyses 26a: Moses
myrcean 21: Mercia
of S(ancte) **Neod** 23: of St Neot's (in Huntingdonshire)
Nicerates wyf 42: Niceratus's wife
Nichanor 42g: Nicanor
for **Nichanor**e 42: for Nicanor
norm(andi) 23: Normandy
Northumb(er)land 23b: Northumberland
Northuuales 23b: Wales (not including Cornwall)
norðanhymbra 10: of the Northumbrians
norðhymbran 21: Northumbria
norðman 21: Northman
æt **ólan íg**e 21: at Alney
Omer 42: Homer
Om(er)i 42g: of Homer
of **ongelþeod**e 10: from England
pægina læh 10: unidentified place
pandare 56: Pandar or Pandarus
Pandarus 56: Pandarus or Pandar
Penalopee 42: Penelope
Penolopes 42g: Penelope's
on S(ancte) **PET(r**es) messedei 23: on St Peter's day (29 June)
petreius 33: Petreius (in Geoffrey of Monmouth he is Petreius

Cocta, a senator and leader of 10.000 men)
ðes **philip**pus 14: this Philip
ðysne **philipp**u(m) 14: this Philip
Pilat(us) 53: (Pontius) Pilate
pirrus 9: Pyrrhus
Porcia 42: Portia
say(n)t **poule** 35: St Paul
Pounce Pilatt 53: Pontius Pilate
Prothesela(us) 42: Protesilaus (husband of Laodamia)
I de **R** 54: (initials of scribe)
rachel 29: Rachel
Ræchel 28: Rachel
in **Reding**(e) 23: in Reading
Nicholas **Reysby** 52: Nicholas Reysby (recipient of dedicatory letter)
Robertus rex 54: King Robert (see **broys**)
Rodogone 42: Rhodogune (daughter of Darius)
romane 9: the Romans
þan **Romanisc**e 33: the Romans
Rome 33: Rome
romeburg 9: the city of Rome
romleoden 33: the people of Rome
Sankegreal 55: Saint Graal (the Holy Grail)
sarasinz 23b: Saracens
Sat(ur)day 39: Saturday
Saturn 56: Saturn
scald 8: (river) Scheldt
on **sciðia** mægðe 14: in the country of Scythia
scotta ealond 10: island of the Irish
scottorum 54: of the Scots
sealwyda 8: Selwood (then in the border territory with Welsh kingdoms)
s[`e′i]mp(r)y(n)gha(m) 52: Sempringham
septembris 17: of September
Seresb(yr)i 23: Salisbury
sodomam 25: Sodom
strato 42g: Strato or Straton
sumursætna 8: of the people of Somerset
de **syro** sermone 17: a sermon on Cyrus (the Great, of Persia)
syr(us) 57: Cyrus (a tyrant, father of Mary Magdalene)
binnan **tarent**an 9: in Tarentum
tarentine 9: the Tarentini
be **temes**e 8: by the (river) Thames
teofil(e) 39: Theophilus
Teuta queene 42: Queen Teuta (of Ilyria)
Theanam 42g
Theban 42: of Thebes, Theban
Thebanam 42g
victis **Theb**is 42g: Thebes being taken
ad **thimoth**eum 46g: to Timothy
s(an)c(tu)s **thomas** 50: Thomas Aquinas
Thymodia(m) 42g
Troie 42: Troy
Troilus 43, 45: Troilus
tru(m)here 10: Trumhere
tuda 9: Tuda
þurkylle 21: Thorkel
Valence 49: Valence (in France, famed for fine cloth)
Valeria 42: Valeria (wife of Servius the grammarian, refused to marry a second time)
ubbe 35: Ubbe, seneschal of Denmark
ulfkytel 21: Ulfcetel of East Anglia
Vther Pendragon 55: Uther Pendragon (father of King Arthur)
Wales 23b: Wales
uuerfrid bisco`p′ 7: Werferth, bishop (of Worcester) *c.* 872-915
weogerna ceastre 7: Worcester
westseaxan 21: Wessex
on **westseax**u(m) 8: among the West Saxons (i.e. in Wessex)
to **westsex**an 21: to Wessex
æt **weþmor** 8: at Wedmore
wilsætan 8: the people of Wiltshire
Wincestr(e) 23b: Winchester
wulfsie 21: Wulfsige (abbot of Ramsey)
wulfsige 7: Wulfsige, a reeve leased land by Bishop Werferth
wynferð 10: Winfrith
ysaac 17: Isaac
ysaie 39: Isaiah

People named in the commentaries to the plates

(For quite a few of the users and owners of English vernacular manuscripts from the dissolution to the eighteenth century, biographical information is to be found in the *Oxford DNB*, and some further sources are noted. A quick way into recent work in this area is provided by the collection of papers in Graham 2000[3]; Adams 1917 and Wright 1958[2] remain valuable introductions.)

ABBA: dubious reading.

(9) Anglo-Saxon name read by some at foot of f. 48v of Add. 47967 (Orosius).

ÆLFRIC:

(6) 'ælfric clericus' is a tenth-century addition on f. 98v of the Hatton Pastoral Care.

ÆLFRIC BATA: (*fl. c.* 1010). A monk and teacher at Christ Church, Canterbury, in the early eleventh century. He was a pupil of the more famous Ælfric, whose *Colloquy* he enlarged; and he composed other such teaching materials. (Gwara with Porter 1997; *Oxford DNB*).

(20) His name appears on f. 117r of Tiberius A. iii.

ÆLFSTAN:

(12) Anglo-Saxon name written in the margin of Royal 7 C. xii, f. 109r.

ÆTHELWALD: (*d.* 830). Or Aedeluald. Bishop of Lichfield 818-30. (Two other early bishops of this name were the bishop of Lindisfarne (721 × 724-40) and the bishop of Dunwich (845 × 870), both also sometimes associated with the Book of Cerne.)

(4) The bishop of Lichfield is the likeliest referent for the acrostic poem on f. 21r and name on f. 87v in the Book of Cerne.

ÆTHELWOLD: (904 × 9-984). Abbot of Abingdon and later bishop of Winchester. A teacher and scholar, the Benedictine Rule was among the texts he translated into English. (*Oxford DNB*).

(8) Special attention is given to his appointment as bishop (963) on f. 28r of the Parker Chronicle.

ALINGTON, SIR GILES: (*d.* 1573). Grandson of Ursula, daughter of Sir Robert DRURY. (David 1995).

(42) Henry PAYNE left him the Ellesmere Chaucer in 1568/9.

ALLEN, THOMAS: (1540-1632): Mathematician, from Staffordshire. Spent most of his long life in Oxford University, where Fellow of University College. Amassed a large collection of manuscripts. (Watson 1978 [2004]; *Oxford DNB*).

(19) Owned first part of Titus A. iv and may therefore have owned the second part, which contains Rule of St Benedict.

(31) Owned the first part of Titus D. xviii, but not necessarily the second part, which contains an *Ancrene Riwle* text.

(46) Fly-leaf note of his misidentification of contents in Harley 674 (*Cloud*).

ALTERMONGER:

(30) 'Iohn Altermonger the worste that euer' is written on f. 22v of Bodley 34.

ASHBURNHAM, BERTRAM: (1797-1878). The fourth earl Ashburnham would seem to have been the buyer of the York Plays manuscript.

(53) A Lord Ashburnham bought the York Plays manuscript in 1847; British Museum purchased this manuscript at the sale of the Ashburnham library 1899.

AVERIL, WILLIAM:

(50) Ownership inscription 'Guilielmus Auerelus: | Londiniensis' at top of f. 78r Harley 1197, Part II.

BACON, FRANCIS: (1561-1626). Baron Verulam, Viscount St Albans. Philosopher, statesman, and essayist. Lord chancellor of England. (*Oxford DNB*).

(16) Perhaps borrowed Nero A i (Wulfstan) from Cotton by 1613, or, more likely, had on loan Julius C. ii, into which excerpts from Nero A. i were entered.

BARDEL, JOHN: An owner's name at the back of the Sloane Lyrics manuscript. Greene (1962: 173-74) suggests linking him with the inscription 'Liber dompni Joannis Berdwell monachi sancti E' he reports from Holkham Misc. 37, f. 197v; he also reports an inscription on f. 19r 'Eadmundo sancto pertinet iste liber' and the name of another monk, John Wulfspett, in the Holkham manuscript. Arguing that Bardwell (or Bradel or Bardel) is a Suffolk name, he notes a parish named Bardwell near Ixworth.

(40) A name is entered on f. 36v both as 'bardel' and 'bradel'.

BARN, R:

(52) name on f. 122v of Add. 36704 (Capgrave).

BASSET: 'Margaret basset' and 'anna basset'. Have been identified as great-granddaughters of Sir Thomas More and maids-in-waiting to Queen Mary (Seymour 1995-97: II. 267-68).

(45) Among names scribbled on f. 120v of St John's College L.1 (Chaucer's *Troilus*). Other names scribbled on f. 120v are Wylliam, Thomas, and John.

BATMAN, STEPHEN: (*c.* 1543-1584) Translator and author, from Somerset. After Cambridge, was one of MATTHEW PARKER's domestic chaplains, helping build up collection of manuscripts. (Parkes 1997; *Oxford DNB*).

(43) Owned Corpus Christi College Cambridge 61 (Chaucer's *Troilus*) from 17 December 1570; apparently gave it to Matthew Parker.

BATTELEY, JOHN: (*bap.* 1646, *d.* 1708) Antiquary; prebendary and archdeacon of Canterbury. From Suffolk. Part of his collection of books was sold by his nephew, John Batteley, Master of the Augmentation Office, to ROBERT HARLEY, 5 November 1723. (Wright 1972; *Oxford DNB*).

(36) Harley 2253 (Harley Lyrics) among manuscripts in his collection.

BEAUCHAMP: see under NEVILLE (a).

BEALE, ROBERT: (1541-1601). Clerk to the Privy Council 1572-1601. Member of the Society of Antiquaries. Collector of manuscripts. (Brewerton 1998; *Oxford DNB*).

(12) An erased name read as Robert Beale is on f. 4 (a fly-leaf) of Royal 7 C. xii (Ælfric's Catholic Homilies).

BERDWELL, JOHN: see BARDEL.

BLOMEFYLDE, MYLES: (1525-1603). From Bury St Edmunds, Suffolk. Educated at Cambridge, where licensed (1552) to practise medicine. Lived in Chelmsford from 1560s to death. Possibly related to WILLIAM BLOMEFYLDE, from whom he could have obtained the Digby plays (Myles did have a copy of one of William's books). Johnston (1995: 109) notes a William Blomfeld associated (1509) with the Fraternity of St Nicholas and the Merchant Guild of Norwich a generation earlier and, tantalized by Myles Blomefylde's report that 'dutch' was among the languages known to the later William Blomfeld, speculates on connections with a possible family background of merchants and the influences from the Low Countries in the *Mary Magdalen* play. (Baker and Murphy 1967, 1976; *Oxford DNB*).

(57) Initials 'MB' in Digby 133, f. 95r (*Play of Mary Magdalen*).

BLOMEFYLDE, WILLIAM: (*fl.* 1529-1574). Alchemist and preacher. Before the Dissolution a monk at Bury St Edmunds, but must have left Bury by 1529, when charged with heresy at Tunstal. Later vicar of St Simon and St Jude, Norwich. Perhaps a relation of MYLES BLOMEFYLDE. (Baker and Murphy 1967, 1976; *Oxford DNB*).

(57) Was William an intermediary owner of Digby 133 (*Play of Mary Magdalen*) between Bury and Myles?

BLYTH, HUGH: (*d.* 1455). Rector of Abbess Roding, Essex, is likely identification.

(39) First recorded owner of Add. 41175 (Glossed Gospels): ownership inscription and requests for prayers on ff. 1v, 2r and 164.

BODLEY, SIR THOMAS: (1545-1613). Scholar and diplomat. Born in Exeter. Educated at Magdalen College Oxford and Geneva. In 1599 refurnished the library of the University of Oxford library, which had fallen into decay, and restored its roof. The Bodleian Library was formally opened to readers in 1602. Made the University of Oxford the chief beneficiary of his will. (*Oxford DNB*).

BO(W)YER, ROBERT: (*c.* 1560-1621). Politician. Clerk of the Parliaments. Also served as keeper of the records in the Tower of London in 1604. Second son of WILLIAM BOW(Y)ER. Educated at Oxford; Clifford's Inn; Middle Temple. (*Oxford DNB*).

(5) According to CAMDEN he had Cotton Nero D. iv (Lindisfarne Gospels) perhaps as early as 1603. The manuscript could even have passed to him from his father.

BO(W)YER, WILLIAM: (*d.* 1569/70). Bailiff of Westminster and keeper of the records in the Tower of London by 1563. (*Oxford DNB*).

(5) If HICKES's statement is to be believed, that Nero D. iv (Lindisfarne Gospels) was consulted by John Day and John Foxe in work towards their *Gospels of the fower Evangelistes* (1571), the manuscript could already have been in London and possibly therefore in William Bowyer's possession. If so, could have been consulted by Nowell and Joscelyn in London.

(21) JOSCELYN's note 'in lib. Mr Boyer. et hist. petrob.' in pl. 21 (Cotton Tiberius B. iv) is evidence for his ownership of another Anglo-Saxon Chronicle manuscript, Cotton Tiberius B. i.

BRIDGEWATER: place-name in titles borne by members of the Egerton family. See under Thomas EGERTON.

(42) Name sometimes associated with Huntingdon Library, EL 26 C 9. The manuscript is commonly known as the Ellesmere Chaucer.

BRIGHT, B.H: mid-nineteenth-century bookseller.

(53) The York Plays manuscript passed through his hands.

CAMDEN, WILLIAM: (1551-1623). Historian and antiquary. Second master at Westminster when ROBERT COTTON a schoolboy there; headmaster from 1593. His *Britannia* was first published in 1586 (translated into English 1610 under his supervision), about the time he was one of the founding figures of the Elizabethan Society of Antiquaries; other editions and further writings on the antiquities of Britain followed. (Lutz 2000; *Oxford DNB*).

(5) Knew, possibly by 1603 (the date of the volume's dedicatory letter to Sir Robert Cotton), that Nero D. iv (Lindisfarne Gospels) was then 'in the hands of my good friend M. Robert Bowyer' (Brown 2003: 136).

CARYE, William: (*d.* 1572-73). Or Cari. Of the parish of St Mary Magdalen, Milk St, London. Described as a clothworker, but a man of some standing. Book collector. Known to members of MATTHEW PARKER's circle, especially to Bale and JOSCELYN. (Watson 1965 [2004[1]]; Parkes 1997; Watson 2004[2]: 4-5).

(43) BATMAN acquired Corpus Christi College Cambridge 61 (Chaucer's *Troilus*) from Carye on 'the xvij of decemb(er) | an(n)o / 1570 /'.

CASSIODORUS: (*c.* 490-585). Historian, statesman, monk. Founded the monasteries Vivarium and Castellum in his estates in southern Italy, important for the making and transmission of manuscripts.

(2b) Author of prayer on f. 141v of the Vespasian Psalter.

CAXTON, WILLIAM: (1415 x 24-1492). Born in Kent. Merchant, working in Bruges, Cologne and Ghent from the 1440s. Printer and translator. Set up the first known printing-press in Britain near Westminster Abbey by 1476. (Blake 1969; *Oxford DNB*).

(55) The Winchester Malory manuscript was in Caxton's workshop *c.* 1480-83.

CECIL, WILLIAM: (1520/21-1598). Lord Burghley. Politician, Minister of state, Lord Treasurer. Born Bourn, Lincolnshire. Educated St John's College Cambridge; Gray's Inn. (*Oxford DNB*).

(2), (23) Owned Vespasian A. i (Vespasian Psalter) and Laud Misc. 636 (Peterborough Chronicle).

(11) Could have had the Exeter Book on loan in London (Graham 1994).

CEOLWULF: (*d.* 764). A king of Northumbria (729-737) who retired to monastic life. Dedicatee of Bede's *Ecclesiastical History*. (*Oxford DNB*).

CHANNOIS: Maybe Chaunois; Charmois also suggested.

(56) Name with date 1592 on f. 231v of Arch. Selden. B. 24.

CLERKE, JOHN: (1510-1580) Scrivener, active in updating the York Plays register. (Beadle and Meredith 1983: xxi-xxiii; Meredith 1987).

(53) Scribe C in the York Plays, not only did he enter new plays but he added much information about texts, performance, organization and other subsidiary matter.

CLYNTON: There were Clintons of Castleditch in Eastnor in the 1569 Visitation of Herefordshire. (Ker 1960: xiv).

(30) 'Thomas clynton clericus' is written on f. 74v of Bodley 34.

COLDVELL, HENRY:

(43) Name in Corpus Christi College Cambridge 61, f. 151r (Chaucer's *Troilus*).

COLEMAN: Writer of signed marginalia in eleventh-century Worcester. (Ker 1949[2]).

(22) Added chapter titles on ff. 84v, 85, and a signed note on f. 87v of the 'Ca' copy of Bede's *Historia*.

COLMORE:

(15) The name 'elysabet colmore', perhaps a sixteenth-century owner of at least this part of this composite volume, is on f. 11 of Vitellius C.iii (Herbal).

CORBET, ROBERTUS:

(16) Author of a letter drafted on f. 124 of Nero A. i.

COTTON, JOHN: (1621-1702). Politician. Only son of Sir Thomas Cotton (1594-1662) and grandson of Sir ROBERT COTTON, he carried out his grandfather's wishes for the collection, ensuring its transfer to the nation. Friend of Dr Thomas Smith, who first catalogued Sir Robert's library.

COTTON, SIR ROBERT BRUCE: (1571-1631) Politician and antiquary, his collection of books, shelved in bookcases (distinguished by the busts of major figures from the Roman world placed on them) was open to many users. Proud of his connection to the Scots royal line, he added Bruce to his name. Through the agency of his grandson, JOHN COTTON, the library passed to the nation. In 1731, when in Ashburnham House, Westminster, over 200 manuscript books were lost or badly damaged by fire. The Cotton library formed one of the foundation collections of the British Museum Library in 1753. (Tite 1984, 1992, 1994, 2003; Wright 1997; *Oxford DNB*).

(23) Peterborough Chronicle may at one time have belonged to him. Note that plates come from fourteen Cotton manuscripts (2, 5, 14, 15, 16, 17, 18, 19, 20, 21, 25, 31, 33 and 37).

CRANMER, THOMAS: (1489-1556). Educated Cambridge. Archbishop of Canterbury 1532-56. Henry VIII's negotiator in marriage dealings. Composed a litany for the reformed church (1545) and supervised preparation of the first and second prayer-books of 1549 and 1552 (*The Book of Common Prayer*). Burned at the stake in the reign of Mary I. (*Oxford DNB*).

(28) Name entered on f. 3 of London, British Library, Royal 1 A. xiv.

CRASHAW, WILLIAM: (*bap.* 1572, *d.* 1625/6). Puritan divine. Born in Handsworth, Yorkshire. Matriculated at St John's College Cambridge 1588, graduating 1592. Elected Fellow 1594, MA 1595, BD 1603. Left Cambridge *c.* 1600. Preacher at the Temple 1604-13, where he accumulated more books and manuscripts than he could house. Pastor at Burton Agnes, Yorkshire, 1613. In London again from 1618, as vicar of Whitechapel. Father of the poet Richard Crawshaw. (Wallis 1954; *Oxford DNB*).

(54) Owned 167 manuscripts which HENRY WRIOTHESLEY, third earl of Southampton, arranged (1618) to buy for use at Southampton House in London; the collection, including St John's G. 23 (Barbour's *Bruce*) sent to Cambridge after Wriothesley's death.

CROMPTON, THOMAS: (1558-1602). Lawyer and politician. (*Oxford DNB*).

(16) Apparent owner of Nero A. i (Wulfstan) after LAMBARDE.

CROWLOND, JOHN: (*d.* 1493). Fellow of Queens' College Cambridge and parson of South Ockendon, Essex (Hudson 1988: 423).

(39) Among early owners of Add. 41175 (Glossed Gospels). May have given book to Queens' College.

CRVSSCANKE: ?Or Cruickshank.

(56) Name on f. 230r of Arch. Selden. B. 24 is read variously, e.g. 'villem crvsscan?ke', 'Villem Grisseance'.

CURTEYS, ALICIE: of Tunsted, Norfolk?

(52) Named with 'Will(elmu)s' on f.121v of Add. 36704 (Capgrave).

CURTEYS, WILLIAM: (*d.* 1446). Abbot of Bury St Edmunds in Lydgate's day. (*Oxford DNB*).

(49) His name is on f. 43v of Harley 2255 (Lydgate), which he may have owned.

CUTLER, THOMAS:

(53) A name (*c.* 1600) occurring in the opening pages and on the last verso in Add. 35290 (York Plays); the initials TC (f. 89r) are associated with 'The Barbours' play.

DAVIDSON, ANDREW:

(31) The signature 'Andreas Davidsonus' appears on f. 1 of the first booklet of Titus D. xviii.

DAVYSOUN, JOAN:

(9) Name (sixteenth century?) on f. 1r of Add. 47967 (Orosius).

DEE, JOHN: (1527-1609). Mathematician and astrologer. Amassed over 3000 books, at that time a huge library. (Roberts and Watson 1990: 75-78; *Oxford DNB*).

(9) According to Hickes he owned Add. 47967 (Orosius), but it is not in the catalogue of Dee's library.

DE DRISTON, WALTER:

(16) Intended recipient of a letter drafted on f. 124 of Nero A. i.

D'ESCURES, RALPH: (*c.* 1068–1122). Bishop of Rochester 1108–14 and archbishop of Canterbury 1114–22. (*Oxford DNB*).

(25) Presence of a translation in Vespasian D. xiv from one of his homilies provides dating evidence.

D'EWES, SIR SIMONDS: (1602–1650). 1st baronet. Antiquary and bibliophile. Worked towards a dictionary of Old English; also had plans to publish Joscelyn's dictionary. His grandson, 3rd baronet, sold the collection to ROBERT HARLEY in 1706, mainly through WANLEY's agency. (Watson 1966; Heyworth 1989: 228–32; *Oxford DNB*).

(13) Junius 11 perhaps in his library *c.* 1637 (evidence of binding).

(23) Borrowed the Peterborough Chronicle from the Bodleian in 1647.

DE FOIX, GASTON: (1331–1391). Or Phoebus or Fébus or Phébus. Author of the *Livre de chasse* (1387–89), a work popular into the seventeenth century. (Thomas and Avril 1998).

(44) *The master of game* (Douce 335) is translated from de Foix's book.

DE HARLAY, ACHILLE: (1639–1712).

(1) Owned St Petersburg Bede; left by his son Achille to St Germain des Prés in Paris.

DE LAET, JOHANNES: (1581–1649). Merchant and scholar. Born in Antwerp. Attended the University of Leiden, defending his thesis in 1599. Polymath, interested in geography, history and language. Director of the Dutch West-India Company from 1621. Had many learned friends throughout Europe. Visited England frequently and also sent his son Samuel to transcribe manuscripts on his behalf. Engaged in writing a dictionary of Old English. (Bekkers 1970; Hetherington 1980: 97–101; Bremmer 1998; Hoftijzer 1998; *Oxford DNB*).

(13) Had Junius 11 in Leyden in the 1640s.

(15) Made use of Vitellius C. iii when in England in 1641, borrowed for his use by LE NEVE.

DE LICHE: The note of purchase made by Sparwenfeldt in the Codex Aureus in 1690 refers to buying it 'from the famous collection of the illustrious Marqués de Heliche'. The actual seller at this date is likely to have been Catalina de Haro, eighth Marquesa de Heliche. (Belsheim 1878: xviii n. 1; Breeze 1996; Campos Vilanova 1997).

(3) The de Liche collection is recorded as the source for this manuscript in Madrid in 1690.

D'ORLÉANS, CHARLES: (1394–1465). Duke of Orleans from 1408. Captured at the battle of Agincourt 1415 and a prisoner in England to 1440. Poet in English and French. (Arn 1994, 2000).

(43) One of the many contenders put forward as the figure in gold in the frontispiece of the Corpus *Troilus*.

DE THORP: (*fl.* 1360–1370). William de Thorp, made free in 1368–69; in 1376 left 'my books of the play' to a Richard de Yedingham. (Johnston 2002).

(53) The link may be to another York Plays manuscript. See 'VIII. The Gothic System of Scripts: Secretary', pp. 211–12.

DE VERE family: John de Vere, 12th earl of Oxford, and his son Aubrey were executed in 1462 on Tower Hill. Aubrey's brother John made peace with Edward IV. Sir ROBERT DRURY was an executor of the thirteenth earl (David 1995; Hanna and Edwards 1995).

(42) A poem about the house of Vere was written into the Ellesmere manuscript (verso of f. ii to recto of f. iv) late in the fifteenth century and signed 'p(er) Rotheley'. The Ellesmere manuscript was perhaps in the 'chestfull of frenshe and englisshe bokes' left by the 13th earl when he died in 1513 (Doyle 1955–58).

DEWLLYNS, WILLIAM BENSON:

(57) Owner of Digby 133 in late sixteenth or early seventeenth century.

DIGBY, SIR KENELM: (1603–1665). Author, naval commander, and diplomatist. Educated at Gloucester House (now Worcester College) Oxford, where tutored by Thomas ALLEN. In exile in Paris 1649–60. A member of the Royal Society from 1660. Allen gave Digby quite a few books in the 1630s. (Watson 1978; *Oxford DNB*).

(57) Possible owner of Digby 133 after STOW and ALLEN.

DOMNALL GORM': see MACDONALD.

DOUCE, FRANCIS: (1757–1834). For a time a keeper of manuscripts at the British Museum. An inheritance in 1823 gave him the means to buy freely. Left his books, manuscripts, coins, and prints to the Bodleian. (de la Mare 1984; *Oxford DNB*).

(47) Owned Douce 335 (*Master of Game*).

DOWNES, GEOFFREY: Fellow of Queens' College Cambridge 1490–94. For this Geoffrey Downes and a London layman of the same name, probably a relation who established the chantry, see Swanson 2002.

(39) Left instructions on f. 1 for Add. 41175 (Glossed Gospels) to go after the death of his brother, James Downes ('post mortem Maiestri Jacobi Downes donetur capelle de Potte') to the chantry chapel at Pott Shrigley, Cheshire.

DRURY, Sir Robert: (*b. before* 1456, *d.* 1535). London barrister. Privy councillor. Acquired property in Hawstead, Suffolk. The Ellesmere manuscript passed down through his family, passing in 1557 to Henry PAYNE and returning to Ursula Drury's grandson Sir Giles ALINGTON. (David 1995; *Oxford DNB*).

(42) Wrote 'Robertus drury miles William drury miles Roberus drury miles domina Jarmin domina Jarningan dommina Alington' on the verso of f i, naming his two sons and three daughters *c.* 1528–36. The 'HD' (f. 11) and 'Henricus Drury Miles' (f. 147v) must be of a later generation. The 'domina Jarmin' or Anna Drury was married first into the family of 'Edwarde Waldegrave' (verso of f. i), who had a cousin Margery St John (verso of ff. i, iv 'Margery seynt John ys a shrew'). The 'dommina Alington' or Ursula Drury was Sir Giles ALINGTON's grandmother. The 'Thomas Calthorpp' of the verso of f. i was perhaps Sir Robert's great-nephew (Sir Robert's first wife Anna was the daughter of Sir William Calthorpe of Norwich).

DUBROVSKY, PETER: (1756–1816). Graduate of Kiev Ecclesiastical Academy. Appointed to the Russian Church in Paris in 1778 and at the Russian Embassy in Paris from 1780 until 1792. Took his collection of manuscripts to St Petersburg in 1804, passing them on in 1805 to the Imperial Library, where he was appointed curator to a newly established department of manuscripts.

(Logutova 2001).

(1) Acquired the St Petersburg Bede, probably *c.* 1791.

DUGDALE, SIR WILLIAM: (1605-1686). Garter king-of-arms. Historian: among his publications was the *Monasticon Anglicanum* (1655-73), three volumes still consulted. From Warwickshire. Educated at home and at school in Coventry. A friend of Spelman, HATTON, etc., he had access to records in the Tower, to the Cottonian manuscripts and more widely. (*Oxford DNB*).

(6) In 1644 consulted Hatton 20, then owned by Christopher, Lord HATTON.

(15) Borrowed Vitellius C. iii in 1653.

(16) Borrowed Claudius B. iv (Hextateuch) in 1653.

DUNCAN, JOHN:

(56) Name on f. 229 of Arch. Selden. B. 24.

EADFRITH: (*d.* 721?). Bishop of Lindisfarne. (*Oxford DNB*).

(5) Scribe of the Lindisfarne Gospels.

EADUI BASAN: (*fl. c.* 1030). Or Eadwig. Noted scribe, based at Christ Church, Canterbury. (Heslop 1990; *Oxford DNB*).

(2a) Wrote the additional leaves added to the Vespasian Psalter in the eleventh century, evidence perhaps for its presence then in Christ Church rather than St Augustine's.

(20) Perhaps owner at one time of Tiberius A. iii.

EASTRY, HENRY OF: (*d.* 1331). Prior of Christ Church, Canterbury, from 1285. By chance, the list of about 1830 volumes he drew up during the annual inspection of the Christ Church library 1337-38 has survived. (*Oxford DNB*).

(17) Old English Hexateuch identified with no. 95 in Eastry's catalogue (James 1903).

(20) Cotton Tiberius A. iii identified with no. 296 in Eastry's catalogue (James 1903).

(28) Royal 1 A. xiv (Gospels) identified with no. 314 in Eastry's catalogue (James 1903).

EDWARD III: (1312-1377). King of England from 1327. Established the Order of the Garter (1347). Succeeded by his grandson, Richard II. (*Oxford DNB*).

(37) A connection with his court is argued for the *Pearl* manuscript (Nero A. x).

EDWARD PLANTAGENET: (1373-1415). Duke of Aumale, 2nd duke of York. Known also as Edward of Langley. Grandson of Edward III. Translated *The master of game* (see commentary to pl. 47) while confined to Pevensey Castle under suspicion of treachery. Died at the battle of Agincourt. (*Oxford DNB*).

(48) Possible recipient for a presentation copy of Hoccleve's *Regement of Princes*.

EGERTON, THOMAS: (1540-1617). 1st viscount Brackley; baron Ellesmere. Lord Chancellor. Educated Brasenose College Oxford and Lincoln's Inn. Founder of the collection of Egerton manuscripts. His son John Egerton (1579-1649) became the first earl of Bridgewater. When Francis Egerton, 3rd duke of Bridgewater, died in 1803 without a direct heir, the Bridgewater Library went to his nephew, the earl of Stafford, whose second son, also named Francis, assumed the Egerton name, becoming first earl of Ellesmere in 1846. (David 1995; Seymour 1995-97: II. 234-35; *Oxford DNB*).

(42) May have owned the Ellesmere Chaucer. His son John wrote the pressmark 'Q: 3' on f. ii, to which the second earl appended '/3'. Manuscript in family library until sold to Henry E. Huntington in 1917.

ELLESMERE: place-name in titles borne by members of the EGERTON family.

(42) Name traditionally associated with Huntington Library, EL 26 C 9 (the Ellesmere Chaucer).

ELMHAM, THOMAS (OF): (*b.* 1364, *d.* in or after 1427). Monk of St Augustine's Abbey, Canterbury, and author of its chronicle entitled *Speculum Augustinianum*, composed 1414-18 and now Cambridge, Trinity Hall MS 1. In a chapter on books ('De Libris'), Elmham describes eight books, giving a coloured illustration which shows six of them on the altar. (Budny 1999; *Oxford DNB*).

(2) The Vespasian Psalter is identified with the second psalter 'aliud Psalterium' described as kept on the high altar.

EWYNE (?GWYNE): This neat hand also wrote six christian names on f. 49v of Bodley 34.

(30) 'Will(el)m(us) Ewyne de Magna Cowarne' is written on f. 65r of Bodley 34.

FAIRFAX, CHARLES: (1597-1673). Antiquarian and genealogist. From Denton, Yorkshire. Son of Thomas, 1st baron Fairfax. Educated at Trinity College Cambridge and Lincoln's Inn. (*Oxford DNB*).

(58) Bought Fairfax 16 in Gloucester, 8 September 1650, 'meaninge to exchange itt for a beter booke'.

FAIRFAX, HENRY: (*d.* 1708). Second son of Henry, 4th baron Fairfax.

(53) Owned the York Plays (Add. 35290) by date of inscription on f. 3r 'H: Fairfax's Book 1695'; record of his giving it to Thoresby on f. 3v.

FAIRFAX, THOMAS: (1612-1671). 3rd baron Fairfax. Born at Denton, Yorkshire. Parliamentary general. Nephew of CHARLES FAIRFAX. (*Oxford DNB*).

(58) Bequeathed Fairfax 16 to the Bodleian Library in 1671.

FINDLASON, AGNES:

(56) Name 'Agnes Findlason | w^t my hand' and 'A Findlason' on f. 229r of Arch. Selden. B. 24.

FITZALAN, HENRY: (1512-1580). 12th earl of Arundel. Recipient of many of the books and manuscripts belonging to Thomas CRANMER. FitzAlan's books passed to his son-in-law John LUMLEY. (*Oxford DNB*).

(28) Could supply ownership gap between Cranmer and Lumley for Royal 1 A. xiv.

FOLLOWELL, RICHARD: of Litchborough , where a Malory family lived; and Litchborough was about twenty miles from Newbold Revel (Malory's home).

(55) Made notes in Add. 59678 before 1535.

FOUNTAINE, ANDREW: Probably the Andrew Fountaine who died in 1873. For Sir Andrew Fountaine (1676-1753) of Narford,

Norfolk, virtuoso and noteworthy collector of coins, china, pictures, books, see *Oxford DNB*. His property went to his sister's family, whose grandson assumed the name of Fountaine. Did the earlier Sir Andrew next own Capgrave's *Life of St Gilbert* after the KEMP family?

(52) Ownership note 'Andrew Fountaine| Sept. 29 1817' on f. 120r of Add. 36704 (Capgrave).

FRANTON, EDWARD:

(43) His name, spelled backwards, appears in the pages of the Corpus *Troilus*.

FRITHESTAN: (*d.* 932/3). Became bishop of Winchester in 909. (*Oxford DNB*).

(8) Attention is drawn to his name in f. 20v of the Parker Chronicle, and 'FRIÐESTAN diacon' is written over an erasure on f. 57r.

GEORGE I: (1660-1727). King of England 1714-27. (*Oxford DNB*).

(4) Cambridge, University Library, Ll.i.10 in library of John MOORE bought by the king and presented to Cambridge in 1715.

GOWER, HUMPHREY: (1638-1711). Master of St John's College Cambridge. (*Oxford DNB*).

(45) St John's College, L.1 (Chaucer's *Troilus*) was one of fifty books (mostly printed) given by him to the college in 1683.

GRAYE, JAMES: (*d.* 1490). Priest and notary public.

(56) Formerly falsely identified as the scribe of Arch. Selden B. 24.

GRINDAL, EDMUND: (1516 x 20-1583). Educated at Cambridge. Churchman, successively bishop of London and archbishop of York before succeeding MATTHEW PARKER as archbishop of Canterbury 1575-83. (*Oxford DNB*).

(50) Name on f. 385 of Harley 1197, and connected therefore with ff. 385-401.

GRYLLES, WILLIAM: Fellow of Exeter College Oxford 1541-51.

(39) Name erased from f. 1 of Add 41175 (Glossed Gospels).

HARE, ROBERT: (*c.* 1530-1611). Antiquary. Clerk of the Pells. From Suffolk. Educated at Gonville Hall (and Caius) College Cambridge and Inner Temple. MP for Dunwich 1563. Many of his books went to Trinity Hall Cambridge. (Wright 1972; Watson 2000 [2004[1]]; *Oxford DNB*).

(50) Note 'Roberti hare 1563' (?3) above Wolsey's arms on Harley 1197, f. 402r, so may have owned ff. 402-413.

HARLEY, EDWARD: (1689-1741). 2nd earl of Oxford. From *c.* 1711 had day-to-day control of the library his father founded. His widow Henrietta sold the manuscripts to the nation in 1753 for £10,000. (Wright 1962; Wright and Wright 1966; *Oxford DNB*). Note that six plates are from Harley manuscripts (36, 41, 46, 48, 49 and 50).

HARLEY, ROBERT: (1661-1724). 1st earl of Oxford. Politician. Founded important collection of books known as the Harleian Library and carried on by his son EDWARD HARLEY. WANLEY was introduced to Harley in 1701 and worked for father and son from 1703 to 1726. (Wright and Wright 1966; Wright 1972; *Oxford DNB*).

HATTON, CHRISTOPHER: (*bap.* 1605, *d.* 1670). 1st Baron Hatton. Antiquary. Educated at Jesus College Cambridge. (*Oxford DNB*).

(6), (29) Owned Hatton 20 (*Cura Pastoralis*) and Hatton 38 (Gospels).

(24) Among manuscripts not sold at his death; presented to the Bodleian Library by the 2nd lord Hatton in 1678.

HAUARD: A family of this name was important in Hereford, which had a mayor named 'Thomas Havard' in 1528, 1539, 1552, and an alderman of the same name in 1569 (Ker 1960: xiv).

(30) 'Thomas Hauard esquier' is written on f. 73v of Bodley 34.

HEDGEMAN, John: 'of Hawkedoun in the Countie of Suff''.

(42) Inscription Manly and Rickert read on f. 175 of the Ellesmere *Canterbury Tales* by ultraviolet.

HEMMING: (*fl. c.* 1095). Worcester monk, second half of the eleventh century. He played a part in drawing together the eleventh-century collections of charters and other records of Worcester, now Cotton Tiberius A. xiii and commonly known as Hemming's Cartulary. (Ker 1948 [1985]; *Oxford DNB*).

(22) The 'Ca' copy of the translation of Bede's *Historia* was written by Scribe 2 of Hemming's Cartulary.

HENRY, PRINCE OF WALES: (1386/7-1422). Shakespeare's Prince Hal. As Henry V, was king of England 1413-22. For discussion of his books, see Cavanaugh 1980: 412-21, Krochalis 1988-89. (*Oxford DNB*).

(47) Dedicatee of the translation *The master of game*.

HENRY FREDERICK, PRINCE OF WALES: (1594-1612). Eldest son of James I, he died before his father. His books, including the collection given to him by Lord Lumley, became part of the Royal Collection, which was one of the foundation collections of the British Museum in 1757. (*Oxford DNB*).

(28) Royal 1 A. xiv (Old English Gospels) is no. 109 in the catalogue Henry had made of Lumley's collection in 1609.

HEPBURN, MARGARET: see under Henry SINCLAIR.

HICKES, GEORGE: (1642-1715). Historian and philologist. Author of *Linguarum veterum septentrionalium thesaurus* (I. 1703; WANLEY's catalogue is volume II. 1705). A central figure in Anglo-Saxon scholarship. (Douglas 1939: 93-119; *Oxford DNB*).

(5) Notes that Cotton Nero D. iv (Lindisfarne Gospels) was used by Day and Foxe in the preparation of their *Gospels of the fower Evangelistes* (1571).

(9) While chaplain to John Maitland, duke of Lauderdale in 1677-78 saw Add. 47967 (Orosius); states it had belonged to John Dee.

(11) Prints runic passages from the Exeter Book in *Thesaurus* (1703).

HOLYNGBORNE, WILLIAM: monk of St Augustine's Abbey, Canterbury, late fifteenth century. (Kane 1960).

(41) Name entered in Harley 6041, f. 96v (*Piers Plowman*).

HOLLAND, JOSEPH: (*d.* 1605). Member of the Elizabethan Society of Antiquaries. (Caldwell 1943; *Oxford DNB*).

(58) John STOW notes (f. 82v) that Fairfax 16 'Here lacketh ·6· leves| that are in Josephe| Hollands boke'. This does not square with Cambridge

University, Gg. 4. 27, which Holland owned *c.* 1600. Fairfax's note (f. 1r) that 'Joseph Holland' had another such manuscript 'intendinge to exchange itt for a better booke' is probably based on Stow's note.

HOLLOND, RICHERD: Identified wrongly by Cockayne as Admiral Richard Holland, *d.* 1401. (Flom 1941).

(15) Ownership signature 'Richerd Hollond thys boke', perhaps sixteenth-century, on f. 76 of Vitellius C. iii.

HON(E)YWOOD, MICHAEL: (1596-1681). Educated at Christ's Church College, Cambridge. Dean of Lincoln 1660-81. Responsible for the construction of the library designed by Sir Christopher Wren. (Thomson 1989: xix-xx; *Oxford DNB*).

HOO FAMILY: Bedfordshire (Kane 1960; Wright 1972).

(41) Evidence of shields of arms in margins suggests that Harley 6041(*Piers Plowman*) was written for some member of the Hoo family.

HORN, CHARLES:

(50) Name Carolus Hornus on f. 385 and again f. 401 of Harley 1197, a separable booklet of this manuscript.

HOWARD, HENRY: (1540-1614). Earl of Northampton. Educated at King's College Cambridge, and taught at Trinity Hall. Scholar, courtier. Earl Marshal of England. (*Oxford DNB*).

(16) Borrowed Nero A. i (Wulfstan) from the Cotton collection *c.* 1612.

HOWARD, HENRY: (1628-1684). 6th duke of Norfolk. Grandson of THOMAS HOWARD. Gave Arundel collection to the Royal Society in 1667. (*Oxford DNB*).

(34) Arundel 292 among manuscripts transferred by the Royal Society to the British Museum in 1831.

HOWARD, THOMAS: (1585-1646). 14th earl of Arundel. Collector and patron of the arts. Educated at Westminster School and Trinity College Cambridge. JUNIUS was his librarian. (*Oxford DNB*).

(34) Owned Arundel 292 (*Bestiary*).

HUGO DE:

(37) Name in *Pearl* manuscript (Nero A. x, f. 95r).

JAMES IV: (1473-1513) king of Scotland. Married to Margaret Tudor, daughter of Henry VII, a union that led to the 1603 accession of the Stewarts to the English throne. Died on the battle-field at Flodden. (*Oxford DNB*).

(56) Report of date and place of his birth provides evidence for history of Arch. Selden. B. 24.

JAMES, RICHARD: (*bap.* 1591, *d.* 1638). Scholar. Educated Newport Grammar School, Exeter College Oxford, Corpus Christi College Oxford. ROBERT COTTON's librarian from *c.* 1625, remaining with Sir Thomas after Sir Robert's death. Thus had access to all the Cotton manuscripts. (Watson 1978: 300; *Oxford DNB*).

(19) His extracts from Titus A. iv in Bodleian, MS James 6, were made while this manuscript still belonged to ALLEN.

(23) Note his use of the Peterborough Chronicle manuscript.

JERARD, WILLIAM:

(50) Late-fifteenth-century ownership note in Harley 1197, Pt I, f. 77r.

JOHN OF LANCASTER: (1389-1435). 3rd son of Henry IV; duke of Bedford. From 1422 regent of France. Literary patron and collector of books. No evidence indicating ownership or patronage of English vernacular writings. (Cavanaugh 1980: 468-73; Stratford 1987, 1993; *Oxford DNB*).

(48) Suggested as a possible recipient for a presentation copy of Hoccleve's *Regement of Princes*.

JOSCELYN, JOHN : (1529-1603). Or Josselin. Educated Queens' College Cambridge. Held a prebend in Hereford between 1560 and 1570. MATTHEW PARKER's Latin secretary, he had easy access to the Parker and Cotton collections. Also made significant use of Canterbury, Exeter, and Worcester collections. Compiler of an unpublished Old English dictionary. (Graham and Watson 1998; Graham 2000[2]; *Oxford DNB*).

(16), (21) Owned Nero A. i; probably owned Tiberius B. iv.

(20) Provides evidence for John Twyne's ownership of Tiberius A. iii; note in his hand on f. 176v.

Among the other manuscripts he used are (5) Lindisfarne Gospels, (6) Hatton 20, (8) Corpus Christi College 173, (11) Exeter Cathedral 3501, (19) Titus A. iv, (22) Cambridge, University Library, Kk.3.18, (23) Laud Misc. 636 and (25) Vespasian D. xiv.

JUNIUS, FRANCIS(CUS) or François Du Jon: (1591-1677). Scholar and antiquary. Born in Heidelberg; later education in Holland, to which he often returned. For part of his life THOMAS HOWARD's librarian; at times tutor to Thomas Howard's son, his grandchildren and his ward, the earl of Oxford. Left some 122 books and manuscripts to the Bodleian Library. (Breuker 1998; Rademaker 1998; Stanley 1998; *Oxford DNB*).

(13) Received Junius 11 from Archbishop USSHER by 1652; published edition (Amsterdam, 1655).

(24) Hatton 116 among the manuscripts returned to the Bodleian shortly before his death.

(27) Owned Junius 11 (*Ormulum*).

(29) Used Hatton 38 for the edition he and Thomas MARSHALL published of the Anglo-Saxon gospels at Dort in 1665.

Among the many other manuscripts he consulted or made copies from are (5) Lindisfarne Gospels, (6) Hatton Pastoral Care, (14) Julius A. x (Old English Martyrology), (16) Nero A. i (Wulfstan), (19) Titus A. iv, (20) Tiberius A. iii and (21) Tiberius B. iv (Chronicle).

KAYLE:

(45) Written in hand of later fifteenth or early sixteenth century at foot of f. 120r (formerly a pastedown) of St John's *Troilus*; perhaps an owner's name.

KEMP, SIR ROBERT: (*d.* 1647). Of Gissing, Norfolk. Lucas (1972; 1997:142) shows that a Thomas Gybbons saw a manuscript of Capgrave's 'Life of St Gilbert' and 'Tretis' in Kemp's possession, probably between 1641 and 1647.

(52) Owned Capgrave's *Life of St Gilbert* (Add. 36704).

KEWE, IOH'.: of Reydon, Suffolk?

(52) Note of payment for prayers on behalf of himself and his wife 'Matild'' on f. 121v of Add. 36704 (Capgrave).

KNYGHTLY, FERDINAND: of Fawsley, Northants. Son of Sir Richard Knyghtley (1533-1615). Ferdinand 'saw much foreign military service and was highly favoured by the electress'. (DNB Archive in *Oxford DNB*).

(58) One of three names with mottoes and date 14 October 1612 on f. 33v of Fairfax 16.

KNYVETT: a Norfolk gentry family of this name is recorded as owning books in the fifteenth century. A sister of JOHN SHIRLEY's second wife married John Knyvett (1416-91), the son of Sir John Knyvett of Southwick and Mendlesham, and other family links have been established with Shirley. (Connolly 1998: 63, 109). In the next century, Sir Thomas Knyvett (*c.* 1539-1618) of Ashwellthorpe, Norfolk, had a large collection of books (McKitterick 1978), among them Cambridge University Library MS Ff. 1. 6 (Harris 1983: 307).

(43) 'Knyvett' on f. 108r of Corpus *Troilus*.

KOENWALD:

(6) 'koenwald monachus' is a tenth-century addition on f. 98v of the Hatton Pastoral Care.

LAMBARDE, WILLIAM: (1536-1601). Educated at Lincoln's Inn. Historian of Kent. His *Archaionomia* (1568) was the first printed edition of Anglo-Saxon law. (Warnicke 1973; *Oxford DNB*).

(16) Copied extracts from Nero A. i into Julius C. ii.

(21) Copied extracts from Tiberius B. iv (Chronicle) into Canterbury Cathedral, MS E. 1.

LANGBAINE, GERARD: (1608/9-1658). Provost of Queen's College Oxford 1646. Active cataloguing and making notes about Oxford manuscripts in the 1640s. (*Oxford DNB*).

(57) Digby 133 probably in DIGBY's 1634 bequest to the Bodleian Library.

LAUD, WILLIAM: (1573-1645). Archbishop of Canterbury and Chancellor of the University of Oxford. Educated at Reading Free School and St John's College Oxford. Beheaded at Tower Hill. (*Oxford DNB*).

(23) Gave Laud Misc. 636 to the Bodleian Library in 1639.

(35) By 1633 owned Laud Misc. 108 (the *South English Legendary* manuscript into which the romances *Havelok* and *King Horn* were incorporated).

LAUDERDALE, see MAITLAND.

LEE: 'William lee(?De B(*or* k) (et) Johan(nes) [ ] portera(n)t vn br' de Wast.,'.

(45) Scribble in St John's *Troilus*, f. 1r.

LEE-DILLON, HAROLD ARTHUR: (1844-1932). 17th viscount Dillon of Ditchley, Oxfordshire. Antiquary. First curator of the armouries of the Tower of London. Fellow of the British Academy from its foundation in 1902. (*Oxford DNB*).

(39) Gave Add. 41175 (Glossed Gospels) to British Museum.

LELAND, JOHN: (*c.* 1503-1552). Antiquary. Returned to England *c.* 1529. Reconnoitred monastic collections, and by 1533 had some sort of commission from Henry VIII to examine monastic and collegial libraries. Travelling around libraries and writing until 1547, when he became insane. (Carley 1999: 275-76; *Oxford DNB*).

(2) Probably saw the Vespasian Psalter in Canterbury Cathedral, 1533-34.

(38) Saw Peterhouse 75.I at Peterhouse in 1542.

LE NEVE, SIR WILLIAM: (*bap.* 1592, *d.* 1661). Herald and genealogist. Son and heir of William Le Neve of Aslacton, Norfolk. This would seem to be the appropriate person. (*Oxford DNB*).

(15) Borrowed Vitellius C. iii for use by DE LAET in 1641.

(17) Borrowed Claudius B. iv (Hexateuch) in 1641.

LEOFRIC: (*d.* 1072). Scholar and lover of books. Educated in Lotharingia. Chaplain to Edward the Confessor in 1041, when Edward returned from exile. 1st bishop of Exeter 1050-72. (Lloyd 1967; *Oxford DNB*).

(11) Of the sixty-six books Leofric gave Exeter Cathedral, only the Exeter Book is in the cathedral library today.

LISLE, WILLIAM (or L'isle): (*c.* 1569-1637). Educated at Eton and Cambridge. Antiquary and Fellow of King's College, Cambridge. Had a particular interest in Old English biblical materials. (Lee 2000; Graham 2000[1]; Pulsiano 2000; *Oxford DNB*).

(8) Consulted the Parker Chronicle, entering collations from it into the Peterborough Chronicle.

(17) Borrowed Claudius B. iv from Cotton in 1621.

(22) Consulted Laud Misc. 636.

(23) Annotated the Peterborough Chronicle with collations from the Parker Chronicle.

(25) Vespasian D. xiv borrowed from Cotton.

LUMLEY, JOHN: (*c.* 1533-1609). Lord Lumley. Acquired many of CRANMER's books through his father-in-law Henry FITZALAN, earl of Arundel. The large collection of books and manuscripts he inherited formed the nucleus of his library, which passed to HENRY FREDERICK, prince of Wales, eldest son of James I. Prince Henry had a catalogue made in 1609. Thus the books entered the Royal Collection and were part of the gift made by George III to the British Museum. (Jayne and Johnson 1956; *Oxford DNB*).

(28) His name is on f. 3 of Royal 1 A. xiv (Old English Gospels), together with Cranmer's.

LYE, EDWARD: (*bap.* 1694, *d.* 1767). Lexicographer. Oxford. Consulted many manuscripts and transcripts made from them. His large two-volume dictionary (1772) was supervised through press by Owen MANNING. (Clunies Ross 1997; *Oxford DNB*).

(11) Allowed to borrow the Exeter Book, which was in his possession 1759-62.

MACDONALD, DONALD GORM': (*d.* 1617). Chief of the MacDonalds of Sleat from 1585

(56) Two lines of Gaelic verse with signature 'Misi Domnall Gorm'' below them appear on f. 231v of Arch. Selden. B. 24. Bannerman (1979/80: 26 and fn. 3 suggests that he was the owner until the manuscript left Scotland in 1592 (i.e. the date accompanying the signature CHANNOIS).

MADDEN, SIR FREDERIC: (1801-73). Among the most distinguished of Keepers of Manuscripts in the British Museum. His notebooks (in the British Library) and diaries (in the Bodleian Library, Oxford, with a copy held in the British Library) are a valuable resource both for manuscript studies and life in Victorian England. (Caygill 2001; *Oxford DNB*).

(51) Had the Lincoln Cathedral 91 on loan in 1832; manuscript also lent to J.O. Halliwell in 1845.

(53) Probably responsible for identification of contents in Sotheby's catalogue for sale 18 June 1844. His notes record the sale of the York Plays to THORPE for RUSSELL in 1844 and afterwards to Lord ASHBURNHAM. This was a manuscript Madden wanted for the national collection.

MAIDWELL:

(30) A late-sixteenth-century hand wrote in bottom margin of f. 52r of Bodley 34 five lines of verse that paraphrase the last five lines of *Seinte Iuliene* (immediately above) and end 'Q(uod) Maidwell'; another note in this hand further up on this page.

MAITLAND, JOHN: (1616-1682). 1st duke of Lauderdale. Married widow of Sir Lionel TOLLEMACHE. No heir, so property passed to wife's son by first marriage. (*Oxford DNB*)

(9) According to HICKES, owned Add. 47967 (Orosius).

?MAN(ERS): see under RYTCHYNE.

MANNING, OWEN: (1721-1801). Scholar, at Queens' College Cambridge. Historian of Surrey. (*Oxford DNB*).

(11) Allowed to borrow the Exeter Book when seeing LYE's dictionary through the press.

MARSHALL, THOMAS: (1621-1685). Dean of Gloucester. Rector of Lincoln College, Oxford. A friend of JUNIUS. (*Oxford DNB*).

(9) Annotated Junius's transcript of Tiberius B. i (Old English Orosius) with notes taken from Add. 47967.

MOORE, JOHN: (1646-1714). Bishop of Norwich and later of Ely. After Moore's death, King GEORGE I bought his library and in 1715 presented it to Cambridge University. (*Oxford DNB*).

(4) Book of Cerne in Moore's library by 1697.

MOYELLE, THOMAS: (*b. before* 1500, *d.* 1560). Or Moyle. One of the General Surveyers of the Court of Augmentation to Henry VIII and Edward VI. Speaker of the House of Commons. His mother was a daughter of Sir Robert DRURY. (*Oxford DNB*).

(58) Signature of ownership on f. 321v of Fairfax 16 possibly his.

NANDICKE, RICHARDE:

(53) A name (*c.* 1600) that occurs in the opening pages of the York Plays, Add. 35290; the initials RN (f. 92r) are associated particularly with 'The Smithis' play.

NEVE, JOHN: 'of Oxenborowe', in Norfolk.

(42) Wrote eight lines of Virgil's *Georgics* into f. 48r of the Ellesmere Chaucer manuscript.

NEVILLE, ANNE:

(a) Anne: (1426-1492). Daughter of Richard Beauchamp, earl of Warwick, and Isabel Despenser. Married Richard Neville, 'the kingmaker', in 1439 and, after his death in 1471, kept in custody. Her estates restored to her in 1487.

(b) Anne: (1456-1485). Daughter of Anne and Richard Neville, earl of Warwick. First married Edward, Prince of Wales, and afterwards Richard III. (*Oxford DNB*).

(c) Anne: (*d.* 1480). Daughter of Joan Beaufort and Ralph Neville, Earl of Westmorland, she became Duchess of Buckingham (1424). Her daughter Joanna's second husband was Sir William KNYVETT of Norfolk.

(43) Name on f. 101v of Corpus *Troilus* could be any one of the above. Knyvett link makes (c) likely. Yet (a) possible because Beauchamp was John Shirley's patron and (b) because this Anne was heiress of the Beauchamp family. And, as pointed out by Doyle (1970: 125-27), these were not the only women of this name.

NICHOLAS, OLIVER: from Aubrey, Wiltshire. Matriculated at Magdalen Hall Oxford in 1602. At Lincoln's Inn 1606.

(58) One of three names with mottoes and date 14 October 1612 on f. 333v of Fairfax 16.

NORTH, ROGER: (1531-1600). Lord North (2nd baron). Treasurer of Queen Elizabeth's household. Of Kirtling in Cambridgeshire, about six miles away from where Sir Giles ALINGTON lived. (*Oxford DNB*).

(42) Signed '1 DVRVM 5 PATI 68' together with the date 1 May 1568 and a motto on the verso of f. iv; added two English poems on ff. ii and v signed 'R North' and 'RN'.

NOWELL, LAURENCE: (1530-*c.* 1570). Antiquary. Cousin of Laurence Nowell, dean of Lichfield, with whom he used erroneously to be identified. Matriculated at Christ Church Oxford by 1550, Fellow 1552-53 -?54. Travelled, returning to England by 1559. In Cecil's household by 1562-63 as 'servant' or 'secretary'. Left his library to LAMBARDE in 1567, when he left for the continent. (Flower 1935; Warnicke 1974; Berkhout 1998; *Oxford DNB*).

(5), (11), (23) Used Lindisfarne Gospels, Exeter Book, Peterborough Chronicle (just possibly in London in Parker's household: see Graham 1994).

(21) Copied extracts from Tiberius B. iv into Add. 43704.

(25) Owned Vespasian D. xiv , from which he excerpted words for a dictionary of Old English.

PALMERE, WILLIAM: (*d.* 1400). Recorded as a clergyman in Sussex and Leicestershire in 1390s. Rector of St Alphege, Cripplegate, in London, 1397-1400. In his will left 'my book called Piers Plowman' to a woman, Agnes Eggesfeld. (Wood 1984).

Not associated with any extant manuscript. See 'VII The Gothic System of Scripts: Anglicana', p. 103.

PARFRE: a family name that crops up in records of Thetford, Norfolk, from 1490s to the middle of the sixteenth century. Sloane 446 has a John Parfre as father of William. (Baker and Murphy 1967).

(57) 'Jhon Parfre ded wryte thys booke' on f. 157v of Digby 133.

PARKER, SIR JOHN: (1548-1618). Son of MATTHEW PARKER. Helped JOSCELYN in making lists of words, etc. (Strongman 1997).

(29) His signature in red pencil is on f. 1 of Hatton 38.

PARKER, MATTHEW: (1504-1575). Dean of college of secular priests at Stoke-by-Clare 1535; chaplain to Anne Boleyn. Master of Corpus Christi College Cambridge 1544. Archbishop of Canterbury from 1559. Amassed collection left to Corpus Christi

College in 1575. (*Oxford DNB*).

(2) Borrowed Vespasian Psalter from CECIL in 1556.

(3) Gameson (2001-02) argues that the red foliation suggests Parker intervention in Codex Aureus, and that it was still in England *c.*1600.

(8), (17), (22) Owned Corpus Christi College 173 (Parker Chronicle); Claudius B. iv (Hexateuch); Cambridge, University Library, Kk.3.18 (Bede); Claudius B. iv (Gospels).

(11) Could well have had the Exeter Book on loan in London (Graham 1994).

(23), (25) Consulted both the Peterborough Chronicle and the Vespasian D. xiv homiletic collection.

(29) Ownership note 'Matthæs Cantuar: 1572' on f. 3r of Hatton 38 (Gospels).

(43) The words 'ex dono' in his note on f. 150v suggest that BATMAN gave the Corpus 61 *Troilus* to Parker.

(50) Red marks in Harley 1197 through to final part need investigation.

PASTON family: Norfolk landowners. Letters written by members of the family from 1425-95 give unparalleled insights into eight decades of English life. (*Oxford DNB*).

(42) Phrase 'demeuz enmeuz' connected with the Paston family is recorded on the verso of ff. i and vii of the Ellesmere Chaucer.

PAYNE, HENRY: Member of Lincoln's Inn. Of Nowton, near Hawstead. Member of Lincoln's Inn. A neighbour of the DRURY family, he witnessed Sir William Drury's will in 1557.

(42) On f. 130 'per me henricum Payne'. Left 'my Chaucer written in vellum and illumyned w[t] golde' by his will (PCC 3 Sheffield) proved 2 February 1568/9 to Sir Giles ALINGTON (Seymour 1995-97: II. 235).

PENNELL', DOROTE:

(43) A name written on f. 63r of the Corpus *Troilus*, probably early in the sixteenth century.

PENNELL, WILLIAM:

(53) A name entered in the last verso of the York Plays (Add. 35290).

PERUEYS, HENRY: A London draper. An apprentice to Simon Eyre, draper, 1437. Still alive 1476. (Smithers 1987: xiii-xiv).

(35) Owned Laud Misc. 108 (the *South English Legendary* manuscript into which the *Havelok* and *King Horn* booklet was incorporated).

POKYSFEN, JOH.:

(50) Wrote Harley 1197, ff. 144-203, in the fifteenth century. (Watson 1973 [2004[1]]).

RAMSAY, JOHN: Prior of Charterhouse at Perth and scribe of a second copy of Barbour's *Bruce* (1489).

(54) Sometimes falsely identified with the scribe (I. de R.) of St John's College MS G. 23.

REDE, JOHN: priest.

(35) Attests to Perueys's ownership of Laud Misc. 108 (the *South English Legendary* manuscript into which the romances *Havelok* and *King Horn* were incorporated).

REYNOLDS, WALTER: (*d.* 1327). Bishop of Worcester from *c.* 1308 and archbishop of Canterbury 1313-27. Godfather to Edward III, whom he crowned at Westminster. (*Oxford DNB*).

(31) His name is on a list tucked into Titus D. xviii.

ROTHELEY: Unidentified; possibly had some connection with the household of the earls of Oxford (DE VERE family). A John Rotheley from Westchester (?West Caistor), Norfolk, was in the retinue of Edmund, marquis of Suffolk in 1448, and is identified as the likeliest of six possible Rotheleys found in public records at appropriate dates. (Hanna and Edwards 1995).

(42) A poem in a late-fifteenth-century hand, composed and/or copied 'p(er) Rotheley', appears from the verso of f. ii to the recto of f. iv in the Ellesmere *Canterbury Tales*; its content suggests a de Vere connection.

ROTHELEY, WILLIAM: A London goldsmith. Warden of the Goldsmiths' Company 1444, 1450, 1459, 1465. Latest record names him as a city tax collector 1480. (Smithers 1987: xiii-xiv).

(35) Attests to PERUEYS's ownership of Laud Misc. 108 (the *South English Legendary* manuscript into which the romances *Havelok* and *King Horn* were incorporated).

RUDD, THOMAS: Or Rodd? Mid-nineteenth-century London bookseller.

(53) York Plays passed through his hands.

RUSSELL, THOMAS: (*c.* 1781-1846). Thomas Cloutt, a dissenting minister and inveterate buyer of books. Russell, a pseudonym, was officially his name from 1823. (Cawley 1980; *Oxford DNB*).

(53) The evidence for Cloutt's ownership between Thorpe's 1844 purchase and Ashburnham's in 1847 depends on a note made by MADDEN which states that the York Plays manuscript was sold to Thorpe for the Rev. Thomas Russell. Cawley 1980 suggests that at Cloutt's death (1846) Thorpe again bought the York Plays manuscript, selling it on to ASHBURNHAM.

RYTCHYNE:

(53) 'R Rytchyne man(?ers)' is among the names entered in the York Plays register (Add. 35290).

SAVILE, HENRY (1568-1617): Of Banke, Yorkshire. Henry Savile graduated from Oxford, was licensed as a physician, and spent most of his life in St Martin-in-the-Fields. The Savile family lived in the Halifax area, and the collection was begun by his grandfather and father. (Watson 1969 [2004[1]]; *Oxford DNB*).

(37) Nero A. x (*Pearl* manuscript) in his collection.

SCHINER, PATRIK:

(56) Name on f. 230v of Arch. Selden. B. 24.

SCHINER, VILLEM:

(56) Name on f. 230v of Arch. Selden. B. 24.

SCOT(T), ROBERT: (*b.* in or before 1632, *d.* 1709/10). London bookseller and publisher. (Rostenberg 1965: II. 281-313; *Oxford DNB*).

(6), (29) Among books bought after Hatton's death 1670 and sold to the Bodleian Library in 1671.

(26) Handled Theyer's books, among them Royal 4 A. xiv.

SCROPE family: Richard (le) Scrope (*c.* 1350-1405) was archbishop of York, 1398-1405; William (le) Scrope (1351?-1399) was earl of Wiltshire. (*Oxford DNB*).

(43) The single illumination on f. 1v of the Corpus *Troilus* is attributed to a limner who completed commissions for members of the Scrope family.

SEBOURNE: Seabournes of Sutton are in the 1569 Visitation of Herefordshire (Ker 1960: xiv).

(30) 'Richard Sebourne of' and 'Willelmus Sebourne This indent' are to be found respectively on ff. 26r and 38r of Bodley 34.

SELDEN, JOHN: (1584-1654). Matriculated at Oxford from Hart Hall in 1600; left without a degree, entering Clifford's Inn in 1602. MP in 1621, representing Oxford University from 1640 to 1653. Left his collection of over 8000 manuscripts and printed books to the Bodleian Library, where they were received in 1659. (*Oxford DNB*).

(16) Extracts from Nero A. i (Wulfstan) in his *History of Tithes* (1618). (Tite 2003: 130).

(17) Borrowed Claudius B. iv (Hextateuch) in 1621 or later.

(20) Made use of the in Tiberius A. iii *Regularis Concordia* text in his *History of Tithes* (1618). (Tite 2003: 130).

(56) Owned Arch. Selden. B. 24.

SHIRLEY, JOHN: (*c.* 1366-1456). A member of the household of Richard Beauchamp, earl of Warwick, he very likely had access to royal circles. Although often represented as playing a part in book trade in fifteenth-century London, it is more likely that the texts he copied and translated were for his own use and for use within the Beauchamp household. Family connexions with the KNYVETT family have been traced. (Edwards 1997; Connolly 1998; *Oxford DNB*).

(43) Wrote two lines from Lydgate's *Prayer for King, Queen and People* on f. 1r of Corpus Christi College Cambridge 61 (*Troilus*).

SINCLAIR, HENRY: (*d.* 1513). 3rd lord Sinclair, earl of Orkney; in 1489 married Margaret Hepburn, daughter of Lord Hailes. Other Sinclair names written into manuscript include: f. 79 'Maurius Synclar'; f. 230r 'Elezabeth synclar, '?Jen Sinclar' (his daughters).

(56) Arms, assumed only in 1489, on f. 118v; ownership note on f. 230v.

SLOANE, SIR HANS: (1660-1753). Physician and collector. Born in Killyleagh, Co. Down, Ireland. Widely travelled. Succeeded Newton as president of the Royal Society. Left his manuscripts, books, and other collections to the nation on condition that his two daughters be paid £20,000. Like the Harley and Cotton collections, his was one of the foundation collections of the British Museum library. (de Beer 1953; *Oxford DNB*).

(40) Sloane 2593 first known in his collection.

SMITH, JOHN: (*bap.* 1659, *d.* 1715). Treasurer of Durham. Editor of Bede's *Historia ecclesiastica,* both Latin and Old English. Edition completed and published in 1722 by his son George. (*Oxford DNB*).

(10) Wanley saw books on loan from Tanner in Smith's lodgings in 1715, among them very possibly the Tanner Bede.

SMOLO, LAWRENCE:

(56) Name on f. 230v of Arch. Selden. B. 24.

SOMER, JOHN: (*d.* in or after 1409). Astronomer and mathematician. A Franciscan (or Friar Minor or Minorite or Grey Friar) at the Bridgewater house; probably at Oxford in 1380. The most famous manuscript associated with him is a calendar with astronomical tables (Royal B. viii) written by him for Joan, Princess of Wales, mother of Richard II. (*Oxford DNB*).

(38) Calculations given in Peterhouse 75. I, f. 63v, are attributed to him.

SOWSCH, JACOBY:

(50) Name among scribbles on f. 140, in Part II of Harley 1197.

SPARWENFELDT, JOHN GABRIEL: (1655-1727). Swedish ambassador in Madrid, Spain, late in the seventeenth century.

(3) Bought (inscription, f. 3) the Codex Aureus for the Swedish royal collections in 1690.

STANLEY, ISOBEL: recorded as having married a Walter Moyle in the sixteenth century. Was she a relation of John STANLEY?

(58) Did she own Fairfax 16?

STANLEY, JOHN: (1400-*c.* 1469). Courtier and M.P. for Surrey. From Hooton in the Wirral. Lived in Battersea. Usher of the Chamber and Serjeant of the Armoury 1431-60.

(37) No hard evidence underpins the argument that the *Pearl* manuscript was written for some Stanley family in Staffordshire and Cheshire.

(58) John Stanley probably commissioned Fairfax 16.

STILLINGFLEET, EDWARD: (1635-1699). Bishop of Worcester 1689-99. Educated at Cranbourne Grammar School and St John's College Oxford. Amassed a large collection of manuscripts and rare books. His manuscripts were bought by ROBERT HARLEY; Narcissus Marsh, archbishop of Armagh, bought his books. (*Oxford DNB*).

(46) Owned Harley 674 (*Cloud*).

STOW(E), JOHN: (1525-1605). Chronicler and antiquary. Admitted Freeman of the Merchant Taylors' Company in 1547. His books went with the D'EWES library to ROBERT HARLEY. (Dorsch 1959; Hudson 1984; *Oxford DNB*; Gadd and Gillespie 2004; Edwards 2004).

(57) Thought to have acquired Digby 133 from Myles Blomefylde, on evidence of very short note on f. 146r (Baker and Murphy 1967).

(58) Note in his hand in Fairfax 16 (Edwards 2004).

TALBOT, ROBERT: (1505/6-1558). Prebendary of Norwich from 1547. Educated at Winchester College and New College Oxford. One of the earliest to read Old English in modern times. (GRAHAM 2000[1]; *Oxford DNB*).

(16) Probably the first owner of the Old English Hexateuch after the dissolution of the monasteries.

(17) Used Nero A.i (Wulfstan).

(22) May have owned the 'Ca' version of the Old English Bede.

(25) Used Vespasian D. xiv (Old and early Middle English homiletic materials, etc.).

TANNER, THOMAS: (1674-1735). Educated at Queen's College Oxford, and Fellow of All Souls. Various church appointments; bishop of St Asaph from 1732. (*Oxford DNB*).

(10) Tanner 10 Bede was among his manuscripts acquired by the Bodleian in 1736.

TATE, FRANCIS: (1560-1616). Member of the original Society of Antiquaries. Lawyer; Member of Parliament. (*Oxford DNB*).

(15) Provides evidence that Nero A. i (Wulfstan), which he may once have owned, was in Cotton's library by 1613. Had manuscript on loan 1612-16.

(17) Borrowed Claudius B. iv (Hexateuch) by 1612.

(21) Borrowed Tiberius B. iv (Chronicle) in 1606 (Lutz 2000: 21, fn. 46).

THEYER, JOHN: (*bap.* 1598, *d.* 1673). Antiquary. Born in Brockworth, Glos.; lived for much of his life in Cowper's Hill, Glos. Inherited manuscripts from his grandfather Thomas Theyer, who married a sister of Richard Hart, last prior of Llanthony. Gathered up books in the west of England. Left his books to his grandson Charles; collection went to a London bookseller, ROBERT SCOTT, from whom bought by Henry Compton, bishop of London, for King Charles II. (*Oxford DNB*).

(26) In *c.* 1678 Charles II bought 312 volumes that had been Theyer's for the Royal Library, among them Royal 4 A. xiv.

THORESBY, RALPH: (1658-1725). Antiquary and topographer. From Leeds. (Cawley 1980; *Oxford DNB*).

(53) Given the York Plays (Add. 35290) by Henry Fairfax sometime between 1695 and 1708. His collection went to auction at the death of his oldest son.

THORNTON, ROBERT: (*b.* in or before 1392, *d.* in or before 1465). Lord of the manor of East Newton in 1418, in the North Riding of Yorkshire; dead by 1465, when widow remarried. Two large manuscripts were compiled by him for reading by family and friends: Lincoln Cathedral 91, popularly known as the Thornton Manuscript (see pl. 51), and London, British Library Additional MS 31042. (Brewer and Owen 1977; Thompson 1982, 1983, 1987; *Oxford DNB*).

THORPE: Bookseller.

(53) Bought York Plays manuscript in 1844 at Sotheby's, selling it to ASHBURNHAM in 1847.

THYNNE, WILLIAM: (*d.* 1546). Member of the royal household in the early Tudor period. His 1532 edition of Chaucer, dedicated to Henry VIII, did much to establish the canon for the next two centuries. (Blodgett 1984; *Oxford DNB*).

TOLLEMACHE family:

(9) Inherited Add. 47967 (Orosius) from the MAITLAND family. Signature of John, 1st baron Tollemache, 1876, on f. 1. The British Museum acquired the manuscript in 1953 from the trustees of the then Lord Tollemache.

TRENTHALL:

(45) Fifteenth-century note on pastedown now f. 120r says that 'Joh(anni) Trenthall' (but '-nt-' could be read as *ut* or *nc* or *uc*) was given Cambridge, St John's L. 1 (Chaucer's *Troilus*) by 'R.C./ M-'.

TURNER, WILLIAM: (1509/10-1568). Dean of Wells. Born at Morpeth in Northumberland; his widow owned some Anglo-Saxon books. (*Oxford DNB*).

(5) His name was once identified with the scrawled inscription on f. 211 of the Lindisfarne Gospels (Nero D. iv), where only 'Thomas' is safe.

TWYNE, JOHN: (*c.* 1505-1581). Probably taught at St Augustine' s Canterbury before the Reformation. Master of King's School Canterbury from its new foundation in 1541. Sheriff, mayor, and MP at various times. (Watson 1986 [2004[1]]; *Oxford DNB*).

(20) According to Joscelyn, owned Tiberius A. iii, f. 178 (a stray from Tiberius A. vi).

TWYNE, THOMAS: (1543-1613). Or Twine. Scholar and writer. Son of John TWYNE. Educated Oxford and Cambridge. Fellow of Corpus Christ College, Oxford. Physician at Lewes, Sussex. (*DNB*; Watson 1986 [2004[1]]).

(30) Gave Bodley 34 to the Bodleian Library, Oxford, in 1612.

VAN VLIET: (1620?2-1666). Educated at Leyden University. Visited an uncle in England in 1641, and accompanied diplomatic visits to England in 1651-2 and 1660-61. Held major administrative posts in Breda. An enthusiast pioneer in comparative linguistics. Interested also in Old English, and in the early 1660s JUNIUS lent him the Old English-Latin dictionary he had constructed for his own use. According to Holt 1878: I. lvi, van Vliet's library was auctioned at The Hague in 1666 (no. 107 in catalogue = Junius 1). (Brouwen and Campbell 1939; Ker 1940; Dekker 2000: 341-42.

(27) Ownership note 'Jani Vlisii Bredæ 1659 6 Febr. const. f. 18' in Junius 1, f. 2r.

VNET: Unetts of Castle Frome and Ledbury are in the 1569 Visitation of Herefordshire. A Richard Unett 'gent' acted as godfather at christenings in Ledbury in 1563. (Ker 1960: xiv).

(30) 'I Richard Vnet of ledbury In the Com'' is written on f. 6r of Bodley 34.

VOSSIUS, JOHANNES:

(50) Author of the *Encomium in laudem Thomae Wolsey* in the final pages of Harley 1197.

USSHER, JAMES: (1581-1656). Archbishop of Armagh. Educated Trinity College Dublin. (*Oxford DNB*).

(2) Borrowed the Vespasian Psalter (Vespasian A. i) in 1625.

(13) However he came by Junius 11 (from D'EWES? DE LAET?), he gave it to JUNIUS by 1652 (according to Christoph Arnold of Nuremburg, in a letter to Junius).

(16) Borrowed Nero A. i (Wulfstan) in 1646 or 1647, writing extracts into Bodleian Library, MS Rawlinson D. 290.

WALKER, EDWARD:

(56) Note 'By me Edward Walker' on f. 155 of Arch. Selden. B. 24.

WALPOLE, HORACE: (1717-97). 4th earl of Orford. Writer and politician. (*Oxford DNB*).

(53) Bought Add. 35290 (York Plays) for £1.1.0 in 1764 sale of THORESBY's library. His Strawberry Hill library was sold in 1842, when Thomas

RUDD paid £220.10.0 for the York Plays, selling the manuscript on for £235.

WANLEY, HUMFREY: (1672-1726). Palaeographer and librarian, most famed for his great catalogue of Old English and early Middle English manuscripts (vol. II of HICKES's *Thesaurus*, 1705). Main shaper of HARLEY collection across the years 1703-1726. Saw and described all but about twelve manuscripts containing sizeable amounts of Old English. (Douglas 1939: 120-47; Wright 1960[2]; Wright and Wright 1966; Heyworth 1989; Gatch 1990; *Oxford DNB*).

(9) Whereas notes for other people specify manuscripts they are thought to have seen, for Wanley it is more appropriate to note that one of the few sizeable Old English manuscripts he did not see was Add. 47967 (Orosius).

WARE, SIR JAMES: (1594-1666). Irish antiquary and historian. Graduate of Trinity College Dublin, where encouraged in antiquarian pursuits by USSHER. (*Oxford DNB*).

(16) Extracts from Nero A. i (Wulfstan) written into his notebook, Oxford, Bodleian Library, MS Rawlinson B. 479. (Tite 2003: 130).

WERFERTH: (*d.* 907 x 15). Bishop of Worcester from *c.* 872. A Mercian, he was among the men King Alfred involved in his literary activities. Asser attributes the Old English translation of Gregory's *Dialogues* to Werferth. (*Oxford DNB*).

(6) Alfred's preface to the Hatton *Cura Pastoralis* is addressed to Werferth.

(7) As bishop, agrees a three-life lease with his reeve Wulfsige.

WHELOCK, ABRAHAM: (*c.* 1593-1653). Educated at Trinity College Cambridge. Appointed to the first Anglo-Saxon professorship at Cambridge (1638); also held a professorship in Arabic. Editor of the first edition of the Old English Bede, together with parts of the Anglo-Saxon Chronicle (1643). (*Oxford DNB*).

(8) Took readings from the Parker Chronicle for his Old English Bede edition (1643).

(23) Cambridge, University Library MS Kk. 3. 18 was the copy-text for Whelock's edition (1643).

WILKINS, THOMAS: (1625/6-1699). Historian and authority on the Welsh language. Rector of Llanvair, Llantrissant, Glamorganshire. (Hill 2003).

(32) Jesus 29 (both parts) was one of three manuscripts he gave to Jesus College Oxford in 1693.

WILLIMOT:

(6) A twelfth-century hand declares 'Willimot wrote thus or better' on f. 53v of the Hatton Pastoral Care.

WILLSON, JOHN:

(53) A name entered in the last verso of Add. 35290 (York Plays).

WINGFIELD, ROBERT: of Northants.

(58) One of three names with mottoes and date 14 October 1612 on f. 333v of Fairfax 16.

WOLSEY, THOMAS: (1470/1-1530). Statesman. Cardinal from 1515. (Wright 1972; *Oxford DNB*).

(12) Name on f. 3 (fly-leaf) of Royal 7 C. xii (Ælfric's Catholic Homilies).

(31) Name on list folded into back of Titus D. xxviii.

(50) Harley 1197, ff. 402-13, final booklet of manuscript, presented to him by Johannes VOSSIUS; f. 402r contains the cardinal's arms.

WOTTON, NICHOLAS: (*c.* 1497-1567). Secretary of State. Later dean of Canterbury and York. (*Oxford DNB*).

(8) Owned Corpus Christi College 173 (Parker Chronicle).

WRIOTHESLEY, HENRY: (1573–1624). 3rd earl of Southampton. Educated at Cambridge. Courtier at Queen Elizabeth's court. Patron of Shakespeare and other writers. Statesman, soldier, explorer, he died fighting in the Netherlands against Spain. (*Oxford DNB*).

(54) Bought William CRASHAW's books, meaning them to go to St John's College, Cambridge, after his death. St John's College G. 23 (Barbour's *Bruce*) among his legacy.

WRIOTHESLEY, THOMAS: (1608-1667). 4th earl of Southampton and second son of HENRY WRIOTHESLEY. Lord High Treasurer from 1660. (*DNB*; P[revité-]O[rton] 1918; *Oxford DNB*).

(54) Gave the Crashaw books to St John's College by 1635. St John's College G. 23 (Barbour's *Bruce*) among the collection.

WULFSTAN: (*d.* 1023). Bishop of Worcester and archbishop of York. Author of *Sermo Lupi* (see pl. 16). (*Oxford DNB*).

(6) Added notes to the Hatton Pastoral Care.

WYSSHAM: Wyshams of Tedstone Delamere are in the 1569 Visitation of Herefordshire (Ker 1960: xiv).

(30) Entries in Bodley 34: f. 39r 'In the name of god amen I george Wyssham of Tedeston' in the Com''; f. 44v 'I george Wyssham de Tedestorne in the Com' of Herff' yeoman doethe'; f. 53v 'Thomas Wysham de Tedestorne in com' hereff' gent in ducentis sterlingorum soluend''.

YOUNG, PATRICK: (1584-1652). Biblical scholar. Born in Seaton, in Lothian. His father was tutor to James VI of Scotland (late James I, king of England). Royal Librarian from *c.* 1609. (*Oxford DNB*).

(24), (26) Young's catalogue of Worcester manuscripts, *c.* 1622, provides evidence that Hatton 116 and Royal 4 A. xiv were then still at Worcester.

Index of manuscript pages discussed

Index of other manuscript pages reproduced

Inscriptions on casket

Tables